To John Shafer
For all your contributions
to the Bear Valley Cultural
History Project.
Thank You!

Don Hanna + Crew
10/2/95

THE DESERT'S PAST

THE DESERT'S PAST

A NATURAL PREHISTORY OF THE GREAT BASIN

DONALD K. GRAYSON

Smithsonian Institution Press
Washington and London

Editor and typesetter: Peter Strupp/Princeton Editorial Associates
Production editor: Jack Kirshbaum
Designer: Janice Wheeler

Library of Congress Cataloging-in-Publication Data

Grayson, Donald K.
The deserts' past: a natural history of the Great Basin / Donald K. Grayson
p. cm.
Includes bibliographical references and index.
ISBN 1-56098-222-5
1. Geology, Stratigraphic—Pleistocene. 2. Geology, Stratigraphic—Holocene. 3. Geology—Great Basin. 4. Paleontology—Great Basin. 5. Indians of North America—Great Basin—Antiquities. 6. Paleo-Indians—Great Basin. 7. Great Basin—Antiquities. I. Title.
QE697.G8 1993
979'.01—dc20 2-25065

British Library Cataloguing-in-Publication Data is available.

Manufactured in the United States of America
99 98 97 96 95 94 93 5 4 3 2 1

∞ The paper used in this publication meets the minimum requirements of the American National Standard for Permanence of Paper for Printed Library Materials Z39.48-1984.

TO MY PARENTS

○○○

Contents

○○○

Figures

○○○

Tables

○○○

Preface

Most North Americans grow up knowing that parts of our continent were once covered by glaciers, that now-extinct mammoths and sabertooth cats walked the same ground on which we now walk our dogs, that people lived in North America long before Columbus stumbled across it. Most of us acquired this knowledge so casually that, if we happen to be asked when these things occurred, we have no real answer. We might know that mammoths looked like elephants, but not that they became extinct about 11,000 years ago. We might know about Ice Age glaciers and still not know that the maximum expanse of the most recent glaciation of North America occurred about 18,000 years ago. To judge from a recent radio advertisement, in which a mammoth expresses bewilderment over the meaning of the word "man," it might even come as a surprise to know that mammoths were hunted by people in the New World.

These kinds of things are easy to learn: it takes no great insight, and little effort, to register the fact that mammoths looked a lot like elephants and became extinct in North America about 11,000 years ago. It is, however, harder to grasp the nature and magnitude of the change that has occurred during and since the end of the Ice Age throughout North America.

We tend to assume that landscapes and the life they support are relatively permanent unless human activity modifies them. We are not surprised when the farmland that surrounds the town in which we grew up gives way to subdivisions and shopping malls: that kind of change we are used to, and have come to expect. But it is very surprising to learn how ephemeral the assemblages of plants and animals that surround us today really are, and, in most cases, how recently those assemblages came into being. The brevity of our lives easily misleads us into thinking that the way things are today is the way they have been for an immense amount of time. It is even easier to be misled into thinking that things are the way they are now because they have to be that way.

Until recently, life scientists attributed far greater stability, longevity, and predictability to biological communities than those communities actually possess. One of the great scientific gains of the past two decades or so is the recognition of the very major role that history has played in forming the plant and animal communities that now surround us, the recognition of how unpredictable changes in those communities can be, and the recognition of how fleeting their existence often is. Plant and animal communities appear stable and real to us only because we do not live long enough to observe differently. Bristlecone pines, which do live long enough, know better.

Today, most life scientists whose work has any significant time depth also know better. Although we may not live as long as bristlecone pines, we do have techniques for extracting information about earth and life history that can tell us not only what specific landscapes were like in the past, but also precisely when in the past they were like that. Even though we have made less progress toward understanding why they may have been that way, we have come a long way in this realm as well. We now know enough about at least the late Ice Age and the times that followed to be able to provide fairly detailed environmental histories for many parts of North America.

In this book, I provide such a history for the Great Basin. I define the "Great Basin" in multiple ways in Chapter 2, but here suffice it to say that the Great Basin covers some 165,000 square miles, centering on the state of Nevada, but also including substantial parts of adjacent California, Oregon, and Utah. My goal is simple: to outline the history of Great Basin environments from the time of the last maximum advance of glaciers in North America to the arrival of Europeans and their written records. In so doing, I hope to convey the dynamic nature of the landscapes and life of this region.

During the late Ice Age, there were camels living near what is now Pyramid Lake in northeastern Nevada; there were massive glaciers in the high mountains of eastern Nevada; there were substantial lakes in settings as far flung as Death Valley and the Great Salt Lake Desert; there were trees in the valleys of the Mojave Desert of southern Nevada. The camels, glaciers, lakes, and low-elevation trees are now gone. Today, piñon-juniper woodlands are draped across millions of mountain-flank acres in the Great Basin, and shadscale vegetation is common in many of the valleys that lie beneath the woodlands; to the south, creosote bush becomes a dominant shrub in the valley bottoms. This is a remarkably recent state of affairs, and a prime goal of this book is to document these facts and to discuss why they are so.

It was not hard for me to decide what to cover in this book: glaciers and lakes, shrubs and trees, mammals and birds, the people. Others might have chosen a different set of topics, in some cases broader, in others narrower. The set I have chosen, however, not only strikes me as important but also reflects my background as a scientist trained in both archaeology and vertebrate paleontology. It also reflects the fact that it has been my good fortune to know, and to work with, most of the people whose work is discussed in this book.

Deciding on the temporal coverage was more difficult. That this book would deal with the last 10,000 years was clear from the outset, as was the fact that it would also cover the waning years of the Ice Age or Pleistocene. These are, after all, years that were critical to the formation of the plant and animal communities of the Great Basin as we know it today. They also happen to be the years on which my own work has focused. In the end, I decided to begin my coverage at about 25,000 years ago, albeit, depending on the specific topic, sometimes earlier and sometimes later. I made that decision both because the selection of this starting date allows me to discuss the Great Basin prior to and during the last glacial maximum and because our knowledge of Great Basin environments tails off sharply before that date.

Today, the term "natural history" is often used in a very general way to refer to the things that life and earth scientists study. That is the way I use it here, modifying it in the title to indicate that this book deals primarily with events that took place prior to the times for which written records are available. Thus, this book is very much a "natural prehistory," dealing with the landscapes of the Great Basin, and the life it supported, during the past 25,000 years or so.

In a recent essay, Don and Kay Fowler have discussed the fact that American Indians and other non-western peoples became incorporated into western notions of "natural history" not because all human life was so incorporated, but because non-westerners were perceived as being more primitive, as "closer to nature" (D. D. Fowler and Fowler 1991:47), than western peoples.

It is hard to shake the deeply embedded, pejorative implications of including non-western peoples in a "natural history" of anyplace, but the shaking is needed. The fault lies not in the inclusion of non-westerners in the examination of natural history, but in the exclusion of western peoples. The natural history I present includes not only the prehistoric archaeology that deals solely with the native peoples of the Great Basin, but also the historic archaeology that deals with all peoples within the Great Basin after written records become available. The prehistoric peoples of the Great Basin were, in fact, "closer to nature" than the contemporary peoples of Reno or Salt Lake City are now, not in the nineteenth century sense that they were further removed from God or closer to the beasts of the earth, but in the very real sense that they had to cope far more directly with the environmental challenges that nature dealt them. The very same is true for the early historic human occupants of the Great Basin, whether native or not, as the history of the Donner Party shows, and as I discuss in Chapter 10.

I would be pleased to discover that Great Basin archaeologists, geologists, paleobotanists, and paleozoologists had read and learned something, no matter how minor, from this book. But the truth is that I did not write it for my professional colleagues. Instead, I wrote it for those who know little if anything about the environmental history of the Great Basin, or even about the modern Great Basin. Although I have worked in this region for well over twenty years, I have yet to lose the excitement that comes from identifying the bones of an extinct horse or camel from Ice Age deposits. I continue to be awed by the Bonneville Basin, from its salt flats to the high terraces carved on its mountains, both products of Pleistocene Lake Bonneville. I will never forget the moment I discovered the remains of a 5,300-year-old heather vole in the deposits of central Nevada's Gatecliff Shelter, not because it was a vole, but because of what it meant for our understanding of mammal history in the Great Basin. I am still excited by our developing knowledge of the human prehistory of the Great Basin, not so much because of the impressive nature of the artifacts themselves, but because of the varied environmental challenges these people successfully met. I wrote this book because I wanted to share all of this with those who know little or nothing about it.

As a result, I have assumed that the readers of this book come to it with little knowledge of such things as radiocarbon dating, pollen analysis, packrat middens, equilibrium-line altitudes, and projectile point chronologies. I explain them all here. I also assume that readers will know little about the modern Great Basin (Chapter 2), about North America during the Ice Age, and of the initial peopling of the New World (Chapters 3 and 4). In the first two parts of this book, I have spent a good deal of time providing that essential background. Those already in the know might skip these parts, though I depend heavily on them in later sections of the book.

Some technical comments are needed. I have generally given the scientific names for plants and animals only at the first significant mention of the species involved. An appendix provides a concordance of the common and scientific names of plant species. Concordances for the names of vertebrates that are used more than once are given in tables that accompany the text. Standard deviations for radiocarbon dates are not provided: these can be found in the original references.

It is standard in academic works to provide citations to the work of others in the text, as that work is called upon. With one exception, I have not done that here, because I do not want to interrupt the text with lengthy lists of the works on which I have depended so heavily. Instead, each chapter ends with a set of notes. Those notes provide the references I have used, often with comments on them. I have also used the notes to describe places that I think are worth visiting, from archaeological sites to local museums. The notes are an integral part of the book, but using them to provide the references has left the text far less cluttered than it otherwise would have been. The one exception involves direct quotations: there, the source of the quotation is provided in the text itself.

If visitors to Great Basin National Park, Death Valley National Monument, Malheur National Wildlife Refuge, the Bonneville Salt Flats, Arc Dome Wilderness, Pyramid Lake, or any of the almost endless number of remarkable places the Great Basin has to offer, find that their trips are made more meaningful by this book, I will be pleased: it is for them that it has been written. If my scientific colleagues find it of value as well, then I will be happier still.

Donald K. Grayson
Seattle, Washington

○○○

Acknowledgments

A list of the people who have taught me about the Great Basin may quite literally be found in the References section of this book. In addition, however, there are many people who discussed Great Basin issues with me (sometimes at great length), provided me with everything from references and manuscripts to reprints and maps, allowed me access to museum collections, and accompanied me on various field trips that were crucial to the preparation of this book. These friends and colleagues include Mel Aikens, Charlotte Beck, Larry Benson, Glenn Berger, Jim Brown, Fred Budinger, Angela Close, Don Currey, Bob Davis, Margot Dembo, Robert Dunnell, Bob Elston, Don Fowler, Mary Ann Graham, Russ Graham, Ann Haniball, Don Hardesty, Kim Harper, Gene Hattori, Vance Haynes, Roger Johnson, Tom Jones, Joe Jorgensen, Stephanie Livingston, Margaret Lyneis, Brigham Madsen, Dave Madsen, Jim Mead, Dave Meltzer, Bob Musil, Fred Nials, Jim O'Connell, Lori Pendleton, Anan Raymond, Dave Rhode, Stan Shockey, Steve Simms, Dick Taylor, Dave Thomas, Bob Thompson, Claude Warren, and Peter Wigand. Thanks to Lee Greenstreet as well; his friendship and help have made years of work in northern Nevada and south-central Oregon even more pleasant than they otherwise would have been (and the Denio Burgers are pretty good, too).

Stephanie Livingston, Jim O'Connell, and Bob Thompson read nearly the entire manuscript of this book at an early stage; their reactions were critical in formulating the final version. Peter Strupp, of Princeton Editorial Associates, did a remarkable job of editing the entire manuscript. Equally important were the comments given me on individual chapters by Kim Harper (Chapter 2); Don Currey (Chapter 5); Bob Thompson (Chapters 6 and 8); Stephanie Livingston (Chapters 7 and 11); Charlotte Beck, Bob Elston, and Tom Jones (Chapter 9); and Don Hardesty (Chapter 10). Vance Haynes, Dave Madsen, and Dave Thomas kindly provided illustrations that appear in Chapters 3, 9, and 10; Tim Hunt prepared the artifact illustrations that appear in Chapter 9. My thanks to all who helped.

PART ONE

○○○

The Great Basins

CHAPTER ONE

○○○

Discovering a Great Basin

It was July 13, 1890, and the first Republican candidate for the presidency of the United States lay dying in his New York City hotel room, his son by his side, his celebrated wife Jessie in Los Angeles, a continent away. Seventy-seven years old, John C. Frémont had come to New York from Washington, where he had finally obtained a $6,000 yearly pension for his military service. That sum, Frémont hoped, would secure his family from the poverty that had marked their recent life. But he had not counted on dying so soon, and Congress had made no provision for continuing a pension in the absence of a pensioner.

The events that took place in Washington and New York that spring and summer echoed sequences that seemed to mark everything Frémont had ever done: grand successes followed by remarkable failures. Born to loving parents but illegitimate; a hero in the Bear Flag Revolt of 1846 that led California to independence, but court-martialed and convicted for what General Stephen Watts Kearny claimed was mutiny; nominated for President but defeated by James Buchanan; a millionaire in California but soon bankrupt; a Californian in the end but buried in New York because so many Californians opposed the use of public funds to bring him west for one last time. Ironies everywhere, but especially in his final resting place, overlooking a river named for the great explorer Henry Hudson—second place in death for one who desperately wanted first place in life but could never quite hold on to it. Buried in New York, where not one significant place carries his name, and not in California, where he himself named so many significant things—Walker River, Owens Valley, and even Golden Gate, above which he might have been buried. Denied the final trip west by Californians, citizens of the very state his efforts had helped swing from Mexican to American control, citizens (or the sons and daughters of citizens) who had been spurred to come west by his *Report of the Exploring Expedition . . . to Oregon and North California in the Years 1843–'44.* Buried not in California, where he had once been a hero, but in New York, the state to which he and Jessie had retreated in personal defeat after his twice-failed role as a Union general in the Civil War.

Of Frémont's successes, perhaps the grandest was his second expedition for the U.S. Bureau of Topographical Engineers. His first, in 1842, had gone from St. Louis to just beyond South Pass in the northern Rocky Mountains of Wyoming, an expedition that he made with Kit

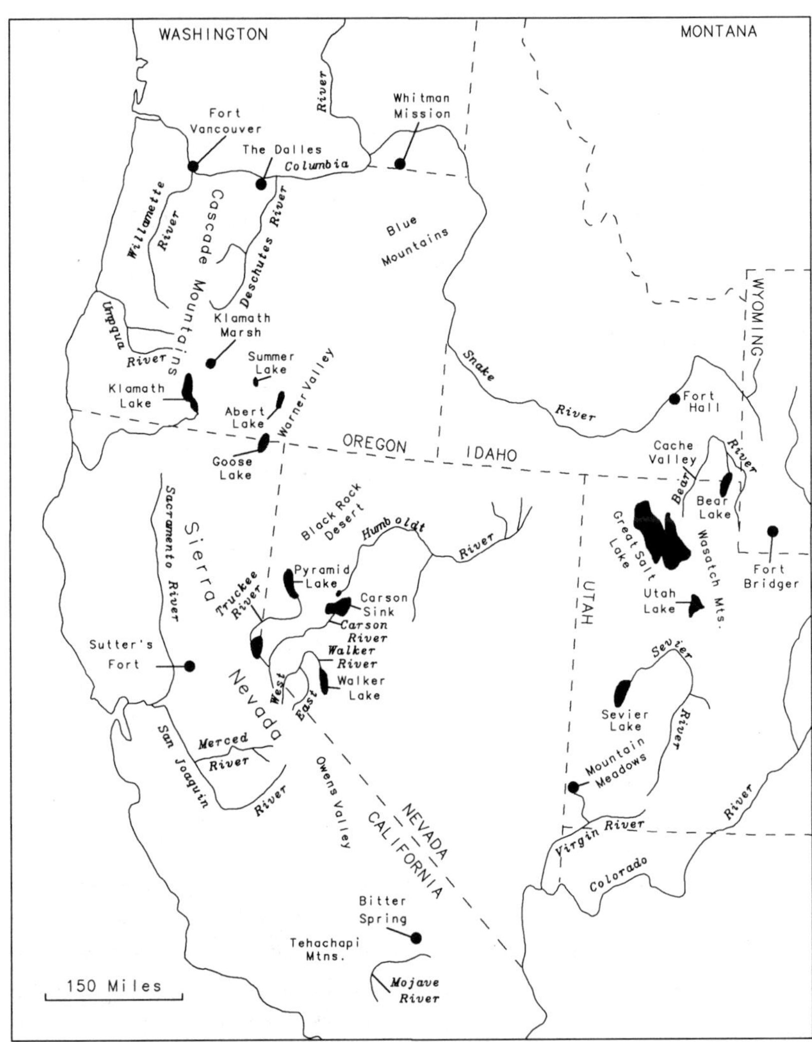

Figure 1-1. The American West, showing locations mentioned in Chapter 1.

Carson—whom Frémont turned into a legend—as one of his guides. The second expedition was to go much further.

Although the expedition clearly followed from, and was funded as a result of, the expansionist dreams of Thomas Hart Benton, the powerful senator from Missouri and Frémont's father-in-law, it is not clear what unwritten goals Frémont carried with him on this second excursion deep into the American west. What is clear is that he went further than his written orders allowed, wintering in Mexican California even though he was a representative of the American military. It is also clear that he had no written authorization to bring along a 12-pound mountain howitzer, the famous Frémont cannon.

He left St. Louis on May 13; three months later, Frémont was back at South Pass, the terminus of his first expedition, but now simply the jumping-off point for the work that was to make him famous (Figure 1-1). Accompanied once again by Kit Carson, Frémont made his way south to the Bear River, his description of which was to be crucial in guiding the Mormons to Salt Lake Valley in 1847. On September 6, the expedition reached Great Salt Lake, Frémont's "Inland Sea, stretching in still and solitary grandeur far beyond the limit of our vision" (Frémont 1845:151).

Great Salt Lake was a major target of their work, and they spent nearly a week here, exploring its shores by foot and its waters by boat. The expedition renewed its journey on September 12, heading north to Fort Hall on the Snake River, then down along the Snake to Fort Boise in western Idaho. From here, they cut across the Blue Mountains of northeastern Oregon, reaching Marcus Whitman's mission just east of the Columbia River near modern Walla Walla in southeastern Washington on October 24. They then traveled west along the Columbia River, arriving at Fort Vancouver on November 8.

Fort Vancouver moved several times during its history, but when Frémont arrived it was on the north side of the Columbia River, just north of the mouth of the Willamette River; today, it is within the city limits of Vancouver, Washington, and a reconstructed version exists as the Fort Vancouver National Historic Site. At 300′ wide and 700′ long, it was massive, the Hudson's Bay Company's prime redistributive and administrative center in this part of the world. Ships came up the Columbia River to supply the fort and to be supplied with furs (the British bark *Columbia* was there when Frémont arrived). The fort also served as a stopping-off point for the growing number of American emigrants who were then entering Oregon's Willamette Valley, some 2,400 of them in 1843 and 1844.

Frémont was well treated at Fort Vancouver, as were all others who came here, but he stopped only long enough to stock up for the return home. His orders for that return were clear and simple. "Return by the Oregon road," Colonel J. J. Abert had ordered, "and on again reaching the mountains, diverge a little and make a circuit of the Wind river chain" (D. Jackson and Spence 1970:160). But taking the "Oregon road" was pretty much how Frémont had come to be where he was, and he was not about to return the way he had come. When Frémont stocked up, he stocked up for a far more rigorous journey, and by the time he had returned to The Dalles, on the eastern edge of the Columbia River's passage through the Cascade Mountains, he had three months' worth of supplies for his 25 men, along with a herd of cattle and 104 mules and horses. And, rather than heading east from The Dalles, as Abert's orders clearly indicated he should, he headed south.

Leaving The Dalles on November 25 in the midst of flurrying snow, Frémont moved south along the eastern flank of the Cascades, past the Metolius River, past the headwaters of the Deschutes, and south to Klamath Marsh.

Arriving at the marsh on December 10, Frémont used his cannon for the first time, discharging it to impress the Indians whose fires were visible across the water. These were Klamath Indians, Frémont knew, but he was incorrect in thinking that this was Klamath Lake, and that the river he had found here—the Williamson—was the Klamath River. In fact, Klamath Lake was still 30 miles to the south. But, thinking he had found the lake, Frémont spent several days here, resting his horses and exploring. Once satisfied with what he had seen, he headed east, leaving on December 13 through thickening snow. Three days later, after the men forced themselves, their animals, and the howitzer through deep and crusted snow, the woods suddenly ended:

> we found ourselves on the vertical and rocky wall of the mountain. At our feet—more than a thousand feet below—we looked into a green prairie country, in which a beautiful lake, some twenty miles in length, was spread along the foot of the mountains, its shores bordered with green grass. . . . Not a particle of ice was to be seen on the lake, or snow on its borders, and all was like summer or spring. . . . Shivering on snow three feet deep, and stiffening in a cold north wind, we exclaimed at once that the names of Summer Lake and Winter Ridge should be applied to these two proximate places of such sudden and violent contrast. (Frémont 1845:207)

These places still bear the names Frémont gave them, a highway marker on Oregon State Route 31 pointing out where Frémont and his men suffered their way down Winter Ridge on the evening of December 15, 1843, leaving the howitzer halfway up, to be retrieved the next day. Frémont had entered the Great Basin.

From here, the group continued south and east, further into the Oregon desert. Lake Abert came next, so named by Frémont "in honor of the chief of the corps to which I belonged" (Frémont 1845:209). Then they headed further south and east to Warner Valley, where Christmas Day was celebrated with a blast from the howitzer. Crossing the 42nd parallel, which today marks the boundary between Nevada and Oregon but which then saw them entering Mexican territory, they moved deeper into northwestern Nevada—High Rock Creek it seems, then Soldier Meadow, next, on New Year's Day, along the Black Rock Desert through what is now Gerlach, Nevada, and next, on January 10, to Pyramid Lake, "a sheet of green water, some twenty miles broad [that] broke upon our eyes like the ocean" (Frémont 1845:216).

Here they rested, trading for cutthroat trout with the Northern Paiute who occupied the shores of the lake, allowing their horses to feed, killing the last of their cattle, and getting their howitzer unstuck from the steep shores of the Lake Range that forms the eastern edge of Pyramid Lake. The lake itself they named from the "very remarkable rock" they saw jutting from it, a rock that to them "presented a pretty exact outline of the great pyramid of Cheops" (Frémont 1845:217). Once recuperated, they followed the Truckee River south, and then left it as it swung west toward the Sierra Nevada, instead heading south and hitting the Carson River, named by Frémont for the scout whose legend he had begun.

It was here, in the Carson Valley on January 18, that Frémont said he made his decision to cross the Sierra Nevada into California, though there are indications that the decision had been made well before. Faced with horses in poor condition and with no means of making shoes for them, Frémont observed, "I therefore determined to abandon my eastern course" (Frémont 1845:220) and to cross the Sierra Nevada into California.

The exact route they took has never been clear. Frémont himself became lost, knowing mainly that they had to go west and that they had to go up. They first crossed the East, then the West, Walker River, and they surely saw Lake Tahoe from a peak to the south. They then forced their way over the top, eating horses and mules as they went, stumbling and crawling through the snow, emerging into the green California spring on February 24, all of them alive. On March 6, they finally reached the American River, only a mile from the Sacramento River and Sutter's Fort. They had left The Dalles with 104 horses and mules; they had begun their ascent of the Sierra Nevada with 67; they arrived at Sutter's Fort with 33 exhausted and nearly useless animals. Another, less animate, loss was the howitzer: this they had abandoned on January 29, somewhere along the western flank of the Sweetwater Mountains, its whereabouts still a debated mystery.

Three weeks at Sutter's Fort saw both men and animals revived. They left on March 24, this time with 130 horses and mules and some 30 cattle. Rather than moving north and out of Mexico, they went south and deeper into it, following the San Joaquin Valley to southern California's Tehachapi Mountains, crossing over them and into the Mojave Desert a few miles south of Tehachapi Pass. Back in the Great Basin again, they moved mostly east, hitting the Mojave River near what is now Victorville, California, and roughly following the Spanish Trail across southern California and southern Nevada into Utah. At Bitter Spring in southern California's Mojave Desert, Kit Carson and his companion Alexis Godey revenged the death of a party of Mexicans by tracking down and scalping two of the Indians who had done the killing, a sign of the savage ferocity for which Carson was to later become infamous. And along the Virgin River near Littlefield, Arizona, one of Frémont's own—Baptiste Tabeau—was killed by Indians, the first of his men to die.

Leaving the scene of Tabeau's death, the expedition moved northward, reaching Mountain Meadows on May 12. Thirteen years later, this site, on the very fringe of the Great Basin in southwestern Utah, was to become the location of a Mormon-engineered massacre of some 100 immigrants from Arkansas and Missouri. For Frémont, however, it was simply a "noted place of rest and refreshment" (Frémont 1845:271). Equally important, as the expedition left Mountain Meadows, it was joined by Joseph Walker, one of the most famous of western backwoodsmen. It was Walker who guided the group north to the Sevier River, and then to Utah Lake, south and east of Great Salt Lake. Finally, on May 27, Frémont and his men headed east into the Wasatch Range and out of the Great Basin. On August 6, nearly 15 months after his departure, Frémont was once again in St. Louis.

Frémont had thus struggled his way south from the Columbia River deep along the western edge of the Great Basin, and then over the Sierra Nevada in the dead of winter. He had then moved even further south in the interior valleys of Mexican California, and then east across one of the most challenging deserts in North America, ultimately swinging north to nearly rejoin his original diversion into the Great Basin at Great Salt Lake.

His orders, however, had directed him to return by the Oregon Trail, not by the Spanish Trail, some 500 and more miles to the south, and those orders had said nothing about California. He explained his entry into California by considering the situation in which he had found himself in January 1844. Why, however, did he swing so far south from the Columbia River, and from the Oregon Trail, in the first place? Just as Frémont used his *Report* to justify his decision to enter California, he also used it to justify making this move.

There were, he said, three prime geographic reasons for making this "great circuit to the south and southeast." The first was to find Klamath Lake and explore the Klamath country, then poorly known. The second was to find and explore Mary's Lake, the sink into which the Humboldt River flows in western Nevada, now called Humboldt Lake. Third, he wished to locate, if it existed, the Buenaventura River, "which has had a place in so many maps, and countenanced the belief of the existence of a great river flowing from the Rocky mountains to the bay of San Francisco" (Frémont 1845:196).

Of these goals, Frémont approximated achieving the first, but failed at the second. He explored the Klamath country, but never found Klamath Lake, having mistaken it for Klamath Marsh to the north and east. This was hardly his fault, since he also referred to the "imputed double character" of Klamath Lake as "lake, or meadow, according to the season of the year" (Frémont 1845:196), a description that applies not to the deep and permanent Upper Klamath Lake but that fits Klamath Marsh well.

After having explored the Klamath country, however, his movements south from Warner Valley and past Pyramid Lake brought him well west of Humboldt Lake, and his *Report* provides no clarification of the location and nature of the sink of the Humboldt, except that it could not be found the way he went.

Ironically, even though Frémont himself was to name the river "Humboldt" during his next expedition in 1845, he saw neither lake nor river until the summer of 1847. And, when he finally saw Humboldt Lake, he was in the forced tow of Stephen Watts Kearny, who soon had him arrested and court-martialed for the role he had played in the acquisition of California for the United States.

The Klamath country and Humboldt Lake existed, and in that sense were quite different from the Buenaventura, one of the most enduring myths that the geography of North American deserts was to provide, a myth that has its roots in the earliest entry of Europeans into the intermountain west. In 1775, the Franciscan Father Francisco Garcia, part of Juan Bautista Anza's second expedition to forge overland routes linking the settlements of Sonora and New Mexico with those of coastal California, traveled up the Colorado River to somewhere near the current location of Needles, California. Garcia then headed west, reached and followed the Mojave River westward, and crossed into the San Joaquin Valley.

While there, he gained the impression that the Kern River cut through the Sierra Nevada; he was told of the San Joaquin River, and thought that this cut the Sierra Nevada as well. Indeed, Anza himself reached San Francisco Bay in 1776, and his diarist, Father Pedro Font, mistook the rivers that flowed into this bay for a large body of fresh water that reached east of the Sierra Nevada. So the myth began.

On July 29, 1776, Fathers Francisco Dominguez and Francisco Escalante left Santa Fe to find an acceptable overland route to Monterey, which had been established in 1770. They headed north through western Colorado and hit the Green River. This they named the San Buenaventura, after the biographer of St. Francis. From here, they moved west, crossing the mountains and reaching Utah Lake. While at Utah Lake, they were told of Great Salt Lake, and assumed, from its salinity, that it had an outlet to the sea. Moving south, they crossed the Sevier River, which they thought was part of the San Buenaventura. Abandoning the idea of reaching Monterey on this trip—a wise decision, given the way they had gone—they continued south and returned to Sante Fe in January 1777.

Maps were soon produced that incorporated and compounded these errors. By the early 1800s, influential maps showed the Buenaventura River flowing from Sevier Lake in the far eastern Great Basin to San Francisco Bay. Zebulon Pike's map in 1810, Alexander von Humboldt's in 1811, and Lewis and Clark's in 1814 all provided for such a river.

A river that flowed from the Rockies to the Pacific Coast in this region would be of tremendous economic importance, since it would provide a means of transportation of people and goods to and from California. Moving the former was important if the United States was to stretch from coast to coast. Moving the latter was important if the United States was to become a major player in trade with Asia. If the Buenaventura were real, it had to be discovered and charted.

But the Buenaventura was not real, and seasoned explorers of the west soon became aware of that. In 1826, Jedediah Smith had traveled from Cache Valley to Great Salt Lake, then south to the Colorado, turning west across the Mojave Desert to reach the San Bernardino Valley. Denied permission from the Mexican governor to travel north to San Francisco, he did so anyway, since he wanted to return by following "some considerable river heading up in the vicinity of the Great Salt Lake" (G. R. Brooks 1989:77–78).

He did not find that river, and in May 1827 he left his men along the Stanislaus River and, accompanied by two others, became the first non-Indian that we know to have crossed the Sierra Nevada. Apparently passing through Ebbett's Pass south of Lake Tahoe, his return trip to Great Salt Lake took him south of Walker Lake and through south-central Nevada. He headed back to his men almost immediately, taking the southern route via the Colorado River and Mojave Desert to the San Bernardino Valley.

Late in 1827, he and his men began the move north up the Sacramento Valley to the Trinity and Klamath rivers, then north up the Pacific coast to the Umpqua River, where 15 of his men were killed by Indians; Frémont referred to this episode to explain why he fired his cannon at Klamath Marsh. By the time Smith reached Fort Vancouver in August 1828, he knew that there was no river south of the Columbia that cut through either the Cascades or the Sierra Nevada.

Smith did not keep that information to himself, writing to William Clark (of Lewis and Clark, then Superintendent of Indian Affairs) to tell him of his travels, and thus informing him that the Buenaventura did not exist. "By Examination and frequent trials," he wrote, he "found it impossible to cross a range of mountains which lay to the East" (Morgan 1964:340).

Although Smith died before he could complete his projected book on his travels, William Clark and Thomas Hart Benton were good friends and fellow expansionists who routinely discussed what was known of the geography of western North America. Surely if by no other route than this, Frémont would have known that the Buenaventura was fiction. Indeed, in 1829 and 1830, Frémont's friend and guide, Kit Carson, had crossed the Mojave Desert from the east and traveled up the interior valleys of California. As Carson noted on seeing the Sacramento Valley with Frémont in 1844, "I had been there seventeen [*sic*] years before, and knew the place well" (Quaife 1966:79).

Arrayed next to such information, however, was the fact that many contemporary maps did continue to show such a river. As Frémont noted, the Buenaventura formed "agreeably to the best maps in my possession, a connected water line from the Rocky mountains to the Pacific ocean" (Frémont 1845:205). If Frémont really did not know that the river was fictitious, then finding it could have been a legitimate and major goal of his intermountain explorations, and an excellent reason to move so far south from the Columbia River and the Oregon Trail. If he knew it did not exist, he did not let on, and the river became a prime justification for being where he had not been told to go, and it certainly became a major literary device in reporting the results of his explorations.

By the time Frémont reached southern California, he knew that there was no such river. In his *Report* entry for April 14, 1844, the day his party crossed over the Tehachapis, Frémont let his readers know as well:

> It had been constantly represented . . . that the bay of San Francisco opened far into the interior, by some river coming down from the base of the Rocky mountains, and upon which supposed stream the name of Rio Buenaventura had been bestowed. Our observations of the Sierra Nevada . . . show that this neither is nor can be the case. No river from the interior does, or can, cross the Sierra Nevada. (Frémont 1845:255)

The Columbia was the only river that led from the deep interior to the Pacific Ocean, and this was far to the north. Frémont had followed the mountains south from the Columbia to southern California and he knew this to be the case. Although other explorers had known for over a decade that the Buenaventura did not exist, Frémont's *Report* brought the news to a wide audience, and finally put the myth to rest.

But among scientists who work in the Desert West, Frémont is far better known for a very different pronouncement, since his *Report* carries an entry for October 13, 1843, that first introduced the term that is now used to characterize much of this region:

> The Great Basin—a term which I apply to the intermediate region between the Rocky mountains and the next range [the Sierra Nevada], containing many lakes, with their own system of rivers and creeks, (of which the Great Salt is the principal,) and which have no connexion with the ocean, or the great rivers which flow into it. (Frémont 1845:175)

The *Great Basin:* John C. Frémont's term for the area of internal drainage in the arid west. Between the crest of the Rocky Mountains on the east and that of the Sierra Nevada on the west, from the edge of the Columbia River drainage on the north to the edge of the Colorado River drainage on the south, all waters that fall end up in enclosed basins that may, or may not, contain lakes; none of those waters reaches either the Atlantic or the Pacific oceans. The "Great Basin" is an ideal name for this area, and that is what it has been called ever since Frémont introduced the phrase in his 1845 *Report.*

Frémont is often credited not only with having named this region, but also with having established the fact of internal drainage. He certainly did establish to his own satisfaction that no water flowed from the Great Basin across the Sierra Nevada and southern Cascades. However, his outbound route left a vast portion of the northern Great Basin and southern Columbia Basin unexplored by him. He could not have known by his own efforts that no waters flowed from this region into the Columbia system.

In fact, Frémont never claimed to have established the fact of internal drainage. Indeed, he made it clear that the information that allowed him to be sure that he was dealing with a "Great Basin" came from Joseph Walker.

Born in Tennessee in 1798, Walker began his explorations of the Great Basin in 1833, when he led a fur-trapping group down the Bear River to Great Salt Lake. After exploring the western shore of the lake and discovering that it had no outlet, he headed west across the desert, reached the Humboldt River, and followed it down to the Humboldt Sink. Moving south from the Sink, he passed Carson Lake, Carson River, and, it appears, Walker Lake. From here, Walker crossed the Sierra Nevada to the Merced River in California; on the way, his party became the first whites to see Yosemite Valley, on or about October 30, 1833.

Walker wintered in California, beginning the trip back in February 1834. From the Tubatulabal Indians, he learned of a pass through the southern Sierra Nevada, and took what is now called Walker Pass to reach Owens Valley. From here, they generally followed the east flank of the Sierra Nevada northwards, back to the Humboldt Sink. They then retraced their steps back along the Humboldt, leaving it to head north to the Snake and out of the Great Basin.

Although Walker himself left no detailed account of this trip, his clerk, Zenas Leonard, did, and it is primarily from Leonard's published travels that Walker's 1833–1834 crossings of the Great Basin are known. Leonard's *Narrative,* which appeared in book form in 1839, notes again and again that the lakes they saw—Great Salt Lake, Humboldt Lake, Carson Lake—had no outlets. By the time they had completed their journey, the general nature of the desert they had crossed had become completely clear, and Leonard himself came close to defining the Great Basin just the way Frémont was to do a few years later:

> This desert . . . is bounded on the east by the Rocky mountains, on the west by the Calafornia [*sic*] mountain, on the North by the Columbia [Snake] river, and on the south by the Red, or Colorado river. . . . There are numerous small rivers rising in either mountain, winding their way far towards the centre of the plain, where they are emptied into lakes or reservoirs, and the water sinks in the sand. Further to the North where the sand is not so deep and loose, the streams rising in the *spurs* of the Rocky and those descending from the Calafornia mountains, flow on until their waters at length mingle together in the same lakes. The Calafornia mountain extends from the Columbia to the Colorado river, running parallel with the coast about 150 miles distant, and 12 or 15 hundred miles in length with its peaks perpetually covered with eternal snows. There is a large number of water courses descending from this mountain on either side—those on the east side stretching out into the plain, and those on the west flow generally in a straight course until they empty into the Pacific; but in no place is there a water course through the mountain. (Quaife 1978:212–213)

Walker thus knew in 1834 not only that there was no Buenaventura cutting through to the Pacific, but also that a vast amount of the intermountain area appeared to be of internal drainage. Unlike Frémont, he had traveled both the Humboldt and the area between the Humboldt and Snake rivers.

On May 12, 1844, while at Mountain Meadows, Frémont "had the gratification to be joined by the famous hunter and trapper, Mr. Joseph Walker" (Frémont 1845: 271), who then became the group's guide. Frémont thus had the opportunity to discuss geographical and topographical matters with the older and more experienced explorer. That the hydrology of the area Frémont called the Great Basin was discussed is clear, since Frémont gives Walker full credit for confirming what Frémont may have suspected but certainly had not proved: that this vast area lacks any outlet to the sea.

The existence of the "Great interior Basin," Frémont observed,

> is vouched for by such of the American traders and hunters as have some knowledge of that region; the structure of the Sierra Nevada range of mountains requires it to be there; and my own observations confirm it. Mr. Joseph Walker, who is so well acquainted in those parts, informed me that, from the Great Salt lake west, there was a succession of lakes and rivers which have no outlet to the sea, nor any connexion with the Columbia, or with the Colorado of the Gulf of California. He described some of these lakes as being large, with numerous streams, and even considerable rivers, falling into them. In fact, all concur in the general report of these interior rivers and lakes. . . . The structure of the country would require this formation of interior lakes; for the waters which would collect between the Rocky mountains and the Sierra Nevada, not being able to cross this formidable barrier, nor to get to the Columbia or the Colorado, must necessarily collect into reservoirs, each of which would have its little system of streams and rivers to supply it. (1845:275)

Frémont could not have been clearer in giving credit where credit was due, to Walker and the other "American traders and hunters" whose knowledge of the region far exceeded his own. Indeed, although Frémont argued that the small size of the streams that he saw coming into the Columbia from the south suggested that they did not reach very far south, and hence that the Columbia drainage must provide the northern edge of the Great Basin, even here he noted that "all accounts" concurred that the waters of the Great Basin were separated from those of the Columbia.

As extensive and impressive as they were, and as important as they were to be in bringing others west—in forwarding Thomas Hart Benton's dreams—Frémont's explorations in 1843 and 1844 were too limited to demonstrate on their own that no water flowed from this huge area. What he did do was build on the travels and knowledge of others, most notably of Joseph Walker. He confirmed what they had found, coined a felicitous term—the Great Basin—to encapsulate that confirmed knowledge, and presented it all in one of the most readable, and most widely read, volumes of exploration ever published in and on North America, a book that made public both what he had learned and the private knowledge of those who had preceded him.

Notes

On Frémont, see Egan (1985), Herr (1987), D. Jackson and Spence (1970), and Frémont himself (Frémont 1845, 1887). Cline (1988) provides an excellent discussion of early explorations of the Great Basin in general and of the Buenaventura River myth in particular. For Kit Carson's autobiography, see Quaife (1966); on the route of the Oregon Trail, Hill (1986). Among other places, Frémont's cannon is discussed in D. Jackson and Spence (1970), Townley (1984), and Reveal and Reveal (1985); on the Mountain Meadows massacre, see J. Brooks (1962). On Walker, see B. Gilbert (1983) and, for Leonard's *Narrative,* Quaife (1978); on Smith, Morgan (1964) and G. R. Brooks (1989). Morgan (1985) provides a fascinating discussion of the Humboldt River as a historic route across Nevada.

CHAPTER TWO

○○○

Modern Definitions of the Great Basin

The Hydrographic Great Basin

If scientists had just stuck with Frémont's fully appropriate definition, the Great Basin would be a well-defined hydrographic unit, applying only to that huge area of the arid west that drains internally. That definition, in fact, remains a common one, though few people working in the Great Basin follow it slavishly.

When it is so defined (Figure 2-1), the Great Basin covers some 165,000 square miles, from the crest of the Sierra Nevada and southern Cascades to the crest of the Wasatch Range, and from edge to edge of the Columbia River and Colorado River drainages. In terms of modern political units, the hydrographic Great Basin centers on the state of Nevada, but also includes much of eastern California, western Utah, and south-central Oregon, and small portions of southeastern Idaho and adjacent Wyoming. Precipitation that falls in this vast region drains neither to the Pacific nor to the Atlantic, but instead generally flows into streams that empty into low, saline lakes or that simply disappear by evaporation and absorption into the ground, Frémont's "fetid salt lakes" (Frémont 1845:209) or Smith's "plains whose sands drank up the waters of the river and spring where our need was the greatest" (G. R. Brooks 1989:96).

The hydrographic Great Basin does have many bodies of water that are called rivers (Figure 2-2). The nature of Great Basin internal drainage can quickly be seen by following any of them downstream.

The Donner und Blitzen River, for instance, is a beautiful stream that rises in Oregon's Steens Mountain and flows into Malheur Lake, helping to create one of North America's finest wildlife refuges. When the waters of Malheur Lake rise, they flow into nearby Harney Lake, but these lakes now have no outlet.

To the south and west, the Walker River rises in two branches—the East and West Walker—from the eastern flanks of the Sierra Nevada south of Lake Tahoe, and runs, through a curious course that I will discuss in Chapter 5, into Walker Lake. Walker Lake, however, also has no outlet.

The Carson River rises on the flanks of the Sierra Nevada closer to Lake Tahoe, and then flows north and east into Carson Lake and the Carson Sink. "Sink" says it all. Further north, the Truckee River rises in Lake Tahoe, and until recently flowed north and east to fill

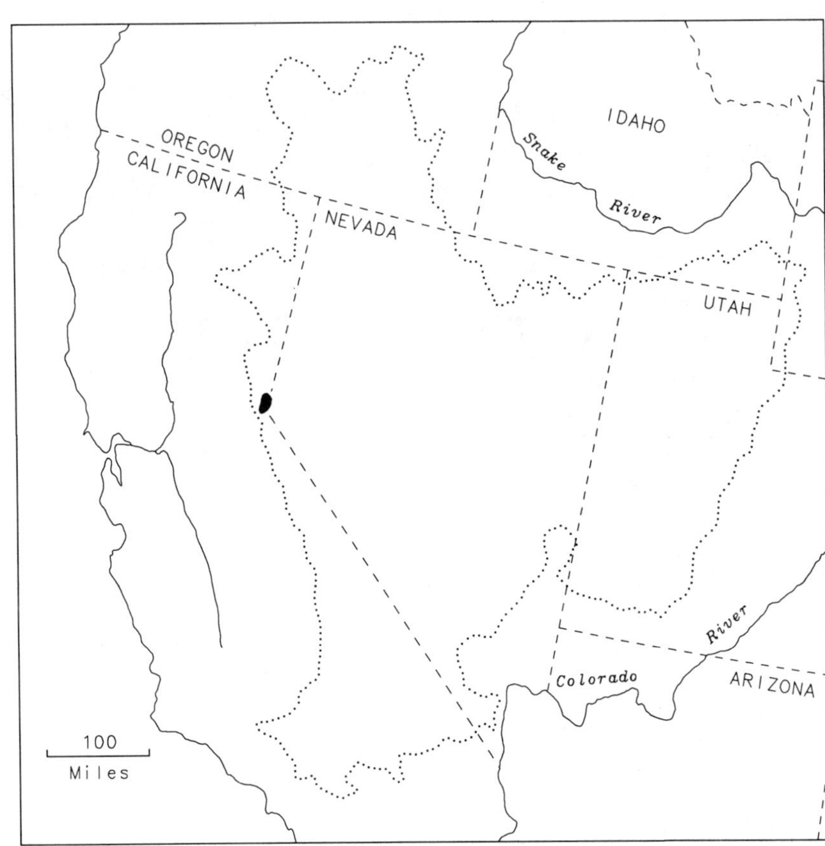

Figure 2-1. The hydrographic Great Basin. After G. I. Smith and Street-Perrott (1983).

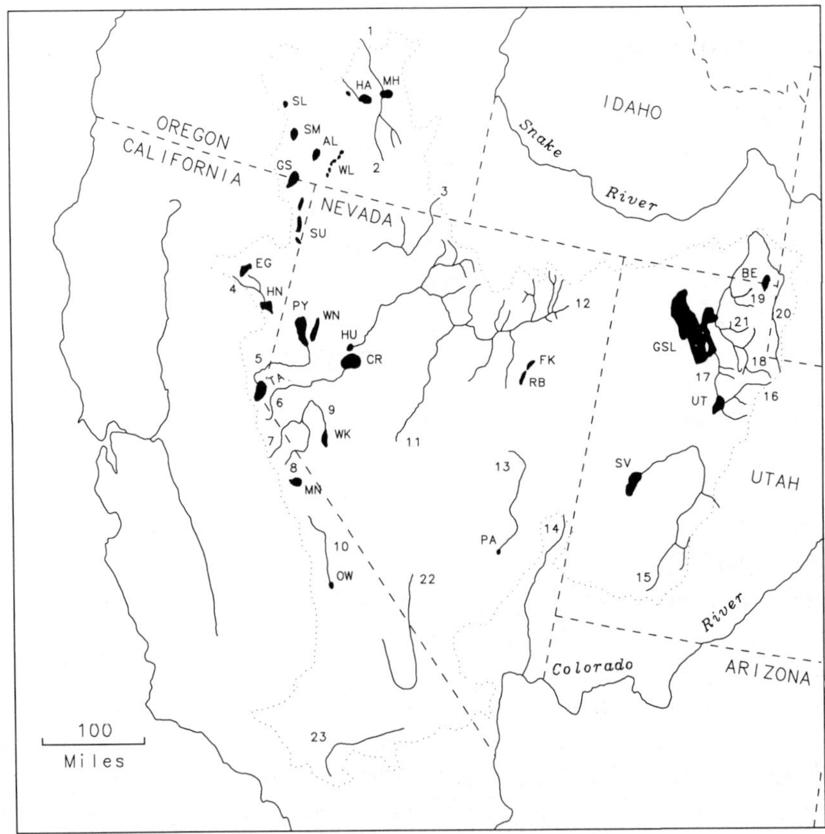

Figure 2-2. Major rivers and lakes of the Great Basin. *Key to rivers:* 1, Silvies; 2, Donner und Blitzen; 3, Quinn; 4, Susan; 5, Truckee; 6, Carson; 7, West Walker; 8, East Walker; 9, Walker; 10, Owens; 11, Reese; 12, Humboldt; 13, White; 14, Muddy River/Meadow Valley Wash; 15, Sevier; 16, Provo; 17, Jordan; 18, Weber; 19, Logan; 20, Bear; 21, Ogden; 22, Amargosa; 23, Mojave. See Figure 5-1 and Table 5-1 for key to lakes.

Figure 2-3. The Black Rock Desert; the Jackson Mountains are in the background.

both Pyramid and Winnemucca lakes. By 1939, the use of the Truckee's water for irrigation, and the construction of a highway across the inlet of Winnemucca Lake, had turned Winnemucca Lake into a playa. Today, a diminished Truckee feeds only Pyramid Lake, which, as Frémont learned, has no outlet. The Quinn River rises in northern Nevada from the confluence of many small streams and ends in the Black Rock Desert: only in good years does it form even a shallow lake (see Figure 2-3).

The Humboldt—the longest of Great Basin rivers—begins in northeastern Nevada, then flows generally southwest across the northern part of the state. Because of its length and location, the Humboldt was extremely important in the Americanization of California, serving as the prime transportation route across the state during the nineteenth century. The Bidwell-Bartleson party came this way on their way to California in 1841. The Donner-Reed party followed the river dangerously late in 1846, on their way to disaster in the Sierra Nevada (see Chapter 10). Thousands more followed during the next decade, on their way, they hoped, to gold or to land. But the Humboldt runs only as far as Humboldt Lake and Humboldt Sink—"sink" again—and emigrants were faced with a wicked stretch of desert beyond that point.

The eastern Great Basin has its share of rivers as well. The Logan flows into the Bear, and the Bear into Great Salt Lake. The Ogden joins the Weber, which also feeds Great Salt Lake. The Provo flows into Utah Lake, and overflow from Utah Lake spills into Great Salt Lake via the Jordan River. Frémont was wrong in thinking that Utah Lake was part of Great Salt Lake, but he certainly knew that neither had an outlet to the sea. To the south, the Sevier River runs into Sevier Lake. This lake would still have water in it were it not for irrigation demands on the Sevier River, but it, too, lacks an outlet.

In the southwestern Great Basin, the Amargosa River rises in western Nevada and then flows—when it has any water in it at all—south along the east side of the Amargosa Range and then north into Death Valley, where any water it might have simply disappears. The Mojave River begins in the San Bernardino Mountains of southern California and runs north and east until it, too, just disappears. The Owens River drains Owens Valley into Owens Lake. Its waters now reach the Pacific, but only because the city of Los Angeles has appropriated them. All Great Basin streams drain internally, and it is this fact that leads to the definition of a hydrographic Great Basin.

The Physiographic Great Basin

There are three other Great Basins to go along with the one defined by hydrographers, each created by a different set of scientists focusing on a different aspect of the Desert West. For those who like crisp regional boundaries, these other Great Basins can be frustrating, since only the hydrographic Great Basin allows any real certainty as to where the Great Basin starts and stops. Scientists defining one of the other Great Basins can draw the edges of each of their Great Basins differently, depending on the precise definitional criteria they use, and on whether or not they think a given patch of the Desert West matches those criteria. Only for the most compulsive is this haziness of boundaries problematic, since in all cases the haziness reflects the continuum on the ground.

Physiographers, those who study the evolution and nature of the earth's surface, focus not on the drainages of the Intermontane West, but instead on the fact that much of this area has a very distinctive topography: wide desert valleys flanked by often massive mountain ranges that run roughly north-south, and that generally parallel one another. Topography of this sort covers an area much broader than the Great Basin itself no matter how it is defined. This "Basin and Range Province," as it is called, runs from southeastern Oregon and southern Idaho deep into northern Mexico, including much of the southern Southwest on its way. But the northernmost part of this complex geological area is called the Great Basin Section of the Basin and Range Province, and provides the second common definition of the Great Basin (Figure 2-4).

So defined, three of the borders of the physiographic Great Basin are well marked: the Sierra Nevada and southern Cascades on the west, the Rocky Mountains on the east, and the Columbia Plateau on the north. In all three cases, the borders coincide fairly well with the edges provided by the hydrographic definition. The same, however, is less true for the southern end, which is defined somewhat arbitrarily.

South of a line that runs roughly from Las Vegas on the east to just north of the Mojave River on the west, topographic relief becomes much less than it is in the north, and the mountains become smaller and more irregular in outline. This line marks the southern edge of the physio-

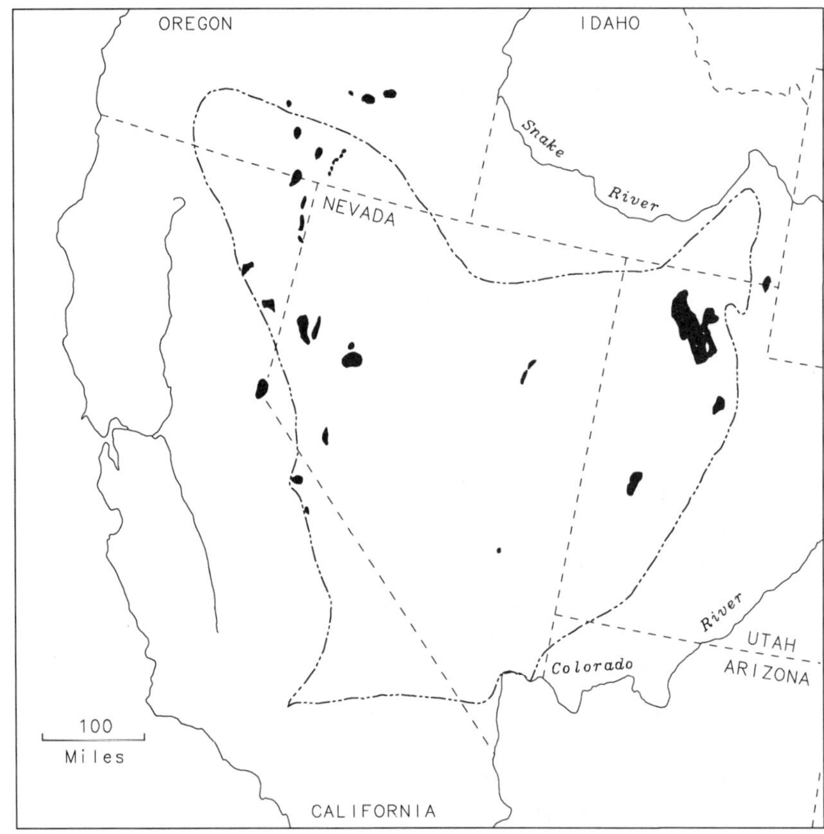

Figure 2-4. The physiographic Great Basin. After Hunt (1967).

Table 2-1. Great Basin Mountain Ranges with Summits above 10,000′[a]

Range	Summit	Elevation (feet)	Summit county
Antelope Range (AN)	Ninemile Peak	10,104	Nye, NV
Bodie Mountains (BM)	Potato Peak	10,235	Mono, CA
Carson Range (CR)	Freel Peak	10,881	Alpine, CA
Cherry Creek Range (CH)	Unnamed	10,458	White Pine, NV
Deep Creek Range (DC)	Ibapah Peak	12,087	Juab, UT
Diamond Mountains (DM)	Diamond Peak	10,614	Eureka/White Pine, NV
Duck Creek Range	Unnamed	10,328	White Pine, NV
East Humboldt Range (EH)	Hole-in-the-Mountain Peak	11,306	Elko, NV
Egan Range (EG)	South Ward Mountain	10,936	White Pine, NV
Grant Range (GR)	Troy Peak	11,298	Nye, NV
Hot Creek Range (HC)	Morey Peak	10,246	Nye, NV
Independence Mountains (IN)	McAfee Peak	10,439	Elko, NV
Inyo Mountains (IY)	Mount Inyo	11,107	Inyo, NV
Jarbidge Mountains (JB)	Matterhorn	10,839	Elko, NV
Monitor Range (MN)	Unnamed	10,888	Nye, NV
Oquirrh Mountains (OQ)	Flat Tap Mountain	10,620	Utah, UT
Panamint Range (PM)	Telescope Peak	11,049	Inyo, CA
Pequop Mountains (PQ)	Spruce Mountain	10,262	Elko, NV
Pilot Range (PR)	Pilot Peak	10,716	Elko, NV
Quinn Canyon Range (QC)	Unnamed	10,185	Nye, NV
Roberts Mountains (RC)	Roberts Creek Mountain	10,133	Eureka, NV
Ruby Mountains (RB)	Ruby Dome	11,387	Elko, NV
Schell Creek Range (SC)	North Schell Peak	11,883	White Pine, NV
Shoshone Mountains (SH)	North Shoshone Peak	10,313	Lander, NV
Snake Range (SN)	Wheeler Peak	13,063	White Pine, NV
Spring Mountains (SP)	Charleston Peak	11,912	Clark, NV
Stansbury Mountains (ST)	Deseret Peak	11,031	Tooele, UT
Sweetwater Mountains (SW)	Mount Patterson	11,673	Mono, CA
Toiyabe Range (TO)	Arc (Toiyabe) Dome	11,788	Nye, NV
Toquima Range (TQ)	Mount Jefferson, South Summit	11,941	Nye, NV
Wassuk Range (WK)	Mount Grant	11,239	Mineral, NV
White Mountains (WM)	White Mountain Peak	14,246	Mono, CA
White Pine Range (WP)	Currant Mountain	11,513	White Pine, NV

[a]Range abbreviations identify mountains in Figure 2-5.

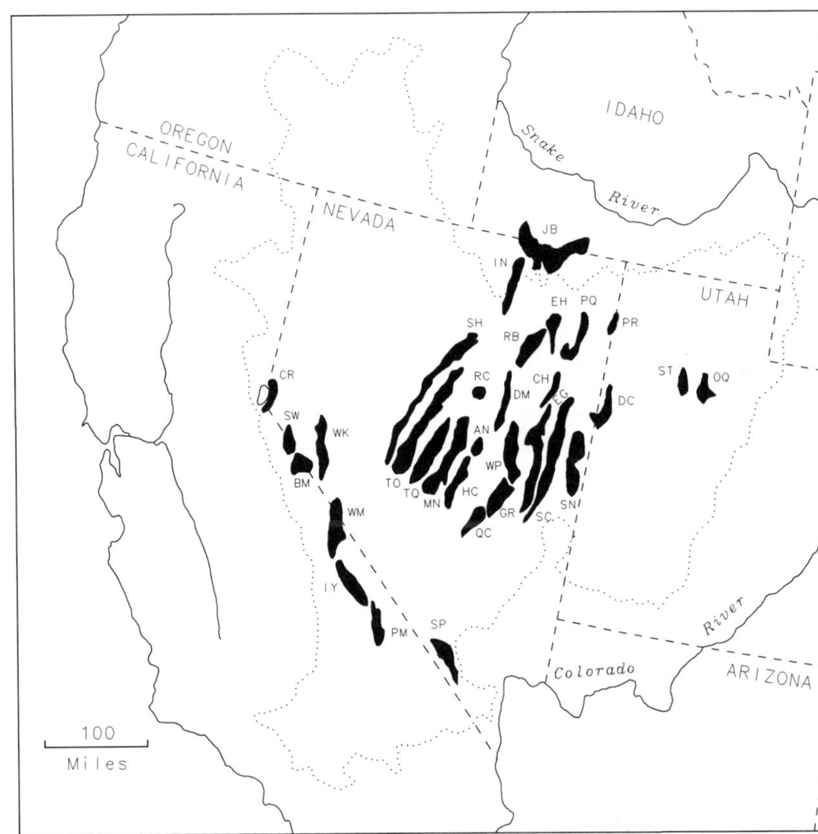

Figure 2-5. Great Basin mountain ranges with summit elevations greater than 10,000′. See Table 2-1 for key; the Duck Creek Range, which lies between the Schell Creek and Egan ranges, is not drawn.

Table 2-2. A Transect across Nevada at 39° N Latitude: The Mountains from East to West[a]

Range	Summit elevation (feet)	Length (miles)	Maximum width (miles)
Snake	13,063	68	19
Schell Creek	11,883	133	16
Egan	10,936	110	15
White Pine	11,513	52	18
Pancake	9,240	24	15
Antelope	10,104	41	7
Monitor	10,888	106	14
Toquima	11,941	78	13
Toiyabe	11,788	126	18
Shoshone	10,313	106	13
Paradise	8,657	29	13
Wassuk	11,239	65	14
Singatse	6,778	28	6
Pine Nut	9,450	39	20
Carson	10,881	51	11

[a]Maximum length and width figures primarily from McLane (1978).

graphic Great Basin. Although the northern, eastern, and western edges of this Great Basin match the drainage divide reasonably well, the southern boundary lops off a small part of the hydrographic Great Basin.

The mountains of this second Great Basin can be truly impressive. How many of them there are depends on how a "mountain" is defined, and I will simply point out that the physiographic Great Basin contains 33 ranges whose summits reach above 10,000′ (Figure 2-5). Of these 33, 16 have peaks that reach above 11,000′, whereas the summits of three—the Deep Creek Range of western Utah, the Snake Range of eastern Nevada, and the White Mountains of eastern California—rise above 12,000′. The highest point on the tallest of these mountains, White Mountain Peak in the White Mountains, reaches 14,246′ (Table 2-1).

In addition to being tall, these mountains are long, relatively narrow, and generally oriented north-south. A transect across Nevada at 39° N latitude, for instance, cuts 15 Great Basin ranges. On the eastern edge of this transect, the Snake Range runs 68 miles from north to south and includes Wheeler Peak (13,063′), the second highest point in the Great Basin. The Schell Creek Range to the immediate west runs 133 miles from north to south. After it, the Egan Range runs 110 miles in the same direction, and so on (Table 2-2). In fact, even the smallest of the ranges encountered along this transect—the Pancake Range in central Nevada—is 24 miles long. The spines of all 15 of these ranges run in the same general direction; hiking each of them would require that we walk 1,056 miles, an average of 70 miles per range.

Even though the mountains rise high above sea level, the elevations of the summits do not give a good indication of how far they rise above the surrounding valleys, because Great Basin valleys themselves tend to be quite high.

The highest valleys are in the central Great Basin of central and eastern Nevada, where valley bottoms tend to lie between 5,300′ and 6,000′, though some are higher still. From here, valley bottom elevations fall in all directions: to between about 3,800′ and 5,800′ in northwestern Nevada;

Figure 2-6. Valley bottom elevations in the Great Basin according to 1:250,000 scale U.S. Geological Survey maps.

Table 2-3. Valley Elevations used in Figure 2-6

Map	Valley	Elevation (nearest 100′)
Adel	Catlow	4,500
Alturus	Surprise	4,500
Brigham City	Great Salt Lake	4,200
Burns	Malheur Lake	4,100
Caliente	Delamar	4,400
Cedar City	Escalante Desert	5,100
Crescent	Fort Rock	4,300
Death Valley	Death Valley	–300
Delta	Sevier Desert	4,500
Elko	Ruby Valley	5,900
Ely	Steptoe	6,000
Goldfield	Sarcobatus Flat	4,000
Kingman	Eldorado	1,800
Klamath Falls	Lake Abert	4,300
Las Vegas	Dry Lake	2,000
Lovelock	Smoke Creek Desert	3,900
Lund	White River	5,200
McDermitt	Paradise	4,300
Mariposa	Owens	4,000
Millett	Reese River	5,700
Ogden	Cache Valley	4,500
Preston	Cache Valley	4,500
Reno	Carson Sink	3,900
Richfield	Escalante Desert	5,000
Salt Lake City	Utah Lake	4,500
San Bernardino	Lucerne Valley	2,900
Susanville	Honey Lake Valley	4,000
Tonopah	Monitor	6,800
Tooele	Great Salt Lake Desert	4,200
Trona	Searles	1,600
Vya	Black Rock Desert	4,000
Walker Lake	Walker Lake	4,000
Wells	Humboldt River	5,400
Winnemucca	Reese River	4,500

to between about 3,800′ and 5,000′ in western Utah; to 2,500′ and lower in the far southern Great Basin. In the far southwestern corner of the physiographic Great Basin, Death Valley's Badwater Basin falls to –282′, the lowest surface in the United States.

If the elevations of Great Basin valleys are plotted on graph paper, the diagram that results looks very much like an arch, with the peak of that arch lying in the central Great Basin. Figure 2-6 also illustrates the arch-like construction of the physiographic Great Basin. This illustration was built using the 34 1:250,000 scale U.S. Geological Survey topographic maps that cover this region, each of which displays 2° of longitude and 1° of latitude. To create this figure, I chose the largest sizable intermountain valley nearest to the center of each map, and recorded the lowest point in that valley (the only exceptions are for maps covering areas along the edges of the Great Basin; here, I simply selected the largest valley still within the Great Basin). The figure shows the results, rounded to the nearest 100′ (Table 2-3 lists the valleys and the associated elevations that are plotted in the figure). The high valleys of the central Great Basin emerge clearly, as do the decreasing valley elevations met in all directions from here, with the steepest decline to the south.

A return to the 39° N latitude transect across Nevada provides an even better feel for the mountain and valley structure of the physiographic Great Basin, and also helps place the high-elevation summits in better relief. Table 2-4 compares the lowest elevations in the valleys that intervene between the 15 ranges along this transect with the highest points on the adjacent mountains. Valley bottom to mountain top relief varies from 3,800′ (between Little Smoky Valley and the top of the Antelope Range, and between Ione Valley and the top of the Shoshone Range) to 7,600′ (from the bottom of Spring Valley to the summit of the Snake Range). Average maximum relief between valley floor and mountain top along our transect is 5,800′—over a mile.

The relief record for adjacent valley bottoms and mountain tops in the Great Basin is not set by any of the reliefs encountered along this transect. Instead, it is set by Death Valley and the adjacent Panamint Range: 11,331′ of relief from the –282′ depths of Badwater Basin to the 11,049′ summit of nearby Telescope Peak. The elevational difference between the highest (White Mountain Peak at 14,246′) and the lowest (Badwater at –282′) points in the Great Basin is an impressive 14,528′ (see Figure 2-7).

Marked by often massive north-south–trending mountain ranges with wide desert valleys between, the physiographic Great Basin coincides fairly closely with the hydrographic except in the south, where it excludes the southernmost extent of the area of internal drainage. A third approach to defining the Great Basin, however, excludes even more of the south.

Table 2-4. A Transect across Nevada at 39° N Latitude: Maximum Relief between Valleys and Adjacent Mountains

Range	Summit (feet)	Intervening valley	Basin (nearest 100′)	Maximum relief (nearest 100′)
Snake	13,063			
		Spring	5,500	7,600
Schell Creek	11,883			
		Steptoe	6,000	5,900
Egan	10,936			
		White River	5,400	6,100
White Pine	11,513			
		Railroad	5,100	6,400
Pancake	9,240			
		Little Smoky	6,300	3,800
Antelope	10,104			
		Antelope	6,300	4,600
Monitor	10,888			
		Monitor	6,500	5,500
Toquima	11,941			
		Big Smoky	5,500	6,500
Toiyabe	11,788			
		Reese River	6,200	5,600
Shoshone	10,313			
		Ione	6,500	3,800
Paradise	8,657			
		Walker River	4,100	7,100
Wassuk	11,239			
		Mason	4,300	6,900
Singatse	6,778			
		Smith	4,500	5,000
Pine Nut	9,450			
		Carson	4,700	6,200
Carson	10,881			

Figure 2-7. Death Valley from the Panamint Range; the Black Mountains, part of the Amargosa Range, are in the distance.

The Floristic Great Basin

The third approach to defining the Great Basin is biological, drawing its line around relatively distinctive assemblages of plants. This floristic or botanical Great Basin encompasses an area whose lower elevations are characterized by plant communities in which shadscale and sagebrush are the dominant shrubs, and in which the mountain flanks are marked by some combination of piñon and/or juniper woodland.

The western boundary of the floristic Great Basin is set by the appearance of the forests of the Cascades and Sierra Nevada, forests dominated by such trees as grand fir (*Abies grandis*), red fir (*Abies magnifica*), incense-cedar (*Calocedrus decurrens*), and a variety of pines—jeffrey pine (*Pinus jeffreyi*), western white pine (*P. monticola*), sugar pine (*P. lambertiana*), and ponderosa pine (*P. ponderosa*). This boundary is well defined; as botanist Dwight Billings (1990:78) has noted, "the phytogeographic boundary between the Sierra Nevada and the Great Basin is about as sharp as one finds anywhere between two large biological regions."

The eastern edge is a little more problematic. Ecologist Forrest Shreve once included all of Utah except the state's highest mountains, as well as parts of adjacent Colorado and southwestern Wyoming, in his easternmost Great Basin. Since Shreve's definition appeared in 1942, however, ecologists have tended to end the Great Basin in central Utah, along the Wasatch Range and the high Colorado Plateau. Here, Great Basin vegetation is interrupted by montane forests of white fir (*Abies concolor*), blue spruce (*Picea pungens*), Engelmann spruce (*P. englemannii*), and Douglas-fir (*Pseudotsuga menziesii*)—all trees of the Rockies.

The most widely used definition of the floristic Great Basin, that by Noel Holmgren and his colleagues, draws the northern boundary at the base of the Ochoco and Blue mountains of eastern Oregon, and just north of the Snake River Plain in eastern Idaho (see Figure 2-8). At this point, the edge of the floristic Great Basin is marked by the appearance of ponderosa pine forests, and by the occurrence of trees that do not occur to the immediate south, including grand fir and white pine. The match with the hydrographic Great Basin here is not perfect: much of

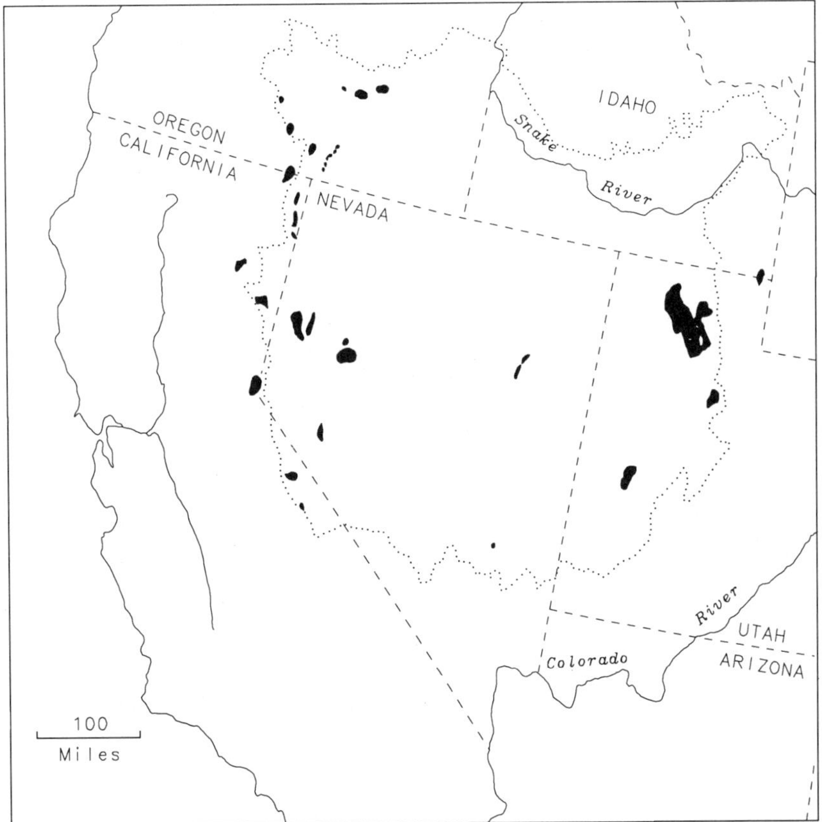

Figure 2-8. The floristic Great Basin. After Cronquist et al. (1972).

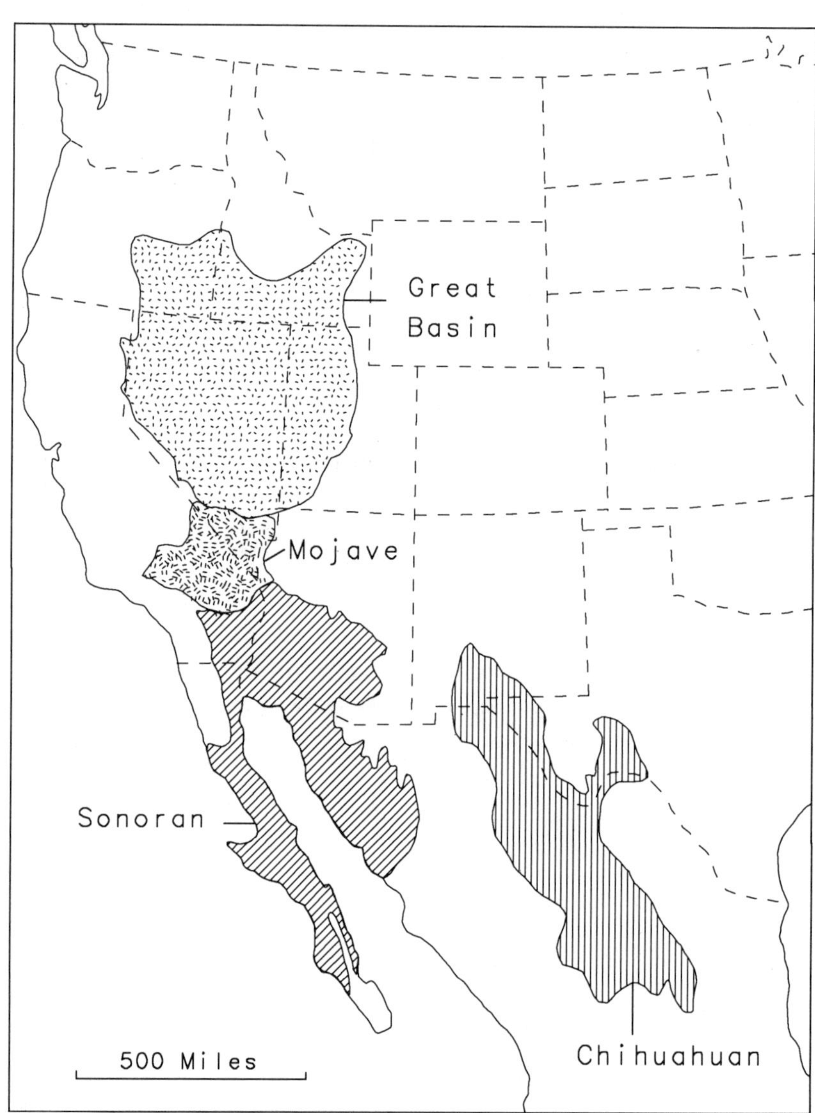

Figure 2-9. The four biologically defined North American deserts. After Spaulding et al. (1983).

southeastern Oregon and southern Idaho drains to the Snake River, and ultimately to the Pacific.

What the floristic Great Basin gains in the north, however, it loses in the south. There are four biologically defined North American deserts—the Chihuahuan, Sonoran, Mojave, and Great Basin deserts (see Figure 2-9). The Great Basin is the coldest of these, the other three all having warmer winters and hot summers. The three warm deserts also have in common the fact that, no matter how much they differ from one another in other ways, they all have creosote bush (*Larrea tridentata*).

Creosote bush, however, is not found in the botanical Great Basin. By definition, the botanical Great Basin derives its southern boundary from the northern limit of the distribution of creosote bush, a boundary that roughly follows the 4,000′ contour through southern Nevada and adjacent California.

The transition is easy to see in any part of the southern Great Basin. U.S. Highway 395, for instance, cuts through Owens Valley in eastern California. Near Big Pine, the valley floor is covered by Great Basin shrubs, including shadscale (*Atriplex confertifolia*), four-winged saltbush (*A. canescens*), and big sagebrush (*Artemisia tridentata*). Once one approaches the dry bed of Owens Lake, however, scattered individuals of a tall, wispy, dark green shrub begin to appear. Soon after, just south of the Owens Lake playa and the town of Olanche, plants that look like oddly shaped, almost deformed, trees begin to appear. The spind-

Figure 2-10. Joshua trees in Joshua Flats, eastern Inyo Mountains, California; sagebrush and rabbitbrush dominate the understory.

ly, dark green shrub is creosote bush, the presence of which marks the southern boundary of the Great Basin as a botanical unit, and the northern edge of the Mojave Desert. The strangely shaped plant is the Joshua tree (*Yucca brevifolia*). This plant, one of the most famous in the North American deserts, is confined to the higher elevations of the Mojave Desert. In the space of a few miles, the trip from Big Pine to Little Lake moves from the botanical Great Basin into the botanically defined Mojave Desert (see Figure 2-10).

This well-accepted delineation of the Great Basin as a botanical unit reduces Shreve's 1942 definition by eliminating eastern Utah and adjacent Colorado and southwestern Wyoming, but includes, as Shreve did, the Owyhee Desert of southeastern Oregon and the Snake River Plain of southern Idaho. Many botanists, however, note that the Owyhee Desert and Snake River Plain do not fall within either the hydrographic or physiographic Great Basin: the water drains to the Snake River, and there are no massive north-south–trending mountains. These botanists also note the relative simplicity of the sagebrush-grass steppe vegetation here. Seeing all that, they eliminate these two areas from the floristic Great Basin.

If that is done, a Great Basin emerges that is well defined botanically and whose borders also match very well those drawn by reference to hydrography and physiography, with the exception of the south. Here, the Mojave Desert is botanically quite distinct (creosote bush and Joshua trees are just two of the reasons), yet incorporates large areas, including Death Valley and southern Owens Valley, that drain internally and that are within the physiographic Great Basin.

Noting that valleys within the floristic Great Basin are marked by either sagebrush or shadscale and that the lower elevations of the mountains are often covered with woodland composed of piñon pine or juniper does not say very much about the vegetation of the Great Basin. A better feel for the botanical Great Basin can be gained by observing the nature of the vegetation from the bottom of a Great Basin valley to the top of an adjacent mountain.

A BOTANICAL WALK FROM MONITOR VALLEY TO MOUNT JEFFERSON

Mount Jefferson (11,941′) is the highest point in central Nevada's Toquima Range (see Figure 2-5). The bottom of Monitor Valley due east of here falls at about 6,830′, the elevation alone showing that we are in the high part of the Great Basin arch.

The vegetation of Monitor Valley at this point is dominated by two shrubs: the low black sagebrush (*Artemisia arbuscula*) and the yellow-flowered rabbitbrush (*Chrysothamnus*). Although abundant at this spot, however, these shrubs do not dominate the entire valley bottom. A dozen miles to the north, for instance, the frequently dry lake bed or playa called Monitor Lake, which sits in the lowest part of the valley at an elevation of about 6,090′, is surrounded by a dense stand of bright green big greasewood (*Sarcobatus vermiculatus*), a shrub highly tolerant of alkaline soils. Immediately adjacent to the playa, the greasewood is accompanied by saltgrass (*Distichlis spicata*), a plant whose name describes its habitat well. As one moves away from the edge of the playa, dwarf sagebrush and rabbitbrush become increasingly abundant, and soon replace the greasewood entirely.

Both shadscale and four-winged saltbush can also be found in Monitor Valley. Where they appear, these shrubs are low, widely spaced, drab gray affairs that typically cover only some 10% of the ground's surface. In other, lower-elevation, Great Basin valleys, shadscale and saltbush often dominate the vegetation.

Shadscale looks like the kind of plant one might expect to see growing in sediments that are high in salts and low in moisture. Indeed, up to 40% of the dry weight of shadscale leaves may be salt, with most of that found near the surface of the leaves themselves: the salt accumulation increases the ability of shadscale leaves to reflect sunlight. Although this adaptation is impressive, equally impressive is the life that shadscale supports.

As a group, kangaroo rats are almost ideal desert mammals. Short front feet and legs combined with large rear ones and a long tail for balance make them excellent jumpers in open desert settings. An extremely large and efficient ear apparatus provides them with an effective means of detecting predators. Their ability to extract water from their food and to concentrate their urine allows desert-dwelling kangaroo rats the luxury of never having to find free-standing water to drink.

There are five species of kangaroo rats in the Great Basin, of which four are primarily seed-eaters. Only the chisel-toothed kangaroo rat (*Dipodomys microps*) habitually eats leaves, and the leaves it eats are from shadscale. The chisel-toothed kangaroo rat is well adapted to desert conditions, but shadscale leaves are so high in salt that living on them seems nearly impossible, even for such a well-adapted creature. How do they accomplish this?

Some years ago, my colleague Jim Kenagy both posed and answered this question. The lower incisor teeth of chisel-toothed kangaroo rats are flat in cross section with a chisel-like cutting surface (hence the name of the animal); all other kangaroo rats have rounded lower incisors with more awl-like cutting edges (Figure 2-11). That fact had been known for a long time; it was Kenagy who showed why it is only these kangaroo rats that have such teeth.

They have them because they use them to strip off the outer, salt-bearing portion of shadscale leaves. Holding the leaf in their forepaws, they strip first one side, then the other, of the leaf. They leave behind a pile of leaf shavings, but eat the starchy and moist leaf interior, whose salt content can be as low as 3% of that near the leaf's surface. As a result, they are able to survive on a diet that is essentially pure shadscale leaves, although they can also survive in settings that lack this plant.

Work done on the mammals of the Monitor Valley has shown that there are two species of kangaroo rats that live in the Monitor Lake area: Ord's kangaroo rat (*Dipodomys ordii*) and the chisel-toothed kangaroo rat. They can both be found in the same set of shrubs, but they certainly do not compete intensely for food. Ord's kangaroo rat feeds primarily on seeds, whereas the chisel-toothed kangaroo rat is mainly eating the leaves from Monitor Valley's shadscale.

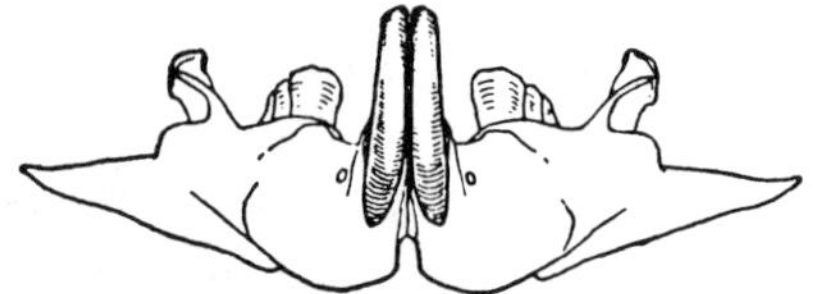

Figure 2-11. The lower incisors of chisel-toothed (right) and Ord's kangaroo rats. From E. R. Hall (1946). Copyright © 1946 Eugene Hall, courtesy of the University of California Press.

As one moves above the floor of Monitor Valley and onto the lower slopes of the Toquima Range, or into the wide canyon bottoms that emerge from the mountains, the dominant plants of the valley bottom give way to big sagebrush as the salt content of the soil decreases and as its moisture content rises. Slightly above 7,000′, the vegetation becomes dominated by big sage and a series of other shrubs with which it is often found—Nevada Mormon tea (*Ephedra nevadensis*), for instance, and two species of rabbitbrush. A variety of grasses are to be found here as well, unfortunately including downy brome or cheatgrass (*Bromus tectorum*), an introduced Eurasian species that has replaced many of our native grasses (see Chapter 11).

As one moves higher, especially in and near the gentler canyons, the sage gets thicker and taller. Although shadscale supports its share of life, the sagebrush community, with its greater plant cover, supports even more: there are, for instance, more vertebrates to be found in the sage than in the shadscale.

A fair number of Utah junipers (*Juniperus osteosperma*) descend from the mountains onto the upper slopes of Monitor Valley. Junipers, in fact, are routinely the first conifers met along the flanks of Great Basin mountains, since these trees can exist in habitats drier and colder than those tolerated by singleleaf piñon (*Pinus monophylla*).

The lowest piñon pines are generally found at slightly higher elevations than the lowest junipers. At the mouth of Pine Creek Canyon, east of Mount Jefferson, the first, lone juniper is encountered at about 7,050′ in elevation, but the piñons begin at about 7,180′. From this point, the piñon-juniper woodland continues up the canyon to an elevation of about 8,200′. By that elevation, however, the junipers are stunted, and the piñons are thriving only on the canyon's south-facing slope. Just as the first juniper was encountered lower than the first piñon, piñon continues above the point where juniper meets its elevational match. From top to bottom here, the piñon-juniper woodland is some 800′–900′ in elevational thickness, slightly narrower than its average elevational width of 1,150′.

The plants that accompany the piñon and juniper in the Toquima Range vary from place to place, but sagebrush and grasses are common members of the understory, as are Mormon tea and rabbitbrush; in wetter areas, snowberry (*Symphoricarpus*) and silver buffaloberry (*Shepherdia argentea*) take over. As in all piñon-juniper woodland, the trees rarely grow beyond 20′ in height, and their branches rarely touch—this is woodland, not forest—and the most common shrub in the understory is big sagebrush, continuing up from below.

The piñon in the Toquima Range piñon-juniper woodland is singleleaf piñon, but there are two species of piñon pine in the Great Basin. The other, Colorado piñon (*Pinus edulis*), has a wide distribution, centering on the four corners area of the Southwest, but entering the Great Basin only along its eastern edge, making it as far west as the southern end of the Schell Creek Range in southern Nevada. Where the two piñons meet, they hybridize, but throughout most of the Great Basin, the piñon in piñon-juniper woodland is *Pinus monophylla*.

Both piñons produce an extremely nutritious nut—10% protein, 25% fat, and 55% carbohydrate for singleleaf—that provided a crucial food for many Great Basin native peoples, as I will discuss shortly. Not for all Great Basin peoples, however, since piñon barely makes it north of the Humboldt River in Nevada. And, of course, without piñon, piñon-juniper woodland cannot exist north of the Humboldt, although juniper alone does.

Rocky Mountain juniper (*Juniperus scopulorum*) can also be found in piñon-juniper woodland. This tree is common in the eastern Great Basin, making it as far west as central Nevada, and both it and Utah juniper are found within the piñon-juniper woodland in the Toquima Range. This tree, however, never forms an integral part of the piñon-juniper assemblage; it seems less drought resistant than Utah juniper, and it is generally a tree of higher elevations than those in which piñon-juniper woodland is found. When Rocky Mountain juniper is found in piñon-juniper woodland, it has often followed streams and washes down from above, and this is what it does in the Toquima Range.

Given that Colorado piñon is found only along the far eastern edge of the Great Basin and that Rocky Mountain juniper descends into the piñon-juniper woodland from above, it follows that almost all of the piñon-juniper woodland in the Great Basin is assembled from singleleaf piñon and Utah juniper. Over 17,000,000 acres of the Great Basin are covered by this woodland, all on the lower and middle flanks of the mountains. Usually, piñon-juniper woodland falls between 5,000′ and 8,000′ in elevation, and it usually occurs where mean annual precipitation is between 12″ and 18″.

It is, however, not just precipitation that dictates where piñon-juniper woodland occurs. Many years ago, Dwight Billings discovered that, in the Virginia Range southeast of Reno, temperatures above and below the piñon-juniper belt were colder than they were in the belt itself. Indeed, he found that valley bottom temperatures could be as much as 15°F or so cooler than those in the woodland, and that these temperature differences lasted year-round. This belt of warmer temperatures is created by the downslope movement of colder, heavier air into the valley bottom. Such thermal belts are common—the rule rather than the exception—in the Great Basin, and Billings was cautiously impressed by the correlation he found between the placement of the thermal belt on the Virgina Range and the placement of the piñon-juniper woodland here. Later work has confirmed Billings's observations.

Neil West and his colleagues have shown that, although the average elevational thickness of the piñon-juniper woodland is 1,150′, the width declines to both the north and west in the Great Basin. Woodlands more than 1,300′ in elevational thickness are confined to the southern half of the Great Basin. To the north in Nevada, the piñon-juniper woodland tends to cover narrower elevational bands, and eventually disappears.

West and his co-workers suggest that the disappearance of the woodland is related to the disappearance of the inversion-caused thermal belts. The frontal systems that move into the Great Basin from the Pacific strengthen toward the northern reaches of this region (see Chapter 5). These frontal storms break up thermal inversions, and it is this process, they suggest, that leads first to the diminishing elevational thickness, and then to the disappearance, of piñon-juniper woodlands in the northern Great Basin. In fact, even in areas where piñon-juniper woodland generally does exist, this process seems to be at work. The west face of the northern Ruby Mountains of eastern Nevada, for instance, has no piñon-juniper woodland, apparently because there are no mountains west of here to break up inversion-destroying storm systems coming in from the west: no inversions, no woodlands.

North of the Humboldt River, there is virtually no piñon. Utah juniper makes it further north than piñon, but it, too, finally gives way, apparently because it cannot take the increased summer drought encountered in the north. So, in far northern Nevada, some ranges are devoid of piñon but still within the range of Utah juniper, and these have Utah juniper woodlands—the Granite Range, for instance, in northwestern Nevada, and the Independence, Bull Run, and Jarbidge mountains to the east. Just a little further north, there are ranges that have neither piñon nor juniper—the Santa Rosa and Pine Forest ranges, for instance.

But just a little further north of here, western juniper (*Juniperus occidentalis*) assumes the role filled by Utah juniper to the south. Unlike Utah juniper, however, western juniper is essentially a Californian species, coming from the Sierra Nevada into the lower elevations of the mountains of far northeastern California and northwestern Nevada, and spreading across southern Oregon into southwestern Idaho. It is this juniper that is seen in the arid lands of south-central Oregon (see Figure 2-12). Although it is sometimes said that western juniper never occurs with piñon in the Great Basin, the two species can occasionally be found together, as in the Panamint Range of southeastern California.

Climbing through the piñon-juniper woodland into higher elevations can be surprising, because once the trees begin to be left behind, the vegetation looks a lot like what was encountered before the woodland was entered in the first place. In the Toquima Range, the elevations at which this transition occurs vary, but, along Pine Creek beneath Mount Jefferson, the piñon becomes confined to the canyon's south-facing slope by about 8,200′ in elevation.

Here, the vegetation above the canyon bottoms is once again dominated by sagebrush, in some places much denser than that beneath the woodland, but accompanied by the same plants found with it before its dominance was interrupted by piñon and juniper. There are additions, of course, perhaps the most notable of which is curlleaf mountain mahogany (*Cercocarpus ledifolius*), which occurs individually and in small clusters in and just above the piñon-juniper woodland. Not a true mahogany at all but rather a member of the rose family, this tree is widespread in the Great Basin. Curlleaf mountain mahogany can reach great heights—well over 30′—but it was so heavily used as a source of charcoal during the mining booms of the nineteenth century that such large examples are now hard to come by.

Although there are plants like mountain mahogany that occur in the sagebrush above, but not beneath, the piñon-juniper, the upper and lower sagebrush assemblages are quite similar to one another, both on the Toquima Range and elsewhere. Seeing these similarities, Dwight Billings observed in 1951 that it almost looks as if the piñon-juniper woodland has simply been superimposed on a continuous sagebrush-grass zone, and he looked to the area north of the Humboldt Range to support this notion. Here, he noted, in places like the Santa Rosa Range where neither piñon nor juniper exists, the sagebrush-grass vegetation begins in the valleys and continues virtually uninterrupted

Figure 2-12. Paulina Marsh from the Connley Hills in south-central Oregon's Fort Rock Basin. The trees in the foreground are western juniper; the photograph was taken from just above the Connley Caves, which are discussed in later chapters.

to elevations of nearly 10,000′. Subsequent research not only has shown that the piñon-juniper assemblage does appear to have been superimposed on a more continuous sagebrush and grass plant community, but also suggests when this happened (see Chapter 8).

In the Toquima Range, as the piñon becomes confined to the south-facing slopes of Pine Creek Canyon, starting at an elevation of roughly 8,200′, another conifer begins to makes its appearance on the uppermost parts of the north-facing slopes, and along drainages cutting down those slopes. This conifer is limber pine (*Pinus flexilis*), one of a number of subalpine conifers characteristic of the upper elevations of many of the highest Great Basin mountain ranges. As higher elevations are reached, the limber pines become taller and move lower down the slopes. By the time 9,100′ has been reached, these trees cover north-facing slopes, and have begun to cover the upper reaches of the south-facing wall of the canyon as well. Another 500′ higher, and the limber pines have descended both slopes almost to the borders of the stream. We are now in subalpine conifer woodland.

On the Toquima Range, limber pine is the only subalpine conifer, growing here in number from about 9,600′ to just over 11,000′ in elevation (see Figure 2-13). There are much lower limber pines in the Toquima Range, since they follow cold air drainages thousands of feet downward, and I have seen limber pine as low as 8,000′ or so in this range, in the heart of piñon-juniper woodland. But these are special situations, and most of the limber pine on the Toquima Range is restricted to 9,600′ or so and above—nearly the uppermost parts of the mountain.

The higher elevations of other Great Basin mountains may have other subalpine conifers; many, in fact, have several of them. In ranges some distance from both the Sierra Nevada and the Wasatch Range, these additional subalpine conifers include bristlecone pine (*Pinus longaeva*), whitebark pine (*P. albicaulis*), Englemann spruce, and subalpine fir (*Abies lasiocarpa*).

Any of these trees can actually be found at surprisingly low levels. There is, for instance, a very healthy 75-year-old bristlecone pine sitting at 5,800′ on the eastern edge of the Snake Range in far eastern Nevada. Located in the bottom of a canyon that drains both air and moisture from above, this tree looks starkly out of place, but the only threat to its continued existence would appear to be botanists, who, unaware that its existence has been reported, break off

Figure 2-13. Treeline and alpine tundra in the Toquima Range, central Nevada, at approximately 11,000′. The trees are limber pine; the archaeological site of Alta Toquima, discussed in Chapter 9, lies just above and adjacent to the trees.

pieces to take as voucher specimens. But even though bristlecone pine can descend to 5,800′ in the Snake Range, and limber pine can penetrate well into the piñon-juniper woodland in the Toquima Range, these trees do not occur in any number on these mountains beneath an elevation of 9,500′ or so. Above that point, they can form anything up to and including true subalpine forests.

These five subalpine conifers do not occur only in the Great Basin, of course, and their other locations have been used to suggest a general truth about the affinities of the montane floras of the Great Basin as a whole.

The Sierra Nevada rises to the west of the Great Basin; the Rockies rise to the east. Both highlands would seem to provide an excellent potential source of plants for the mountains that fall in between. In fact, however, Sierran and Rocky Mountain contributions to the Great Basin flora differ greatly from one another. For instance, the five subalpine conifers I have mentioned are found in both the Rocky Mountains and the Great Basin, but only two of them also occur in the Sierra Nevada. That is, the affinities of the subalpine trees of the Great Basin appear to be to the east, not to the west: to the Rockies and not to the Sierra Nevada.

We can take this analysis one step further and look not just at subalpine conifers, but at all conifers that occur in the Great Basin well above the piñon-juniper woodlands. There are 11 of these, all listed in Table 2-5, which I have taken from the work of botanist Philip Wells. As Table 2-5 shows, all 11 are found in the Rockies; only three are shared with the Sierra Nevada. Just as important, none of the montane conifers in the Great Basin is found only in the Sierra Nevada, but eight of them are found only in the Rockies. These relationships are impressively unequal.

This is not to say that no Sierran conifers make it into the Great Basin. Western juniper is Sierran and makes it all the way across southern Oregon into southwestern Idaho, as well as into the Panamint Range. Nor is it to say that no truly Sierran montane conifers make it into the Great Basin at all; the table lists only those that make it some distance into the area. There are a number that penetrate a short distance into the western Great Basin from the Sierra Nevada. Incense-cedar and Washoe pine (*Pinus washoensis*) make it to the Warner Mountains. Western white pine makes it into the Virgina Mountains, the Pine Nut Range, and the Warners. Jeffrey pine is in the White Mountains, the Wassuk Range, the Virginia Range, the Bodie Hills, and

Table 2-5. Sierran and Rocky Mountain Montane Conifers Also Found in the Great Basin[a]

Great Basin conifer	Sierra Nevada	Rocky Mountains
White Fir (*Abies concolor concolor*)		+
Subalpine Fir (*Abies lasiocarpa*)		+
Common Juniper (*Juniperus communis*)	+	+
Rocky Mountain Juniper (*Juniperus scopulorum*)		+
Englemann Spruce (*Picea englemannii*)		+
Whitebark Pine (*Pinus albicaulis*)	+	+
Lodgepole Pine (*Pinus contorta latifolia*)		+
Limber Pine (*Pinus flexilis*)	+	+
Bristlecone Pine (*Pinus longaeva*)		+
Ponderosa Pine (*Pinus ponderosa scopulorum*)		+
Douglas-fir (*Pseudotsuga menziesii glauca*)		+

[a]After P. V. Wells (1983).

elsewhere. The Sierran form of ponderosa pine is found 35 miles east of Reno. But no Sierran conifer gets very far east into the Great Basin, whereas Rocky Mountain conifers make it all the way across.

This pattern applies to Great Basin montane floras as a whole. From grasses to sages to buttercups and pines, the affinities of the floras of Great Basin mountains are closer to the Rockies than to the Sierra Nevada. K. T. Harper and his colleagues have shown that plant species from the Rockies appear to have been about four times more successful in reaching Great Basin mountains than have species from the Sierra Nevada. Indeed, even the floras of the mountains closest to the Sierra Nevada have a greater affinity to the Rocky Mountain flora than to that of the Sierra Nevada. In the sample amassed by Harper and his co-workers, only the White Mountains, just across the Owens Valley from the Sierra Nevada, violate this rule. In fact, the Rocky Mountain affinities of Great Basin montane floras remain even when plants that disperse in different ways are looked at separately: wind-dispersed plants, plants that disperse by sticking to animals, those with fleshy parts that are eaten—all behave the same way.

Why should this be? Why should mountain ranges a few dozen miles downwind from the massive Sierra Nevada and hundreds of miles away from the Rocky Mountains have their affinities to the latter and not to the former?

A number of factors appear to account for this seemingly odd relationship, factors that have been suggested by such botanists as K. T. Harper, Philip Wells, and James L. Reveal. First, Sierran species as a group are at a climatic disadvantage in any attempt to colonize the Great Basin. These species are adapted to wetter, more maritime conditions than their Rocky Mountain counterparts, which are adapted to drier, more continental conditions that are far more like those encountered in the Great Basin. In addition, the soils of the Sierra Nevada are often acidic, developed as the result of the weathering of igneous rocks. The soils of the Rockies are often basic, developed from the weathering of calcareous rocks. Since the soils of Great Basin mountains are often basic, Rocky Mountain plants, adapted to the conditions such soils present, do much better here than do Sierran plants.

In a classic study of the distribution of Sierran ponderosa and Jeffrey pines in the ranges just east of the Sierra Nevada, Dwight Billings showed that, in every instance, these trees grow on acidic soils developed from volcanic rocks affected by heated waters charged with sulfur: acidic soils, Sierran plants. More recent work, done by E. H. DeLucia, W. H. Schlesinger, and Billings, has shown that these altered sites are deficient in nutrients, particularly phosphorus, and that it is this deficiency that prevents colonization by typical Great Basin vegetation, including sagebrush. The Sierran conifers, on the other hand, are excluded from adjacent, unaltered soil because their seedlings cannot compete with Great Basin grasses and shrubs for moisture.

Beyond considerations of climate and soil, time and geographic barriers have probably also played a role in determining the unequal affinities of the plants of the Sierra Nevada and Rocky Mountains to those of the Great Basin mountains. The Rocky Mountains are older than the mountains of the Great Basin, whereas the Sierra Nevada is younger. As a result, plants from the east have had more time to colonize this area than plants from the west. Rocky Mountain species may have been well established in the Great Basin by the time Sierran plants were able to make the attempt.

And, in making that attempt, they would have had to deal with a structural barrier that did not exist to the east. With rare exceptions, the entire western edge of the floristic Great Basin, from its boundary with the Mojave Desert on the south to its junction with the Columbia Plateau on the north, lies below 6,600′. This relatively low area divides the Sierra Nevada and its immediate mountainous outliers—the White Mountains and the Wassuk Range, for instance—from the massive ranges of central Nevada.

James Reveal has called this low-lying region the "Lahontan Trough." Although this trough seems to have acted as a conduit for some Mojavean species to move north, it may also have functioned as a barrier to at least reduce the rate at which propagules of Sierran plants reached the mountains to the east. Reduced rates of dispersal translate into reduced chances of success. Rocky Mountain species encountered no such low-elevation barrier. Although the huge Bonneville Basin, in which Great Salt Lake sits, occupies the northern half of much of western Utah, and although much of the southern half of the Great Basin in Utah is below 6,600′ in elevation, stepping-stones in the form of major mountain masses exist at both the northern and southern ends of this eastern trough. These mountainous stepping-stones provide high-elevation areas of access to the Great Basin from the Rockies. Comparable montane bridges simply do not, and did not, exist for Sierran plants.

For all of these, and undoubtedly for other, reasons, Great Basin mountains are stocked with plants whose affinities are to the east rather than to the west. This situation pertains not just to the subalpine conifers with which I began this discussion, but to most aspects of Great Basin montane floras. Indeed, it even seems to apply to birds. Ornithologist William Behle has pointed out that there is greater evidence for Rocky Mountain birds having penetrated deep into the Great Basin than there is for Sierran birds having done so. The ebb and flow of life in Great Basin mountains appears to have been east to west, not west to east, and nowhere is this more evident than for the montane plants of the Great Basin. Even though this appears to be the case, however, there are arguments against it, drawn largely from paleontology, and these I will discuss in Chapter 6.

No matter where the trees came from, as we move upward through the subalpine conifers on a Great Basin mountain—for instance, through the limber pine on the Toquima Range—a number of things may happen, depending largely, though not entirely, on the elevation and mass of the mountain. The trees may go all the way to the top. This, in fact, is what happens on parts of the Toquima Range due west of Monitor Lake. The mountain is simply not tall enough at this point to provide conditions that exceed the tolerance limits of limber pine. On truly massive mountains, however, as higher elevations are reached, the subalpine conifers ultimately give way to treeless vegetation—true alpine tundra and alpine desert above a true timberline (see Figure 2-13).

Timberlines are never as sharp and are rarely as horizontal as they appear to be from a distance. The upper edge of tree distribution is generally caused by decreased summertime temperatures, and in particular by a growing season that has decreased beyond the point at which successful reproduction can occur. Indeed, both arctic and alpine timberlines (one latitudinal, one elevational) tend to fall at the 50°F July isotherm. Aspects of topography that increase summer temperatures on a given mountain also increase the local elevation of the timberline, and those that decrease summer temperatures decrease that elevation. Thus, on Northern Hemisphere mountains, trees rise higher on southern and western exposures than they do on northern and eastern ones, since it is the southern and western slopes that gain the full benefits of the summer afternoon sun. Similarly, trees rise higher on ridges, and tundra descends lower in hollows, because of cold air drainage, and also because snow accumulation can be so great in canyon heads as to prevent tree reproduction during the warmer months.

As a result, timberlines are generally ragged, swinging upslope and down depending on local topography. The nature of the trees themselves may vary as we approach timberline, often becoming dwarfed and stunted, and at times taking on the peculiar form known as krummholz (see Figure 2-14).

Formed as the result of intense wind, krummholz trees are often low and matted; they are frequently single-tree

Figure 2-14. Krummholz limber pine at 11,000′ on the Toiyabe Range; Arc Dome, the summit of the range, is in the background.

thickets up to about 3′ tall, sometimes taller, that can cover a patch of ground 50′ or more wide. Small krummholz trees can also exist in the lee of rocks and in other sheltered places, but it is generally the shrubby thickets that catch the eye at the upper timberline.

Not all trees form krummholz, but in the Great Basin all five subalpine conifers—limber pine, bristlecone pine, Engelmann spruce, whitebark pine, and subalpine fir—do. Engelmann spruce krummholz, for instance, occurs on Mount Moriah in the Snake Range; subalpine fir krummholz on Willard Peak on the eastern flank of the Great Basin; limber pine krummholz on the Toiyabe Range; whitebark pine krummholz on the Carson Range; and bristlecone pine krummholz on Mount Washington in the southern Snake Range (the only place in the Great Basin where this is known to happen). There is even piñon pine krummholz on the Panamint Range.

Mechanical abrasion by winter winds and their pelting loads of ice and snow can be important in dictating the form of krummholz. However, those winds play an even more important role in krummholz formation by desiccating exposed needles at a time when stems and roots are frozen and so cannot replace lost water. Hence, krummholz height mirrors winter snow cover, since the covered needles are protected from the wind.

Botanist John Marr has even shown that winds can cause a single krummholz tree to walk across the landscape, as the upwind edge is battered and destroyed by wind dessication, while the downwind end roots its branches and reproduces vegetatively. If downwind growth exceeds upwind destruction, the plant can move into an area where it could not have begun life in the first place, leaving behind a trail of dead wood as it advances. In his study of Engelmann spruce and subalpine fir krummholz in the Front Range of the Colorado Rockies, the largest such trails Marr found were over 50′ long; the nearest sheltered site at which one of these might have gotten its start was some 165′ away. Given that the most rapid growth downwind that Marr could document was on the order of 23″ per century, this krummholz tree may have taken 700 years to get where Marr found it a few years ago.

On the Toquima Range, there is only limber pine, and the interface between it and alpine tundra begins at about 11,000′. Limber pine krummholz, however, extends up to some 11,500′ on Mount Jefferson in the central Toquima

Figure 2-15. The central Toquima Range, as seen from the Monitor Range; piñon-juniper woodland forms the lower band of trees, and limber pine woodland forms the upper band.

Range, whereas alpine tundra extends beneath 11,000′ in topographic concavities that act as cold air traps and that accumulate massive quantities of snow in the winter. Indeed, just as the first limber pines we encountered on the way up the Toquima Range were on the north-facing slope of Pine Creek Canyon, the last ones found here are on the south-facing slope. The Toquima Range timberline is jagged, as timberlines usually are.

Once above the trees, the vegetational landscape is distinctly different. Not only are the trees gone, but so are the shrubs that have accompanied us since we entered the foothills of the mountains. These above-timberline environments are marked by the dominance of low, perennial herbaceous vegetation and by dwarf shrubs. Not surprisingly, these are among the least well known of Great Basin environments, not so much because they can be inhospitable, even in the summer, but because they are so inaccessible.

Just as with plants from lower elevations in Great Basin mountains, Rocky Mountain alpine tundra species are found further west in the Great Basin than Sierran alpine tundra plants are found east. Work done by Dwight Billings suggests that strong similarities between the alpine floras of the Sierra Nevada and the Great Basin exist only with the closest Great Basin ranges, such as the White Mountains. Rocky Mountain similarities, on the other hand, extend deep into the west, to include the Deep Creek and Ruby mountains.

Other affinities extend to the true arctic tundra of the far north, the similarities here reflecting the opportunities for north-south movement along high-elevation routes. In the Beartooth Mountains of the Rockies, Billings has shown, nearly half of the plant species in the alpine vegetation are found in the arctic as well, but that number drops dramatically as the Great Basin is entered. In the Deep Creek Range, 30% of the alpine species are shared with the arctic; in the Ruby Mountains, 25%; in the Toiyabe Range, 23%. The numbers reflect the poor long-distance colonizing abilities of tundra plants, as well as the route that the Rockies provide to the direct north. Indeed, many Great Basin alpine tundra plants seem derived not from the west, east, or north, but instead from lower-elevation desert forms.

On the Toquima Range, alpine tundra vegetation is found from the upper timberline to the top of Mount Jefferson's South Summit (11,941′), the highest point on the mountain. From the edge of the Mount Jefferson plateau, the Monitor Lake playa, some 5,000′ below, is clearly visible. Also clearly visible is the vegetation encountered on the way up, vegetation that appears as if it had been layered in zones (see Figure 2-15).

These zones were named by Billings in 1951. Even though a much more detailed set of names now exists to describe the plant associations of the Great Basin, the names Billings provided remain appropriate, and I will use them here. In the valley bottom is Billings's *Shadscale Zone,* although it is poorly developed in high-elevation Monitor Valley. Slightly higher, the *Sagebrush-Grass Zone* is visible as a grayish-green apron on the upper valley and lower mountain flanks; above it occurs the first stripe of timber—the *Piñon-Juniper Zone,* sitting in the thermal inversion belt, and looking far more ragged from above than it looked from the valley bottom. The upper edge of the Piñon-Juniper Zone is marked by another grayish-green interruption in the trees, the *Upper Sagebrush-Grass Zone.* Then the second stripe of timber, here composed only of limber pine, but generally called the *Limber Pine–Bristlecone Pine Zone,* reflecting the fact that limber pine is not always the only conifer in this subalpine belt (in fact, the Monitor Range, directly to the east, has both limber and bristlecone pines).

The upper edge of the limber pine provides the second Toquima Range timberline, the first created by piñon pine some 2,500′ down ("double timberlines" Billings called them). From above, we can again see how ragged the interface between subalpine conifers and alpine herbaceous vegetation really is. Then, finally, the vegetation that characterizes the uppermost reaches of the Toquima Range, Billings's *Alpine Tundra Zone.* In a little more than 5,000′ in elevation, we have passed through the six classic vegetation zones to be found in the heart of the Great Basin.

Although these zones exist in the central part of the Great Basin, they do not exist everywhere in the region. There are a number of ways in which this is true. Some mountains, for instance, are not tall enough to reach above the Upper Sagebrush-Grass Zone, or even above the Piñon-Juniper Zone. The Piñon-Juniper Zone does not make it north of the Humboldt River, and there are even massive, tall mountains, like Steens in south-central Oregon, that have no subalpine conifers on them. More important, however is the fact that, as either the Rocky Mountains to east or the Sierra Nevada to the west is approached, the montane vegetational zones become distinctly different.

On the east, a chaparral of Gambel oak (*Quercus gambelii*) and bigtooth maple (*Acer grandidentatum*) lies above the sagebrush and grass on the flanks of the Wasatch Range overlooking Great Salt and Utah lakes. This chaparral is, in turn, surmounted by forests of Douglas-fir, white fir, and blue spruce. Above 10,000′, subalpine conifers—Engelmann spruce, subalpine fir, and, on drier sites, limber pine—extend to timberline; above timberline, alpine tundra is once again encountered.

I have discussed the weak penetration of Sierran conifers east into the Great Basin. Sierran montane plant zones per se, as opposed to individual species of trees that have moved eastward, are well represented only on the Carson Range, between Lake Tahoe and Reno, and, of course, on the eastern flank of the Sierra Nevada itself. On the Carson Range, yellow pines—ponderosa and jeffrey—and white firs begin above the piñon-juniper woodland and extend upward to about 7,500′ in elevation. Then come the red firs, often alone, but often with lodgepole pine (*Pinus contorta*), western white pine, and mountain hemlock (*Tsuga mertensiana*). Above about 8,300′, the lodgepole pines and mountain hemlocks become dominant, but these give way to, or actually join, the subalpine conifers—whitebark pine and limber pine. Timberline falls at about 10,300′ on the Carson Range; above this, alpine vegetation takes over.

THE VERTEBRATES OF THE FLORISTIC GREAT BASIN

While the hydrographic Great Basin is an abstraction, seen only by circling it and following its waters and ultimately realizing that none flow out, the botanical Great Basin is the one that seems to impinge most directly on the senses. It is certainly interesting, as well as both geologically and economically important, that Great Basin waters flow inward, but it is the plants and the things that live in, on, and around them that form the immediacy of the Great Basin when you are in it.

Although the floristic Great Basin is defined on the basis of its plants, the vertebrates that live here are equally remarkable. There are, for instance, nearly 100 species of mammals known from the Great Basin. The Malheur National Wildlife Refuge lists 230 species of birds recorded in this part of south-central Oregon; the Ruby Lake National Wildlife Refuge lists 225. Both of these lists reflect only those birds seen in and around the particular low-elevation wetlands that led these places to become refuges. Gordon Alcorn lists 456 species of birds recorded from, or probably to be found in, the state of Nevada alone. Add the native snakes, lizards, frogs, turtles, and fishes, and there are well over 600 species of vertebrates living in the Great Basin.

How most of these animals reached, or reach, the Great Basin poses no mystery. The greater scaup (*Aythya marila*) breeds in the far north and winters on both the Atlantic and the Pacific coasts; it is occasionally found in the Great

Basin as it makes its way from wintering to breeding grounds or vice versa. The northern shrike (*Lanius excubitor*) and snowy owl (*Nyctea scandiaca*) both breed north of the Canadian border; during winter, the shrikes frequently, and the owls occasionally, move as far south as the Great Basin. The western patch-nosed snake (*Salvadora hexalepis*) and the western ground snake (*Sonora semiannulata*) apparently moved north into Nevada (and into Oregon for the western ground snake) by following the Lahontan Trough out of the Mojave Desert. Merriam's kangaroo rat follows the shadscale up the same trough, reaching far northwestern Nevada.

Other vertebrates appear to pose real mysteries. The Devil's Hole pupfish (*Cyprinodon diabolis*) exists only one place on earth: in a pool in a rock-bound hole only some 23′ across in Ash Meadows, southern Nevada. How did it get here? The Salt Creek pupfish (*Cyprinodon salinus*) is a Death Valley specialty: how did it come to be in one of the hottest and driest places on earth?

Mammals provide equally intriguing questions. Pikas (*Ochotona princeps*) are small, short-eared mammals closely related to jack rabbits and cottontails. They are generally restricted to higher latitudes, but they are also found at high elevations in western North America. Desert environments are absolutely inimical to pikas: they simply cannot take the summer heat of lower elevations, and die in a few hours if they are exposed to it. So it is no surprise that there are no pikas in Great Basin valleys. However, there are pikas in a number of Great Basin mountains, each of which is surrounded by valleys in which no pika can or does live. In southeastern California, there are large populations of pikas on the White Mountains; in central Nevada, they live on the Desatoya, Toiyabe, Toquima, Monitor, and Shoshone ranges. In eastern Nevada, they are found on the Rubies. How could this have happened? And, equally intriguing, given that it did happen, why are there no pikas on apparently similar mountains, like the Snake, Egan, and Schell Creek ranges?

Other mammals show very similar distributions. Yellow-bellied marmots (*Marmota flaviventris*) occur in many Great Basin mountains south of the Humboldt River, but in none of the valleys. How did they get to these mountains? The same is true for bushy-tailed packrats (*Neotoma cinerea*) and some dozen others. All of these animals provide distributional mysteries, the likely solutions to which I will discuss in Chapters 7 and 8.

The Ethnographic Great Basin

The hydrographic, physiographic, and botanic Great Basins look to drainage, landforms, and plants, respectively, to define three different Great Basins. These definitions are known to one degree or another to almost every geologist or life scientist who works in the area. The fourth and last Great Basin, however, is defined on the basis of the native peoples who lived in the area at the time Europeans first arrived. It is far less well known than the other three, primarily because the native peoples of the Great Basin are no longer a highly visible part of the landscape, Euroamericans having taken over from them in that role.

For over a century, anthropologists have divided the peoples of the world into groups based on the similarity of the cultures possessed by those peoples. These "culture areas" cluster peoples who are behaviorally more similar to one another than they are to peoples outside of that unit. Culture areas do not take into account how the peoples involved perceive each other, or how they get along with one another. Nor are the borders drawn around single sociopolitical entities like "tribes." Instead, culture areas group together sets of people on the basis of similarities in such things as the nature of their subsistence pursuits, their sociopolitical organization, their material manufactures, and their religion.

The Great Basin Culture Area of anthropologists provides yet another Great Basin, a spatial grouping of peoples far more similar to one another than they were to peoples in adjacent culture areas. Although large-scale groupings of people based on cultural similarities do not often coincide well with groupings independently derived from considerations of linguistic relationships, the Great Basin is one place where the match between language and culture was nearly, though not quite, perfect.

When linguists classify languages into groups that reflect their historical relatedness, they do so hierarchically. A language—generally composed of a set of mutually intelligible dialects—is lumped with other, similar languages into a higher-order unit, generally called a language family. Similar language families are then grouped into an even higher-order unit, generally called a phylum. Among European languages, for instance, Italian, French, Portuguese, Provençal, and Romanian are grouped into a Romance family, all the members of which are derived from Latin. English, German, Yiddish, Dutch, Swedish, Danish, and others are grouped into a Germanic family.

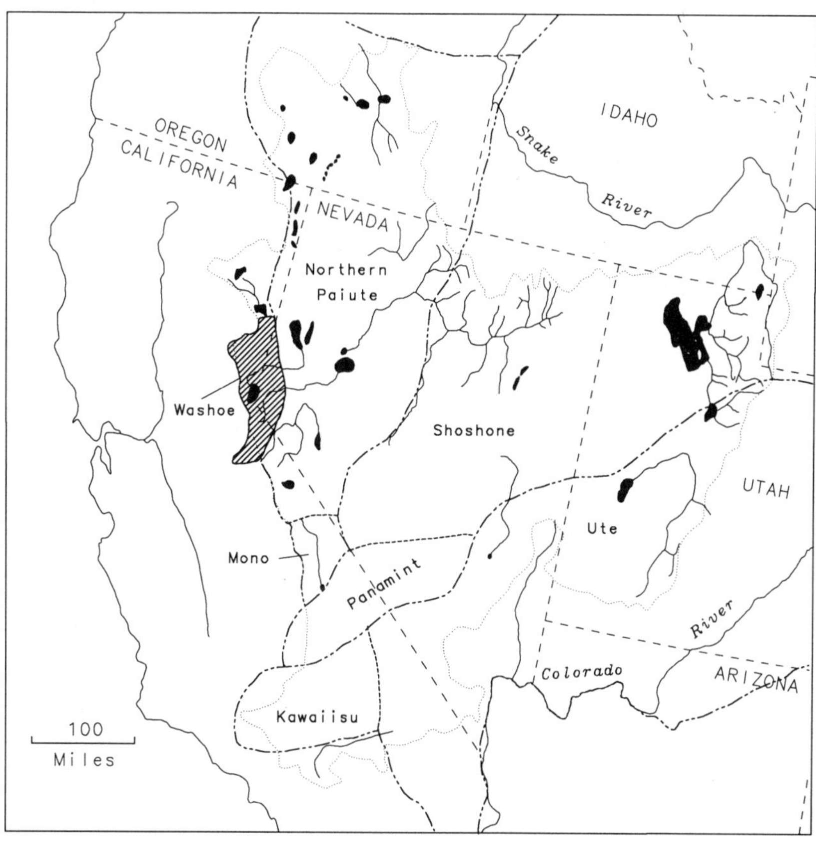

Figure 2-16. The Great Basin as a culture area. After d'Azevedo (1986).

Ukranian, Polish, Russian, Serbo-Croatian, and others are grouped into Slavic. Although the languages within each of these families show strong similarities to one another, the families themselves are also similar to one another and quite clearly share a common ancestor. As a result, the Germanic, Slavic, and Romance languages are grouped into a higher-order category called Indo-European. Other language families in this group include Celtic (which in turn includes Gaelic and Welsh) and Baltic (Latvian and Lithuanian), and, in its own family, Greek. Such groupings directly reflect history because they directly reflect commonality and closeness of descent.

It is not clear how many languages were spoken in North America at the time of the first European contact, but there were hundreds of them; one influential study listed 221 that were sufficiently well known to attempt to classify. The ties of historical relatedness indicated by analyses of those languages are fascinating. The speakers of languages belonging to the the Uto-Aztecan language family, for instance, lived, and live, from southeastern Oregon to Panama. Nahuatl, the language of the Aztecs and their modern descendants, is Uto-Aztecan, as is the language of the Hopi of Arizona. If the languages are related, the people are related, and so it is with the Hopi and the Aztec, just as it is with the French and the Italians. And so it is as well with nearly all of the native peoples of the Great Basin: with one exception, they were and are Uto-Aztecan speakers, and thus are closely related to both Aztecs and Hopi.

There are six Uto-Aztecan languages in the Great Basin, all extremely similar to one another, and all grouped into a single branch of Uto-Aztecan called Numic (see Figure 2-16). The similarities and differences among Numic languages show them to fall into three natural groups, each consisting of two languages. These three subdivisions are often simply called Western, Central, and Southern Numic, though linguists will also call them by the names of the languages of which they are composed: Mono-Paviotso, Panamint-Shoshone, and Kawaiisu-Ute.

Even more interesting, perhaps, is the fact that the first language in each one of these pairs occupied a very small part of the far southwestern Great Basin, whereas the second in each pair spread out over vast distances to the north and east. Mono speakers, for instance, occupied the

Owens River valley in southeastern California; Paviotso (Northern Paiute), its match in the pair, spread from about Mono Lake well into southeastern Oregon. The speakers of Kawaiisu lived in an area running from the Mojave River to the mountains bordering the San Joaquin Valley. The speakers of Ute spread out from their border with the Kawaiisu, east and north across southern Nevada, much of Utah, and ultimately into Colorado. The area between the Mono and Kawaiisu, focusing on Death Valley, was occupied by the Panamint; the speakers of the second in this language pair, Shoshone, spread out from here through central Nevada and across northern Utah into southern Idaho and adjacent Wyoming.

Languages are often composed of several mutually intelligible dialects, and the Numic languages are no exception. The pattern of Numic dialectical variation, however, is intriguing, since most of it occurs in the far southwestern corner of the Great Basin. Although Kawaiisu (with only 30 elderly speakers left by the early 1980s) has not been shown to have any dialects, dialectical variation within both Mono and Panamint is greater than that within the far more widespread Paviotso, Shoshone, and Ute. In addition, dialectical variation within these three widespread Numic languages is greatest where they approach the borders of Mono, Paviotso, and Kawaiisu.

Given that dialectical variation develops as a result of diminished opportunities for contact between peoples, and that such divergence often reflects distance in both time and space, one might guess that those languages that are most widespread would also have the greatest dialectical diversity. This is not the case in the Great Basin. The fact that most of the linguistic diversity in the Great Basin is found in its southwestern corner has led some to argue that this corner—roughly centered on Death Valley—represents the homeland of Numic speakers, from which they have spread out across the Great Basin, perhaps in relatively recent times. This notion, of relatively recent Numic expansion across the Great Basin, accounts very well for the geographic distribution of linguistic variation in the Great Basin, since the longer residence times in the southwestern part of the area explain why linguistic divergence is greater here. Whether or not such relatively recent expansion actually occurred, however, is a different issue, as I will discuss in Chapter 9.

One group of Numic speakers most certainly did expand outward in relatively recent times, although this movement has nothing to do with the hypothesized late prehistoric Numic expansion. During the eighteenth and nineteenth centuries, Ute and Shoshone speakers on the edge of central and southern Numic territory obtained the horse from the Spanish and began to hunt bison on the western Plains. One of the Shoshonean groups, the Comanche, moved deep into the southern Plains, breaking contact with their Great Basin relatives. As a result of their linguistic isolation, the language spoken by the Comanche diverged sufficiently from Shoshone that it is now treated as a separate, seventh, Numic language. The Comanche, however, diverged culturally as well, and belong to the Plains, not to the Great Basin, culture area.

In addition to Numic speakers, the anthropological Great Basin includes another group of people, the Washoe, whose territory roughly centered on Lake Tahoe, but also extended along a 100-mile-wide strip on and adjacent to the eastern flanks of the Sierra Nevada. Today, both Reno and Carson City sit in territory once occupied by the Washoe. Although the Washoe are culturally very similar to the Numic speakers of the Great Basin, their language is quite distinct. Along with a variety of primarily Californian and Southwestern languages, it is placed in a phylum called Hokan. Linguistically, the Washoe are far more closely related to a number of Californian groups than they are to Numic speakers, even though their life-style allies them with the Great Basin and not with California.

The classic picture of native American lifeways in the Great Basin was drawn by the ethnographer Julian Steward. Steward's description and analysis of Great Basin peoples depended not only on the observations of other ethnographers, but also on fieldwork that he conducted among these peoples during the 1920s and 1930s. Although he published a variety of papers and monographs dealing with the Great Basin, Steward's most influential work, his *Basin-Plateau Aboriginal Sociopolitical Groups,* appeared in 1938. Over 50 years old, this volume is the key reference to the aboriginal lifeways of Great Basin native peoples.

Steward argued that the sparse, scattered, and unpredictable nature of resources in the Great Basin dictated that the basic economic unit in this area be the nuclear family—parents, children, and sometimes grandparents, averaging about six people in size. Throughout much of the Great Basin, plants in general, and seeds in particular, were of extreme dietary importance, and a highly sophisticated technology, from stone grinding tools to basketry seed-beaters and winnowing trays, existed to harvest and process plant foods. The gathering and preparation of plant foods was the realm of women, and their economic contribution was essential to the well-being of any family.

Plant foods formed the core of the diet; but animal products were important for the nutrition they provided and for such things as skins for clothing, bone for tools, and sinew for a wide variety of purposes. Although both men and women took smaller game, the larger mammals—antelope, deer, mountain sheep, and, in some areas, bison—were hunted by the men. The economic efforts of male and female were essential to the success, even survival, of both sexes. Accordingly, Steward argued, groups smaller than the nuclear family could not exist for long.

Steward also argued that, with rare exceptions, the food resources of the Great Basin were too meager to support large groups on a routine basis. In much of the area, Steward maintained, the largest single settlement was the winter village, where families gathered when new stores of plant foods could no longer be obtained. The location of a winter village was determined by ease of access to a series of critical resources. Perhaps most importantly, the villages were located near sites where foods gathered earlier in the year had been stored. Since piñon nuts usually provided the prime overwintering resource, winter villages were typically located in an area where substantial amounts of these nuts had been cached. In addition to stored foods, access to water and wood, for construction and fuel, was also critical. Within the list of places that met these needs, the winter village would also be located in such a way as to avoid the coldest temperatures winter might have to offer.

Given these requirements, it is probably no surprise that the winter settlements were often placed at the lower edge of the piñon-juniper woodland. Such a placement minimized the costs that would be incurred in transporting large quantities of pine nuts elsewhere. In addition, because of the thermal inversions that develop in the Great Basin—the same inversions that seem to be so important to the development of the piñon-juniper zone in the first place—locating the winter villages at the base of the piñon-juniper woodland provided a setting that was as much as 15°F or so warmer than the valley bottoms. Those inversions, however, are destroyed by storm systems coming in from the west, especially on mountains that are not protected to the west by other ranges. The temperature advantage, then, would be greatest on the east flank of a range, and Steward's 1938 maps of winter village locations show that most of those that were in the mountains were indeed on the east sides of those mountains.

Winter villages, however, could also be located in other places—in the mouths of canyons, for instance, or along valley bottom streams that could provide fish. In Owens Valley, to take one example, the decision as to whether to winter in the valley or in the piñon-juniper zone depended heavily on the nature of the fall piñon crop. If that crop were large, and the transportation costs involved in moving it down to the valley correspondingly high, people might winter in the mountains. If it were poor, and the transportation costs correspondingly low, greater advantages were to be had by remaining in the valley.

The decisions made in Owens Valley concerning winter village location were similar to those made elsewhere in the Great Basin in that the location of these villages depended heavily on resource availability and resource productivity in a given year. As those things changed from year to year, so did winter village locations change. With rare exceptions, Steward argued, people did not know during any given winter exactly where or with whom they would be spending the next one.

How many people a winter village held in a particular year depended on the abundance of the resources that were available near that village. If stored resources were meager, a single family might winter alone, but if it had been a good year and resources were truly abundant, then as many as 15 or 20 families—some 100 people—might pass the winter months together. Although many kinds of foods could be stored—from roots and seeds to dried fish, bird, and mammal meat—in most parts of the Great Basin, piñon nuts provided the key overwintering resource. More than any other single item, these nuts approached the status of a true staple in those parts of the Great Basin that had piñon trees in abundance.

As I have mentioned, piñon nuts are extremely nutritious. Singleleaf piñon, the species found in most of the Great Basin, provides a nut that is 10% protein, 25% fat, and 55% carbohydrate; Colorado piñon has a nut that is about 15% protein, 65% fat, and 20% carbohydate. In both cases, the protein includes all 20 amino acids.

A given stand of piñon will not produce every year: a good crop from a particular stand will probably be followed by several lean years in that stand, presumably because the trees need to replenish the resources used to produce both cones and nuts. Fortunately for the people who depended on them, the general nature of a piñon crop could be predicted well in advance, since the cones that bear the nuts are visible well over a year before the crop matures. Because many things could intervene to destroy a developing crop, exactly where the crops would be best could not be predicted a year in advance. However, one could predict, as archaeologist David Thomas has pointed out, where they would be bad.

Julian Steward estimated that a family of four people working a good crop for four weeks could gather enough nuts to last them about four months, or about the whole winter. Hence the importance of piñon: this resource was critical to surviving the harshest and leanest time of the year. The larger the piñon crop, the easier it would be to survive the winter, and the larger the winter village became.

Those villages remained occupied only from the end of the piñon season to the onset of spring, when new foods became available. As spring approached, the winter village would begin to break up, with individual families or, most often, small groups of families going their own way. The small groups of people that traveled together tended to be interrelated by marriage. According to Steward, it was rare that more than four or five such families—25 or 30 people—would stay together for any length of time. His data suggest that the usual cluster was on the order of two or three families, or 15 to 20 people. After leaving the winter village, those small groups spent the months from spring to fall moving from resource to resource, the length of time spent at any one place dictated by the abundance of the resources at that place.

Communal activities involving sets of related families did take place outside of the winter village. Many of those communal activities involved hunting. A wide variety of animals, from coots and ducks to jack rabbits and antelope, could be taken far more efficiently in cooperative hunts than by single individuals or by small groups of people. Sage grouse (*Centrocercus urophasianus*), for instance, congregate in large flocks from late fall to spring and could be taken en masse, sometimes in the hundreds, by hunters cooperating to drive them into nets or other surrounds. Indeed, Thomas has described a complex series of low, intersecting rock walls extending for over 1,300′ on central Nevada's Monitor Range that may have been a communal sage grouse hunting facility.

Although a number of different animals could be taken cooperatively, it was the communal hunting of antelope (more correctly pronghorn, but *Antilocapra americana* either way) and jack rabbits (species of *Lepus*) that seems to have been of greatest importance. Many descriptions of these communal hunts are available. Details differ from account to account, but the general picture of how they were performed remains the same. Communal antelope hunts, for instance, were conducted under the leadership of a shaman, who held supernatural powers over the animals. Under his direction, people worked the animals in a given valley, forcing them between huge V-shaped wings that led into corrals, where they would be killed by waiting hunters, men and women alike. At times, the facilities that funneled and corralled the animals were made of fairly substantial materials—rock and wood—but, more commonly, they were of sagebrush. The V-shaped wings leading to the corral might be long—over a mile long in some cases—but they were not particularly high, since antelope rarely jump significant heights.

Communal antelope hunts of this sort were often so efficient that a dozen years might pass before a given valley would see another one. Some have suggested that these hunts were purposely staggered in time in order to allow the animals to recover in number, but it is far more likely that they were staggered simply because it took years for populations to rebound.

Jack rabbit drives were conducted in much the same fashion, though here the animals were driven into huge nets, each of which was some three feet high and several hundred feet long. Robert Lowie described one such drive among the Washoe, in which 200 people took between 400 and 500 jack rabbits a day.

Both jack rabbit and antelope drives could be held at various times of the year. If they were held during the winter months, people from different winter villages would join together, returning to their villages after the hunt had ended. If they were held at other times of the year, different families or family groups would band together for the duration of the hunt, and then continue on their separate ways.

At times, communal hunts coincided with another communal aspect of Great Basin life—the festival or "fandango." These gatherings took place two or three times a year. How long they lasted depended on how long the food lasted, food that was routinely provided by a jack rabbit or antelope drive, or by the fall pine nut harvest. Indeed, a fall jack rabbit drive was often conducted by people who had gathered to harvest pine nuts, making both sets of resources available to support a fairly substantial fall festival. Lasting about a week, the purpose of these gatherings was strictly social—dancing, games, courting, gossiping, and, no doubt, the sharing of information about local resources all took place.

Although communal activities of this sort did happen, most time outside the winter months was spent in small groups, a few families moving across the landscape together in search of food. As fall approached, these small groups would move toward areas likely to produce a substantial piñon crop, and a significant fraction of autumn would be occupied by gathering, processing, and storing these nuts. And the winter, as I have discussed, would be spent at a winter village.

In Steward's own words, Great Basin native culture "was stamped with a remarkable practicality . . . starvation was so common that all activities had to be organized toward the food quest, which was carried on mostly by independent families" (1938:46). But to this basic description must be added one important caveat and a major modifier. Steward would have agreed with the modifier; he himself suggested it. However, the caveat he emphatically rejected.

The caveat first. Steward conducted his fieldwork during the 1920s and 1930s. The people he talked to described conditions and lifeways that had existed during the last half of the nineteenth century and during the first few decades of the twentieth. In addition to describing things they themselves had done, the people he interviewed also recalled what they had been taught by their elders. But none of these people came even close to knowing with any certainty what life had been like prior to the monumental disruptions caused, directly or indirectly, by the arrival of Europeans in North America.

In 1962, the anthropologist Elman R. Service attacked Steward's description of Great Basin lifeways on just these grounds. He argued that what Steward was describing was a system in disarray as a result of European contact. On all but the western edge of the Great Basin, Service contended, many Great Basin peoples had had their lifeways completely disrupted by Indians who had adopted the horse. Elsewhere, he suggested, Europeans themselves directly destroyed Great Basin cultures, by usurping the resources on which they depended: cutting down piñon for food, occupying critical springs and canyon mouths, disrupting the animals they hunted, and so on. Great Basin natives quickly became peripheral hangers-on in American towns; indeed, the very people Steward interviewed generally occupied just such a position.

For Service, Steward's ethnographic Great Basin—a Great Basin founded on more or less independent nuclear families moving across the landscape, now coming together into larger groups, now fissioning once again—represented a lifeway that reflected disruption caused by the European arrival, not a lifeway that had existed before that event.

The arrival of Europeans was, of course, disastrous to native American lifeways throughout North America. Recent archaeological work has shown that, with rare exceptions, massive cultural change generally preceded actual face-to-fact contact with Europeans by many years, with that change due to population declines caused by such diseases as whooping cough, smallpox, and measles. In some areas, population losses were so huge that, by the time Europeans made their physical arrival, there were no human occupants to be found. Given our increasing understanding of these issues, Service's concerns over the meaning of Steward's descriptions are even more appropriate now than they were when he first raised the issue over three decades ago. I return to this important issue in Chapter 9.

The modifier needed to Steward's general description of Great Basin lifeways is not controversial. In fact, that modifier gave Steward's work on Great Basin native lifeways tremendous theoretical import.

Steward observed that the complexity of the societies he had studied varied across the Great Basin, and that this variability was keyed to the distribution, abundance, and predictability of the resources to which people had access. Peoples who lived in settings in which diverse, predictable, and abundant resources were packed into relatively small areas were marked by a sociopolitical organization far more complex than that of peoples living in areas in which resources were sparse, widely scattered, and unpredictable. At times, Steward almost seems to have thought of Great Basin peoples as having been divided into those living in resource-rich areas and who possessed a relatively complex sociopolitical organization, and those living in areas of lesser abundance, whose sociopolitical complexity was therefore less. But as Kay Fowler and others have pointed out (and certainly this was clear to Steward as well), organizational complexity formed a continuum in the Great Basin, a continuum keyed to resource distribution, predictability, and abundance.

Steward used the Owens Valley Paiute to exemplify the upper end of his continuum. These people lived, and live, in a well-watered, environmentally complex territory that includes not only the Owens Valley itself, but also the

Sierra Nevada to the west, and the Inyo and White mountains to the east. The resources of this area were extremely rich. The mountain flanks to the east held good stands of piñon; mountains to both the east and the west were well stocked with a wide range of mammals; the valley provided fish, rabbits, antelope, and rich seed and root crops. Other parts of the Great Basin might provide the same set of resources, but only rarely were they so densely packed. As a result, Owens Valley held permanent villages—perhaps some three dozen of them, some of which may have held as many as 200 people. Indeed, at one person per 2.1 square miles, Owens Valley had the highest estimated population density known for the Great Basin. (The average may have been on the order of one person per 16 square miles, and the lowest as low as one person per 35 or so square miles, this for the Gosiute of the Bonneville Basin in Utah; we have, however, no way of knowing what pre-European population numbers were like.)

Owens Valley itself was divided into districts, with each district having one or more villages and the people of the district communally owning the rights to hunt, fish, and gather plant foods in that district. The people of each such district cooperated with one another in communal hunting and fishing, in holding ceremonies, and, in some areas, in irrigating plots of wild seeds. These communal activities were routinely directed by one individual, a headman, chosen largely for his leadership abilities; the sons of headmen might inherit that position if they showed the same leadership qualities.

All this was very different from the sociopolitical organization seen in many other parts of the Great Basin, where permanent villages did not exist, where land ownership or at least land control did not exist, where there were no leadership positions that might be inherited, and where resources were not routinely thought of as owned.

Although the Owens Valley Paiute provided Steward with his example of the sociocultural complexity that developed as resources increased in density, abundance, and predictability, it has become clear that such complexity likely developed wherever the resources allowed. This is the case even though we have no detailed, written descriptions for these other areas that can compare with the description that Steward provided for the Owens Valley Paiute. Comparable complexity appears to have existed in the Carson and Humboldt basins of western Nevada, in the Malheur Basin of south-central Oregon, and along the western flanks of the Wasatch Range, in all instances driven by the availability of rich riverine and marsh resources. In all these areas, substantial late prehistoric villages are known from archaeological work—the prehistoric analogue of historic ethnographic accounts.

It is clear that the ethnographic Great Basin was characterized by a resource-driven continuum in organizational complexity. Indeed, perhaps nowhere in North America south of the Arctic is the relationship between the organizational complexity of native American lifeways and resource availability quite so clear. This will remain true even if it turns out that some aspects of Great Basin cultures as described by Steward reflect the negative impacts of European contact. The developing late prehistoric archaeological record for the Great Basin strongly suggests, if it does not already show, that, had Steward been able to talk to late prehistoric peoples, the continuum of organizational complexity would have been more, not less, evident.

The cultural Great Basin is larger than the Great Basin defined in other ways, since the peoples that make up this area extended well into Idaho (the Northern Shoshone and Bannock), Wyoming (the Eastern Shoshone), and Colorado (the Ute). Although it is the largest of the several Great Basins, the cultural Great Basin is, in two separate senses, also the most poorly known. Scientifically, this is so because what characterized it—native American lifeways in latest prehistoric times—no longer exist to be directly studied. It is also the most poorly known in the sense that what is known—and there is quite a bit—is primarily known to anthropologists and archaeologists, and not to others.

Choosing a Great Basin

Since this is a book about the natural prehistory of the Great Basin, it might seem that I should choose just one of these four Great Basins to examine. There are, however, some simple truths that constrain this choice, and that place it in its proper perspective. The ethnographic Great Basin as anthropologists have so carefully defined it may not have existed 2,000 years ago. Indeed, as I will discuss in Chapter 9, some believe that Numic speakers may not even have been in much of the Great Basin at that time. The floristic Great Basin as it now exists did not come into being until some 4,500 years ago or so, as I will explore in Chapters 6 and 8. The hydrographic Great Basin as it now exists has greater time depth, but it sprang leaks in a number of places between 25,000 and 10,000 years ago, spilling its waters into the Pacific, as I will discuss in Chapter 5. In fact, the Great Basin's hydrographic boundaries have been breached since that time as well (see Chapter 5), but such violations were far less significant than the major leaks that occurred during the late Ice Age.

The only Great Basin that has actually continuously been here for the last 25,000 years and more is the physiographic Great Basin. Even though this Great Basin has not stood still over these years—as anyone who was there for the 1954 earthquake in Dixie Valley, central Nevada, or for the 1915 quake in Pleasant Valley to the north, can attest—at least the general boundaries of the physiographic Great Basin remained very much the same for the entire period of time with which I will be dealing. Adopting this Great Basin, though, would exclude much of the Mojave Desert, and doing that would make it far harder to fathom some major issues involved in understanding the development of the botanical Great Basin.

The whole thrust of this book is to watch the Great Basins develop and change over the past 25,000 years or so. Since that is the case, there is nothing wrong with using all four definitions at the same time, which is what I shall do. The boundary of the Great Basin that you will see drawn on many of the maps in this book, however, is the boundary of the hydrographic Great Basin. It is that boundary that I used, by and large, in deciding what to include, and what to exclude, in the narrative that follows.

Notes

The Great Basin as a physiographic unit is discussed in detail by Hunt (1967). McLane (1978) provides an excellent, historically oriented discussion of Nevada's mountain ranges. Stewart (1980), Baldwin (1981), and Hintze (1988) provide detailed accounts of the structural history of Great Basin mountains.

The best general overview of the natural history of the modern Great Basin is Trimble (1989). For general reading on the plants of the Great Basin, see Lanner (1981, 1983b), Mozingo (1987), and Gleason and Cronquist (1964). Shreve (1942) provides his classic botanical look at the deserts of North America. For a more detailed discussion of the plants of the intermountain west as a whole (and the basis of much of my discussion) see Cronquist et al. (1972), and especially Noel Holmgren's lengthy article on the plant geography of the intermountain region in that volume. The superb collection of papers in Osmond et al. (1990) focuses on physiological adaptations of Basin and Range plants, and thus supplements the essentially distributional approach taken in Cronquist et al. (1972). Dwight Billings recently won the Nevada Medal for scientific contributions to our understanding of what that state contains; those of his contributions that I have used in this chapter are Billings (1950, 1951, 1954, 1978, 1988, 1990). West (1988) provides a superb discussion of the plant communities of the intermountain west as a whole. A brief, but excellent, discussion of the plants that characterize the Mojave Desert is presented by Benson and Darrow (1981). MacMahon (1988) provides a far more detailed discussion, and places the Mojave Desert in the more general context of the North American warm deserts. DeDecker (1984) presents a detailed discussion of the distribution of the plants of the northern Mojave Desert.

The best reference to the mammals of Nevada remains E. B. Hall (1946); my work on the mammals of Monitor Valley is discussed in Grayson (1983). Zeveloff and Collett (1988) provide a general discussion of Great Basin mammals as a whole. Alcorn (1988) provides an avian counterpart to Hall's detailed treatment of mammals; for fish, see Sigler and Sigler (1987). Information on the vegetation of Monitor Valley and the Toquima range is taken both from my own work and from R. S. Thompson (1983); on the alpine tundra of this area, see Charlet (1993). On salt accumulation in shadscale, see S. D. Smith and Nowak (1990); on chisel-toothed kangaroo rats, see Kenagy (1972, 1973) and Hayssen (1991). On the invasion of the Great Basin by cheatgrass, see Chapter 11. My discussion of Great Basin biogeography draws on P. V. Wells (1983), Reveal (1979), West et al. (1978), Behle (1978), Harper et al. (1978), and Tanner (1978). West et al. (1978) expand on the role of thermal inversions in the development of piñon-juniper woodland; see also Hidy and Klieforth (1990). Timberlines in general are discussed in an excellent book by Arno and Hammersly (1984); see also Stevens and Fox (1991). For more on krummholz, see Marr (1977), LaMarche and Mooney (1972), and W. K. Smith and Knapp (1990).

DeLucia and Schlesinger (1990) present an excellent review of the research that has been done on the disjunct distribution of Sierran conifers on altered soils in the western Great Basin. The full details of that research are to be found in DeLucia et al. (1988, 1989), Schlesinger et al. (1989), and DeLucia and Schlesinger (1991). Billings (1950) was the first to observe and interpret these Sierra "tree islands."

Native American languages are discussed in Greenberg (1987a), a book that linguists find highly controversial (see the lengthy multiple-author review in Greenberg (1987b); see also Ruhlen (1991). On Great Basin languages, see W. H. Jacobsen (1986) for Washoe and W. R. Miller (1986) for Numic; W. R. Miller (1983, 1984) provides a more general discussion of Uto-Aztecan languages; further references are provided in Chapter 9. W. R. Miller et al. (1971) discuss dialectical variation within Panamint. On the distribution of Great Basin languages and the implications it may have for the history of Great Basin native peoples, see Lamb (1958) and Chapter 9. On the Kawaiisu, see Zigmond (1986). Julian Steward's classic statement of Great Basin lifeways is contained in Steward (1938); see also Steward (1937, 1970). Steward (1933) provides his ethnography of the Owens Valley Pauite. David Thomas's analysis of the predictability of piñon yields is in Thomas (1972b); see also Lanner (1981, 1983b). The Monitor Range sage grouse communal hunting facility is discussed and illustrated in Thomas (1988). Kay Fowler's discussions of Great Basin subsistence and settlement patterns are found (among other places) in C. S. Fowler (1982, 1986, 1989); see also Janetski (1991). Lowie (1939) discusses the Washo. Service's challenge to Steward appears in Service (1962). Thomas (1986) provides an extremely handy compilation of some of the most valuable sources that exist on Great Basin ethnography. On the impact of disease on native Americans, see Ramenofsky (1987) and the references therein, especially the references to the work of S. F. Cook and H. Dobyns. Substantial late prehistoric Great Basin villages in areas marked by rich riverine and marsh resources are now known from the Carson Sink (S. T. Brooks et al. 1988; Raven and Elston 1988; Raven and Elston 1989; Raven 1990), the Humboldt Sink (Livingston 1986, 1988b), the Lake Abert and Chewaucan Marsh basins (Oetting 1989, 1990; Pettigrew 1985), and elsewhere (see the papers in Janetski and Madsen 1990).

On major twentieth-century earthquakes in the Great Basin, see Page (1935), Slemmons (1957), Stewart (1980), Wallace 1984), and Bell and Katzer (1987).

Both Badwater Basin and Telescope Peak are in Death Valley National Monument. Badwater can be reached by car. Reaching the top of Telescope Peak requires a seven-mile hike during which 2,916′ of elevation are gained, but the trail is remarkably good and the hike a relatively easy one (see Foster 1987 for a discussion of the walk). The view from the top is magnificent, and includes Badwater 11,331′ below. The upper end of the road to the Telescope Peak trailhead is poorly maintained, and a vehicle with good clearance is essential.

PART TWO

○○○

Some Ice Age Background

CHAPTER THREE

Glaciers, Sea Levels, and the Peopling of the New World

Archaeology deals with the entire time span of our existence, from our earliest tool-using ancestors in sub-Saharan Africa some 2.5 million years ago, to contemporary peoples from Tanzania to Tucson. Much archaeological research is fairly routine and, although important, causes little heated debate. But there are certain issues, as in all sciences, that become the focal point of loud argumentation and of lasting disagreement.

The archaeology of the Americas was once marked by many such debates. Did contact across the Pacific Ocean stimulate the development of the high civilizations of South and Middle America? Were the prehistoric pueblos of the American Southwest founded by immigrants from Mexico, or in some other way directly caused by cultural developments to the south? Both of these questions have now been answered in the negative, as archaeological research has clearly shown ancient and local antecedents for all of the New World peoples involved.

These debates have been replaced by others, two of which I address in this and the following chapter. When did people first arrive in North America? And what impact did they have on the native fauna when they got here?

The Bering Land Bridge and the Human Arrival

Pleistocene Glaciation

There is a chance that people first reached the New World by some lucky accident that saw them drift across the Atlantic or Pacific oceans. However, the chances of that occurring with a group large enough to have become established are so slim that no one has given the idea more than a passing thought. Instead, the earliest Americans are presumed to have come from northeastern Siberia, crossing from Old World to New in the vicinity of Bering Strait (Figure 3-1).

Here, mainland Alaska and mainland Siberia are slightly less than 60 miles apart. When the fog lifts long enough, one side can be seen from the other. Eskimos found crossing Bering Strait in the large, open boats called umiaks to be easy enough that a fairly routine trade developed between groups on both sides, hampered only by the fact that contacts were sufficiently close that these trading partners also became enemies.

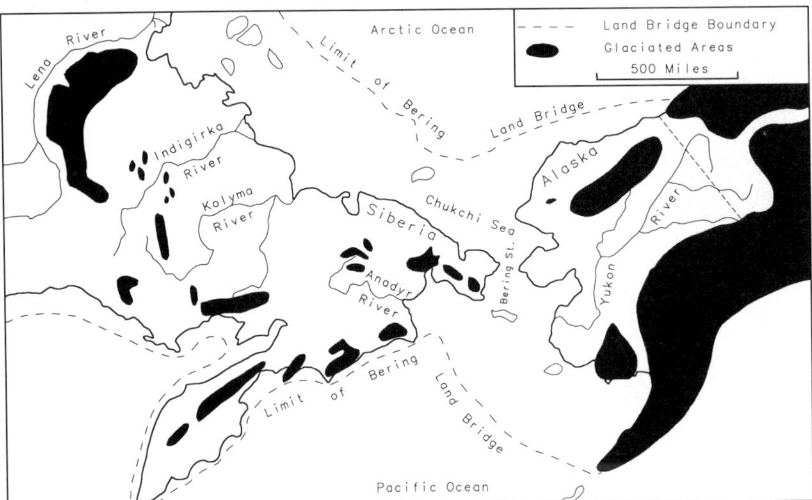

Figure 3-1. Beringia during full-glacial times. After Morlan (1987).

The Eskimo, however, are a modern people with a sophisticated technology for dealing with their environment, and there is no reason to suppose that the first movement of people into the New World had to be made by boat. Instead, the surmise is that the crossing was made when sea levels were lower, Bering Strait did not exist, and people, as well as a wide variety of other mammals, could have walked across. To understand how that could have happened requires some knowledge of geology.

The "Ice Age" is a popular name for the epoch in earth history that geologists call the Pleistocene, falling by definition between 1.65 million and 10,000 years ago. The Pleistocene saw the alternate expansion and retraction of glacial ice over vast portions of the earth's surface. The last 10,000 years, since the end of the Pleistocene, is referred to as the Holocene: it is the epoch we are in now.

The latest, or Wisconsin, glaciation occurred between 122,000 and 10,000 years ago and is the best known of all North American glacial advances and retreats. Although best known, the Wisconsin glaciation was merely the last in a lengthy series of glaciations—more than 20—that actually began before the geological Ice Age itself. It might be comforting to think that the Ice Age ended, and the Holocene began, 10,000 years ago. However, that date, like the date for the beginning of the Pleistocene, is merely a geological convenience: no one who studies the Pleistocene thinks that it is over. Instead, it is clear that we are now in one of the periods of glacial retreat that is as characteristic of the Ice Age as are the glacial advances.

The effects of Ice Age climate, and of glaciation itself, were considerable. Much of the landscape of North America, including vast expanses that were never beneath glacial ice, cannot be understood without knowledge of those effects. Some of these I will discuss in the following chapters. For now, I want to explore how it is that people could have walked from Siberia to Alaska on dry ground.

During the Wisconsin glaciation, two massive ice sheets formed in the north, ultimately covering most of Canada and parts of the northern United States. In the east, the Laurentide Ice Sheet extended from Labrador to the eastern foothills of the Rocky Mountains, reaching a maximum thickness of about 11,000′—a pile of ice over two miles high. To the west, the Cordilleran Ice Sheet covered all but the highest pinnacles of the Canadian Rockies and Coast Range, sending its ice south beyond where Seattle now sits and reaching a maximum thickness of approximately 8,000′. To the south of these huge ice sheets, many mountains harbored their own, alpine glaciers. The distinctive sawtooth ridges that mark the skylines of many parts of both the Sierra Nevada and the Rocky Mountains were largely formed by glacial action, while isolated mountains as far south as south-central Arizona and New Mexico were glaciated as well.

The timing of the earliest advances and retreats of glacial ice is not particularly well known, though glacial advances in the Sierra Nevada seem to have occurred as early as 2.4 million years ago. We know far more about the latest Pleistocene advances and retreats.

During the earliest Wisconsin, from about 122,000 to 80,000 years ago, glacial advances are well documented only for some far western mountains, in Alaska, and in the Yellowstone area of the Rocky Mountains. It is clear, however, that both the Laurentide and Cordilleran ice sheets had begun to expand by 75,000 years ago or so, reached their maximum southern extent some 5,000 years later, and then retreated into Canada. Some 30,000 years ago, they began to grow once again, pushing south of the Canadian border, and reaching their maximum Late Wisconsin extent in most areas about 18,000 years ago. (In some areas, like the Canadian Arctic, maximum late-Wisconsin glacial growth does not seem to have been reached until later in time, perhaps even as late as 11,000 years ago.) In all areas, glaciers were waning rapidly as the Pleistocene came to an end 10,000 years ago.

A NOTE ON TERMINOLOGY

Throughout this volume, I will use the term "late Wisconsin" to refer to the period of time between about 25,000 and 10,000 years ago. That interval includes the last glacial maximum and ends with the end of the Pleistocene. The "late Pleistocene" is officially defined as the period that includes both the last interglacial and the Wisconsin glaciation, roughly 132,000 to 10,000 years ago. In this volume, however, I will use the phrase "late Pleistocene" as a rough equivalent to "late Wisconsin."

THE BERING LAND BRIDGE

The total amount of water on the earth is virtually constant. Today, about 97.6% of the earth's water resides in the oceans, with only a trace present in the atmosphere. The remainder is found on land—some 0.6% as rivers, lakes, and groundwater, the rest—1.7%—as glacial ice. Nearly all of the water locked up in ice is found in the Greenland and Antarctic ice sheets. Were the glaciers to expand again, the water they would convert into ice would come from the oceans. As the glaciers expanded, the oceans would fall; as they retreated, the oceans would rise. Indeed, there is enough water frozen in the ice sheets of Greenland and the Antarctic that, if they were to melt, sea levels would rise some 250′.

Melting glaciers cause sea levels to rise; expanding glaciers cause them to fall. Estimates for the drop in sea level at the time of the last glacial maximum, at about 18,000 years ago, run between about 330′ and 490′. A drop to either end of this range of estimates would create a wide expanse of dry land between Alaska and Siberia.

Obviously, as sea level drops, more and more land is exposed along coastlines. Dozens of teeth from extinct North American elephants, for instance, have been dredged up off the Atlantic coast. These teeth did not get washed offshore from contemporary land surfaces. Instead, they are the remains of now-extinct mammoths that at one time trudged along the exposed continental shelf along our east coast, exposed because the water that now covers this area was, prior to 11,000 years ago (by which time mammoths were becoming extinct), dry land. In fact, the shoreline receded some 60 miles or more along the east coast; along the west coast, where the continental shelf tends to be far narrower, the shoreline receded some 30 miles.

Bering Strait connects the Bering Sea to the south with the Chuckchi Sea to the north (Figure 3-1). The floor of the northeastern Bering Sea, Bering Strait, and Chukchi Sea forms a flat shelf running from the Siberian to the Alaskan coasts, and covered by between 100′ and 500′ of water. A sea level reduction of 330′ would result in a land bridge 1,000 miles wide, and data from Bering Strait itself suggest that this is precisely where things stood 18,000 years ago.

However, the land bridge as a whole is so shallow that nothing approaching the volume of ice that covered the earth's surface during the last glacial maximum is needed to expose huge parts of it. A sea level decrease of 150′, for instance, would create a land bridge 200 miles wide. The shallowness of the land bridge, combined with the volume of water that was locked up in ice during much of the Wisconsin glaciation, appears to have led to the existence of a land bridge exposed to one degree or another during much of the time between 75,000 and 14,400 years ago, although it may have been entirely under water one or more times between 45,000 and 35,000 years ago. As the Wisconsin glaciers began to wane, the bridge narrowed, but when the entire land bridge became inundated is not clear. Until recently, it was thought that this occurred about 14,400 years ago, but new information strongly suggests instead that the final flooding happened approximately 11,000 years ago.

Essentially, then, a land bridge between Siberia and Alaska existed from about 75,000 to perhaps 11,000 years ago. It is difficult to know precisely what the vegetation of this land bridge was like, for the simple reason that it is now covered by water. Studies on the adjacent mainland, however, strongly suggest that the land bridge had a tundra-steppe plant cover: low shrubs and grasses, with cottonwoods, willows, and alders in locally favorable spots.

There is no reason to think that people who were adapted to the Siberian side of the land bridge would have had any particular difficulties coping with the challenges presented by the bridge itself.

It is an assumption that people crossed from the Old World to the New at the point where the two come closest together, but this is an assumption that has no serious competition.

It is also an assumption that people crossed when the land bridge existed, but it is true that a crossing could have been made on sea ice, as perilous as that might have been. And although umiaks, used by Eskimos to cross Bering Strait in recent times, may not have existed when people first entered the New World (no later than about 12,000 years ago), boats sufficient to do the job existed in some parts of the world very early on. What we know about the archaeology of Australia shows this very clearly. The earliest securely dated archaeological sites in Australia are nearly 40,000 years old, and it is widely assumed that the first peoples arrived here 50,000 years ago or so. If that were the case, then perhaps they arrived around 53,000 years ago, when sea levels in this part of the world were at the lowest point they have reached during the last 60,000 years. Even if they crossed at this time of minimum water levels, an open sea voyage of at least 55 miles would have been necessary, a distance comparable to that between Alaska and Siberia today.

Nonetheless, the assumption that people crossed when the land bridge was exposed appears to be a reasonable one, since our species was only one of many that made the crossing in one direction or another during the Pleistocene. Among other things, North America gained the mammoth, muskox, bison, moose, and caribou, as well as wolves, grizzly bears, and, amazingly enough, lions (see Chapter 4). In fact, of the 22 species of mammals, excluding people, known from paleontological sites of late Wisconsin age in northeastern Siberia, 21 are also known from Alaska. The movement of our own kind across the Bering Land Bridge was part of a general faunal interchange between the Old and New worlds. What people accomplished in making the crossing was nothing special, and it is far more parsimonious to assume that they came across as part of this interchange than to think that they walked across sea ice or came by boat. In fact, it is harder to understand why the woolly rhinoceros, alone among the 22 Siberian species, did not make it across, than it is to understand why people did.

The fact that the crossing likely took place at a time of glacial advance suggests a simple question. Would the first Americans not have been in for a rude shock, crossing the land bridge only to be confronted by glacial ice?

In fact, the geography of Alaska is such that that is not what happened. Glaciers, of course, need precipitation to form. In Alaska, that precipitation was borne by air masses moving north and east from the northern Pacific Ocean onto the southern Alaskan mainland. However, the entire southern front of Alaska, from the Aleutians to the British Columbia border, is marked by high mountain ranges, reaching their 20,300′ pinnacle at Mount McKinley. As wet air moving out of the North Pacific encountered these mountains, it was forced upward, cooled, and condensed. The resultant precipitation allowed the formation of massive glaciers on the mountains themselves, glaciers that ultimately coalesced and formed the northwestern arm of the Cordilleran Ice Sheet.

But by the time these storm systems got much beyond the crests of the mountains, they had been wrung nearly dry. Central Alaska, low in elevation, was never glaciated, nor was the adjacent Yukon. Further north, the high Brooks Range, whose peaks reach beyond 8,000′ in elevation, saw the development of a massive glacial complex, but the low plains north of the Brooks Range also remained unglaciated.

Central and far northern Alaska—some two-thirds of the state—were thus never covered by ice. No matter when people first entered the New World via the Bering Land Bridge, they may have passed by Pleistocene glaciers, but they would not have had to deal with them. Central Alaska was ice free.

Ice free, however, does not necessarily mean livable. Environments cold enough to contain glaciers may be cold enough to be miserable for people, and glaciers themselves can modify surrounding environments tremendously. For one thing, when air is forced over glacial ice, it is rapidly cooled, and, because it is cooler, becomes heavier as well. The resultant cold, heavy air rushes downslope, creating drainage or catabatic winds that can chill areas far beyond the glacier itself. A similar, though far less pronounced, phenomenon is experienced by people who camp in the mouths of desert mountain canyons in the summer months. As the air in the high elevations of the mountain is cooled, it rushes downslope, funnelled through the canyon itself, creating strong and relatively chilly winds that last until the temperature imbalance between the higher, colder, and lower, warmer air has lessened. This phenomenon is one reason why subalpine conifers can follow canyons to lower elevations in places like the Toquima and Snake ranges.

In addition to creating their own winds, glaciers also shatter and grind the rock over which they pass. Some of the finely ground material remains beneath the ice until the glacier finally melts and exposes it to the surface. Some is washed out from beneath the ice by glacial waters, to be deposited in front of the glacial mass as outwash alluvium. No matter which of these mechanisms exposes the finely ground rock on the surface, once it is there, it can be picked up by winds to form rock-dust clouds. Such material, called loess, blankets huge portions of the American midwest, the ultimate source having been the outwash deposits from Laurentide ice. Loess deposits over five feet thick are common in such states as Illinois and Kansas.

It is fully possible that, while the eastern terminus of the Bering Land Bridge was ice free, the environments here were inhospitable for people. Unfortunately, the nature of the environments that the first peoples would have encountered here is not fully clear, and an active debate continues between those who believe that during full-glacial times, say 22,000–18,000 years ago, central Alaska and adjacent Canada would have been a bleak and barren place and those who argue very much the opposite.

On one side of this argument are those who believe that much of the area from Siberia, across the Bering Land Bridge, and into the Yukon—the region referred to as Beringia—was covered by a spatially complex arid grassland. This hypothesized grassland is argued to have been so productive that it was able to support a diverse set of large mammals, many of which made their living by grazing, and the rest of which survived by eating the grass-feeders.

This position has been most forcefully developed by paleontologist Dale Guthrie, whose novel ideas are largely derived from the kinds of mammals that have been found in the paleontological sites of interior Alaska. Guthrie has observed that Pleistocene-aged faunas here were dominated by large grazers, some of which—including mammoth, horse, and bison—are now extinct. The same sites have yielded a diverse set of far less common mammals. Among the less common grazers are elk and mountain sheep, as well as the extinct American camel and the saiga, an antelope that no longer occurs in the New World, but that is doing well on the Russian steppe. The nongrazers from these sites include moose, caribou, muskox, and the extinct mastodon, as well as an impressive series of carnivores, from coyotes and wolves to lions and brown bears.

Guthrie counted the number of animals from these sites, and observed that the ratio of grazing to nongrazing ungulates was at least 20 to 1, whereas in the same area today the ratio is on the order of 1 to 100. From this, Guthrie concluded that interior Alaska must have supported a productive grassland during the Wisconsin glaciation.

This hypothesized productive grassland, with its mammoth, horses, and bison, has come to be called the "mammoth steppe," not only for its postulated size, but also for one of its most characteristic animals. Guthrie argues that the mammoth steppe covered virtually all of Wisconsin-aged Beringia, and extended well across Eurasia.

Guthrie's thoughtful analyses of the paleontological faunas from Beringian sites have led him to speculate about many of the details of this biome. He has observed, for instance, that these sites contain horse, saiga, and mountain sheep, animals that do not do well in deep snow. From this finding, he infers that, although the winters of Alaskan Beringia might have been cold, they must also have been marked by light, and frequently wind-swept, snows. Many of the grazers had large antlers, tusks, and horns; Guthrie infers from this that the growing season must have been long. The longer the growing season, he argues, the bigger such body parts can become. Hence, he suggests that the cold winters of the mammoth steppe were short, hemmed in on one side by late and moderately warm autumns, and on the other by early springs and attendant early thaws.

Guthrie's Wisconsin-aged Beringia is thus fairly lush, with high densities of huge grazing mammals that had to contend with cold but short winters, and that fed on abundant grasses fostered by a long growing season. From the point of view of human hunters, such a landscape may well have been extremely appealing.

Guthrie is a zoologist, and almost all of his arguments are drawn directly from the animals themselves, whether he is addressing himself to the density of mammals on the landscape, the vegetation that covered that landscape, or the length of the growing season and the depths of the snows. There are other sources of information on some of these matters, sources that in some cases are much more direct than the mammals. Most important among these other avenues into the past is the evidence provided by the remains of the plants that grew in Beringia during the Wisconsin glaciation.

In eastern Beringia, our direct knowledge of the vegetation of the deeper past comes primarily from the study of pollen grains that have accumulated in the sediments of the lakes and bogs that abound in the area.

Most wind-pollinated plants, and even some that depend on animals to do the job, produce pollen abundantly. Those tiny particles—a single pollen grain from an alder or a willow weighs only some 20 billionths of a gram—can be carried far and wide by wind. Some pollen grains end up doing what they were meant to do, but most end up scattered across the landscape. When this "pollen rain" brings pollen to environments that protect it from oxidation and abrasion, as in lakes and bogs, it preserves beautifully. Samples of sediments from these protected environments can then provide a long sequence of vegetational history as represented by the changing pollen rain through time. Because the places that preserve pollen well are often good places for organic preservation in general, the deposits that provide the pollen can usually be dated by the carbon-14 method, as discussed later in this chapter. Indeed, it has recently been shown that modern radiocarbon dating technology can even date samples of the pollen grains themselves. Pollen analysis is time-consuming, even tedious, but the results can tell us the nature of the vegetation on the landscape at a given and known time in the past, and can also tell us how, if not always why, that vegetation changed through time.

The results of such exacting work in eastern Beringia have produced reasonable accord among pollen workers, virtually none of whom sees anything resembling Guthrie's mammoth steppe. A review by Thomas Ager and Linda Brubaker suggests that, during early Wisconsin times, before about 55,000 years ago, unglaciated Alaska was a cold and dry place whose vegetation was primarily sparse herbaceous tundra. During the Middle Wisconsin, when glacial retreat occurred and the Bering Land Bridge may have been briefly flooded once or twice, tundra remained widespread, but spruce forest and interspersed forest and tundra occupied the valleys of central Alaska as the glaciers reached their mid-Wisconsin minimum. When the glaciers expanded again, with the onset of the Late Wisconsin, so did cold and dry conditions. Spruce, which now blankets much of interior Alaska, may have been displaced from the entire state, not to return until some 9,500 years ago. Herbaceous tundra, with shrubs in locally favorable areas, seems to have characterized virtually all of unglaciated Alaska between about 26,000 and 14,000 years ago. Not until this latter date, as Alaska became wetter and warmer and the Bering Land Bridge began to go under for the last time, did the herbaceous tundra become shrubbier, and not until 11,000 years ago do the trees seem to have begun their return—first, trees of the genus *Populus* (which includes the balsam poplar, cottonwood, and quaking aspen), and, much later, spruce.

Not only does the pollen work suggest that Guthrie's mammoth steppe did not exist, it also shows that no uniform vegetation existed across this huge area in glacial times. For instance, my colleague Patricia Anderson recently analyzed the pollen sequences provided by two lakes in the Kotzebue Sound drainage of southwestern Alaska, north of the Seward Peninsula. Her results show that the full-glacial vegetation here may have been fairly rich in places, dominated perhaps by grasses and sedges, but also containing such shrubs as sagebrush and dwarf forms of birch and willow in favorable areas. On the other hand, James Ritchie and Les Cwynar have documented that, in the northern Yukon during the Late Wisconsin, upland sites were marked by sparse and discontinuous herbaceous tundra, whereas in lower areas sedge and grass meadows existed at least locally. It appears that the full-glacial vegetation of eastern Beringia was a complex mosaic of different kinds of plant associations.

The ecologist Paul Colinvaux has characterized Late Wisconsin eastern Beringia as a bleak place: "Frozen ground; clouds of loess; catabatic winds from glaciers; short summers, in places drier or warmer than now" (Colinvaux 1986:9). These words present a picture of interior Alaska and the adjacent Yukon that contrasts in almost every significant way with Guthrie's mammal-based reconstruction. Whether things were really this bleak we do not know, but the pollen work establishes that, although the Beringian tundras were a complex matter, they were, in fact, tundra, and not the productive grassy steppe called for by Guthrie.

If Guthrie is wrong, is there an obvious explanation of how he might have been led astray? In fact, there is. The paleontological sites that led Guthrie to argue what he has argued were not pristine sites that had been carefully excavated layer by layer by professional paleontologists. Instead, they had formed as a result of placer mining, in which bone-bearing sediments were washed away in the search for gold. Even though thousands of specimens came to light in this fashion, the deposits themselves had accumulated over thousands of years. As a result, there is no convincing evidence that a rich large mammal fauna occupied eastern Beringia during the Wisconsin. A small number of animals accumulating over a large number of years can give the impression that there had been an African savannah of large mammals, even though such a thing never existed. It is possible that Guthrie's assumption that these animals existed contemporaneously has led him astray.

We do not yet know when people first crossed the Bering Land Bridge into the New World, but the archaeological records on both sides of the land bridge suggest that it must have been some time during the Wisconsin glaciation. With the exception of a brief interlude during Middle Wisconsin times, when spruce and a forest-tundra mix invaded the lowlands of interior Alaska, the new human arrivals would have arrived in a country not that different from the one that they, or their immediate ancestors, had left behind: a relatively unproductive, primarily herbaceous tundra with a thin, but perhaps locally rich, scattering of large mammals.

AN "ICE-FREE CORRIDOR"?

The term "Beringia" is routinely used to encompass the vast area that lies between the Kolyma River in eastern Siberia and the Mackenzie River in the Northwest Territories of Canada. During the Wisconsin glacial maximum, the western or Siberian end of Beringia was open to traffic into and out of the rest of Eurasia. But as mountain or alpine glaciers grew and finally coalesced to form the Cordilleran Ice Sheet in northwestern North America, and the Laurentide Ice Sheet grew to its maximum to the east, eastern Beringia became increasingly isolated from the rest of North America. During a significant part of the Wisconsin glaciation, Beringia is more accurately thought of as part of Asia than as part of the New World.

This is true for the simple reason that, whereas movement into western Beringia was always possible, whether by people or by beasts, movement out of eastern Beringia into more southerly North America might have been blocked, to one degree or another, by glacial ice and attendant inhospitable conditions during a significant part of the Wisconsin. As a result, a human presence in eastern Beringia—the interior of Alaska, the Yukon, and the adjacent Northwest Territories—during the Wisconsin did not necessarily and quickly lead to a human presence further south.

I said that eastern Beringia might have been blocked "to one degree or another" during a significant part of the Wisconsin because we do not yet know exactly what conditions were like at the possible junction of Cordilleran and Laurentide ice, roughly along the eastern edge of the Mackenzie and northern Rocky mountains in the Yukon, British Columbia, and Alberta.

The possible presence of a glacial maximum "ice-free corridor" running between the two major ice sheets from eastern Beringia into areas south of glacial ice has been discussed for decades. Unfortunately, the glacial history of the area in which an ice-free corridor might have existed is extremely complex. Laurentide ice entered the area from the north and east, whereas both Cordilleran ice and that contributed by smaller montane glaciers entered the area from the west. Although deposits laid down by these glaciers clearly overlap in many areas, the fact that they overlap may mean little, since the expansion and retreat of the glaciers involved may not have been synchronous. Making matters worse is the fact that later glaciation tends to obliterate deposits laid down during earlier glacial episodes. The result of all this is that the glacial history of this area remains poorly understood.

Most geologists now feel that there either was an ice-free corridor during the entire Wisconsin glaciation, or that, if Laurentide and Cordilleran ice did come into contact, the contact lasted only a few thousand years. In either view, there would have been a corridor running between the ice sheets from at least 75,000 years ago to the end of the Pleistocene, with the possible exception of a single, relatively brief, interval. The exact location of that corridor would have shifted as the ice masses themselves shifted, but that would not alter the fact that such a corridor seems to have existed.

Even though that may have been the case, the presence of a physical gap between the ice sheets does not mean that conditions between the ice masses would have been particularly pleasant. Cold air must have rushed off the glaciers, creating frigid conditions; glacial meltwater would have created extensive lakes; the little evidence that is available suggests that the vegetation was likely a sparse herbaceous tundra with scattered shrubs. Indeed, recent work by Carole Mandryk suggests that the part of the corridor that ran through west-central Alberta was characterized by vegetation no more productive than current arctic tundras, and that these conditions lasted from at least 18,000 years ago to about 14,000 years ago.

A POSSIBLE COASTAL ROUTE

Even if midcontinental northern North America did not provide a particularly hospitable set of environments for people for a significant part of the Wisconsin glaciation, there is another option for moving people southward during times of maximum glacial expansion, although this option requires technology and motivation that may or may not have been available. Knut Fladmark and others have suggested that early North Americans might have moved southward not by a midcontinental route between the glaciers, but instead along the Pacific Coast.

Noting how inhospitable any possible midcontinental route would have been for human travelers during much of the Wisconsin, Fladmark observed that there may have been many ice-free areas along the North Pacific coast, areas that could have been utilized by people on their southward movement. If, he suggested, the earliest occupants had any form of steerable watercraft, they could have boated from ice-free zone to ice-free zone, living on the potentially rich resources of the coast on the way south. In that fashion, they could have readily moved from the eastern terminus of the land bridge down along the coast, ultimately reaching the unglaciated shores of southern Washington and Oregon.

Unfortunately, it is not yet possible to stipulate exactly how formidable the coastal environment would have been during full-glacial times. Because the Wisconsin was a time of greatly lowered sea levels, the coast that might have been used by early peoples is now deep beneath the waters of the Pacific, as is much of the evidence that would tell us exactly how far the glaciers reached toward the glacial-age shoreline from the mountains that edge this entire region. What we do know is that, at the glacial maximum, glaciers reached the sea along substantial parts of the coasts of Alaska and British Columbia. Some of these glaciers made sea contact for as much as 60 miles, some for perhaps even longer distances. These would have presented daunting obstacles to peoples who were not truly well equipped. How long that situation lasted, however, is simply not known, and it is possible that the coast presented far less of a challenge during substantial parts of the Wisconsin.

The coastal possibility may deserve as much attention as the more frequently discussed midcontinental route, but it does not get it. It probably does not get it because, as Fladmark pointed out, many have interpreted the earliest secure archaeological record of North America as having been left by people who made their living hunting large land mammals, as I will discuss. As a result, it is widely assumed that the earliest people entering North America were large-mammal hunters, and thus would have had to use the midcontinental route. Even if people could skirt coastal ice by boat, mammoth could not.

However, if early peoples in the New World were adept at utilizing the resources from a wide variety of environments, and there is little reason to think otherwise, then the resources offered by the coast may have been rich for them. There is no reason to exclude the coastal route as a possible avenue into North America south of glacial ice, even though at times of maximum glacial advance the odds that such a route would have been used appear slim.

THE HUMAN OCCUPATION OF WESTERN BERINGIA

Fossil data suggest that morphologically modern peoples originated in sub-Saharan Africa prior to 100,000 years ago, from whence they ultimately spread throughout the world. At the moment, the earliest evidence for such peoples in Eurasia is from the Middle East, where they had arrived by about 90,000 years ago. Western Europe saw the arrival of morphologically modern peoples—"Cro Magnon Man"—about 35,000 years ago, replacing the earlier and far less modern Neanderthal populations. In much, but not all, of the Old World, these spreading populations of morphologically modern peoples replaced earlier forms, such as Neanderthals, although precisely how that happened is anything but clear.

In some areas, however, these modern peoples were the first arrivals, and that appears to have been the case in far northern Eurasia. For some reason—low populations densities, a behavioral inability to cope with the far north, or something else—northern Eurasia simply does not seem to have been occupied by Neanderthals or Neanderthal-like populations. Instead, the initial human occupation of this region seems to have occurred after 40,000 years ago, presumably as part of the same process that brought morphologically modern peoples into western Europe.

The earliest known archaeological sites in far northern Eurasia are thus fairly recent, and were clearly created by peoples who were in every way modern. The archaeological sequence in the Lena River drainage in western Siberia may begin by about 35,000 years ago, but the early materials are not well dated and may in fact be younger than 20,000 years. The earliest known archaeological sites close to or in western Beringia are on the central Kamchatka Peninsula, south and west of the land bridge itself, and date to about 14,000 years ago. Earlier sites have yet to be found, even though an impressive amount of archaeological work has been done in this region.

If this view of the archaeology of far northern Eurasia is accurate, and if the earliest North Americans entered via the Bering Land Bridge, then the earliest North American archaeological sites will postdate 40,000 years ago, and may be significantly younger than that date, depending on how long modern peoples took to reach this remote part of the world.

On a global scale, then, it seems most likely that the New World was first occupied by morphologically modern peoples (that is, by *Homo sapiens sapiens*) and that that occupation did not occur until after 40,000 years ago.

But what seems most likely may or may not have happened. In truth, no event of far northern North America or of the Old World can appropriately be used to set limits on the age of the earliest archaeological sites in the New World. The timing of the initial entry or entries of people cannot be determined by when the Bering Land Bridge was open or closed, because there are other ways of passing from Siberia to Alaska, and there are even other possible avenues of entry, no matter how unlikely they may appear. The date or dates of entry south of glacial ice cannot be determined by examining when an ice-free corridor was available, because we do not really know the history of that corridor, above and beyond the fact that it was clearly available by 11,500 years ago, and because there were other ways of arriving south of the ice. The timing of the earliest entry cannot even be determined by the timing of the earliest entry of people into western Beringia, since we do not really know when that occurred, and, again, there is some slim chance that the earliest entry occurred by some other route.

On the other hand, once we know when people first got here, then we may be able to use our knowledge of such events as the first peopling of western Beringia, the opening and closing of the land bridge, and the chronology of an ice-free corridor or the nature of North Pacific coastal ice chronologies to explain why the archaeology looks the way it looks. But the question of the timing of the entry of people into the New World can be answered only by doing archaeology in the New World.

Identifying the Earliest New World Archaeology

So what are the earliest archaeological sites in the New World and what do they look like? I have already mentioned that the answer to this question is one of the most hotly debated issues in the archaeology of the Americas. This debate relates to the often slippery nature of simpler forms of archaeological data, as well as to the difficulties associated with the methods used to date archaeological sites. The debate also relates to the fact that so many New World sites once thought to have been extremely old have been shown to be something else entirely. Because of all this, archaeologists use a straightforward set of criteria to judge whether or not a potentially ancient archaeological site really is ancient, or that it really is archaeological.

IS THE SITE REALLY ARCHAEOLOGICAL?

Early in their careers, archaeologists learn that the results of human handiwork called artifacts fall on a continuum of recognizability. On one end of that continuum are objects so complex that there can be no doubt that human hands played a role in their manufacture—a decorated bowl, for instance, or a finely made stone arrow point.

On the other end of the continuum are objects so simple that it can be extremely difficult, or even impossible, to know with certainty that people had anything to do with producing them. People break stones to manufacture tools, but a wide variety of natural processes, from alternate freezing and thawing to tumbling in stream beds, break stones as well. The results of simple stone tool use or manufacture can be so similar to the results of natural stone fracture that the products of the two kinds of processes may be indistinguishable.

Most of the time such similarities cause no major problems, since the context of simple stone tools gives them away. If they are found among more complicated objects that clearly resulted from human behavior, there is usually no question. If they are found outside such settings, however, problems arise, and if they are found in the kind of setting that is known to produce stone mimics of simple artifacts—in, for instance, a stream bed—caution is appropriate. Hence the first criterion for any archaeological site to be accepted as such, including any early archaeological site, is that it must contain undoubted artifacts or human bones.

IS THE SITE REALLY THAT OLD?

Dating can be a tricky matter in any archaeological setting. A wide variety of dating techniques can be used to place archaeological materials in time, some of which I will discuss in other contexts. However, the prime technique used to date materials from the past 40,000–50,000 years or so is radiocarbon dating. Most of the dates that I discuss in this book, whether or not they relate to the archaeological record, were derived from this approach.

RADIOCARBON DATING

Of the three isotopes of carbon that occur in nature, two (abbreviated ^{12}C and ^{13}C) are stable; one, ^{14}C, is radioactive. Carbon-14 is produced as a result of the bombardment of our atmosphere by cosmic rays. That bombardment produces neutrons, which in turn react with nitrogen-14 to produce radioactive carbon-14.

The radioactive carbon produced in this fashion combines with oxygen to form carbon dioxide, and in that form is widely distributed throughout the atmosphere, some ending up in plants and animals. During the lifetime of an organism, its carbon-14 content remains in equilibrium with that of the surrounding atmosphere, though there are some pernicious exceptions (the shells of both marine and, especially, terrestrial molluscs, for instance, can incorporate older carbonates). When the organism dies, the balance between atmospheric and organismic carbon-14 is lost, and the carbon-14 begins to decay without being replaced.

The half-life of carbon-14 is about 5,730 years; every 5,730 years, half of it disappears, decaying into a beta particle and nitrogen-14. Because the half-life of carbon-14 is known, measuring the amount of it left in the remains of an ancient organism provides a means of measuring exactly when that organism died: after 5,730 years, half is gone; after 11,460 years, another half, and so on. In fact, the limit of conventional radiocarbon dating is set by the fact that after enough years pass—40,000 years is about the standard limit—the amount of carbon-14 left is so minute that it is difficult to measure accurately.

Radiocarbon dating of tree rings of known age has shown that "radiocarbon years" are not always the same as calendrical years. A comparison of radiocarbon dates and calendrical dates for tree ring series extending back nearly 10,000 years shows that the two can diverge by as much as 800 years, the maximum deviation occurring at about 7,000 years ago. Other techniques suggest that, during the last 30,000 years, the maximum difference between radiocarbon and calendar years falls at about 20,000 years ago; here, the radiocarbon method gives ages that are about 3,500 years too young. For my purposes, these deviations are minor (and can be corrected), but it is worth recalling that radiocarbon years and calendrical years are not neccessarily identical, even though they are generally extremely similar. Throughout this book, I have, with rare exceptions, used radiocarbon years.

Although radiocarbon dating works much the way it is supposed to, it is not always an easy matter to obtain valid radiocarbon dates. In the archaeological context, the older the site, the harder it is to get good dates, because the older the site, the poorer the preservation of organic materials tends to be, and the greater the chances that any organic material still present will be contaminated or will have moved from its original position. Indeed, some organic material is relatively easily contaminated and great caution is required in using such materials as a source of radiocarbon dates. Bone is a prime example, since carbonates from ground water can easily make radiocarbon dates obtained from bone appear significantly earlier or later than the actual time of death of the animal.

Even with easily contaminated material, however, valid radiocarbon dates can often be obtained. Bone again provides a good example. About two-thirds of the composition of a fresh, dry bone is inorganic. The remaining organic fraction primarily consists of small fibers called collagen. The organic content of bone may be quickly lost after an animal dies and its bones are scattered across the landscape. However, if the bone is deposited in an environment conducive to the preservation of organic material, as might be provided by a dry cave, the organic fraction of the bone may be preserved. If so, the collagen can be extracted and the individual amino acids that make up that collagen can be isolated. Using newly available technology, those individual amino acids can be radiocarbon dated. Because the chances of contamination of certain amino acids in bone are quite small, the chances of getting an inaccurate date are correspondingly small. Indeed, to increase the odds of getting an accurate date, different amino acids from the same specimen can be dated, and the results compared.

That new technology uses an atomic particle accelerator and an ion counter to count the number of individual carbon-14 atoms in a sample directly. Conventional radiocarbon technology, in contrast, relies on counting the beta particles emitted as carbon-14 atoms decay.

Because the new approach counts the number of carbon-14 atoms directly, a number of benefits result. First, accelerator (or AMS) dating can date truly minute samples of carbon, on the order of a milligram, as opposed to the 10- to 100-gram samples of carbon routinely required by the conventional process. Second, accelerator dating opens the possibility of dating organic material well beyond the range of conventional dating, perhaps back to as far as 100,000 years ago.

There are other ways of dating archaeological sites, but for early New World sites, radiocarbon dating is essential, unless the site is so old that the radiocarbon technique cannot be used. The second criterion, then, is that an archaeological site felt to be ancient must be provided with trustworthy radiocarbon dates, or, if the site is too old for that, that it be provided with equally trustworthy dates produced in some other way. As we will see, however, there are no known sites in the New World that are clearly archaeological that may be so old as to be beyond the range of radiocarbon dating.

IS THE SITE UNDISTURBED?

In the best of all possible situations, archaeologists would be able to date the earliest New World archaeological sites by dating human bones found in those sites, or by dating wood or bone artifacts found through careful excavation. Unfortunately, such situations have proved difficult to come by. The oldest potential archaeological sites in the New World tend to be marked by stone tools, not by organic ones, and they lack human bones. As a result, these sites must be dated using organic material associated with the artifacts—bits of wood or seeds or animal bones so tightly associated with the stone tools that a strong argument can be made that they were laid down at the same time.

In many archaeological settings, it is not difficult to make that strong argument. A fireplace or hearth associated with living debris, for instance, can provide charcoal that, when dated, will provide an excellent estimate of the age of that fireplace. But many, perhaps most, archaeological sites are disturbed in one way or another. Burrowing rodents; digging by people; the roots of trees and shrubs; alternative freezing and thawing; even the trampling of large mammals (including people): all can move artifacts and other material horizontally across a site and vertically into sediments older and younger than those in which they were initially deposited. Some disturbances of this sort—Coke cans next to the bones of Pleistocene animals, for instance—are easy to detect. Harder to detect are disturbances in which subtle processes have moved single objects up or down.

The depositional layering, or stratigraphy, of many sites can be so complex that modern excavations are routinely conducted by a team of scientists that includes geologists or geologically trained archaeologists whose job it is to unravel the depositional history of the debris that forms the site. The complex nature of most archaeological sites, no matter what their age, leads to a third criterion for evaluating a possibly early site. To be considered seriously, that site must have been excavated with exquisite care, the stratigraphy of the site carefully unraveled, and possible means of disturbance eliminated.

CAN THE RESULTS BE EVALUATED?

In order to provide secure information on the earliest peoples of the New World, then, an archaeological site must have undoubted artifacts or human bones—that is, it must beyond a doubt be an archaeological site. It must have radiocarbon (or other) dates that have been carefully extracted from either human bone or organic artifacts, or from material so tightly associated with the artifacts that contemporaneity cannot be doubted. And the deposits of the site must be free of gross disturbances and have been excavated in such a way that the integrity of the deposits cannot be questioned.

To these three prime criteria, a fourth must be added. The results of the work that led to the conclusion that a given site meets these criteria must be published in such a way that others can conduct the same evaluation. This last criterion, of course, exists in all sciences.

Given these criteria, what does the earliest New World archaeology look like? I will explore this issue in four steps. First, I will look at some notable misses—sites and specimens that some thought were truly ancient, but that are now recognized as not being so at all. The story of these sites shows how easy it is to be wrong in this context. Second, I will take a quick look at a notable site in the Great Basin that some dedicated workers think is both ancient and archaeological, but that most archaeologists do not accept as having anything to with people. Third, I will take an even quicker look at two sites that are now the best candidates for the earliest New World archaeological sites south of glacial ice. Finally, in Chapter 4, I will quickly review the nature of the earliest secure archaeology in

North America, in order to provide an essential backdrop for understanding what we know about the latest Pleistocene and earliest Holocene archaeology of the Great Basin.

Some Notable Misses

THE OLD CROW BASIN

The lead article in the journal *Science* for January 26, 1973, carried a riveting title: "Upper Pleistocene Radiocarbon-dated Artefacts from the Northern Yukon." The one-line synopsis beneath the title was even more surprising: "Man was in Beringia 27,000 years ago."

The contents of the story were straightforward, even though the site that had provided the date was not. Working in the Old Crow Basin in the northern Yukon—the eastern fringe of unglaciated Beringia—the paleontologist C. R. Harington had found a fossilized caribou tibia whose end had been carefully serrated to produce a tool identical to fleshing implements used by recent Subarctic peoples to work hides. What was intriguing about the flesher was that it had been found among the bones of extinct Pleistocene mammals, including mammoth, suggesting by this placement that it might be extremely old.

Unfortunately, rather than having been found buried in an undisturbed context, the artifact had been found on the surface, leaving open the possibility that it was a recent tool lying among ancient bones. To Harington and his archaeological colleague W. N. Irving, this seemed unlikely, but the only way to be sure was to date the artifact itself. This they did, and *Science* reported the results: the tool was approximately 27,000 years old, and people had been in Beringia even before the last glacial advance.

Or had they? Geologist C. Vance Haynes had challenged the presumed antiquity of the flesher even before the radiocarbon date appeared. The challenges multiplied after 1973, however, because the crucial date had been run on the radiocarbon content of the carbon dioxide gas that had been produced by treating the inorganic fraction of the bone with acid. After the flesher was dated, scientists became increasingly aware of the fact that this fraction of bone can be readily contaminated through contact with either older or younger carbonates in groundwater. In this case, the suspicion in the archaeological community was that the artifact was far younger than the radiocarbon date implied. At the time, nothing could be done about this, because all of the tool but its serrated end had been destroyed to produce the original date.

That situation changed with the development of accelerator dating, and its ability to date milligram samples of carbon. In 1986, a tiny sample—0.3 grams—was removed from the flesher. The protein was extracted from that sample and then dated. The results were as stunning as the original date, and once again *Science* brought the news. The caribou flesher was only 1,350 years old. The flesher *looked* just like a modern tool because it *was* a modern tool.

In addition to the flesher, three other artifacts that had been made from caribou antler and that had been found with the bones of extinct mammals were also dated: the oldest was only some 3,000 years old. The title of the *Science* paper said it all: "New Dates on Northern Yukon Artifacts: Holocene not Upper Pleistocene."

CALIFORNIA BONES

The second significant miss—or more accurately, group of misses—was provided by a set of human bones obtained from sites ranging from San Diego on the south to San Francisco Bay on the north. The sites take their names from their locations, so listing them reveals where they are to be found: Scripps, Del Mar, Laguna Beach, Los Angeles, and Sunnyvale (San Francisco Bay). In all but one instance, the original context of the bones is poorly known; the exception is Sunnyvale, which was professionally excavated in the 1970s. Laguna Beach gives a feel for the problem, since this skull was dug out of a road cut by two teenagers in 1933. Similarly, the Los Angeles skull was turned up by WPA workers digging a storm sewer in 1936.

The problem arose in 1967, when archaeologist Louis Leakey became so intrigued by the Laguna Beach skull that he asked that it be radiocarbon dated. The results appeared in 1969: collagen from the skull dated to 17,150 years ago. The situation became more intriguing two years later, when collagen from the Los Angeles skull was dated to older than 23,600 years (there was too little collagen left to get any more precise information than that). Here were two human skulls dating to well within the Pleistocene, when most other aspects of the New World archaeological record suggested that people had not arrived here until the very end of the Pleistocene.

Things became even more interesting during the mid-1970s, when Jeffrey Bada of the University of California (San Diego) and his colleagues applied a new dating technique to these bones, and to those from Del Mar, Sunnyvale, and Scripps.

This technique, called amino acid racemization, depends on the fact that amino acids undergo chemical changes (the process is called racemization) after the death of an organism. If the rate at which these changes occur can be established, the time of death of the organism can be inferred. Of the many tricks involved in doing amino acid racemization dating properly, one is that the rate of change must be established for each area in which the technique is to be used. Establishing that rate in turn depends on having trustworthy radiocarbon dates for organic material from the area.

In dating the California human bones, Bada used the Laguna Beach skull, with its date of 17,150 years, to calibrate his amino acid racemization curves. The results he got were astonishing: Sunnyvale was estimated to be some 70,000 years old; the Del Mar bones, between 41,000 and 44,000 years old; the Scripps bones averaged some 40,000 years old; the Los Angeles skull, 26,000 years. Bada published his results in a highly respected journal, *World Archaeology;* the Laguna Beach skull was on the cover.

Rarely have such spectacular results done so much to harm the faith placed in a new dating technique. Although archaeologists wondered about the 17,150-year radiocarbon date for Laguna Beach, few wanted anything to do with the amino acid racemization dates, and many assumed that the technique, rather than its application in this instance, was fatally flawed. Sunnyvale provided excellent ammunition for such a view. While the Sunnyvale skeleton provided an estimated age of 70,000 years by amino acid racemization, radiocarbon dates from beneath the archaeological deposits fell at about 10,300 years ago, and charcoal from the archaeological deposits themselves dated to 4,460 years ago. Something was seriously wrong.

Accelerator dating has now solved the problem. All of these specimens were younger than 6,500 years old. The oldest, one of the Scripps specimens, has been dated to 6,300 years. The Los Angeles skull rang in at 3,560 years; Laguna Beach, the one that started it all, and that was used to calibrate the racemization curve, fell at 5,100 years (see Notes). At the moment, there are no well-dated human bones from the New World that are over 11,500 years old.

A Great Basin Miss

In the case of the Old Crow and California sites, there was no doubt that the sites were archaeological. The debates were over their age, and the outcome of those debates shows why archaeologists place so much stress on the dating criterion I discussed earlier. The Calico site, located in the central Mojave Desert of southeastern California, and thus on the southern edge of the hydrographic Great Basin (Figure 3-2), illustrates the problems that result when dealing with a site that appears to be reasonably well dated, but whose archaeological nature is not clear.

Louis Leakey's request that the Laguna Beach skull be dated was not his first attempt to push back the date of entry of people into the New World. In the early 1960s, Leakey became deeply impressed by a series of large, clumsy-looking artifacts from the Mojave Desert that had been shown to him by Ruth D. Simpson of the San Bernardino County Museum. Simpson thought that these materials were ancient, dating well into the Pleistocene, but she had been unable to demonstrate such an antiquity because all of her potentially ancient objects had been found on the surface, and there was no way she could date them.

During a 1963 field trip to the area, Leakey and Simpson found what they thought was a buried archaeological site of tremendous antiquity exposed in a road cut. Leakey, flush from his epochal successes in Olduvai Gorge, was convinced that they had hit archaeological pay dirt. The following year, with funding from the National Geographic Society, and with Leakey as overall project director and Simpson leading the fieldwork, excavations began at the Calico site, so named for the nearby Calico Mountains. Although outside funding for the project ran out in 1970, and although Leakey himself died in 1972, work by a dedicated group of volunteers has continued at Calico ever since.

Four years after the work had begun, Leakey and his colleagues reported that they had discovered over 170 artifacts at Calico, and they estimated that the deposits that provided these artifacts were between 50,000 and 80,000 years old. The true age of the deposits became clearer in 1981, when the results of the application of the uranium-thorium dating technique to materials in these deposits were published.

Like radiocarbon dating, uranium-thorium (U-Th) dating is a radiometric technique, relying on the breakdown

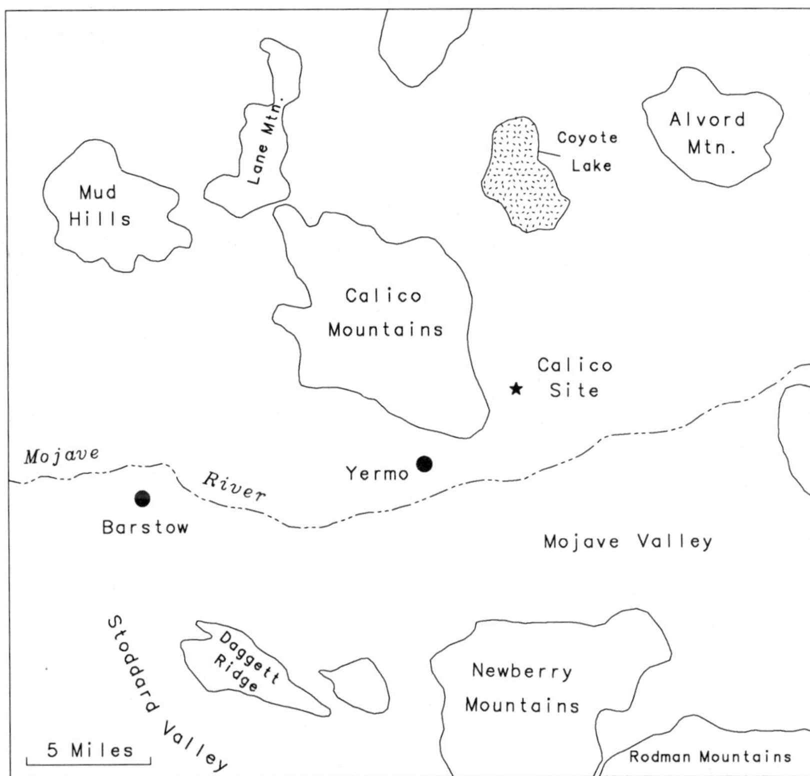

Figure 3-2. The location of the Calico site.

of a radioactive isotope—in this case uranium-234—into a "daughter" isotope—in this case, thorium-230. The half-life of radiocarbon is 5,730 years, limiting the current applicability of this approach to the last 40,000 years or so; but the half-life of uranium-234 is 75,000 years, thus allowing much older material to be dated. And, whereas radiocarbon dating must be applied to organic materials, U-Th dating can be applied to the calcium carbonate crusts that form on rocks as a result of groundwater activity.

The U-Th age for the deepest Calico deposits felt to have provided artifacts turned out to be 203,000 years. That is, the basal levels of this site predate the last interglacial. Leakey would have been pleased.

He also would have been pleased with the latest report on the number of artifacts Calico is thought to have provided. In 1983, archaeologist Fred Budinger reported that over 11,000 objects thought to be artifacts had been collected.

Budinger, as well as all other scholars who have worked on the Calico materials, knows full well what it means if he and his colleagues are right. As Budinger puts it, "The implications of a 200,000 year date for hominids in the New World are significant and far-reaching, and will certainly effect our understanding of both New and Old World populations during the Pleistocene Epoch. For one thing, the Calico evidence has made apparent the probability of pre–*Homo sapiens sapiens* man in the Western Hemisphere" (Budinger 1983:82).

If Budinger and his colleagues are right about Calico, that is exactly what it means, even opening the possibility that modern peoples may have evolved from earlier stock in the New World as well as in the Old. There is no reason to question the Calico dates: the site does appear to be that old. But is it archaeological?

Many Calico specimens are fairly crude: cobbles of chert, jasper, limestone, and other kinds of rock that have had flakes removed from one or more edges and from one or more sides. Some, however, look very much like undoubted artifacts, and would likely be accepted as such if they came from an archaeological site in a very different context. These specimens include slender, parallel-sided stone flakes, as well as flakes that appear to have been worked along one edge.

Unfortunately, looking like an artifact and being an artifact can be two very different things. The context of the Calico site is one that is known to produce artifact mimics.

The Calico specimens have been meticulously excavated from an alluvial fan, deposits that were brought by water, mud, or debris flows from the Calico Mountains up to four miles away. Archaeologists have long known that rocks tumbled as such fans are being formed can look much like artifacts. It is this fact that leads nearly all archaeologists to conclude that the specimens from Calico are far more likely to be what Vance Haynes has called "geofacts"—"artifact-like phenomena of geological origin" (Haynes 1973:305)—than they are to be artifacts.

Indeed, the archaeologist Louis Payen has applied a time-worn test to 83 Calico specimens that Leakey selected as among the best produced by the site. The test Payen used measures the angles at the edges of stone tools, and assumes that true stone tools will have edge angles that are more acute than those on stones that have been flaked by nature. Payen used a huge control sample of undoubted stone tools from sites other than Calico, and found their edge angles to average 72°. He then measured the same angles on the Leakey sample of prime specimens, and found them to average 87°. Finally, he measured edge angles on a sample of Calico specimens that Leakey had rejected as artifacts. They averaged 88°. Payen concluded that the specimens selected by Leakey, and by extension all Calico specimens, were geofacts, not artifacts.

Scholars supporting the validity of the Calico site have responded vociferously to Payen's analysis, as well as to Haynes's critique, but the context of the Calico site is such that natural rock breakage that produces specimens that look like true stone artifacts is to be expected. As a result, Calico has found almost no support among archaeologists. Even though we cannot demonstrate that none of these objects are artifacts, it is virtually impossible to prove that any of them are. Calico fails to meet one of the prime criteria: it does not contain undoubted artifacts.

Two Possible Hits

The sites that I have discussed to this point are either archaeological but not old, or old but not archaeological, and so illustrate the importance of the criteria with which I began this discussion. There are, however, two New World sites that may meet three of these criteria, and thus are accepted by many archaeologists as providing the earliest secure evidence for people in the New World, even though they do not at the moment meet the fourth criterion—that the results of the work be fully published. Because because ample amounts of information have been published on both places already, I discuss them briefly here, even though neither is close to the Great Basin.

MEADOWCROFT ROCKSHELTER

Located on a small tributary of the Ohio River some 30 miles southwest of Pittsburgh in far southwestern Pennsylvania, Meadowcroft Rockshelter is not huge by rockshelter standards—only some 700 square feet protected by the rock overhang—but the deposits within were some 15′ deep. It is probably no accident that the archaeological potential of the site was tapped by an archaeologist, James Adovasio, whose training was in the Great Basin. Great Basin archaeologists are always alert to the possibilities presented by cave deposits, whereas those working in northeastern North America rarely get to deal with such sites, and, when they do, they are often disappointed in the results.

Adovasio and his team began to work at Meadowcroft in 1971. His excavations continued for seven years, by which time they had carefully revealed what may be one of the two oldest known archaeological sites south of glacial ice in the New World.

The deepest Meadowcroft deposits appear to date to about 31,000 years ago, but those sediments, as well as the ones that immediately overlie them, contain no suggestion of human activities. Artifacts do not appear until just above the deepest part of the depositional unit called Stratum IIA. Those oldest artifacts were found alongside fireplaces or hearths that in turn provided organic materials that could be dated. Indeed, Meadowcroft is one of the best-dated archaeological sites in the world, Adovasio having obtained 52 radiocarbon dates for the site, dates that range from 175 years ago at the top (Stratum XI) to 31,000 years ago at the bottom.

These dates produce a consistent picture of the accumulation of deposits in Meadowcroft, since, with extremely rare exceptions, as the deposits get deeper, the dates get older, just as should happen. Lower Stratum IIA, which contains the earliest artifacts, has six radiocarbon dates, the oldest of which falls at 16,175 years ago, the youngest at 12,800 years ago. Averaged, the dates for the artifact-bearing parts of lower IIA suggest that the accumulation of this material centered on a date of 14,000 years ago.

The several hundred artifacts that come from deepest Meadowcroft have yet to be fully described in print, but, in addition to the waste flakes that resulted from stone tool manufacture, the assemblage includes a number of small blades. Blades are stone flakes that are twice as long as they are wide and that, in this instance, must have been struck from carefully prepared cores of raw material.

In addition to these, a single projectile point, made from chert, was found in the uppermost part of lower Stratum IIA, bracketed between dates of 11,300 and 12,800 years ago. Archaeologists use the term "projectile point" to refer to the points that tipped spears, darts, and arrows, since it is not always easy to tell the three kinds of points apart. The early Meadowcroft point, however, could not have been an arrowpoint, because it is too big (the earliest known use of the bow and arrow in North America postdates 2,000 years ago).

This fairly simple stone tool assemblage is not convincingly similar to anything else known from North America. The lack of strong similarities to anything else south of glacial ice is not surprising, given how small this collection of material is, and given that it is also older than anything else known from North America as long as the dates are correct.

"As long as the dates are correct" is an important caveat, since not everyone is convinced that they are. There are some anomalies in the Meadowcroft data, and it is on these that the skepticism has focused.

Two of the anomalies are straightforward. Carefully excavated archaeological sites routinely provide not only artifacts, but also the remains of contemporary plants and animals. Meadowcroft, excavated with tremendous care, provided both floral and faunal materials throughout its deposits. There are not many identified organic items from lower Stratum IIA, but those that exist could have come right out of the modern flora and fauna of the area.

The biggest problem is presented by plant material. Associated with radiocarbon dates that fall between about 13,000 and 14,000 years ago, the plants represented in this sample include oak, hickory, and walnut. These are all components of the modern vegetation.

Paleobotanical work, however, has shown that, between 13,000 and 14,000 years ago, the vegetation surrounding Meadowcroft was likely to have been spruce woodland, not deciduous forest. Indeed, hickory does not appear to have arrived in southwestern Pennsylvania until well after 10,000 years ago, and there are no remains of spruce woodland plants at all at the bottom of Meadowcroft. The plants are bothersome.

There are three obvious ways to explain the nature of the Stratum IIA plant assemblage. First, it is possible that small enclaves of deciduous forest trees existed in sheltered areas in southwestern Pennsylvania during late Wisconsin times. The possibility that that was the case, however, is seeming more and more unlikely as our knowledge of Wisconsin-age environments in this part of the world improves. Second, it is possible that the tiny fragments of nutshells, seeds, and wood of deciduous trees from the depths of Meadowcroft represent contaminants from upper levels. This would not be surprising: the remains of these plants are not uncommon in higher levels of the site, and contamination of this sort may be virtually impossible to detect.

Vance Haynes, however, has targeted a third possibility: bad radiocarbon dates. Haynes suggests that the lower levels of Meadowcroft may have been contaminated by ancient, soluble organic material carried into the shelter by groundwater. He supports this argument by pointing out that there are two specimens from lower Stratum IIA from which the soluble organic material was partially removed and dated separately from the remainder of the specimens. The soluble organic material turned out to be much older—4,600 years in one case, 10,000 years in the other—than the rest of the specimen. If all the soluble organic material had been removed from all the specimens, Haynes implied, the radiocarbon dates might all be post-Pleistocene in age, and thus be in line with the organic remains from Stratum IIA.

To test this possibility, Adovasio took the last datable specimen from the very bottom of Meadowcroft and sent it to the accelerator dating laboratory at Oxford University in England. At Oxford, dates were obtained from both the soluble organic material and the remaining insoluble part of the sample. The two dates were virtually identical: 31,400 and 30,900 years old. These dates also matched a conventional radiocarbon date for the same level—30,710 years—that had been obtained from a different specimen earlier in the project.

It is hard to know what to make of the twin problems posed by the dates and the plant remains in lower Stratum IIA. Perhaps, as Adovasio argues, it is no big deal, and there were people living in Meadowcroft between 12,000 and 16,000 years ago. Perhaps, as Haynes has argued, it is a huge deal, and the material that provided many of the dates was contaminated with ancient soluble organics.

MONTE VERDE

The Monte Verde site is located in the Central Valley of south-central Chile, some nine miles from the modern coastline. The site was discovered in 1976; work at the site began in that year and continued until 1985, all under the direction of archaeologist Tom Dillehay of the University of Kentucky.

Monte Verde sits on two sides of a small creek; Dillehay estimates that the occupied area covers some 8,600 square feet, of which some 4,600 square feet were excavated. In addition to its age, which I will discuss shortly, what makes this site remarkable is the superb preservation of the organic remains it contains. The archaeological materials are capped by peat, and then by a layer of cemented gravels. This, plus the high water table, has kept the cultural deposits continuously wet, and has led to excellent preservation of the organic items in the archaeological layer.

Monte Verde contained a cluster of at least 12 roughly rectangular structures ranging from 8′ by 10′ to 13′ by 15′ in size. The foundations of these structures were made from logs; the superstructures were appparently poles draped with animal skins: fragments of skin still adhere to some of the poles. Inside the structures were plant remains, stone tools, and clay-lined pits that had once held fires. Wooden mortars and grinding stones were found near some of those hearths. There are also other structures on the site, one of which is a wishbone-shaped feature made of sand and gravel that had upright wooden posts located every few inches along both wings, apparently the remains of a pole frame. Adjacent to the structure, Dillehay found a concentration of stone tools, piles of wood, and the bones of an extinct mastodon-like mammal.

Dillehay has obtained nine radiocarbon dates for this material, dates that fall between 11,800 and 12,800 years ago. A single additional date falls at 13,565 years ago. An additional nine dates have been obtained for older and younger deposits at the site, all of which are consistent with the dates for the archaeological material.

Until recently, many people questioned whether Monte Verde was really an archaeological site, and whether the dates were really trustworthy. In 1989, however, the Smithsonian Institution published the first of two volumes on this site. That volume, which deals with the geological context and chronology of the site, strongly suggests that the human occupation at Monte Verde dates to around 12,000 years ago. As such, this site becomes the first well-documented human occupation of the New World prior to 11,500 years ago, and suggests that even earlier sites are to be expected. Meadowcroft Rockshelter might be one, but this question cannot be answered until full documentation of that site is available.

Notes

The information on Eskimo movements across Bering Strait comes from E. W. Nelson (1983). General information on the Pleistocene is found in Imbrie and Imbrie (1979); I have drawn on Elias, Short, and Phillips (1992), Flint (1971), Porter (1988), Richmond and Fullerton (1986b), McManus and Creager (1984), Hopkins (1982), and Porter et al. (1983) for my discussion of the North American Pleistocene in general, and on the Bering Land Bridge in particular. Faunal exchange across the land bridge is treated in Harington (1980). Definitions of subdivisions of the Pleistocene are presented by Richmond and Fullerton (1986a).

It is worth pointing out that the greenhouse effect, caused by the accumulation of such gases as carbon dioxide (from the burning of fossil fuels) and methane (from the bacterial decomposition that occurs in landfills, garbage dumps, and the insides of cows) in the atmosphere, may cause a sea level rise of as much as 5′ during the next century (see Schneider, 1989). That increase will come both from the expansion of sea water as it warms and from the melting of existing glaciers. Indeed, sea level has already risen 5″ in the last 100 years, as global temperatures have risen 1°F and greenhouse gases have increased by some 25%. A 5′ rise in sea level would be disastrous for many low-lying areas. On the same theme, Flaschka et al. (1987) discuss the potential effects of a 2°C (3.6°F) increase in average annual temperature on the surface water resources of the Great Basin, but they do not take into account the potential of increased summer temperatures to strengthen monsoonal precipitation in this region.

On the debate over the nature of Beringia during the Wisconsin glaciation, see Guthrie (1968, 1982, 1985), Colinvaux (1986), Ager and Brubaker (1985), P. Anderson (1985), Ritchie and Cwynar (1982), and Ritchie (1984). Hopkins et al. (1982) provide a thorough and detailed account of many aspects of Beringian history. T. A. Brown et al. (1989) discuss the radiocarbon dating of pollen. On the "ice-free corridor," see J. M. White et al. (1985), Porter (1988), Burns (1990), Mandryk (1990), and Catto and Mandryk (1990). For the coastal route, see Fladmark (1979).

See R. Jones (1989) for a review of the early prehistory of Australia, and J. P. White and O'Connell (1979) and R. Jones (1989) for a discussion of the means by which people first reached Australia.

On the criteria used to evaluate archaeological sites for validity, I have followed Haynes (1980b) closely. The best introduction to radiocarbon dating in an archaeological context is presented by Taylor (1987). For recent discussions of accelerator dating, see Stafford et al. (1991) and D. E. Nelson (1991). Calibration of the radiocarbon time scale using dated tree rings (as well as other approaches) is discussed in a series of papers in Stuiver and Kra (1986). On the relationship between radiocarbon and calendrical years during the past 30,000 years, and on calibrating the radiocarbon time scale across this period, see Bard et al. (1990).

An excellent discussion of the human fossil and archaeological record is presented by Klein (1989). Vigilant et al. (1991) provide a recent, technical discussion of the genetic data suggesting an African origin for modern peoples about 200,000 years ago, but the approach they used has been shown to be flawed: see the recent review and references in Gibbons (1992) and Maddison et al. (1992).

For general statements on the peopling of the New World, see Grayson (1988b) and Meltzer (1989). B. M. Fagan (1987) provides a readable overview of this issue. On the archaeology of Beringia as a whole, see Morlan (1987). On the earliest archaeology of western Beringia, see Dikov (1978, 1990), and Yi and Clark (1985); on Siberia as a whole, see Larichev et al. (1988, 1990). Archaeological material felt to be more than 30,000 years old has recently been reported from the Chukotka Peninsula (Laukhin and Drozdov, 1991), but the artifacts involved come from a bore hole, and no excavations have been conducted at this site.

The Old Crow debate began with Irving and Harington (1973) and ended with D. E. Nelson et al. (1986). The amino acid racemization dates for the California human bones are found in Bada and Helfman (1975) and the radiocarbon dates that put an end to this debate, in Bada et al. (1984), Taylor et al. (1985), and, most recently, Stafford and Tyson (1989) (but see also Stafford et al. 1990). Bada (1985) has noted that if the 5,100 year AMS date for Laguna Beach is used to calibrate the racemization curve, Holocene ages for the once-contested human bones are provided by this method as well: it was the calibration, not the technique, that was flawed. Calico can be pursued in Haynes (1973), Patterson (1983), Budinger (1983), Bischoff et al. (1981), Simpson (1989), Taylor and Payen (1979), and Grayson (1986); this last reference takes a deep historical look at Calico and Calico-like enigmas and what they do to archaeologists. Meadowcroft is discussed in Adovasio and Carlisle (1988), Adovasio et al. (1988), Carlisle and Adovasio (1982), Adovasio et al. (1980, 1992), Haynes (1980a, 1991b), and Tankersley and Munson (1992), among other places. The title of Adovasio et al. (1980) indicates the depths at which some of these debates are felt. For the Pleistocene and early Holocene distribution of the plants found at Meadowcroft, see T. Webb et al. (1987). My discussion of Monte Verde is based on Dillehay (1989).

The Calico site is easily visited. The Bureau of Land Management has designated this site an "Area of Critical Environmental Concern," and, in conjunction with a private group called the Friends of Calico, keeps the site open year-round for public visits. On site, there are a small museum, visitor center, and library, all staffed by volunteers. There is a self-guided trail, as well a guided tour of the meticulous excavations that have been underway here for more than 25 years. These tours are well worth the time. Even if the archaeological issues are not of interest to you, the geology itself—a carefully excavated 200,000-year-old alluvial fan—is fascinating. At last check, the site was open from 8:00 A.M. to 4:30 P.M. from Wednesday through Sunday, with tours offered every hour on the half-hour, excluding 12:30, from 8:30 A.M to 3:30 P.M. There is no camping on the site itself, but ample facilities are available nearby. The California Desert Information Center in Barstow, run by the Bureau of Land Management [831 Barstow Road, Barstow, California 92311; (619) 256-8617] can provide a map of BLM campgrounds in the nearby Mojave Desert; both Owl Canyon (10 miles from Barstow) and Afton Canyon (41 miles from Barstow) are within easy reach of the Calico Site. The center has a small but excellent museum, and provides information on visiting Calico (see also Foster 1987).

The Calico site is 15 miles northeast of Barstow on Interstate 15. Take the Minneola Road exit (look for the "Calico Early Man Archaeological Site" sign), then follow the signs north for 2.5 miles until you reach the site. The road is dirt, but, the last time I was there, in excellent condition. In 1985, over 6,000 people made the visit.

CHAPTER FOUR

○○○

The End of the North American Pleistocene

Extinct Mammals and Early Peoples

The end of the Pleistocene in North America was a time of remarkable change. Throughout much of this region, plant communities were reorganized, as separate species of plants responded in their own individual ways to new climatic conditions. Huge glacial lakes that had formed in the Great Basin desiccated, some apparently with great speed. A substantial set of large and, from our modern perspective, exotic mammals became extinct. In addition, people spread throughout a landscape that had apparently been occupied by only scattered human groups at best. I explore the late Pleistocene lakes and plants of the Great Basin in subsequent chapters, but the mammals and people require a broader perspective.

The Mammals

The end of the Pleistocene in North America saw an episode of extinction that was astonishing in its breadth and depth, seeing the loss of 35 genera of mammals and some 19 genera of birds in a remarkably brief period of time. Some of the mammals are well known to most Americans: the mammoth and sabertooth cat, for instance. Some, however, remain known only to scientists who specialize in this time period, even though these animals are no less fascinating. Many of these mammals lived in the Great Basin toward the end of the Pleistocene, and there is little doubt that the earliest human occupants of the Great Basin encountered them (see Table 4-1).

THE XENARTHRANS

The order called the Xenarthra (at one time known as the Edentates) includes the modern sloths, vermilinguas (often called anteaters), and armadillos. Today, the only native North American representative of this group is the nine-banded armadillo, *Dasypus noveminctus.* During the late Pleistocene, however, seven genera of now-extinct xenarthrans occupied North America, especially across the southern United States.

The northern pampathere (*Holmesina septentrionalis*) ranged from Florida to Texas and Mexico, and as far north as Kansas. Like living armadillos, pampatheres were covered with a flexible armor of bony platelets, but the northern pampathere was some 6′ long and 3′ tall. A second species, the southern pampathere (*Pampatherium*), was also found in North America, but it is known from only one site in Texas.

Table 4-1. Genera of Extinct Late Pleistocene North American Mammals

Order	Family	Genus	Common name
Xenarthra	Dasypodidae	*Pampatherium*	Southern pampathere
		Holmesina	Northern pampathere
	Glyptodontidae	*Glyptotherium*	Simpson's glyptodont
	Megalonychidae	*Megalonyx*	Jefferson's ground sloth
	Megatheriidae	*Eremotherium*	Rusconi's ground sloth
		Nothrotheriops	Shasta ground sloth
	Mylodontidae	*Glossotherium*	Harlan's ground sloth
Carnivora	Mustelidae	*Brachyprotoma*	Short-faced skunk
	Canidae	*Cuon*★	Dhole
	Ursidae	*Tremarctos*★	Florida cave bear
		Arctodus	Giant short-faced bear
	Felidae	*Smilodon*	Sabertooth cat
		Homotherium	Scimitar cat
		Miracinonyx	American cheetah
Rodentia	Castoridae	*Castoroides*	Giant beaver
	Hydrochoeridae	*Hydrochoerus*★	Holmes's capybara
		Neochoerus	Pinckney's capybara
Lagomorpha	Leporidae	*Aztlanolagus*	Aztlan rabbit
Perissodactyla	Equidae	*Equus*★	Horses
	Tapiridae	*Tapirus*★	Tapirs
Artiodactyla	Tayassuidae	*Mylohyus*	Long-nosed peccary
		Platygonus	Flat-headed peccary
	Camelidae	*Camelops*	Yesterday's camel
		Hemiauchenia	Large-headed llama
		Palaeolama	Stout-legged llama
	Cervidae	*Navahoceros*	Mountain deer
		Cervalces	Elk-moose
	Antilocapridae	*Capromeryx*	Diminutive pronghorn
		Tetrameryx	Shuler's pronghorn
		Stockoceros	Pronghorns
	Bovidae	*Saiga*★	Saiga
		Euceratherium	Shrub ox
		Bootherium	Harlan's muskox
Proboscidea	Mammutidae	*Mammut*	American mastodon
	Elephantidae	*Mammuthus*	Mammoths

★Genus survives outside North America.

The North American glyptodont (*Glyptotherium floridanus*) is known mainly from near-coastal settings in South Carolina, Florida, and Texas, south into Mexico. Enclosed in a turtle-like shell or carapace with an armored tail and skull, this remarkable animal had huge limbs and a pelvic girdle that was fused to its carapace. Some 10′ long and 5′ tall—roughly the size of a Volkswagen Beetle—the North American glyptodont probably weighed between about half a ton and a ton, and may have been semiaquatic.

Far better known than the North American pampatheres and glyptodont are the extinct ground sloths of North America. Modern sloths are arboreal; fat ones may weigh 20 pounds. During the late Pleistocene, four genera of ground-dwelling sloths occupied various parts of North America, the smallest of which (Jefferson's ground sloth, or *Megalonyx jeffersoni,* first described by Thomas Jefferson) was the size of a bison and is known from Florida to Alaska. The largest of the North American sloths, Rusconi's ground sloth (*Eremotherium rusconii*), was roughly the size, but not the shape, of a mammoth, probably weighed some three tons, and is known only from the southeast and Texas. Harlan's ground sloth (*Glossotherium harlani*), characterized in part by the presence of pebble-like bones in its skin, was larger than Jefferson's ground sloth, and is the most abundant sloth in the asphalt deposits of Rancho La Brea, in what is now Los Angeles.

The best known of the ground sloths, however, is the Shasta ground sloth (*Nothrotheriops shastensis*), known from northern Mexico, the western United States, and Alberta. A number of dry caves in the southwestern United States contain the well-preserved dung of this bear-sized sloth. Detailed analyses of this dung have shown that the Shasta ground sloth ate plants still common in parts of the Southwest, suggesting to some that the diet may live on without the animal, although others disagree.

THE CARNIVORES

The smallest of the carnivores that became extinct were the two species of short-faced skunk (*Brachyprotoma*). This apparently highly carnivorous skunk was widespread, found in boreal settings from the eastern United States to the Yukon.

Today, the highly carnivorous dhole (*Cuon alpinus*), which belongs to the same family as dogs and wolves, is found through much of Asia, where it appears to subsist primarily on large mammals. Dholes were also found in North America during the late Pleistocene, their remains known from Alaska and the Yukon in the north and from northern Mexico in the south. It is reasonable to assume that they also occurred in intervening areas, but at the moment there are no records to show that this was the case.

The extinct dire wolf (*Canis dirus*) belongs to the same genus that includes the coyote (*Canis latrans*) and the gray wolf (*Canis lupus*). It has been argued that dire wolves, widespread in North America south of glacial ice, may have been heavily dependent on scavenging for their diet.

Two genera of bears are known to have become extinct in North America toward the end of the Pleistocene. The Florida Cave Bear (*Tremarctos floridanus*) was most common in the southeastern United States, but is also known from as far west as New Mexico, and south into northern Mexico. Today, the less powerfully built and smaller spectacled bear (*Tremarctos ornatus*) occupies the mountains of northwestern South America. In contrast, the giant short-faced bear (*Arctodus simus*) is known from northern Mexico, much of the contiguous United States, Saskatchewan, the Yukon, and Alaska. Long-limbed and some 30% larger than the North American grizzly, the short-faced bear was at one time thought to have been a powerful predator, but recent studies, based on skeletal remains from the Great Basin, strongly suggest that it was omnivorous or perhaps even largely herbivorous.

The sabertooth cat (*Smilodon fatalis*) is one of North America's most famous Pleistocene mammals. Known from Alberta in the northwest to Florida in the southeast, this lion-sized cat had upper canine teeth that were laterally compressed and serrated on both front and back edges, forming effective cutting tools. Recent analyses of the teeth of this animal show that little contact was made between those teeth and the bones of their prey. That, in turn, suggests that sabertooth cats probably left a good deal of meat on the carcasses of their victims, and so probably provided significant feeding opportunities for scavengers, including dire wolves. Perhaps this is why the distributions of dire wolves and sabertooth cats were so similar, and why their remains are often found together in the same sites.

The more lightly built scimitar cat (*Homotherium serum*) is not nearly as well known as the sabertooth, but appears to have been widely distributed, with fossils known from as far north as Alaska and the Yukon and as far south as Texas. Although this cat had smaller teeth than the sabertooth, they were also laterally compressed and serrated in front and back.

There were also cheetahs in North America toward the end of the Ice Age. Known from Wyoming, Colorado, and Nevada, the American cheetah (*Miracinonyx trumani*) differs from its Old World counterpart (*Acinonyx jubatus*) in a number of ways, including the fact that it was bigger and had fully retractable claws. Although some have argued that cheetahs evolved in the New World and reached the Old World via the Bering Land Bridge, the relationships between these animals are not at all clear.

Lions were also widespread in North America during the late Pleistocene, found from California to Florida, and from Alaska to Mexico and beyond. The fact that these animals have never been found in the forested east suggests that they were similar to modern lions in their preference for open habitat.

THE RODENTS

Only three genera of rodents were lost from North America toward the end of the Ice Age, but those three were impressive. The giant beaver (*Castoroides ohioensis*) ranged from New York to Florida in the east to Alaska in the northwest, but appears to have been most common in the Great Lakes region. Roughly the size of a black bear, these animals frequented marshes, lakes, and ponds. Detailed analyses of their skeletal remains, however, shows that, unlike their modern relatives, they did not build dams.

The other two genera of rodents that became extinct were capybaras. Today, the single species of capybara (*Hydrochoerus hydrochoerus*) provides the world with its largest living rodent, adults weighing over 100 pounds and reaching a length of well over 3′. Found from Panama to Uruguay, capybaras inhabit dense vegetation near water and use their excellent swimming abilities to escape danger. Similar habits seem to have characterized both late Pleistocene North American capybaras. Holmes's capybara (*Hydrochoerus holmesi*), known only from Florida, was somewhat larger than its modern counterpart, but Pinckney's capybara (*Neochoerus pinckneyi*), known from South Carolina and Florida, was half again larger.

THE RABBITS

Only one member of the order to which pikas, rabbits, and hares belong (the Lagomorpha) is known to have become extinct toward the end of the North American Pleistocene. The tiny Aztlan rabbit (*Aztlanolagus agilis*), which had jack rabbit-like adaptations for running, is known from the Chihuahuan Desert of New Mexico, Texas, and northern Mexico. Unlike many of the other mammals I am discussing here, the Aztlan rabbit does not seem to have survived the Wisconsin glacial maximum, some 18,000 years ago.

THE HORSES AND TAPIRS

Horses (the genus *Equus*) evolved in the New World and crossed into Asia via the Bering Land Bridge. They became extinct in the New World at the end of the Pleistocene, only to be reintroduced by Europeans during early historic times. Horses were extremely widespread in North America toward the end of the Ice Age; they appear to have been among the most abundant of all the larger Ice Age mammals here. Today, wild horses are so abundant in many parts of the arid west, including the Great Basin, that their numbers are artifically controlled.

Tapirs (the genus *Tapirus*) also live on outside North America. During the late Pleistocene, there were two species of North American tapirs, known from Pennsylvania and Florida in the east to California in the west.

THE ARTIODACTYLS

The losses among North America's late Pleistocene even-toed ungulates, or artiodactyls, were enormous: thirteen genera of these animals became extinct, ranging from peccaries to muskoxen.

Today, the collared peccary (*Tayassu tajacu*) ranges north into the southwestern United States and Texas, but it appears to be a recent arrival, and peccaries were far more widespread in North America during the late Pleistocene. The long-nosed peccary (*Mylohyus nasutus*) is well known from the eastern half of North America, and apparently occupied wooded enviroments, much like the more massive European wild boar (*Sus scrofa*). The flat-headed peccary (*Platygonus compressus*) was even more widely distributed, known from coast to coast, and from the edge of glacial ice on the north into Mexico on the south. The discovery of multiple, tightly associated skeletons of flat-headed peccaries suggests that they were gregarious, unlike the long-nosed peccary, which appears to have been more solitary in habits. Also unlike long-nosed peccaries, flat-headed peccaries appear to have preferred open environments.

Like horses, camels are New World natives, evolving here and then entering the Old World via the Bering Land Bridge. Unlike horses, however, some members of the camel family—llamas (the genera *Lama* and *Vicugna*)—survived in the New World. During the late Pleistocene, North America supported one genus of camel and two of llamas. The camel (*Camelops hesternus*) was widespread in North America; in life, it would have looked much like a large version of a dromedary (*Camelus dromedarius*), although its legs were longer, its head narrower and longer, and its single hump placed somewhat further forward. The large-headed llama (*Hemiauchenia macrocephala*) was widespread in the more southerly United States, known from southern California to Florida. This long-limbed animal appears to have been relatively speedy and adapted to open terrain. The stout-legged llama (*Palaeolama mirifica*) is known primarily from near-coastal settings in Florida, Texas, and California, though a nearly complete skeleton is also known from southern Missouri. Compared to the large-headed llama, this animal was of stockier build, and seems to have been adapted to more rugged terrain and to a more mixed diet.

The mountain deer (*Navahoceros fricki*) was a stout-legged animal intermediate in size between black-tailed deer (*Odocoileus hemionus*) and elk (*Cervus elaphus*), and closely related to the caribou (*Rangifer tarandus*). This was an alpine deer; its remains have been found only in or near the Rocky Mountains and in the mountains of northern Mexico. Remains of the elk-moose (*Cervalces scotti*), on the other hand, come mainly from the central and eastern United States and from the Yukon and Alaska. The size of a moose, this was a long-limbed animal that had complexly palmate antlers.

Today, the pronghorn is doing well in arid western North America, although it nearly became extinct during the early twentieth century. Toward the end of the Pleistocene, however, three genera of pronghorn did become extinct. All three had four-pronged horncores (the bony support for the horn itself), which distinguishes them from their living relative, whose horncores have only two prongs. The smallest of these extinct forms, the diminutive pronghorn (*Capromeryx minor*), stood only some 2′ tall at the shoulder, probably weighed about 20 pounds, and is known from California to Texas. Shuler's pronghorn (*Tetrameryx shuleri*) was about the size of its modern relative, and has been reported securely only from Texas, although it is probably known from Nevada as well. The final genus of extinct pronghorn, *Stockoceros*, has two named species (although these may actually refer to the same animal) and is known from Texas, Arizona, New Mexico, and northern Mexico.

Three genera of animals related to cattle (family Bovidae) also became extinct in North America toward the end of the Pleistocene. One of these, the saiga (*Saiga tatarica*) now thrives on the arid steppes of the Soviet Union; during the late Pleistocene, its range extended into Alaska and the Northwest Territories. The shrub ox (*Euceratherium collinum*) has been reported from late Pleistocene deposits from California to Iowa, and from as far south as central Mexico. Apparently related to muskoxen, but with distinctly different horncores, these animals seem to have been grazers that occupied hilly, but not mountainous, terrain. The last of the three, Harlan's muskox (*Bootherium bombifrons*) is known from nearly all of unglaciated North America, except for the far southeast and southwest. Able to cope with warmer climates than the living muskox (*Ovibos moschatus*), this animal appears to have occupied fairly open terrain, and was longer limbed and taller than its modern relative, although shorter from head to tail.

The mountain goat (*Oreamnos americanus*) is now doing well in northwestern North America. However, Harrington's mountain goat (*Oreamnos harringtoni*) failed to survive the end of the Pleistocene. Known from a variety of sites in the southern arid west, Harrington's mountain goat occupied environments ranging from open juniper woodlands to subalpine coniferous forests. Although some 30% smaller than its modern relative, Harrington's mountain goat was in many ways similar to modern mountain goats, including the fact that it had a white coat, as shown by preserved hairs from cave sites in the southwestern United States.

THE MAMMOTHS AND MASTODON

The American mastodon (*Mammut americanum*) was widespread in unglaciated North America, known from coast to coast and from Alaska to Mexico, but seems to have been most abundant in the woodlands and forests of the east. The upper tusks of these animals projected more or less horizontally from their skulls, then curved gently outward and, finally, back in. Their distinctive cheek teeth had large cusps arranged in pairs to form ridges that ran at right angles to the main axis of the tooth. These animals were browsers, apparently thriving in late Pleistocene open spruce woodlands. They were also massive, stockier in build than both modern elephants and extinct late Pleistocene mammoths. They were, however, shorter than mammoths, standing some 9 to 10′ at the shoulder.

The remains of mastodons are usually found as single individuals, suggesting that they were solitary. In this way, they differ from mammoths, whose remains are often found in groups of several individuals, suggesting that they were gregarious. Mammoth and mastodon differed in many other ways as well. More closely related to modern elephants than are mastodons, late Pleistocene North American mammoths had flat, high-crowned teeth in their jaws, each composed of a series of enamel-bordered plates running at right angles to the main axis of the tooth. Unlike the browsing mastodons, mammoths were primarily grazers, and their teeth reflect this dietary difference. Their distributions also reflect this difference: although mammoths are known from throughout unglaciated North America, their remains are most abundant in environments that were open grasslands. Also unlike mastodons, the tusks of mammoths point downward as they leave the skull, then curve down, out, and back in.

Of the two species of late Pleistocene North American mammoth, the woolly mammoth (*Mammuthus primigenius*) was more northern in distribution, and is well known not only from its bones and teeth, but also from frozen carcasses found in Alaska and Siberia. The Columbian mammoth (*Mammuthus columbi;* also called Jefferson's mammoth, *Mammuthus jeffersoni*) has been found from the far north into Mexico, and reached a height of over 11′, comparable to the size of an African elephant.

The Timing of the Extinctions

This was an astounding assemblage of mammals, next to which the current North American mammalian fauna appears dramatically impoverished, not so much in terms of the numbers of individual animals (there were probably 100,000,000 bison and pronghorn alone when Europeans first arrived here), but in terms of the kinds of animals. All of them, however, were gone by 10,000 years ago.

We can feel fairly certain about that date because, of the thousands of well-dated archaeological sites known from North America that are younger than 10,000 years old, none contains the remains of any of the extinct mammals, with rare and detectable exceptions caused by the incorporation of older bone into younger deposits. The lack of remains of these animals in deposits dating to the last 10,000 years makes it clear that the extinctions were over by that time, or that, if they were not over, the animals had dwindled in number to the point that they had become archaeologically and paleontologically invisible.

For years, it was assumed that, although the extinctions were over by 10,000 years ago, they had not begun until about 12,000 years ago. This was assumed for a fairly simple reason. By 1969, excellent dates falling between 12,000 and 10,000 years ago had become available for six of the extinct mammals: mammoth, mastodon, camel, horse, tapir, and Shasta ground sloth. Since six of the animals had clearly become extinct during this 2,000-year period, it seemed reasonable to assume that all or virtually all of the others had succumbed at the same time.

Rcently, however, assessments of the timing of the extinctions have suggested that this assumption may have been wrong. Most telling is the fact that, although it was easy to place six of the genera between 12,000 and 10,000 years ago, it has been extremely difficult to place any more in that time span. In the more than 20 years that have passed since 1969—when the last of the six was placed between 12,000 and 10,000 years ago—we have been able to date only three more—the sabertooth cat, the giant short-faced bear, and the stout-legged llama—to that 2,000-year slot.

As a result, it is beginning to look more and more as if scientists dealing with the extinctions were too hasty is assuming that all 35 genera of mammals became extinct within a narrow 2,000-year time span. At the very least, if the extinctions did occur that quickly, we cannot show it, and it appears equally likely that the extinctions were spread over a much longer period of time, perhaps on the order of several thousand years longer.

At the moment, all we can be sure of is that at least nine of the genera became extinct after 12,000 years ago, and that the extinctions were over by 10,000 years ago. This is unfortunate, since all of the recent detailed attempts to explain the losses have assumed that they all happened during the last 2,000 years of the Pleistocene.

The People

No matter when the first people arrived south of glacial ice in North America, it is certain that they were here by about 11,500 years ago. You have to look far and wide to find archaeological sites that might be older than 11,500 years, and everything that has been found has been argued about. Beginning between about 11,500 and 11,000 years ago, you have to look far and wide to find a significant patch of ground that was both inhabitable and that *lacks* traces of human occupation.

This change at 11,500 years ago or so may be real, or it may simply reflect tricks played on us by the archaeological record. Since the earliest secure archaeological sites in the Great Basin fall within this time slice, understanding those sites requires that we understand as well something about the archaeology of western North America as a whole during this time.

CLOVIS AND SOME CLOVIS SITES

In 1952, Ed Lehner was thinking about buying a ranch in the San Pedro Valley in Cochise County, far southeastern Arizona. Walking across property that he was soon to purchase, Lehner noticed bone protruding from the base of the steep bank of a dry streambed, some eight feet beneath the surface. In the first of many moves that were to give him a place in the history of North American archaeology,

Lehner removed some of the bones and brought them to the Arizona State Museum, where they were identified as belonging to a mammoth. Archaeologist Emil Haury of the University of Arizona soon visited the site, and realized that, although no artifacts were visible in the streambank, the age of the deposits was such that they might well be there. Haury and Lehner decided to keep a close eye on what was then simply an interesting paleontological site.

Three years later, Lehner got in touch again: heavy summer rains had exposed much more of what was there. Haury returned and decided it was worth a closer look.

Excavations began in late November of 1955, and, soon after the first dirt had been moved, the first artifact appeared. Indeed, the Lehner site, as it came to be called, proved to be so important that work here, work on the collections the site provided, and work on similar sites subsequently discovered in the area has continued ever since. Thanks ultimately to Ed Lehner, we have learned a tremendous amount about the late Pleistocene prehistory of the Southwest. Thanks to the generosity of both Ed and Lyn Lehner, the site itself is now part of the San Pedro Riparian National Conservation Area, and is strictly managed by the Bureau of Land Management.

The deposits at the Lehner site are fairly simple. At the base of a deep set of Holocene sediments, there is a black, organic clay that is routinely called the "black mat." This mat is widespread in the San Pedro Valley, and represents an ancient marsh. The base of the black mat at Lehner has been dated to about 10,800 years ago, and the artifacts at the Lehner site lie directly beneath it. When Haury worked his way through the black deposits, he came upon the decaying remains of 9 mammoths and a single bison; later work at the site has brought the total number of mammoths here to 13.

Haury also discovered what he interpreted as being two hearths, along with the mandible of a mammoth and bones from both tapir and horse. Recently, work by Vance Haynes has suggested that these hearths may be natural stains and not archaeological at all, but that does not affect the main part of the site, since, along with the mammoths, Haury found 21 stone artifacts. Of these, eight appeared to be simple cutting tools, perhaps used to butcher one or more of the mammoths. The other 13 were projectile points, 11 of which were found in the immediate vicinity of mammoth or bison bone.

Because of the care with which Haury worked, and because of the research that has been done here since that time, the setting for what appears to represent a series of ancient mammoth kills is fairly well known. At the time the site was forming, this area was a sand- and gravel-floored streambed bordered on the south by a nearly vertical clay wall about six feet high; the nature of the north wall is unknown, but it probably looked much the same. The analysis of pollen taken from dirt samples along the arroyo has shown that the area surrounding the ancient stream—appropriately called Mammoth Kill Creek—was desert grassland, slightly wetter and cooler than today, but not dramatically different. Haury suggested that mammoths probably walked up the streambed to reach a watering spot—the Lehner site—where they were attacked and killed by human hunters. Haury also argued that these mammoths had not been killed all at once, but represented instead a series of kills that had extended over some fairly short period of time. It is also possible that a combination of the killing of mammoths and the scavenging of those that had died naturally was involved in the formation of this site, but the age of the site is quite clear. Lehner dates to almost exactly 10,900 years ago.

The projectile points from Lehner are truly distinctive. They range in size from about one to four inches long, but it is their form that makes them distinctive. They are all lanceolate, with slightly concave bases, and nearly all have thin flakes removed from both sides, producing a very characteristic fluting that begins at the base and extends less than halfway toward the tip. The fluting appears to have aided in hafting the point to a spear or to a foreshaft that then fit into a spear. The edges just above the bases of the points are dulled by grinding; this was probably done either to prevent the sinew that held the point in place from being cut, or to remove irregularities in the point that would otherwise have hastened breakage.

Lehner is not the only site to have provided fluted points of this very distinctive style. Indeed, when Haury first visited Lehner, he was fresh from his work at the Naco site, 12 miles southeast of Lehner and just north of the Mexican border. Here he had found the remains of a single mammoth that had fallen on a sand bar adjoining a streambed. Among the bones of this mammoth were eight fluted points virtually identical to those from Lehner (see Figure 4-1). It has been pointed out that the Naco mammoth may have been one that got away, since there are no artifacts other than the points here.

Not far from these two sites, but discovered and excavated much later, are Murray Springs and Escapule, both of

Figure 4-1. The Clovis points from the Naco site, Arizona (the longest measures 4.6″). Photograph by E. B. Sayles, courtesy of the Arizona State Museum.

which have mammoths and the same kind of fluted points. Further afield, there are the Miami site in Texas, Dent in Colorado, Domebo in Oklahoma, Blackwater Draw in New Mexico, Lange/Ferguson in South Dakota, and a number of others, all of which have both mammoths and the points. Not all sites with the points have mammoths: the Sheaman site in Wyoming substitutes bison; the Kimmswick site in Missouri has mastodon. Although the animals may change, the dates do not. Whenever they have been well dated, these sites fall between 11,200 and 10,900 years ago. Some may be slightly older, but none are younger.

The points, and the whole cultural complex they represent, take their name from the town of Clovis, New Mexico, because it was near here, at the Blackwater Draw site, that they were first found and recognized to be ancient. There is, of course, more to Clovis than just the distinctive points and large mammals. Clovis sites have provided a variety of stone tools made on both flakes and blades, and there are also a small number of bone tools, including what are either bone projectile points or spear foreshafts. There are also Clovis sites known that are not large-mammal kill sites. The Anzick site in Wyoming, the Simon site in Idaho, and the Wenatchee site in eastern Washington all appear to be caches of fluted points and a variety of other objects. Nonetheless, even though there is more to the Clovis toolkit than the Clovis points themselves, it is the points that allow Clovis sites to be recognized as such, because it is the points that are so distinctive and that, unlike the bone tools, preserve in and on the ground.

Even with the hints that are now available concerning pre-Clovis occupations in the New World, the origins of Clovis remain unclear. There are no fluted points known from the Asiatic side of the Bering Land Bridge, and, although there are fluted points from Alaska and the Yukon, none are known to predate Clovis points from south of glacial ice. The best guess is that Clovis points originated exactly where they are found—south of glacial ice in North America.

On the other hand, Alaskan archaeological assemblages assigned to what is called the Nenana complex, which dates to around 11,300 years ago, do show many similarities to Clovis assemblages, as long as the projectile points are excluded. Based on detailed assessments of the stone tools in these two sets of assemblages, Ted Goebel and his colleagues argue that Nenana and Clovis may represent the northern and southern archaeological remnants of the same initial peopling event. If so, we may finally be beginning to understand Clovis origins.

At the moment, Clovis sites provide the earliest securely dated, noncontroversial sites in the New World south of glacial ice. Monte Verde appears to be changing that, but, even so, Clovis will still stand as distinctive because there are so many sites that fall into this early cultural complex, all of which date to between about 11,200 and 10,900 years ago.

There are, however, several fairly serious ways in which we can be misled by Clovis as we try to understand the early peoples of North America.

The first of these involves big-game hunting. As soon as the first fluted point was found with the remains of an extinct large mammal, it began to be widely assumed that the people who made the points gained a significant part of their livelihood by hunting big game. Even though many have discussed the possibility that the hunting of large mammals may have been a relatively rare event in a Clovis life, sites such as Naco and Lehner provide such a compelling picture of cunning human hunters taking massive game that many have found it difficult to think of Clovis in any other way.

But the fact that Clovis peoples were capable of taking such mammals as mammoths simply does not mean that big-game hunting provided a critical part of their diet, or that it was even an important part of their lives. The apparent importance of mammoths to Clovis people may result instead from the very biased way in which our sample of Clovis sites has accumulated. With the exception of the very rare cache sites, in almost every case buried Clovis sites have been discovered because someone—often an astute rancher like Ed Lehner—saw large bones protruding from the ground. Subsequent excavations showed that there were artifacts associated with these bones. Sites that cannot be found in this way have a much reduced chance of being discovered: eroding projectile points are much less visible than eroding mammoth bones, Clovis sites tend to have small numbers of artifacts anyway, and most people would not recognize a Clovis artifact as such to begin with.

As a result, if Clovis peoples in the west spent most of their time hunting mice and gathering berries, we probably would not know it. As archaeologist James Griffin said years ago, the restriction of the Clovis diet to large mammals has been by archaeologists, not by the makers of the fluted points themselves.

This is not to say that Clovis peoples were not big-game hunters. Sites like Lehner suggest that Clovis peoples took elephants in situations that required considerable skill. What I am saying is that because of the way we have learned about most of our Clovis sites—bones found first—our sample may be so biased that we have gotten a very mistaken impression of the role that large mammals played in their subsistence. It may well be true, as the archaeologist Richard MacNeish once said, that a typical group of Clovis peoples may have taken only a mammoth or two in their lifetime, and never stopped talking about it.

Clovis may also mislead us into thinking that human population densities in North America took a major jump upward shortly after 11,500 years ago. This potential problem results from the fact that Clovis points are both readily recognizable and well dated. When archaeologists find one, they know what it is, and they know how old it is. In addition, because it is a Clovis point, and because Clovis is both old and relatively rare, many, perhaps most, discoveries of these points end up getting published. Although nearly all later North American projectile point styles also have a fixed and known range in time, each and every discovery of these later points is not published because we know so much more about these later periods.

Clovis points provide the earliest recognizable artifact type in North America south of the ice. Even if both Meadowcroft and Monte Verde are as old as the dates suggest, neither contains any artifact types sufficiently distinctive that they would be recognized as ancient outside of a datable context—if, for instance, they were found lying on the surface. Because Clovis is so easily recognized, and because we know of nothing earlier that is, Clovis may mislead us into thinking that there was a major population increase in North America shortly after 11,500 years ago, when all that really happened was the invention of an easily recognized artifact type.

The difficulty is clear. Even so, I suspect that a population increase really did occur, the real question being how big that increase was. That is the only way I can reconcile the large number of buried sites that begin to appear between 11,500 and 11,000 years ago with the vanishingly small number that we may know about before that time.

Finally, it is also important to realize that, although nearly all Clovis points are fluted (there are rare unfluted Clovis points as well—Lehner had three), not all fluted points are Clovis. Clovis in the Great Plains, for instance, is followed by a cultural complex called Folsom. Folsom sites date from about 10,900 to 10,200 years ago, and contain not mammoth but bison as the prime large mammal in kill sites. Folsom points are fluted, but, unlike the Clovis version, the flutes run all the way from the base to the tip. Many eastern fluted points are superficially most similar to Clovis points from the Plains and Southwest: they are lanceolate with concave bases and flutes that extend less than halfway up from the base. But although they are similar, these eastern points are not identical to the Clovis version. In the northeast, where they have been well dated, they are often between 10,600 and 10,000 years old. That is, they tend to be contemporary with Folsom, not with Clovis.

Eastern archaeologists no longer automatically think, as they once did, that superficial similarites between their fluted points and Clovis points mean similarity in time, since they clearly do not. Western archaeologists have not always been so careful: when they see fluted points superficially similar to Clovis points, they often call them Clovis, and thus assume that they are the same age as Clovis. They may in fact be the same age, but they may also be older or younger.

What Caused the Extinctions?

It is hard not to be struck by the fact that, just as the large Pleistocene mammals were breathing their last, Clovis peoples were busy creating the sites marked by fluted points and mammoths. For some animals the correlation between the dates for Clovis (11,200 to 10,900 years ago) and the dates for extinction are just too close to be attributed to coincidence.

The dates for the Shasta ground sloth in the Southwest provide an excellent example. Thanks largely to the painstaking efforts of Paul Martin of the University of Arizona, large numbers of excellent radiocarbon dates are now available for ground sloth dung and soft tissue from Southwestern sites. Of the 38 dates in this series, the youngest falls at 10,500 years ago.

Harrington's mountain goat provides a second example. The remains of this animal are fairly well known from caves within Arizona's Grand Canyon. Detailed work by Jim Mead of Northern Arizona University provided 37 radiocarbon dates from the remains of Grand Canyon goats. Of these 37, 35 fall before 11,000 years, two fall between 11,000 and 10,000 years, and none are more recent. These animals were becoming extinct while Clovis peoples and other fluted point makers were spreading across the landscape.

There are two prime explanations for the extinction of so many mammals toward the end of the Pleistocene in North America. One of these emphasizes the fact that many of the extinctions occurred while Clovis peoples seem to have been spreading across the landscape, and argues that human hunting caused the extinctions. The other explanation targets climatic change.

Paleontologists Russell Graham and Ernest Lundelius have developed one version of the climatic argument in detail. They focus on evidence that changing seasonal swings in temperature were at the root of it all. Put simply, this argument maintains that, although the late Pleistocene may have seen colder annual temperatures, it was also a time when temperature swings from winter to summer were dampened, in part because Arctic air masses were blocked from moving south into central North America by the massive ice sheets that covered Canada. As the Pleistocene ended, they suggest, average annual temperatures rose, but seasonal differences in temperature increased dramatically. These increased seasonal temperature swings caused massive changes in North American plant communities, leading to habitats that were structurally far less complex than those that supported the Pleistocene mammals. In this view, the reorganization of vegetational communities caused increased competition among herbivores and decreased the availability of the plant foods utilized by these animals. This severe ecological disruption caused tremendous range changes for many smaller mammals and extinction for many larger ones.

There are many other climatically oriented attempts to explain late Pleistocene mammal extinctions in North America. Dale Guthrie, for instance, attributes the demise of those mammals in many areas to the demise of the mammoth steppe. As I have discussed, however, Guthrie's mammoth steppe has not found much support among paleobotanists, whose data indicate that it did not exist. Recently, Vance Haynes has presented intriguing evidence that much of North America south of glacial ice may have undergone a brief but significant pulse of drought at about 11,000 years ago. In this view, the black mat that overlies the Clovis deposits at such sites as Lehner and Murray Springs indicates a rise in the water table immediately following that episode. To Haynes, one of the effects of this drought might have been to concentrate larger mammals at water holes, where they became easy prey for Clovis hunters. He suggests that the combination of drought and human predation helped cause the extinction of at least some of the late Pleistocene mammals.

The alternative view has been built in a remarkable series of papers by Paul Martin, who is impressed by the correlation between the timing of the extinctions and the spread of the makers of fluted points throughout much of North America. Martin argues that the large mammals fell prey to human hunters, and that the mammoths we see in Clovis sites document part of the process.

Put so starkly, Martin's position may seem weak, but in fact he has pointed to a wide variety of mysteries for which he can account but for which the climatic school as yet cannot. Horses, for instance, became extinct in North America at the end of the Pleistocene. They thrived, however, when reintroduced by Europeans during early historic times; today, an estimated 32,000 wild horses live in Nevada and western Utah alone. If climate caused the extinctions some 11,000 years ago, why do horses do so well now? Further, he asks, if climatic change provides the cause, why do we not see comparable extinctions at the end of earlier North American glaciations? Only people, Martin argues, can account for the depth and breadth of the losses that occurred.

This is not the place to delve deeply into this complex matter. Instead, I simply observe that Martin's overkill explanation fails on a number of grounds. As I have discussed, only nine of the genera that became extinct can be securely shown to have been contemporaneous with the users of fluted points. But even if we could show that all of the mammals survived until the end of the Pleistocene, attributing the extinctions to human predation requires that we make yet another major assumption: that people really hunted all the large mammals that became extinct. As time goes on, it is seeming increasingly unlikely that that was the case.

A number of years ago, Lundelius and his colleagues compiled a large list of paleontological sites in the United States. Horses and camels are the first and third most frequently reported mammals in the sites on that list; mammoths and mastodon are second and fourth, respectively. Horses and camels, however, have never been reported in secure "kill" association in fluted point sites. Indeed, although a few kill associations are known for mastodon, the only extinct mammal that shows up in such a context in any number is the mammoth.

The climatic models account not only for the extinction of the large mammals, but also for huge changes in the ranges of many small mammals that occurred at the same time. These facts, coupled with the evident weaknesses of the overkill explanation, lead most scientists to believe that the answer to this mystery is to be found in climatic change, not in the behavior of the late Pleistocene human occupants of the New World, even if human predation might have been critical in insuring that a few genera that might otherwise have had a chance to survive did not.

No matter what caused the extinctions, however, when the Pleistocene ended, the mammals were gone, and the people were here.

Notes

On the Pleistocene mammals of North America, see Kurtén and Anderson (1980), the best and standard reference. A more recent, but far less detailed, review of these mammals can be found in Grayson (1991b); this source, from which parts of this chapter were taken, also provides references to the literature on the North American extinct mammals. Stuart (1991) reviews both North American and northern Eurasian extinctions. On horses in the American West, see Berger (1986). On the chronology of the extinctions, see Grayson (1987a, 1989b, 1991b). Martin and Klein (1984) is the best reference to the debate over the causes of the extinctions; Grayson (1991b) provides a succinct overview of these issues. Graham and Lundelius (1984) develop their views in detail; see also Graham (1985a,b, 1986, 1990), and Lundelius (1988, 1989). Guthrie (1984, 1990a,b) outlines his position on late Pleistocene extinctions. Paul Martin has developed his position in a lengthy series of fascinating papers: a selection of the most important would include Martin (1967a,b, 1973, 1984, 1990a,b), and Mosimann and Martin (1975).

On the Lehner site, see Haury et al. (1959), Mehringer and Haynes (1965), N. Allison (1988), and Haynes (1991a). On the dates for Clovis, see Haynes (1987, 1991a, and, especially, 1992); on edge grinding, see Titmus and Woods (1991). Powers and Hoffecker (1989) discuss the early archaeological sequence now available for interior Alaska; Goebel et al. (1991) discuss the similarities between Nenana and Clovis stone tool assemblages. Griffin (1964) provides his statement on Clovis diet; see MacNeish (1964) for his statement on Clovis hunting. Meltzer (1988) provides a wide-ranging exploration of fluted point users in eastern North America. My dates for Folsom follow Haynes (1992). The dates for ground sloth and Harington's mountain goat extinction in the Southwest are in Martin et al. (1985) and J. I. Mead et al. (1986). The sample of paleontological sites south of glacial ice compiled by Lundelius and his colleagues is in Lundelius et al. (1983).

PART THREE

○○○

The Late Ice Age Great Basin

CHAPTER FIVE

○○○

The Late Pleistocene Physical Environment

Lakes and Glaciers

The fastest anyone has ever officially gone on land is 633.468 miles per hour, a speed hit by Richard Noble in the *Thrust 2* on October 4, 1983, on northwestern Nevada's Black Rock Desert. That accomplishment broke the record set by Gary Gabelich on October 23, 1970, when his *Blue Flame* hit 622.287 miles per hour on the Bonneville Salt Flats, western Utah. Kitty O'Neil, who holds the land speed record for women, clocked 524.016 miles per hour on December 6, 1976, driving her *Motivator* on the Alvord Desert in eastern Oregon. The fastest bicycle ever pedaled was pedaled 152.284 miles an hour by ex-Olympian John Howard, drafting behind a car on the Bonneville Salt Flats.

Virtually all land speed records have been set at the Bonneville Salt Flats or at places just like it. The attributes these places have in common are fairly obvious: they are big, flat, and salt-encrusted. Although the shared attributes are obvious, the reason those attributes are shared is less so. All of these places were once at the bottom of lakes that formed during the Pleistocene, and it was deposition within, and the desiccation of, those lakes that created the almost perfectly level surfaces on which land speed records are now set. The Alvord Desert was once beneath Pleistocene Lake Alvord. The Black Rock Desert was once beneath Pleistocene Lake Lahontan. Australia's Lake Eyre, the scene of Donald Campbell's setting of the speed record for wheel-driven turbines (429.311 miles per hour), was once beneath Pleistocene Lake Dieri. The Bonneville Salt Flats, as well as the rest of the Great Salt Lake Desert, were once beneath Pleistocene Lake Bonneville.

Modern Great Basin Lakes

Lakes are rarely the first thing to come to mind when traveling through the Great Basin today. Although ranges like the Ruby and East Humboldt mountains have their share of alpine lakes, lakes, as oppposed to ephemeral sheets of water, are harder to come by in the valleys. It can even be hard to know what to call a real lake, since bodies of water in the valley bottoms that appear to be truly substantial—Goose Lake, straddling the Oregon-California border, for instance, or Lake Abert in south-central Oregon, or Malheur Lake to the east—have all been completely dry during historic times. One of the remarkable things about today's Great Basin is how variable lakes in the valleys are. In any given year, a list of lakes made in the spring and

Table 5-1. Valley Bottom Lakes in the Great Basin[a]

Lake	Pleistocene system	Area (acres)[b]	References
Oregon			
Abert (AL)	Chewaucan	36,540	1,2
Summer (SM)	Chewaucan	25,000	1,2
Goose (GS)	Goose	97,390	1,2
Harney (HA)	Malheur	26,400	1,2
Malheur (MH)	Malheur	49,700	1,2
Agency (AG)	Modoc	9,300	1
Upper Klamath (UKL)	Modoc	61,540	1
Anderson (WL)	Warner	410	12
Bluejoint (WL)	Warner	6,920	12
Campbell (WL)	Warner	2,340	12
Crump (WL)	Warner	7,680	1,2
Fisher (WL)	Warner	300	12
Flagstaff (WL)	Warner	3,580	12
Hart (WL)	Warner	7,230	1,2
Mugwump (WL)	Warner	210	12
Pelican (WL)	Warner	230	12
Stone Corral (WL)	Warner	1,000	12
Swamp (WL)	Warner	850	12
Turpin (WL)	Warner	300	12
Upper Campbell (WL)	Warner	980	12
California			
Eagle (EG)	Acapsukati	24,100[c]	5
Adobe (AD)	Adobe	110	11
River Spring (RS)	Adobe	140	11
Honey (HN)	Lahontan	57,600[d]	10
Lower Klamath (LKL)	Modoc	30,000[e]	9
Tule (TL)	Modoc	96,000[e]	15
Owens (OW)	Owens	71,000[f]	7
Mono (MN)	Russell	54,900[g]	5
Tahoe (TA)	Tahoe	121,000	4
Nevada			
Ruby (RB)	Franklin	9,000	4
Humboldt (HU)	Lahontan	4,200	4
Pyramid (PY)	Lahontan	142,000[h]	5
Soda Lakes (SD)	Lahontan	260	6
Upper Carson (CR)	Lahontan	25,600[i]	11
Walker (WK)	Lahontan	65,000[i]	5
Winnemucca (WN)	Lahontan	61,000[j]	5
Summit (SM)	Summit	530	4
Washoe (WA)	Washoe	4,100	4
Artesia (AT)	Wellington	1,000	4
Lower Pahranagat (PA)	White River	585	4
Upper Pahranagat (PA)	White River	370	4
Utah			
Bear (BE)	Bonneville	70,400	13
Great Salt (GSL)	Bonneville	1,152,200	3
Sevier (SV)	Bonneville	120,320	14
Utah (UT)	Bonneville	94,100	8
Total		2,543,415	

Notes: a, Lake abbreviations identify lakes in Figure 5-1; *b,* areas in acres may be converted to square miles by dividing by 640; *c,* 1960 level; *d,* 1867; *e,* ca. 1905; *f,* 1872; *g,* 1930–1939 average; *h,* 1891–1902 average; *i,* 1882; *j,* 1891–1902 average.

References: 1, D. M. Johnson et al. 1985; 2, Phillips and Van Denburgh 1971; 3, Currey et al. 1984; 4, Smales 1972; 5, Harding 1965; 6, Rush 1972; 7, Gale 1915; 8, R. H. Jackson and Stevens 1981; 9, Sweet and McBeth 1942; 10, Russell 1885b; 11, Planimetric measurement from USGS 1:24,000 series map; 12, planimetric measurement from USGS 1:100,000 series map; 13, Sigler 1962; 14, G. K. Gilbert 1890, Oviatt 1989; 15, Sweet and McBeth 1942; Bob Davis, Bureau of Reclamation (Klamath Falls, Oregon), personal communication.

early summer will be long, recording as lakes what are actually playas temporarily filled with runoff from adjacent mountains. The same list made in late summer or early fall will be far shorter.

Not only does any list of lakes vary seasonally, it also varies across the years. During wet years, like the middle 1980s, existing lakes expand and flood areas previously thought secure, and playas fill with water year-round. During dry spells, as occurred from 1928 to 1935, lakes that seem permanent shrink and dry. Outside of alpine settings, Great Basin lakes that have not disappeared completely during historic times are rare—Great Salt Lake, Utah Lake, Pyramid Lake, Mono Lake, Walker Lake. Not coincidentally, these lakes lie close to either the Wasatch Range or the Sierra Nevada, and all lie at the terminus of streams that flow from these mountains, streams whose catchments tend to be both high and large.

Added to all these natural variations are fluctations that have occurred because of human intervention during historic times. Owens and Mono lakes provide good, if disturbing, examples. Owens Lake is now dry, a result not so much of the diversion for irrigation that began during the 1870s and 1880s, but of the withdrawal of water from Owens Valley for use in Los Angeles, beginning with the completion of the Los Angeles–Owens Valley Aqueduct in 1913. Mono Lake waters began to be diverted by the Los Angeles Department of Water and Power in 1941. By 1989, the level of the lake had fallen 42′, increasing the salinity of the lake and allowing predators to reach previously isolated colonies of breeding birds on the lake's islands. The current struggle to save Mono Lake is a continuation of the battle that was waged earlier in the century by the residents of Owens Valley to reserve access to a fair share of their own resources.

Winnemucca Lake used to receive its waters from the Truckee River when the river was high. Completion of the Derby Dam on the Truckee in 1905, diversion of Truckee River water into the Carson River basin, and other uses of Truckee water spelled the end of Winnemucca Lake. Today, the channel that used to carry water from the Truckee to Winnemucca Lake is closed by highway fill. Sevier Lake in central Utah was dry by 1880, a result of diversion of water from the Sevier River for irrigation; not until 1983 did the lake begin to fill again, the result of extremely high precipitation in the high plateaus and mountains of central Utah.

All of this variation—natural changes in lake levels from season to season and from year to year, and changes that we have caused—makes the compilation of a simple list of Great Basin valley bottom lakes a difficult affair. I have done it anyway, and the results are in Table 5-1 (see also Figure 5-1).

In compiling this table, I generally included all those valley bottom lakes that are indicated as "permanent" on the U.S. Geological Survey 1:250,000 scale topographic maps, while eliminating those that are usually dry during the summer (for instance, Franklin Lake in Ruby Valley). The second column in the table, "Pleistocene system," provides the name of the Pleistocene lake that filled the basin in which the modern lake sits. The Pleistocene lakes themselves I will discuss later in this chapter.

The third column claims to show the area of the lakes in acres, but it should already be clear that such areas change dramatically from season to season and from year to year. In some cases, I have provided figures that predate major modification of the drainage system—Owens, Mono, Winnemucca, and Sevier lakes are examples. In some cases, the areas represent historic average levels—Great Salt Lake and Utah Lake are examples. In other cases, I simply measured lake areas from 1:24,000 or 1:100,000 U.S. Geological Survey topographic maps.

This table includes a few lakes—most notably Tahoe and Summit—that are not true valley bottom lakes at all; these I have included because their basins held significant Pleistocene lakes. In addition, there are four lakes on my list—Agency (which could just as well have been treated as part of Upper Klamath Lake), Upper Klamath, Lower Klamath, and Tule—that actually fall outside of the hydrographic Great Basin, since they drain to the Pacific via the Klamath River. These I include both because they all fall within the basin of a large Pleistocene lake (that likewise drained to the Pacific), and because the area in which they are located falls within the botanical Great Basin.

My list has 45 lakes on it, with a total area of some 2,500,000 acres. Of that acreage, almost half is contained in Great Salt Lake, the rest differentially scattered across the remaining systems. A better idea as to how this water is distributed can be gained from Figure 5-2, which shows the acreage of Great Basin lakes that fall within each of the 1:250,000 scale maps that cover the Great Basin. It would have been convenient if each lake fell squarely within a given map, but, although most lakes do fall that way, some are divided among maps. Goose Lake, for instance, is shared between the Alturas and Klamath Falls sheets. In all such cases, I simply assigned the entire lake to that Great

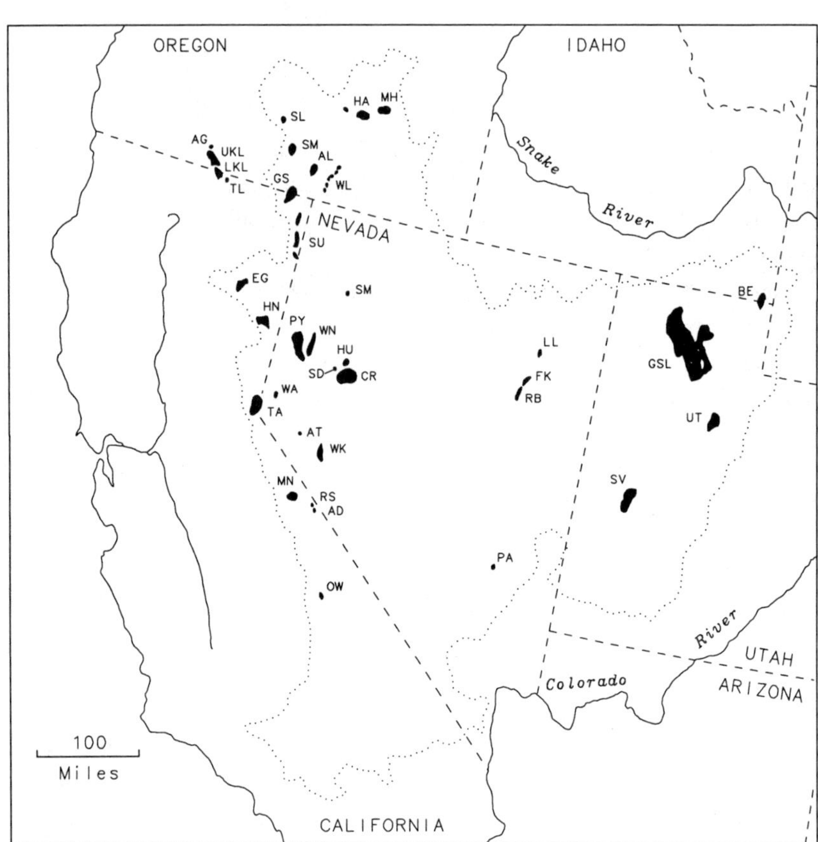

Figure 5-1. Great Basin lakes. *Key:* FK = Franklin Lake; SL = Silver Lake; SU = Surprise Valley (Alkali) lakes; LL = Little Lake. See Table 5-1 for key to other lakes.

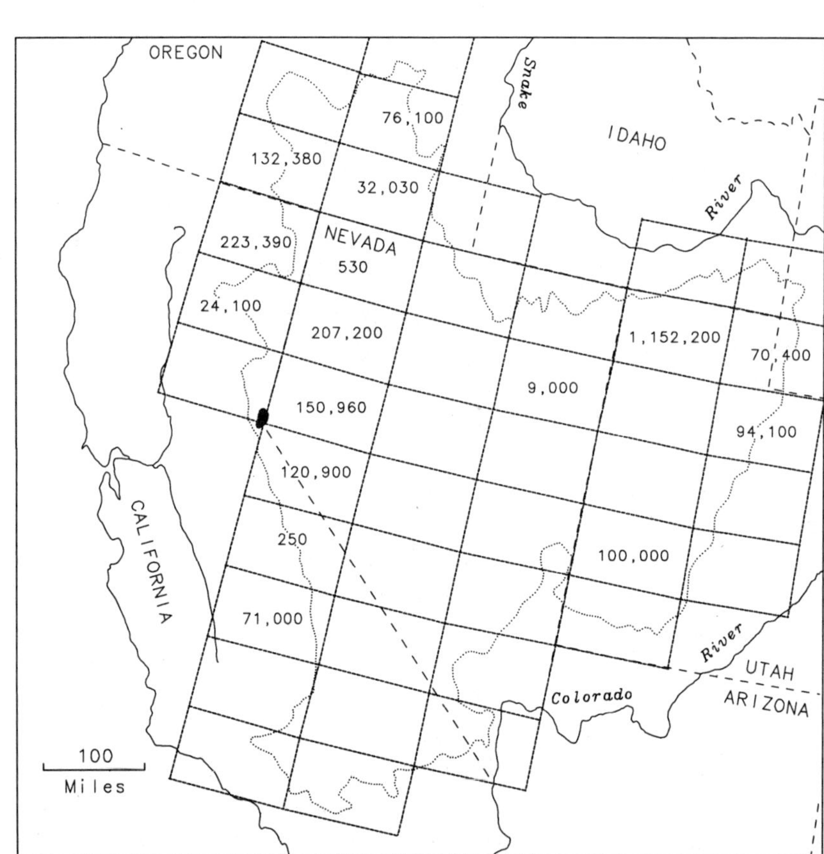

Figure 5-2. Total areas of Great Basin lakes (in acres) according to 1:250,000 scale U.S. Geological Survey maps.

Basin map that contains most of it. Alturas thus got all 97,390 acres of Goose Lake, even though roughly one-third of it (and even more if measured in terms of drainage area) falls on the Klamath Falls map. This way of assigning lake areas does not affect the simple points I want to make from this figure. Great Basin lakes of any permanence are primarily found on the eastern, western, and northern fringes of this region. Lakes become rarer toward the heart of the Great Basin, and toward the south. The reasons for this are simple.

Great Basin Climate and Modern Lakes

The distribution and amount of rainfall received by the Great Basin is, of course, determined by the nature of the air masses that carry moisture into, and within, the region. In an important analysis of Great Basin rainfall patterns, meteorologist John Houghton has documented how three main sources of precipitation interact to establish those patterns.

Most important of all sources of precipitation here are the low-pressure storm systems that are brought into the Great Basin by westerly winds moving off the Pacific Ocean. During the warmer months of the year, those westerlies lie far to the north. The cold water on the surface of the Pacific Ocean along Oregon and California chills the air that comes into contact with it, slowing evaporation and creating a layer of cool, stable air over the water itself. As a result, moisture-bearing westerlies rarely penetrate into the Great Basin during summer.

During winter, however, the westerlies move southward and bring storm systems—Pacific fronts—onto the coasts of Oregon and California, where they soon encounter the Sierra Nevada and Cascade Mountains. Forced upward, these air masses are cooled and condensed, and as a result drop often massive amounts of precipitation on the western (windward) sides of these ranges. How much of their moisture the air masses lose in this way, and that is thus lost to the Great Basin, depends not only on their initial moisture load, but also on the mass and elevation of the parts of the Sierra Nevada and Cascades they encounter.

Although the Pacific component of Great Basin rainfall is the most important component of precipitation in this region, it plays the heaviest role in the western and northern Great Basin, since the former area is closest to the Pacific source, and the latter receives the greatest number of Pacific frontal storms. In addition, Pacific moisture is an important source of rainfall wherever the frontal systems encounter massive mountain ranges. The Wasatch Range, for instance, receives its maximum precipitation in the winter from Pacific storm systems, although it benefits as well from the fact that it lies downwind of Great Salt Lake.

The Pacific component of Great Basin precipitation comes mainly between October and April. In the summer months—July and August—the westerlies are far weaker, and precipitation from this source is at its minimum. It is during these warm months that monsoonal storms, driven by the temperature differential between air masses over the gulfs of California and Mexico on the one hand, and those over the land on the other, enter the Great Basin from the south. Although the southeastern Great Basin is the major recipient of precipitation from these storms, receiving some 35% of its annual rainfall in this way, much of the southern and eastern Great Basin benefits from these southerly rains. Indeed, some two-thirds of all summer rain in the Great Basin is derived from the Gulf component of Great Basin precipitation.

The spring and fall months see a third source of precipitation rise in importance. Between April and June on the one hand, and October and November on the other, low-pressure systems develop over the Great Basin itself, often east of the most massive parts of the Sierra Nevada. These systems—the Great Basin or Tonopah lows—draw their moisture from a number of sources. However, they generally drop more precipitation in the spring than in the fall, suggesting that a prime source of the moisture they carry lies in the snowpacks of Great Basin mountains and in the low-elevation lakes of the area: both snowpacks and lake levels are at their seasonal highs during the spring and early summer. Rains from this Continental component are most important in an area that roughly straddles the Utah-Nevada border. Here, about half the average annual precipitation comes from this source, with nearly all the rest contributed by the Pacific storms of winter.

Figure 5-3 shows the contributions of these three precipitation regimes—Pacific, Gulf, and Continental—to the annual total rainfall received in the Great Basin. The average annual rainfall from all these sources combined is illustrated in Figure 5-4. These rainfall patterns alone go far to explain why lakes are found where they are in the Great Basin. All other things being equal, areas of decidedly low precipitation have no lakes.

However, it is the precipitation that falls on bordering mountains that accounts for many Great Basin lakes. The

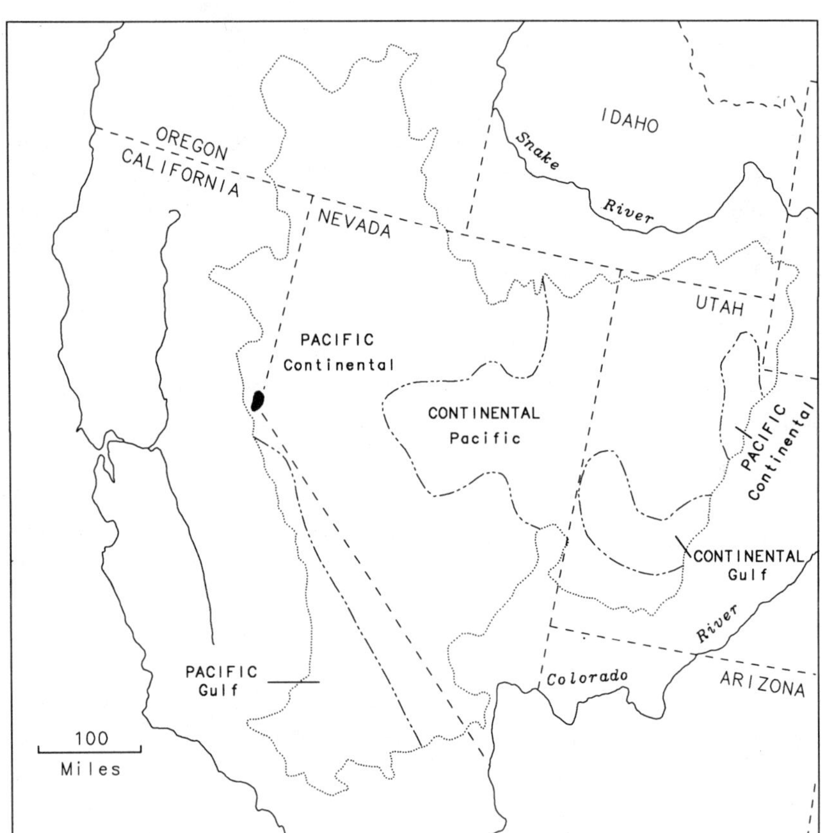

Figure 5-3. The contributions of Pacific, Gulf, and Continental sources to annual precipitation in the Great Basin; upper name in each pair is the primary, lower name the secondary, precipitation source. After Houghton (1969).

Figure 5-4. The distribution of average annual rainfall (in inches) in the Great Basin. After U.S. Department of Commerce (1983).

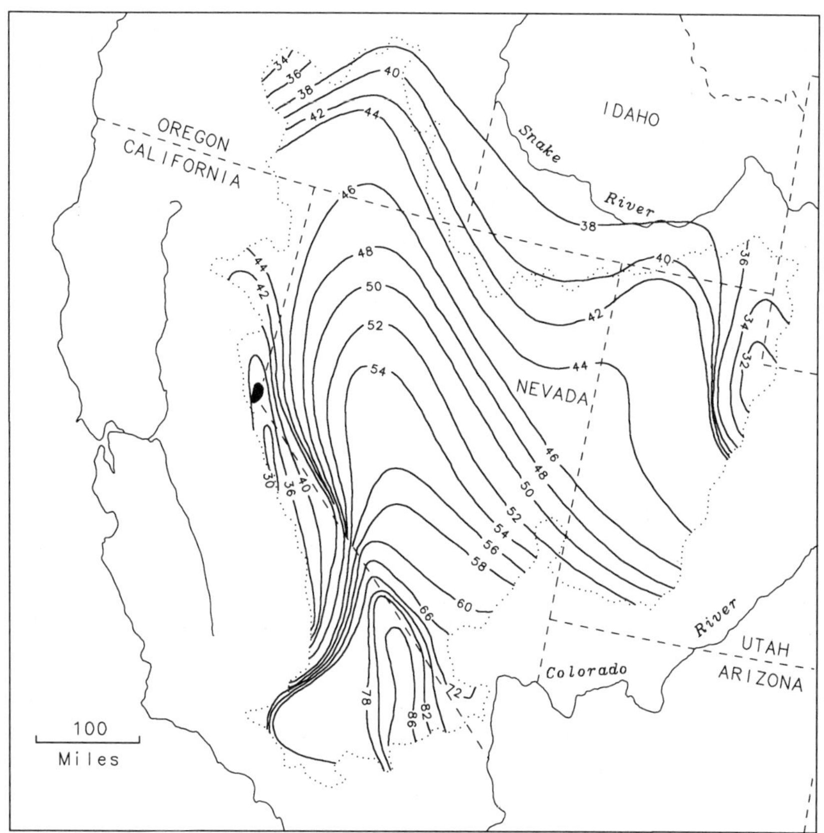

Figure 5-5. Lake evaporation rates (in inches per year) in the Great Basin. After U.S. Department of Commerce (1983).

Sierra Nevada receives over 50″ of precipitation a year, whereas the Wasatch Range receives over 40″. On the west, Lake Tahoe lies on the eastern edge of the Sierra Nevada, whereas the sources for the major lakes flanking the western Great Basin—Pyramid, Winnemucca, Upper Carson, Walker, Mono, and Owens—all lie within the Sierra Nevada. On the east, Great Salt Lake, Utah Lake, and Sevier Lake have their sources in rivers that flow from the Wasatch Range. Ultimately, these lakes are fed primarily by precipitation brought by winter storms coming from the Pacific. These storms bring their moisture at a time when evaporation is at a minimum and when moisture is readily stored in the mountains in the form of snow. Precipitation directly on the lakes is important, but it is the mountain-born rivers that sustain the sizable lakes that fringe the far eastern and far western edges of the Great Basin.

For instance, precipitation provides 31% of the input to Great Salt Lake but surface streams provide 66% (the remaining 3% is provided by groundwater). Of this 66%, nearly all comes from rivers that flow directly or indirectly from the Wasatch Range and the western Uinta Mountains: 59% from the Bear River, 20% from the Weber, and 13% from the Jordan. On the other side of the Great Basin, Walker Lake receives 83% of its input from the Walker River, which in turn flows from the Sierra Nevada. Only 11% of Walker Lake inflow comes directly from precipitation, the remaining 6% coming from groundwater and local runoff.

Thus, lakes fringe the eastern and western edges of the Great Basin because they are fed by streams that originate in adjoining, massive uplands—the Sierra Nevada and Wasatch Range. These uplands, in turn, receive their precipitation from winter storms moving off the Pacific.

The Great Basin is also fairly lake rich in its northern reaches. The Ruby and Warner valleys and Harney Basin, for instance, all have substantial lakes, but the waters that feed them come neither from the Sierra Nevada/Cascades nor from the Wasatch Range. All do have major uplands nearby—the Ruby, Warner, and Steens mountains in these three cases—but even more substantial uplands are found to the south, where comparable lakes do not exist.

There are two prime reasons for the existence of these northern lakes. First, the Great Basin north of 40° N latitude—that is, north of a line that runs through Pyramid and Humboldt lakes, through the Ruby Valley south of Ruby Lake, and just south of Utah Lake—receives a greater share of Pacific frontal storms than do areas that lie south of that latitude. The northern Ruby Mountains, for example, lie directly in the path of these storms; the upper reaches of the Rubies may receive nearly 50″ of precipitation a year as a result. Further south, a high-pressure system, the "Great Basin High," often prevents Pacific frontal storms from entering; it is when this high-pressure system weakens that Pacific storms sweep across this area as well. The greater frequency of winter storms originating in the Pacific helps account for the greater number of lakes in the northern Great Basin.

Evaporation rates also play a key role, however. These rates are far higher in the southern Great Basin than they are to the north. In the north, mean annual lake evaporation rates are on the order of 40″ to 45″ a year. On the southern edge of the Great Basin, they are on the order of 70″ a year or more (Figure 5-5). These differences are largely a function of the increased temperatures encountered in moving from north to south. The mean annual temperature in Las Vegas, for instance, is 66°F; in Elko, in the northeastern part of the state, it is 45°F. Decreased evaporation, coupled with increased precipitation, accounts for the relative abundance of lakes in the north, and for their absence in the south.

So the distribution of lakes in the Great Basin can be accounted for by modern Great Basin geography and climate. Pacific storms moving into the Great Basin between October and April provide much of the precipitation. On the western and eastern edges of the area, that water collects in the high mountains—the Sierra Nevada and Wasatch Range—and is ultimately deposited in the lakes. On the north, the water is also largely deposited in the fringing mountains, but here the existence of lakes is assisted by the increased frequency of Pacific storms north of 40° N latitude, and by evaporation rates that are far lower than those to the south. The distribution of lake areas shown in Figure 5-2 makes good sense when seen in climatic and geographic perspective.

Pleistocene Lakes in the Great Basin

Geologists use the term "pluvial lake" to refer to Pleistocene lakes whose levels were higher because of altered ratios between precipitation and evaporation. Later, I will discuss current estimates of late Pleistocene temperatures and precipitation in the Great Basin. For now, I merely note that these estimates routinely suggest that late Ice Age temperatures were lower, and average annual precipitation levels higher, than those of today. Pluvial lakes were the result.

When lake basins that have outlets to the sea receive greater amounts of water or lose less to evaporation, or both, excess water can flow outward through swollen stream channels. Because the separate basins of which the Great Basin is composed have no outlets, they respond in a predictable way to increased amounts of water. Basins that have no lakes get them, just as ephemeral lakes appear today in many Great Basin playas when runoff is high. Basins that have lakes get bigger ones. Since lake levels cannot be controlled by simply increasing outflow through drainage channels, lakes continue to rise until one of a number of things happens.

In most basins, as lakes rise, their surface areas increase. As that happens, more water is exposed to evaporation, so more is lost to this process. In some cases, the lakes can rise to the point that increased evaporation balances increased input, and the lake stabilizes at this level.

If that does not happen, the increased flow leads inexorably to the point at which the lake will overflow, a situation no different from what happens when you forget to turn off the water in your bathtub. Water will then pour into an adjacent basin. If increased evaporation from that process does not lead to an equilibrium between water loss and water gain, then the adjacent basin—probably filling on its own anyway—can fill as well. Given enough water, these now conjoint basins can overflow yet again. The process will not stop until evaporation balances or exceeds precipitation, or until the altered precipitation/evaporation ratios that led to the lake level rise in the first place change once again. Alternatively, the lake can rise until it finds a way to spill to the sea. Goose Lake, for instance, rose so high in 1868 that it overflowed into the Pit River system, thus stabilizing its level at 4,716′ (in typical Great Basin fashion, Goose Lake also became completely dry in 1926).

Although it is easy to state the general principles involved in the rise and fall of Great Basin lakes, the details can be extremely complex. For instance, lake basins can lose water through underground flow to other basins. To take but one example, eastern Nevada's northern Butte Valley provides groundwater to Ruby Valley to the north. In addition, the increased evaporation that occurs as lakes expand their surface areas can be partially offset by the fact

Table 5-2. Pluvial Lakes of the Great Basin[a]

Pluvial lake	Location	Area (square miles)	Pluvial lake	Location	Area (square miles)
California			Nevada *continued*		
Acapsukati★	Eagle Lake Basin	62	Groom	Emigrant Valley	36
Adobe★	Black Lake	6	Hawksy Walksy★	Hawksy Walksy Valley	12
Cuddeback	Cuddeback Lake	35	High Rock★	High Rock Basin	12
Deep Spring	Deep Springs Valley	17	Hubbs	Long Valley	195
Harper★	Harper Lake Basin, Mojave River	54	Jakes	Jakes Valley	63
Horse★	Horse Lake Basin	8	Kawich	Kawich Valley	22
Koehn	Fremont Valley	42	Kumiva	Kumiva Valley	15
Le Conte	Salton Sea	1,776	Labou★	Fairview Valley	20
Madeline★	Madeline Plain	300	Lahontan	Lahontan Basin	8,610
Manix★	Troy Lake, Coyote Lake	157	Laughton	Cold Spring Valley	7
Manly	Death Valley	600	Lemmon	Lemmon Valley	13
Modoc★	Modoc Lake	1,095	Lunar	Sand Spring Valley	6
Mojave★	Soda Lake, Silver Lake	77	Macy	Macy Flat	9
Owens★	Owens Lake	205	Maxey	Spring Valley	81
Panamint★	Panamint Valley	300	Meinzer	Long Valley	344
Russell	Mono Lake Basin	267	Mud	Ralston Valley	133
Searles★	China and Searles Lake basins	384	Newark	Newark Valley	302
Surprise	Surprise Valley	568	Paiute★	Bawling Calf Basin	4
Tahoe★	Lake Tahoe Basin	211	Parman★	Summit Lake Basin	7
Thompson★	Antelope Valley	215	Railroad	Railroad Valley	375
Idaho			Reveille★	Reveille Valley	41
Thatcher★	Bear River Basin	100	Rhodes	Rhodes Salt Marsh	13
Nevada			Spring	Spring Valley	233
Antelope	Antelope Valley	48	Toiyabe	Big Smoky Valley	203
Bristol	Dry Lake Valley	35	Tonopah	Big Smoky Valley	90
Buffalo★	Buffalo Valley	77	Waring	Goshute and Steptoe valleys	541
Carpenter	Lake Valley	134	Washoe★	Washoe Lake Basin	23
Cave	Cave Valley	69	Wellington★	Smith Valley	117
Clover	Clover and Independence valleys	352	Yahoo	Stevens Valley	2
Coal	Coal Valley	69	Oregon		
Columbus	Columbus Salt Marsh	79	Alkali★	Alkali Lake Basin	212
Corral	Little Smoky Valley	9	Alvord	Alvord Desert	491
Crooks★	New Year Valley	5	Catlow	Catlow Basin	351
Desatoya	Smith Creek Valley	168	Chewaucan	Abert and Summer Lake basins	480
Diamond★	Diamond Valley	392	Fort Rock★	Fort Rock Basin	905
Dixie	Dixie Valley	276	Goose★	Goose Lake Basin	368
Edwards	Edwards Creek Valley	102	Malheur★	Harney Basin	950
Franklin	Ruby Valley	483	Warner	Warner Valley	505
Gale	Butte Valley	159	Utah		
Garfield	Garfield Flat	3	Bonneville★	Great Salt Lake; Great Salt Lake and Sevier deserts	19,970
Gilbert	Grass Valley	155			
Gold Flat	Gold Flat	26	Pine	Wah Wah Valley	41
Granite	Granite Springs Valley	40	Utaho	Pocatello Valley	42

★Lake overflowed into an adjacent basin at maximum levels.

[a]From Snyder et al. (1964), Mifflin and Wheat (1979), Dicken (1980), G. I. Smith and Street-Perrott (1983), J. R. Williams and Bedinger (1984), and Benson and Thompson (1987a,b).

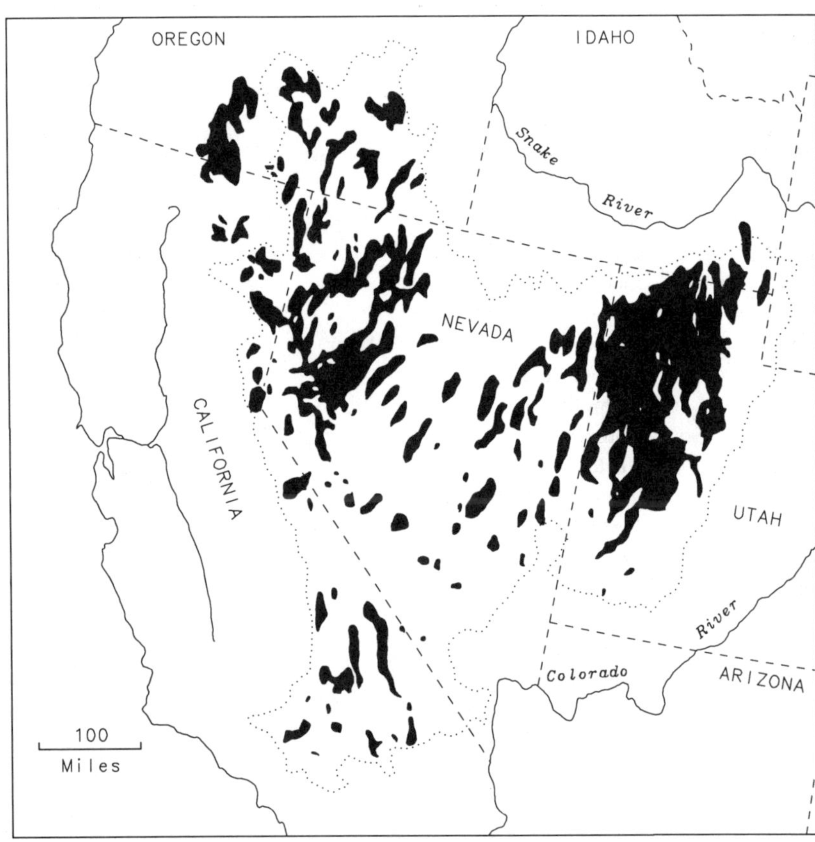

Figure 5-6. Pluvial lakes in the Great Basin. After G. I. Smith and Street-Perrott (1983) and T. R. Williams and Bedinger (1984).

that expanded lake surfaces can now catch greater amounts of precipitation. As lakes rise and fall, their salinity changes, and changing salinities also alter evaporation rates. Nonetheless, the general principles are clear and fairly simple. Increased precipitation or decreased evaporation or both lead to higher lake levels. Since both things happened in the Great Basin during the Pleistocene, pluvial lakes were abundant, and in some cases huge.

Today's Great Basin has—or would have were waters not diverted for other purposes—some 2,500,000 acres of lakes that at least tend to be there more often than they are not (see Table 5-1). During the late Pleistocene, the Great Basin held at least 27,800,000 acres of lakes, a figure that is likely to be conservative because small, ancient lakes are difficult to detect long after the fact. That is, at least 11 times more of the Great Basin's surface was covered by water during parts of the Pleistocene than is so covered today (see Table 5-2 and Figure 5-6).

Although the Great Basin held some 80 pluvial lakes during the Pleistocene, the largest of these lakes, Lahontan and Bonneville, are also the best known, and it is these on which I focus here.

PLEISTOCENE LAKE BONNEVILLE

In mid-April 1846, 22 members of the families of George and Jacob Donner and James Reed left Springfield, Illinois, headed for disaster in the snows of the Sierra Nevada (see Chapter 10). On August 22, they, and 65 other members of what has come to be known as the Donner Party, emerged from the mouth of Emigration Canyon in the Wasatch Range to enter the far eastern edge of the basin of Pleistocene Lake Bonneville (Figure 5-7). Continuing west, they passed south of Great Salt Lake, a Lake Bonneville remnant, and to the north of Utah and Sevier lakes, the only other lakes that still occupy the Bonneville Basin. They had well over 100 miles to go before they would finally be out of the largest of all Great Basin Pleistocene lake basins. East of Floating Island, they mired their wagons and lost many of their cattle, but were still about ten miles north and east of the Bonneville Salt Flats, the home of so many of today's land speed records. Some 30 miles to the north and west lay the Pilot Range, whose Pilot Peak provided the visible target for those coming this way, and whose Pilot Springs provided the water that was so des-

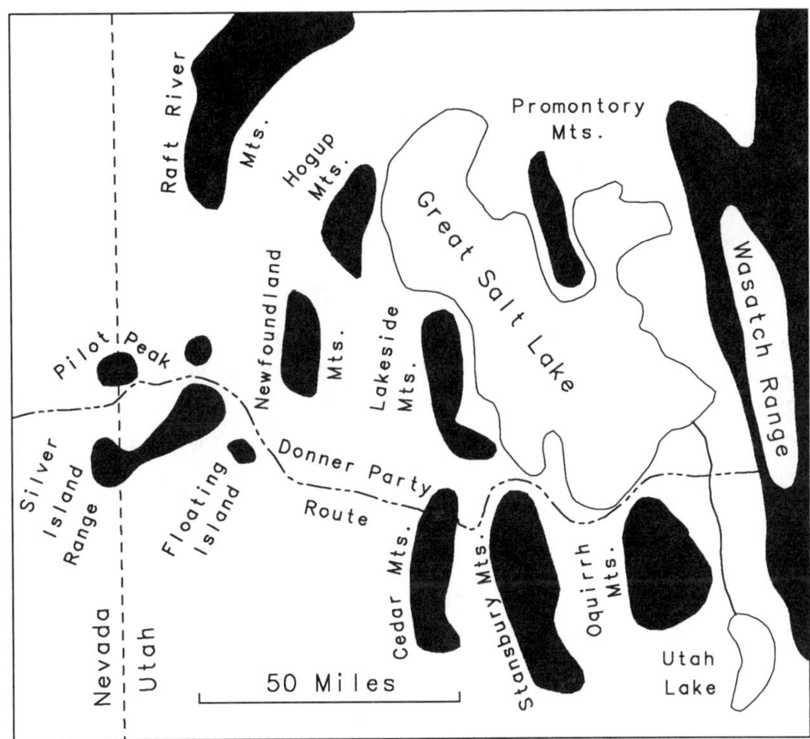

Figure 5-7. The Donner Party route across the Bonneville Basin. After Hawkins and Madsen (1990) and Stewart (1960).

perately needed after the crossing. The end of the Bonneville Basin lay a few miles beyond this range.

Had the Donner party attempted to cross the Bonneville Basin some 150 years earlier, around the year 1700, they would have found much of the Great Salt Lake Desert, including the Bonneville Salt Flats, under shallow water. Floating Island—which actually appears to be a floating island from a distance—was at the end of a small peninsula jutting into the waters of a much-expanded Great Salt Lake.

Had they tried to make the same trip some 16,000 years earlier, however, they would not have even gotten out of the lower reaches of Emigration Canyon. Instead, they would have seen almost nothing but water facing them to the west, with some of today's mountains emerging from the blue as islands—the Cedar, Lakeside, and Newfoundland mountains, for instance, and the Silver Island and Pilot ranges.

Great Salt Lake is one of the most saline permanent lakes on earth. Nearly 20% of the weight of the lake's contents is dissolved solids, some five billion tons of them, with sodium chloride—common table salt—leading the way and making Great Salt Lake some seven times saltier than the ocean. Some of these salts are there because they are derived from the waters of the much larger Lake Bonneville that preceded Great Salt Lake in this basin, but, as new waters reach the basin today, new salts are added as well. Recently, dissolved solids have been added to the lake at a rate of some two million tons a year.

Exactly how saline the lake is varies from season to season and from year to year: the higher the lake level, the lower the salinity. In 1873, when the lake reached one of its historic elevational highs, the proportion of dissolved minerals dropped to slightly below 12%. In 1963, when the lake retreated to its historic low of 4,191′, dissolved solids formed nearly 30% of the lake's contents. It is always easy to float in Great Salt Lake, but how easy it is depends on how high the lake is.

The level of Great Salt Lake depends, of course, on the balance between evaporation and inflow. The latter, as I have mentioned, is provided by streams, precipitation, and groundwater, with Wasatch-derived streams by far of greatest importance. Great Salt Lake is in the northern latitudes of the Great Basin; Ted Arnow and Doyle Stephens have calculated that, at an average elevation of 4,196′, evaporation from the surface of the lake is about 45″ a year, roughly the same as it is for Pyramid Lake (48″ a year) and Walker Lake (about 49″). During historic times, the average elevation of the surface of Great Salt Lake has been about 4,200′, at which point the lake has an area of about 1,700 square miles (official flood stage lies at 4,202′). At its historic low, 4,191.35′ in 1963, the lake had an area of about 950 square miles and a maximum depth of about 25′. The historic high, at 4,211.85′, was reached in June 1986 (and again in March 1987), at which point the lake has an area of approximately 2,300 square miles and a maximum depth of about 45′.

Although the historic low and high levels of Great Salt Lake are separated by only 23 years, the increase to 4,211.85′ did not take nearly that long. In response to both increased precipitation and decreased evaporation, the lake rose 12.2′ between September 18, 1982, and June 3, 1986. Indeed, the rise would have been some 2.5′ greater were it not for the fact that water is withdrawn from feeding streams for human use. Even so, the economic loss from this unexpected rise in the level of Great Salt Lake approached $300 million (far higher losses were caused in higher-elevation areas by the increased precipitation). Rapid fluctuations in levels of this sort are fully typical of Great Basin lakes.

Great Salt Lake lies in the eastern part of the Bonneville Basin, the Great Salt Lake Desert, in the western. The lowest thresholds between lake and desert lie just south and southwest of the Newfoundland Mountains between 4,214′ and 4,216′ in elevation. Were Great Salt Lake to rise above this level, the Great Salt Lake Desert would begin to be flooded, the magnitude of the flooding depending, of course, on the magnitude of the rise. The last time this happened, which appears to have been around A.D. 1700, the lake increased its size abruptly, to about 3,700 square miles, as a large part of the Great Salt Lake Desert was flooded.

The late prehistoric high, however, was nothing compared to Lake Bonneville during its late Pleistocene heyday. At its greatest extent, Pleistocene Lake Bonneville covered three major intermontane subbasins in Utah, Nevada, and Idaho—the Great Salt Lake Desert and Great Salt Lake subbasins in the north, and the much smaller Sevier subbasin in the south (Figure 5-8). Lake Bonneville then had an area of about 19,970 square miles, roughly the size of Lake Michigan (22,400 square miles), and was about 1,220′ deep. Indeed, the only reason the lake did not get any bigger than that is that it began to overflow into the Snake River drainage in southern Idaho. When it did this, it was no longer a part of the hydrographic Great Basin, but instead belonged to the Columbia River system.

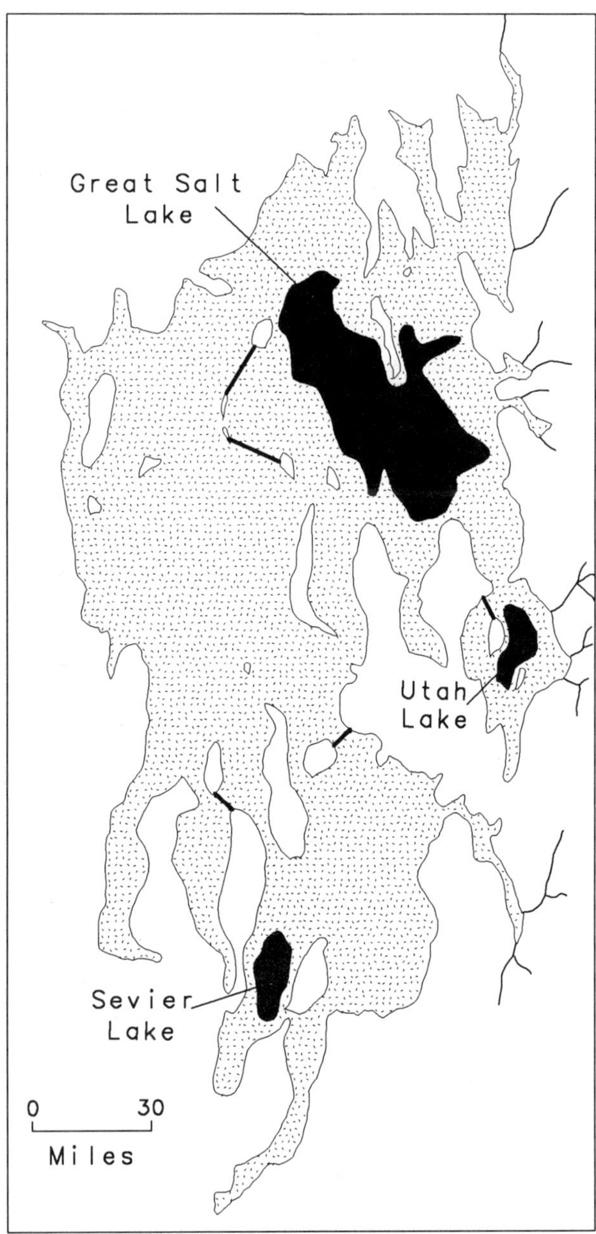

Figure 5-8. Lake Bonneville at its maximum; divides between subbasins are marked by bars. After Benson and Thompson (1987a,b).

Driving through the Bonneville Basin today, it is impossible not to be impressed by the terraces that have been carved into the mountains on the edges of, and within, the basin (see Figure 5-9). Standing on the salt-encrusted floor of the old lake and looking toward terraced hills, it does not take much imagination to picture the body of water that must have been here, even though it has taken tremen-

Figure 5-9. Lake Bonneville terraces on Table Mountain, adjacent to the Old River Bed connecting the Sevier Lake and Great Salt Lake subbasins of Pleistocene Lake Bonneville.

dous imagination to work out the history of the lake that carved those terraces.

There are four major shorelines in the Bonneville Basin, each of which consists of a number of beach ridges at roughly the same elevation. The names and approximate elevations of these are shown in Table 5-3, but these elevations are truly approximate. The weight of the water that made up Lake Bonneville depressed the entire basin as much as 240′. Once the water began to recede, the basin began to rebound, but it has done so differentially, so that the elevations of a given shoreline vary from place to place. In the vicinity of Great Salt Lake, for instance, the Provo shoreline varies between 4,790′ and 4,925′ in elevation; the Gilbert shoreline here varies from about 4,240′ to about 4,300′ in elevation. It is this differential rebound that explains why the Bonneville Salt Flats are not in the lowest part of the modern Bonneville Basin.

The major shorelines, and the separate beach ridges of which they are composed, mark the rises and falls of Pleistocene Lake Bonneville toward the end of the Pleistocene. Although the precise dates of all these events are not yet fully clear, the general picture is quite clear, due in large part to major advances in our understanding of the history of this lake that have been made during the past decade.

The Bonneville Basin appears to have been dry or nearly so before about 32,000 years ago. Indeed, at this

Table 5-3. Lake Bonneville Shorelines[a]

Shoreline	Age (years ago)	Elevational range (feet above sea level)	Surface area (square miles)
Stansbury	22,000–20,000	4,420–4,520	9,300
Bonneville	16,000–14,500	5,090–5,335	19,970
Provo	14,500–14,200	4,740–4,930	14,400
Gilbert	10,900–10,300	4,240–4,300	6,600
Great Salt Lake	Modern	4,200	1,800

[a]From Currey et al. (1984), Benson et al. (1990), and Oviatt et al. (1990).

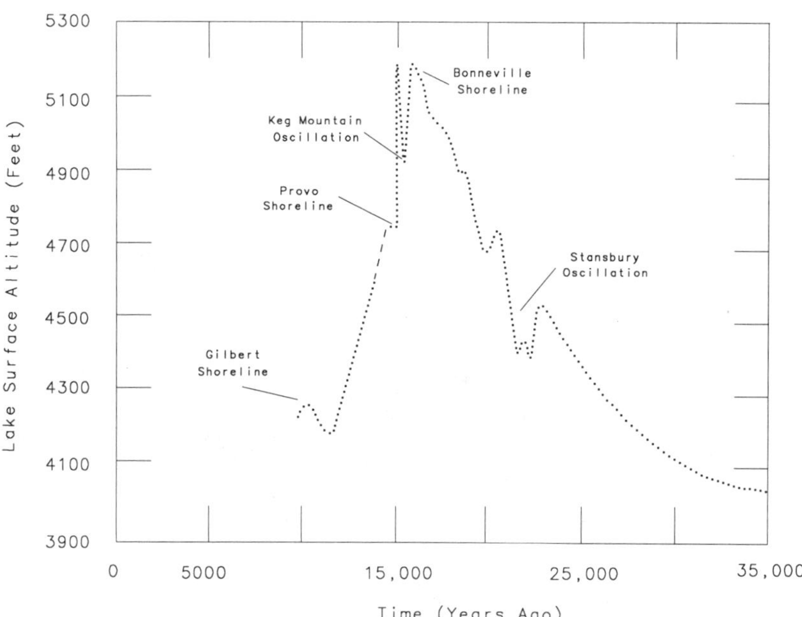

Figure 5-10. Lake Bonneville surface levels through time. After Benson et al. (1990).

time, the bed of Great Salt Lake itself may have been a water-veneered playa, or at best occupied by a shallow, saline lake. Soon thereafter, the lake began to rise and, by 26,000 years ago, had reached an elevation of about 4,315′ (Figures 5-8 and 5-10; for comparison, the 4,220′ contour crosses the main runway at the Salt Lake City Airport). The lake continued to rise, and by about 22,000 years ago, had reached an elevation of approximately 4,500′, at which point it had an area of about 9,300 square miles. For the next 2,000 years or so, the lake stayed at roughly this level, albeit rising and then falling some 150′ during this interval (the "Stansbury Oscillation"), and creating the complex of erosional and depositional features known as the Stansbury shoreline.

At around 20,000 years ago, the lake rose above the Stansbury terraces and continued to rise to its peak, with only a few beach-forming pauses along the way. Soon after 16,000 years ago, it had reached its maximum elevation at about 5,090′, cutting the Bonneville Shoreline and covering some 19,970 square miles of Utah, Nevada, and Idaho with water.

This was the highest the lake was to reach, not because there was insufficient water to drive it higher, but because it had become so high that it reached the threshold that separated it from the Columbia River drainage system. Sometime after 16,000 years ago, Lake Bonneville began to overflow into the Snake River drainage, controlled by a threshold near Zenda, in southern Idaho. For a relatively short period of time, perhaps on the order of a few hundred years, the lake continued to overflow, but, at about 15,000 years ago, it dropped beneath the overflow level, only to rise again (the "Keg Mountain Oscillation"). By 14,500 years ago, it had risen once more to the Bonneville shoreline and the Zenda threshold.

This time, however, it did not simply overflow as it had done before. It cut through the threshold at Zenda and unleashed one of the two largest floods known to have occurred in earth history (see Notes for the largest known flood). The upper 340′ of Lake Bonneville passed through Red Rock Pass in southern Idaho, rushing first into the Snake River—which was flooded in places to depths of over 400′—and then into the Columbia. Although the size of Lake Bonneville is easy to imagine from within the Bonneville Basin, the magnitude of the Bonneville Flood is anything but easy to visualize. Geologists Robert Jarrett and Harold Malde have estimated that, at its peak discharge, water tore through Red Rock Pass at the rate of some 33,018,000 cubic feet per *second*. University of Utah geomorphologist Donald Currey, whose work has done so much to elucidate the history of Lake Bonneville, has pointed out that, at this rate of discharge, Lake Bonneville would have declined some 6′ per day. By the time it was all over, not only had Lake Bonneville declined from the Bonneville shoreline, at about 5,090′, to the Provo level, 4,740′, but 1,130 cubic miles of water had been discharged into the Snake River basin, and the lake had decreased from some 19,970 square miles to some 14,000 square miles in area.

How long Lake Bonneville took to unleash all of this water is unknown. At the peak flood rate of 33,018,000 cubic feet of water per second, the flood would have lasted only a few months, but there is no reason to think that the peak discharge would have lasted this long. Best guesses put the duration at sometime between two months and one year.

The flooding stopped when the lake reached resistant rock at Red Rock Pass, stabilizing its levels at the Provo shoreline. During the flood, a volume of water almost equal to that contained within Lake Michigan (1,169 cubic miles, compared to the 1,130 cubic miles disgorged through Red Rock Pass) had been shunted into the Snake River basin.

Because it is extremely difficult to visualize what such a flood would have been like, a few comparisons might help provide some perspective. The average discharge rate for the Amazon River is 6,180,000 cubic feet per second—approximately one-fifth of the peak discharge rate of the Bonneville Flood. The largest known flood in historic times occurred in 1953, when the Amazon discharged 13,595,000 cubic feet per second—only 41% of the peak discharge of the Bonneville Flood. Nothing in historic times comes even remotely close to what happened at Red Rock Pass some 14,500 years ago. Indeed, the average discharge rate of all the world's rivers to the oceans is 42,376,000 cubic feet per second; the peak discharge rate for the Bonneville Flood is 78% of that figure!

With the level of Lake Bonneville now established by the new threshold at Red Rock Pass, some 1.5 miles south of the old threshold at Zenda, the lake stabilized at an elevation of about 4,737′. Here the lake stood for only a few hundred years, producing the Provo shoreline. Sometime after 14,200 years ago, however, the lake began a climatically induced decline. Between 13,000 and 12,000 years ago, it shrank to at least historic levels in the two northern subbasins, and may have even dried up entirely. How fast this retreat might have been depends on how the radiocarbon dates for Lake Bonneville for this period are interpreted: one detailed assessment suggested that this climatically induced drop proceeded at the rate of some 20′ a century, or 2.4″ a year. A faster decline is most certainly possible.

It is curious, however, that this decline may not have equally affected the Sevier subbasin, to the south. This subbasin is separated from the more northerly parts of the Bonneville Basin by what is called the Old River Bed, an abandoned river channel that sits at an elevation of 4,580′ between Keg Mountain and the Simpson Mountains, some 55 miles north of today's Sevier Lake. Work in this area by geologist Charles Oviatt suggests that, when Lake Bonneville declined to beneath the elevation of the Old River Bed, the waters in the Sevier subbasin may have remained high enough to flow north for some 2,000 years, from 12,000 to 10,000 years ago. The late Pleistocene lake in the Sevier Basin has been given its own name, Lake Gunnison, after Lieutenant J. W. Gunnison, a U.S. government surveyor who lost his life in the Sevier River valley in 1853.

If Lake Gunnison really was this high for this 2,000-year period, why it was becomes something of a mystery. Today, the streams that feed Sevier Lake originate well south of those that feed Great Salt Lake (see Figures 2-2 and 5-8). Oviatt has cautiously suggested that the high-water levels in the Sevier Lake basin between about 12,000 and 10,000 years ago might have resulted from a strengthening of the southwestern monsoons—Houghton's Gulf Component of Great Basin precipitation. In Oviatt's view, these summer rains, and accompanying clouds, may have intruded far enough north to have fed the lake that existed in the Sevier basin at this time, but not far enough north to have maintained Lake Bonneville itself. On the other hand, Larry Benson of the U.S. Geological Survey suspects that, since the chronology of Lake Gunnison is based on a relatively small number of radiocarbon dates, the overflow detected by Oviatt may, in fact, have occurred only at the very end of the Pleistocene. If this is true, then Lake Gunnison becomes less perplexing.

It becomes less perplexing because the northern Bonneville Basin was flooded once again between about 10,900 and 10,300 years ago, reaching the 4,260′ Gilbert level. We know that Sevier Lake overflowed to the north at this time; Benson suggests that the overflow of Lake Gunnison was confined to this period.

This latest episode in the history of Lake Bonneville is intriguing for a number of reasons. First, unlike previous episodes in the lake's history, we know that people saw Lake Bonneville when it was at the Gilbert level. Second, this final rise of Lake Bonneville correlates remarkably well with a climatic event first defined from northwestern Europe, an event called the Younger Dryas.

The Younger Dryas takes its name from a herbaceous tundra plant, the mountain avens, genus *Dryas*. This plant is a marker for the apparently rapid replacement of forest by tundra that took place in northwestern Europe shortly after 11,000 years ago. Not only did forest give way to arctic grasses, herbs, and shrubs here, but glaciers expanded in Norway and Scotland, and temperatures, at least as inferred from studies of the Greenland ice cap, fell nearly 11°F. This North Atlantic cold snap lasted only some 800 years; by 10,000 years ago, it was over. Similar events seem to have occurred in northeastern North America and in the Southern Hemisphere. Although we seem to be getting closer to an explanation for it, we are not there yet. One thing, however, is clear: the Younger Dryas occurred at almost exactly the same time as the rise of Lake Bonneville to the Gilbert level.

Since we do not fully understand why the Younger Dryas occurred, we obviously cannot fully understand the relationship between it and the contemporary rise and fall of Lake Bonneville. As regards the Gilbert phase of Lake Bonneville itself, however, Donald Currey has suggested that this roughly 600-year highstand might reflect the results of general atmospheric warming. That warming, he notes, may have strengthened monsoonal systems moving into the Great Basin from the Gulf of Mexico, an argument very similar to that made by Oviatt to account for the existence of Lake Gunnison. Currey thinks that this period of time in the eastern Great Basin may have seen cloudy and humid, though not warm, summers, with greater amounts of Gulf-derived moisture feeding the Bonneville Basin (and recall that the eastern Great Basin today is the prime recipient of Gulf moisture in the summer months, as Figure 5-3 shows). Increased cloudiness during the summer months would, of course, decrease evaporation during the warmest months of the year, and the combination of decreased evaporation and increased precipitation might, Currey argues, account for the Gilbert rise of Lake Bonneville.

Whether or not it does, however, is a far different question, and how this rise might be linked to the Younger Dryas is an even far broader issue. Lake Lahontan may record a similar event at about the same time, as I will discuss, but here the evidence is not nearly as strong as it is for the Bonneville Basin.

No matter how this short episode in the life of Lake Bonneville is to be explained, when the lake retreated from the Gilbert level, Lake Bonneville came to an end. The retreat of Lake Bonneville from the Gilbert level saw the birth of the Great Salt Lake Desert, the Bonneville Salt Flats, and Great Salt Lake itself. Later fluctuations in water levels were minuscule compared to what happened during the Pleistocene.

PLEISTOCENE LAKE LAHONTAN

When land speed records are set on the Bonneville Salt Flats, they are set on the dry bed of Pleistocene Lake Bonneville. When they are set on the Black Rock Desert, they are set on the dry bed of Pleistocene Lake Lahontan, the second largest of the Great Basin's pluvial lakes (see Figure 5-11).

At its maximum, Lake Lahontan covered 8,665 square miles of western and northwestern Nevada, as well as a small part of adjacent California, reaching a maximum depth of about 900′ at the site of today's Pyramid Lake. In historic times, lakes in the Lahontan Basin have had a maximum surface area of about 600 square miles. Thus, the Pleistocene lake at its largest was some 14 times larger in surface area than the modern lakes at their largest.

The Lahontan Basin is far more complicated than the Bonneville Basin, in large part because six major rivers drain into it from different directions. As I discussed in Chapter 2, these six are the Humboldt, which terminates in Humboldt Lake and the Humboldt Sink; the Truckee, which flowed into Pyramid and Winnemucca Lakes; the Carson, which flowed into the Carson lakes and Carson Sink; the Walker, ending in Walker Lake; the Susan, flowing into Honey Lake; and, the Quinn, ending in the Black Rock Desert.

With the exception of the Quinn, each of these rivers flows into a more or less substantial lake. Given that the sinks of the Humboldt and Carson rivers can merge in times of high water today, and that the Truckee River flows into two separate basins (Pyramid and Winnemucca), these rivers provide six separate subbasins within the Lahontan Basin as a whole. In addition, there is a seventh, the Buena Vista subbasin, to the northeast of Carson Sink, that has no river at all (Figure 5-12).

These seven separate drainages were once united beneath the waters of Lake Lahontan. However, since each of these basins is separated from every other by a threshold at a different level, the rates of rise and fall of water within each are independent of those rates in every other, unless the water rises high enough to connect one or more of them. When that occurs, of course, the waters in the connected basins form a single lake.

Figure 5-11. Lake Lahontan shorelines on a spur of the Virginia Mountains, just west of Pyramid Lake.

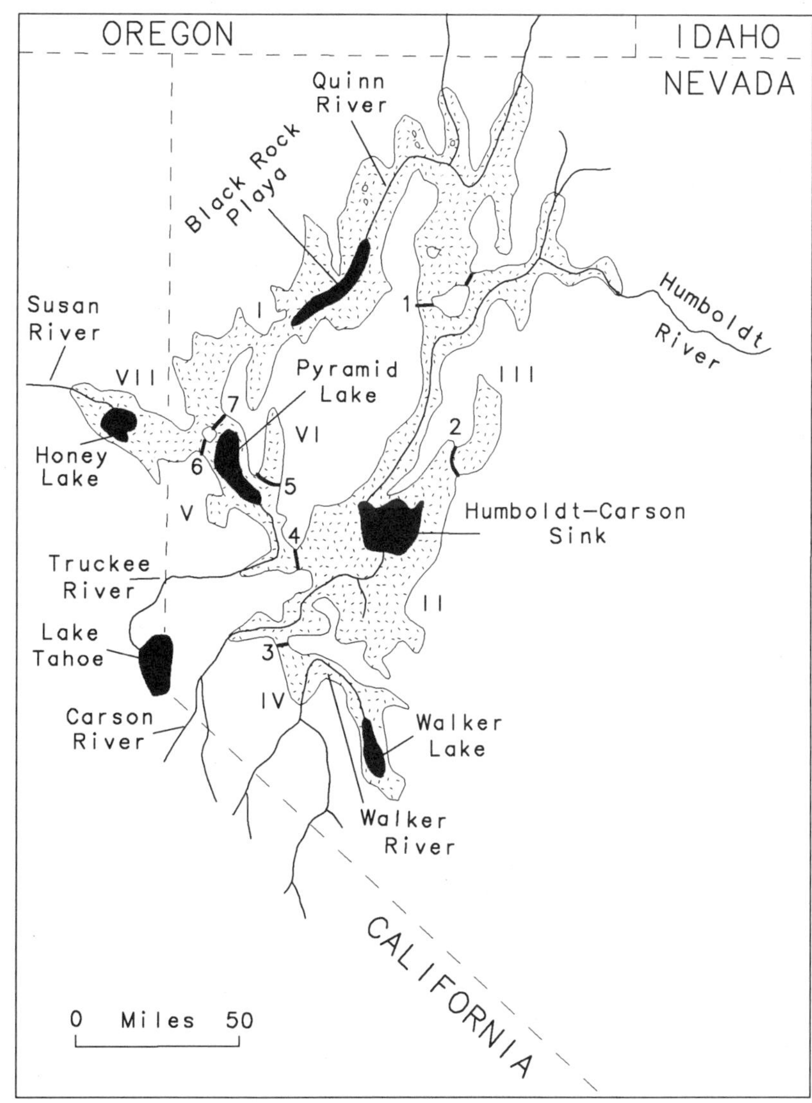

Figure 5-12. Lake Lahontan at its maximum; divides between subbasins are marked by bars. After Benson and Thompson (1987a,b).

Table 5-4. Lake Lahontan Subbasin Thresholds and Their Elevations[a]

Threshold	Elevation (feet)
Adrian Valley	4,291
Pronto	4,239
Darwin Pass	4,150
Chocolate	4,140
Astor Pass	4,009
Emerson Pass	3,960
Mud Lake Slough	3,862

[a]From Benson and Thompson (1987a,b).

Table 5-4 shows the elevations of these thresholds. The highest threshold in the system connects the Walker Lake basin to the Carson Sink, and lies at an elevation of 4,291′. Only above this level are all the separate subbasins connected into a single Lake Lahontan. As a result, geologist Jonathan Davis has noted, there really is no single Lahontan chronology; there is instead a family of chronologies and lake histories, fewer in number when the lake is high, greater in number when the lake is low. Only when the waters rise above 4,291′ does a single, united lake form.

To make matters even more complex, not all of the rivers that empty into the Lahontan Basin have stayed put during the last 100,000 years or so. Jonathan Davis has suggested that, sometime during the later Pleistocene, the Humboldt River did not flow into Humboldt Lake as it does today, but instead ran well north of what is now Rye Patch Reservoir in north-central Nevada, and into the Black Rock Desert. Whether or not this actually occurred still needs to be established; if it happened, then when it happened is not at all clear, and it may have occurred prior to 70,000 years ago.

No such uncertainly surrounds Walker River, whose fickle nature is far better documented. The geography of the river alone suggests that odd things might happen here. The east and west branches of Walker River flow north and east out of the Sierra Nevada, to join in Mason Valley just south of Yerrington, Nevada (see Figure 5-12). The enlarged river then flows almost due north, to the end of Mason Valley, then turns in the opposite direction and flows almost due south, along the east side of the Wassuk Range, to end up in Walker Lake. The abrupt turn taken by the river is curious, not only because it is so abrupt, but also because there is an old river channel heading off to the northwest, out of Mason Valley and, by a nearly level pass called Adrian Valley, into the Carson River drainage. Indeed, Adrian Valley contains the threshold between the Walker Lake and Carson Lake drainage systems. There is absolutely no doubt that in the past the Walker River has occupied this channel, flowing north into the Carson drainage. Whenever that occurred, the effect on Walker Lake would have been devastating. As I have mentioned, Walker River provides 83% of the inflow to Walker Lake. Without that source, Walker Lake would be a puddle. The challenge is not to figure out if this happened: the challenge is to figure out when and why.

How complicated the Lake Lahontan system is should now be obvious. There are six different rivers feeding that system, of which four come from the Sierra Nevada, and provide 61.2% of the modern river inflow into the basin. The two others come from the mountains of northern and eastern Nevada, and provide the remaining 38.8% of river inflow (Table 5-5). There are seven different subbasins within this area, each separated from the others by thresholds that fall at different elevations. There is even a river, the Walker, known to have flowed both north into one of these basins and south into another, and a second river, the Humboldt, that may have been similarly fickle in the past. Even with these complexities, however, a tremendous amount of progress has been made during the past decade or so toward gaining at least a general understanding of the history of Lake Lahontan and its separate parts.

Although attempts have been made to reconstruct the history of Lake Lahontan between about 25,000 and 50,000 years ago, there is little secure information about this period of time, other than the fact that moderate-sized lakes appear to have existed in the western subbasins of the

Table 5-5. River Discharge into the Lahontan Basin[a]

River	Percent of total discharge	Source area
Carson	16.9	Sierra Nevada
Humboldt	37.5	Northern and eastern Nevada
Quinn	1.3	Northern and eastern Nevada
Susan	3.2	Sierra Nevada
Truckee	27.0	Sierra Nevada
Walker	14.1	Sierra Nevada
Total	100.0	

[a]From Benson and Paillet (1989).

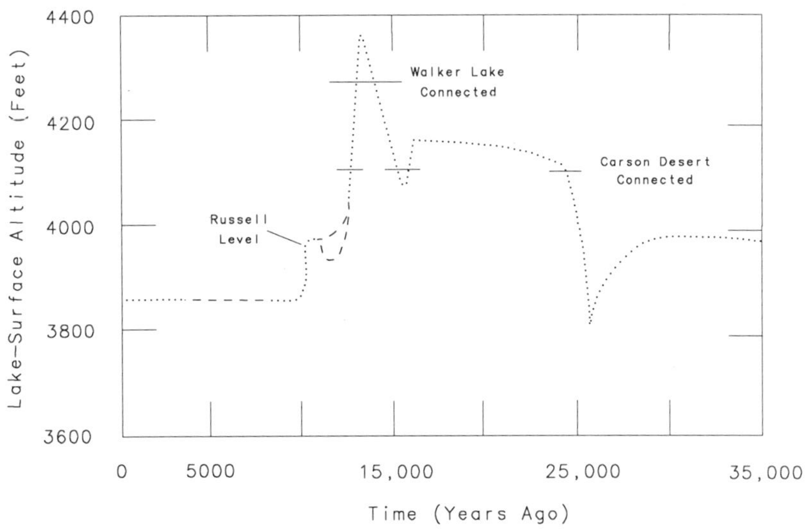

Figure 5-13. Lake Lahontan surface levels through time. After Benson et al. (1990).

Lahontan drainage. By 24,000 years ago, however, the water had risen to at least 4,135′, enough to connect the Pyramid Lake, Winnemucca Lake, and Black Rock Desert subbasins beneath the waters of a single lake, and perhaps connecting with the Carson Sink as well. Water levels seem to have remained high for some 8,000 years, then fell briefly between about 16,000 and 15,700 years ago (Figure 5-13).

Soon after this fall, however, the lake began to rise once again, on its way to its late Pleistocene high. The exact time that it reached this highstand is by no means clear, but the event occurred sometime between 14,500 years ago (the date of the Bonneville Flood far to the east) and 13,000 years ago. The most detailed attempt to date this episode has been made by Larry Benson. His results strongly suggest that, by about 14,200 years ago, the surface of Lake Lahontan had risen to an elevation of about 4,300′, thus joining all the subbasins into a single lake. His work also suggests that the lake reached its highstand, with a surface elevation of about 4,363′, by about 13,800 years ago. It was at this point that Lake Lahontan covered 8,665 square miles and was about 900′ deep. How long it remained here is not yet clear, but Benson estimates that it may have been at this level for no longer than 50 years or so, and argues that it had receded to about 4,300′ within a century after it had reached its highstand.

By 12,000 years ago, the lake had fallen at least 330′, and perhaps more. "Perhaps" because there is very little information available on the levels of the lakes within the separate subbasins between about 12,500 and 10,000 years ago, so precisely how far and how fast the lake fell from its highstand at about 14,000 years ago is simply not known. It does, however, appear that by 10,000 years ago the total surface area of lakes in the Lahontan Basin was no greater than it was during the mid-nineteenth century.

In the Bonneville Basin, a short-lived lake reached the Gilbert level between about 10,900 and 10,300 years ago, as I have discussed. The evidence that supports the existence of this lake is so strong that there can be no doubt that it existed. There is also evidence that a substantial lake existed in the Lahontan Basin after Lake Lahontan had declined from its highstand.

Some two decades ago, the geologist Roger Morrison argued that a large lake that postdated the highstand of Lake Lahontan had existed in the Carson Desert. He called it the First Fallon Lake, and suggested that it was most likely late Holocene in age. Recently, however, Donald Currey has argued that it might be of the same age as the lake that filled the Bonneville Basin to the Gilbert shoreline. To emphasize the possible parallel with Lake Bonneville history, Currey called the shoreline left by this latest Pleistocene lake in the Carson Desert the "Russell" shoreline: Israel C. Russell was the pioneer nineteenth-century geological explorer of the Lahontan Basin, just as Grove Karl Gilbert was of the Bonneville Basin. The problem with the Russell shoreline, however, is that its age is poorly controlled, only a very small number of radiocarbon dates suggesting that it might, in fact, be latest Pleistocene in age. Indeed, those few dates suggest that the Russell lake may have existed at about 11,300 years ago, a date that, if correct, would make it earlier than the Gilbert shoreline in the Bonneville Basin. Clearly, far more work will have to be done before we can be certain that a substantial lake existed in the Carson Desert at the same time as Lake Bonneville reached the Gilbert level.

One of the most-studied subbasins within the Lahontan Basin as a whole is the Walker Lake Basin. I have not said much about Walker Lake up to this point for two reasons. First, changing levels of this lake may reflect either regional climatic change or the diversion of the Walker River into the Carson Sink. Second, what we know about the history of Walker Lake does not make a lot of sense.

For a number of years, the Walker Lake Basin has been the focus of intense investigation by a U.S. Geological Survey scientific team, in the hopes that a long-term climatic record could be developed that would help in making decisions about the suitability of Yucca Mountain, in southern Nevada, as a long-term nuclear waste storage site. The interdisciplinary team conducting this project was led by Larry Benson, and focused on extracting and dating lake sediment cores, and on studying virtually everything in those cores that might provide information on the history of the lake. Diatoms (phytoplankton) from the cores have been studied by Platt Bradbury, ostracodes (small crustaceans) by Richard Forester, and pollen by Robert Thompson.

There is some evidence that the Walker Lake basin held a deep lake between at least 32,000 and 25,000 years ago, and even better evidence that Walker Lake was not a lake at all between about 22,000 and 14,000 years ago, when the basin was occupied by a saline marsh. During this interval, it appears that the Walker River was flowing not into Walker Lake, but instead north into the Carson Basin, where a sizable lake then existed.

The most puzzling aspect of the Walker Lake picture involves the next 10,000 years, since the sediment cores extracted by the USGS team have supplied no convincing evidence that a lake existed in this basin between about 14,000 and 4,700 years ago, suggesting that the Walker River must have flowed northward during this entire interval. The difficulty, of course, is that this simply could not have been the case if the reconstruction of Lake Lahontan that I have just presented—much of which has been derived by the same people (and particularly by Benson and Thompson)—is correct. That reconstruction has Lake Lahontan so high at 14,000 years ago that it incorporated the Walker Lake Basin. In fact, radiocarbon-dated shorelines within the Walker Lake Basin itself imply that a deep lake existed here at about that time. Given this situation, the Walker River could not have flowed north even if it had wanted to, but must instead have flowed directly into an expanded Lake Lahontan.

How this discrepancy is to be resolved is unclear, though there are some obvious possibilities. As Benson has noted, it is possible that the lake sediments laid down during the 14,000-year-old Lake Lahontan highstand were subsequently eroded, presumably by wind action, from the places sampled by the USGS team. It is also possible that the lake that existed at the Lahontan maximum simply did not leave much of a sedimentary record, though this seems extremely unlikely. No matter what the explanation, there must be one, since it is impossible that Lake Lahontan rose so high as to enter the Walker Lake Basin at a time centering on 14,000 years ago, at the same time as the Walker River flowed north, and there was no lake here. Worse, if the 14,000-year-old highstand did exist (as seems most likely) and the USGS team missed it, then the arguments that they have made that there was no lake here anytime between 14,000 and 4,700 years ago cannot be given too much faith either. If the highstand could be missed, then certainly other, lower lake levels could be missed as well.

Comparing what we know in general about the histories of Lake Lahontan and Lake Bonneville shows that those histories are roughly, though not perfectly, synchronous during the past 35,000 years or so. Both lakes seem to have been low at around 35,000 years ago, and both appear to have been growing between about 25,000 and 16,000 years ago. Both seem to have oscillated briefly during the next 1,000 years: the Keg Mountain Oscillation in the Bonneville Basin at around 15,000 years ago, and an unnamed fall and rise in the Lahontan Basin at about 15,500 years ago. At or soon after 14,500 years ago, both lakes were very high—the Bonneville Flood occurred in the Bonneville Basin at this time, and all seven separate subbasins were united beneath the waters of Lake Lahontan at the time of this flood, or soon thereafter. Both lakes then underwent a severe decline, though no good case can now be made that these declines were truly synchronous. Lake Bonneville began its decline from the Provo level shortly after 14,200 years ago, and appears to have been quite low by 13,000 years ago or so. The timing of the decline of Lake Lahontan is not nearly as well-controlled, but it, too, appears to have been low by 13,000 years ago or so. Both basins remained relatively dry until about 11,000 years ago. The Bonneville Basin refilled to the Gilbert level between about 10,900 and 10,300 years ago, and then declined to at least historic levels. Weak evidence suggests that the Lahontan Basin may also have seen deeper water during this interval, but this evidence is so weak that much more research is needed to tell whether this was truly the case. However, even if a lake did exist in the Lahontan Basin at this time, it would still remain to be shown that this lake did not result from the behavior of the Walker River. If it did, then the similarities between the latest Pleistocene histories of lakes Bonneville and Lahontan would be entirely coincidental.

Regardless of how the most recent end of the Bonneville and Lahontan stories turn out, the parallels between the histories of the lakes that occupied these basins are too great to be accidental. It is important to realize that these similarities exist even though the water supply for Lake Bonneville lies entirely in the eastern Great Basin, and largely in the Wasatch Range and western Uinta Mountains, while 62.2% of the river flow into the Lahontan Basin today comes from the Sierra Nevada. Given such different sources of inflow, the similarities must reflect broad, regional climatic control over the sizes of these lakes.

It is, however, one thing to conclude that climate did it, which seems quite clear, and quite another to specify exactly what it was about late Pleistocene climates that not only caused the growth of pluvial lakes in the Great Basin, but also caused the general synchroneity in the histories of the two largest lakes. An answer to this question seems to be at hand.

PLUVIAL LAKES AND LATE PLEISTOCENE CLIMATES

During the mid-1980s, much of the northern Great Basin saw increased precipitation and a corresponding increase in the size of the lakes that the region holds. Great Salt Lake reached its historic high in June 1986, and matched that high in March 1987; it would have risen even further were it not for the fact that human activities now divert so much water from its feeding streams. Malheur Lake flooded roads, ranches, and critical wildlife habitat on the Malheur National Wildlife Refuge. Humboldt Lake likewise flooded roads and other human constructions, and then overflowed into the Carson Sink.

Eventually, the high rate of precipitation that fed these increases ended, and the lakes began to retreat. But, what if the precipitation had not declined? In the Lahontan Basin, for instance, incoming rivers discharged at a maximum rate nearly 2.5 times their historic averages in 1983. If this discharge rate had continued, while evaporation rates remained the same, would Lake Lahontan have reappeared?

The answer, Larry Benson has shown, is no. Had water input into the Lahontan Basin remained at 1983 values with the same evaporation rates, lakes in the Lahontan Basin would have grown substantially, ultimately covering 2,672 square miles, but this is only 31% of the area of Lake Lahontan at its maximum (8,665 square miles). The extremely high precipitation rates experienced in the Lahontan Basin in the mid-1980s would not have recreated anything like Lake Lahontan if evaporation rates remained unchanged.

Today, evaporation rates in the Lahontan Basin are on the order of 48″ a year. What if the 1983 water inflow figures were combined with the lowest monthly evaporation rates known to have occurred during historic times? Those lowest known rates yield 24.8″ of evaporation a year, roughly half the average amount. Given the 1983 inflow rates (2.5 times the average) and the minimum monthly evaporation rates (about 0.5 times the average), Benson showed that Lake Lahontan could, in fact, reappear.

So combining known precipitation maxima with known evaporation minima over a sufficient amount of time can recreate a Lake Lahontan at its peak. But, even though such a combination could bring back the lake, there is no guarantee that this is actually the way it worked. Evaporation rates may have declined even more dramatically, or precipitation rates risen to even higher levels, to create the lake. What we do seem to know about is temperature.

Estimates of late Pleistocene temperatures derived from the study of late Pleistocene vegetation (see Chapter 6) and glaciers (see later in this chapter) in the Great Basin provide fairly consistent results, implying a mean annual temperature decrease on the order of 9°F to 13°F. Decreased temperatures would, of course, decrease the evaporation rate. Benson calculated the decreased rate to lie between 25″ and 28″ a year, the exact figure depending on how the temperature decreases were distributed seasonally. If the temperature decreases were combined with an increase in cloudiness, which would decrease evaporation beyond that expected from a temperature decline alone, little mystery would remain in the growth of Great Basin pluvial lakes.

But where would the increased precipitation and cloudiness come from? Here the answer seems to lie in the effects of the huge glacial mass that blanketed much of northern North America during the Wisconsin maximum. Today, the winter jet stream, which marks the boundary between cold and warm air masses, passes over the west coast of North America at about 50° N latitude. Climatic modeling of atmospheric circulation during the late Pleistocene by climatologist John Kutzbach and his colleagues strongly suggests that one effect of the vast northern ice mass was to split the jet stream in two, with one arm skirting the northern edge of that ice, the other swinging far south of it in western North America.

One effect of the more southerly location of the jet stream would be to increase the frequency of Pacific storms reaching the Great Basin, bringing both increased precipitation and increased cloud cover. Therein, it now seems, lies the origin of pluvial lakes in the Great Basin: decreased temperatures (on the order of 11°F), coupled with increased precipitation and cloudiness. Decreased temperatures alone would decrease evaporation rates. In fact, by increasing ice cover on lakes, decreased temperatures would likely decrease evaporation rates well beyond those expected from the temperature drop alone, as Benson and Thompson have pointed out. Increased cloudiness would enhance these effects, and increased precipitation would provide the lakes with the stuff of which they are made.

If all this actually occurred, then Great Basin pluvial lakes should have declined as the continental glaciers shrank, and this is exactly what did happen. The climatic models suggest that the jet stream was no longer split at 12,000 years ago, and that it had moved well north of the position it held before the ice mass had begun to disintegrate, though it still remained south of glacial ice. The more northerly position of the jet stream at 12,000 years ago suggests that lakes Lahontan and Bonneville should have been gone by that time. In fact, they were. Charles Oviatt and his colleagues have even observed that the Stansbury Oscillation, which occurred at about 21,000 years ago in the Bonneville Basin, may be associated with a brief glacial retreat in the far north at about this time.

We thus seem to be on the verge of a good explanation for the rise and fall of lakes Lahontan and Bonneville. But "on the verge of" is an important qualifier here. As I will discuss shortly, the histories of glaciers and lakes in the Great Basin are discordant: advances and retreats in the two systems are not well correlated. If the jet stream explanation is correct, then it remains to be explained why this is the case. This I will return to shortly, after discussing the glaciers themselves.

NOTES ON OTHER GREAT BASIN PLEISTOCENE LAKES

LAKE CHEWAUCAN

Because they have been most heavily studied, the histories of lakes Bonneville and Lahontan are the best understood among the histories of all Great Basin pluvial lakes. Unfortunately, the histories of many Great Basin lakes have hardly been studied at all, and little can be said about them, above and beyond their maximum sizes and depths. But in some areas, the potential for unraveling lake histories has been shown to be so high that it seems unlikely that those histories will remain unresolved for much longer.

Lake Chewaucan in south-central Oregon provides an excellent example. At its maximum, this lake covered some 480 square miles to a maximum depth of about 375′. Today, two lakes, Summer and Abert, are found within its basin, covering about 96 square miles (Figure 5-14), but there have also been times during the past 100 years when these lakes were virtually dry.

In 1982, geologist Ira Allison provided basic descriptions of Lake Chewaucan and its basin. Soon after, Jonathan Davis of the Desert Research Institute demonstrated that sediments of Pleistocene Lake Chewaucan that have been exposed by erosion just north of Summer Lake contain 54 separate layers of volcanic ash or tephra.

Volcanic ashes from different sources, and often even those that originate from the same source at different times, have different chemical compositions. As a result, they can be identified wherever they are found. The ashes can also be dated in a variety of ways. Those that were deposited within the past 40,000 years, for instance, can be placed in time by obtaining radiocarbon dates for organic materials above, below, or within the ash. Older tephras can be dated using a method that depends on the decay of radioactive potassium to inert argon (K/Ar dating), and many can be dated using thermoluminescence (TL dating).

This latter method depends on the fact that in many minerals that undergo natural irradiation, electrons become trapped by flaws in the crystalline structure of those

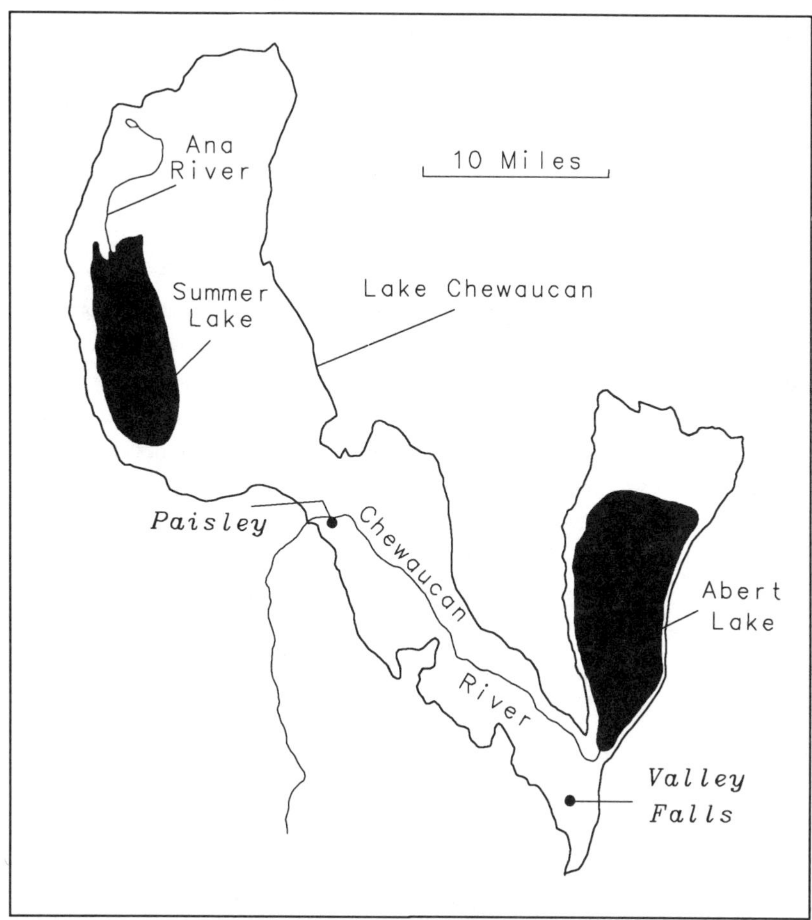

Figure 5-14. The Lake Chewaucan basin. After J. O. Davis (1985a).

minerals. These electrons, along with light, are released when the material is heated. The rate at which electrons are trapped in a given setting can be calculated, and the amount of light released on heating is proportional to the number of trapped electrons. As a result, materials that have been heated in the past, and exposed to radiation, can be dated either by measuring the amount of light given off on reheating, or by measuring the number of accumulated electrons directly. The event dated is the time of last heating, which resets the TL clock. TL dating has wide application in archaeology. It can, for instance, be applied to ceramics or to stone tools that had been heated as part of the manufacturing process. It can also be used to date tephras. The combination of radiocarbon dating, K/Ar dating, TL dating, and other techniques can allow tephras of a wide variety of ages to be dated.

Because tephras are scattered explosively and then quickly settle from the air, they mark a virtual instant in time, and so allow far-flung deposits to be correlated with tremendous precision. Equally important, once they have been dated, identifying a given ash in a depositional sequence also reveals exactly how old that part of the deposit is.

The detailed characterization and dating of tephras—tephrochronology—is still a relatively young science, but a lot has been accomplished during the past few decades. Davis was able to build on this accumulated knowledge, a good deal of which he had provided through his own efforts in the Lahontan Basin.

Davis securely identified six tephras in the exposed Lake Chewaucan sediments that fell during the past 35,000 years. The youngest of these covers much of the surface here, and was erupted from Mount Mazama at about 6,800 years ago (the eruption of Mount Mazama, some 65 miles due west, created the caldera in which Crater Lake now sits). The Mount St. Helens M tephra that is represented in these deposits fell some 19,000 years ago; this came from the same Mount St. Helens in southwestern Washington that erupted in 1980, 180 miles north and slightly west of

Summer Lake. The precise origin of the two Trego Hot Springs tephras Davis identified here is not known, but they came from somewhere in the Cascade Mountains. The more recent of the two fell some 23,400 years ago, with the earlier one falling not long before. The earliest two members of the series identified by Davis are the Wono tephra, about 25,000 years old, which also probably originated in the Cascades (and perhaps from Mount Mazama), and the Marble Bluff tephra, which erupted from Mount St. Helens about 35,000 years ago.

In his initial investigation, Davis made no attempt to extract lake history from these deposits, since that was not the focus of his work. A few years later, however, he returned to the Summer Lake Basin with Robert Negrini of California State University, Bakersfield. Whereas Davis brought his expertise in Pleistocene geology to the analysis of the deposits of Lake Chewaucan, Negrini brought his expertise in the study of variations in the declination, inclination, and intensity of the earth's magnetic field through time.

It is well known that the declination (the difference between magnetic north and true north at any one point on the earth's surface) and inclination (the vertical component of the earth's magnetic field at any one point) change through time. These variations are often well recorded in fine-grained sediments that contain magnetic minerals, since those minerals align themselves with the magnetic field as they are being deposited. For many areas, curves have been built showing the precise nature of these variations through time.

One such curve is available from the Mono Lake Basin of California, and covers the period from 36,000 to 12,000 years ago. Negrini and Davis hoped that they would be able to detect paleomagnetic variations in the fine-grained deposits of Lake Chewaucan, and then correlate those variations with the well-dated sequence developed for the Mono Lake Basin. Such correlations would then allow them to infer precise dates for the Lake Chewaucan deposits, above and beyond those already available from the volcanic ashes.

They were remarkably successful in doing this. The sediments of Lake Chewaucan proved to contain a paleomagnetic record very similar to that of the Mono Lake Basin, albeit not nearly as continuous. The detailed similarities between these curves allowed them to provide a much finer-grained chronology for the Lake Chewaucan deposits than Davis had been able to provide from his analysis of the tephras alone.

Combining their new chronology with an analysis of the sediments in the section they analyzed, Negrini and Davis concluded that the latest Pleistocene highstand of Lake Chewaucan occurred no earlier than 16,800 years ago, and that water levels were low between 27,400 and 23,200 years ago, and between 21,700 and 19,300 years ago.

Negrini and Davis suggest that chronological correlations based on paleomagnetic variations may ultimately be found to have a resolution of 500 years or less. Although the history of Lake Chewaucan is not understood in any more than a gross way, the work that Davis and Nigrini have done, and that Allison did before them, demonstrates that this basin holds a detailed record not only of Lake Chewaucan, but also of regional volcanic history, and that this record can be dated with great precision. Indeed, Kenneth Gobalet and Negrini have recently shown that the deposits here also contain well-preserved fish fossils.

In addition, Glenn Berger of Western Washington University has now provided thermoluminescence dates for a number of the previously undated ashes at Summer Lake. The oldest of the tephras that he dated using TL is approximately 200,000 years old; several undated ashes lying beneath this one are older yet. It is clear that the Summer Lake Basin provides a tremendous opportunity to clarify the later Pleistocene history of Lake Chewaucan, and it will probably not be too long before someone takes advantage of this fact.

THE OWENS LAKE–DEATH VALLEY SYSTEM

Searles Lake is part of a complex system of lakes and rivers that begins in the Mono Basin and ends in Death Valley (Figure 5-15). When this system was operating at its maximum, the Pleistocene lake in the Mono Basin overflowed into Lake Adobe in Adobe Valley. Lake Adobe, in turn, overflowed into the Owens River, where it joined more direct Sierran runoff to flow into Owens Lake. Once Owens Lake had reached a depth of about 200′, it overflowed into China Lake. When China Lake reached a depth of about 40′, it overflowed into Searles Lake. Once Searles Lake had reached a depth of about 660′, it both coalesced with China Lake and overflowed into Panamint Lake, in the Panamint Valley. And, once Panamint Lake filled to overflowing, it dumped into Death Valley's Lake Manly. Death Valley, not surprisingly, was the end of the line in this interconnected system of rivers and lakes that

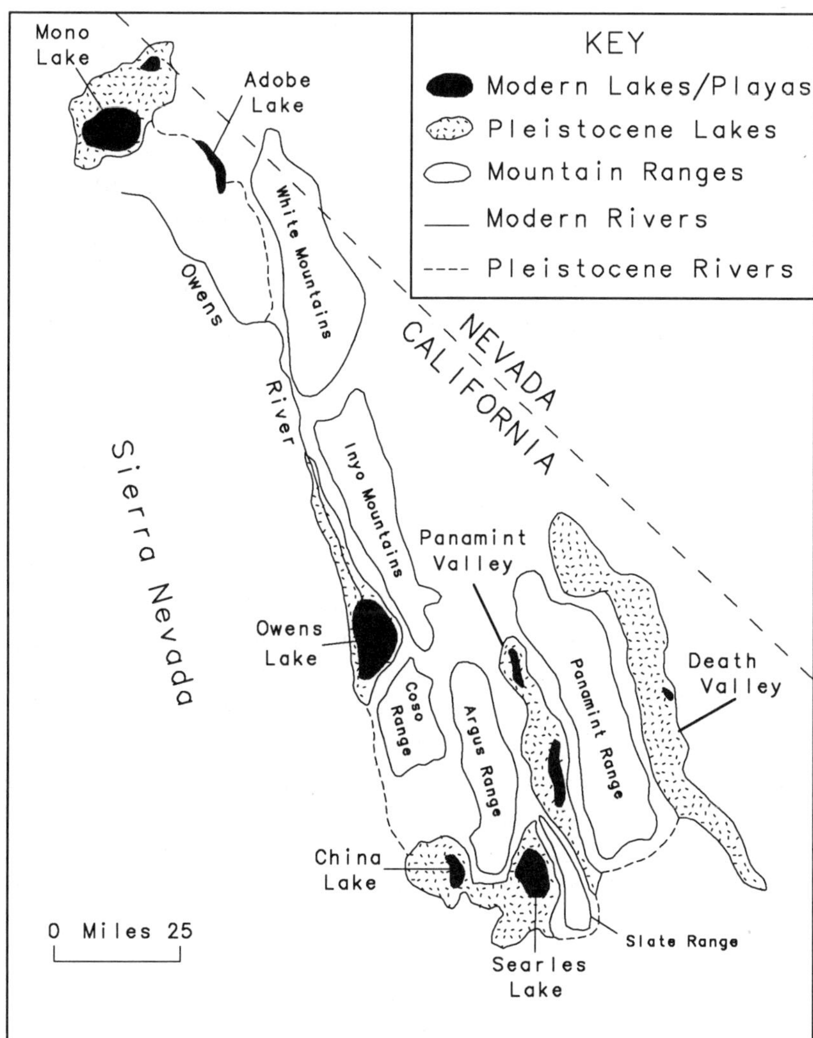

Figure 5-15. The Owens River system during the late Pleistocene. After Benson et al. (1990).

ran some 350 miles. Death Valley, however, received water not only from the Owens River–Death Valley system, but also from the Amargosa River, whose headwaters are to the east of the valley, and from the Mojave River system, to the south. I will discuss Death Valley's Lake Manly in more detail in Chapter 6; here, I focus only on Searles Lake.

During the last 35,000 years or so, the Pleistocene lake that filled the Mono Basin (Pleistocene Lake Russell) does not seem to have risen high enough to have participated in this complicated system. Unfortunately, of all the lakes downstream from Lake Russell in this series, only Searles Lake has received detailed attention, and it is not possible to infer the history of the entire set of potentially interconnected lakes from what we know of this single lake.

The history of Searles Lake has been the target of a lengthy series of important studies by George I. Smith of the U.S. Geological Survey. Smith's work has focused on the analysis of deep cores taken from deposits within the Searles Lake Basin. The deepest of these cores not only penetrated 2,274′, and some 3.2 million years, to the bottom of lake-deposited sediments here, but then penetrated an additional 728′ through sands and gravels deposited by intermittent streams prior to the formation of Searles Lake, and then through nearly 50′ of bedrock.

Smith's analysis of the latest Pleistocene history of Searles Lake has been constructed by combining information gained from a large number of cores. A chronology for these sediments has been built by extracting and dating a fairly wide variety of materials provided by these cores, and the nature of the lake at any given point in the past has been inferred from the nature of the sediments themselves. Smith has used the general nature of these sediments to build an outline of lake history, alternating muds and salt beds, for instance, presenting a picture of alternating deeper and shallower lakes. In addition, he has conducted highly detailed analyses of the chemical and mineral content of the various depositional units revealed by the cores. He has thus been able to use the chemistry and mineralogy of the deposits to attempt to refine our understanding of the history of Searles Lake.

Unfortunately, different interpretations of the hydrological meaning of the chemistry and mineralogy of the late Pleistocene deposits of Searles Lake provide different, and sometimes radically different, interpretations of lake depth. As a result, whereas Smith's work on these sediments has demonstrated the tremendous potential of his approach for extracting a detailed history of Searles Lake, it is also clear that we are far from having a secure understanding of the information contained in the deposits of that lake.

On the other hand, the various reconstructions of Searles Lake history do not differ radically for the past 16,000 years. These reconstructions suggest that the lake had risen dramatically by 16,000 to 15,000 years ago, and remained at a very high level until shortly after 14,000 years ago, at which time it began to decline precipitously. This highstand and subsequent decline correlate well with similar events in both the Lahontan and Bonneville basins. To the more immediate north, Lake Russell, in the Mono Lake basin, also appears to have reached a late Pleistocene highstand between about 15,000 and 13,000 years ago.

Searles Lake differs from these other lakes, however, in that, sometime at or soon after 13,000 years ago, it appears to have risen once again, remaining fairly high until about 11,300 years ago. This relatively late highstand has no correlate in the basins to the north. The final Pleistocene increase in Searles Lake appears to have occurred between 11,000 and 10,500 years ago, virtually identical in time to the rise of Lake Bonneville to the Gilbert level, and, perhaps, of Lake Lahontan to the Russell level.

What we know of the history of all Great Basin pluvial lakes during the past 16,000 years ago or so is beginning to suggest that major changes in lake levels were strongly synchronous. The best understood of these lake histories, however, is that for Lake Bonneville. Lake Lahontan may have major surprises in store for us, especially as regards the poorly understood history of Walker Lake itself. A tremendous amount has also been learned about the history of Searles Lake during the past 15 years or so, but sufficient differences exist between the various reconstructions of the history of this lake to make it clear that much remains to be done here. Many other lake basins provide untapped potential for learning about the past: Lake Chewaucan provides a superb example because Jonathan Davis and his colleagues have begun the process of tapping that potential, but an enterprising Quaternary geologist could find truly rich ground in any of the Oregon Pleistocene lake basins, or, for that matter, in any of dozens of unstudied lake basins in Nevada.

Great Basin Glaciers

The mountains that fringe the Great Basin on three sides—the Sierra Nevada to the west, the Wallowa Mountains to the north, and the Rocky Mountains to the east—support active glaciers today. Within the Great Basin, however, there is but a single glacier, on the north-facing slope of Mt. Wheeler in the Snake Range at an elevation of about 11,200′. Covering some 50 acres, it may not even be active. Given that glaciers formed as far south as the mountains of south-central Arizona and New Mexico during the Pleistocene (see Chapter 3), and given that the Great Basin has 33 mountain ranges with peaks above 10,000′ (see Table 2-1 and Figure 2-5), it will probably come as no surprise that substantial numbers of Great Basin mountains were glaciated during the Pleistocene.

The Pleistocene glaciers of the Great Basin have been the focus of surprisingly little work. Geologists interested in alpine glaciers have had richer peaks to climb in the American West, including those of the Sierra Nevada, the Cascades, and the Rocky Mountains. And rather than focusing their attention on the glaciated mountains, Great Basin geologists interested in the Pleistocene have understandably focused instead on the valley bottoms, and on the more accessible, more tractable, and more unique information they provide on Pleistocene lake histories. In fact, for a number of Great Basin mountains, the only indication we have that they were glaciated comes from a series of reports, based on relatively brief field trips, by glacial geologist Elliot Blackwelder during the early 1930s. It is telling that the two most recent and thorough reviews of Pleistocene glaciation in the mountains of the western United States, published in 1983 and 1986, provide just three paragraphs, out of a total of nearly 70 pages, on the Pleistocene glaciers of the Great Basin. This does not reflect some kind of bias on the parts of the authors of

Table 5-6. Great Basin Mountains Glaciated during the Pleistocene

Range	Elevation (feet)	Reference
Carson Range	10,881	G. A. Thompson and White (1964)
Deep Creek Range	12,087	Ives (1946)
East Humboldt Range	11,306	Wayne (1984)
Independence Mountains	10,439	Blackwelder (1934)
Jarbidge Mountains	10,839	Coats (1964), Coats et al. (1977)
Monitor Range	10,888	Dohrenwend (1984)
Oquirrh Mountains	10,620	Ives (1946)
Pine Forest Range	9,458	Rennie (1987)
Ruby Mountains	11,387	Wayne (1984)
Santa Rosa Range	9,732	Dohrenwend (1984)
Schell Creek Range	11,883	Willden (1964)
Shoshone Mountains	10,313	Dohrenwend (1984)
Snake Range	13,063	Whitebread (1969)
Stansbury Mountains	11,031	Ives (1946)
Steens Mountain	9,733	Lund and Bentley (1976)
Sweetwater Mountains	11,673	Halsey (1953)
Toiyabe Range	11,788	Osborn (1989)
Toquima Range	11,941	Dohrenwend (1984)
Wassuk Range	11,239	Dohrenwend (1984)
White Mountains	14,246	LaMarche (1965), Elliot-Fisk (1987)
White Pine Range	11,513	Piegat (1980)

these reviews, but instead reflects the state of our knowledge.

The work that has been done shows that at least 21 Great Basin mountain ranges were glaciated during the Pleistocene (Table 5-6). With only three exceptions, all of these ranges have peaks in excess of 10,000′ high, and all three exceptions—Steens Mountain in south-central Oregon, and the Pine Forest and Santa Rosa ranges in northern Nevada—are in the northerly reaches of the Great Basin, where temperatures and evaporation rates are lower, precipitation higher.

Of these 21 glaciated ranges, the Ruby and East Humboldt mountains have received by far the most attention. As early as 1931, Blackwelder had presented evidence that these ranges had been the scene of two separate episodes of glacial expansion and retreat, episodes that he called the Lamoille and Angel Lake stages, named for Lamoille Canyon in the northern Ruby Mountains and for Angel Lake in the East Humboldt Range. Not long after, Robert Sharp confirmed Blackwelder's arguments, and more details on these two episodes have been provided recently by William Wayne.

That the Ruby Mountains and East Humboldt Range were glaciated is obvious even to those with only general knowledge of the effects that glaciers have on the landscape. The existence of U-shaped valleys provides an excellent example. Unless something intervenes, stream-cut valleys generally have a V-shaped profile, produced by stream incision. Glaciers flowing down a valley, however, pluck and grind rocks from valley sides and bottoms, often exposing bedrock, and typically producing a valley that, in cross section, looks like a huge U. Kiger and Big Indian gorges in Steens Mountain are textbook examples (see Figure 5-16), but the northern Ruby Mountains and East Humboldt Range have superb instances as well, including both Lamoille and Rattlesnake canyons on the west side of the northern Rubies (see Figure 5-17). The U-shaped profile of upper Lamoille Canyon is particularly easy to see, since a paved road follows the canyon nearly to its top.

The term "moraine" refers to the materials accumulated by glaciers, whether at their sides (lateral moraines), at their ends (terminal moraines), or beneath themselves (ground moraines). In the northern Ruby Mountains, both lateral and end moraines emerge from Lamoille Canyon (see

Figure 5-16. Kiger Gorge, a glacially carved valley in Steens Mountain.

Figure 5-18) and a number of valleys to the south; the outermost moraines fronting Lamoille Canyon sit a full mile from the edge of the mountain itself. All of these moraines were deposited during the Lamoille glaciation, the earliest of the two known glaciations in this area. Although some moraines from the later Angel Lake glaciation descend far down the canyons, none get as far as the Lamoille moraines, and none emerge from the canyons onto the broad valley floor fronting the mountain itself. Indeed, Sharp estimated that Lamoille moraines reached an average altitude 500′ lower than that reached by Angel Lake moraines.

Sharp also estimated that the Lamoille-age glacier in Lamoille Canyon was about 12 miles long, whereas the Angel Lake glacier that formed here was some eight miles long. To the south, in Rattlesnake Canyon, the Lamoille-age glacier covered roughly eight miles of the valley, whereas the Angel Lake glacier covered less than four. Sharp estimated that, in the northern Rubies and East Humboldts together, Angel Lake glaciers covered only 80% of the area occupied by Lamoille-age glaciers. Even though this was the case, Angel Lake glaciation was impressive. By mapping the upper limit of the glacier-scoured wall in Lamoille Canyon, Sharp showed that the Angel Lake glacier here reached a maximum thickness of some 900′; the Lamoille glacier must have been thicker yet.

In addition to the end moraines, lateral moraines, and U-shaped valleys, both the northern Rubies and East Humboldts show a wide range of other glacial phenomena, from glacially polished bedrock to glacial outwash deposits that extend well into Huntington Valley to the west of the northern Rubies. Perhaps the most obvious of these other remnants of glaciation, however, are the numerous high-elevation cirques, or amphitheater-shaped depressions carved by glacial ice. These features are found at the heads of many of the higher valleys in both ranges. Wayne mapped approximately 50 of them for that part of the northern Rubies centering on Lamoille Canyon.

Each of these cirques marks the head of a glacier. In the northern Rubies, the cirques lie at an average elevation of

Figure 5-17. Lamoille Canyon, Ruby Mountains. The glacier that carved this canyon originated in the cirque that now holds Lamoille Lake (see Figure 5-19); the subalpine conifers in this view include both whitebark and limber pines.

Figure 5-18. Terminal and lateral moraines emerging from the mouth of Lamoille Canyon, Ruby Mountains.

Figure 5-19. Lamoille Lake, developed in a glacial cirque in the northern Ruby Mountains.

about 9,385′, but the average elevations decrease toward the north, and cirques in the northern reaches of the East Humboldt Range lie at an average elevation of about 8,890′. Many of these cirques are readily visible to those who hike the Ruby Crest Trail here. In fact, many now contain lakes that form one of the scenic highlights of the trail. Both on and off the trail, these cirque lakes include Verdi Lake just north of Verdi Peak, Echo Lake at the head of Echo Canyon, Lamoille Lake at the head of Lamoille Canyon, and Liberty Lake just south of Liberty Pass (see Figure 5-19).

Since these lakes most likely formed soon after deglaciation, the chances are good that the sediments contained in their basins can provide a partial environmental history of the area since the ice retreated (see Chapter 6). If nothing else, dating the earliest sediments in these lakes should provide an excellent indication of when the ice retreated. On Steens Mountain to the north, for instance, analyses of the deepest sediments within Wildhorse Lake, a cirque lake lying at 8,480′, shows that this cirque was free of glacial ice by 9,400 years ago (see Figure 5-20); lower on Steens Mountain, Fish Lake (7,380′) was free of ice by about 13,000 years ago.

Although detailed analyses of the sediments contained within the cirque lakes of the northern Ruby Mountains and the East Humboldt Range would undoubtedly repay the effort, that work has yet to be done. Robert Thompson tried, but the sediments he encountered were too rocky to be penetrated by his coring equipment. He did extract a core from Upper Dollar Lake, a noncirque lake in the upper reaches of Lamoille Canyon, but he hit Mazama ash, deposited some 6,800 years ago, and was unable to go deeper.

In fact, there is only one radiocarbon date from either the northern Ruby or East Humboldt mountains that pertains to the chronology of glaciation and deglaciation here. That date comes from a small bog that sits on a moraine at an elevation of 8,660′ in Lamoille Canyon, and indicates that this part of the canyon had become ice free by 13,000 years ago. Beyond that, estimates of the ages of

Figure 5-20. Wildhorse Lake, developed in a glacial cirque, Steens Mountain. Peter Mehringer has shown that this cirque was ice free by 9,400 years ago.

the Lamoille and Angel Lake glacial episodes depend on more subjective criteria, and on correlation of these glaciations with better-dated sequences in the Rocky Mountains and Sierra Nevada.

Since Blackwelder's work in 1931, it has been clear that the Lamoille glaciation was the older of the two. For instance, Angel Lake moraines sit on top of areas that had already been glaciated during the Lamoille episode. In addition, Lamoille glacial deposits are far more heavily eroded than those of the Angel Lake episode. To take but one example, the end moraines of Angel Lake glaciers are cut by streams running through narrow passages, but those of the Lamoille episode are cut by far wider stream channels, as both Sharp and Wayne observed.

Wayne's detailed consideration of the relative weathering of the deposits associated with these two episodes of glaciation, coupled with an analysis of glaciation in both the Sierra Nevada and Rocky Mountains, led him to argue that the Lamoille glaciation is not Wisconsin in age at all. Instead, he argues, it correlates with the preceding North American Pleistocene glaciation, the Illinoian, and occurred at about 150,000 years ago. The Angel Lake glaciation, on the other hand, he attributes to the Wisconsin glacial maximum, between about 20,000 and 13,000 years ago. As such, both of these episodes correlate with far better-known episodes of glacial advance in both the Rocky Mountains (termed the Bull Lake and Pinedale glaciations, respectively), and in the Sierra Nevada (the Tahoe and Tioga glaciations, respectively, although the age of the Tahoe glaciation is still debated). In addition, they correlate well with what we know of glacial history on the eastern edge of the Bonneville Basin.

As impressive as the glaciers of the Ruby Mountains and East Humboldt Range are, an even more impressive sequence of glacial events seems to have taken place on the White Mountains of eastern California, the most southerly

Table 5-7. The Glacial Sequence in the White Mountains[a]

Stage	Glaciation	Estimated age (years ago)	ELA (feet)	Glacier length (miles)
I	Chiatovich Flats	2–2.5 million	—	—
II	Dyer	1.0 million	7,244	8.3
III	Indian	0.4–0.6 million	8,868	3.4
IV	Perry Aiken	140,000	9,944	2.5
Va	Early Middle Creek	20,000	10,442	1.7
Vb	Late Middle Creek	14,000	10,882	1.1
VI	Chiatovich Cirque	10,000	12,303	—

[a] After Elliot-Fisk (1987).

glaciated range in the Great Basin. This sequence has been developed by Deborah Elliot-Fisk of the University of California (Davis). Her work documents that at least fifteen valleys and five high-elevation plateaus in the White Mountains have been glaciated, and suggests that there have been at least six major episodes of glaciation in these mountains (see Table 5-7).

The earliest of these glacial episodes, the Chiatovich Flats Glaciation, dating to perhaps 2–2.5 million years ago, seems to have been associated with the growth of an icecap on the summit plateaus of the White Mountains, and it is possible that the subsequent Dyer Glaciation also saw the growth of such an icecap.

Later glaciations in the White Mountains appear to have been confined to valley settings. Radiocarbon dates from two separate valleys show that the maximum advance of the Early Middle Creek Glaciation was over by about 18,000 years ago (the actual dates are 17,780 and 18,510 years ago). Dates from the same pair of valleys also show that the Late Middle Creek glacial advance had ended by about 12,700 years ago (the actual dates are 12,710 and 12,510 years ago). And there is a single date for the Chiatovich Cirque Glaciation that shows that it occurred sometime before 9,740 years ago. The Chiatovich Cirque Glaciation, in fact, may well be contemporary with the well-dated rise of Lake Bonneville to the Gilbert level, and with the hypothesized rise of Lake Lahontan to the Russell level.

The Relationship between Pleistocene Glaciers and Lakes in the Great Basin

Given that both glaciers and lakes expanded in the Great Basin during the late Wisconsin, it seems obvious to wonder about the temporal relationship between the two. Such wondering has, in fact, gone on since the nineteenth century.

Logically, there are three possible relationships between the highstands of pluvial lakes and the maximum expansion of the glaciers. The glaciers might have reached their maximum extent well before the lakes reached theirs, and have been in retreat when the lakes were at their high points. Alternatively, the lakes may have peaked before the glaciers, and have been in retreat as glaciers reached their maximum extent. Finally, both glaciers and lakes may have peaked at the same time, highstands of the lakes matched by maximum expansion of the glaciers. In fact, our current knowledge of the Great Basin during the Pleistocene shows that the glaciers peaked well before the lakes.

There are two prime direct means available for deciphering the relationship between lake and glacier histories in the Great Basin. First, exceedingly well-dated lake histories could be coupled with exceedingly well-dated glacier histories. Then the relationship between the two could simply be read from time charts. This cannot be done now, since the glacial chronology is not available.

Second, we might look for situations in which glacier and lake deposits were laid down in the same place, and study the temporal relationship between the two on the ground. There are only two places known in the Great Basin where lakes rose high enough, and glaciers descended low enough, for their deposits to occur together: the Mono Lake basin in the west, where deposits from Sierran glaciers occur with deposits laid down by Lake Russell, and the Bonneville basin in the east, where deposits from glaciers that emerged from the Wasatch Range are found with deposits laid down by Lake Bonneville.

In the Mono Lake basin, geologist K. R. Lajoie has argued that Lake Russell reached its last highstand (circa

15,000–13,000 years ago) well after glaciers had receded from elevations within reach of the lake. Far better known, however, is the relationship between glacial and lake deposits on the eastern edge of the Bonneville Basin, an area that has been studied for a century.

Little Cottonwood and Bells canyons drain part of the Wasatch Range some 15 miles south and a little east of Salt Lake City. Little Cottonwood Canyon is a familiar place to Utah skiers, since State Road 210 goes from the floor of Pleistocene Lake Bonneville, at an elevation of about 5,000′, to the ski lifts of Alta, some 4,000′ higher. Like many other west-draining canyons in the Wasatch Range, Little Cottonwood Canyon was glaciated during the Pleistocene. But it was only here, and in Bells Canyon to the immediate south, that glaciers were of sufficient magnitude to reach beyond the mouths of the canyons and to come within the elevational range of the waters of Lake Bonneville.

The glaciers in both Little Cottonwood and Bells canyons were fed from north-facing cirques on the canyons' south sides, some ten of them in Little Cottonwood Canyon alone. At least twice during the Pleistocene, these glaciers grew massive enough to reach nearly a mile beyond the front of the Wasatch Range, forming moraines that now have houses built on them (risky, since the Wasatch Fault Zone runs through here).

The deposits of the earlier of these two glacial advances have been called the "Dry Creek till," so I will call this the Dry Creek glaciation. Although this episode is not well dated, the deposits that it left are very heavily weathered, and it is obviously quite old. The best guess is that it correlates with the Bull Lake glaciation of the Rocky Mountains, which occurred about 150,000 years ago. If so, then the Dry Creek advance probably happened at much the same time as the Lamoille glaciation in the Ruby Mountains and East Humboldt Range.

The age of the second, far more recent, glaciation in Little Cottonwood and Bells canyons is much better known. The deposits left by this episode of glacial advance are called the "Bells Canyon till," so I will call this the Bells Canyon glaciation. Glaciers reached the mouths of both Little Cottonwood and Bells canyons during this episode. A number of years ago, David Madsen and Donald Currey made a joint effort to understand the glacial and vegetational history of Little Cottonwood Canyon during latest Pleistocene and Holocene times, and as part of that effort obtained radiocarbon dates that bracket the Bells Canyon glacial episode. They obtained a date of 26,000 years on organic material from beneath Bells Canyon till at the mouth of Bells Canyon, showing that the advance did not occur until after that time. They were also able to show that, by 12,300 years ago, glacial ice had retreated from an elevation of 8,100′, far up the canyon. The last glacial episode, then, must fall between these two dates.

Those dates suggest that the Bells Canyon advance correlates with the Pinedale glaciation of the Rocky Mountains, a glaciation that peaked between 22,000 and 18,000 years ago. Madsen and Currey suggested that the actual dates for the peak of the Bells Canyon glaciation fall at about 19,000 to 20,000 years ago.

Certainly, the glaciers in both Little Cottonwood and Bells Canyon had retreated by 16,000 years ago, since by the time Lake Bonneville had risen high enough to cut a shoreline on the moraines here, the glaciers were already gone from the mouths of the canyons. We can be sure of that because lake sediments from the Bonneville highstand cover deposits left by the glaciers. Given that the lake did not become high enough to reach this area until 16,000 years ago, and was gone from here by 14,000 years ago, it is certain that the glaciers had retreated from the mouths of these two canyons by that time.

Where we have good evidence as to the relationship between glacial expansion in the mountains and lake expansion in the valleys, it is clear that the glaciers were already on the wane when the lakes were hitting their peaks. Why should this have been?

It is perhaps tempting to think that the relationship is a simple mechanical one: that it was the melting of the glaciers that fed the lakes and that allowed their tremendous increase. After all, the water had to go somewhere once it was no longer ice. Just as sea levels fell as glaciers expanded and rose as glaciers melted, perhaps lakes in the Great Basin were driven to great heights as a result of glacial melting.

But although the logic behind such a simple relationship is appealing, things did not work this way. As G. K. Gilbert pointed out a century ago, there was simply not enough water locked up in the glaciers to account for the size of Great Basin lakes at their maximum. In addition, everything we know about the sequence of glaciers and lakes in the Bonneville basin suggests that glaciers reached their peak several thousand years before Lake Bonneville reached its peak. Although the waters provided by melting glaciers certainly did not cause the lakes to become any smaller, the retreat of the glaciers themselves cannot account for the highstands of the lakes. The answer must lie in the nature of late Pleistocene climatic change.

LATE PLEISTOCENE CLIMATES: ESTIMATES FROM GLACIAL PHENOMENA

The net budget of a glacier is determined by calculating the difference between the amount of ice and snow that is added to it and the amount that is lost from it. In glaciers that have reached a steady state, the net budget is zero, with new material added at the same rate as the old is lost. In such steady-state glaciers, the line that divides the area of snow and ice accumulation from the area of snow and ice loss is called the equilibrium line, and the altitude at which this line falls is called the equilibrium line altitude, or ELA.

During the past decade or so, geologists have spent a good deal of time calculating modern ELAs, studying why they fall where they fall, and comparing modern ELAs with their Pleistocene counterparts. My colleague Stephen Porter, for instance, has taken a very detailed look at the factors that determine the elevation at which glaciers form in the Cascade Range of Washington State, and, although these elevations (called the glaciation threshold) are not identical to ELAs, they are very close to them. Porter found that 90% of the variance in these elevations is accounted for by two factors: mean annual temperature and the amount of precipitation that falls between October and April (the months when accumulation of these glaciers exceeds the losses they suffer, or the "accumulation season").

Given that we appear to know why ELAs (and similar elevational parameters) fall where they do, this understanding can be coupled with our knowledge of the position of late-Pleistocene ELAs to infer various aspects of full-glacial climates. Porter used paleobotanical data from the Olympic Peninsula to infer that accumulation-season precipitation was probably no more than 20%–30% greater than that of today. Were that the case, he observed, then a decrease in mean annual temperature of about 7.6°F would be needed to account for the fact that full-glacial ELAs were some 2,950′ lower than modern ELAs in the Washington Cascades.

John Dohrenwend of the U.S. Geological Survey has conducted a similar analysis of Pleistocene ELAs in the Great Basin. For several reasons, the results of his study have to be taken somewhat more cautiously than the results of Porter's Cascade analysis. First, there are very few weather stations in the Great Basin that provide information on precipitation and temperature for the mountains themselves. Second, the modern ELAs must largely be inferred from glaciers in surrounding areas, since there is only one glacier in the Great Basin today.

Even so, Dohrenwend's careful estimates of modern ELAs and climatic variables seem sound, and indicate that the full-glacial ELA was approximately 2,430′ beneath the modern ELA. That position, he observed, implies a full-glacial reduction in mean annual temperature of 12.6°F, assuming no change in the amount of accumulation-season precipitation. If accumulation-season precipitation had been about 1.5″ greater than it is today, then the full-glacial temperatures would have been 9.9°F lower than today's mean annual temperature. Dohrenwend's estimate for the full-glacial reduction in average annual temperature is in line with other estimates derived from a variety of approaches, most of which indicate that that reduction was on the order of 9°–13°F (see Chapter 6).

Deborah Elliot-Fisk has conducted a similar analysis for the Middle Creek Glaciation in the White Mountains. Her analysis suggests that, toward the end of Late Middle Creek times, roughly 12,700 years ago, the snowline here was depressed some 3,900′ beneath its current location, corresponding to a summer temperature decrease of about 15.3°F. This value is somewhat higher than might have been expected, since it is similar to summer temperature decreases estimated for full (not late) glacial times that have been derived from the distributions of Pleistocene plants (see Chapter 6).

Since, as Elliot-Fisk has noted, the White Mountains have the longest visible record of glaciation in the Great Basin, and perhaps even in North America, it is worth noting that she calculated ELAs for her glacial stages II–VI. As can be seen in Table 5-7, these increase significantly over time. Elliot-Fisk attributes this increase to the progressive uplift of the Sierra Nevada during the roughly 2.5-million-year history of glaciation in the White Mountains. Since the Sierra Nevada lies to the immediate west of the White Mountains, she argues that the increasing height of the Sierra Nevada placed the White Mountains in an increasingly severe rain shadow, causing the ELA to rise as time passed. Had the Sierra Nevada not been there, glaciers on the White Mountains should have become more massive as time passed, as the White Mountains themselves were uplifted. Instead, exactly the opposite happened.

AN EXPLANATION FOR THE DIFFERENTIAL GROWTH OF LAKES AND GLACIERS?

The most compelling argument to account for the growth of Pleistocene lakes suggests that the presence of huge ice masses across Canada pushed storm tracks southward, bringing increased precipitation to the Great Basin. That precipitation, along with increased cloud cover and decreased temperatures, led to the formation of huge Pleistocene lakes in the Great Basin. What we know of the chronology of glaciation in the Great Basin, however, suggests that the maximum expansion of glaciers predated the maximum expansion of lakes by a significant amount of time, probably on the order of several thousand years. Why should this have been the case?

As yet, there is no fully convincing answer. It is, however, possible that, during the maximum expanse of continental ice, at about 18,000 years ago, the jet stream was pushed far south, and that it was not until after continental ice began to melt that the jet stream moved north to bring increased precipitation to the Great Basin. If this were the case, then the pluvial lakes of the Southwest should have reached highstands before the pluvial lakes of the Great Basin hit their peaks, and the peaks in southwestern lakes should coincide with the maximum expansion of glaciers in the Great Basin. In addition, southwestern lakes should have been lower when their Great Basin counterparts were at their maximum. In fact, recent studies of pluvial San Agustin Lake, in west-central New Mexico, suggests that this lake was high at 18,000 years ago, and was at much lower levels between 16,000 and 11,000 years ago. If future studies confirm that this was the case, and that other southwestern pluvial lakes had similar histories, then ice-caused movements of the jet stream will have gained major support as a cause of the differential growth of glaciers and lakes in the Great Basin.

William Scott has suggested that Great Basin glaciers reached their maximum when the Great Basin was both cold and dry, and that the lake expansion that followed occurred under a warmer, wetter climatic regime. This fairly straightforward reading of the record is fully consistent with the possibility that the jet stream was forced further south during full-glacial times, retreating north as the continental glaciers waned.

All of these hypotheses are essentially reasoned guesses. But we are at least beginning to know fairly accurately what happened when, and to have some reasonable ideas as to why these events occurred. Most importantly, our hypotheses can readily be tested—for instance, by pairing lake and glacier histories in the Great Basin with lake histories in the Southwest. We are, as a result, immensely better off than we were just a few years ago, when we had very little reliable information about the history of either lakes or glaciers in the Great Basin.

Notes

The land speed records are taken from the *Guinness Book of World Records;* on the Bonneville Salt Flats, see Turk (1973).

For an excellent account of the diversion of Owens Valley waters to Los Angeles, see Reisner (1986); this disturbing volume discusses the "development" of water resources in the western United States as a whole, and is required reading for all interested in the resources of the west in general. For a local account of the Owens Valley story, see Chalfant (1975).

The recent history of Mono Lake is told in many places; excellent, though often highly technical, access is provided by the Mono Basin Ecosystem Study Committee (1987). Botkin et al. (1988) provide a readable, succinct scientific summary of the Mono Lake situation, whereas Gaines (1989) reviews not only the issues involved, but also provides a guide to the lake basin as a whole. The late David Gaines was one of the founders of the Mono Lake Committee, an organization that, since 1978, has fought to prevent the Los Angeles Department of Water and Power from destroying a lake that not only is one of western North America's scenic gems, but also provides critical habitat for many organisms, including California gulls (*Larus californicus*) and eared grebes (*Podiceps nigricollis*): Mono Lake supports the world's second largest breeding colony of the California gulls, and 30% of North American eared grebes use the lake during migration. Visitors to Owens Valley will find themselves confronted with slick pamphlets produced by the Los Angeles Department of Water and Power (e.g., Los Angeles Department of Water and Power 1989a,b). These pamphlets carefully ignore the destruction that the diversion of Mono Lake and Owens Valley waters has caused, and would have us believe that Los Angeles is to be thanked for preserving the natural beauty of eastern California. Instead of purchasing these pamphlets, consider joining the Mono Lake Committee (P.O. Box 29, Lee Vining, California 93541). If you are in the area, stop in at the Mono Lake Visitor's Center in Lee Vining.

On the Truckee and Carson River basins, see Townley (1977); on water history in the western Great Basin in general, see Harding (1965), though parts of this reference are now dated. Table 5-1 contains the references I used for lake area estimates. The information I have presented on Great Basin climates is drawn largely from Houghton (1969) and Houghton et al. (1975); see also Hidy and Klieforth (1990) and Benson and Thompson (1987a,b). Data on precipitation in the Ruby Mountains come from R. S. Thompson (1984); water budgets for Great Salt Lake and Walker Lake are presented in Arnow (1980, 1984), Everett and Rush (1967), and Rush (1972). Evaporation rates for Nevada are presented in B. R. Scott (1971).

Interbasin groundwater flow in the Great Basin is mapped in a number of places, including Division of Water Resources, State of Nevada (1972), Bedinger et al. (1984), and Harrill et al. (1988). References on the Pleistocene lakes of the Great Basin are included in Table 5-2. The best map of Pleistocene lakes in the Great Basin is that by T. R. Williams and Bedinger (1984), which supplants the earlier effort by Snyder et al. (1964). Mifflin and Wheat (1979) on the Pleistocene lakes of Nevada is an indispensable source; the most recent general discussions of Great Basin Pleistocene lakes are found in Benson and Thompson (1987a,b), G. I. Smith and Street-Perrott (1983), and Benson et al. (1990); Morrison (1965) also provides an important, though now largely dated, discussion of those lakes.

On the modern Great Salt Lake, see Arnow (1980, 1984), Sturm (1980), and the other papers in Gwynn (1980). The recent fluctuations of Great Salt Lake are discussed by Arnow (1984), Lindskov (1984), Mabey (1986, 1987), and Arnow and Stephens (1990). The economic damage caused by the increased precipitation received by Utah in 1983 is detailed by Kaliser and Slosson (1988) and Kaliser (1989).

There is an immense literature on Lake Bonneville; an excellent place to start is with the historical overview provided by Sack (1989). The classic reference on Lake Bonneville is G. K. Gilbert (1890); my presentation has depended heavily on Currey (1980, 1988), Currey and Oviatt (1985), Currey et al. (1984), Oviatt et al. (1990), W. E. Scott et al. (1983), G. I. Smith et al. (1989), R. S. Thompson et al. (1990), Benson et al. (1990), the papers in Machette (1988), and, to a lesser extent, on Spencer et al. (1984) [this last reference is clearly incorrect on some scores (e.g., Grayson 1988a)]. Oviatt (1988) provides an intriguing discussion of the history of Lake Gunnison; I have drawn heavily on that paper here (see also Oviatt 1987, 1989, and Oviatt and McCoy 1988). The Lake Bonneville shoreline elevations used in the text are primarily from Currey and Oviatt (1985) and Oviatt et al. (1990); different elevations are to be found in Benson et al. (1990; see their Figure 7). The figures I have used for the elevation of Lake Bonneville at the Gilbert level (4,260′) and for the maximum extent of Lake Bonneville (19,970 square miles) were kindly provided to me by Donald Currey. For recent discussions of the Keg Mountain Oscillation, see Burr and Currey (1988), Currey and Burr (1988), and Oviatt (1991b).

Information on the Bonneville Flood is drawn from Malde (1968) and Jarrett and Malde (1987). On the Younger Dryas, see Ruddiman (1987), Paterson and Hammer (1987), Harvey (1989), Broecker and Denton (1990), and Peteet et al. (1990).

The largest geologically documented flooding in earth history issued periodically from glacial Lake Missoula. This lake formed in northern Idaho and northwest Montana when an extension of Cordilleran ice, called the Purcell Trench lobe, dammed the Clark Fork valley, creating a body of water that had a volume of approximately 600 cubic miles. The floods occurred as the dammed water broke through the ice that held the lake; the erosion caused by this massive flooding created the Channeled Scabland of eastern Washington. The volume of water released in this way was only about half of that released in the Bonneville Flood, but the peak discharge rates of the Missoula Floods have been estimated to have been between 97,000,000 and 484,000,000 cubic feet of water per second—some three to fourteen times the peak discharge rates of the Bonneville Flood. The precise timing and number of Missoula Floods are not yet clear. One appears to have occurred some 18,000 years ago, another at about 13,000 years ago. That there were multiple floods that drained Lake Missoula is not in question; it is the exact number that is currently being debated. Not all, however, would have been of tremendous magnitude. When, during the 1920s, J. Harlan Bretz first proposed that eastern Washington's Channeled Scabland was created by monstrous floods, geologists strongly objected. Today, it is clear that the world's largest scientifically documented floods did just what he said they did. For discussions of the Missoula Floods, see Baker (1973, 1983), Waitt (1984, 1985), Clarke et al. (1984), and Atwater (1987); see also Steele (1991). A popular account of these floods, along with a helpful guide to the features produced by them, is found in Allen et al.

(1986), but do not believe what they say about human prehistory in arid western North America.

Key sources on Lake Lahontan include the classic by Russell (1885b), and recent analyses by Benson (1978, 1991), Benson and Thompson (1987a,b), Benson and Paillet (1989), Benson et al. (1990), J. O. Davis (1982, 1983), Lao and Benson (1988), Morrison (1964), and R. S. Thompson et al. (1986, 1990); for an alternative view of the last highstand of Lake Lahontan, see Bradbury et al. (1989). On the diversion of the Humboldt River, see J. O. Davis (1982, 1987). The dates I have used for the Lake Lahontan highstand are from Benson (1993). Important analyses of Walker Lake and Walker River, including their histories, are found in the Lake Lahontan references cited previously, as well as in G. O. King (1978), Benson (1988), Bradbury (1987), and Bradbury et al. (1989). Data on stream inflow into the Lahontan Basin as a whole are taken from Benson and Paillet (1989); this reference also discusses what would have happened in the Lahontan Basin had inflow rates remained at 1983 levels. Morrison (1964) is a key reference on the geology of the southern Carson Desert, and of Lake Lahontan in this area; it also contains his definition and discussion of the First Fallon Lake. Currey (1988) and Elston et al. (1988) argue that this lake might be contemporary with the rise of Lake Bonneville to the Gilbert level, as do Benson et al. (1990); see also Dansie et al. (1988).

For discussions of the displacement of the jet stream and the effects that might have had on Great Basin lakes, see COHMAP Members (1988), Kutzbach (1987), Kutzbach and Guetter (1986), Benson and Thompson (1987a,b), Oviatt et al. (1990), and R. S. Thompson et al. (1992).

I. S. Allison (1982) provides an excellent introduction to the Summer Lake Basin and to Lake Chewaucan. J. O. Davis (1985a) analyzes the tephra layers in the deposits of Lake Chewaucan; Negrini and Davis (1992) discuss the Lake Chewaucan paleomagnetic record, and Gobalet and Negrini (1992) discuss the remains of tui chub (*Gila bicolor*) recovered from the sediments of this lake, estimated to be 98,000 years old. Excellent discussions of TL dating are presented by G. W. Berger (1988) and Aitken (1989). On paleomagnetic variations see the overview by Verosub (1988). The TL dates for Summer Lake tephras are presented by G. W. Berger (1991) and Berger and Davis (1992).

The key references for Searles Lake are G. I. Smith (1979, 1984) and G. I. Smith et al. (1983); see also G. I. Smith and Street-Perrott (1983), G. I. Smith et al. (1989), and Benson et al. (1990). Searles Lake is not alone in providing a record that spans some 3,000,000 years in or near the Great Basin: for a similar record at Tule Lake, northeastern California, see Adam et al. (1989). On Lake Russell, see Benson et al. (1990).

The first mention of the glacier on Wheeler Peak (then called Jeff Davis Peak) is in Russell (1885a); see also Ferguson (1992) and, for a more poetic account, Heald (1956). References to the Pleistocene glaciers of the Great Basin are provided in Table 5-6; the two recent reviews of Pleistocene alpine glaciation in western North America to which I refer are Porter et al. (1983) and Richmond (1986). Blackwelder (1931) reports his pioneering work. My discussion of glaciation in the Ruby Mountains and the East Humboldt Range relies heavily on Sharp (1938) and Wayne (1984). Deglaciation of Steens Mountain is discussed by Mehringer (1986); R. S. Thompson (1984) discusses his attempt to core lakes in the Ruby Mountains. See Hart (1991) on hiking the Ruby Crest Trail; this excellent little book also provides detailed information on hiking many other Great Basin mountain ranges. Elliot-Fisk (1987) discusses the glacial sequence in the White Mountains; both this paper and Dorn et al. (1990) present radiocarbon dates for the most recent episodes in this sequence.

On the general relationship between lakes and glaciers in the Mono Lake Basin, see Benson and Thompson (1987b). For the Mono Lake basin, see Benson et al. (1990). On Little Cottonwood and Bells canyons, see D. B. Madsen and Currey (1979), Richmond (1964, 1986), W. E. Scott et al. (1983), Morrison and Frye (1965), and W. E. Scott (1988); Gilbert (1890) also discussed the relationship between Lake Bonneville and the glaciation of nearby mountains. For definitions of such terms as "equilibrium line altitude" see Meier (1962). On ELAs, see Porter (1977) and Porter et al. (1983); Porter (1977) provides the information I have used on the Cascade Range, whereas Dohrenwend (1984) provides the ELA analysis for the Great Basin (see also Zielinski and McCoy 1987, but this paper is overly dependent on Blackwelder's early data on glaciation in the Great Basin). W. E. Scott (1988) provides his ideas on the cause of the differential growth of lakes and glaciers in the Great Basin; see also Benson and Thompson (1987a,b). The late Pleistocene history of pluvial San Agustin Lake is discussed in Markgraf et al. (1984); Phillips et al. (1986) also present evidence for increased precipitation in northwestern New Mexico between 24,000 and 21,000 years ago.

CHAPTER SIX

○○○

The Late Pleistocene Vegetation of the Great Basin

Learning about Ancient Vegetation

William Lewis Manly and his traveling companions spent the Christmas of 1849 in Death Valley. Manly's companions did not escape the valley until mid-February, and then only because Manly and his friend John Rogers walked out, returning with supplies, directions, and hope. Not until March 7 did the whole group reach Rancho San Francisco, near Los Angeles, and full safety. On their way out, they gave Death Valley its name, even though only one of their immediate group had actually died there: "we took off our hats, and then overlooking the scene of so much trial, suffering and death spoke the thought uppermost saying:—'*Good bye Death Valley*!' then faced away and made our steps toward camp" (Manly 1894:216).

Manly and his group had been lured into Death Valley by talk of a cutoff that would save them many days on the trip from Salt Lake City to California. The shortcut they tried left the Old Spanish Trail in southwestern Utah, and then cut southwest across southern Nevada, leading the travelers to Ash Meadows, and then into the heart of what is now Death Valley National Monument.

Seventy miles northwest of Las Vegas, Manly's group passed by Papoose Lake, now close to the boundary between Nellis Air Force Base and the Nevada Test Site. Realizing that continuing west might see them die of thirst, the small band of travelers headed south:

> we turned up a cañon leading toward the mountain and had a pretty heavy up grade and a rough bed for a road. Part way up we came to a high cliff and in its face were niches or cavities as large as a barrel or larger, and in some of them we found balls of a glistening substance looking something like pieces of varigated [*sic*] candy stuck together. The balls were as large as small pumpkins. It was evidently food of some sort, and we found it sweet but sickish, and those who were so hungry as to break up one of the balls and divide it among the others, making a good meal of it, were a little troubled with nausea afterwards (Manly 1894:126).

Manly guessed that what they had found was a food cache belonging to Indians, and was concerned that what they had done might cause them serious problems. "I considered it bad policy to rob the Indians of any of their food," he went on to say, "for they must be pretty smart people to live in this desolate country and find enough to keep them alive . . . they were probably revengeful, and might seek to have revenge on us for the injury" (Manly 1894:126).

The Manly party was not the only one to take notice of this "glistening substance," although they may have been the only ones to mistake it for food. In 1843, Frémont found the same stuff. Exploring the canyon of a small tributary of the Bear River in far southern Idaho on August 29 of that year, Frémont found "several curious caves" on the roofs of which he noted "bituminous exudations from the rock" (Frémont 1845:141).

Sixteen years later, the U.S. Army's Corps of Topographical Engineers assigned Captain James H. Simpson the task of discovering a better wagon route across the Great Basin. Simpson gladly accepted the task—no surprise, since he had suggested it in the first place—and traveled from Salt Lake City to Genoa, Nevada, and back during the spring and summer of 1859. By the time he was done, not only had he found a better wagon route, but he had also blazed a path that the Pony Express was to follow closely in 1860, that the telegraph was to use in completing its transcontinental service in 1861 (putting the Pony Express out of business), and that U.S. Highway 50 follows closely today.

On July 16, 1859, Simpson was exploring Dome Canyon in the House Range, just west of the Sevier Desert and south of what is now Fish Springs National Wildlife Refuge. He found the "walls of the cañon full of small caves, and as usual showing a great deal of the resinous, pitchy substance, that seemingly oozes out of the rock" (J. H. Simpson 1983:125). Unlike Manly's party, however, Simpson did not taste it; he guessed that it might have been "the dung of birds or of small animals" (1983:125).

Simpson was very close to being right. These hard, shiny deposits that are so often found cemented to the walls of caves and rock crevices in the Great Basin are made by a group of house-rat–sized rodents that belong to the genus *Neotoma.* These active little mammals are found throughout much of North America, but they are especially common, and rich in species, in the arid West. The first members of the genus to be described scientifically were from the woodlands of the East: they were given the scientific name *Neotoma floridana,* and came to be called the woodrat. That common name was well established for these animals by the time the western species came to be described, so the western forms are often called woodrats as well. Western "woodrats," however, may or may not live in woodlands, so other common names have come into use for them. The most widely accepted of these names is "packrat," which comes from the fact that these rodents often pick up whatever small items they find interesting, packing them off to their dens. Because they use their mouths to do this, they often leave behind whatever it was they were carrying when they found the new item they wanted more. The third common name applied to them, "trade rat," comes from this behavior.

Today, there are three species of packrats in the Great Basin. One of these, the white-footed packrat (*Neotoma fuscipes*), is essentially a far western species, found along the West Coast from Oregon to Baja California. It enters the Great Basin only on its far northwestern edge, in northeastern California and adjacent south-central Oregon. The desert packrat (*Neotoma lepida*), on the other hand, is found almost throughout the Great Basin. The bushy-tailed packrat (*Neotoma cinerea*) also occupies much of the Great Basin, but it is missing from large parts of southern Nevada and southeastern California.

Although the ranges of these two packrats overlap, the desert packrat tends to live in and adjacent to the valleys of the Great Basin, whereas the bushy-tailed packrat is essentially an animal of higher altitudes. Only in the northern Great Basin—south-central Oregon, for instance—are bushy-tailed packrats able to live at elevations low enough that their ranges routinely overlap those of desert packrats. Yet even here competition between the two is lessened by the fact that they tend to focus their attention on different habitats. Desert packrats routinely den beneath isolated boulders, though they will also build dens at the bases of shrubs and trees. Bushy-tailed packrats, on the other hand, prefer caves and crevices. They also take readily to buildings: the altitude record for bushy-tailed packrats in the Great Basin was provided by an animal living in the summit hut on White Mountain Peak in eastern California, at an elevation of 14,246′.

What Manly and his friends ate, and what Simpson guessed may have had something to do with the dung of small mammals, was part of a packrat midden. Packrats bring a wide variety of materials back to their dens. These objects routinely include twigs, leaves, seeds, stones, and bones, but they may include anything that piques a packrat's interest, and that is small enough to be carried or dragged along. Much of what they retrieve is plant material, and much of this is either consumed or used in den construction. A good deal of it, however, simply accumulates, along with everything else, in the areas near their dens. The accumulated detritus of a packrat's life grows to often substantial heaps of litter. These heaps are packrat middens.

If this were all there were to it, packrat middens would appear comparable to our basements, attics, or garages: places in which the detritus of our lives tends to accumulate. However, unlike most people I know, packrats also urinate and defecate on their middens. If the midden on which a packrat is urinating is in the open, then the urine just washes away. But if the midden is in a sheltered spot—in a dry cave or crevice, for instance—the urine will crystallize and become about as hard as rock candy (recall Manly's description).

This crystallized material is called amberat, referring both to its consistency and to its source. Because the urine saturates the midden, everything in the midden becomes encased in this hardened material. As long as the midden does not become wet, it can last for tens of thousands of years. As Geoffrey Spaulding and his colleagues have put it, many old, hardened packrat middens "resemble blocks of asphalt with the consistency and mass of an unfired adobe brick" (Spaulding et al. 1990:60). The oldest known middens are too old to date by the radiocarbon method—that is, they are over 40,000 years old.

Manly and his friends were thus not eating food that had been carefully stored by people, but were instead eating a packrat midden—a mass of plant fragments, bones, stones, dirt, fecal pellets, and other items cemented together by crystallized packrat urine. There is no way of knowing how old the midden that they ate was, but it is the potential age of these middens, coupled with their contents, that has earned them significant amounts of scientific attention during the past few decades.

That ancient packrat middens could teach us a tremendous amount about the past was dramatically demonstrated by botanist Philip V. Wells and zoologist Clive D. Jorgensen. In 1961, Wells and Jorgensen had gone to the Nevada Test Site, in southwestern Nevada. Hiking down Aysees Peak, near Frenchman Flat, Jorgensen broke off a piece of packrat midden and found that it was full of juniper, even though Aysees Peak is too hot and dry for juniper today. One of the advantages of packrat middens is that packrats do not go far from their dens to accumulate the material that ends up in the middens: a few hundred feet is their normal cruising range. As a result, the juniper in the Aysees Peak midden that Jorgensen had found must have grown on that peak, even though it was no longer there.

Wells and Jorgensen ended up collecting, analyzing, and dating the material from nine packrat middens in the Frenchman Flat area. All of them proved to contain Utah juniper. They were able to show that the youngest of these middens dated to 7,800 years ago, whereas the oldest was over 40,000 years old. One of the middens, from Mercury Ridge on the Spotted Range, even held a marmot skull, dated to 12,700 years ago. Like the juniper, the marmot was out of place: today, marmots are found no closer than 100 miles away (see Chapters 7 and 8).

Wells and Jorgensen published their results in *Science* in 1964. In this short paper, they documented the facts that packrat middens can contain ancient plant and animal remains, that these remains can often be readily identified, and that the middens themselves can be dated by the radiocarbon method. They also used the data they had obtained to discuss what the late Pleistocene vegetation of the Frenchman Flat area must have been like, an issue I will return to later in this chapter.

Wells and Jorgensen had made a truly major contribution. They had discovered a novel source of readily dated ancient plant material. The years since the appearance of their paper have seen an explosion of interest in this source of information about plant, and, through the plants, climate history in the Desert West. Much of this work has been done either by Wells or by the students of Paul S. Martin of the University of Arizona. Martin's students, in particular, have been avid analysts of packrat middens, especially those in the southwestern United States and in the central and southern Great Basin. As a result, a tremendous amount has been learned about plant history in the arid West.

This is not to say that we were totally ignorant of the late Pleistocene and Holocene history of Great Basin vegetation prior to Wells and Jorgensen's discovery. There are, in fact, two prime sources of information about plant history in the Desert West: the ancient seeds, leaves, twigs, and other larger parts of plants (called "plant macrofossils") that are found in such abundance in packrat middens, and pollen. Packrat middens also contain pollen, but the best source of ancient pollen in the Great Basin is provided by the sediments of lakes that have continually held water since those sediments were deposited (see Chapter 3). Other sources also exist: the sediments that surround springs, for instance, and those that fill caves. Even the deposits of playa lakes have some potential for providing ancient pollen.

Palynologists (scientists who study pollen and spores) prefer to study the pollen from the deposits of lakes that have been continually wet for simple reasons. If a lake in the arid West dries, the exposed deposits of that lake will inevitably be eroded by wind, leaving often-massive gaps in the sequences represented by those deposits. Sometimes the gaps created in this fashion are obvious; sometimes, they are extremely difficult, if not impossible, to detect. In addition, the pollen in lake deposits that have been continually wet will likely be better preserved than that in sediments that have been alternately soaked and dried. As a result, if palynologists have a choice, it is a lake that has continually been a lake that draws their attention.

Detailed analyses of pollen from Great Basin contexts began in the 1940s, with now-classic work by Henry P. Hansen, then of Oregon State University. It has continued ever since, and we now have lengthy pollen-derived vegetational histories from areas as far-flung as Tule Springs (west of Las Vegas) in the south and Steens Mountain (Oregon) in the north, and from the Wasatch Mountains in the east to the Tahoe Lake Basin in the west.

When Wells and Jorgensen introduced packrat midden analysis to the scientific community, they modestly noted that "*Neotoma* middens may have unique value as a check on the palynological approach to Pleistocene ecology" in the Desert West (P. V. Wells and Jorgensen 1964:1172). They felt that such a check was important because the pollen of many wind-pollinated plants disperses widely, producing a "pollen rain" that reflects not the plants of the particular patch of ground on which it fell, but of the regional wind-pollinated vegetation as a whole. In addition, pollen that ends up in lakes comes not just from the air, but also from all the tributaries that feed that lake, adding another regional aspect to the pollen in the deposits of that lake. In the Great Basin, most valley bottom lakes receive water from streams that originate in the surrounding mountains; as a result, the pollen in those lakes often reflects the vegetation of higher elevations.

It is now clear, with nearly 30 years of work behind us, that Wells and Jorgensen could have claimed far more for the approach they pioneered. The analysis of pollen from the stratified deposits of lakes, springs, caves, and other settings provides a fundamentally different kind of information than the analysis of the plant macrofossils provided in abundance by packrat middens. Each approach has strong advantages and some disadvantages; the two together provide a powerful means of unraveling plant history.

The study of well-preserved pollen from deep, stratified deposits results in a reconstructed vegetational sequence that is virtually continuous, unless erosion has removed part of the sequence. Further, since the pollen that becomes embedded in ever-deepening layered deposits often reflects the vegetation of fairly broad areas, the effects of strictly local phenomena—for instance, the local extinction of one species of packrat with one set of dietary preferences and its replacement by another species with a different set—can be muted. In addition, in favorable depositional environments, pollen can be truly abundant: it is not uncommon for a single cubic centimeter of lake deposits to contain tens of thousands of pollen grains. In the right kind of setting, pollen analysis can provide continuous, detailed records of plant history over substantial amounts of time, records that are based on rich samples of the pollen produced by that vegetation.

Packrat midden analysis does not come close to doing that. Although generations of packrats may occupy the same area and their middens may thus accumulate over long spans of time, the deposition of those middens is not continuous in the same way that sedimentation in a lake basin is continuous. In addition, many middens represent only brief periods of time. In some cases, middens that began to grow tens of thousands of years ago may have been inactive for thousands of subsequent years before new material began to be deposited on them. As a result, each plant assemblage, and sometimes each species of plant, has to be radiocarbon-dated if the time it was deposited is to be known accurately.

Unlike pollen in lake or cave sediments, plant fragments in packrat middens represent the vegetation that was growing in the area within a few hundred feet of that midden. Packrats do not travel as far as the wind, nor are they routinely blown across the landscape, or washed into the areas in which their middens accumulate, mouths full of pieces of plants.

So, in sharp distinction to most pollen records from places like lakes and springs, the plant assemblages from packrat middens represent "spot samples," snapshots of the vegetation at a particular place at a particular time. As a result, much labor is required to build long sequences of vegetational change from packrat middens. First, middens of the right age have to be found and collected. Then the plants of those middens have to be extracted and identified. Then they have to be dated. And many middens, representing the appropriate times, have to be analyzed if vegetational change on a regional basis is to be understood.

If pollen sequences can provide a continuous picture of vegetational change through time with far less effort, then why bother with middens at all? There are, in fact, many reasons to bother. First, the pollen of many plants often cannot be identified beyond the genus level; indeed, pollen often cannot be identified beyond the family level. However, well-preserved plant fragments from packrat middens can frequently be identified to the species level. Thus, whereas pollen analysts can discuss whether the abundance of pine trees in an area decreased or increased through time, midden analysts can tell you whether the pine involved was singleleaf piñon, Colorado piñon, or limber pine. Having access to the species of plant involved opens up the possibility of extracting species-by-species plant histories in the arid West. Indeed, midden analysts have been phenomenally successful at doing just that.

In many ways, it is also a benefit that the plants in packrat middens almost necessarily represent local vegetation. Pines, for instance, are notoriously prolific producers of easily dispersed pollen. As a result, an ancient pollen assemblage from lake sediments that is composed of 20% pine pollen does not necessarily imply that pine trees were growing around that lake. But a plant assemblage from an ancient packrat midden that is composed of 20% pine leaves, twigs, and seeds does mean that pines were growing nearby—and you would know what species they came from.

In a splendid example of long-distance wind transport of pollen, Louis Maher of the University of Wisconsin once demonstrated that the pollen of Mormon tea (genus *Ephedra*) can be found in the Great Lakes region, at least 700 miles from its nearest possible source. On the other hand, if you find an *Ephedra* seed in a packrat midden, you can be sure that it was growing nearby at the time it was deposited. With the right material, you can also tell what species of *Ephedra* it was, and the *Ephedra* fossils can even be radiocarbon-dated directly. Although it has recently been shown that pollen grains can also be directly dated (see Chapter 3), that is an extremely laborious and expensive process that is unlikely to come into common use. In contrast, it is easy to date seeds, leaves, and twigs.

Pollen analysis of sediments from lakes, springs, and caves, and the analysis of plant macrofossils from packrat middens, can, just as Wells and Jorgensen noted, serve as checks on one another. But, even better, these approaches provide two complementary, independent sources of information about past vegetation. Each used alone is powerful. When used together, they provide an extremely sensitive means of learning about the past history of vegetation in the Desert West.

This point is driven home even more clearly when it is realized that packrat middens routinely occur on different parts of the landscape than do most of the deposits that provide pollen. Ancient packrat middens are not often found on the floors of Great Basin valleys, since those valleys rarely provide the rocky outcrops that the rodents prefer, and that the middens need if they are to survive the centuries.

Our knowledge of the late Pleistocene and Holocene vegetational history of the Great Basin thus comes primarily from the analysis of pollen from stratified lake and cave deposits, and from the analysis of plant macrofossils from packrat middens. The Great Basin is a vast place, the number of paleobotanists working here fairly small, and the number of truly acceptable lakes for pollen work low. Middens are abundant, but intense midden-based investigations of the plant history of this area go back no more than 20 years or so. That there is much to be learned is clear, as is the fact that there are probably huge surprises in store for us. In fact, piñon pine provided one not long ago (see Chapter 8).

But we do know enough to have a general picture of the late Pleistocene and Holocene vegetation of the Great Basin. In the pages that follow, I focus on the late Pleistocene part of that picture, reserving the Holocene for Chapter 8. To provide a feel for the late Pleistocene vegetation of this region, I begin by reviewing three very different areas that have been the focus of recent studies: Death Valley in the Mojave Desert, the Carson Sink in the Lahontan Trough, and Ruby Valley in the central Great Basin.

Three Regional Pictures

THE MOJAVE DESERT: DEATH VALLEY

Death Valley is one of the hottest and driest places on earth (see Figure 6-1). On July 13, 1913, the air temperature at Death Valley's Furnace Creek reached 134°F, the highest ever recorded in the Western Hemisphere, and the second highest ever recorded on the planet. The only higher reading comes from Tripolitania, in Libya's Sahara Desert. Even January is warm in Death Valley; the average January *minimum* temperature is 37°F, and temperatures as high as 85°F have been recorded here during this month. In Death Valley's hottest month, July, temperatures average 102°F, and the average maximum July temperature is 116°F. The

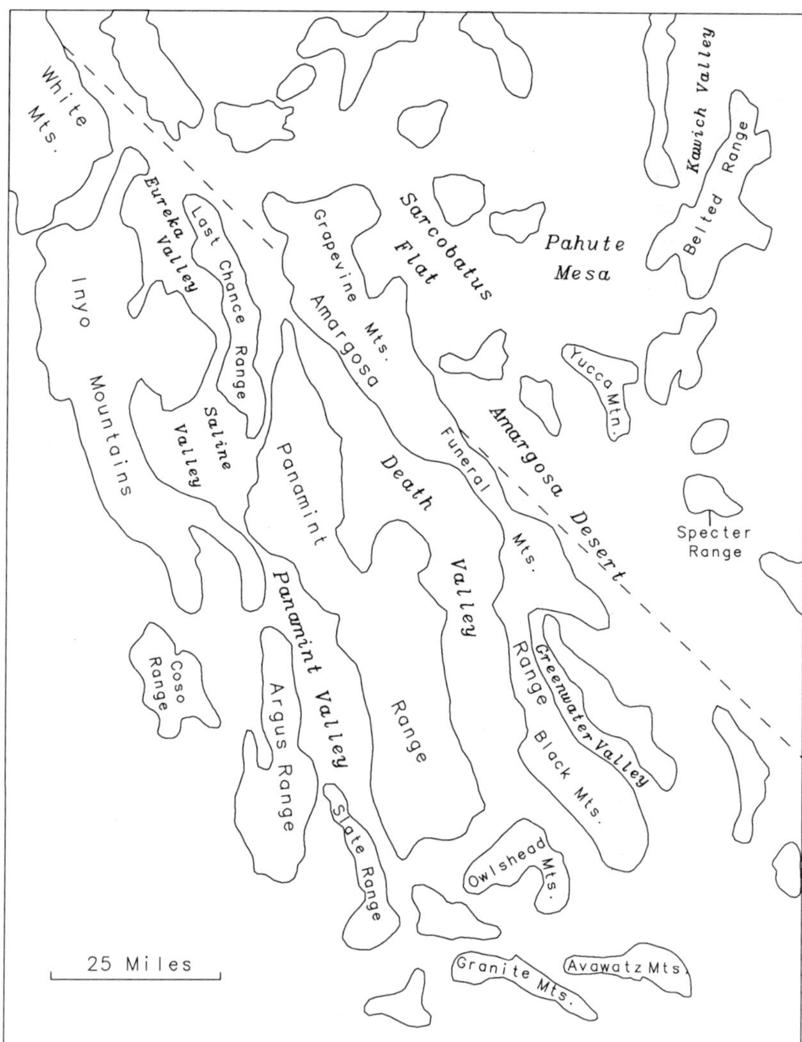

Figure 6-1. The Death Valley region.

difference between the lowest and highest temperatures in a given year can easily exceed 100°F. Even these readings, however, are glacial compared to the heights that can be reached by ground temperatures: those have been measured as high as 190°F, and may go beyond that.

Precipitation is as low as the temperature is high, averaging a meager 1.65″ a year. On top of that, the evaporation rate is extraordinarily high: 155″ of evaporation was measured at the National Park Service Headquarters on Cow Creek between May 1, 1958, and May 1, 1959, the highest evaporation rate ever measured in the United States. Even the highest elevations of the lofty Panamint Range, which forms the western border of the valley and which reaches 11,049′, receive only some 12–15″ of precipitation a year.

High temperatures and low precipitation combine with soils that are often extremely saline to limit greatly the kinds and densities of plants that can now survive in Death Valley. In fact, some 200 square miles of the central part of the valley are covered by a playa that has ample water for plants, but whose salinity is so high that they simply do not grow there. Detailed studies by George B. Hunt of the U.S. Geological Survey have shown that, as plants descend toward this saltpan, their advance stops fairly abruptly as groundwater salinity exceeds 6%.

A series of gravel fans, whose permeability to water varies but which generally allows water to pass readily, slopes toward the saltpan from the adjacent mountains. Between the toes of these fans and the saltpan itself, there is a zone about a mile wide where, Hunt has shown, the ground is sandy, the water table fairly high, and salinity levels do not exceed 6%. Most of the plants that occur here depend on the availability of groundwater to survive (such plants are called phreatophytes). Their precise distribution in this zone is dictated largely by their tolerance for the salinity of the water they utilize. The most tolerant of them is pickleweed (*Allenrolfea occidentalis*), a greenish succulent that covers large areas just above the playa, often growing on large mounds.

Moving back from the saltpan, other plants appear, most of which also appear to be dependent on the availability of groundwater: saltgrass, Torrey inkweed (*Suaeda torreyana*), alkali sacaton grass (*Sporobulus airoides*), arrow weed (*Pluchea sericea*), and four-winged saltbush. There are even trees in this zone, most notably honey mesquite (*Prosopis juliflora*), but also introduced tamarisks (*Tamarix*).

These plants are quickly left behind as one moves above the sandy substrate that surrounds the saltpan and onto the gravel matrix of the fans. Here, most plants survive without access to the water table, and instead use moisture made available by surface runoff. Toward the northern end of the valley, the lower parts of the gravel fans are covered by stands of desert holly (*Atriplex hymenelytra*).

To the south, the lower parts of the gravel fans are marked by desert saltbush or cattle spinach (*Atriplex polycarpa*). Creosote bush makes its appearance on the fans as well. As I discussed in Chapter 2, creosote bush is one of the most widespread plants of the Mojave Desert and is also the species whose northern boundary marks the border between this desert and the botanical Great Basin. In Death Valley, it is found from near the bases of the fans, as low as –240′ in elevation, up onto the flanks of the mountains themselves, to elevations as high as about 4,000′.

Whereas creosote bush covers much of the fans, two other shrubs tend to be found only along their upper reaches. In the north, white bursage (*Ambrosia dumosa*), a common Mojave Desert shrub also known as burro weed, replaces desert holly along higher elevations of the fans. To the south, brittle bush (*Encelia farinosa*) tends to replace desert saltbush in the same fashion. Creosote bush can be found with them all.

Springs that emerge on the gravel fans often support dense vegetation, including plants that otherwise grow in the valley bottom where they have access to groundwater—arrow weed, alkali sacaton grass, and four-winged saltbush, for example. Mesquite is found here as well, both honey mesquite, and, at higher elevations, screw bean mesquite (*Prosopis pubescens*).

The mountains bordering Death Valley have not been the subject of botanical studies as detailed as those made by Hunt for the valley itself. To the east and west, the creosote bush of the gravel fans is replaced by shadscale in the Panamint, Black, and Funeral ranges. In the Panamint Range, well-developed piñon-juniper woodland occurs between elevations of about 6,000′ and 9,600′. As is common elsewhere in the piñon-juniper woodlands of the Great Basin, Utah juniper both appears and disappears first with increasing elevation. For instance, along the road from Wildrose Campground to Mahogany Flat, on the west slope of the Panamint Range, the first Utah junipers occur at an elevation of about 5,850′, whereas the first singleleaf piñons occur at 6,100′. By the time Mahogany Flat (so named because it is covered with mountain mahogany) has been reached, at an elevation of 8,133′, the junipers are gone. The piñons, however, continue upward to an elevation of about 9,600′, at which point krummholz piñons can be seen.

The juniper in this woodland includes not only the familiar Utah juniper, but also, as botanist Frank Vasek has shown, the primarily Sierran western juniper. Western juniper is not common here, but it is found at the very upper reaches of the piñon-juniper zone, and in the lower reaches of the bristlecone pine-limber pine association, which comes next. The shrubs in the piñon-juniper zone include plants that would be entirely at home in the botanical Great Basin to the north: green rabbitbrush (*Chrysothamnus viscidiflorus*), Mormon tea (*Ephedra viridis*), black sage, and cliffrose (*Cowania mexicana*).

Even though the Panamint Range borders Death Valley, it is sufficiently massive and tall to support subalpine conifers on its higher elevations. Limber pine is found above 9,600′, bristlecone above 9,800′, with big sage and green rabbitbrush as accompaniments. The uppermost 80′ or so of the slopes of the ridge along Telescope Peak, for instance, are marked by both of these subalpine conifers, although, as the top of the Panamints is approached here, limber pines become more and more scattered while bristlecones become thicker. There are even scattered pockets of white fir in the moister, more sheltered, and higher canyons of the Panamint Range.

Toward its northern end, Death Valley narrows considerably. Here, the Panamint Range trends northward, while the Grapevine Mountains trend toward the northwest. Toward the far northern tip of the Panamint Range, the two mountains come within a few miles of one another, a narrow strip of Death Valley wedged in between.

Along the western flank of the Grapevine Mountains, creosote bush, along with desert holly at lower sites and white bursage at higher ones, dominates up to elevations of about 4,400′. Above about 5,000′, big sagebrush becomes the dominant shrub, accompanied by green rabbitbrush and Mormon tea. Singleleaf piñon makes its appearance at about 5,800′, accompanied by shrubs from the sagebrush zone beneath, including green rabbitbrush and Mormon tea. There is Utah juniper among the piñon here, but, unlike the situation in the Panamint Range to the west, it is rare in the Grapevine Mountains. The piñon thins considerably above 8,000′; by 8,200′, limber pine makes its appearance, and continues upward to the summits of both Grapevine (8,738′) and Wahguyhe (8,628′) peaks.

The floor of Death Valley is so inhospitable to plants that not even creosote bush can survive there. Excluding mesquite, whose roots can penetrate 150′ or more in search of water, and the introduced tamarisk, there are no trees on the valley floor, on the gravel fans, or even on the lower flanks of the mountains. Trees do not begin to appear until elevations of about 6,000′ have been reached, 6,300′ above the valley bottom itself.

What was the late Pleistocene vegetation of this area like? The answer, in two words, is "very different."

THE LATE PLEISTOCENE VEGETATION OF DEATH VALLEY

Our knowledge of the late Pleistocene vegetation of Death Valley comes primarily from the work of Philip Wells and his student Deborah Woodcock, who have analyzed a series of packrat middens from the flanks of the valley (see Table 6-1). Augmenting that work are excellent analyses done by Geoffrey Spaulding on middens from Eureka Valley to the immediate west of Death Valley, and from the Amargosa Desert to the immediate east.

To date, nine dated late Pleistocene samples, from four packrat middens, have been analyzed from Death Valley itself, and from its adjacent mountains. Table 6-1 lists key plant species from these samples; many more species have

Table 6-1. Late Pleistocene Pack Rat Midden Plant Assemblages from Death Valley and Adjacent Mountains[a]

Location	Elevation (feet)	Date (years ago)	Key plant species
Amargosa Range	4,200	11,600	Curlleaf Mountain Mahogany
			Utah juniper
			Whipple yucca
	3,700	9,680	Utah juniper
			Joshua tree
Panamint Range	2,540	13,060	Shadscale
			Utah juniper
		11,210	Beavertail cactus
			Whipple yucca
		9,455	Brittle bush
			Beavertail cactus
		9,090	Beavertail cactus
	1,395	19,550	Shadscale
			Utah juniper
			Beavertail cactus
			Joshua tree
			Whipple yucca
		17,130	Shadscale
			Beavertail cactus
			Whipple yucca
		10,230	White bursage
			Brittle bush

[a]From P. V. Wells and Berger (1967), Van Devender (1977), P. V. Wells and Woodcock (1985), and Woodcock (1986).

been identified from these middens than are listed here, but these are the ones on which I will focus (the others are discussed in the papers by Wells, Woodcock, and Spaulding that are referenced in the Notes). The table presents this information according to the elevation of the midden, and then, within each midden, by the age of the samples from oldest to youngest.

Look first at the Panamint Range sample that is both lowest in elevation (1,395′) and oldest (19,550 years). The midden that provided this sample is on a south-facing slope whose vegetation today is dominated by creosote bush and white bursage, a classic Mojave Desert combination. However, this midden sample suggests—and a wealth of other data confirm—that neither of these two widespread Mojave Desert plants were here during full-glacial times. Instead, at 19,550 years ago, this site was surrounded by shadscale, Joshua trees, Utah juniper, and Whipple yucca, among other things. The next-youngest assemblage from this midden (17,130 years old) still has the shadscale and Whipple yucca, but the Joshua trees and juniper are gone.

Today, Joshua trees occur no lower than about 4,000′ in elevation in the Death Valley area, some 2,600′ higher than this site. Juniper occurs as low as 4,700′ in the northern Panamint Range today, but it is generally found no lower than about 6,000′ in this region, some 4,600′ higher than the 19,550-year-old sample.

Because this midden is on a south-facing slope, the packrats that built it occupied a warmer and drier setting than they would have occupied had they chosen a north-facing slope. Perhaps this is why neither Joshua trees nor juniper are present in the 17,130-year-old sample from this midden, which retains the shadscale and Whipple yucca but loses the trees. That is, it is possible that these trees were still present on north-facing slopes at this elevation 17,000 years ago, but gone from south-facing ones. However, it is also possible that the loss of juniper here reflects a general upslope movement of trees sometime after 19,000 years ago.

Whether the loss of juniper at this spot is a local or a regional phenomenon, the 19,550-year-old sample from the Panamint Range shows that juniper extended down to 1,395′. The fact that juniper was not abundant in this midden suggests that this site may have been near the lower elevational reaches of this tree at that time. The 4,600′ elevational displacement for Utah juniper, from full-glacial times to today, that this midden documents is impressive. As Wells and Woodcock have pointed out, this represents one of the most extreme late Pleistocene-to-modern elevational shifts known for any plant in North America.

Juniper woodland thus descended nearly to the floor of Death Valley during the full glacial, after which it began to move upward. Exactly when it reached its current elevational limits is not yet known, but that clearly did not happen until the Holocene, and perhaps well into the Holocene.

Wells and Woodcock have suggested that the upslope movement of juniper was slow, in opposition to earlier arguments that the loss of woodland toward the end of the Pleistocene or during the early Holocene may have occurred quite rapidly. Although this may have been the case, we do not have enough middens from this area to know. As Spaulding has observed, it has not been possible to fix the time of the loss of woodlands at any one site because the transition from the presence to the absence of trees is routinely lost in the large temporal gaps that characterize the midden samples.

What is absent from the Death Valley middens is as interesting as what is in them. Today, white bursage, brittle bush, and creosote bush are abundant on the gravel fans that connect the mountains to the valley floor. The late Pleistocene middens, however, contain no trace of these plants until the Pleistocene is essentially over. The earliest midden date for white bursage and brittle bush here falls at 10,230 years ago. The earliest record for creosote bush is at 1,990 years ago, but that is undoubtedly because there are no earlier Holocene middens known from this area: it is known from just northwest of Death Valley at 5,400 years ago (see Chapter 8).

There is little reason to think that the Pleistocene absence of these plants reflects bias on the part of the packrats who were collecting the plants. There is a chance, and perhaps a good one, that the species of packrats doing the collecting shifted as the Pleistocene came to an end (see Chapter 7). Since different species of packrats are known to have different dietary preferences, such a shift could make vegetational change look more pronounced than it was. However, there is no reason to think that, if white bursage and brittle bush were in the area at the time the earlier middens were accumulating, local packrats would not have at least occasionally introduced the remains of those plants into their middens, no matter what species of packrat was involved.

There is, perhaps, a slightly better chance that these two species of plants were in Death Valley during the late

Pleistocene, but beneath the elevations from which the middens come. That middens are generally restricted to sheltered areas above valley floors is one of the difficulties with which packrat midden analysts must contend. However, during at least some of the late Pleistocene, the lower elevations of Death Valley were covered by water.

Death Valley's Pleistocene lake, Lake Manly (see Figure 5-15), has not been studied in detail; its chronology is poorly known, and the geomorphic features that it left behind are indistinct. In fact, the record left by this lake has been called "one of the least distinct and most incomplete records of any Pleistocene lake in the Great Basin" (Hunt and Mabey 1966:A71).

Lake Manly reached a maximum depth of about 600′, and so reached a maximum elevation of about 300′ above sea level. Recent work, however, has shown that this level was reached well before 100,000 years ago. This conclusion agrees with independent work in Panamant Valley to the immediate west, which demonstrates that Lake Panamint overflowed into Death Valley, through Wingate Pass, prior to 110,000 years ago. In fact, recent research by Ronald Dorn and his colleagues demonstrates that, during the latest Pleistocene, Lake Manly had a maximum depth of about 300′, only half of its earlier peak.

When that latest Pleistocene highstand was reached is not fully clear. Fortunately, the available dates from both Death Valley and other areas that contributed their waters to Lake Manly are beginning to narrow down the interval when it could have been reached, and a few dates are now available from Death Valley itself.

Searles Lake, upstream on the chain of lakes that helped to feed Lake Manly, appears to have been very high between 16,000 and 14,000 years ago, and again between 13,000 and 11,000 years ago, as I discussed in Chapter 5. Research in Panamint Valley suggests that Lake Panamint may have become high enough to overflow during the late Wisconsin, and perhaps early in the interval that falls between about 24,000 and 10,000 years ago. Perhaps, then, these are the times to focus on in estimating when Lake Manly was full.

On the other hand, much of the water that filled Lake Manly may have come not from the Owens River system, but from the Mojave River system to the south. If that is true, then the chronology of Lake Manly cannot simply be inferred from the chronology of Searles Lake.

Two major late Pleistocene lakes formed along the course of the Mojave River: Lake Manix, which reached a maximum depth of 380′ and a maximum area of about 160 square miles; and, downstream, Lake Mojave, which covered some 60 square miles to a maximum depth of about 36′ (see Figure 6-2). Recent work in the Lake Mojave basin by William Brown, Stephen Wells, and their colleagues strongly suggests that this lake was high between about 18,000 and 16,000 years ago (the Lake Mojave I phase), and between about 13,700 and 11,400 years ago (the Lake Mojave II phase). Although the lake became high enough to spill toward Lake Manly during the first of these phases, the major overflow toward Death Valley was during the Lake Mojave II phase.

Significantly, the estimates for the interval when Lake Mojave overflowed into Death Valley coincide with the estimates of the timing of a significant event in the Lake Manix Basin. Geologist Norman Meek has shown that, sometime after about 14,230 years ago, Lake Manix cut through its outlet, causing its waters to pour downstream. Not only did this downcutting create today's Afton Canyon, which reaches depths of over 490′, but the waters of Lake Manix also emptied into Lake Mojave. Since the Lake Mojave Basin was far too small to contain this water, it must have reached Death Valley as well.

The Amargosa River may have also provided Death Valley with substantial amounts of water during the late Pleistocene, but its history is so poorly known that no help is to be had from this source. The histories of Searles Lake, Lake Manix, and Lake Mojave, however, suggest that Lake Manly may well have been high between about 16,000 and about 11,000 years ago. Given events in both the Searles Lake and Lake Manix basins, this highstand was most likely reached between about 14,000 and 11,000 years ago.

The small amount of chronological work that has been done in Death Valley itself supports this possibility. Lake sediments here have been radiocarbon-dated to between 12,000 and 13,000 years ago. This finding, in conjunction with other data, led geologist Robert LeB. Hooke to conclude that a perennial lake may have existed in Death Valley from before 26,000 years ago to about 10,000 years ago. When the lake actually reached its highest levels toward the end of the Pleistocene is not known, but radiocarbon dates obtained by Dorn and his colleagues show that Lake Manly was beneath its highstand by 13,000 years ago.

Whenever the lake was here, its presence limited the lowest elevation that plants could reach in the valley. This

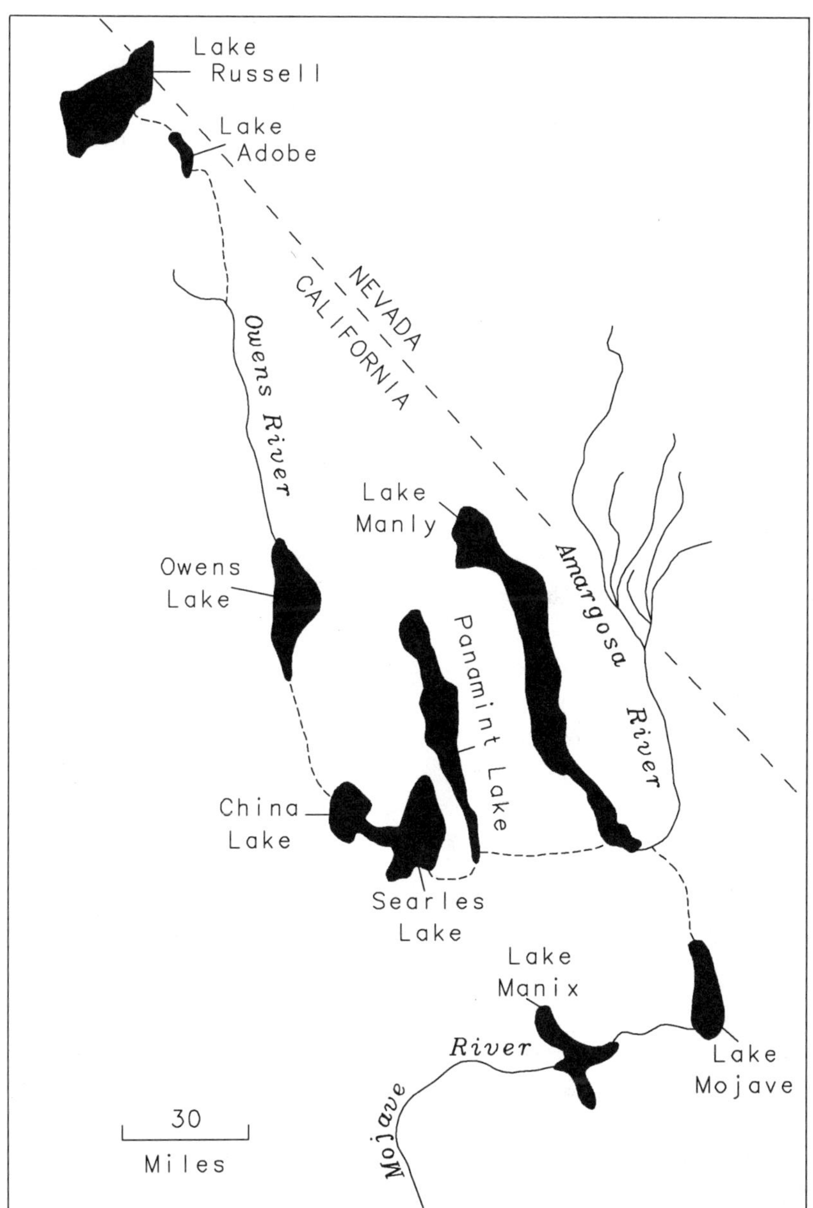

Figure 6-2. The Death Valley drainage system during the late Pleistocene. After J. R. Williams and Bedinger (1984). For key, see Figure 5-15.

in turn means that, for at least some, and perhaps a substantial, period of time, plants like white bursage and brittle bush would have been limited to a narrow strip between the lowest middens that lack them (for instance, at 1,395′ between 19,550 and 17,130 years ago) and the water itself (which reached an elevation of at least 10′ above sea level). If the plants were in that strip at that time, finding evidence for them will be quite a challenge.

However, the information on plant history that is available for areas near Death Valley, amassed by Spaulding, matches that assembled by Wells and Woodcock for the valley itself, and there is no reason to doubt the arguments that all three of these scientists make. White bursage and brittle bush, characteristic plants of the modern Mojave Desert, are not found in these middens because they were not here during the late Pleistocene.

The same thing is clearly true for creosote bush. A glance at Table 6-1 shows that there are no records for creosote bush in Pleistocene Death Valley. The widespread abundance of this plant in this part of the world is a remarkably recent phenomenon, as I will discuss in Chapter 8. In fact, of all the plants listed in Table 6-1, the only one that actually seems to have stayed put during the 20,000 years between the earliest dated Death Valley midden and today is *Opuntia basilaris*—the beavertail cactus.

Of the five Death Valley midden samples older than 11,000 years, four provided the remains of Whipple yucca (*Yucca whipplei*). These samples range from 11,210 to 19,550 years old, and from 1,395′ (the oldest) to 4,200′ in elevation. This plant does not grow in the Death Valley area today. In fact, the closest it comes is the far western fringe of the Mojave Desert on the west (on the Pacific slope of California, it is called chaparral yucca), and the Grand Canyon on the east (where it is called desert Spanish bayonet). Nonetheless, it was clearly fairly common in Death Valley during the late Pleistocene. It does not, however, appear to have survived here beyond the Pleistocene/Holocene transition, some 10,000 to 11,000 years ago.

Deborah Woodcock examined the temperature extremes of the areas in which Whipple yucca now grows, and found that it only survives in areas with average July temperatures that fall between 64° and 84°F. In Death Valley today, July temperatures average about 102°F. The lowest midden that contains Whipple yucca falls at 1,395′, where July temperatures are lower than 102°F, but still substantially higher than 84°F (Woodcock estimated that they are something on the order of 93°F). The implications are clear: to occur here, Whipple yucca probably needed summer temperatures much cooler than they are now. Woodcock, in fact, estimated that they were between about 11° and 15°F cooler.

It also appears that this plant may have needed warmer winter temperatures than are now found in Death Valley. Woodcock found that the coolest average January temperatures in areas in which Whipple yucca now lives fall at about 39°F. This is above the 37°F average for the floor of Death Valley, but Whipple yucca was growing at an elevation of 4,200′ at 11,600 years ago, very close to the modern line of winter snow accumulation.

The implications seem fairly clear: the late Pleistocene summers of Death Valley were cooler, and perhaps substantially so, than they are now, and the winters at least somewhat warmer. Compared to today, in other words, Death Valley's climate was not only more tolerable from the perspective of Whipple yucca, it was also far more equable.

Woodcock made similar calculations using the known climatic values associated with the modern distribution of Utah juniper. This allowed her access not only to late Pleistocene temperatures, but also to late Pleistocene precipitation. In the end, she estimated that the summer temperature decline was on the order of 14° to 21°F, whereas precipitation levels were on the order of three to four times higher than those of today. The ensemble of Woodcock's calculations would suggest an average annual temperature decrease of some 8°F. This annual decrease, I note, is slightly lower than the lower end of the estimates derived from late Pleistocene glacial data from further north within the Great Basin (see Chapter 5).

When did these conditions end? From the fact that white bursage and brittle bush appear at 1,395′ by 10,230 years ago, Woodcock infers that a shift to far more modern climatic conditions in Death Valley occurred sometime between 11,000 and 10,000 years ago. Given that the youngest sample that contains Whipple yucca dates to 11,210 years ago, that argument appears fully reasonable.

Although four middens, and nine separate samples from those middens, is not a lot on which to base a regional vegetational reconstruction spanning some 10,000 years, Spaulding's work to the east and west of Death Valley provides results that are fully in line with those obtained by Wells and Woodcock.

The far northern end of Death Valley is bounded on the west by the Last Chance Range. Just across this range is Eureka Valley, famed for its massive sand dunes, which, at a height of about 682′, are the tallest in the Great Basin (see Figure 6-3). Eureka Valley is the Mojave Desert's northernmost intermountain basin; creosote bush, and with it the Mojave Desert itself, dwindles and disappears in the hills to the immediate north.

Spaulding worked at the northern end of Eureka Valley, in the Horse Thief Hills. He extracted a single late Pleistocene assemblage (and several Holocene ones) from the far southern end of these hills at a locality he called Eureka View (see Figure 6-4). The vegetation of this area is now dominated by creosote bush and shadscale, but that was not the case when the late Pleistocene Eureka View midden accumulated. That midden, at an elevation of 4,690′ and dated to 14,720 years ago, is marked by an abundance of Utah juniper twigs and seeds. Today, the closest this tree gets to Eureka View is in the Last Chance Range to the east, at elevations some 1,600′ higher than the midden. Of the two dominant plants in the area today—creosote bush and shadscale—Spaulding found only shadscale in the midden. Just as in Death Valley, creosote bush does not seem to have been here during the Pleistocene; in fact, it does not appear in Spaulding's middens until 5,400 years

Figure 6-3. The Eureka dunes, southern Eureka Valley.

ago. White bursage, which also grows in the midden locality today, was likewise missing from the late Pleistocene assemblage; it does not show up until 8,800 years ago.

Alongside the shadscale and juniper, the late Pleistocene Eureka View midden also contained a number of plants that today are characteristic not of the Mojave Desert, but of the floristic Great Basin to the north. Perhaps most surprising, however, is the fact that the sample also provided a few needles of what appears to be limber pine, suggesting that this subalpine conifer might have grown nearby as well.

Figure 6-4. The northern end of Eureka Valley. The Last Chance Range is to the right, the Horse Thief Hills (the location of Spaulding's Eureka View midden) in the distance.

Spaulding examined a second late Pleistocene midden sample, dated to 10,690 years ago, from a few miles north of the Eureka View locality, at an elevation of 5,300′. The site that provided this midden is just north of the local edge of the Mojave Desert, the vegetation dominated by shadscale and green rabbitbrush and lacking creosote bush. The most common plant fossils in the midden sample, however, are from Utah juniper; shadscale was not far behind in abundance, but there was no rabbitbrush at all.

Spaulding has also done an impressive amount of work along the eastern edge of the Amargosa Desert, east of Death Valley. Among other places, he has analyzed Pleistocene middens from the Specter Range (see Figure 6-1), and, to the immediate west, the Skeleton Hills. The rich picture of late Pleistocene vegetation that Spaulding has developed here is based on over a dozen midden samples from locales that range in elevation from 2,600′ to 3,900′, and that range in time, according to several dozen radiocarbon dates, from 36,600 years ago to the end of the Pleistocene.

Spaulding's work here shows once again that sites that are now dominated by Mojave Desert plant associations were, from full-glacial times to the end of the Pleistocene, marked by Utah juniper, rabbitbrush, and shadscale. Although lower-elevation samples contain higher proportions of desert shrubs and other xeric plants (those preferring warm and dry settings) than do higher-elevation middens, Utah juniper grew at elevations as low as 2,600′ and perhaps lower (this is where the middens run out), and did so at some sites until beyond the end of the Pleistocene. Singleleaf piñon even shows up in full-glacial age samples from both the Specter Range and the Skeleton Hills: a record from the Skeleton Hills, at 3,035′ in elevation, provides the northernmost, lowest full-glacial record for this species yet known.

As in areas to the west, the junipers along the eastern edge of the Amargosa Desert were accompanied by plants that are not here today—snowberry, for instance, which now grows only at far higher elevations or in more northerly places. And, as elsewhere, some of the most characteristic plants of the modern Mojave Desert are absent from Spaulding's middens: white bursage does not appear in his Skeleton Hills samples until 8,800 years ago; creosote bush does not make its appearance until later yet.

All of this information—from Death Valley, from Eureka Valley, and from the eastern edge of the Amargosa Desert—provides a fairly firm, though as yet insufficiently detailed, picture of the late Pleistocene vegetation of this region.

What we would see in Death Valley during full-glacial times, say 19,000 years ago, would be dramatically different from what we would see today. The ground on which the National Park Service headquarters now sits may well have been under water then. The flanks of the mountains to both east and west would have been covered not with such xerophytic shrubs as creosote bush, but instead with Utah juniper, shadscale, and scattered Joshua trees and Whipple yucca. It is hard to know what plants would have been in the valley itself, but the typical plants that now extend toward the toes of the gravel fans—white bursage, brittle bush, and creosote bush—were absent. Shadscale was probably prominent in the lower elevations at that time, most likely accompanied by a series of plants that now grow only to the north or at higher elevations.

Even toward the end of the Pleistocene, at, say, 11,000 years ago, we would not see a botanical landscape anything like that of today. The white bursage and brittle bush would still be missing—they will not appear for another 800 years or so—as would the creosote bush, for which we will have to wait longer yet. The trees would have moved well upslope, but Utah junipers would still be living several thousand feet lower than they do now, and would be easily visible from the valley floor. Scattered Whipple yucca would probably be here as well, though not for long.

If we could actually visit Death Valley 19,000 years ago, or even much closer to the end of the Pleistocene than that, we would probably not have to worry nearly as much as we do now about the proper time of year to go. Winters, mild today, appear to have been even milder yet during the late Pleistocene. Summers, scorching today, may have been marked by temperatures similar to those of Seattle on a hot July day—80° or 85°F, perhaps, but perhaps also associated with frequent cloud cover. Unless we happened to recognize the physical features of the landscape—Telescope Peak, for instance, or Grapevine Peak—we might not even realize that we were in Death Valley. Death Valley, hell in '49, was a far different place during the late Pleistocene.

THE LAHONTAN TROUGH: CARSON SINK

During the mid-nineteenth century, emigrants to California crossed Nevada by following the Humboldt River west as far as they could, to Humboldt Lake and the Humboldt Sink. Once here, they had two choices. They could con-

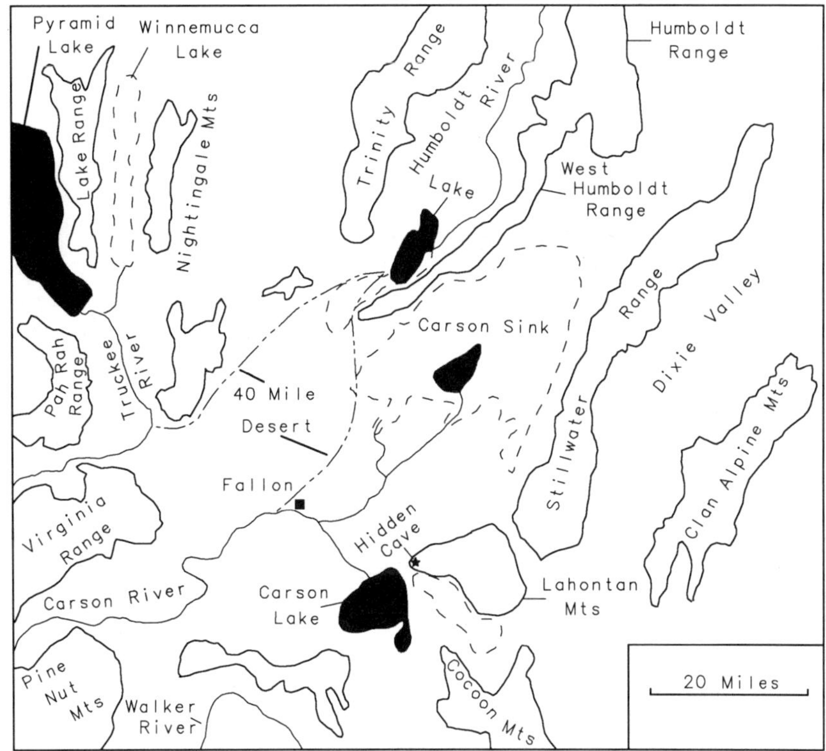

Figure 6-5. The Carson Desert and its region.

tinue to the southwest and cross 40 miles of desert to reach the Truckee River near modern Wadsworth, Nevada (and along the route now followed by Interstate 80). Or they could drop south to cross 40 miles of desert to reach the Carson River near modern Fallon (and close to the route followed by Highway 95; see Figure 6-5).

Neither choice was pleasant. Both of these Forty Mile Deserts not only were hot, but, far more important, also lacked any predictable source of potable water. In addition, they became so heavily used that they were routinely without food for livestock. Emigrants' diaries are full of the horrors encountered here:

> We now begin to meet with the destruction of property and stock; the road being almost lined with wagons, the dead and dying horses, mules, and cattle . . . we went to victory, stalking our way through indescribable scenes of suffering and want . . . hundreds of horses, mules and cattle dead, dying, and suffering, are laying thick around, and wagons, carts, and carriages line both sides of the road . . . the worst of it all now is to see, every few hundred yards, the grave of some kind brother, father or mother, and even some who have not been buried, but have probably been foresaken when sick or faint, and left to die and waste away in the winds and rains of heaven (John Wood in the Carson Desert, 1850; from Curran, 1982:182–183).

The southerly route passed by the west end of the West Humboldt Range, then continued through the Carson Desert to the Carson River (named, by Frémont, after Kit Carson). This area is, of course, within the basin of Pleistocene Lake Lahontan. It is also part of Reveal's Lahontan Trough, that relatively low-lying area along the western edge of the Great Basin that I discussed in Chapter 2.

Vast expanses of the Carson Desert region, and in particular the well-drained sediments of Lake Lahontan and the surrounding hills above the valley floor, are covered by shadscale, the small and grayish Bailey's greasewood (*Sarcobatus baileyi*), and the low, spiny bud sage (*Artemisia spinescens*). Dwight Billings has shown that this association of plants replaces big sagebrush and its companions in this region where annual rainfall drops below about 7″ (today, Fallon receives about 5″ a year). He has also shown that Bailey's greasewood provides about 50% of the shrubby cover within this complex of plants, and shadscale provides an additional 20%. Winterfat (*Ceratoides lanata*), an important winter food plant for cattle and deer, can be found in this association as well, as can Indian ricegrass (*Oryzopsis hymenoides*), an important source of edible seeds for native Americans throughout the Great Basin.

Stabilized sand dunes in the Carson Desert region often support significant stands of smokebush (*Psorothamnus polydenius*), a plant that had a variety of medicinal uses among the Northern Paiute of western Nevada. Four-winged saltbush is commonly found with smokebush on these dunes, as are two species of horsebrush (*Tetradymia*).

But more obvious to the casual observer are the plants that surround the edges of the playas in this region. Here, big greasewood is common, often in almost pure stands. This branchy, light green shrub is the one that most travelers notice from their cars as they drive on roads that cut through through or next to playas, not only in the Carson Desert, but also in much of the Great Basin. When big greasewood occurs with another shrub in the Carson Desert, that companion is often yet another species of *Atriplex,* the large-leaved Torrey saltbush (*Atriplex torreyi*), though in certain settings, big greasewood can be found alongside shadscale and bud sage as well.

Even today, after more than a century of diversion of the waters that flow into the Carson Sink, substantial marshes usually exist in the sink and elsewhere in the area. The watercourses that feed these marshes support cottonwoods (*Populus fremontii*—named for Frémont, who discovered it near Pyramid Lake in 1844); the marshes themselves support significant stands of both bulrush (*Scirpus*) and cattail (*Typha*).

The Carson Desert region ranges from about 3,900′ in elevation (for instance, at Carson Lake) to about 4,900′ in the bordering hills. Hills not much further removed reach above 5,000′, and the West Humboldt Range, which borders the Carson Desert to the north, reaches 6,349′. All parts of this region that lie beneath an elevation of about 4,363′ were beneath the waters of Lake Lahontan at its highstand. And much of it is now marked by plants that belong to just two genera—*Atriplex* and *Sarcobatus,* the genera to which shadscale and greasewood belong.

THE LATE PLEISTOCENE VEGETATION OF THE CARSON SINK

Our knowledge of the late Pleistocene vegetation of the Carson Desert is not nearly as good as it is for the Death Valley area. Attempts to extract pollen-rich sediment cores from Carson Lake by the U.S. Geological Survey have so far come to naught, and late Pleistocene packrat middens have yet to be found in this area, though there is a good chance they are here somewhere. Instead, what we know of the vegetation of this part of the Lahontan Basin toward the end of the Pleistocene comes from detailed analyses, by paleobotanists Peter Wigand and Peter Mehringer, of pollen from the deep sediments of Hidden Cave.

Hidden Cave sits on the northern edge of Eetza Mountain, one of a series of low (maximum elevation 4,281′) hills that form the enthusiastically named Lahontan Mountains in the southern Carson Desert (see Figures 6-5 and 6-6). The site is aptly named: the opening to the cave is simply a small hole in the face of Eetza Mountain. The site is so hidden that it was not until the mid-1920s that it was discovered, by a group of boys searching for stolen money that had reportedly been stashed in a cave somewhere in the area. Even today, the opening to the site can be difficult to find, though the task is made much easier by the fact that a well-marked trail now leads to it (see Figure 6-7).

Although the opening is small, the cave itself is quite large—approximately 150′ long and 95′ wide. Prior to the scientific excavations that removed much of the sediments that it contained, the distance from the floor to the ceiling was about 15′. Today, after several archaeological projects, that distance is much greater.

The first of these projects took place in 1940, conducted by S. M. and Georgia N. Wheeler, of the Nevada State Parks Commission. Norman Rouse and Gordon Grosscup, of the University of California (Berkeley), conducted additional archaeological work within the cave in 1951, but the most important excavations took place here in 1979 and 1980, directed by David Thomas of the American Museum of Natural History (see Figure 6-8).

These recent excavations were interdisciplinary in nature, as is characteristic of modern archaeology in general. The team assembled by Thomas included geologists, whose job it was to guide the stratigraphic excavations of the site and to interpret the geological history of those deposits; archaeological zoologists, whose task was to identify and analyze the animal remains from the site; paleobotanists, whose goal was the identification and interpretation of the plant remains recovered by the excavations; and, of course, a series of archaeologists whose interests focused on the cultural material the site provided.

Geological work on the sediments revealed by Thomas's excavations showed that Hidden Cave was formed some 21,000 years ago, presumably as a result of wave action by the waters of Lake Lahontan. Because the mouth of the cave sits at 4,104′, well beneath the 4,363′ highstand reached

Figure 6-6. Eetza Mountain in the northern Carson Sink. Hidden Cave is located in the canyon to the left, just above the light-colored patch.

Figure 6-7. The hidden Hidden Cave. The entry to the cave is not visible, but is located just above the bare spot, formed by sediments removed from Hidden Cave during the 1979–1980 American Museum of Natural History excavations.

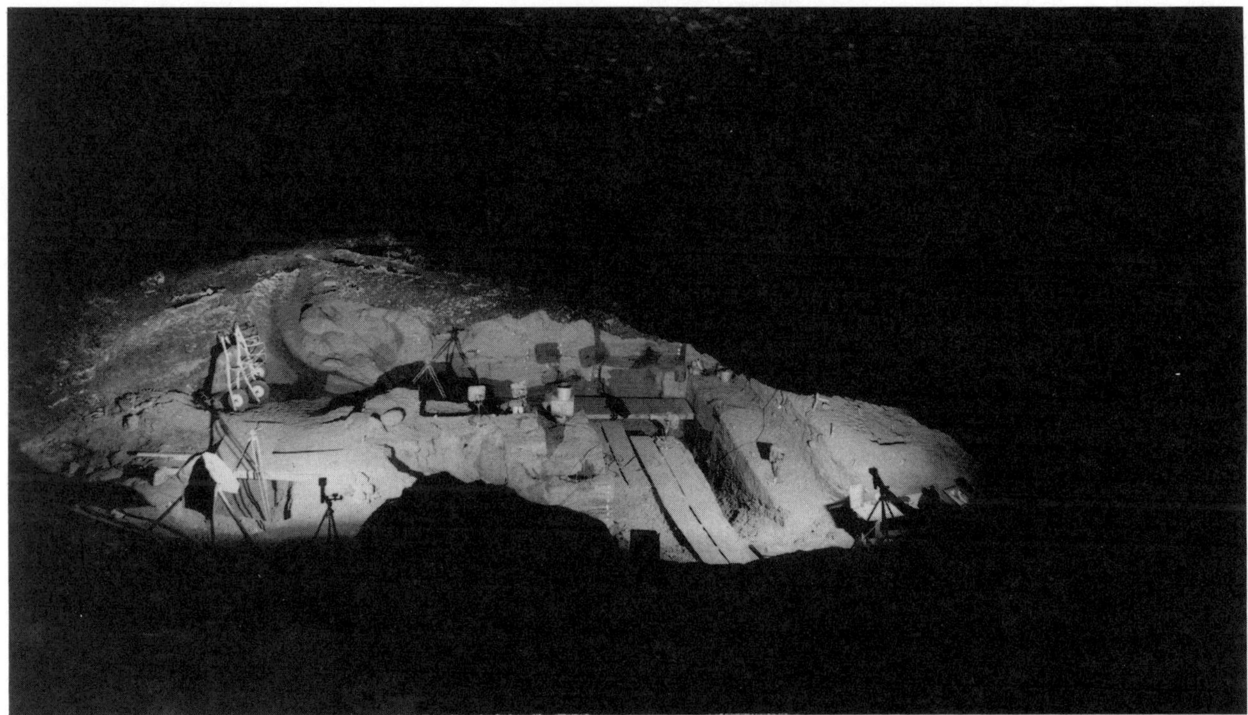

Figure 6-8. The interior of Hidden Cave during excavation. Photograph by Albert A. Alcorn, courtesy of David H. Thomas.

by Lake Lahontan, much of the Pleistocene-aged depositional sequence within the cave consists of water-deposited sands and clays and water-worn gravels.

In later chapters, I will discuss the faunal and archaeological materials provided by Hidden Cave. Here, I am concerned only with the plant remains provided by the late Pleistocene deposits of the site, which dated to between about 18,000 and 10,000 years ago.

Those remains proved to be fairly scanty, in contrast to the richer pollen and seed record provided by the younger, Holocene-aged sediments of the cave. Indeed, many of the Pleistocene samples so carefully extracted and studied by Wigand and Mehringer proved to be so devoid of pollen that they could not be used to say anything secure about the late Pleistocene vegetation of the area. Others, however, were richer, and those more productive samples suggest that the late Pleistocene vegetation of this area was very different from what it is now.

Today, the vegetation of the Eetza Mountain area is much like that which I described for the Carson Desert in general. The slopes and rolling crest of Eetza Mountain are covered by bud sage, Bailey's greasewood, and four-winged saltbush. In the playa beneath Hidden Cave, big greasewood is abundant both on the flats and on the low dunes, with Torrey saltbush sharing the dunes. The late Pleistocene Hidden Cave samples analyzed by Wigand and Mehringer, however, contained as much as 50%–60% pine pollen, and another 30% or so was contributed by sagebrush.

The sagebrush pollen from the late Pleistocene deposits of Hidden Cave could only be identified to the genus level, as *Artemisia*. It would be of great value to know whether this was bud sage, which grows on the slopes of Eetza Mountain today, or big sage, which is absent, or some other species entirely. As I discussed, Billings has observed that big sage now grows only in those parts of the Carson Desert region that receive more than 7″ of precipitation a year. Today, the Carson Desert itself receives only some 5″ of precipitation annually, with evaporation above 50″ a year. There are slight hints from the remains of the birds and mammals that were excavated from Hidden Cave that the sage so well represented in Wigand and Mehringer's late Pleistocene samples at least includes big sage. The pollen itself, however, cannot tell us that.

Pines, as I have noted, can produce copious quantities of pollen, which can then be spread far and wide by the wind.

As a result, high frequencies of pine pollen in cave or lake sediments do not necessarily mean that pines grew in the immediate neighborhood. In the Holocene deposits of Hidden Cave, pine never contributed much more than about 30% of the total amount of pollen in Wigand and Mehringer's samples, compared to over 50% in some of the late Pleistocene samples. The contrast may suggest that pines grew far closer to Hidden Cave during the late Pleistocene than they do today. Because of the difficulties involved in identifying species of pine from their pollen, the species of pine represented in the deposits of Hidden Cave is not known. Even more problematic, however, is the fact that, insofar as the pine pollen in the Pleistocene levels of Hidden Cave came from sediments associated with the waters of Lake Lahontan, it may have been derived from great distances. As a result, the high levels of pine pollen in those sediments may say little about the local distribution of pine trees.

The high representation of pine and sagebrush pollen in the late Pleistocene deposits of Hidden Cave is of high interest, but equally interesting is what is not represented. Here, the chenopods stand out.

The saltbushes (*Atriplex*), greasewoods (*Sarcobatus*), and pickleweed (*Allenrolfea*) belong to the Chenopodiaceae, or goosefoot, family. The pollen of the genera that comprise this family are often extremely difficult to tell part. Indeed, they are also often difficult to separate from the pollen of the related amaranths. These similarities in pollen morphology lead pollen analysts to place those that cannot be distinguished in a broad group often referred to informally as "cheno-ams."

Because *Atriplex* is one of the most abundant genera in the Hidden Cave area today, it is unfortunate that the pollen from this plant cannot be identified to at least the genus level. On the other hand, Wigand and Mehringer were able to identify the *Sarcobatus* pollen from their late Pleistocene samples. This they removed from the rest of the cheno-ams, and they were thus able to show the history of cheno-ams in the Hidden Cave deposits with one of the major contributors of such pollen removed. As a result, the cheno-am pollen they reported was probably largely from *Atriplex*.

That remaining cheno-am pollen suggests that *Atriplex* was not very abundant during the late Pleistocene in the Hidden Cave area, perhaps in part a reflection of the fact that a significant fraction of the potential saltbush habitat was under the waters of Lake Lahontan during much of this time. All the cheno-ams combined (excluding *Sarcobatus*) provided only about 10% of the pollen grains in Wigand and Mehringer's late Pleistocene Hidden Cave samples. In contrast, the late Holocene samples they analyzed ran to about 40% cheno-ams (again without *Sarcobatus*), much of which is undoubtedly from *Atriplex*.

What does all this suggest about the vegetation of the southern Carson Desert during the time represented by Wigand and Mehringer's late Pleistocene samples, between about 18,000 and 10,000 years ago? First, it may suggest that pines extended to much lower elevations than they do today. Second, it suggests that sagebrush—species unknown, but I would guess that it at least included big sage—was common on the slopes surrounding the site, and perhaps extended well toward Lake Lahontan itself. Finally, it suggests that saltbushes, now such an important component of the local vegetation, were at best rare. In short, the late Pleistocene vegetation of the Lahontan Mountains and adjacent Carson Desert during the late Pleistocene appears to have been a sagebrush-dominated steppe, perhaps with pines not far off. That, of course, is quite different from what is here now.

THE CENTRAL GREAT BASIN: RUBY VALLEY

Once the Donner party had crossed the Great Salt Lake Desert in 1846, they reached the Pilot Range, on what is now the Utah-Nevada border (see Figure 10-1). When they left the Pilot Range, they headed west, across the Toana and Pequop ranges, past the southern end of the East Humboldt Range, and into the northern end of Ruby Valley. From here, they moved south past Franklin and Ruby lakes, the massive Ruby Mountains blocking their way west. Just beyond the southern end of Ruby Lake, they found Overland Pass, the first major hollow allowing easy wagon passage from Ruby Valley, on the east, to Huntington Valley, on the west (see Figure 6-9). They then headed north along Huntington Creek, and soon hit the Humboldt River (see Figure 6-10 for locations). Had they passed this way only a week or two earlier, their names would now be no better known to nonhistorians than are those of Samuel Young and George Harlan, who came this way not long before the Donners and their companions.

At least, though, Ruby Valley did not present the Donner Party with the horrors they had encountered in the Bonneville Basin. The Ruby Mountains rise to 11,387′ to form the western edge of the valley, and intercept sig-

Figure 6-9. Ruby Valley from the eastern end of Overland Pass.

nificant amounts of moisture brought by the Pacific westerlies. These westerlies travel relatively unimpeded along the Humboldt Valley until they meet the massive Rubies, which wring the moisture out of them. The uppermost elevations of the Rubies may, as a result, receive as much as 50″ of precipitation a year, nearly all of which falls in the winter.

Because of the Ruby Mountains, Ruby Valley is well watered, containing two lakes as well as substantial marshes. Although Franklin Lake often dries up during the summer, Ruby Lake (also called the Ruby Marshes) has remained wet even during most historic droughts. Indeed, Ruby Lake forms the heart of the 37,600-acre Ruby Lake National Wildlife Refuge, which borders most of the southern Ruby Mountains (see Figure 6-11).

Only about 25% of the water that supports the 15,000 acres of Ruby Lake and its marshes is provided by precipitation directly on the lake. Instead, Ruby Lake, which lies at an elevation of 5,965′, is primarily maintained by a large series of springs that issue from the east side of the southern Ruby Mountains. The springs do not maintain the lake by flowing directly into it so much as they maintain it by providing copious amounts of groundwater. It is this spring-fed groundwater that charges the lake, water that ultimately results from the wintertime Pacific westerlies intercepted by the Ruby Mountains.

The vegetation of Ruby Valley and the adjacent Ruby Mountains has been well described by hydrologist R. F. Miller and his colleagues, by botanist Lloyd Loope, and by Robert Thompson of the U.S. Geological Survey.

Miller and his colleagues have shown that the nature of the valley bottom vegetation is sensitively determined by the local position of the water table. In those parts of the valley floor where the water table periodically rises to the surface and causes flooding, the dominant plants include saltgrass, shrubby cinquefoil (*Potentilla fruticosa*), and baltic rush (*Juncus balticus*). Wet meadows commonly contain beaked sedge (*Carex rostrata*) and silverweed (*Potentilla anserina*), whereas the marshes themselves support both hardstem bulrush (*Scirpus acutus*) and common cattail (*Typha latifolia*).

A very different set of plants is found where the water table is too low to reach the surface, but is nonetheless high enough for water to rise to the surface by capillary action. Saltgrass also occurs here, but its companions now include big greasewood, rubber rabbitbrush (*Chrysothamnus nauseosus*), and Great Basin wildrye (*Elymus cinereus*).

Where the water table is still further removed from the surface, but capillary action is able to carry water to the roots of plants, yet another plant association is found. Rubber rabbitbrush and big greasewood occur in this setting as well, but they are now accompanied by big

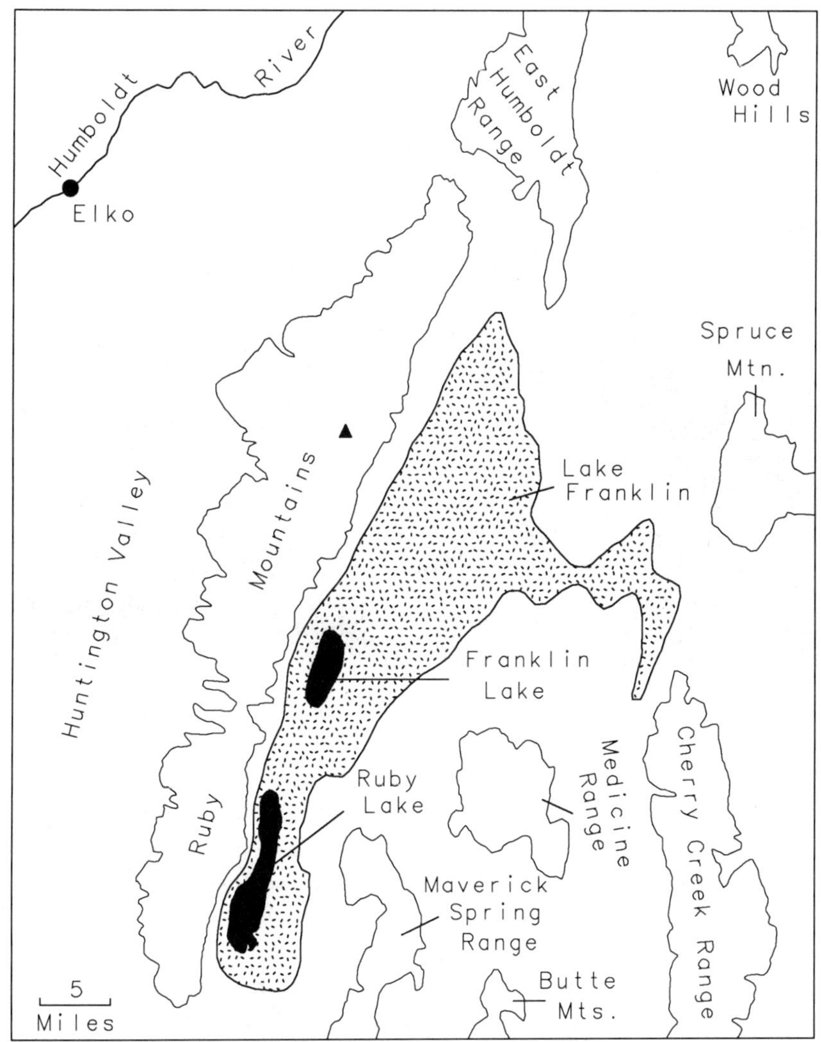

Figure 6-10. Ruby Valley. The triangle marks the location of Upper Dollar Lake. After R. S. Thompson (1984).

sagebrush or shadscale, the exact combination of plants depending on how finely textured the sediments that make up a given patch of ground happen to be.

Finally, when the water table becomes so far removed from the surface that plants must receive all their moisture from precipitation, a different set of shrubs appears. Gravel bars that were produced by Pleistocene Lake Franklin are marked by black sage and winterfat. In lower settings between the bars, big sage, shadscale, winterfat, and yet another species of saltbush, the low Nuttall's saltbush (*Atriplex nuttallii*), are common.

To the west of Ruby Lake, along the eastern flanks of the Ruby Mountains, big sagebrush is abundant, and continues to be so into the piñons and junipers. The piñon-juniper here extends from about 6,100′ to about 8,200′ in elevation, and is often dense. Mountain mahogany becomes increasingly common within the piñon-juniper as elevation increases, and then continues, often in virtually pure stands, to an elevation of about 9,500′.

The northern Ruby Mountains support an impressive number of subalpine conifers—limber pine, whitebark pine, Engelmann spruce, white fir, and a small stand of bristlecone pine. The southern Rubies, however, have only limber pine and bristlecone pine. Both of these occur as low as 8,000′ in elevation, but most are found above 8,500′, and both continue to elevations in excess of 10,500′, above which true alpine vegetation can be found in parts of the southern Rubies.

In a very general sense, the vegetation of Ruby Valley and the southern Ruby Mountains is well characterized by

Figure 6-11. The Ruby Marshes.

Billings's set of six Great Basin plant zones (see Chapter 2). The Shadscale and Sagebrush-Grass Zones are present in the valley bottom and along the lower flanks of the Ruby Mountains; a Piñon-Juniper Zone occurs in the mid-elevations of the eastern slope of the southern Rubies; an Upper Sagebrush-Grass Zone occurs above it, followed by a Limber Pine–Bristlecone Pine Zone, and then, finally, by a fairly weakly developed Alpine Tundra Zone.

THE LATE PLEISTOCENE VEGETATION OF RUBY VALLEY

These plant zones, however, did not exist here during the late Pleistocene. Our most direct knowledge of the late Pleistocene vegetation of Ruby Valley and the adjacent Ruby Mountains comes from the work of Robert Thompson. Thompson's efforts to understand the vegetational history of this area were multipronged: he collected packrat middens from the southern Ruby Mountains, he attempted to core upland lakes, and he extracted two sediment cores from Ruby Lake itself. Of these multiple approaches, however, only one of the Ruby Lake cores reached the Pleistocene. Thompson found more than 100 packrat middens, but those he had dated were at the most 3,000 years old. Of the upland lakes he attempted to core, only Upper Dollar Lake provided a lengthy vegetation record, but it did not reach the Pleistocene, and even the Holocene sediments he retrieved here had been significantly disturbed, perhaps by landslides.

The sediment core that Thompson pulled from Ruby Lake, however, reveals quite a bit about the late Pleistocene. He extracted a core 23.5′ long from the deposits of this lake, and obtained 17 radiocarbon dates on the organic materials contained within that core. Those dates, plus the fact that the core also contained 6,800-year-old Mazama ash at a depth of 6.2′, provide good temporal control over the information on lake and vegetation history that his core revealed.

Ruby Valley contained a substantial lake during the Pleistocene, called Lake Franklin. Although poorly studied, Lake Franklin appears to have reached a maximum depth of about 130′, and covered some 485 square miles (see Figure 6-10). Thompson's Ruby Lake core provided some of the first detailed information available on the history of this substantial lake. That information comes not only from the pollen contained within the core, but also from the remains of green algae and ostracodes that it contained.

Although changing frequencies of green algae through time in ancient lake sediments can be difficult to interpret securely, the analysis of changing abundances of ostracodes is more straightforward. Ostracodes are tiny—roughly 0.05″ across—crustacea that live near the junction between water and sediment at the bottom of streams, lakes, and oceans. These minute animals have bivalved shells, as if they were tiny molluscs. They are not molluscs, however, but crustacea, and as such, they molt as they grow, replacing their old shells with new ones. Because their shells, composed largely of calcium carbonate, preserve extremely well in congenial settings, and because their habitat requirements are becoming fairly well known, the study of the history of ostracodes has become an important tool in understanding Pleistocene and Holocene lake histories.

Richard Forester of the U.S. Geological Survey identified and analyzed the ostracodes from Thompson's Ruby Lake core. Between the ostracodes, on the one hand, and the algae and pollen (identified and analyzed by Thompson), on the other, Thompson was able to reconstruct a significant part of the late Pleistocene history of the Ruby Lake basin.

The base of the Ruby Lake core, 23.5′ down, dated to about 37,000 years ago. The algae and ostracodes—or, more exactly, the lack thereof—strongly suggest that, from this time until about 28,000 years ago, the Ruby Lake basin was at most seasonally wet, and perhaps received only groundwater discharge onto a playa surface. Between 28,000 and 23,000 years ago, the water deepened somewhat, to form a shallow, saline, and perhaps ephemeral lake. Not only do the ostracodes suggest such a lake, but so does the high abundance of the pollen of ditchgrass (*Ruppia*), a plant that thrives in brackish or saline water.

Sometime after, and perhaps soon after, 23,000 years ago, ditchgrass pollen virtually disappeared from the Ruby Lake core. This finding, combined with the information provided by algae and ostracodes, suggests that the water level had risen to create a permanent, yet still highly saline, lake. This episode is not well dated, but clearly falls between 23,000 and 18,500 years ago.

When, then, did Lake Franklin rise to flood nearly 500 square miles of Ruby Valley to a depth of some 130′? Algae and ostracodes both show that that happened soon after 18,500 years ago. Fresh, deep water filled the basin at this time, and, with the possible exception of a brief interlude when the lake may have declined substantially, deepwater conditions lasted until at least 15,400 years ago.

This was Lake Franklin, but how long it lasted beyond 15,400 years ago is not clear. For some reason, the period between about 15,400 and 10,800 years ago is not well represented in the Ruby Lake core. This 4,600-year gap may have happened because the lake dried up, causing sedimentation to stop, and perhaps allowing existing deposits to be eroded. Alternatively, the gap may represent some local depositional quirk. When the record kicks back in, at 10,800 years ago, the fossil record continues to suggest the presence of a freshwater lake, perhaps moderate in size. By 10,400 years ago, this lake had declined to low levels, and had become increasingly saline.

It is unfortunate that the Ruby Lake core contains a gap between about 15,400 and 10,800 years ago. It is possible, though, that the gap itself is telling us quite a bit. Ruby Valley is two lake basins west of the Bonneville Basin: only Pleistocene Lake Waring, which filled parts of Goshute, Antelope, and Steptoe valleys, intervened between Lake Franklin and Lake Bonneville. Since that is the case, it may well be meaningful in this context that Lake Bonneville retreated dramatically between 13,000 and 12,000 years ago, and remained extremely low until about 10,900 years ago (see Chapter 5). It is very possible that the substantial gap in Thompson's Ruby Lake core correlates with the post-13,000-year desiccation of Lake Bonneville. If so, then the observation that the gap begins over 15,000 years ago might simply reflect the fact that substantial deposits were eroded from the surface of the playa that developed when Lake Franklin desiccated.

A second possible parallel with the later history of Lake Bonneville may be found in the fact that Lake Franklin was clearly fairly high between 10,800 and 10,400 years ago. Recall that, after Lake Bonneville shrank toward the end of the Pleistocene, it rose once again, to the Gilbert level, between 10,900 and 10,300 years ago. The history of lakes Bonneville and Franklin may match perfectly here, though more information on the history of Lake Franklin during the time represented by the gap is needed to be certain.

The entire Pleistocene sequence from the Ruby Lake core, from 37,000 to 10,000 years ago, is dominated by two terrestrial plants—pine and sagebrush. As was the case at Hidden Cave, the species of pine and sage represented by this pollen cannot be identified. Whatever the species were, however, at least one of them was clearly fairly abundant.

Sagebrush contributed about 50% of all the pollen present in the Pleistocene levels of the core. Pine contributed about 30%, sometimes more, sometimes less. As with Hidden Cave, what is not abundant in the pollen profiles is as interesting as what is. Greasewood provided less than 5% of the late Pleistocene pollen identified by Thompson, whereas the remaining chenopods, including *Atriplex,* provided less than 10%. The pollen group that includes the junipers also contributed less than 5% of the total.

How do these numbers compare to the modern pollen rain in the Ruby Marshes? Thompson collected surface pollen from the marsh in order to answer this question. He found that these modern samples contained about 25% sagebrush pollen (compared to 50% in the late Pleistocene), and about 45% pine pollen (compared to about 30% in the late Pleistocene). Greasewood acounted for about 1.5% of the modern pollen rain in the marsh (compared to less than 5% during the late Pleistocene); cheno-ams, minus greaswood, for about 6% (compared to less than 10%); and the juniper group, 15% (compared to the late Pleistocene total of less than 5%).

Thompson was as cautious as Wigand and Mehringer were when it came to deciphering the meaning of the late Pleistocene pine pollen represented in his core. Thompson observed that modern marsh samples contain more pine pollen than the late Pleistocene lake samples. This is the case even though there are now no pines in Ruby Valley itself; they are confined to elevations above 6,100′ on the eastern flanks of the Ruby Mountains. As a result, Thompson argued that, while pines must have existed somewhere in the region, they certainly did not approach the edge of the lake, and they may not have been very common, or even present, in the southern Ruby Mountains as a whole. In addition, he suggested that woodland junipers, now abundant in the southern Rubies, must have been rare here during the late Pleistocene, and may even have been absent.

Thompson pictures the late Pleistocene vegetation of Ruby Valley as having been a sagebrush steppe that was in existence from at least 37,000 years ago to, and beyond, the end of the Pleistocene. In the absence of Pleistocene-age packrat middens, or some other source of equally ancient plant macrofossils, it is not possible to know what species of sagebrush is represented in the Ruby Lake core. It is, however, fully reasonable to suggest that big sage was heavily involved in producing the pollen that is so abundant in the late Pleistocene sediments of the Ruby Lake core.

Thompson's data thus show that pines were probably less abundant, and perhaps far less abundant, in the Ruby Valley region during the late Pleistocene than they are today, that junipers were rare and perhaps even absent, and that the vegetation of Ruby Valley at this time is best characterized as having been a sagebrush steppe. The saltbushes (*Atriplex*), so common here today, must have been in the area, but they, too, appear to have been rare compared to their abundance during much of the last 10,000 years.

Thompson suggests that the long period during which sagebrush steppe dominated this region implies a stable, cold, and dry climatic regime. He also suggests that this entire period, from 37,000 years ago to beyond 10,000 years ago, was marked by precipitation that fell mainly in the winter. This latter view conflicts with Donald Currey's argument that the rise of Lake Bonneville to the Gilbert level at the very end of the Pleistocene was caused by strengthened monsoonal systems moving inland during the summer months from the Gulf of Mexico (see Chapter 5). However this conflict is resolved, it is clear that Ruby Valley was marked by sagebrush steppe vegetation during the late Pleistocene. Thompson's call for a stable, cold, and relatively dry climatic regime is fully consistent with that vegetation.

Thus, Billings's six Great Basin plant zones did not exist in Ruby Valley and the adjacent Ruby Mountains during the late Pleistocene, although they exist here today. Admittedly, we do not know much about the vegetation of the mountains themselves, but there was clearly no well-defined Shadscale Zone in the valley bottom, and perhaps hardly any shadscale at all. There was clearly no Piñon-Juniper Zone in the mountains, and perhaps hardly any juniper at all. Indeed, as we will see in Chapter 8, there was probably no piñon either. Of Billings's six modern plant zones, only the Sagebrush-Grass Zone flourished here during the late Pleistocene, and this it did for at least some 20,000 years.

A General Look at Late Pleistocene Great Basin Vegetation

During the late Pleistocene, Utah juniper and Joshua trees were not far from the floor of Death Valley, but there was no desert holly, no white bursage, and no creosote bush. In the southern Carson Desert, there was abundant sage, and presumably big sage, with, perhaps, pines nearby, but little in the way of *Atriplex*. In Ruby Valley, there was an expansive sagebrush-grass steppe above the lake itself, but not much in the way of saltbushes, and perhaps no piñon or juniper at all.

Nearly all the plants that were in these areas are still fully at home in the hydrographic Great Basin. Today, for instance, Joshua trees and Utah junipers grow side by side in the lower elevations of the northern Pahranagat Mountains. Sagebrush-grass steppe characterizes much of the northern Great Basin of south-central Oregon. But whereas the plants are now common within the hydrographic Great Basin, during the late Pleistocene they were often in what seem to be the wrong places, and often in combinations not seen today. Had I chosen examples other than Death Valley, the Carson Sink, and Ruby Valley, the results would have been much the same.

THE NORTHERN MOJAVE DESERT

The most detailed knowledge we have of the late Pleistocene vegetation of the Great Basin is not for the botanical Great Basin itself, but for the northern Mojave Desert just to the south (see Figures 6-1 and 6-12 for locations mentioned in this section). In part, those who accumulated this knowledge were spurred on by the pioneering Mojave Desert packrat midden work of Philip Wells, and by insightful early packrat and pollen work in this area by Peter Mehringer. This work not only revealed the unsuspected nature of the botanical history of the Mojave Desert, but also showed the potential of this area to yield its secrets to paleobotanical efforts.

In more recent years, it has been Geoffrey Spaulding and Peter Wigand who have done the most to develop this record. Much, but not all, of their work has been done as part of the research conducted to determine whether or not Yucca Mountain, in the Mojave Desert of southwestern Nevada, would be an appropriate long-term repository for nuclear waste. Given that "long-term" in this context means 10,000 years, knowledge of future climatic change, and the potential that such change has for altering groundwater characteristics, is essential. And, to understand future climatic change, knowledge of past climatic changes is equally essential. One of the ways to get at past climatic change is by studying past vegetational change, and much of our detailed knowledge of the vegetational history of the northern Mojave Desert has developed in response.

The results of this work are remarkably consistent. Between about 19,000 and 12,000 years ago, woodlands composed of Utah juniper, or of juniper and singleleaf piñon, were widespread throughout the Mojave Desert, from elevations as low as 2,000′ to those as high as 6,000′. The understory of this xeric woodland included plants now common at higher elevations, or in the Great Basin to the north—Mormon tea, rabbitbrush, and shadscale.

Juniper woodland also extended beneath these elevations during this period, but, on the driest sites, treeless desert vegetation thrived, with such plants as shadscale, Mormon tea, and rabbitbrush again important. Death Valley and, to the east, the Amargosa Desert, have both

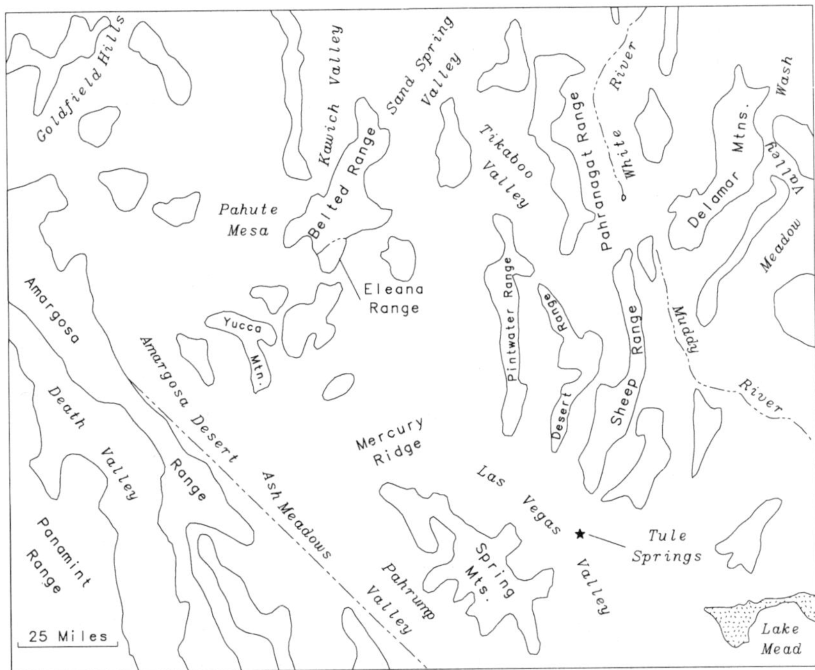

Figure 6-12. Mojave Desert locations mentioned in the text (see also Figure 6-1).

provided examples of this low-elevation, glacial-age desert vegetation. Plants that today thrive in this zone, and that are fully characteristic of the modern Mojave Desert—white bursage and creosote bush, for example—were then absent or extremely rare. Given the tremendous abundance of these plants in the Mojave Desert today, this is remarkable.

There is also ample evidence that subalpine conifers descended to very low elevations. Wigand, for instance, has shown that limber pines were present at an elevation of 5,500′ in the Pahranagat Mountains between 18,000 and 19,000 years ago. This is some 3,000′ beneath the lower limit of limber pine here today, and it is at the lower limit of the current distribution of juniper here. Wigand has also shown that limber pine grew at 5,000′ on the southern edge of Pahute Mesa, east of the Amargosa Range, 18,000 years ago. Spaulding has shown that, at 16,500 years ago, limber pine co-occurred with Joshua trees, Utah juniper, and shadscale at 6,100′ on the western flank of the Sheep Range. If this assemblage of plants can be duplicated anywhere in the world today, I am not aware of it.

Move back slightly earlier in time, and there are equally impressive records for the downslope movement of a number of other subalpine conifers. In the late 1960s, Peter Mehringer and tree-ring expert C. W. Ferguson of the University of Arizona showed that, at 23,600 years ago, bristlecone and limber pines, along with white fir and Utah juniper, grew on the south side of Clark Mountain, in southeastern California some 50 miles southwest of Las Vegas. The midden that provided this record sat at an elevation of 6,270′. Bristlecone pine does not occur on Clark Mountain today, though it does occur on the massive Spring Range to the north. In the Spring Range, however, it is found at an elevation 5,600′ higher than that at which it was growing on Clark Mountain during the late Pleistocene! White fir does occur on Clark Mountain today, but on the north, not the south, side. It would have to descend some 1,650′, and survive a south-facing exposure, to reoccupy the position it held here 23,600 years ago.

The bristlecone pine was gone from here by 12,500 years ago. By this time, the midden site studied by Mehringer and Ferguson was within a Utah juniper–singleleaf piñon woodland, though white fir and limber pine still existed near enough that they, too, were represented in the younger midden sample.

These are not isolated records. Wigand has 20,300-year-old white fir, limber pine, and Utah juniper at 5,500′ in the Pahranagat Range, 3,000′ beneath the closest white fir now to be found in this range. Spaulding has shown that, at 21,700 years ago, bristlecone pine, limber pine, white fir, and singleleaf piñon existed at an elevation of 6,500′ in the southeastern Sheep Range. Today, limber pine and white fir are found 1,400′ higher, and bristlecone 1,700′ higher, in the same range.

In short, prior to 19,000 years ago or so, such now-subalpine conifers as bristlecone pine and white fir extended to remarkably low elevations, in some cases more than a mile beneath their current lower elevational limits in nearby settings, and existed on ranges where they are now extinct. Such extremely low elevation records have yet to be found after 19,000 years ago, but limber pine remained well downslope for at least several thousand years after this date. Beneath it, and sometimes with it, grew a woodland composed of Utah juniper or of both Utah juniper and singleleaf piñon, with an understory of shrubs whose affiliation is not to the Mojave Desert, but to more northern, or higher-elevation, settings.

Only in the driest of settings did true desert shrub vegetation exist. Indeed, the juniper and piñon-juniper woodlands of the late Pleistocene Mojave Desert were so widespread that, for a number of years, it was thought that true desert vegetation might not have existed at all here during the late Pleistocene. As Spaulding has put it, "that desertscrub was present at all [in the Mojave Desert] during the last glacial age is a revelation" (1990b:195).

Since piñon pine was fairly widespread in the Mojave Desert during the late Pleistocene, it might seem to follow that it must also have been widespread in the botanical Great Basin just to the north. In fact, however, it was not. Although there are many late Wisconsin records for singleleaf piñon in the Mojave Desert, there is not a single twig, needle, nut, or piece of wood to document the presence of this tree during the Pleistocene any distance north of what is now the border between the botanical Great Basin and the Mojave Desert. Surprises may be in store for us, but at the moment there is not a shred of evidence to show that singleleaf piñon, now abundant in the botanical Great Basin, successfully sank a single root in this region during the late Pleistocene. This, too, came as a revelation. The earliest singleleaf piñons known from the botanical Great Basin are securely Holocene in age.

One of the frustrations midden analysts must learn to accept is that their plant records click in and out through time. As a result, and as I have discussed, major transitions between kinds of vegetation can be lost unless the sample of available middens is extremely fine grained temporally. A sample of that sort may eventually become available for the Mojave Desert, but it is not available yet. On the other hand, one of the advantages of the pollen record, as I have also discussed, is that it is often chronologically detailed, even though the species or even genera of plants that are being so carefully tracked through time may be unknown. When both kinds of information are available, these frustrations can disappear.

It is fortunate, then, that work done by Peter Mehringer at Tule Springs has provided a detailed pollen record that shows the replacement of a juniper woodland with a sagebrush understory by desert shrub vegetation dominated by sagebrush and *Atriplex*. That transition occurred about 12,000 years ago. Which species of sage and saltbush were involved is, of course, unknown, but there can be no doubt that this was not a shift to modern vegetation: today, this area is dominated by white bursage, creosote bush, and *Atriplex*. As we will see later, the establishment of something like the modern vegetation of this area did not occur until well into the Holocene.

At Tule Springs, the low-elevation juniper woodland seems to have met its demise around 12,000 years ago. A wide range of packrat midden samples confirms that significant vegetational change was taking place in many part of the northern Mojave Desert at about this time. Spaulding, for instance, has analyzed a series of middens from the Eleana Range, on the southern flank of Pahute Mesa (actually just north of the northern edge of the Mojave Desert). Between 17,100 and 13,200 years ago, one of his middens, located an an elevation of about 5,900′, contained abundant limber pine, along with such shrubs as rabbitbrush and sagebrush. At 11,700 years ago, the shrubs were still here, but the limber pine was essentially gone, replaced by a Utah juniper–singleleaf piñon woodland, which still exists nearby. On the eastern edge of the Amargosa Desert, Owl Canyon supported a juniper woodland, with Utah agave, at an elevation of about 2,600′, at 12,300 years ago. At 10,300 years ago, the agave was still there, but the junipers were gone. Today, neither juniper nor Utah agave grows here. Instead, the vegetation of this site is dominated by such Mojave Desert shrubs as creosote bush and white bursage, which are not in the middens.

Thus, the low-elevation woodlands of the Mojave Desert had begun to disappear by 12,000 years ago. Two thousand years later, desert vegetation was widespread in low-elevation settings (that is, beneath about 3,500′) in the Mojave Desert, though this vegetation was still significantly different from that which is found in the area today.

The woodlands gave way at different times in different places. The earliest evidence now available for true desert vegetation in the northern Mojave Desert comes from the eastern edge of the Amargosa Desert. Here, Spaulding has shown that a desert community was in place by 14,800 years ago at an elevation of 3,000′. Today, the vegetation of the site that provided this late glacial midden is dominated by creosote bush and white bursage. At 14,800 years ago, however, the desert vegetation that grew here was dominated by shadscale and snowberry (*Symphoricarpos longiflorus*). Snowberry does not grow in this area now. In fact, it does not grow on low-elevation sites in the Mojave Desert at all, though it is in the mountains of the floristic Great Basin to the north.

In contrast to the early "desertification" of this part of the eastern Amargosa Desert is the persistence of Utah juniper woodland in the central Sheep Range to the east. Here, Spaulding has shown that juniper woodland was present at 9,400 years ago in Basin Canyon, at an elevation of 5,340′, on a site now marked by Joshua trees and Mormon tea. And, on the Spotted Range between the Amargosa Desert and the Sheep Range, juniper woodland seems to have lasted up to as late as 7,800 years ago on a site that, today, is also marked by Mojave Desert vegetation.

In short, toward the end of the Pleistocene, low-elevation woodlands gave way to desert vegetation, but when this happened depended on both time and place. Not surprisingly, low-elevation sites tended to lose their woodland earlier than higher ones; drier sites lost woodland earlier than wetter ones. Exposure, elevation, substrate, and other environmental variables all played a role in determining when the woodland disappeared from any particular spot. Most, but not all, of the woodlands were gone by the time the Pleistocene came to an end. In their place was desert vegetation, but even that was distinctly different from the vegetation that occupies most of this area today.

CLIMATIC ESTIMATES FROM MOJAVE DESERT LATE PLEISTOCENE VEGETATION

Spaulding has used the vegetational data he and others have amassed from the northern Mojave Desert, and in particular from the Nevada Test Site and vicinity, to attempt to reconstruct the full-glacial climate of this region.

From the fact that such trees as limber pine and Utah juniper occurred 3,300′ and more beneath their current elevational limits, Spaulding infers that full-glacial summer temperatures were between 11° and 16°F cooler than those of today. He also observes that frost-sensitive plants, including creosote bush and white bursage, did not occur in the northern Mojave Desert during the late glacial. Arguing from the known minimum temperatures of areas in which creosote bush occurs today, as well as from the widespread presence of the relatively cold-tolerant shadscale in the Mojave Desert during the late Pleistocene, Spaulding also suggests that average winter temperatures here were at least 11°F lower than their modern values. His estimates imply an average annual temperature some 12.5°F colder than today's.

Plants that appear to need significant amounts of summer rainfall seem to have been absent from the northern Mojave Desert during the late Pleistocene. On the other hand, plants that are characteristic of the floristic Great Basin were common in the Mojave at that time. This, Spaulding argues, must mean that summer rains were rare here during the full glacial. Arguing from the distribution of limber pine and piñon juniper during the late Pleistocene, he infers that full-glacial precipitation here was some 30%–40% higher than it is today, with most of that precipitation falling during the winter months.

Spaulding's estimate for the full-glacial summer temperature decrease matches that derived from the distribution of Whipple yucca by Deborah Woodcock almost perfectly. On the other hand, whereas Woodcock sees a relative precipitation increase on the order of 300%–400% compared to that of today, Spaulding calls for an increase about one-tenth of this. The differences in these estimates might well be accounted for by the very different position that Death Valley occupies within the Mojave Desert. Woodcock's estimated increase would see an average annual precipitation of at least 7.9″ at an elevation of 1,475′ in Death Valley, whereas Spaulding's estimate would see an average annual precipitation of about 11.8″ at an elevation of about 5,950′ in the Eleana Range. Given the disparate settings, there is no reason to think that both estimates cannot be correct.

Spaulding, however, also calls for a substantial decline in winter temperatures, whereas Woodcock sees winter temperatures as having been slightly warmer than those of today. This major difference seems impossible to reconcile at the moment. It is worth noting, though, that late-glacial plant records from the Sonoran Desert to the south also suggest, as paleoecologist Thomas Van Devender has observed, that winter temperatures in this part of the Southwest could not have been much cooler than those of today. As Van Devender and Wells have both argued, the late Pleistocene vegetation of what are now the warm deserts of Nevada, California, and Arizona seems to support the argument that the climate of this period was equable, with far cooler summers than those of today combined with winter temperatures that were not much, if at all, cooler than those of modern times.

ANOMALOUS LATE PLEISTOCENE PLANT ASSOCIATIONS IN THE NORTHERN MOJAVE DESERT

Not long ago, it was assumed that the plant communities we see around us today are made up of such tightly coadapted species that any given community would respond as a whole to climatic change. The oak-hickory forests of the northeastern United States, for example, or the spruce-fir forests of Canada, were seen as being organic units that had lives of their own. After all, when patches of such communities burned down or were cut, the same association of plants grew back as long as enough time was allowed to elapse. As a result, ecologists talked about the movement of entire plant communities during periods of significant climatic change, believing that those communities moved north or south or upslope or downslope during such periods.

This view has now succumbed to the sheer weight of paleobotanical data demonstrating that it was wrong. We now know that plant communities are not organic entities with lives of their own, but are instead historically constructed assemblages of species, each of which has its own adaptive requirements and its own particular history. In eastern North America, for instance, oaks were confined to the far south at 18,000 years ago, during the full glacial. By 10,000 years ago, they had reached the southern Great Lakes; by 8,000 years ago, they were in the northeast in numbers. Hickory, on the other hand, dispersed much more slowly from the southeast: it did not reach the northeast in any numbers until after 6,000 years ago. Today's northeastern oak-hickory forests were built from the intersecting but separate histories of different species of plants with different adaptive requirements and different migrational histories.

It is also true that the plant communities we see around us today did not have to become what they in fact became.

Historical accident may play a large role in determining the nature of biotic communities, a fact that was well known over a century ago. To take but one example, cattle egrets (*Bubulcus ibis*) were first reported in South America during the 1870s, apparently carried there from Africa by a tropical storm. They had reached Florida by the 1940s, and were breeding in Canada by the early 1960s; they were also in the eastern Great Basin by 1963 and the western Great Basin by 1974. Such dispersal accidents may be quite important: if a plant or animal happens to become well established somewhere, later arrivals may not be able to replace it.

In short, the animal and plant communities that now surround us reflect the results of individualistic responses to climatic change, of differential migrational abilities, of competitive relationships among species, and of sheer chance.

This view has a number of important implications. It implies, for instance, that we cannot predict in any detail what will happen to the members of a given biotic community in the face of future climatic change, although we can predict that each species will react in its own way. This is true because we lack sufficient knowledge of the habitat requirements of those species, because we lack sufficient knowledge of how a given species will react in new competitive settings, and because there is no way to predict the occurrence of chance events.

That species react in individualistic fashion to climatic change helps account for the fact that the late Pleistocene vegetation of the Mojave Desert includes assemblages of plants that are not to be found anywhere today. The combination of limber pine, Joshua tree, Utah juniper, and shadscale some 16,500 years ago in the Sheep Range is but one example. Others abound. Spaulding, for instance, has found that desert almond (*Prunus fasciculata*), white fir, Utah agave, limber pine, and shadscale grew together in the southeastern Sheep Range 24,400 years ago. Three thousand years later, shadscale, white fir, and ocean spray (*Holodiscus dumosus* or *microphyllus*) occupied this same spot. Neither of these combinations is known to occur today, here or anywhere else. These and other "anomalous" plant associations ultimately resulted from the individual responses of separate species to the climatic conditions presented to them during the late Pleistocene.

These facts also provide a very simple answer to the question "where was the Mojave Desert during the Pleistocene?" The answer is that, in terms of the rich plant associations that now characterize it, it simply did not exist.

The Floristic Great Basin

Although far greater in extent, the floristic Great Basin has seen much less packrat midden work than has the Mojave Desert. A map prepared by Robert Webb and Julio Betancourt of the U.S. Geological Survey shows this fairly dramatically (see Figure 6-13). This map depicts the number of radiocarbon dates available for packrat middens in the western United States. The Mojave Desert of southern Nevada is almost blanketed by dated middens. To the north, however, there is only one concentration that comes even close, for the Utah-Nevada border in the vicinity of the Snake Range. To make matters worse, the dated Great Basin middens are by no means equally distributed through time (see Figure 6-14): most are for the latest Pleistocene (14,000 to 11,000 years ago) and the latest Holocene (the past 3,000 years). Pleistocene packrat middens have been analyzed in number for only a relatively small part of the Great Basin, and for only a relatively narrow time frame. And although some excellent late Pleistocene pollen sequences are known, these are not abundant either. As a result, we have neither the geographic nor the temporal control over the late Pleistocene vegetation of the floristic Great Basin that is available for the Mojave Desert.

The large circles along the Utah-Nevada border in Figure 6-13 result from the work of two people, Philip Wells and Robert Thompson. These scientists have analyzed a large series of middens from in and near the Deep Creek, Snake, Confusion, and Wah Wah mountains (Figure 6-15), and have also provided midden-based glimpses of late Pleistocene vegetation to the north and south. Their efforts have raised a series of questions concerning the history of conifers in this area, only some of which can be answered now.

The Snake, Confusion, and Wah Wah range middens document that subalpine conifers, and in particular bristlecone pine and the shrubby common juniper (*Juniperus communis*), occupied very low elevations during the full glacial, and, with limber pine, remained low through the end of the Pleistocene. For instance, Wells's work in the Confusion Range has shown that all three of these species survived until at least 11,900 years ago at elevations as low as 5,250′. For bristlecone pine, this represents an elevational decrease of about 2,200′; for common juniper, the decrease is about 2,800′.

In protected settings, Englemann spruce descends to fairly low elevations today, and bristlecone pine can now

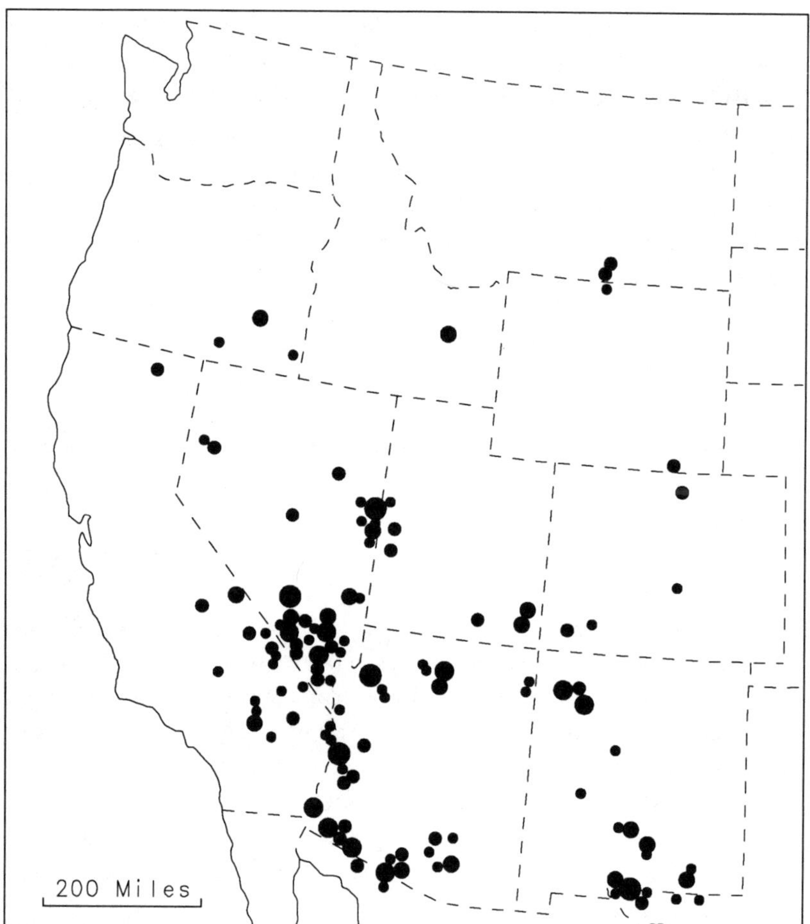

Figure 6-13. The number of radiocarbon dates for packrat midden samples in the western United States. The size of the circle is proportional to the number of dates. After R. H. Webb and Betancourt (1990).

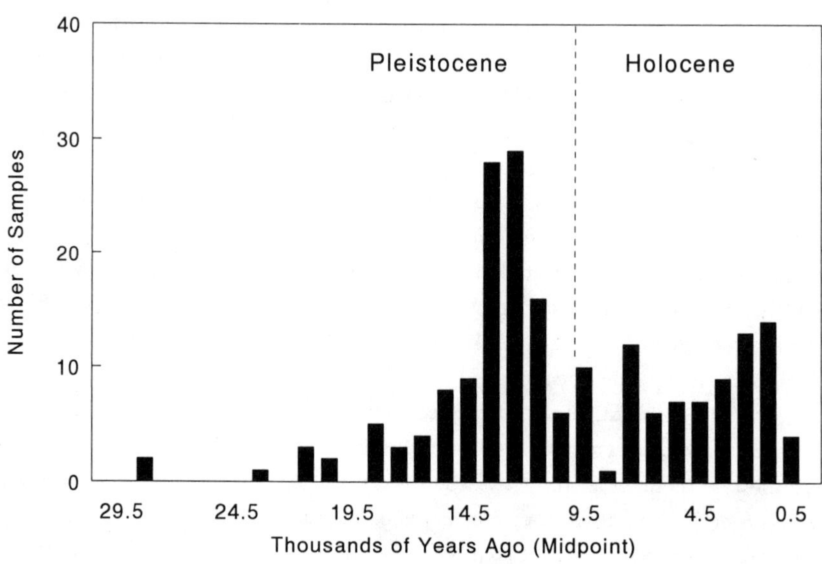

Figure 6-14. The number of dated packrat midden samples in the Great Basin, by age. From R. S. Thompson (1990).

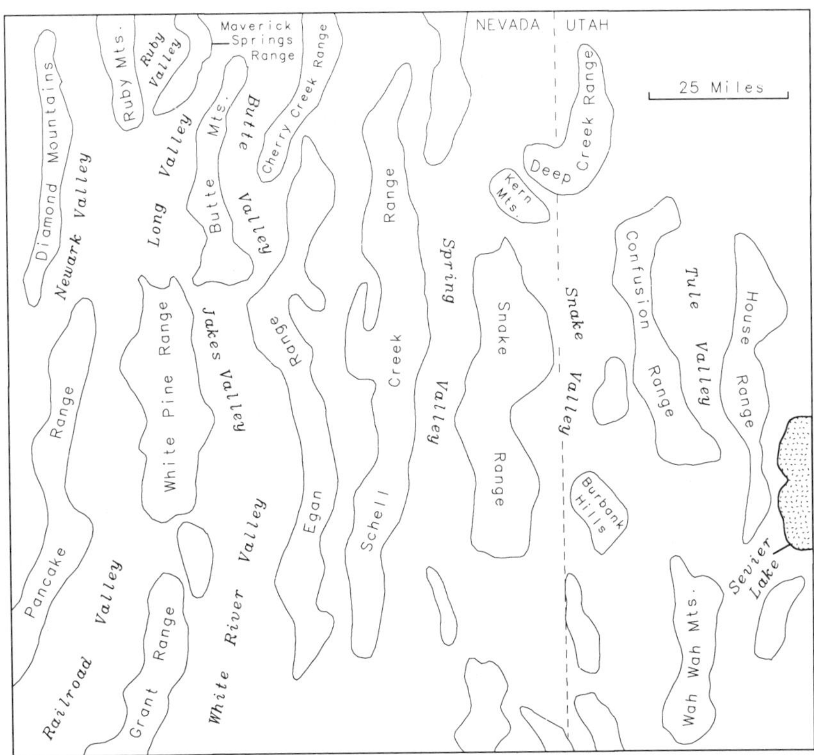

Figure 6-15. Central Great Basin locations mentioned in the text.

be found at 5,800′ in the eastern Snake Range (see Chapter 2). However, this happens only in special settings—in moist canyon bottoms that receive substantial cold air drainage. During full- and late-glacial times, Engelmann spruce descended to elevations as low as 6,100′ in the Snake Range, and remained there until as recently as 10,200 years ago. Although present in only small amounts during latest Wisconsin times, this spruce has been detected in a number of full- and late-glacial low-elevation middens in the Snake Range, and there is no reason to doubt Wells's argument that it was then fairly abundant in the lower elevations of the Snake Range. Bristlecone pine is so abundant in the low-elevation late Pleistocene middens that no question can arise as to its great abundance on the landscape at the time the middens accumulated.

In this part of the central Great Basin, then, subalpine conifers, including bristlecone pine, common juniper, and, on the Snake Range, Engelmann spruce, grew at very low elevations on the mountain flanks. Although Wells has discussed only the conifers in his midden samples, Thompson's detailed analyses have shown that the understory of these subalpine woodlands included plants that still occur near the midden sites—for instance, sagebrush, winterfat, mountain mahogany, and shadscale—as well as those that have now moved upslope—for instance, snowberry and fern bush (*Chamaebatiaria millifolium*).

Thompson has calculated that the low elevations reached by bristlecone pine during the full glacial in this area imply a summer temperature decrease of between 16° and 18°F. This estimate exceeds the upper end of Spaulding's estimate for the Mojave Desert full-glacial summer temperature decline (11°–16°F), while falling within the range of Woodcock's Utah juniper-based Death Valley calculation (14°–21°F). Thompson cautiously speculates that mean annual precipitation in the mountain flanks may have been some 150%–200% greater than that of today, with all or nearly all of that increase falling in the winter months. Unlike Spaulding and Woodcock, Thompson has not attempted to calculate winter temperatures from his data, since the central Great Basin does not contain the variety of frost-sensitive plants found in the Mojave Desert (for a summary of these full-glacial temperature estimates, see Table 6-2).

As we have seen, subalpine conifers also reached low elevations in the Mojave Desert. There, however, the valley bottoms are much lower than they are in the floristic Great Basin, and juniper or piñon-juniper woodlands, and in some cases true desert vegetation, occupied lower altitudes.

Table 6-2. A Summary of Temperature Decrease Estimates for Full-Glacial Times in the Great Basin

	Summer	Winter	Annual
Mojave Desert			
Spaulding	11°–16°F	11°F or more	12.5°F
Woodcock	14°–21°F	0°F or less	ca. 8°F
Great Basin			
Thompson	16°–18°F	—	—
Glaciers	—	—	9.9°–12.6°F

In the central Great Basin, however, valley bottoms are several thousand feet higher than those in the Mojave Desert (see Figure 2–6). Basal elevations in Snake Valley, which lies between the Snake and Confusion ranges, fall at about 4,800′. Basal elevations in Tule Valley, east of the Confusion Range, fall at about 4,500′. Moreover, both Snake and Tule valleys held arms of Lake Bonneville when that lake was at the Bonneville and Provo levels, between about 16,000 and 14,200 years ago (see Chapter 5). Indeed, geologist Dorothy Sack has shown that Tule Valley may have been integrated into the Lake Bonneville system as early as 19,500 years ago.

An intriguing question is raised by the fact that subalpine conifers descended to very low elevations in the central Great Basin, an area of high-elevation valleys that at times held pluvial lakes. Could it be that bristlecone and limber pine woodland were virtually continuous across the mountain flanks from the Wasatch Range to at least the central Great Basin? Is it even possible, as Robert Thompson and Jim Mead (1982:42) have put it, that subalpine conifers "formed a continuous belt from the Wasatch Front to the Sierra Nevada"?

Wells has made this argument in some detail. Observing that bristlecone pine is truly abundant in central Great Basin late Pleistocene midden samples that range from about 5,400′ to about 8,800′ feet in elevation, he has suggested that forests of bristlecone pine may have been virtually continuous from the Rocky Mountains to the central Great Basin. He has also observed that limber pine is found in the Sierra Nevada, in the Rockies, and on a wide range of Great Basin mountains in between. Limber pine is one of only two subalpine conifers that has such a broad distribution, and whose populations across this area are so similar that they are all placed in the same subspecies (common juniper is the other one). As a result, Wells suggests that limber pine may have had a continuous distribution somewhere across the entire Great Basin during the late Pleistocene.

If correct, this notion has important implications for understanding how the modern distributions of Great Basin plants, mammals, and other organisms have come about. At the moment, however, our knowledge of the late Pleistocene vegetation of Great Basin mountain flanks is very limited. There is, as I have noted, no late Pleistocene midden record from the Ruby Mountains, none from the Toquima Range, none from the Monitor Range—none, in fact, from most ranges within the floristic Great Basin. As a result, we do not know how widespread the bristlecone and limber pine woodlands and forests were.

There is, however, another aspect to this argument that can be evaluated. This aspect involves the history of sagebrush steppe and shadscale vegetation within the Great Basin. As Thompson and Mead have pointed out, in order for subalpine woodlands or forests to have been continuously distributed from the Rockies to the Sierra Nevada, or even from the Rockies to the central Great Basin, those trees would have had to have occupied not only the mountain flanks, but also the valley bottoms. Understanding the nature of the vegetation of those valley bottoms is thus critical in evaluating whether or not subalpine conifers were continuously distributed across the Great Basin.

In Wells's view, many valley bottoms in the Great Basin during the late Pleistocene were covered not by sagebrush steppe but by limber and bristlecone pines. In fact, he suggests that "the cold deserts of the central Great Basin are Holocene expansions replacing an immense subalpine forest of bristlecone and limber pines" (1983:379–380). This cold desert flora (the sagebrush and saltbushes) migrated north, he argues, from a glacial-age refuge in the Mojave Desert, putting an end to the continuous distribution of subalpine conifers in the floristic Great Basin.

Fortunately, the nature of the vegetation in the valley bottoms of the floristic Great Basin is becoming increasingly well known. Wigand and Mehringer's work at Hidden Cave shows that the southern Carson Desert supported sagebrush steppe during the late Pleistocene, perhaps with pines nearby. Thompson's work in Ruby Valley has demonstrated that this major valley bottom also supported sagebrush steppe, and supported it at an elevation—roughly 6,000′—above that occupied by bristlecone pine on the slopes of the Snake, Confusion, and Wah Wah ranges to the south.

As a result, it has become clear that at least some valley bottoms supported extensive sagebrush steppe vegetation during the late Pleistocene. Given that, wherever pollen evidence is available from such contexts, it shows the presence of vegetation of this sort, it appears that most valley bottoms in the floristic Great basin were characterized by such shrubs as sagebrush and, in places, shadscale.

Wells was probably led astray by the very source of the information that prompted him to make his intriguing speculations in the first place: packrat middens. By their nature, packrat middens tend to be found in exactly those rocky settings that are colonized by trees. Middens are not found on the fine-grained substrates of valley bottoms, but it is those substrates that support such shrubs as sagebrush and shadscale.

When middens are found in the valley bottoms, it is routinely because they are on bedrock outcrops. In fact, Thompson analyzed a 12,200-year-old midden from a limestone outcrop, at 5,400′ in elevation, in Snake Valley, just east of the Snake Range. That midden contained limber pine, which might seem to support Wells's argument. However, it seems most likely, as Thompson argued, that the limber pine here occupied only the limestone outcrop, not the finer-textured valley bottom sediments that surrounded it. Indeed, other plants in this midden included sagebrush, shadscale, and winterfat, all of which are found on those finer sediments today.

As a result, it is easy to account for the fact that Ruby Valley supported sagebrush steppe vegetation during the late Pleistocene at elevations above those at which subalpine conifers were found, at the same time, to the south. The pines were occupying the rocky substrates of the mountain flanks, while the shrubby desert vegetation was occupying the fine-grained sediments on the floor of Ruby Valley itself.

It must also be noted that Wells's analyses of central Great Basin packrat middens have focused not on the full range of plants preserved in those middens, but instead only on the conifers. Thompson, on the other hand, has analyzed both conifers and shrubs. As Thompson has observed, this critical difference probably goes a long way toward accounting for Wells's belief that such shrubs as sagebrush and saltbushes were not in the valley bottoms during the late Pleistocene.

Combined, the packrat midden and pollen records suggest that the Mojave Desert was not a "refuge" for such cold desert shrubs as sagebrush and saltbushes during the late Pleistocene. All indications are that at least sagebrush, and perhaps a diverse variety of other cold desert shrubs, had a far wider distribution during the late glacial than they do today. The abundance of sagebrush in the late Pleistocene Mojave Desert simply represents a massive increase in their range, not the result of a forced retreat during glacial times.

It seems extremely unlikely that any subalpine conifers were continuously distributed across significant parts of the Great Basin during the late Pleistocene. The distributions of such trees as bristlecone and limber pines were greatly expanded compared to their modern distributions, in many areas extending to the bases of mountain ranges and occupying appropriate bedrock outcrops in the valley bottoms. Nonetheless, as Thompson and Mead have argued, the finer-grained sediments of those valley bottoms supported sagebrush steppe, along with plants that today occur in the Shadscale Zone, including shadscale itself. The late Pleistocene populations of bristlecone and limber pines in the mountains of the floristic Great Basin may have been far closer to one another than they are today, but it appears that, in many areas, substantial amounts of desert shrub vegetation intervened, occupying the lowlands between the mountains themselves.

Many studies elsewhere in the Great Basin have shown that conifers were far more widely distributed during the late Pleistocene than they are now. For instance, several analyses of the sediments of Pleistocene Lake Bonneville have shown elevated levels of conifer pollen, but those analyses are hampered by poor chronological control over the sediments involved. Such is not the case, however, for the sediments of Swan Lake, southeastern Idaho, analyzed by R. C. Bright of the University of Minnesota.

Swan Lake (elevation 4,765′) is located at the north end of Cache Valley, and about 4.5 miles south of Red Rock

Pass, the Lake Bonneville spillway into the Snake River drainage (see Chapter 5). Today, the vegetation surrounding the lake is dominated by big sagebrush, rabbitbrush, and grasses, with big greasewood common as well. Bright showed that the deepest sediments within Swan Lake were laid down between about 12,100 and 10,200 years ago, at which time the local vegetation was distinctly different from the sagebrush steppe that marks the area today.

Pine—perhaps limber and lodgepole—and spruce together account for up to some 90% of the pollen deposited during this interval. Exactly where these trees were is not clear, but the fact that no conifer leaves were found in the lake sediments suggests that they were not growing adjacent to the lake itself. Instead, they probably occupied the surrounding hills, much closer than these trees are found today.

Sagebrush pollen occurs only in low percentages in the late Pleistocene deposits of Swan Lake, perhaps because it was swamped by the copious pollen produced by the nearby pines. It is present, however, and Bright suggested that sagebrush steppe must been nearby, albeit in limited amounts. (That argument gains support from recent work done at Grays Lake, some 60 miles to the northwest and outside the Great Basin itself; here, sagebrush remained abundant during the late Pleistocene, even as conifers expanded in the surrounding uplands.) At Swan Lake, the abundance of sagebrush pollen increased, and that of pine and spruce decreased, dramatically as the Pleistocene came to an end, leaving no doubt that sagebrush steppe expanded markedly here at this time.

Far to the west, Thompson has shown that sagebrush, presumably big sagebrush, grew alongside western juniper and desert peach (*Prunus andersonii*) in the Winnemucca Lake Basin between 12,000 and 11,000 years ago. Neither big sage nor desert peach grow this low here today, and western juniper no longer occurs in the Winnemucca Basin. Instead, the dominant plants surrounding Thompson's midden sites include shadscale and bud sage.

Far to the southeast, plant remains from a series of packrat middens in Meadow Valley Wash, near Caliente, Nevada, have been analyzed by David Madsen, Geoffrey Spaulding, Thomas Van Devender, and Philip Wells. These middens, ranging from 4,400′ to 5,000′ in elevation, contained Douglas-fir, Rocky Mountain juniper, and limber pine between 20,000 and 12,600 years ago. It is not clear when those plants retreated from this area, since the next midden in the series, which does not contain them, is only 6,600 years old. Today, the only nearby conifers are singleleaf piñon and Utah juniper; these occur at surprisingly low elevations—down to about 4,400′—in this relatively cool and moist valley. Douglas-fir is found no closer than about 60 miles to the east.

Although our knowledge of the late Pleistocene vegetation of the Great Basin is spotty, the information we do have is consistent. Subalpine conifers extended to extremely low elevations in the floristic Great Basin during this time, down to basal elevations in the mountains, and even occupying bedrock outcops on the valley floors themselves. In some areas, subalpine and montane conifers have become locally extinct since the end of the Pleistocene, as the glacial-age Douglas-fir in Meadow Valley Wash illustrates. Sagebrush steppe was widespread beneath the mountain flanks, making it unlikely that subalpine conifers were continuously distributed across the Great Basin, or even from the Rocky Mountains into the central Great Basin. Indeed, the plants that comprised this sagebrush steppe extended well upward into the mountains, where they formed the understory in the subalpine conifer woodlands and forests.

During the late Pleistocene, valley bottoms that are today dominated by the vegetation that led Billings to define a Shadscale Zone were dominated instead by sagebrush steppe. At the moment, there is no evidence that a "Shadscale Zone," in Billings's sense, existed in the Great Basin during the late Pleistocene. Shadscale itself is amply documented within the region at that time, however, and the lack of evidence for a true Shadscale Zone may simply reflect the nature of our paleobotanical sample. As with big sagebrush, no late Pleistocene "refuge" is needed to explain the presence of shadscale in the Great Basin during the Holocene: it was here all along.

Although the upslope movement of subalpine conifers was underway as the Pleistocene came to an end, some subalpine and montane conifers remained at low elevations into the early Holocene (see Chapter 8). In addition, there was no Piñon-Juniper Zone in the Great Basin during the late Pleistocene, since there is no evidence that piñon was here during full- and late-glacial times. As far as we know, the closest piñon came was along the modern boundary between the Mojave Desert and the floristic Great Basin. Spaulding's Eleana Range record, at 10,600 years ago, is the northernmost record for late Pleistocene piñon in the entire region.

GREAT BASIN CONIFERS IN HISTORICAL PERSPECTIVE

As I discussed in Chapter 2, the montane conifers of the Great Basin have their closest affinities to those of the Rocky Mountains. Many species of montane conifers found in the Rockies are also found scattered across Great Basin mountains far to the west (see Table 2–5). On the other hand, very few of what Wells appropriately calls "the magnificent array of Sierran conifers" (1983:349) make it very far east into the Great Basin. The affinities of the montane conifers of the Great Basin are clear, and are debated by no one.

Since this is the case, many scientists assume that the Great Basin must have received its montane conifers from the Rockies or from mountains to the south, and not from the Sierra Nevada. In this view, the wooded mountain masses of the Great Basin, surrounded by vast expanses of desert shrub vegetation, are true habitat islands that had to receive their high-elevation conifers from elsewhere. Thus, the mountains of the Great Basin become targets for dispersing montane conifers, and the trick becomes understanding how and when those plants got there.

A good deal of thought has gone into mapping potential dispersal routes to Great Basin mountains, most particularly by Wells, though Thompson and others have also considered the issue in some depth.

There can be no question that some conifers did disperse into the Great Basin during or after full glacial times. Singleleaf piñon provides an excellent example: this pine does not appear to have been in the floristic Great Basin during the Pleistocene, but it is widespread here now.

Utah juniper might provide another example. Wells did not find the remains of this tree in his central Great Basin late Pleistocene middens, but they were abundant in samples that dated to less than about 5,000 years old. He concluded that this tree was a middle Holocene immigrant into this region, and presumably into much of the floristic Great Basin. Thompson, on the other hand, found Utah juniper in nine of his late Pleistocene Snake Range and Snake Valley midden samples, dated to between 34,000 and 27,000 years ago, and to between 13,200 and 10,500 years ago. To Thompson, these dates suggest that Utah juniper was in the Snake Range before and after, but not during, the full glacial. However, he also observes that his dates come not from the juniper fossils themselves, but instead from plants associated with them. As a result, it is possible that the Utah juniper specimens in his late Pleistocene middens represent contamination by younger material (though this seems unlikely, since it shows up in nine of his middens, while piñon pine is absent).

Either way, singleleaf piñon appears to be a recent immigrant into the Great Basin. But even though this is the case, it is not at all clear that we need to look to the Rockies or to the Southwest as a source for most high-elevation Great Basin conifers. Instead, it is possible that these conifers were in the Great Basin all along.

This argument has been made by paleontologist Daniel Axelrod and botanist Peter Raven. They observe that montane conifers first appeared in the region ranging from the Sierra Nevada to the Rockies (what they call the Cordilleran region) during the middle Miocene, some 45 million years ago. This appearance seems to have been an evolutionary response to massive volcanism that produced cold upland habitats in this region. For instance, the Upper Bull Run flora, from some 60 miles northeast of Elko, Nevada, is Eocene in age, and contains such genera as fir (*Abies*), spruce (*Picea*), and Douglas-fir (*Pseudotsuga*). Some of the species represented in the flora seem closely related to modern high-elevation conifers. These include red fir, today a Sierran species, and Engelmann spruce, today abundant in the Rocky Mountains and also found in the central Great Basin and in the Cascade Mountains of Oregon and Washington, but not in the Sierra Nevada.

During the past 10 million years, as the Sierra Nevada, Great Basin, and Rocky Mountains were uplifted, Axelrod and Raven argue, lower elevations of the Cordilleran region became increasingly warm and dry. In response, the conifers either moved upslope or became extinct. Those that survived were those adapted to the new environmental conditions. Because these new conditions were more similar between the Rockies and the Great Basin than they were between the Great Basin and the Sierra Nevada (see Chapter 2), the affiliation of Great Basin high-elevation conifers today is to the east, not to the west.

This view of Great Basin conifer history is distinctly different from that held by such paleobotanists as Thompson and Wells. In their view, the distribution of Great Basin montane and subalpine conifers is to be accounted for by relatively recent immigration. In Axelrod and Raven's view, the same distributions are explained by long-term geological and evolutionary processes, including the fragmentation of the distributional ranges of tree species, and the differential extinction of species that could not adapt to new conditions.

There is some intriguing genetic evidence that suggests that bristlecone pine may have been in the Great Basin throughout the Pleistocene. Ronald D. Hiebert and J. L. Hamrick analyzed genetic variation in five isolated populations of bristlecones in the eastern Great Basin (from the Egan, Snake, and White Pine ranges) and from the adjacent Colorado Plateau. They discovered that levels of genetic variability within these populations were greater than they were between them. They argued that, had Great Basin mountains become stocked with bristlecones as a result of the long-distance dispersal of seeds by birds, the genetic pattern should have been exactly the opposite: relatively low variation within populations (a function of the small sizes of the initial populations), coupled with high genetic variation between them (a function of isolation). On the other hand, if bristlecones have a long residence time within the Great Basin, and were able to share genetic material during glacial episodes when the trees were widespread, then high genetic variation within populations, and low variation among populations, are to be expected. Bristlecones, they concluded, may have been in the Great Basin throughout the Pleistocene. This conclusion is consistent with Axelrod and Raven's argument.

It seems most likely that a place will be found for both of these views of Great Basin conifer history, depending on the particular species of high-elevation conifer involved. Fortunately, there is little here than cannot be solved with deeper paleobiological research.

Douglas-fir provides a good example. Today, this tree is widely distributed in western North America, from British Columbia south through the Cascades and the Sierra Nevada, as well as south through the Rockies into Mexico. It is also found in Great Basin mountains in western Utah and eastern Nevada. The Great Basin populations of these trees are similar to the eastern, Rocky Mountain form, not to the Sierran variety.

The northernmost glacial age record for this tree in the Great Basin is from Meadow Valley Wash, near Caliente, Nevada, and dates to about 20,000 years ago. In Wells's Meadow Valley Wash samples, Douglas-fir had increased tremendously in abundance by 12,600 years ago. To the north, the earliest record he found for Douglas-fir in the Confusion Range dated to 11,900 years ago; Bright's work at Swan Lake shows that it was here shortly before 10,000 years ago.

This south-to-north linear progression of dates would seem to provide excellent evidence for the late-glacial dispersal of Douglas-fir into its modern Great Basin range. Axelrod and Raven, however, disagree. They feel that this tree has been here all along, but not in the places sampled by the central Great Basin packrat middens. Calling attention to the possible effects of cold air drainage down mountain slopes during glacial times, they suggest that such trees as bristlecone pine, Engelmann spruce, and common juniper—which today are subalpine in distribution in the Great Basin—were *beneath* the Douglas-firs, the opposite of today's usual situation. The situation they envisage is not unlike the one that accounts for the distribution of piñon-juniper woodland in the modern Great Basin, with this woodland occupying a warm thermal belt above the valley floors. The warm thermal belt they envisage, however, was occupied by such trees as white fir, ponderosa pine, and Douglas-fir, above the subalpine conifers, and perhaps in small numbers. As a result, they suggest, the middens sampled to date are just too low to have revealed the presence of those trees.

This is a puzzle that can be solved. Pleistocene-age deposits in high-elevation lakes should contain Douglas-fir pollen (the trick is to find lakes in basins that have not been glaciated), as should high-elevation packrat middens. But until work of that sort has been done, it seems unlikely that the questions that now exist regarding the origins of the montane conifers of the Great Basin will be convincingly answered. In fact, as we will see in the next chapter, a virtually identical question can be asked about the distribution of montane mammals in the Great Basin.

Notes

Manly (1894) provides his own story in a Desert West classic. L. Johnson and Johnson (1987) provide a detailed discussion of the route taken by Manly and his companions in the California deserts; see also Southworth (1987). Lingenfelter (1986) provides a fascinating discussion of the history of Death Valley as a whole.

See E. R. Hall (1981) for the distribution of North American packrats; the best place to learn about packrats and the analysis of the residues they leave behind is the superb book edited by Betancourt et al. (1990b). In that volume, Betancourt et al. (1990a) discuss the history of packrat midden studies, T. A. Vaughan (1990) and Finley (1990) discuss packrat ecology, and Spaulding et al. (1990) discuss the composition and analysis of packrat middens. The seminal paper by P. V. Wells and Jorgensen (1964) remains fascinating reading; the synthesis by P. V. Wells (1976) is now somewhat dated, but helps document the development of packrat midden studies. On packrats in the White Mountains, see Grayson and Livingston (1989) and H. V. Carey and Wehausen (1991).

H. P. Hansen's earlier work in the Great Basin is readily accessed through Hansen (1947). A list of his later works is presented in Grayson (1975). The Tule Springs and Steens Mountain work to which I refer is by Mehringer (1965, 1967, 1985, 1986) and Blinman et al. (1979); I discuss this work in detail in Chapter 8. The pollen analysis of Searles Lake sediments is presented by Roosma (1958); for pollen work in the Lake Tahoe area and the Wasatch Mountains, see Adam (1967, 1985) and D. B. Madsen and Currey (1979), respectively. For an introduction to pollen analysis, see Moore et al. (1991). Maher (1969) discusses *Ephedra* pollen in the Great Lakes region.

My presentation of the vegetation of the lower elevations of Death Valley depends heavily on Hunt (1966); see also his more popular book on the geology, ecology, and prehistory of Death Valley (Hunt 1976). I have, at times, followed Benson and Darrow (1981) and used common names for plants other than those used by Hunt. Information on precipitation and evaporation in Death Valley is from Hunt et al. (1966); see also Hunt and Mabey (1966). On the prehistoric use of pickleweed and its seeds, see Jennings (1957) and Aikens (1970); on mesquite, see B. B. Simpson (1988). My discussion of the plants of the Panamint, Black, and Funeral ranges is based on Vasek (1966), Schramm (1982), Vasek and Thorne (1988), and Barbour (1988); see also R. H. Webb et al. (1987). The information on the Grapevine Mountains is drawn from Kurzius (1981); see also A. H. Miller (1946).

My discussion of the late Pleistocene plants of Death Valley is based on P. V. Wells and Woodcock (1985) and Woodcock (1986); see also P. V. Wells and Berger (1967) and Van Devender (1977). The record for Joshua trees at 4,000′ in the Death Valley area is from Grapevine Canyon and is given by Kurzius (1981); the record for Utah juniper at 4,700′ in the northern Panamint Range is provided by Peterson (1984). Spaulding (1990b) presents a summary of the Death Valley data, and places it in the broader context of the late Pleistocene vegetational history of the Mojave Desert as a whole. That different species of packrats have different diets, and that these differences may introduce bias into our midden-derived understanding of ancient vegetation, is discussed by Finley (1990) and Dial and Czaplewski (1990).

The features left behind by Lake Manly are discussed by Hunt and Mabey (1966); see also the references to the Searles Lake system in Chapter 5. Information on Lake Panamint is drawn from R. S. U. Smith (1978) and G. I. Smith et al. (1989). My discussion of Pleistocene Lake Mojave has relied heavily on S. G. Wells et al. (1987, 1990) and W. J. Brown et al. (1990); see also Blackwelder (1954), Ore and Warren (1971), McFadden et al. (1989), and Dorn et al. (1989, 1990). Meek (1989) presents compelling evidence for the rapid emptying of Lake Manix and the accompanying incision of Afton Canyon; W. J. Brown et al. (1990) argue that the downcutting was not catastrophic. On the Lake Manix Basin, see Jefferson (1987), Jefferson et al. (1982), and McGill et al. (1988). Dates on lake sediments within Death Valley itself are presented and discussed by Hooke (1972). Dorn et al. (1989, 1990) provide radiocarbon dates on rock varnish from the shorelines of Searles Lake, Lake Manly, and Lake Manix.

On the Eureka Valley sand dunes, see Bagley (1988), Norris (1988), and G. Smith (1988); on visiting Eureka Valley, see Foster (1987). Spaulding's work on the vegetational history of Eureka Valley and the eastern Amargosa desert can be found in Spaulding (1980, 1983, 1985, 1990a,b), and in Spaulding et al. (1983), on all of which I have relied in my presentation. Spaulding's arguments against equable late Wisconsin climates can be found in these references, and in Spaulding and Graumlich (1986); see also the discussion in Chapter 8.

The emigrant trails through both Forty Mile Deserts are carefully plotted in E. W. Harris (1980); see also Curran (1982). The plants of the Carson Desert region are discussed by Billings (1945). The history of water projects in this part of Nevada as a whole is presented by Townley (1977); see also Reisner (1986). A succinct discussion of the vegetation of the Carson Desert area, and of historic modifications to that vegetation, is provided by Kelly and Hattori (1985). As elsewhere, my discussion of the trees and shrubs of the Great Basin has benefited from Lanner (1983b) and Mozingo (1987).

The history and archaeology of Hidden Cave are discussed in detail by Thomas (1985), from which I have drawn freely. A brief biographical sketch of S. M. Wheeler, whose life remains essentially unknown, is presented by D. D. Fowler (1973). The geology of the deposits of Hidden Cave was analyzed by J. O. Davis (1985b). Wigand and Mehringer (1985) provide a detailed analysis of the pollen and seeds from Hidden Cave; my discussion of the late

Pleistocene vegetation of the Carson Desert is fully dependent on that paper. My description of the vegetation in the Hidden Cave area is based on my own fieldwork; the precipitation and evaporation figures are from Roger Morrison's classic monograph on the southern Carson Desert (Morrison 1964); see also Kelly and Hattori (1985).

Hidden Cave is on land that is under the stewardship of the Bureau of Land Management. The site is easy to visit. Follow highway 50 south from Fallon; after about ten miles, you will see an excellent dirt road, marked by a "Hidden Cave" sign, on the left (east) side of the highway. Turning left here, you will pass a broad opening in Eetza Mountain to the south (note the Lake Lahontan terraces here), and will then come to a second, far smaller, opening. Hidden Cave is on the east side of this opening; the trail will take you there.

The Bureau of Land Management has closed the cave by means of a substantial gate across its mouth. For those who wish to do more than simply see where the site is, the Churchill County Museum provides free tours of the site. Currently, these tours are provided on the second and fourth Saturdays of each month, at 10:00 A.M. The tours leave from the museum; participants are required to provide their own transportation. Tours for twelve people or more may also be arranged through the Carson City District Office of the BLM at (702) 885-6000.

The Churchill County Museum is located at 1050 South Maine Street, in Fallon, telephone (702) 423-3677. Whether or not you opt for the Hidden Cave tour, this excellent museum is well worth the visit, with excellent displays on regional prehistory (Hidden Cave), native Americans, and local history.

My discussion of the vegetation of Ruby Valley and the Ruby Mountains is based on Loope (1969), R. S. Thompson (1984, 1992), R. F. Miller et al. (1982), Critchfield and Allenbaugh (1969), and my own fieldwork. The most recent synthesis of the plants of the Ruby Mountains alpine zone is provided by Charlet (1991). The Ruby Lakes cores are discussed in detail in R. S. Thompson (1984, 1992), and in R. S. Thompson et al. (1990). The depth and area of Lake Franklin provided in the text are from Mifflin and Wheat (1979). See Delorme (1969), Delorme and Zoltai (1984), and Forester (1987) for discussions of ostracodes and their use in paleoenvironmental analysis. On Lake Waring, see Currey et al. (1984).

My discussion of the late Pleistocene vegetation of the Mojave Desert has drawn heavily on Mehringer (1965, 1967), Mehringer and Ferguson (1969), Mehringer and Warren (1976), Spaulding (1977, 1981, 1985, 1990a,b), and Wigand (1990b). The Owl Canyon middens were originally analyzed by Mehringer and Warren (1976); in my discussion, I have used the dates for their samples provided by Wigand (1990b). Both Spaulding (1990b) and Wigand (1990b) provide excellent reviews of Mojave Desert vegetation during this period, and I have drawn heavily on those presentations; see also Van Devender et al. (1987). Van Devender (1977) and Van Devender and Spaulding (1979) argued that the Mojave and adjacent Sonoran deserts did not become deserts until the Holocene; they later helped demonstrate that this view was incorrect.

Spaulding (1985) provides his detailed assessment of the climatic meaning of the northern Mojave Desert late-glacial vegetation data. Van Devender (1990b) presents his argument for a more equable late glacial in at least parts of the Sonoran Desert; P. V. Wells (1983) presents a similar argument for the Mojave Desert.

An excellent discussion of the individualistic nature of the responses of plant species to climatic change is provided by T. Webb (1988); for a discussion focusing on the Great Basin, see R. S. Thompson (1988). Data on the history of oaks, hickories, and many other tree species in the east can be found in T. Webb (1988), as well as in G. L. Jacobsen et al. (1987). On cattle egrets, see Palmer (1962), Godfrey (1966), Hayward et al. (1976), Blake (1977), and Ryser (1985). A list of "anomalous" plant associations in the Sheep Range is provided by Spaulding et al. (1983).

R. H. Webb and Betancourt (1990) analyze the geographic and temporal distribution of the packrat midden samples now available from the Desert West. R. S. Thompson (1990) presents data on the chronological distribution of dated middens from the floristic Great Basin. R. S. Thompson (1978, 1984, 1990) and P. V. Wells (1983) discuss the late Pleistocene midden data from the Deep Creek, Snake, Confusion, and Wah Wah ranges. Sack (1990) outlines the Quaternary history of Tule Valley; see also Oviatt (1991b). The late Pleistocene distribution of conifers and desert shrub vegetation is discussed and debated in R. S. Thompson and Mead (1982), R. S. Thompson (1984, 1990), and P. V. Wells (1983). R. S. Thompson (1984) presents his climatic estimates; see also R. S. Thompson (1990).

Bright (1966) presents the analysis of the Swan Lake sediments; the Grays Lake analysis is in Beiswenger (1991);

analyses of pollen from Lake Bonneville sediments are presented by Mehringer (1977) and Madsen (in Spencer et al. 1984); see also Mehringer (1985, 1986). R. S. Thompson et al. (1986) discuss the Winnemucca Lake middens; the Meadow Valley Wash middens are presented in D. B. Madsen (1972, 1976), Spaulding and Van Devender (1980), and P. V. Wells (1983).

Axelrod (1990) and Axelrod and Raven (1985) are key references to their arguments concerning the history of Great Basin montane conifers; see also Reveal (1979). For the other view, see R. S. Thompson (1990) and P. V. Wells (1983). On the Pliocene vegetation and climates of the Great Basin, see R. S. Thompson (1991). Hiebert and Hamrick (1983) analyze genetic variability within five populations of eastern Great Basin and western Colorado Plateau bristlecones; for a broader view of genetic variation within western conifers, see Critchfield (1984).

CHAPTER SEVEN

○○○

The Late Pleistocene Vertebrates of the Great Basin

The Extinct Late Pleistocene Mammals

The extinction of an amazingly diverse variety of North American mammals toward the end of the Pleistocene has provided paleontology with one of its most hotly debated mysteries (see Chapter 4).

The Great Basin, however, has been largely peripheral to this debate. This is not because the Great Basin is lacking in late Pleistocene vertebrate faunas. Several dozen fossil-bearing sites of this age have been reported from here (see Table 7-1), and uncounted hundreds of other Great Basin localities have provided isolated bones and teeth of extinct Pleistocene mammals.

To some extent, the Great Basin's low profile in the extinction debate follows from the fact that so few paleontologists have focused their research on this area. That does not account for all of it, however, since some superb work has been done in the Great Basin, and one late Pleistocene site from this region—Fossil Lake, in south-central Oregon—is internationally known. Instead, the low profile stems primarily from the fact that Great Basin late Pleistocene sites have proved so difficult to date accurately.

There are a number of reasons for this situation. Some Great Basin sites—for instance, Gypsum Cave in southern Nevada's Frenchman Mountains, and Smith Creek Cave in eastern Nevada's Snake Range (see Figure 7-1 for locations)—were excavated early in the century, at a time when the need for careful, fine-grained stratigraphic excavations had yet to be recognized. Others—Astor Pass, northwest of Pyramid Lake, for instance—were described on the basis of fossil material for which no precise locational information at all was obtained.

However, problems of this sort, in which work done 50 or more years ago is inadequate by today's standards, are by no means confined to the Great Basin. They exist wherever paleontology has a long history. Indeed, there are probably fewer problems of this sort in the Great Basin than elsewhere, simply because fewer people have been interested in the late Pleistocene paleontology of this region.

More to the point is the fact that even paleontological sites that have been collected recently, and with exquisite care, have often been impossible to date with any real accuracy. This is because most Great Basin sites known to

Table 7-1. Great Basin Faunas with Extinct Late Pleistocene Mammals[a]

Site	Location	Setting	Extinct mammals	References
Oregon				
1. Fossil Lake	Fort Rock Basin	Lake deposits	Harlan's ground sloth, giant short-faced bear, horse, flat-headed peccary, camel, large-headed llama, mammoth	I. S. Allison (1966a), Howe and Martin (1977)
2. Paisley Five-Mile Point Cave	Summer Lake Basin	Cave	Horse	Cressman (1942)
Nevada				
3. Astor Pass	Pyramid Lake Basin	Lake gravels	American lion, horse	Merriam (1915)
4. Black Rock Desert (East arm)	Black Rock Desert	Alluvial deposits	Sabertooth, camel, mammoth	Dansie et al. (1988), Livingston (1992)
5. Centennial Parkway	Las Vegas Valley	Pond/marsh deposits	Horse, camel, mammoth	Reynolds et al. (1991)
6. Crypt Cave	Winnemucca Lake Basin	Cave	American cheetah	Orr (1952, 1956, 1969, 1974), R. S. Thompson et al. (1987), Van Valkenburgh et al. (1990)
7. Devil Peak	Spring Mountains	Fissure	Shasta ground sloth	Reynolds et al. (1991)
8. Falcon Hill Caves	Winnemucca Lake Basin	Caves	Horse, shrub ox	Hattori (1982), R. S. Thompson et al. (1987)
9. Fishbone Cave	Winnemucca Lake Basin	Cave	Horse, camel	Orr (1956, 1974), R. S. Thompson et al. (1987)
10. Gypsum Cave	Frenchman Mountains	Cave	Shasta ground sloth, horse, camel, large-headed llama	Stock (1931), Harrington (1933)
11. Hidden Cave	Carson Desert	Cave	Horse, camel	Grayson (1985)
12. Labor of Love Cave	Schell Creek Range	Cave	Giant short-faced bear	Emslie and Czaplewski (1985)
13. Mineral Hill Cave	Sulphur Spring Range	Cave	Horse, large-headed llama, shrub ox	McGuire (1980)
14. Nevada State Prison	Carson City	Lake deposits	Harlan's ground sloth	Stock (1920, 1925)
15. Owl Cave Two	Snake Range	Cave	Horse, camel	Birnie (1986), Turnmire (1987)
16. Rye Patch Dam	Humboldt River	Spring deposits	Horse, camel, mammoth	Firby et al. (1987)
17. Smith Creek Cave	Snake Range	Cave	Horse, camel, Harrington's mountain goat	Stock (1936), S. J. Miller (1979), J. I. Mead et al. (1982)
18. Snake Creek Burial Cave	Snake Range	Cave	Horse, camel	J. I. Mead and Mead (1985), Heaton (1987), E. M. Mead and Mead (1989)
19. Tule Springs	Las Vegas Valley	Alluvial deposits	Jefferson's ground sloth, Shasta ground sloth, American lion, horse, camel, mammoth	Mawby (1967)
20. Wizards Beach	Pyramid Lake Basin	Lake deposits	Horse, camel, mammoth	Dansie et al. (1988)
Utah				
21. Crystal Ball Cave	Snake Valley	Cave	Short-faced skunk, sabertooth, horse, camel, large-headed llama	W. E. Miller (1982), Heaton (1985)
22. Eastern Lake Bonneville	Bonneville Basin	Lake deposits	Horse, camel, Harlan's muskox, mammoth (multiple localities)	D. B. Madsen et al. (1976), M.E. Nelson and Madsen (1978, 1980, 1983)

Table 7-1 ***(continued)***

Site	Location	Setting	Extinct mammals	References
23. Monroc	Bonneville Basin	Lake deposits	Giant short-faced bear	M. E. Nelson and Madsen (1983)
24. Silver Creek Local Fauna	Wasatch Range	Alluvial/marsh deposits	Harlan's ground sloth, sabertooth, horse, camel, mammoth	W. E. Miller (1976)
25. Tabernacle Crater	Sevier Desert	Cave	Camel	M. E. Nelson and Madsen (1979), Oviatt (1991a), Romer (1928, 1929)
26. Utah Sinkhole	Wasatch Plateau	Sinkhole	Mastodon	W. E. Miller (1987)
California				
27. Antelope Cave	Mescal Range	Cave	Horse, camel, large-headed llama	Reynolds et al. (1991a)
28. China Lake	China Lake Basin	Alluvial/lake deposits	Sabertooth, horse, camel, large-headed llama, mammoth	Fortsch (1978)
29. Kokoweef Cave	Kokoweef Peak	Cave	Horse, camel, large-headed llama	Goodwin and Reynolds (1989a), Reynolds et al. (1991b)
30. Mescal Cave	Mescal Range	Cave	Horse	Brattstrom (1958), Jefferson (1991)
31. Mitchell Caverns	Providence Mountains	Cave	Shasta ground sloth, horse, camel	Jefferson (1991)
32. Newberry Cave	Newberry Mountains	Cave	Shasta ground sloth	C. A. Davis and Smith (1981)
33. Salt Springs	Southern Death Valley	Lake deposits	Mammoth	Jefferson (1990)
34. Schuiling Cave	Newberry Mountains	Cave	Horse, diminutive pronghorn	Downs et al. (1959)

[a] Site numbers indicate site locations in Figure 7-1.

date come either from the surface or from caves whose deposits cannot be deciphered stratigraphically.

Fossil Lake is an excellent example of the former, surficial, variety. This site, located in the eastern part of the basin of Pleistocene Fort Rock Lake in south-central Oregon, was brought to scientific attention in 1876. Since that time, dozens of publications on the Pleistocene fishes, birds, and mammals collected from the site have appeared; geologist Ira Allison summarized many of them in an important monograph that appeared in 1966. No one has counted the numbers of fossils that have been scientifically collected and described from this site, but there are thousands. They include the remains of such extinct mammals as Harlan's ground sloth, giant short-faced bear, horse, flat-headed peccary, large-headed llama, and mammoth (descriptions of extinct North American Pleistocene mammals are found in Chapter 4; see Tables 4-1 and 7-2 for the scientific names of those mammals). There are also several thousand well-described bird specimens from this site. Indeed, Fossil Lake was the first paleontological site in North America to have provided significant numbers of Pleistocene bird fossils.

Even though Fossil Lake is a truly important site, and even though it has been studied for over a century, we do not know how old the material from this site is. Most of the specimens are from deflation basins, the fossils having been revealed as a result of wind erosion of the Pleistocene lake sediments in which they were once embedded. Although a few excavations have been undertaken at Fossil Lake, they were done primarily to understand the stratigraphy of the deposits from which the bones are being deflated, not to get large samples of fossils. Getting large samples would require a massive and expensive excavation campaign, and that has not been done.

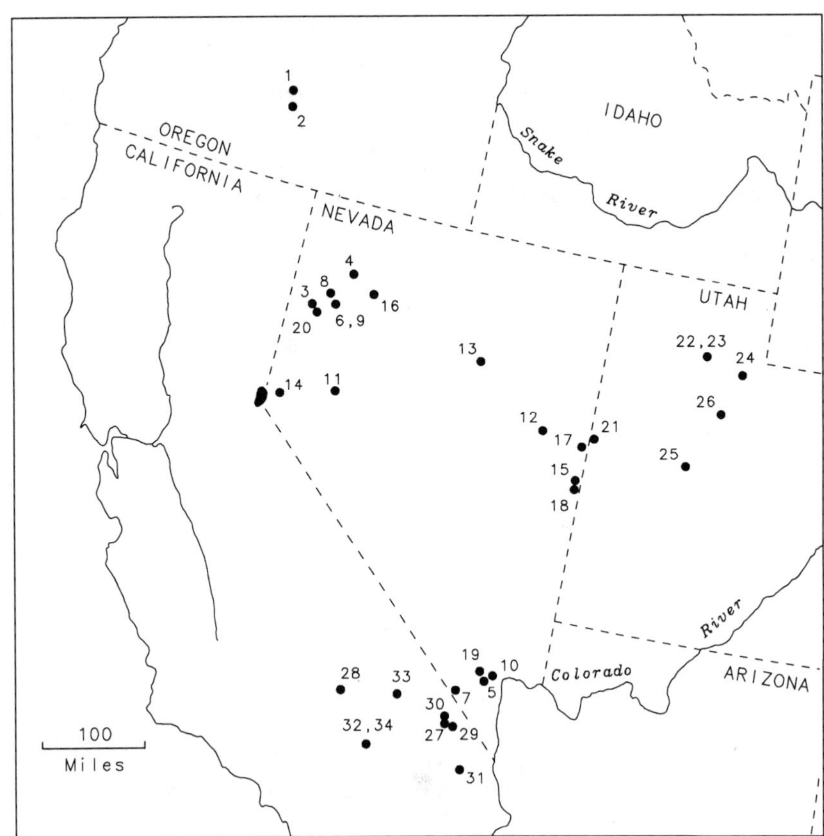

Figure 7-1. The location of Great Basin paleontological sites that have provided the remains of extinct Pleistocene mammals. See Table 7-1 for key to sites.

Nor has there been much of an attempt to get radiocarbon dates from the excavated sediments. One date of 29,000 years was obtained by Allison from snail shells associated with bird bones that he excavated, but land snails often give misleading ages, and there are no other dates to support or refute this one. Even if the date is accurate, it cannot be automatically extended to the thousands of fossils that have come from the surface. Indeed, Allison and his colleague Carl Bond have noted that some of the fish and bird specimens that have been collected here may reflect the existence of a shallow lake in this basin less than 7,000 years ago.

Most of the Fossil Lake specimens are clearly "late Pleistocene" in age, but where they fall in the late Pleistocene is not known. An ambitious paleontologist could certainly help solve this problem: substantial excavations combined with detailed stratigraphic work, much radiocarbon dating, and the careful identification and correlation of the volcanic ashes that are in the Fossil Lake deposits would do the job. Not until that is done, however, will we be able to say anything secure about the age of the materials from this superb site.

The cave sites are a different matter. Many caves were excavated so early that detailed stratigraphic information is not available, whereas others were excavated much more recently but so poorly that the same problems exist. However, some Great Basin caves with late Pleistocene deposits simply do not provide the depositional context needed to provide detailed answers to chronological questions.

Crystal Ball Cave in western Utah's Snake Valley provides an excellent example. Located in Gandy Mountain about three miles west of the small town of Gandy, Utah, Crystal Ball Cave is some 500′ long, with an area of about 20,000 square feet. When it was first discovered in 1956, bones of extinct horses and camels were lying on the surface. These were collected by Herbert Gerisch and Robert Patterson and donated to the Natural History Museum of Los Angeles County, thus making the paleontological potential of the site known to science. Excavations were conducted at the site by Brigham Young University paleontologists Wade Miller and Timothy Heaton in the late 1970s and early 1980s. An excellent discussion of the results of this work was published by Heaton, who reported that the deposits of the site not only contained the remains of extinct horse and camel, but also of large-headed llama, sabertooth, and a new species of short-faced skunk. Literally thousands of bones and teeth came from this site, due to the careful work done here by Miller and Heaton.

Exactly how old is all this material? Unfortunately, in spite of exacting excavations, we do not really know. As rich as they were in bone (some 10% by volume), the sediments of Crystal Ball Cave were only about 18″ deep, and they were completely unstratified. As Heaton (1985: 346) observed, "the cave seems to have been accumulating fossils continuously from some date in the past, when an entrance was formed, to the present." Four radiocarbon dates were obtained, and these range from greater than 23,000 years ago to 12,980 years ago. These dates, however, were on the mineral (apatite) fraction of the bone, which often provides invalid ages. The extinct mammals themselves require a late Pleistocene age for the site, which is consistent with the radiocarbon dates. Beyond this, however, there is no way of knowing precisely how old these specimens are. Given current technology, the only way their ages could be discovered would be by radiocarbon dating the protein, and perhaps the amino acids, from each specimen.

Other cases of this sort abound. Although the Great Basin has provided a good number of late Pleistocene paleontological sites, most of these lack sound chronological control. All we can really say is that they are "late Pleistocene."

Even though the chronology of Great Basin late Pleistocene paleontological sites is not well known, the sites that have been studied show that the Great Basin supported a diverse variety of now-extinct mammals during this period. In fact, of the 35 genera of mammals known to have become extinct in North America toward the end of the Pleistocene, 16 have been reported from the Great Basin.

Those 16 are listed in Table 7-2. The sites that provided them, and the extinct mammals provided by each, are listed in Table 7-1 (I have also included Harrington's mountain goat in Table 7-2, even though the genus to which this extinct mammal belongs is thriving in the Pacific Northwest). The list is substantial: it includes three of the four extinct ground sloths, four of the seven extinct carnivores, one of the two extinct perissodactyls, six of the thirteen extinct artiodactyls, and both of the extinct proboscideans (see Table 4-1).

Table 7-2. Extinct Late Pleistocene Mammals Known from the Great Basin[a]

Genus	Common name
Megalonyx	Jefferson's ground sloth
Nothrotheriops shastensis	Shasta ground sloth
Glossotherium	Harlan's ground sloth
Brachyprotoma brevimala	Short-faced skunk
Arctodus simus	Giant short-faced bear
Smilodon fatalis	Sabertooth cat
Panthera leo★	American lion
Miracinonyx trumani	American cheetah
Equus species	Horses
Platygonus	Flat-headed peccary
Camelops hesternus	Yesterday's camel
Hemiauchenia macrocephala	Large-headed llama
Capromeryx	Diminutive pronghorn
Oreamnos harringtoni★	Harrington's mountain goat
Euceratherium	Shrub ox
Bootherium bombifrons	Harlan's muskox
Mammut americanum	American mastodon
Mammuthus columbi	Columbia mammoth

[a]Species names have been provided if a secure, or reasonably secure, species identification is available; several species of late Pleistocene horses have been identified from the Great Basin.

★Genus still exists in North America.

Even though no complete list of all late Pleistocene sites in the Great Basin exists, it is possible to get a feel for the relative abundance of the Great Basin's extinct Pleistocene mammals by counting the number of sites listed in Table 7-1 in which each extinct mammal occurs (since the eastern Lake Bonneville entry includes many separate sites, I have included each separate site in my tally, but have not listed those sites in Table 7-1).

The results of doing that are shown in Figure 7-2. Although this figure cannot be taken as much more than suggestive, what it suggests is that horses, camels, and mammoths were common on the Great Basin landscape during the late Pleistocene. Although Figure 7-2 makes it appear that Harlan's muskox (see Figure 7-3) was also common in the Great Basin, all of the records for this animal are from eastern edge of Lake Bonneville. It has yet to be reported from other Great Basin locations.

The current list of extinct late Pleistocene mammalian genera known from the Great Basin is probably fairly complete, even though our chronology for those mammals is weak. There is good reason to think that many of the 19

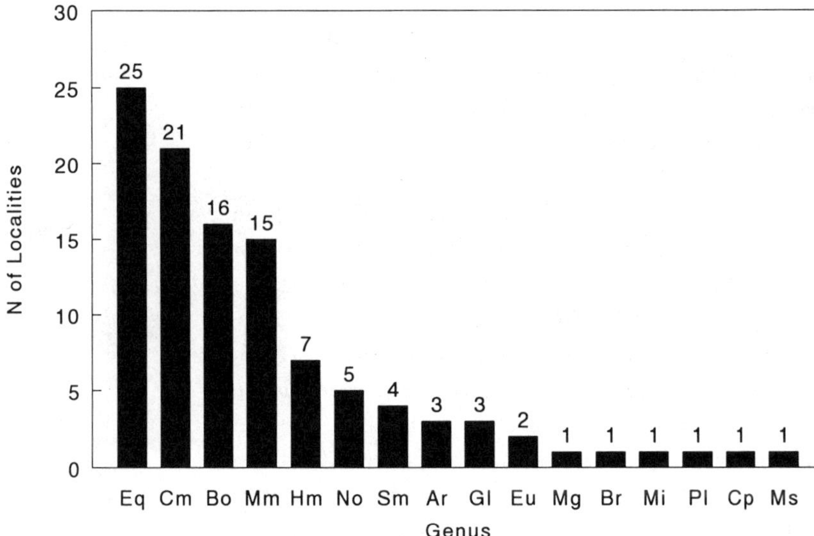

Figure 7-2. The number of localities at which extinct genera of Pleistocene mammals have been reported in the Great Basin. Eq = *Equus;* Cm = *Camelops;* Bo = *Bootherium;* Mm = *Mammuthus;* Hm = *Hemiauchenia;* No = *Nothrotheriops;* Sm = *Smilodon;* Ar = *Arctodus;* Gl = *Glossotherium;* Eu = *Euceratherium;* Mg = *Megalonyx;* Br = *Brachyprotoma;* Mi = *Miracinonyx;* Pl = *Platygonus;* Cp = *Capromeryx;* Ms = *Mammut.*

Figure 7-3. "Musk Oxen Wanted" sign distributed by the Utah State Division of State History. *Symbos cavifrons* is now recognized to belong to the same species as *Bootherium bombifrons,* Harlan's muskox.

extinct genera unknown from the Great Basin did not occur here during the late Pleistocene, since many of the unrecorded extinct mammals do not seem to have lived in what is now the western United States. To take but a few examples, the capybaras *Neochoerus* and *Hydrochoerus* are known only from the southeast; the massive Rusconi's ground sloth is known only from the southeast and Texas; the long-nosed peccary is known only east of about 100° longitude (which marks the eastern edge of the Texas panhandle); the elk-moose is known primarily from the central and eastern United States and Canada, on the one hand, and from the Yukon and Alaska, on the other; the saiga is unknown from the New World outside eastern Beringia. Unless much of what we know about the general distribution of extinct late Pleistocene mammals in North America is wrong, many of the 19 extinct genera that have not been reported from the Great Basin probably did not occur here.

On the other hand, some of them are most certainly to be expected. The Asiatic dhole, for example, is now known only from eastern Beringia and northern Mexico. Clearly, it must have occurred somewhere between these two places, and it is possible that it lived in the Great Basin during the late Pleistocene. The mountain deer is known from localities in or near the Rocky Mountains, and may have entered at least the eastern edge of the Great Basin during the late Pleistocene. There are late Pleistocene records for tapir in the southwestern United States, and

Figure 7-4. Mammoth skull in the process of excavation by the Desert Research Institute at the DeLong Mammoth Site, Black Rock Desert, Nevada.

these animals may have occupied at least the southern edge of the Great Basin.

An almost certain indication that we have yet to record all of the large extinct late Pleistocene mammals of the Great Basin is provided by the dire wolf. As I mentioned in Chapter 4, this animal may have included a large component of scavenged meat in its diet, and was widespread south of glacial ice in North America. The sabertooth appears to have had feeding adaptations that required it to leave substantial amounts of meat on the carcasses of its victims, thus providing opportunities for scavenging carnivores. In fact, a high proportion of sites that have provided sabertooth remains have also provided the remains of dire wolves. For instance, in the large sample of North American late Pleistocene paleontological sites compiled by Ernest Lundelius and his colleagues (see Chapter 4), 15 of the 16 sites that contain sabertooths also contain dire wolves. A 1960 census showed that the late Pleistocene mammals of Rancho La Brea included about two dire wolves for every sabertooth (the actual numbers were 1535 dire wolves and 880 sabertooths). It is very possible that sabertooth feeding behavior accounts for the great similarity in the distribution of these two animals in North America as a whole. Given that this is the case, and given that sabertooth remains are not rare in the Great Basin, the fact that the dire wolf has yet to be securely identified here suggests that our tally of extinct late Pleistocene Great Basin mammals is incomplete.

In Chapter 4, I mentioned that explanations of late Pleistocene mammalian extinctions in North America have focused either on human predation or on climatic change as the cause. I also noted that attempts to explain the extinctions as a result of human hunting appear to fail on a number of grounds. These include the fact that some of the most abundant extinct late Pleistocene mammals (horses and camels, for instance) have never been found in a convincing human-kill context, and that we cannot show that the majority of the extinct mammals actually over-

Table 7-3. Radiocarbon Dates Associated with Extinct Pleistocene Mammals in the Great Basin

Site	Date	Reference(s)
Astor Pass	16,800*	Broecker and Kulp (1957)
China Lake	18,600*	Fortsch (1978), E. L. Davis (1978a,b)
Crystal Ball Cave	12,980*	Heaton (1985)
	18,600*	
	18,820*	
	>23,200*	
East Arm, Black Rock Desert	11,080*	Stout (1986)
East Bonneville Localities:		
City Creek Mammoth	14,150*	D. B. Madsen et al. (1976)
Logan City *Bootherium*	7,080*	M. E. Nelson and Madsen (1980)
Monroc Gravel Pit		
Bootherium	11,690*	M. E. Nelson and Madsen (1980, 1983)
Arctodus	12,650*	
Sandy Mammoth	5,985*	D. B. Madsen et al. (1976)
	7,200*	
	8,815*	
	14,150*	M. E. Nelson and Madsen (1980)
Fishbone Cave	10,900*	Orr (1956)
	11,555*	
	12,280*	R. S. Thompson et al. (1987)
Fossil Lake	29,000*	I. S. Allison (1966a)
Garrison	13,480	J. I. Mead et al. (1982)
Gypsum Cave		
Nothrotheriops	8,527*	Arnold and Libby (1951)
	10,455*	
	11,360	Long and Martin (1974)
	11,690	
	21,470	Thompson et al. (1980)
	23,700	Long and Muller (1981)
	33,910	Thompson et al. (1980)
Equus	13,310	Long and Muller (1981)
	25,000	
Labor-of-Love Cave	5,320*	Emslie and Czaplewski (1985)
Newberry Cave *Nothrotheriops*	11,600*	C. A. Davis and Smith (1981)
Owl Cave Two	8,520*	Turnmire (1987)
Silver Creek Local Fauna	>40,000*	W. E. Miller (1976)
Smith Creek Cave	12,600†	Bryan (1979), J. I. Mead et al. (1982)
	28,650*	
Tabernacle Crater	11,075*	M. E. Nelson and Madsen (1979)
Tule Springs Unit E_1	11,500	Haynes (1967)
	11,900	
	12,270	
	12,300	
	12,400	
	12,400	
	12,450	
	12,650	
	12,920	
	13,000	

Table 7-3 ***(continued)***

Site	Date	Reference(s)
Tule Springs Unit E_1 *(continued)*	13,100	
	13,900*	
	15,920*	
	16,900*	
	17,600*	
	>28,000*	
Tule Springs Unit D	22,600*	
	31,300*	
	>23,000*	
	>31,000*	
	>35,000	
Tule Springs Unit B_2	26,000*	
	>30,000*	
	>32,000	
	>32,000	
	>35,000	
	>37,000	
	>40,000	
Utah Sinkhole	7,080*	W. E. Miller (1987)
	7,590*	
	7,650*	
Wizards Beach	25,470	Dansie et al. (1988)

*Date was obtained from material, or using techniques, now considered to give untrustworthy results, or is not well associated with the extinct mammals.

†Date is from above remains of extinct animals.

lapped in time with the Clovis hunters thought by some to have caused the extinctions.

There are no secure associations between people and the remains of any extinct Pleistocene mammal in the Great Basin, but that may reflect nothing more than the fact that they have not yet been found. Archaeologists would be pleased, but not astounded, by the discovery of human artifacts securely associated with a Great Basin mammoth. Indeed, it is possible that work now being conducted on mammoth sites in the Black Rock Desert by the Desert Research Institute, under the direction of archaeologist Stephanie Livingston, will provide us with just such an association (see Figure 7-4).

The most widely discussed climatic explanation of the extinctions, developed most forcefully by Russell Graham and Ernest Lundelius, attributes the extinctions to the multiple and complex results of the loss of climatic equability at the end of the Pleistocene. During the Pleistocene, they maintain, seasonal swings in temperature were far less than they are now, with summers far cooler and winters possibly somewhat warmer (perhaps as the result of the presence of glacial ice in the north, which prevented the southerly incursion of Arctic air masses). At the end of the Pleistocene, they argue, summer temperatures increased dramatically, whereas winter temperatures may have declined. The result of this shift, possibly mediated in many instances by changes in the nature of the vegetation on which so many of the mammals depended, was extinction.

Unfortunately, because the chronology of the Great Basin late Pleistocene paleontological sites that have provided extinct mammals is so poorly controlled, it is not possible to array the fairly detailed information that is available on late Pleistocene vegetational change here against the chronology of Great Basin mammalian extinction.

Table 7-4. Trustworthy Radiocarbon Dates Associated with Extinct Mammals in the Great Basin[a]

Site	Mammals	Date
Garrison	*Camelops*	13,480
Smith Creek Cave	*Equus*	>12,600
	Camelops	
	Oreamnos harringtoni	
Gypsum Cave	*Nothrotheriops*	11,360
		11,690
		21,470
		23,700
		33,910
	Equus	13,310
		25,000
Tule Springs Unit E_1	*Equus*	11,500–13,100
	Camelops	(11 dates)
	Mammuthus	
Tule Springs Unit D	*Camelops*	>35,000
	Mammuthus	
Tule Springs Unit B_2	*Nothrotheriops*	>32,000–>40,000
	Megalonyx	(5 dates)
	Panthera leo	
	Equus	
	Camelops	
	Mammuthus	
Wizards Beach	*Camelops*	25,470

[a]For details, see Table 7-3.

There actually is a substantial array of radiocarbon dates available for the extinct Pleistocene mammals of the Great Basin. These dates are listed in Table 7-3. (I have not included sites that present clear evidence of stratigraphic mixture, such as Hidden Cave, which contains fossilized camel and horse specimens in late Holocene strata.) The list is substantial; however, the list of dates that can be accepted at face value is much shorter. As I discussed in Chapter 3, many kinds of material, including bone, that were once felt to provide reliable radiocarbon dates are now known to provide results that are often highly misleading. As Table 7-3 shows, the vast majority of dates available for the extinct late Pleistocene mammals of the Great Basin are on precisely that kind of untrustworthy material. Others were run during the earliest days of radiocarbon dating, using methods that are now seen as untrustworthy. Our current understanding of the difficulties involved in dating bone suggests that the only secure way to date such material is by carefully extracting individual amino acids and dating those acids with the AMS method (see Chapter 3). To date, however, there is only a single AMS date for an extinct late Pleistocene Great Basin mammal.

If we eliminate the untrustworthy dates that are listed in Table 7-3, the status of the available chronology for extinct Pleistocene mammals in the Great Basin becomes clear. Trustworthy radiocarbon dates come from only five sites (see Table 7-4). A single date from Smith Creek Cave suggests that the horse and camel remains from here were deposited more than 12,600 years ago. The Garrison packrat midden documents the presence of camels in Utah's Snake Valley at about 13,500 years ago. The Wizards Beach camel, which provides the only AMS age determination for an extinct Great Basin mammal, is about 25,500 years old. At Tule Springs, Vance Haynes's exquisite dating work, along with John Mawby's paleontology, documents the presence of horse, camel, and mammoth between 11,500 and 13,100 years ago, and Shasta ground sloth, Jefferson's ground sloth,

American lion, horse, camel, and mammoth more than 32,000 years ago. Radiocarbon dates of ground sloth dung from Gypsum Cave document that Shasta ground sloths survived in the Las Vegas area until almost 11,000 years ago.

Five sites with trustworthy dates are not much to go on if our goal is to understand the timing and cause, or causes, of late Pleistocene extinctions in the Great Basin. It is worth noting that the four extinct genera that Tule Springs and Gypsum Cave show to have survived in the Great Basin until the tail end of the Pleistocene are among the small number of now-extinct genera we know to have survived this late elsewhere in North America. *Nothrotheriops, Equus, Camelops,* and *Mammuthus* all have excellent dates from outside the Great Basin documenting that they lasted beyond 12,000 years ago.

In short, although our list of now-extinct genera that were in the Great Basin during the late Pleistocene is probably reasonably complete, the weak chronology available for the extinctions here means that the Great Basin can shed very little light on the causes of the extinctions themselves. This is unfortunate, since our understanding of the late Pleistocene climates and vegetation of this region is as good as it is anywhere, and does seem to support the argument that late Pleistocene climates here were more equable than Holocene ones (see Chapter 6). Until far more has been learned about the distribution of the extinct mammals in the Great Basin, however, and until we have much deeper knowledge of the timing of the extinctions here, all we will be able to say is that the Great Basin, like so many other parts of North America, supported a far richer large mammal fauna toward the end of the Pleistocene than it does today. Apparently chief among those mammals were horses, camels, and mammoths.

THE HUNTINGTON MAMMOTH AND THE SINKHOLE MASTODON

In 1988, construction workers turned up the remains of a Columbian mammoth (*Mammuthus columbi*) on central Utah's Wasatch Plateau, about halfway between the towns of Nephi and Price (see Figure 7-1). David Madsen and David Gillette, Utah State archaeologist and paleontologist, respectively, were called in to excavate the site. In addition to the mammoth, they uncovered a fragmentary skull and rib of the giant short-faced bear and a stone tool. These, amazingly enough, were removed from the site by a security guard, and were later retrieved by the U.S. Forest Service. As a result, the relationship between the remains of the bear, the artifact, and the mammoth is unclear.

The Huntington Mammoth site is at the base of the Huntington Reservoir Dam, just east of the Great Basin drainage divide. Huntington Creek drains into the San Rafael River, which drains into the Green River, which drains into the Colorado. Because the site is actually on the Colorado Plateau, it does not appear in Table 7-1. I mention it here because of the elevation at which this mammoth lived or, more accurately, died: 8,990′. Today, the vegetation of the area that provided the mammoth is dominated by Englemann spruce and subalpine fir on nearby north- and east-facing slopes, whereas south- and west-facing slopes are characterized by big sagebrush and quaking aspen (*Populus tremuloides*).

The plant macrofossils of the lake sediments from which the mammoth was recovered were dominated by Engelmann spruce, suggesting that this animal was living in a subalpine environment at the time of its death. Geochronologist T. W. Stafford extracted amino acids from both the mammoth and giant short-faced bear specimens, and had accelerator dates run on them. The mammoth dated to 11,220 years ago, the bear, to 10,870 years ago.

The Huntington mammoth is not the only high-elevation proboscidean known from Utah. A scant two miles to the west and north of the mammoth site, paleontologist Wade Miller discovered the partial remains of two mastodons (*Mammut americanum*) in a sinkhole that had been formed by the collapse of the underlying fine-grained sandstone. The collapse created an opening, or sinkhole, that today is some 120′ by 150′ in dimension. A pond developed in this opening; the mastodon remains were excavated from the sediments that formed within the pond.

Although the Huntington mammoth is just outside the boundary of the hydrographic Great Basin, the sinkhole mastodons are just inside it (hence, they appear in Table 7-1). In fact, these are the only mastodons known from Utah, and the only ones known from the Great Basin. (In 1903, the geologist J. E. Spurr reported mastodon remains from the Tule Springs area, but he never saw the specimens, and was simply reporting something he had been told; later work at Tule Springs has not turned up the animal.) What makes the sinkhole mastodons so interesting is not only the fact that they are the first to be securely documented from the Great Basin, but also the fact that they come from the highest elevation recorded for any mastodon: 9,780′.

The vegetation of the area that surrounds the sinkhole is not unlike the vegetation of the area in which the Huntington mammoth was found: sagebrush in the immediate vicinity, with spruce/fir forest nearby. Paleobotanist Deborah Newman of Brigham Young University identified the pollen from the sediments in which the mastodons were embedded. She found that the vegetation of the area at the time the animal died was very similar to that found here today: sagebrush, spruce, and fir contributed 41% of the identified pollen, with pine contributing an additional 21%. Unfortunately, it is not clear when all of this material accumulated. Radiocarbon dates on the mineral fraction of the bone provided dates of between 7,080 and 7,650 years (see Table 7-3), but this fraction often provides inaccurate results.

Because of the careful work of Gillette, Madsen, and Miller, we now know that mammoths and mastodons occupied surprisingly high elevations in the Great Basin and immediately adjacent areas, and that the vegetation of these mountainous areas then included subalpine conifers, much as it does today. It appears that there is tremendous potential for high-elevation vertebrate paleontology in the Great Basin, something that was not realized up until a few years ago.

The Extinct Late Pleistocene Birds

Extinction at the genus level was not confined to mammals at the end of the Pleistocene in North America: some 19 genera of birds also became extinct at this time (see Table 7-5). The chronology of the avian extinctions is even more poorly understood than the chronology of the mammalian extinctions, but it does seem that they occurred at roughly the same time.

There are very few specialists in avian paleontology, and very little work has been done on the Pleistocene birds of the Great Basin. The work that has been done, however, has been of exceptional quality, much of it the result of the efforts of Hildegarde Howard of the Natural History Museum of Los Angeles County.

This work has documented the late Pleistocene presence of seven now-extinct genera of birds in the Great Basin (see Table 7-6). Of the 35 genera of mammals that became extinct in North America toward the end of the Pleistocene, 16, or 45.7%, are known from the Great Basin, and this list is probably fairly complete. For birds, the comparable figure is 36.8% (7/19), lower than it is for mammals. Since our knowledge of the extinct late Pleistocene birds of the Great Basin is derived from a very small number of sites, there is no reason to think that our list of extinct birds is anywhere near complete. Even as it stands, however, that list shows that the Great Basin late Pleistocene avifauna was in every way as remarkable as its mammalian counterpart.

Today, the Greater Flamingo (*Phoenicopterus ruber*) does not breed north of the Caribbean. Postbreeding flamingos sometimes wander into the far eastern United States, and there are a series of flamingo sightings for Utah and Nevada. Ornithologists J. R. Alcorn and Fred Ryser both suspect that the Great Basin sightings are of escaped birds; somehow, those seen at the artificial lake at the MGM Grand Hotel in Reno seem especially suspicious.

No such uncertainty surrounds the two extinct species of late Pleistocene Great Basin flamingos, both of which have been reported from Fossil Lake. *P. copei,* Cope's Flamingo, appears to have been slightly larger than the modern Greater Flamingo, and had stouter legs; *P. minutus* was, as the name suggests, a smaller version, some 75% of the size of the Greater Flamingo.

Hildegarde Howard has also identified these species from Manix Lake, in the central Mojave Desert of southeastern California. At the time of her work, no absolute dates for the deposits from which this material came were available, and she suggested that the Manix Lake flamingos, and the many other birds she identified from this site, were late Pleistocene in age. However, paleontologist George Jefferson of the George C. Page (La Brea) Museum has now shown that the sediments from which the flamingo remains came are some 300,000 years old, and thus not late Pleistocene at all. Interestingly, the Manix Lake deposits also provided the remains of an immature Cope's Flamingo, suggesting that this large flamingo may have bred in the Great Basin at the time these deposits accumulated.

Most storks of the genus *Ciconia* are Old World in distribution, found from southern Africa north through Europe and Asia. The only exception is the Maguari Stork, which is South American. However, the extinct Asphalt Stork (*C. maltha*), first described from Rancho La Brea, is known not only from the late Pleistocene asphalt deposits or tar pits of southern California, but also from Florida and from Manix Lake, in deposits that are approximately 20,000

Table 7-5. Extinct Late Pleistocene Genera of North American Birds[a]

Family	Genus	Modern relatives
Phoenicopteridae	*Phoenicopterus*★	Flamingos
Ciconiidae	*Ciconia*★	Storks
Anatidae	*Anabernicula*	Shelducks
Cathartidae	*Breagyps*	Condors, vultures
Teratornithidae	*Teratornis*	(Extinct teratorns)
	Cathartornis	
Accipitridae	*Spizaëtus*★	Hawks, eagles
	Amplibuteo	
	Wetmoregyps	
	Neophrontops	Old World vultures
	Neogyps	
Falconidae	*Milvago*★	Caracaras
Charadriidae	*Dorypaltus*	Lapwings
Burhinidae	*Burhinus*★	Thick-knees
Corvidae	*Protocitta*	Jays
	Henocitta	
	Cremaster	Cowbirds, blackbirds
	Pandanaris	
	Pyeloramphus	

★Genus survives outside North America.

[a]After Steadman and Martin (1984) and Grayson (1977b).

years old. Today, only the Wood Stork (*Mycteria americana*) is to be found in the Great Basin, and it appears only occasionally during the summer months.

In contrast to *Phoenicopterus* and *Ciconia,* genera that still exist, the "pygmy goose" genus *Anabernicula* is extinct. Known from late Pleistocene deposits ranging from Texas to California, and from both Fossil Lake and Smith Creek Cave, *Anabernicula* was about the size of a mallard duck. However, it was related not to our common dabbling ducks (genus *Anas*), but instead to the shelducks (genus *Tadorna*). Today, shelducks primarily occupy temperate regions within Europe, Asia, Africa, and the Pacific, though the genus includes one tropical species.

Table 7-6. Extinct Late Pleistocene Bird Genera Known from the Great Basin

Genus	Site and species	Reference
Phoenicopterus	Fossil Lake (*P. copei, P. minutus*)	H. Howard (1946)
Ciconia	Manix Lake (*C. maltha*)	H. Howard (1955), Jefferson (1985, 1987)
Anabernicula	Fossil Lake (*A. oregonensis*)	H. Howard (1946, 1964a)
	Smith Creek Cave (*A. gracilenta*)	H. Howard (1952, 1964b)
Breagyps	Smith Creek Cave (*B. clarki*)	H. Howard (1935, 1952)
Teratornis	Smith Creek Cave (*T. incredibilis*)	H. Howard (1952)
	Tule Springs (*T. merriami*)	Mawby (1967)
Spizaëtus	Fossil Lake (*S. pliogyrps*)	H. Howard (1946)
	Smith Creek Cave (*S. willetti*)	H. Howard (1935, 1952)
Neogyps	Smith Creek Cave (*N. errans*)	H. Howard (1952)

Clark's Condor (*Breagyps clarki*) belonged to the same family group of birds, the Cathartidae, as the Turkey Vulture (*Cathartes aura*) and the California Condor (*Gymnogyps californianus*). Slightly larger than the California Condor, Clark's Condor sported a long but narrow beak, and is known only from the asphalt deposits of southern California and from Smith Creek Cave. The deposits of Smith Creek Cave, however, contained the remains of at least six of these condors, one of which was immature, suggesting that this bird bred in the eastern Snake Range.

Clark's Condor was not the only condor in the Great Basin during the late Pleistocene. The California Condor, which is still barely in existence, has been reported from Antelope Cave in southeastern California's Mescal Range, from Gypsum Cave in southern Nevada, and from Smith Creek Cave. In fact, paleontologist Steven Emslie has obtained excellent radiocarbon dates for condor remains from both Antelope and Gypsum caves: they are 11,080 and 14,740 years old, respectively. California condors from all three sites are, thus, late Wisconsin in age.

Smith Creek Cave also provided a number of specimens of the Western Black Vulture, *Coragyps occidentalis.* This species, well known from Rancho La Brea, is extinct, but the closely related American Black Vulture, *C. atratus,* comes no closer to the Great Basin than southern Arizona. Compared to its modern relative, the late Pleistocene Western Black Vulture was a bulkier bird, with shorter and stouter legs, but probably had much the same adaptations.

The teratorns are closely related to the vultures and condors, but now tend to be placed in their own family, the Teratornithidae. The first of these huge, condor-like birds was discovered at Rancho La Brea; the same species, *Teratornis merriami* or Merriam's Teratorn, is now known from the asphalt deposits of southern California, from Florida, and from northern Mexico. It has also been found in the Great Basin, in the late Pleistocene deposits of Tule Springs, where it is associated with radiocarbon dates that fall between 11,500 and 13,100 years ago. In life, Merriam's teratorn would have looked something like a California Condor, but it weighed half again as much (probably around 35 pounds), had a wingspan of 12′ or more (compared to a maximum of 10′ for the California Condor), and had a hooked, somewhat eagle-like beak.

As impressive as this bird was, however, it was almost dwarfed by the Incredible Teratorn, *T. incredibilis.* First described by Hildegarde Howard on the basis of a single wrist bone from Smith Creek Cave, this bird is now also known from earlier deposits in California. Aptly named, the Incredible Teratorn had a wingspan estimated at 16–17′, nearly twice the size of the California Condor. Although this wingspan places the Incredible Teratorn among the largest flying birds known, place of honor in this category belongs to a much earlier member of the teratorn group, *Argentavis magnificens.* This teratorn, from late Miocene deposits in Argentina, had a wingspan of 25′ and an estimated weight of some 265 pounds.

Detailed analyses of the bones of Merriam's teratorn suggest that these birds were fairly clumsy on the ground, and that their flight was characterized by slow and shallow flapping—not unlike that of herons and pelicans—rather than by soaring. Although it was once assumed that teratorns, which were armed with a hook-like beak, were scavengers, we in fact know virtually nothing about how they obtained their food.

The Errant Eagle, *Neogyps errans,* is known from the tar pits of southern California, from northern Mexico, and from Smith Creek Cave. This bird belongs to the widespread family of hawks and eagles (the Accipitridae), but proper placement within that family is the subject of some debate. Most often, they have been placed with the subfamily of Old World Vultures—with such birds as the Egyptian Vulture (*Neophrons percnopterus*), the Griffon Vulture (*Gyps fulvus*), and the Lammergeier (*Gypaetus barbatus*). Even if this placement is correct, however, aspects of the skeleton of the Errant Eagle—for instance, its eagle-like skull and feet—suggest that it was far more capable of taking live prey than are modern Old World Vultures.

Hawk Eagles, genus *Spizaëtus,* are also accipiters, but they belong to the subfamily that includes the true eagles. Two extinct species of this genus have been reported from the Great Basin, from Fossil Lake and Smith Creek Cave. Today, Hawk Eagles can be found in both the Old World and the New; in the New World, they come no further north than tropical Mexico, where they exist on a diverse variety of small vertebrates. They have never been reported on the wing in North America.

An extinct species of Black Hawk, genus *Buteogallus,* has also been reported from Fossil Lake. The Common Black Hawk (*B. anthracinus*) breeds as far north as central Arizona. Extinct late Pleistocene species of this bird, however, are known not only from Fossil Lake, but also from the asphalt deposits of southern California, from New Mexico, and from Hawver Cave, northern California. Modern Black

Table 7-7. Late Pleistocene Vultures, Condors, and Teratorns Known from the Great Basin

Family	Species	Common name
Cathartidae	*Breagyps clarki*	Clark's Condor
	Coragyps occidentalis	Western Black Vulture
	Gymnogyps californianus	California Condor
Teratornithidae	*Teratornis incredibilis*	Incredible Teratorn
	Teratornis merriami	Merriam's Teratorn

Hawks rely heavily on small animals for their diet, ranging from crabs, lizards, and frogs to small birds.

North America now supports only three species of vultures and condors (birds of the family Cathartidae, or cathartids). These three are the Turkey Vulture, the Western Black Vulture, and, barely, the California Condor. The Great Basin supports only the Turkey Vulture. During the late Pleistocene, however, the Great Basin supported at least three species of vultures and condors: Clark's Condor, the Western Black Vulture, and the California Condor. In addition, this region also supported two species of teratorns, whose dietary adaptations are poorly understood (see Table 7-7).

The Turkey Vulture (*Cathartes aura*) has yet to be reported from the late Pleistocene Great Basin, even though it is common here today. This is probably no accident. Many years ago, Hildegarde Howard and Alden H. Miller observed that the remains of the now-extinct Western Black Vulture far outnumber those of the Turkey Vulture in the late Pleistocene deposits of Rancho La Brea. Turkey Vultures became abundant only as the Western Black Vulture declined in numbers. Although Great Basin data are scanty, the same may well have been true here. Since the Turkey Vulture is present in the late Pleistocene asphalt deposits of southern California, it was probably present, albeit relatively uncommon, in the late Pleistocene Great Basin as well. That it has yet to be found here follows from its relative rarity and from the small sample of late Pleistocene birds that is available from this region: rare things require relatively large samples to be detected.

When the Turkey Vulture is found in the late Pleistocene Great Basin, as it almost certainly will be, that will bring the total number of vultures, condors, and teratorns known from this region to six. Exactly how rich this aspect of the Great Basin avifauna was can be judged from the fact that only seven species of vultures and condors are found in the entire New World today.

It would be valuable to know whether or not the teratorns were scavengers; the fact that they had flapping, as opposed to soaring, flight does not help, since there are Old World vultures that both flap and scavenge. If they were not scavengers, the teratorns themselves might have opened feeding opportunities for at least the vultures by providing carcasses that could be scavenged.

No matter how the teratorns fed, the large number of species of vultures, condors, and teratorns in the late Pleistocene Great Basin raises a number of interesting ecological questions, none of which can be answered now. The fact that there were so many species of these birds here suggests that the mammal fauna of the time was not only rich in species, but also rich in numbers of individual animals. The large size of Clark's Condor and the California Condor suggest the presence of thermal updrafts substantial enough to allow the soaring flight of these birds, unless their soaring depended totally on upslope winds. Since many have suggested that the growth of the pluvial lakes was accompanied by cooler summers and greater cloud cover (see Chapter 5), it would be of interest to know whether the number of vultures and condors decreased as the pluvial lakes grew, and increased as they shrank. It would be of value to know whether there might have been a north-south decline in both the number of species and the number of individuals of these birds, just as there may have been a north-south decline in intensity of cloud cover (if that may be read from the evidence of the pluvial lakes themselves). On the other hand, since intense winds can play the same role as thermals in supporting the flight of these birds, and since thermals are most important to vultures of open terrain, this intriguing question may not have a meaningful answer.

We can but wonder as to the competitive relationships among these birds. Today, as many as six different species of Old World vultures may be found feeding on a single carcass in Nairobi National Park. Could we have viewed a similar scene toward the end of the Pleistocene near what is now Great Basin National Park? The vultures and condors of the late Pleistocene differed dramatically in size, with the smaller Black Vulture and Turkey Vulture (assuming it was there) on the one hand, and the huge Clark's Condor and California Condor on the other. In Africa today, larger vultures take wing later in the day than smaller ones, as they wait for the development of the more substantial thermal updrafts they require. In communal roosts of Turkey and Black vultures in eastern North America, both species wait for the development of thermals before taking flight, but Turkey Vultures leave well before Black Vultures. In addition, dominance among species of vultures tends to be determined by body size. If we waited by the carcass of a camel in the Snake Valley during the late Pleistocene, would the smaller vultures arrive first, followed later by the larger, and probably dominant, condors? If all were present, would their different morphologies lead them to feed on different parts of the carcass, as different species of modern vultures often do? Further research might provide answers to all these questions, answers that might help explain why so many of these birds became extinct.

It is often argued that the decline of the vultures, condors, and teratorns in western North America somewhere near the end of the Pleistocene follows almost automatically from the extinction of the mammals on which they depended for food. Although this line of reasoning most certainly provides part of the answer, I do not think it provides all of it. There were elk and bison in the Great Basin during the Holocene, living in areas they apparently did not occupy historically. There were mountain sheep, pronghorn, and black-tailed deer. Perhaps these sizable mammals could not support six species of vultures and their allies, but why not two or three? Why did the Western Black Vulture become extinct while the Turkey Vulture became abundant? After all, where they occupy the same region today, these birds routinely roost and feed together.

Those who have argued that the decline of the mammals caused the decline of the birds have focused on birds that belong to genera that became extinct, and have probably been misled as a result. If we look only at the extinct genera, then Clark's Condor (*Breagyps*) and the teratorns (*Teratornis*) are all there are to worry about. But if we look at the full range of species that became extinct, we must also account for the retreat of the California Condor from the Great Basin and the extinction of the Western Black Vulture. To say that all of this happened because the large mammals became extinct is too facile an answer. The climates to which these birds were adapted disappeared as well, and a full account of the loss of the vultures, condors, and teratorns will most certainly have to take climatic change into account.

And, finally, what of the dire wolf? I noted earlier that the feeding behavior of the sabertooth was such as to provide ample opportunities for carnivores that scavenged, and that the abundance of sabertooth remains in the Great Basin was hard to reconcile with the fact that the dire wolf has yet to be found here. That, I suggested, implies that our list of extinct Pleistocene mammals in the Great Basin is probably incomplete. In Africa, David Houston has shown that the abundant griffon vultures gain only a small proportion of their diets from predator kills. However, sabertooth feeding behavior appears to have been so inefficient that their kills probably would have helped support scavenging birds as well as dire wolves. The fact that so many species of these birds were here during the Pleistocene makes it all the more likely that the next large, carefully studied paleontological site in the Great Basin will have dire wolves in it, alongside who knows what else.

Altered Late Pleistocene Distributions of Existing Great Basin Mammals

A glance at the distribution of mammals within the Great Basin today reveals a marked oddity. There are a number of small mammals that are found on Great Basin mountains, but not in the valleys that separate them. There are approximately 16 of these species, ranging from pikas and chipmunks to wolverines (see Table 7-8, which provides both common and scientific names for these mammals).

Table 7-8. Montane Mammals of the Great Basin[a]

Species	Common name
Sorex vagrans	Vagrant shrew
Sorex palustris	Water shrew
Ochotona princeps	Pika
Sylvilagus nuttallii	Nuttall's cottontail
Lepus townsendii	White-tailed jack rabbit
Tamias amoenus	Yellow-pine chipmunk
Tamias dorsalis	Cliff chipmunk
Tamias umbrinus	Uinta chipmunk
Marmota flaviventris	Yellow-bellied marmot
Spermophilus beldingi	Belding's ground squirrel
Spermophilus lateralis	Golden-mantled ground squirrel
Neotoma cinerea	Bushy-tailed packrat
Microtus longicaudus	Long-tailed vole
Zapus princeps	Western jumping mouse
Mustela erminea	Short-tailed weasel (ermine)
Gulo gulo	Wolverine

[a]After Grayson (1987b).

If only mammals like wolverines were involved, accounting for their distribution would not pose any great difficulties. Today, wolverines are found in the Great Basin only in the White Mountains, just across Owens Valley from the Sierra Nevada. The infrequent sightings of this carnivore in the White Mountains may reflect animals that cross from the Sierra Nevada during the winter. In fact, mammalogist E. Raymond Hall once suggested that a number of the small mammals that appear isolated on Great Basin mountains may have gotten there by crossing apparently inhospitable valleys during winter. However, it now appears unlikely that this could have been the case in most instances.

The argument that makes this appear unlikely was developed by ecologist James H. Brown. Brown analyzed in detail the distribution of montane mammals (he called them "boreal" mammals) across 19 Great Basin mountain ranges. Brown selected these ranges by applying four criteria. First, he looked only at ranges that had at least one peak above 9,800′ in elevation. Second, he examined only ranges separated from one another by valleys that are at least five miles wide beneath an elevation of 7,500′.Third, he eliminated all those ranges north of the main distribution of piñon-juniper woodland in the Great Basin. Fourth, he included only those ranges whose small mammals faunas appeared to be reasonably well known.

By choosing high and well-separated ranges, Brown hoped to ensure that he was dealing with isolated mountains. By choosing only mountains within the main distribution of piñon-juniper, he hoped to ensure that the ranges he looked at held reasonably comparable habitats, so that differences he saw in the montane mammals of those ranges would not simply reflect differences in major aspects of the vegetation they supported.

The list of 19 ranges that Brown examined is given in Table 7-9; their locations are shown in Figure 7-5 (in 1971, when he first did this analysis, Brown used a 10,000′ criterion, so his earliest list did not include the Desatoya and Sheep ranges). This table also shows the area contained by a given range above 7,500′ in elevation, the highest peak in that range, and the distance to the nearest "continent."

his last variable—distance to nearest "continent"—needs explanation. Brown treated his 19 ranges as if they were true islands. As he observed, much of the Great Basin is "covered by a vast sea of sagebrush desert, interrupted at irregular intervals by isolated mountain ranges" (1971: 467). In this view, the tall, isolated ranges of the Great Basin are true habitat islands, much as oceanic islands are habitat islands. Just as the vertebrates that occupy oceanic islands must have come from somewhere else, Brown assumed that Great Basin mountains must have gotten their montane mammals from the nearest "mainlands"—in this case, the Sierra Nevada and the Rocky Mountains. Thus, distance to the nearest "continent" in Table 7-9 means the distance between a given mountain range and either the Sierra Nevada or the Rockies. The distribution of the montane mammals analyzed by Brown across these 19 ranges is shown in Table 7-10.

Biogeographers routinely divide islands into two types: landbridge islands, which once had a land connection to the mainland, and oceanic islands, which have never been so connected. The Hawaiian islands, for instance, are oceanic islands: they have never been connected by land to any continent. Islands in the Bering Strait, on the other hand, are landbridge islands: they were connected to one another by land during the Pleistocene (see Chapter 3). Analyses of the distribution of vertebrates on islands of both sorts have shown that, other things being equal, larger islands within an island chain have greater numbers of species than smaller ones. There are several reasons why this should be the case, including the fact that larger islands may support more diverse habitats and thus have more species, and that larger islands form larger targets for individuals that are dispersing from elsewhere, and thus have a better chance of being colonized.

Within a set of islands, the relationship between island area and the number of species on those islands takes the form of a curve, and so is called the "species-area curve." That curve is generally well described by an equation of the form

$$S = CA^z$$

where S is the number of species on an island, A is the area of that island, and C is a constant that varies with the region and with the animals involved. The final variable, z, is the slope of the relationship, describing how fast S, the number of species, changes with changes in A, the area of the island. Although this relationship is curvilinear, it becomes linear when both area and numbers of species are expressed logarithmically. It is in this transformed, linear form that the relationships are generally shown (the "log species–log area curve").

In 1971, Brown showed that the relationship between the number of montane mammal species and area in his sample

Table 7-9. Mountain Ranges Examined by Brown (1971, 1978)[a]

Range	Area above 7,500′ (square miles)	Highest peak (feet)	Nearest "continent" (miles)
Toiyabe-Shoshone (1)	684	11,788	110
Ruby (2)	364	11,387	173
Toquima-Monitor (3)	1,178	11,941	114
White-Inyo (4)	738	14,246	10
Snake (5)	417	13,063	89
Oquirrh (6)	82	10,620	19
Deep Creek (7)	223	12,087	104
Schell Creek–Egan (8)	1,020	11,883	114
Stansbury (9)	56	11,031	39
Desatoya (10)	83	9,814	83
Roberts (11)	52	10,133	216
White Pine (12)	262	11,513	150
Diamond (13)	159	10,614	190
Spring (14)	125	11,912	125
Grant–Quinn Canyon (15)	150	11,298	138
Spruce–South Pequop (16)	49	10,262	156
Pilot (17)	12	10,716	114
Sheep (18)	54	9,912	86
Panamint (19)	47	11,049	52

[a]Numbers in parentheses indicate ranges in Table 7-10.

Figure 7-5. The location of the mountain ranges used by J. H. Brown (1971, 1978) in his analysis of the distribution of montane mammals in the Great Basin. DE = Desatoya; SR = Sheep Range. See Table 2-1 for key to other ranges.

Table 7-10. Distribution of Montane Mammals across Great Basin Mountains[a]

	Range																			
Species	**1**	**2**	**3**	**4**	**5**	**6**	**7**	**8**	**9**	**10**	**11**	**12**	**13**	**14**	**15**	**16**	**17**	**18**	**19**	**Total**
Neotoma cinerea	X	X	X	X	X	X	X	X	X	X	X	X	X	X		X	X	X	X	18
Tamias umbrinus	X	X	X	X	X	X	X	X	X	X	X	X	X	X	X	X		X		17
Tamias dorsalis	X		X	X	X	X	X	X	X	X		X	X	X	X	X	X	X	X	17
Spermophilus lateralis	X	X	X	X	X		X	X		X	X	X	X	X	X	X	X			15
Sylvilagus nuttallii	X	X	X	X	X		X	X		X	X	X	X	X	X				X	14
Marmota flaviventris	X	X	X	X	X	X	X	X	X	X	X	X	X							13
Microtus longicaudus	X	X	X	X	X	X	X	X	X	X	X	X			X					13
Sorex vagrans	X	X	X	X	X	X	X	X	X					X						10
Sorex palustris	X	X	X	X	X	X			X		X									8
Mustela erminea	X			X	X	X	X		X											6
Ochotona princeps	X	X	X	X						X										5
Zapus princeps	X	X	X			X					X									5
Spermophilus beldingi	X	X	X																	3
Lepus townsendii		X				X														2
Total	13	12	12	11	10	10	9	8	8	8	8	7	6	6	5	4	3	3	3	

[a]See Table 7-9 for key to ranges and references.

of Great Basin mountain ranges was linear in logarithmic form, just as he suspected it would be. Figure 7-6 shows this relationship not as Brown plotted it, but as we now know it to exist, with 20 more years of fieldwork behind us.

The slope of this line (z = 0.288) is important. The slope suggests how fast species are added as the area of the islands increases: in relationships with similar values for C, higher slopes mean faster increases; lower slopes mean slower increases. In mainland settings, slopes for mammals tend to be much lower (<0.20) than they are in the contexts provided by islands (where they often fall between 0.20 and 0.35). For instance, Brown calculated the log species–log area curve for mammals in four areas of the Sierra Nevada, and found the slope of this relationship to be 0.12, less than half of what it appears to be for Great Basin mountains.

The slope of log species–log area curves for mammals tends to be far higher for landbridge islands than for

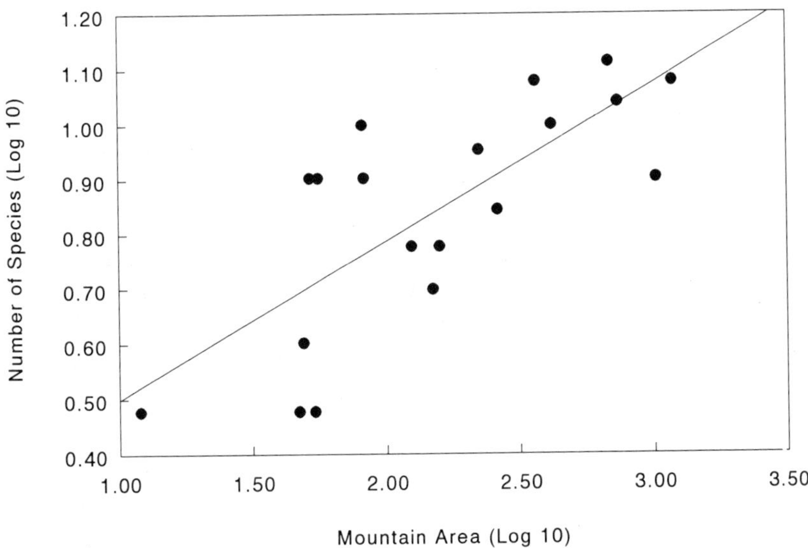

Figure 7-6. The log species–log area curve for montane mammals in the Great Basin, based on current knowledge of the distribution of those mammals. The equation for this relationship is Species = $1.63(\text{Area})^{0.288}$.

mainlands for a simple reason. The probability of extinction for any species in an area is highly dependent on the size of the population of that species. Species with few individuals tend to go locally extinct far more readily than abundant ones. If a rare species goes extinct on a truly isolated patch of habitat, the chances of recolonization are low; if the same species becomes extinct on the mainland, the chances of recolonization are far better, since there are likely to be neighboring populations from which colonists can be drawn.

In short, because the smaller patches of habitat offered by landbridge islands support smaller populations of mammals, extinction rates are higher here. In island settings, recolonization can be extremely difficult. In mainland settings, recolonization is often easy. As a result, species-area curves have higher slopes on landbridge islands than on mainlands.

The slope of the log species–log area curve for montane mammals on Great Basin islands (0.288) is very similar to slopes that have been calculated for islands (generally between 0.20 and 0.35). It is much higher than those generally calculated for mainlands (<0.20). The shape of the species-area curve for these 19 Great Basin mountain ranges, then, suggested to Brown that these mountains are true islands, well isolated from the Sierra Nevada and the the Rockies by the "vast sea of sagebrush desert" that separates them.

Brown did far more than simply calculate the species-area curve for these 19 ranges, however. He also looked at a wide variety of other variables related to the probability of colonization of these ranges by montane mammals.

The nearer an island is to a mainland source of potential colonizers, the greater the number of species it will have, simply because the chances of colonization from the mainland increase as the mainland is approached. Assuming that the mainlands in the Great Basin case are the Sierra Nevada and the Rockies, Brown showed that there is no significant correlation between the number of species on Great Basin mountains and the distances of those mountains to either the Sierra Nevada or the Rockies.

Reasoning that it is possible that Great Basin ranges have obtained their montane mammals from other, nearby, Great Basin ranges, Brown also showed that there was no significant relationship between the number of montane mammal species on Great Basin ranges and the distance to the nearest Great Basin mountain with a greater number of species.

Reasoning that the elevations of the valleys separating the mountains may play a critical role in allowing the mammals to pass from mountain to mountain, with higher valleys allowing easier passage than lower ones, he looked at this variable as well. Again, he found no correlation between the number of montane mammal species on a given mountain and the elevation of the passes that separate that mountain from nearby ones.

These and other variables examined by Brown all seemed to lead to the same conclusions: the montane mammals on Great Basin mountains are now fully isolated from one another. As Brown (1971:475) put it, "at the present time the rate of colonization of the islands is effectively zero . . . the desert valleys of the Great Basin are virtually absolute barriers to dispersal by small boreal mammals." Brown concluded that all of these mammals reached all of the islands during the Pleistocene. Since that time, he argued, there have been extinctions, but no new colonizations.

Brown's 1971 analysis was deeply insightful. From a detailed examination of the modern distribution of montane mammals in the Great Basin, he was able to conclude that these mammals reached the mountains during the Pleistocene, presumably colonizing most or all of them; that the opportunities for colonization ended when the Pleistocene ended; and that, since then, montane mammals have become differentially extinct across the ranges. In this view, for instance, pikas reached both the Toquima Range and the Roberts Mountains during the Pleistocene. They have managed to survive in the Toquima Range, but became extinct in the Roberts.

I will examine the paleontological evidence that can be brought to bear on Brown's argument both in this chapter and in Chapter 8. Before I do that, though, I note that 20 more years of work have suggested that there are two problems with Brown's model. In addition, there are several modifications that need to be made in light of paleontological data. The modifications I will treat later; the problems I deal with now.

The first of these problems stems from the fact that Brown argued that montane mammals colonized the Great Basin during the Pleistocene, and that this colonization came from either the Sierra Nevada or the Rockies. This problem with this argument is parallel to that which I discussed for Great Basin subalpine conifers in Chapter 6. In particular, some Great Basin montane mammals may have been here all along, only to have become isolated, and in some cases extinct, after the Pleistocene ended. In addi-

Table 7-11. Decreasing Value of Slopes for the Log Species–Log Area Curves for Montane Mammals on Great Basin Mountains[a]

Year	Number of ranges	Slope	Correlation[a]	Reference
A. Values as published				
1971	17	0.428	0.822	J. H. Brown (1971)
1978	19	0.326	0.846	J. H. Brown (1978)
1991	19	0.309	0.761	Cutler (1991)
1993	19	0.288	0.744	Grayson and Livingston (1993)
B. Values recalculated for the initial 17 ranges only				
1971	17	0.428	0.822	J. H. Brown (1971)
1978	17	0.319	0.862	J. H. Brown (1978)
1991	17	0.300	0.775	Cutler (1991)
1993	17	0.273	0.756	Grayson and Livingston (1993)

[a] All correlation coefficients have probabilities of <0.01.

tion, it is also possible that, if colonization occurred, it came from the north as well as from the east and west. In fact, I would not be at all surprised to find that Great Basin montane mammals have a complex set of origins: some may be eastern, some western, some northern, and some complete natives.

Second, Brown had to assume that the data he had on the distribution of montane mammals across Great Basin ranges was essentially complete. If life scientists did not make assumptions of this sort, we would get little done.

However, there is good reason to be concerned about the strength of our knowledge of the distribution of montane mammals in the Great Basin. In the summer of 1991, for instance, my colleagues Stephanie Livingston and Peter Wigand, of the Desert Research Institute, and I visited the Roberts Mountains in central Nevada (see Figure 7-5). While Wigand searched for packrat middens, Livingston and I attempted to add to the list of montane mammals known from this range. Without setting a single trap, we added four: Nuttall's cottontail, yellow-bellied marmot, golden-mantled ground squirrel, and bushy-tailed packrat. In a few days, we doubled the known montane mammal fauna of this range, from four species to eight. It is likely that we would have found more if we had trapped as well. After leaving the Roberts, we spent a few hours in the Diamond Mountains. Here, in one afternoon, we discovered two montane mammals that had never been reported from this range: Nuttall's cottontail and yellow-bellied marmot. This increased the number of montane mammals known from this range by 50%, from four species to six.

If we could accomplish this in a few days, without trapping, it is reasonable to worry that much of what has been written about the distribution of montane mammals in the Great Basin—including my own work—reflects gaps in our knowledge of these mammals as much as it reflects actual gaps in their distributions. This is a potentially serious problem.

It is, in fact, fairly easy to show the impact that our slowly increasing knowledge has had on the slope of the log species–log area curve for montane mammals on Great Basin mountains. Table 7-11 shows the dramatic way in which the slope of this relationship has decreased as the years have passed since Brown first presented his argument. Part A of this table shows the slopes as they have been published. To show that the decrease in the magnitude of the slope has not been caused by the increase in the number of ranges that have been used in these analyses, I have recalculated all the slopes using just the original 17 ranges. The results are shown in part B.

As time has gone on, these slopes have decreased tremendously. The current value is not inconsistent with Brown's argument, but it is legitimate to worry that the slope reflects where mammalogists have worked—such tempting, massive ranges as the Toquimas, Rubies, and Whites—as well as it reflects the true distribution of montane mammals on these ranges. Significant amounts of fieldwork will be needed to discover the true nature of the distribution of montane mammals in the Great Basin, with particular attention paid to such mountains as the Diamond, Pilot, Roberts, and Spruce ranges, whose mammal faunas have yet to be well described.

That said, one of the great strengths of Brown's model is that it is eminently testable using data on the past distributions of mammals, whether those data come from paleontological or archaeological sites.

First, his model predicts that montane mammals currently isolated on Great Basin mountains must once have occupied the lowlands that intervene between the mountains. This requirement follows from Brown's assertion that Great Basin mountains received their montane mammals from the Sierra Nevada and the Rockies. Since none of the mammals on this list flies (bats are excluded for just that reason), the valleys must have provided the corridors by which they reached the mountains.

This prediction has a tricky aspect to it. If we are unable to find any of the montane mammals in low-elevation, valley settings during the Pleistocene, then Brown must be wrong. However, if we do discover montane mammals in these settings, then he may be either right or wrong. This is true simply because low-elevation Pleistocene records for montane mammals in low-elevation settings will tell us only that these mammals were in the corridors. They will not tell us where they came from. As with many complex hypotheses, Brown's model will be easier to prove wrong than to show correct.

Second, the model predicts that montane mammals found on only some of the mountains today should have been present on other ranges in the past. This prediction follows from Brown's argument that "all the islands were inhabited by a common pool of species at some time in the past and subsequent extinctions have reduced the number of species to their present levels" (1971:475). In this view, dispersing montane mammals radiated outward from the Sierra Nevada and/or Rockies during the Pleistocene, each species reaching all of the islands. Although it is fully possible that *all* of the species did not reach *all* of the mountains, the prediction is clear. Mountains that only have a subset of the montane mammals today should have had all or nearly all of them in the past.

For instance, of the full set of 14 species analyzed by Brown, the Snake Range has only 10 (see Table 7-10). The missing mammals—assuming they really are missing, and not simply unreported—must have been on these ranges in the past. These missing mammals are pika, white-tailed jack rabbit, Belding's ground squirrel, and western jumping mouse. Excavations in fossil-rich archaeological or paleontological sites must reveal the presence of these mammals here in the past, or Brown must be wrong.

As with the first prediction, this one also cuts deeper in one direction than it does in the other. Failure to find a diverse variety of now-absent montane mammals across a number of Great Basin mountain ranges in the past would clearly show that a major aspect of Brown's model—widespread colonization followed by local extinction—was wrong. Finding that those mammals were present in the past would lend truly strong support to his argument that the ranges were once stocked by a common set of montane mammals, and that differential extinction across the ranges has occurred since the time of isolation. Such a discovery would not, however, provide any insight into the geographic origins of these mammals.

The third prediction that can be derived from Brown's model is that there have been species of boreal mammals on Great Basin mountains in the past that are no longer on any ranges here today. This prediction is actually very similar to the second one, except that it deals with mammals that are not simply missing from some of the ranges, but are missing from all of them.

How this prediction follows from Brown's model can be seen from Figure 7-7. The number of ranges occupied by a given montane mammal varies from 18 down to 2. If white-tailed jack rabbits were to become extinct on the Ruby Mountains and Oquirrh Range, they would represent mammals that once existed on Great Basin mountains, but that no longer do. Thus, this third prediction simply follows from the possibility that there have been montane mammals on Great Basin ranges that have become extinct across all of them.

If this third prediction is not met, then Brown's model is not harmed, since the model does not require that there be species in Great Basin mountains that have become extinct across all the ranges. If the prediction is met, however, then the extinction aspects of Brown's model gain great support.

The fourth prediction is straightforward, but extremely difficult to test. This prediction is that there have been no Holocene colonizations of the mountains by montane mammals. This requirement follows from Brown's argument that the colonizations were Pleistocene in age, and

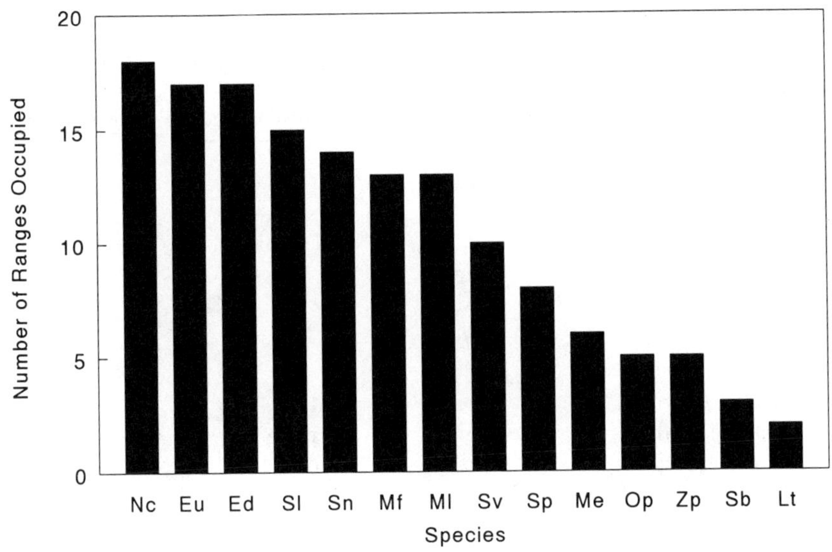

Figure 7-7. The number of mountain ranges occupied by montane mammals in the Great Basin, based on current knowledge of their distributions. Nc, *Neotoma cinerea;* Eu, *Eutamias umbrinus;* Ed, *Eutamias dorsalis;* Sl, *Spermophilus lateralis;* Sn, *Sylvilagus nuttallii;* Mf, *Marmota flaviventris;* Ml, *Microtus longicaudus;* Sv, *Sorex vagrans;* Sp, *Sorex palustris;* Me, *Mustela erminea;* Op, *Ochotona princeps;* Zp, *Zapus princeps;* Sb, *Spermophilus beldingi;* Lt, *Lepus townsendii.*

that the ranges have been isolated since then. As I will discuss further in Chapter 8, this aspect of Brown's model is in need of modification. For many of the montane mammals, the valleys in at least the northern half of the Great Basin remained habitable during the early Holocene, 10,000–7,500 years ago. This is a relatively minor matter, however, and Brown's model really requires that the ranges be isolated now, and that they have been isolated long enough for differential extinction to have taken place across them.

This fourth prediction, then, requires that there be no evidence of the movement of montane mammals between mountain ranges for thousands of years. If there is evidence for significant amounts of movement between mountains, then Brown's model is wrong. Unfortunately, this is an extremely difficult proposition to test.

These are the four predictions with implications for the nature of the late Pleistocene and Holocene faunal record that can be derived from Brown's model. All are directed toward testing that aspect of his argument that maintains that Great Basin ranges were stocked with a common set of montane mammals, that these ranges then became isolated, and that differential extinction of the mammals then occurred across these ranges. None directly addresses the more difficult issue of understanding where these mammals came from in the first place. Here, I will discuss the Pleistocene paleontological evidence that can be brought to bear on these predictions. In Chapter 8, I will discuss the Holocene data that relate to Brown's model.

MONTANE MAMMALS IN PLEISTOCENE LOWLANDS

In 1978 Brown defined a Great Basin "montane island" as a mountain range with at least one peak above 9,800′, and separated from all other such ranges by valleys at least five miles wide below 7,500′ elevation. As a result, I include as Great Basin "lowlands" all areas that do not meet these criteria. Brown excluded from consideration areas north of the Humboldt River and Great Salt Lake, in order to avoid analyzing regions that lacked well-developed piñon-juniper woodland. I will extend my look beyond Brown's, and discuss late Pleistocene montane mammals in lowlands throughout the Great Basin.

So defined, eight species of montane mammals on Brown's list have been securely identified from Pleistocene deposits

Table 7-12. Montane Mammals Known from Late Pleistocene Low-Elevation Settings in the Great Basin

Species	Number of sites
Ochotona princeps	12
Marmota flaviventris	11
Neotoma cinerea	4
Spermophilus lateralis	4
Lepus townsendii	1
Mustela erminea	1
Sylvilagus nuttallii	1
Tamias dorsalis	1
Tamias amoenus	1

Table 7-13. Pleistocene Extralimital Records for Great Basin Montane Mammals: Lowlands[a]

Location	Elevation (feet)	Species	Age (years ago)	Distance (miles)	Reference(s)
Eetza Mountain, NV					
Hidden Cave (1)	4,105	*Marmota flaviventris*	21,000–<1,500	15 SW	7
		Neotoma cinerea		5 NW	
Eleana Range, NV					
ER2–7,10,11r★ (2)	5,940	*Ochotona princeps*	10,800–17,100	40 NE	8, 21
Fort Rock Basin, OR					
Connley Caves (3)	4,445	*Ochotona princeps*	11,200–7,200	20 NW	6
Ivanpah Mountains, CA					
Kokoweef Cave (4)	5,810	*Ochotona princeps*	Late Wisconsin/Early Holocene	170 NW	5, 20
		Marmota flaviventris		155 NW	
		Spermophilus lateralis		60 NNE	
Las Vegas Valley, NV					
Corn Creek PR3★ (5)	3,805	*Ochotona princeps*	14,300	170 W	8, 18, 22
Mescal Range, CA					
Antelope Cave (6)	5,800	*Ochotona princeps*	Late Wisconsin	170 NW	19
		Marmota flaviventris		170 NW	
Mescal Cave (7)	5,085	*Ochotona princeps*	Late Wisconsin?	170 NW	2, 12, 16
		Marmota flaviventris		155 NW	
		Spermophilus lateralis		40 N	
Mormon Mountain, NV					
Mormon Mountain Cave (8)	4,500	*Ochotona princeps*	Late Wisconsin?	140 NE	8, 11
		Sylvilagus nuttallii		65 NW	
		Tamias amoenus		185 NW	
		Marmota flaviventris		85 NE	
		Spermophilus lateralis		85 SW	
		Neotoma cinerea		55 SW	
Newberry Mountains, CA					
Newberry Cave (9)	2,395	*Marmota flaviventris*	Late Wisconsin?	115 NW	3, 4
Providence Mountains, CA					
Mitchell Caverns (10)	4,345	*Marmota flaviventris*	Late Wisconsin/Early Holocene	155 NW	12
Silver Island Mountains, UT					
Danger Cave (11)	4,310	*Marmota flaviventris*	11,000–10,000	70 W	9
		Neotoma cinerea	11,000–9,000[b]		
Snake Valley, NV and UT					
Crystal Ball Cave (12)	5,775	*Ochotona princeps*	Late Wisconsin?	110 SW	10
		Lepus townsendii		80 WSW	
		Marmota flaviventris		15 SW	
		Tamias dorsalis		15 SW	
		Neotoma cinerea		15 SW	
Garrison GA1★ (13)	5,380	*Ochotona princeps*	12,230	60 SE	15, 22, 23
Garrison GA2★ (13)	5,380	*Ochotona princeps*	13,480	60 SE	15, 22, 23
Owl Cave Two (14)	5,600	*Ochotona princeps*	Late Wisconsin?	100 SE	1, 13, 24
		Marmota flaviventris		15 NW	
		Spermophilus lateralis		10 NNW	
		Lepus townsendii		75 NNW	
		Mustela erminea		10 W	

Table 7-13 ***(continued)***

Location	Elevation (feet)	Species	Age (years ago)	Distance (miles)	Reference(s)
Spotted Range, NV					
Mercury Ridge* (15)	4,100	*Marmota flaviventris*	12,700	100 SW	25
Sulphur Spring Range					
Mineral Hill Cave (16)		*Ochotona princeps*	Late Wisconsin?	35 NE	14
Utah Lake, UT (17)		*Thomomys talpoides*	Late Wisconsin	20 NE	17

Notes: a, Numbers in parentheses indicate sites in Figures 7-8 and 7-9. The distance column provides the distance to the nearest known modern populations. *b,* 6 (of 125) specimens from this site are younger than 9,000 years.

*Packrat middens.

References: 1, Birnie (1986); 2, Brattstrom (1958); 3, C. A. Davis and Smith (1981); 4, Goodwin (1989); 5, Goodwin and Reynolds (1989a); 6, Grayson (1977a, 1979); 7, Grayson (1985); 8, Grayson (1987b); 9, Grayson (1988a); 10, Heaton (1985); 11, Jefferson (1982); 12, Jefferson (1991); 13, E. M. Mead and Mead (1989); 14, McGuire (1980); 15, J. I. Mead et al. (1982); 16, Mehringer and Ferguson (1969); 17, M. E. Nelson and Madsen (1980); 18, Quade (1986); 19, Reynolds et al. (1991a); 20, Reynolds et al. (1991b); 21, Spaulding (1985); 22, R. S. Thompson (1984); 23, R. S. Thompson and Mead (1982); 24, Turnmire (1987); 25, P. V. Wells and Jorgensen (1964).

in lowland Great Basin settings (others have been identified less securely, and are not mentioned here). These records are all "extralimital" in the sense that they come from areas outside the current distributions of the species involved. A list of the species for which low-elevation extralimital records are available, as well as the number of sites that have provided those records, is given in Table 7-12; details on the ages and locations of those records are given in Table 7-13. These tables include all the published records of which I am aware. Others may exist, but if they

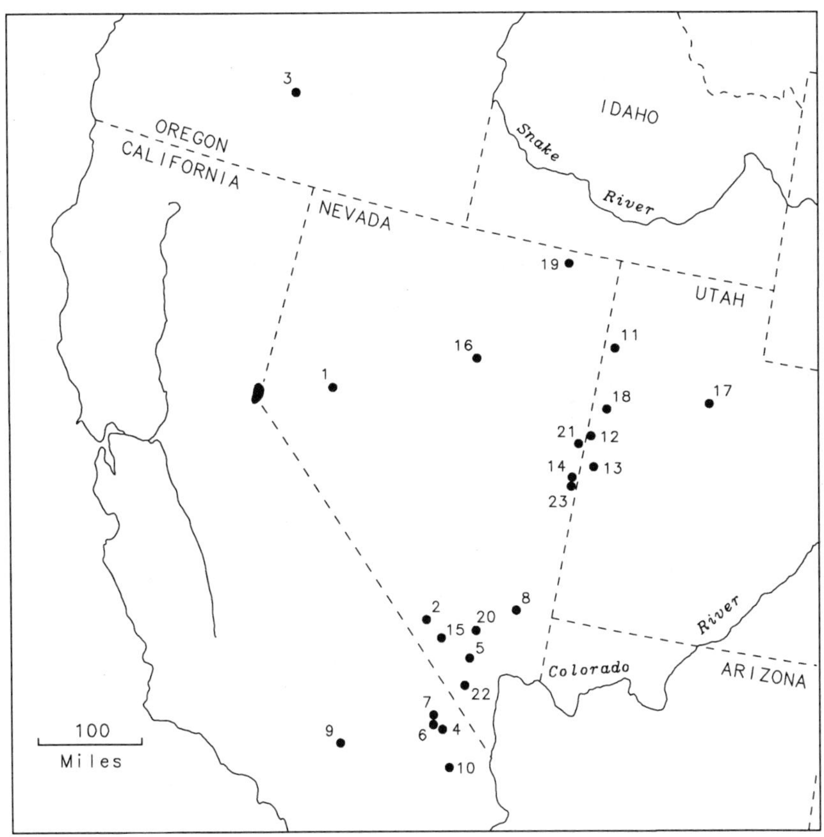

Figure 7-8. The locations of sites that have provided extralimital late Pleistocene records for montane mammals in the Great Basin. See Tables 7-13–7-15 for key.

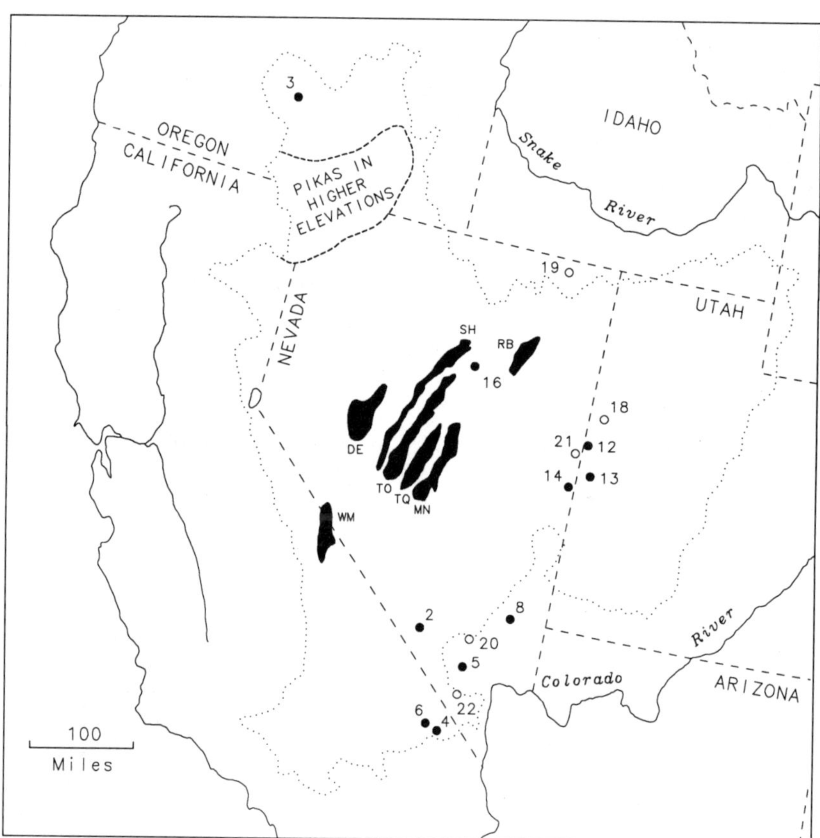

Figure 7-9. The modern distribution of pikas, and of late Pleistocene sites that contain the remains of pikas, in the Great Basin. Sites indicated by closed circles are located in lowland settings; sites indicated by open circles are in mountain settings (see Tables 7-13 and 7-14 for key to sites). Ranges in which pikas occur are shown in black (see Figure 7-5 and Table 2-1 for key). The distribution of pikas in the Sierra Nevada and Rocky Mountains is not shown.

do, there cannot be many of them. Figure 7-8 shows the locations of the sites listed in this table.

The most detailed information exists for pikas. In part, this is because the bones and fecal pellets of these small, rabbit-like animals often become incorporated in packrat middens. As a result, they have been identified and dated during research projects whose prime goal was to decipher Great Basin vegetational history.

The late Pleistocene record documents the fact that low-elevation populations of pikas were widespread in the Great Basin at this time, from the Fort Rock Basin in the north to the Mojave Desert in the south (see Figure 7-9). Not surprisingly, the distance between the now-extinct low-elevation populations and the closest existing populations of pikas increases from north to south. Today, pikas are found within 20 miles of the Connley Caves (Fort Rock Basin), but no closer than 170 miles to Mescal and Kokoweef caves (Mohave Desert).

Yellow-bellied marmots are now discontinuously distributed across much of the Great Basin, but they are rarely found in low-elevation settings, and then primarily in the northern Great Basin; they are entirely absent from large expanses of western Utah and from the Mojave Desert. Eleven late Pleistocene records document that they, too, were widespread in lower elevations, including the Mojave Desert during the late Pleistocene.

Much the same can be said for bushy-tailed packrats and golden-mantled ground squirrels. The records for the golden-mantled ground squirrel are particularly interesting. Mescal and Kokoweef caves both contain what appear to be late Pleistocene-aged specimens of this species (the dating is not secure, and they may be early Holocene). Geographically, these caves fall between two modern, isolated subspecies of golden-mantled ground squirrels, one of which lives in the Spring Range of southern Nevada, the other occupying the San Bernardino Mountains of southern California (see Figure 7-10). The Mescal and Kokoweef cave specimens may well reflect the time when, prior to the isolation of these two recent subspecies, golden-mantled ground squirrels were continuously distributed across this region.

Low-elevation records for other montane mammals included by Brown in his analysis are sparse. Nuttall's

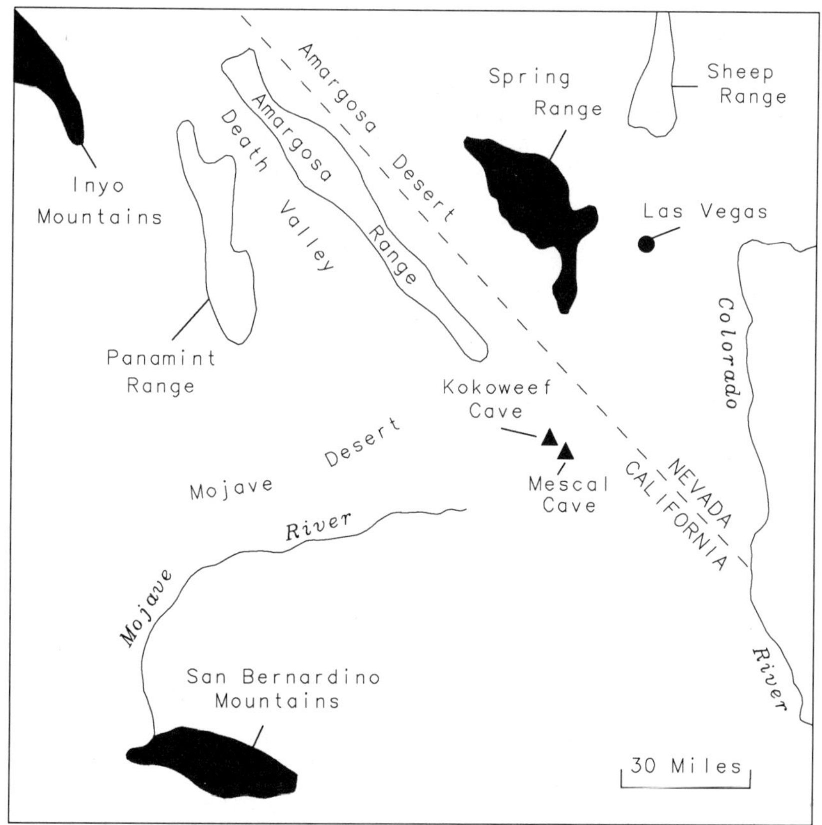

Figure 7-10. The modern distribution of golden-mantled ground squirrels in the southern Great Basin (in black), and the location of Mescal and Kokoweef caves. Distributional data from E. R. Hall (1981).

cottontail, white-tailed jack rabbit, cliff chipmunk, and short-tailed weasel are all known from one site each. However, although the records are sparse, they certainly suggest the presence of these animals in low-elevation areas in which they no longer exist. There is, however, a chance that some may represent animals transported by raptors from higher elevations to the caves in which they were found.

Brown did not include the yellow-pine chipmunk (*Tamias amoenus*) in his analysis. Within the Great Basin today, however, these chipmunks are found only in the White Mountains of eastern California, in the Pine Forest Range of far northern Nevada, and in south-central Oregon. Given this distribution, it is remarkable that the yellow-pine chipmunk has been identified from Mormon Mountain Cave in southern Nevada. Assuming that the identification is correct (fossil chipmunks can be extremely difficult to identify), then the late Pleistocene Mormon Mountain population was living some 185 miles from the closest modern populations, which occur in the White Mountains. This is the largest such range change known among Great Basin montane mammals.

The paleontological record thus documents the presence of a wide variety of now-montane mammals living in low-elevation settings in the Great Basin during the late Pleistocene. Just as Brown's model requires, these mammals were living in the low-elevation corridors between massive mountain ranges before the Pleistocene came to an end.

MONTANE MAMMALS IN PLEISTOCENE MOUNTAINS

Brown's thesis also predicts that montane mammals should have existed on Great Basin mountain ranges where they no longer exist. It is, of course, fully possible that the movement of some or all of these mammals into the mountains from the lowlands occurred as the Pleistocene was ending, or perhaps even later. However, it seems highly likely that, if Brown's view is correct, they would have been on at least the lower flanks of these ranges during the late Pleistocene.

Far less support is available for this aspect of Brown's argument than is available for its lowland counterpart. In fact, only the record for pikas supports this prediction. The

Table 7-14. Pleistocene Extralimital Records for Great Basin Montane Mammals: Mountains[a]

Location	Elevation (feet)	Species	Age (years B.P.)	Distance (miles)	Reference(s)
Deep Creek Range, UT					
Granite Canyon GC1★ (18)	6,790	*Ochotona princeps*	13,620	100 NW	6, 7
Jarbidge Mountains					
Deer Creek Cave (19)	5,800	*Ochotona princeps*	10,085–9,670	60 S	8
Sheep Range, NV					
Flaherty Mesa FM1★ (20)	5,800	*Ochotona princeps*	20,390	135 E	1, 5
Spires SP2★ (20)	6,700	*Ochotona princeps*	18,000	135 E	1, 5
Snake Range, NV					
Arch Cave AC2A★ (21)	6,495	*Ochotona princeps*	34,040	85 NW	6
Council Hall Cave (21)	6,690	*Ochotona princeps*	13,040–23,900	85 NW	4, 7
Smith Creek Cave (21)	6,400	*Ochotona princeps*	>12,600	85 NW	3, 4, 7
Smith Creek Cave SC4,5★ (21)	6,400	*Ochotona princeps*	12,235–13,340	85 NW	6
Streamview Rockshelter SV1,2★ (21)	6,100	*Ochotona princeps*	11,010–17,350	85 NW	6
Spring Range, NV					
Potosi Mountain 2A1,2★ (22)	6,170	*Ochotona princeps*	14,270–14,900	175 WNW	2

Note: a, Numbers in parentheses indicate sites in Figures 7-8 and 7-9. The distance column provides the distance to the nearest known modern population.

★Packrat middens.

References: 1, Grayson (1987b); 2, J. I. Mead and Murray (1991); 3, J. I. Mead et al. (1982); 4, S. J. Miller (1979); 5, Spaulding (1981); 6, R. S. Thompson (1984); 7, R. S. Thompson and Mead (1982); 8, Ziegler (1963).

support it provides, however, is substantial. Twelve sites show that, during the late Pleistocene, pikas existed on 4 of the 19 ranges analyzed by Brown where they do not occur today: the Deep Creek, Sheep, Snake, and Spring ranges. In addition, latest Pleistocene (or perhaps earliest Holocene) pikas are also known from the Jarbidge Mountains, north of the area focused on by Brown (see Table 7-14).

The fact that only pikas have been reported from late Pleistocene deposits in Great Basin mountain ranges probably reflects a strong bias in the way our paleontological knowledge of this region has grown. Very few paleontological or archaeological sites with great time depth have been excavated in these ranges, providing slim opportunities for discovering the past existence of populations of now-montane mammals. On the other hand, a good deal of packrat midden work has been done in these ranges, and it is the middens that have provided most of the data we have for late Pleistocene pikas in the uplands. Of the 13 sites that have provided late Pleistocene pika remains, all but three (Council Hall, Deer Creek, and Smith Creek caves) are packrat middens.

MONTANE MAMMALS EXTINCT IN THE GREAT BASIN

The third paleontological prediction that can be drawn from Brown's hypothesis is that montane mammals may have become extinct throughout the Great Basin. In fact, four such species have been reported: the heather vole (*Phenacomys intermedius*), the northern bog lemming (*Mictomys borealis*), the pine marten (*Martes americana*), and the least weasel (*Mustela nivalis*). The late Pleistocene sites that have provided the remains of these mammals are listed in Table 7-15.

Today, heather voles are found only on the easternmost and westernmost fringes of the Great Basin: in the Carson Range in western Nevada, on the one hand, and in the Uinta and Wasatch ranges of central Utah, on the other. Although these mouse-sized rodents occupy a variety of habitats, they are primarily animals of the coniferous forests, regularly living at and above timberline. Although Smith Creek Cave provides the only late Pleistocene record for the heather vole in the Great Basin, it survived in the Great Basin well into the Holocene, as I discuss in Chapter 8.

Table 7-15. Pleistocene Records for Montane Mammals That No Longer Occur in the Great Basin

Location	Elevation (feet)	Species	Age (years ago)	References
Snake Valley, NV and UT				
Crystal Ball Cave (12)	5,775	*Martes americana*	Late Wisconsin?	1
Snake Creek Burial Cave (23)	5,680	*Martes americana*	Late Wisconsin	2
		Mustela nivalis		
Snake Range, NV				
Cathedral Cave (21)	6,400	*Mictomys borealis*	>24,000–<14,000	3
Smith Creek Cave (21)	6,400	*Phenacomys intermedius* *Synaptomys borealis*	>12,600	4

References: 1, Heaton (1985); 2, E. M. Mead and Mead (1989); 3, J. I. Mead et al. (1992); 4, J. I. Mead et al. (1982).

The northern bog lemming is also primarily northern in distribution, barely entering the far southern United States along the Canadian border. These rodents generally inhabit bogs in spruce forests, but they can also be found in other settings, including subalpine meadows and alpine tundra. For some time, it has been known that northern bog lemmings were found well south of their current distribution during the late Pleistocene, having been discovered in cave deposits in, for instance, Tennessee. Only recently, however, was it discovered that they also occupied the Great Basin during this period.

Jim Mead and his colleagues have shown that two caves in the Snake Range contain the remains of these animals. These caves face one another across Smith Creek Valley: north-facing Cathedral Cave, and south-facing Smith Creek Cave. We know from Robert Thompson's work that, at the time these lemmings lived in Smith Creek Canyon, bristlecone and limber pines descended nearly to the floor of this valley (see Chapter 6), and the well-watered, cool canyon clearly provided excellent habitat for these mammals. How common northern bog lemmings were in the Great Basin during the late Pleistocene is unknown, but it would not be surprising to find that they were widespread.

The remaining two montane mammals that occupied the Great Basin during the late Pleistocene but that are no longer found in this region are both carnivores: the pine marten and the least weasel.

The pine marten is a mink-sized predator of boreal forests. Today, it is found in both the Sierra Nevada and Rocky Mountains, but it has never been seen in the flesh in the Great Basin. The late Pleistocene records come from two Snake Valley sites: Crystal Ball Cave and Snake Creek Burial Cave.

It is probably pushing things to call the least weasel "montane," since it can be found in the farmlands of the northern midwest. In western North America, however, it is found only in the north. Indeed, west of 104° longitude (approximately the eastern border of Wyoming and Montana), it comes no further south than northern Montana. It is this northerly distribution in western North America that leads me to include it here. It has been reported only from Snake Creek Burial Cave, in Snake Valley.

THE EXTINCT NOBLE MARTEN

The pine marten has actually been reported from a third Great Basin site, Deer Creek Cave in the Jarbidge Mountains of northern Nevada. This site, however, does not appear in Table 7-15, since we cannot be certain that this is actually the animal that is represented.

This is not because there is any reason to question the work of zoologist Alan Ziegler, who identified the Deer Creek Cave mammals. There is every reason to believe that what he called a marten really is one. Ziegler, however, identified this material in 1963, before the existence of the very similar, but extinct, noble marten (*Martes nobilis*) was recognized.

In 1926, mammalogist E. R. Hall described a new subspecies of pine marten on the basis of skeletal remains from two caves in northern California. Many years passed before paleontologist Elaine Anderson showed that there were consistent differences between the known remains of the marten Hall had described and the skeletons of living species of martens. In 1970, she assigned the paleontological material to the extinct species *Martes nobilis,* the noble marten.

Today, the noble marten is known from 12 sites in western North America, and from a single site in Nebraska. For more than a decade, it was thought that this animal had become extinct at the end of the Pleistocene. However, a series of sites now suggests that it survived until at least 3,000 years ago or so. Since two of these sites are in the Great Basin, I will return to them in Chapter 8.

The noble marten was also generally thought to have been adapted to cool conditions. This adaptation was inferred from the fact that the remains of this animal have been found in deposits that also yielded the remains of such species as collared lemmings (*Dicrostonyx*), animals of the far north. However, more recent work has shown that the noble marten also existed in settings that are far better described as temperate than as boreal, and it is now clear that this carnivore was adapted to a broad variety of environmental settings. Indeed, the adaptations of the noble marten appear to have been far broader than those of the closely related pine marten, which is, in fact, a boreal mammal.

Recently, Phillip Youngman and Frederick Schueler of the Canadian Museum of Nature have argued that Hall was correct in the first place, and that the noble marten does not differ sufficiently from the pine marten for it to be considered a separate species. Decisions of this sort are often difficult to make with fossil material, but Youngman and Schueler did show that, except for size (the noble marten is the larger of the two), there is quite a bit of overlap in form between noble and pine martens. However, their valuable analysis does not appear to take sufficient account of the differences in the teeth of these two mammals, and it is the teeth, in addition to size, that makes *Martes nobilis* recognizable. Although their argument may well be correct, what they have done to this point has not convinced those who have worked with the remains of these two martens.

I began this section by noting that Deer Creek Cave contained the remains of what Alan Ziegler identified as pine marten, but that we cannot be certain that this is the animal that is represented here. When Ziegler worked, the noble marten was considered to be a form of pine marten, and it was not until seven years later that Elaine Anderson showed that this did not appear to be the case. To be sure of exactly which form of marten is represented here, the Deer Creek Cave material will have to be studied anew. And someone will have to take a very close look at the teeth of pine and noble martens to see if, in fact, they are one and the same animal.

MONTANE MAMMALS IN THE LATE PLEISTOCENE GREAT BASIN

All three paleontological predictions concerning montane mammals that can be drawn from Brown's model and that deal with the late Pleistocene now have substantial support. Montane mammals that now appear to be confined to isolated mountain ranges in the Great Basin were widespread in low-elevation settings here toward the end of the Pleistocene. At least one of these mammals, the pika, was found in ranges where it no longer exists. And at least three (heather voles, northern bog lemmings, and pine martens), and perhaps four (if we include least weasels) were living in the Great Basin toward the end of the Pleistocene, but no longer occur here today.

These discoveries provide substantial support for major parts of Brown's hypothesized history of Great Basin montane mammals. The work conducted to date, however, does not say anything about where the mammals came from in the first place, and does not by itself support the argument that the mammals came from either the Sierra Nevada or the Rocky Mountains. Further, the discoveries do not by themselves shed light on Brown's argument that the montane mammals are now fully isolated from other members of their species on other ranges.

It is important to realize that montane mammals were not the only ones that had altered distributions in the late Pleistocene Great Basin. Thomas Goodwin and Robert Reynolds, for instance, have shown that Townsend's ground squirrels (*Spermophilus townsendii*) and least chipmunks (*Tamias minimus*) occupied low elevations in the Mojave Desert of southeastern California toward the end of the Pleistocene. These squirrels would presumably have lived in the coniferous woodlands that characterized the Mojave at this time (see Chapter 6). Today, both species are widespread in the sagebrush communities of the Great Basin far to the north, but neither occurs in the Mojave Desert. There seems little doubt that, as we learn more and more about the small mammals of the late Pleistocene Great Basin, we will find that many mammals, including far more than just those that are now confined to montane settings, lost their low-elevation or low-latitude habitats after the Pleistocene ended.

WHY THERE ARE FISHES IN DEVILS HOLE, BUT NONE IN GREAT SALT LAKE

THE FISHES OF DEVILS HOLE

Unlike the situation with montane mammals, it takes no deep insight, no detailed quantitative analysis, to realize that the fishes that occupy separate and often minute drainages within the Great Basin are fully isolated from their nearest neighbors in other drainages. Examples can be drawn from any of the 44 species of fishes native to the Great Basin. Indeed, ichthyologists Carl L. Hubbs and Robert Rush Miller wrote a series of classic monographs in which they detailed the distribution of fishes in the modern Great Basin, and used those distributions to reconstruct past relationships among now-isolated Great Basin drainage systems. But the most remarkable instance of isolation among Great Basin fishes is provided by the killifishes and pupfishes that survive in the various drainages that once flowed into Death Valley.

Killifishes and pupfishes belong to the family Cyprinodontidae. Members of this family are extremely widespread, found in Africa, Asia, Europe, and both North and South America. The Great Basin supports, or supported until very recently, eight species of cyprinodonts. Of these eight, one (the White River springfish, *Crenichthys baileyi*) is found in the White River drainage system in eastern Nevada, whereas a second (the Railroad Valley springfish, *C. nevadae*) is known only from seven hot springs in south-central Nevada's Railroad Valley (see Figure 6-15). The remaining six species are, or were, found in drainages that, during the late Pleistocene, contributed their waters to Death Valley's Lake Manly (for a discussion of this drainage system, see Chapters 5 and 6).

These six species, and their locations, are listed in Table 7-16. All six fishes are tiny (1″–2.5″ long), the males often brightly colored and aggressively territorial. Both the bright colors and the territorial aggression of the males appear to be explained by the fact that the habitats of spring-dwelling pupfishes are stable in both time and space, as well as limited in areas suitable for spawning. Indeed, Amargosa pupfishes that live in flowing streams along the Amargosa River itself tend to lose their territoriality and breed in groups.

As fascinating as the adaptations of pupfishes are, the most evident mystery they present is the fact that they are there at all. The most extreme example is provided by the smallest pupfish known, the one-inch-long Devils Hole pupfish. As Edwin Pister has pointed out, this fish occupies the smallest habitat occupied by any viable population of vertebrates in the world.

Devils Hole is a narrow crevice in the Devils Hole Hills, a low range in southwestern Nevada's Ash Meadows, some 30 miles east of Death Valley and within a detached part of Death Valley National Monument (for the location of Ash Meadows, see Figure 6-12). Approximately 50′ beneath the rim of this crevice lies the surface of a pool that measures some 23′ by 10′; the uppermost waters of this pool maintain a nearly constant temperature of about 90°F, making it easy to understand why the old name for Devils Hole pool was the Miner's Bathtub. The Devils Hole pool, fed by a vast underground aquifer, is at least 330′ deep, but how much deeper it may be than this is unknown, since the bottom has never been reached.

The Devils Hole pupfishes, however, care little about the depth of the pool. They descend no further than about 85′, the depth to which sunlight penetrates, and the bulk of

Table 7-16. Pupfishes and Killifishes of the Death Valley Region[a]

Species	Common name	Distribution
Cyprinodon radiosus	Owens pupfish	Owens River
Cyprinodon salinus	Salt Creek pupfish	Salt Creek and Cottonball Marsh, Death Valley
Cyprinodon nevadensis	Amargosa pupfish	Amargosa River Drainage
Cyprinodon diabolis	Devils Hole pupfish	Devils Hole (Ash Meadows)
Empetrichthys latos	Pahrump killifish[b]	Pahrump Valley
Empetrichthys merriami	Ash Meadows killifish[c]	Ash Meadows

Notes: a, After R. R. Miller (1981), Soltz and Naiman (1978), and Sigler and Sigler (1987); *b,* extinct in Pahrump Valley, exists only in refuges; *c,* extinct (last seen in 1948).

their activities are concentrated on a limestone shelf, some 6.5′ by 13′ across, which is covered by a few inches to a few feet of water. It is here that the fishes both feed and breed, and to which they quickly return when disturbed.

Robert Miller has estimated that, in recent times, there have been between about 200 and 700 of these fishes; recent estimates put the maximum sustainable population at around 400 individuals. Late in the 1960s, the pumping of groundwater in the region began to cause a potentially disastrous decline in the Devils Hole pool. Fortunately, a 1976 Supreme Court decision required that the pool be kept sufficiently high to ensure the continued existence of this remarkable fish. Eight more years were to pass before the necessary safeguards were actually in place, but they did come to be. Those concerned with the preservation of biological diversity can only thank those whose work led not only to the 1976 Supreme Court decision but also to the establishment, in 1984, of Ash Meadows National Wildlife Refuge. This refuge helps protect the Devils Hole pupfish and also supports over two dozen kinds of plants and animals that are found nowhere else.

But how did the Devils Hole pupfish get to Devils Hole in the first place? How did the Salt Creek pupfish get to Salt Creek and Cottonball Marsh in Death Valley, the only places it is known to exist? How, in fact, did any of the pupfishes and killifishes that are now found in the isolated springs and streams of the Mojave Desert get to be where they are now?

The answer lies in the fact that the ancestors of these fishes have been in this area far longer than Death Valley itself has existed. Robert Miller has identified a late Miocene pupfish (the short-rayed pupfish, *Cyprinodon breviradius*) from deposits that are perhaps five to ten million years old in the Funeral Mountains, along the eastern edge of Death Valley (Figure 6-1). Although the killifish genus *Empetrichthys* has not been found as a fossil in the Death Valley region itself, it is known from the Piru Mountains, northwest of Los Angeles, some 200 miles to the west. In addition, fishes that appear to be ancestral to *Empetrichthys* are known from Miocene-aged paleontological sites in the Death Valley region itself. All this makes it clear that pupfishes and killifishes have been in what is now the Mojave Desert for what may be at least seven million years, and perhaps far longer. These fishes then become isolated in the Death Valley area as mountains were uplifted, and Death Valley itself warped downward, during the late Miocene, Pliocene, and Pleistocene, in a process that continues today.

The arrival of cyprinodont fishes, then, preceded the Pleistocene by a vast amount of time. There is no known Pleistocene record for any of these fishes here, though the fossils must certainly exist. But, even though we have no direct fossil evidence from the Pleistocene, there can be no doubt that the growth of surface waters in this area during the late Pleistocene played a major role in bringing pupfishes and killifishes to the places where they are now found.

Devils Hole provides an excellent, though not yet fully understood, example. At an elevation of 2,400′, Devils Hole sits some 100′ to 150′ above the adjacent floor of the Amargosa Desert. In 1948, Robert Miller suggested that Devils Hole was once submerged beneath the waters of an ancient lake, perhaps early to middle Pleistocene in age, and that pupfishes became isolated in Devils Hole as the lake waters receded. Indeed, it has been argued much more recently that there was a substantial lake in this area, perhaps of Pliocene age (between roughly two million and five million years ago). It has also been argued that a large marsh filled much of the Amargosa Desert during the Pleistocene. Geologist Fred Nials, however, has recently observed that the deposits that seemed to suggest the existence of these bodies of water actually seem to have been laid down as a result of spring activity. In addition to all this, Alan Riggs has recently suggested that Devils Hole did not even become open to the surface until about 50,000 years ago, and it is certain that no deep lake has existed here since then.

Given that there is no evidence to support the argument that pupfishes were carried to Devils Hole by lake waters, they must have entered by a different route. The existence of Death Valley's Pleistocene Lake Manly not far to the west of Devils Hole documents the increased abundance of surface waters in this region during the late Pleistocene (see Chapters 5 and 6, and Figure 5-15). In 1981, Miller observed that the Devils Hole pool must have overflowed at some time in the past. If, as now seems likely, that overflow took place during the last 50,000 years, the stream involved may well have connected with other bodies of water that existed in what is now the Amargosa Desert during the late Pleistocene. Once Devils Hole was connected to other surface waters in this fashion, pupfishes could have worked their way upward to Devils Hole itself, as long as currents in this stream were not too great for them. As the Pleistocene came to an end, and overflow ceased, the pupfishes would have become totally isolated in the Devils Hole pool. Given that Lake Manly had apparently begun to recede by 13,000 years ago, it is reasonable to speculate that the Devils Hole pupfishes have been isolated here for at least 13,000 years.

The distribution of pupfishes and killifishes in the Death Valley area can thus be explained in a fairly straightforward manner. The ancestors of these fishes were here even before Death Valley as we know it was formed. Many of them reached something like their current locations as a result of the changes in the distribution and amount of surface waters that occurred here during the late Pleistocene. As the Pleistocene came to an end, and as the once-abundant surface waters retreated, many of these fishes became isolated.

Holocene events have also clearly played a role in determining the distribution of these fishes. The pupfishes in Salt Creek and Cottonball Marsh in the heart of Death Valley, for instance, appear to have been isolated from one another for no more than a few hundred years: there is evidence, presented by James LaBounty and James Deacon and drawn from work by Peter Mehringer, that the isolated aquatic habitats now occupied by these fishes were connected as recently as 400 years ago.

Thus, although intriguing, the distribution of pupfishes and killifishes in the Death Valley area does not pose insoluble mysteries. Even the most intriguing of them all—the Devils Hole pupfish—can be explained by the deeper history of these fishes, by the Pleistocene history of surface waters in the region, and by subsequent Holocene isolation.

THE FISHES OF GREAT SALT LAKE AND LAKE BONNEVILLE

It is far easier to explain why there are no fishes in Great Salt Lake. Although there are 20 species of native fishes in the Bonneville drainage as a whole (Table 7-17), and although fish can be found near the mouths of tributaries that drain into Great Salt Lake, the lake itself has none because it is too saline to support them.

This was not the case during the late Pleistocene. Eight species of fishes are known from the deposits of Lake Bonneville. The exact age of the deposits that have provided the identified fish remains is not well controlled, but none seems to be older than the Stansbury terraces, which date to between 22,000 and 20,000 years ago (see Table 5-3).

Table 7-17. Native Fishes of the Modern Bonneville Drainage System[a]

Family and species	Common name
Salmonidae (Trouts)	
Prosopium abyssicola	Bear Lake whitefish
Prosopium gemmiferum	Bonneville cisco
Prosopium spilonotus	Bonneville whitefish
Prosopium williamsoni	Mountain whitefish
Salmo clarki	Cutthroat trout
Cyprinidae (Minnows)	
Gila atraria	Utah chub
Gila copei	Leatherside chub
Iotichthys phlegethontis	Least chub
Rhinichthys cataractae	Longnose dace
Rhinichthys osculus	Speckled dace
Rhinichthys sp.	(Undescribed dace)
Richardsonius balteatus	Redside shiner
Catostomidae (Suckers)	
Catostomus ardens	Utah sucker
Catostomus discobolus	Bluehead sucker
Catostomus platyrhynchus	Mountain sucker
Chasmistes liorus	June sucker
Cottidae (Sculpins)	
Cottus bairdi	Mottled sculpin
Cottus beldingi	Paiute sculpin
Cottus echinatus[b]	Utah Lake sculpin
Cottus extensus	Bear Lake sculpin

Notes: a, From Sigler and Sigler (1987), Minckley et al. (1985), G. R. Smith (1978); *b,* became extinct during the 1930s.

Table 7-18 lists the known late Pleistocene Lake Bonneville species, and also lists the native fishes of Bear Lake, to the northeast, and Utah Lake, to the southeast (see Figure 5-1 for locations). During and after Stansbury times, Bear Lake was connected to, and Utah Lake was part of, Lake Bonneville. As a result, it is perhaps no surprise that of the 10 species of fishes that now exist in Bear Lake, 6 (60%) are also known from the deposits of Lake Bonneville. Of the 11 species that now exist in Utah Lake, 5 (45%) are also known from Lake Bonneville.

The eight species of fishes that we know to have occupied Lake Bonneville include three that now exist only in Bear Lake: the Bonneville cisco, Bonneville whitefish, and Bear Lake sculpin. In addition, they include one species that now exists only in Utah Lake: the June sucker. These four species must have become isolated as Lake Bonneville retreated, and may well have become isolated when

Table 7-18. Native Fishes of Modern Bear Lake, Utah Lake, and Late Pleistocene Lake Bonneville[a]

Species	Bear Lake	Utah Lake	Lake Bonneville
Bear Lake whitefish	!		
Bonneville Cisco	!		×
Bonneville whitefish	!		×
Mountain whitefish	×	×	
Cutthroat trout	×	×	×
Utah chub	×	×	×
Leatherside chub		×	
Least chub		×	
Longnose dace		×	
Speckled dace	×		
Redside shiner	×		
Utah sucker	×	×	×
June sucker		!	×
Mottled sculpin		×	×
Utah Lake sculpin		!	
Bear Lake sculpin	!		×

[a]From Heckmann et al. (1981), Minckley et al. (1985), G. R. Smith (1978), G. R. Smith et al. (1968), and Stokes et al. (1964). The exclamation point (!) indicates a species found only in Bear Lake or Utah Lake.

Lake Bonneville declined precipitously from the Provo level, some 14,000 years ago.

The fact that Lake Bonneville appears to have fallen to or beneath historic levels between 13,000 and 11,000 years ago suggests that a fairly rich fish fauna was lost during this interval. It is also likely that some fishes recolonized the lake when it rose again, to the Gilbert level, between 11,000 and 10,000 years ago, only to undergo yet another round of local extinctions as the Pleistocene drew to an end and Lake Bonneville retreated for a final time. This possible set of multiple local extinctions, however, remains for a future scientist to describe and decipher: nothing is known of the history of Lake Bonneville fishes during this interval.

Other Vertebrates

There were, of course, many vertebrates in the Great Basin during the late Pleistocene in addition to the ones I have discussed here. We are, for instance, beginning to understand the late Pleistocene distribution of amphibians and reptiles in this region. The most obvious animal that I have not discussed, however, is ourselves. People appear to have been widespread in the Great Basin as the Pleistocene drew to a close. Those interested in learning more about the late Pleistocene human occupation of this region might wish to turn to Chapter 9 now, where I discuss that occupation. But because the human prehistory of the Great Basin is best understood in broad sweep, from beginning to end, I will discuss the Holocene environmental history of the Great Basin before dealing with people at all.

Notes

References to the Great Basin paleontological sites that have provided the remains of extinct late Pleistocene mammals are provided in Table 7-1. On early explorations at Fossil Lake, see Cope (1889) and Sternberg (1909). I. S. Allison and Bond (1983) discuss the existence of a Holocene lake in the Fossil Lake area. References to the extinct late Pleistocene mammals of North America, and to explanations of those extinctions, are provided in Chapter 4. The Huntington mammoth is discussed in Gillette and Madsen (1992, 1993), and in Schaedler et al. (1992).

For general discussions of late Pleistocene bird extinctions in North America, see Grayson (1977b) and Steadman and Martin (1984). In discussing the modern distribution of birds in the Great Basin, I have depended on Alcorn (1988), Hayward et al. (1976), and Ryser (1985); other modern distributional information has been taken from Blake (1977), Delacour (1954), and Palmer (1962). I have followed R. Howard and Moore (1991) as regards the classification of modern birds. Information that I have presented on the diet of modern *Spizaëtus* and *Buteogallus* is from Wetmore (1965); see also Blake (1977), Grayson (1977b), and Steadman and Martin (1984).

My discussion of the distribution of extinct birds has depended heavily on Brodkorb (1963, 1964); the common names I have applied to some of these birds come from L. Miller and DeMay (1942). My description of fossil birds has depended in part on H. Howard (1932), Wetmore (1959), Stock (1956), and Rich (1983); my discussion of the teratorns has also drawn on Fisher (1945), H. Howard (1972), and K. E. Campbell and Tonni (1980). Table 7-6 provides references to Great Basin sites that have yielded the remains of extinct late Pleistocene birds. L. Miller

(1931) discusses the California Condor at Gypsum Cave; Jehl (1967) provides additional information on the birds of Fossil Lake. Emslie (1990) presents the radiocarbon dates for the Antelope and Gypsum cave California condors. Those who read the literature on Fossil Lake dating to the 1940s and 1950s will find references to two genera that I have not mentioned here: *Hypomorphnus* and *Palaeotetrix*. *Hypomorphnus* is now treated as a synonym of *Buteogallus* by ornithologists, and Jehl (1967) showed that the material assigned to *Palaeotetrix* is best treated as belonging to the genus to which the Spruce and Blue Grouse belong, *Dendragapus*. The chronology of the Manix Lake birds is discussed by Jefferson (1985); see also Jefferson (1987).

The possible affinities of *Neogyps* are discussed by H. Howard (1932) and Rich (1980, 1983). H. Howard and Miller (1939) discuss the relative abundances of Western Black Vultures and Turkey Vultures at Rancho La Brea; see also Howard (1962). The other late Pleistocene southern California asphalt deposits from which Turkey Vultures have been reported are Carpinteria (DeMay 1941a) and McKittrick (DeMay 1941b).

Information on the behavior of modern vultures that I present is taken from L. Brown (1971), Houston (1983), König (1983), and Rabenold (1983). Those interested in the debate over the affinities of New World vultures (they appear to be more closely related to storks than to such raptors as eagles and hawks) should read Rea (1983).

For J. H. Brown's ideas on the history of montane mammals in the Great Basin, see Brown (1971, 1978) and Brown and Gibson (1983). For tests of Brown's model using archaeological and paleontological data, see Grayson (1987b). For complementary analyses of the montane mammals of the Great Basin, see B. D. Patterson (1990) and Cutler (1991), and Grayson and Livingston (1993); Cutler (1991) did not list *Spermophilus beldingi* in the Toquima Range; Grayson and Livingston (1993) followed Cutler. Tables 7-10 and 7-11 restore this squirrel to its rightful place. Lomolino et al. (1989) provide a parallel analysis of montane mammals in the Southwest. Brown and Gibson (1983) provide a very readable introduction to the island biogeographic theory that formed the basis of Brown's work; for the classic exposition, see MacArthur and Wilson (1967).

I have presented the analysis of the slopes of species-area curves as if those values have a simple meaning. In fact, there is a substantial debate over the meaning of z values, and it is clear that these numbers reflect a diverse variety of factors. Connor and McCoy (1979), Wright (1981), Lawlor (1986), and Lomolino (1989), among others, discuss these issues. Shafer (1990) provides a guide to the literature.

I note that the pronounced decrease in slope that occurred between 1971 and 1978 (see Table 7-11) is due not only to changes in our knowledge of the distribution of Great Basin mammals during that interval, but also, as Jim Brown has mentioned to me, to changes in the list of mammals included in that analysis. Nonetheless, the decrease in slope that has occurred as our knowledge has grown is quite evident (see Grayson and Livingston 1993).

The best sources on the distribution of Great Basin mammals remain Bailey (1936), E. R. Hall (1946, 1981), and Durrant (1952). Updated versions are badly needed. Zeveloff and Collett (1988) provide a general and readable introduction to Great Basin mammals as a whole.

J. I. Mead (1987) reviews all North American Quaternary records of pikas, including those in the Great Basin. Information on the modern distribution of yellow-pine chipmunks in the Great Basin is from E. R. Hall (1946), C. G. Hansen (1956), Moir et al. (1973), and, for the White Mountains, D. A. Sutton and Nadler (1969). On the heather vole in general, see McAllister and Hoffman (1988); on the heather vole in the Great Basin, see Grayson (1981). On the modern distribution and ecology of the pine marten, see Clark et al. (1987). Ziegler (1963) presents his identification of the pine marten from Deer Creek Cave. On northern bog lemmings in Tennessee and elsewhere in the east, see Guilday et al. (1978) and Lundelius et al. (1983).

On the noble marten, see E. Anderson (1970), Graham and Graham (1992), Grayson (1984, 1985, 1987b), and Youngman and Schueler (1991). The distribution of late Pleistocene ground squirrels and chipmunks in the Mojave Desert is discussed by Goodwin and Reynolds (1989b). Force (1991) identified bushy-tailed packrat from Kokoweef Cave, but Reynolds et al. (1991d) do not list this species as extralimital.

The essential reference on the modern fishes of the Great Basin is Sigler and Sigler (1987); my count of the number of native species of Great Basin fishes in the Great Basin comes from that source, though I have added the extinct Ash Meadows killifish to their count. The classic studies on the distribution of Great Basin fishes to which I refer are Hubbs and Miller (1948) and Hubbs et al. (1974); see G. R. Smith (1978) for an important update of these works.

I have followed Sigler and Sigler (1987) in placing *Crenichthys* and *Empetrichthys* in the family Cyprinodontidae (thus I refer to them as cyprinodonts, not as cyprinodontoids); others place them in a separate family, the Goodeidae: see Parenti (1981). Information on the distribution and adaptations of cyprinodont fishes has been taken from Constantz (1981), Kodric-Brown (1981), R. R. Miller (1981), Naiman (1981), Soltz and Naiman (1978), and Sigler and Sigler (1987). Information on the Devils Hole pupfish is drawn from Baugh and Deacon (1983), Deacon and Deacon (1979), Deacon and Williams (1991), La Rivers (1962), R. R. Miller (1948, 1981), Pister (1981), and Soltz and Naiman (1978); on Ash Meadows National Wildlife Refuge, see Deacon and Williams (1991), Pister (1991), and Rolston (1991). For those interested in reading more about these fishes, Soltz and Naiman (1978) provide an excellent introduction. The volume on North American desert fishes, edited by Naiman and Soltz (1981) and directed toward a scientific audience, is superb. On threats to the continued existence of native fishes in the arid West in general, see the excellent volume by Minckley and Deacon (1991). Minckley et al. (1991) treat the current status of cyprinodonts. My discussion of the paleontological record, and deeper history, of cyprinodonts has depended on LaBounty and Deacon (1972), R. R. Miller (1945, 1948, 1981), G. R. Smith (1981), M. L. Smith (1981), Minckley et al. (1985), and Uyeno and Miller (1962). My comments on the geological history of the Amargosa Desert are based on Nials (1990). Riggs (1991) presents evidence suggesting that Devils Hole did not open to the surface until about 50,000 years ago.

On the history of Bonneville Basin fishes, see Minckley et al. (1985), G. R. Smith (1981), G. R. Smith et al. (1968), and Stokes et al. (1964). On the Bear Lake whitefishes, see R. R. Miller (1965).

PART FOUR

○○○

The Last 10,000 Years

CHAPTER EIGHT

○○○

The Great Basin during the Holocene

It is a geological convention that the Pleistocene ended, and the Holocene began, 10,000 years ago. Even though there is no reason to think that the Pleistocene, as an ice age, is truly over, the most recent glacial stage has obviously ended, and did so sometime between 10,000 and 11,000 years ago.

The transition from the last glacial to the current interglacial, however, was just that—a transition. As a result, any date chosen to separate the two has to be arbitrary. In 1975, geologist David Hopkins announced the decision by the Holocene Commission of the International Quaternary Association to place the Pleistocene-Holocene boundary at 10,000 years ago. His comments were fully appropriate: that figure, he said, was chosen "simply because that's a nice round number." And, he added, "no one agreed with me, nor with anyone else" (Hopkins 1975:10). The date was accepted, and is, by definition, the temporal boundary that separates the Pleistocene from the Holocene.

The fact that the boundary is arbitrary, however, does not mean that the date chosen was a bad one. The interval between 11,000 and 10,000 years ago saw the Younger Dryas cold snap (see Chapter 5), the loss of the last Pleistocene mammals, the retreat of Lake Bonneville from the Gilbert level, and a wide variety of other phenomena that seem better associated with the Pleistocene than with the Holocene.

But the boundary is an arbitrary one, not only in the sense that it could have been placed at 11,000 years ago (as some now argue it should be), but also in the sense that crossing it does not cross a divide between "ice age" and modern environments. Indeed, it is not until thousands of years into the Holocene that environments markedly like those of modern times come into being in the Great Basin. It is the Holocene development of these modern environments that I examine in this chapter.

In doing that, I will divide this geological epoch into three parts: the early (10,000 to 7,500 years ago), middle (7,500 to 4,500 years ago), and late (the last 4,500 years) Holocene. These divisions are both unofficial and arbitrary; other divisions of the Holocene are in common use. Nonetheless, Great Basin environments during these times were in many ways distinct. As long as the bounding dates I have chosen are not taken as real edges, they provide a convenient way to examine the history of Great Basin environments during the last 10,000 years.

The Early Holocene: 10,000 to 7,500 Years Ago

SHALLOW LAKES AND MARSHES

Although the pluvial lakes of the Great Basin were gone by 10,000 years ago, many Great Basin valleys that are today dry, or nearly so, supported shallow lakes and marshes during the early Holocene. In addition, many valleys that today contain lakes then contained lakes that were at least as high, and sometimes higher, than they are now.

THE MOJAVE DESERT

The late Pleistocene and early Holocene history of Las Vegas Valley provides an excellent example. This broad valley trends northwest and southeast, between the Sheep Range to the north and the Spring Range to the south (see Figure 6-12); the town of Las Vegas sits toward the southern end of the valley. Today, Las Vegas Valley is drained by Las Vegas Wash, which ultimately connects with the Virgin River, in turn a tributary of the Colorado. The area itself, however, is extremely arid, the wash routinely dry. Work by geologists Vance Haynes and Jay Quade has documented that this was decidedly not the case during the late Pleistocene and early Holocene.

Haynes's work focused primarily on the Tule Springs area, some 10 miles north of Las Vegas (see Figure 6-12). Quade's efforts, on the other hand, were directed toward the upper end of Las Vegas Valley, near Corn Creek Springs, approximately 20 miles northeast of Las Vegas. Although these studies were done some 20 years apart—Haynes's work was published in 1967, Quade's in 1986—and were directed toward different parts of the valley, the results they obtained are entirely consistent.

The picture painted by their research extends well beyond the range of radiocarbon dating, and perhaps to as early as 60,000 years ago. I will begin my discussion, however, with Haynes's geological Unit D, a 16′-thick pile of deposits that is widespread in the valley, and that dates to between about 30,000 and 15,000 years ago.

Near the margin of the valley, Unit D consists of fine-grained sediments, but these grade into "mudstones" (hardened deposits of clays and silts laid down in a moist environment) toward the valley floor. In many places, Unit D is riddled with the casts, or "pseudomorphs," of cicada burrows that were formed as a result of the deposition of carbonates in the original burrows themselves. These burrow casts are so common that, in some places where the deposits of Unit D are exposed, they cover the surface of the ground. The significance of these burrows seems clear: today, cicadas and their burrows are common in the far cooler and moister sagebrush environments of the floristic Great Basin to the north.

Equally clear is the more general environmental picture that can be extracted from Unit D and its contents. Peter Mehringer showed that the mudstones of this unit at Tule Springs contained both cattail and sagebrush pollen (see Chapter 6). This finding, combined with the nature of the sediments themselves, suggests that between about 30,000 and 15,000 years ago, Las Vegas Valley supported small, shallow bodies of water that were often fringed by cattails. Above the marshes and ponds, the alluvial flats supported sagebrush and cicadas. Neither is to be found here today.

In many areas, the top of Unit D is eroded, suggesting that at least some of the marshes and ponds dried up before the next depositional unit, E, began to be laid down some 14,000 years ago. Unit E is divided into two parts, with an erosional break separating the two: E_1 dates to between about 14,000 and 11,700 years ago, whereas E_2 falls between 11,000 and 7,200 years ago. The sediments that make up the two, however, are quite similar: greenish clays, black organic mats, and water-deposited sandy silts that fill depressions created by springs and stream channels.

The black mats here are much like that which overlies the Clovis level at the Lehner site in southeastern Arizona (see Chapter 4), and which dates to about 10,800 years ago. Like the Lehner black mat, those in Las Vegas Valley appear to represent the decay of organic material in a moist environment, but the Las Vegas Valley versions date to between 11,700 and 8,640 years ago.

Although cicada burrows are not as common in Unit E as they are in Unit D, they are nonetheless present. In addition, E_1 contains the bones of extinct Pleistocene mammals, including mammoth, horse, and camel. Unit E_2, on the other hand, does not, and the erosional break between these two depositional units may coincide with the time of extinction of those mammals here.

All of this information suggests that the water table during E_1 and E_2 times (roughly 14,000 to 7,000 years ago, excluding the erosional break that separates the two) was lower than it was when Unit D was deposited: the earlier complex of marshes and ponds had diminished considerably. But the green clays in Unit E show that there was at least some standing water in the valley, the cicadas imply that cool and moist conditions continued, molluscs from these deposits show that marshes continued to exist in the area, and the black mats suggest that these marshes were fairly widespread. Indeed, although Mehringer's work revealed only traces of cattail pollen in the sediments of Unit E, it was there, and his work also showed that other moisture-loving plants grew in the area at this time. Sagebrush, now absent on the valley floor, was also present throughout the deposits that make up Unit E.

Much of E_2 (11,000 to 7,200 years ago) is Holocene in age. The complex of marshes and active springs that characterized Las Vegas Valley while E_1 was accumulating became increasingly smaller during E_2 times, but perennial streams with marshy edges persisted here until about 8,000 years ago. Then, sometime between 8,000 and 7,000 years ago, this cooler and moister regime disappeared. The water table, which was near the surface some 8,500 years ago, dropped dramatically; today, it is some 80′ lower than it was then. The cicadas became locally extinct, the sagebrush retreated, and the deposits of Unit E_1 began to be heavily eroded. Something closer to modern conditions had arrived.

A very similar sequence appears to have characterized the Mojave River drainage. In Chapter 6, I discussed the fact that Pleistocene Lake Mojave reached high levels between 18,000 and 16,000 years ago (the Lake Mojave I phase), and between 13,700 and 11,400 years ago (Lake Mojave II; see Figure 6-2). The end of the Lake Mojave II phase, however, did not see an end to Lake Mojave as a whole.

Today, water rarely travels the entire course of the Mojave River to reach the Lake Mojave Basin. It routinely did so, however, between 11,400 and 8,700 years ago. During that period, a series of shallow lakes formed, leaving behind as evidence blue to green clays (the lake sediments) that are interrupted by cracks caused by desiccation (the drying events that separated these intermittent lakes). Geologist William J. Brown and his colleagues refer to this final stage in the history of Lake Mojave as Intermittent Lake III, previous intermittent lakes having formed just before Lake Mojave I, and between Lake Mojave phases I and II. Although shallow lakes have formed in this basin since 8,700 years ago, none was of the magnitude and duration of those that formed during Intermittent Lake III.

THE FLORISTIC GREAT BASIN

No similarly detailed information exists for now-dry Great Basin valleys in the far northern reaches of the Great Basin. Nonetheless, the information that does exist shows that comparable events occurred here as well. Some of the more intriguing evidence comes from the Alkali Lake Basin of south-central Oregon, and has been developed in detail by archaeologist Judy Willig.

The Alkali Lake Basin is just northeast of the basin of Pleistocene Lake Chewaucan and just southeast of that of Pleistocene Lake Fort Rock (see Figure 8-1). Although no detailed studies have been done on the earlier Pleistocene history of this basin, a large pluvial lake did exist here, covering some 205 square miles to a maximum depth of 275′. Willig's work focused on the latest Pleistocene and early Holocene history of this area, and in particular on the relationship between lake and human history in the north-

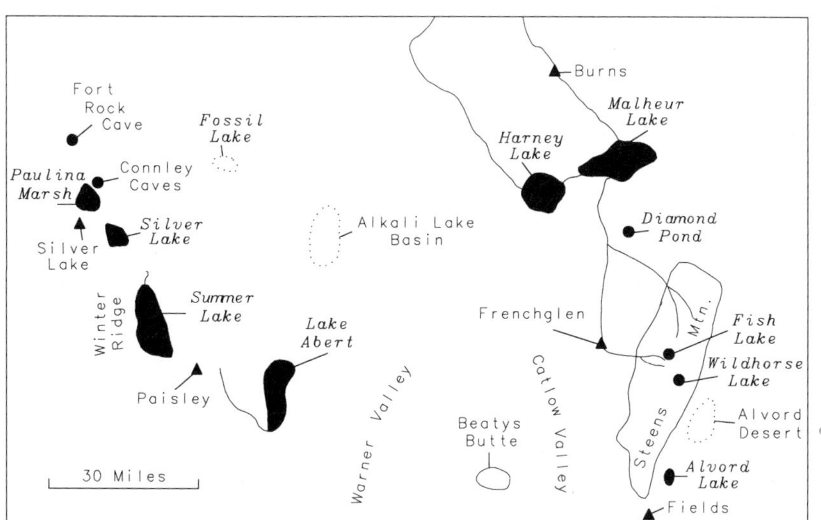

Figure 8-1. Northern Great Basin locations discussed in Chapter 8.

ern Alkali Lake Basin during this interval. I will discuss the archaeology of this area in the next chapter; here, I look only at what Willig discovered about the lakes and marshes of northern Alkali Lake Basin between about 11,500 and 8,000 years ago.

Willig combined analyses of regional geomorphology with stratigraphic excavations to show that, during latest Pleistocene times, perhaps focusing on about 11,000 years ago, the northern Alkali Lake Basin held a shallow (perhaps 20″ deep) lake that covered slightly more than one square mile. This marsh-fringed lake, which appears to have been fairly long lived, she named Lake Koko. Both Willig and geologist Vance Haynes estimate that Lake Koko dried up shortly after 11,000 years ago. That it dried up seems clear: the uppermost deposits of the lake are heavily eroded, even when they are covered by sediments laid down during earliest Holocene times.

These earliest Holocene deposits are associated with the growth of another, larger lake in the northern Alkali Lake Basin. There is good evidence that Sand Ridge Lake, as Willig named it, was nearly 7′ deep, covered approximately 5.5 square miles, and was marsh fringed, permanent, and fresh. That evidence is provided not only by the geomorphological data amassed by Willig, but also by the snails she obtained from the deposits of this lake. Those snails require fresh and permanent water, and also attach themselves to the submerged portions of bulrush and cattail. Although Willig was unable to provide much radiocarbon control over the chronology of the late Pleistocene and early Holocene lakes she defined here, the one date she was able to obtain was for Sand Ridge Lake, and it falls at 9,610 years ago.

Some time after 9,500 years ago, Sand Ridge Lake retreated, forming a lake slightly over 4′ in depth that Willig estimates dates to about 8,500 years ago. Because the deposits of this lake lie beneath Mazama ash, it is clear that this second Holocene lake, which Willig named Lake Delaine, was gone by 6,800 years ago, though exactly when it dried up is not known. Since Mazama ash blanketed this area, only one other sizable lake has formed in the northern Alkali Lake Basin, filling it to a depth of about 4′; this lake was of very brief duration, and nothing secure is known of its age.

The Connley Caves sit on the southwestern slope of the Connley Hills in the western Fort Rock Basin, some 50 miles northwest of northern Alkali Lake Basin and about 10 miles southeast of Fort Rock Cave (see Figure 8-1). A mile to the southwest lies the fluctuating shoreline of Paulina Marsh, now the largest natural body of standing water in the basin as a whole, fed by the only perennial streams that exist in the Fort Rock Basin.

Excavated by archaeologist Stephen Bedwell in 1967, the Connley Caves provided an archaeological sequence that spans the period from 11,200 to 3,000 years ago, with one major exception: the interval between 7,200 and 4,400 years ago is not represented at these sites. Bedwell was primarily interested in the archaeological content of these caves, but, in addition to providing an important series of artifacts, the rockshelters also proved to be fairly rich in bone.

The nature of the fauna deposited in these sites changed dramatically through time. Nearly all the remains of birds that had been deposited here were deposited between 11,200 and 7,200 years ago (95% of them, to be precise). In addition, most of those birds are tightly associated with water—grebes, ducks, shorebirds, and, to a lesser extent, Sage Grouse (*Centrocercus urophasianus;* within their general habitat, these birds are most common in areas with abundant surface water). The steep decline in such birds after 7,200 years ago strongly suggests that the levels of Paulina Marsh were dramatically reduced after that time. Such a reduction is, of course, fully consistent with Willig's evidence for the desiccation of shallow lakes and marshes some time between 8,500 and 6,800 years ago in the northern Alkali Lake Basin, not far to the southeast.

Similar evidence for early Holocene lakes and marshes exists elsewhere in the northern Great Basin. Archaeologist Keith Gehr, for instance, has shown that a series of at least four Holocene lake terraces exists along the southern edge of the Harney Lake Basin within the Malheur National Wildlife Refuge in south-central Oregon, about 40 miles northeast of the northern Alkali Lake Basin (see Figure 8-1). Dates on the earliest, and on the next-to-latest, of these terraces fall at 9,620 and 8,680 years ago, respectively. Although these dates are on snails (which are prone to contamination), the 9,620-year date is virtually identical to that obtained by Willig for Sand Ridge Lake to the southwest.

Although detailed sequences comparable to those from the Mojave River drainage and Las Vegas Valley do not exist for more northerly parts of the Great Basin, the evidence that does exist is convincing. From about 10,000 to between 8,000 and 7,000 years ago, many northern Great Basin valleys supported a series of often substantial lakes and marshes. In some cases (for instance, the northern Alkali Lake Basin), those valleys are now dry. Elsewhere, the lakes and marshes that now exist in these valleys (for instance, Paulina Marsh and Harney Lake) are far smaller than those that existed during the early Holocene.

Between these northern and southern geographic extremes, the data we have come from basins that still contain lakes, and come primarily from the analysis of lake sediments themselves, not from dated shorelines.

Robert Thompson's analysis of sediment cores from the Ruby Marshes, for instance, provided information not only on the late Pleistocene history of Lake Franklin (see Chapter 6), but also on the lakes and marshes that have existed in this area during the last 10,000 years. Basing his arguments primarily on the ostracodes and green algae preserved in the sediments provided by his cores, Thompson showed that, while the lake that occupied this basin had reached fairly low levels by 10,400 years ago, that lake was still deeper than it is today, and that it lasted well into the Holocene. In fact, between about 8,800 and 8,700 years ago, the lake rose briefly, but then began to decline, becoming a sedge-rich marsh by 8,700 years ago. By 6,800 years ago, when Mazama ash fell in Ruby Valley, the basin was nearly dry.

The other information that is available on lake history in the more central part of the Great Basin is less compelling, since it is far less detailed and based on far fewer radiocarbon dates. Geologist Stephen Born has argued that Pyramid Lake was at fairly high levels during the earliest Holocene, but that it had dropped substantially by 8,000 years ago. To the south and west, a series of radiocarbon dates suggest that Mono Lake was far higher between 10,000 and 7,000 years ago than it has been during the last 3,000 years. The only known exception to all this is Walker Lake: it appears to have been dry between about 14,000 and 4,700 years ago (see Chapter 5). The desiccation of Walker Lake, however, seems to have been due to the behavior of Walker River, which, during this 9,000-year interval, apparently flowed north, into Carson Sink, rather than south, into Walker Lake. Unfortunately, there is virtually no direct information available on the early Holocene history of lakes and marshes in the Carson Sink.

What we know about early Holocene lakes and marshes in the Great Basin is remarkably consistent. These bodies of water were widespread in the Great Basin between at least 10,000 and 8,500 years ago, securely documented from the Mojave River drainage and Las Vegas Valley on the south to the northern Alkali Lake Basin on the north. When these shallow lakes and marshes desiccated is somewhat less clear. Although there are suggestions that desiccation occurred at around 8,500 years ago in some areas—the Mojave River drainage, for instance—in other areas, shallow lakes and marshes seem to have existed until after 8,000 years ago, as in Las Vegas Valley and in Ruby Valley. Nowhere, however, is there convincing evidence that valleys that today lack substantial bodies of water maintained these lakes and marshes beyond 7,000 years ago. When Mazama ash fell in such valleys, it routinely fell on ground that was dry or nearly so.

SUBALPINE CONIFERS, SHADSCALE, AND CREOSOTE BUSH

THE FLORISTIC GREAT BASIN

The widespread existence of marshes and shallow lakes in the Great Basin during the early Holocene suggests climates that were cooler or moister, or both, than those of today. What we know of the vegetation of the Great Basin during this interval suggests no different.

Peter Wigand and Peter Mehringer have shown that the pollen from the late Pleistocene sediments of Hidden Cave, western Nevada, is dominated by pine and sagebrush (see Chapter 6 and Figure 6-5). That dominance ended fairly abruptly at around 10,000 years ago, as pine pollen declined to levels no greater than those that characterized the uppermost, latest Holocene, deposits in the site. Pines may have become less abundant on the local landscape at about this time, though this conclusion is clouded by the fact that the pine pollen in the Pleistocene sediments of Hidden Cave may have come from the waters of Lake Lahontan. Sagebrush pollen also declined in the deposits of Hidden Cave at about 10,000 years ago, but the decline it underwent was not nearly as dramatic as that suffered by pine. Sagebrush pollen becomes less abundant at this time than it had been during the late Pleistocene, yet it was still far more abundant between 10,000 and 6,800 years ago or so than it was to be after this interval.

As the amount of pine pollen in the sediments of Hidden Cave dropped substantially and sagebrush pollen declined, cheno-am pollen increased. As I have discussed, much of the cheno-am pollen in Hidden Cave is probably from shadscale (*Atriplex*), and pollen of this sort is not at all abundant in the late Pleistocene deposits of the site. Soon after 10,000 years ago, however, it became so, rising to form some 40% of all Holocene pollen samples.

Today, the vegetation surrounding Hidden Cave is dominated by species of *Atriplex* and greasewood. The rise in cheno-am pollen at 10,000 years ago, however, does not imply that something like the modern vegetation of this area came into being at this time: sagebrush pollen is simply too abundant in the early Holocene strata of Hidden Cave to suggest that. As Wigand and Mehringer note, a more modern vegetational regime does not appear to have become established until shortly after 6,800 years ago, when the abundance of sagebrush pollen drops to levels comparable to those in the latest Holocene deposits of the site. Between 10,000 and about 6,800 years ago, the pollen data from Hidden Cave suggest a cooler, moister environment than is to be found here today, with a far higher sagebrush component in the vegetation than has existed since then.

Some 200 miles to the northeast, Robert Thompson's work in Ruby Valley shows a generally similar sequence. Unlike the Hidden Cave situation, Thompson found no marked decline—no dramatic change at all, in fact—in the pollen of any terrestrial plants at the Pleistocene/Holocene boundary in his Ruby Marsh cores. He did, however, find that sagebrush pollen declined sharply at about 7,700 years ago, ending a period of some 30,000 years of sagebrush dominance in the vegetation of this valley.

Accompanying this decline was a sharp increase in cheno-am pollen. That increase, which probably accompanied the shrinkage of the lake in this basin, was interpreted by Thompson as indicating an expansion of shadscale vegetation in the valley. Although the dates for the transition from vegetation dominated by sagebrush to vegetation in which shadscale played a major role differ between the Carson Sink (about 6,800 years ago) and Ruby Valley (about 7,700 years ago), the sequence of vegetational change is identical, and the difference in timing may in part reflect the 2,000′ elevational difference between these settings.

The distinct nature of early Holocene climates in the Great Basin can be seen in the history of subalpine conifers as well. Not surprisingly, much of the information available on the history of these trees within the floristic Great Basin comes from the Snake Range and nearby mountains, where Thompson and Wells have concentrated so much of their work on late Pleistocene and early Holocene packrat middens (see Chapter 6 and Figure 6-15).

These middens show that some subalpine conifers remained significantly beneath their modern elevational limits well into the early Holocene. In the Snake Range, for instance, both Thompson and Wells have shown that limber and bristlecone pines were widespread, even on south-facing slopes, at elevations as low as 6,500′ as recently as 9,500 years ago. In the massive Snake and Schell Creek ranges, these trees remained at fairly low elevations throughout the early Holocene. Thompson, for instance, has limber and bristlecone pine at 6,500′ on the east slope of the northern Snake Range at 7,350 years ago, and bristlecone pine alone at 6,100′ and 6,500 years ago in Smith Creek Canyon, again on the east slope of the Snake Range. In the Schell Creek Range, he has documented limber pine as late as about 6,500 years ago (and perhaps even somewhat later) at an elevation of 7,700′. All of these sites are in areas that are now dominated by piñon-juniper woodland. In the smaller, lower Confusion Range to the east, however, limber and bristlecone pines, which had occupied sites as low as 5,450′ at 11,880 years ago, were gone from these locations by 8,600 years ago; Thompson has documented a similar sequence, from Carlin's Cave (6,000′), at the southern end of the Egan Range.

In general, the packrat midden record from these ranges suggests that bristlecone pine retreated upslope as the early Holocene progressed, with limber pine following somewhat later. Xeric (warm and dry) sites lost their subalpine conifers first, as did the lower elevations on smaller mountain masses. Lower-elevation mesic (cool and moist) habitats on more massive ranges retained their subalpine conifers far longer. Indeed, they retained them throughout the early Holocene.

As the subalpine conifers moved upward between 10,000 and 7,000 years ago, a variety of plants increased in abundance. Thompson's analyses have shown that plants of the Upper Sagebrush–Grass Zone became common on lower mountain slopes as the subalpine conifers retreated. These shrubs included not only sagebrush but also rabbitbrush and ocean spray. Mountain mahogany became common in these habitats at the same time. A variety of junipers were also present on these lower slopes: most, though not all, early Holocene packrat middens analyzed from these slopes have provided the remains of Utah, Rocky Mountain, or common junipers.

In short, in at least east-central Nevada and west-central Utah, subalpine conifers—limber and bristlecone pines—remained at low elevations in cool and moist settings throughout the early Holocene. In less congenial habitats, they moved upslope during this interval, to be replaced by a variety of shrubs that are now common in the Upper Sagebrush–Grass Zone, and by mountain mahogany and junipers. Although comparable information is not available from other mountain ranges within the floristic Great Basin, there is little reason to think that this picture will change dramatically when such information becomes available.

THE MOJAVE DESERT

The general sequence of vegetational change in the Mojave Desert is quite similar to that in the floristic Great Basin to the immediate north, even though many of the plants involved differ. Instead of subalpine conifers retreating upslope, for instance, it is piñon and junipers that moved upward or that became locally extinct. Instead of sagebrush expanding into areas once occupied by conifers, it is such classic Mojave Desert plants as white bursage and creosote bush. The sequence of change, however, is much the same in both regions.

The woodlands that marked so many low-elevation areas in the Mojave Desert during the late Wisconsin tended to disappear, first from lower-elevation, xeric habitats, and later from higher-elevation, relatively mesic ones. In many areas, piñon and juniper were gone from less congenial settings by 10,000 years ago. In Death Valley, for instance, only a single midden sample documents the continued existence of Utah juniper beneath its modern elevational range after 10,000 years ago, and that single sample, from an elevation of 3,700′, dates to 9,680 years ago. In more favorable settings, these trees lingered longer, though apparently not nearly as long as they lingered in the vicinity of the Snake Range. The latest records for low-elevation conifers in the Mojave Desert are for Utah juniper, and both date to 7,800 years ago: from Mercury Ridge in the north-central Mojave Desert, and from Lucerne Valley in the far southwestern Mojave Desert. Today, both sites support creosote bush and other shrubs, but not junipers.

As these "pygmy conifers" moved upslope, plants that are fully characteristic of the modern Mojave Desert began to arrive, though at different times at different places. White bursage and creosote bush provide excellent examples.

Both of these shrubs are now widespread within the Mojave Desert, but neither of them appears to have been here before, or much before, the end of the Pleistocene. The earliest record for white bursage in the Mojave Desert is from Death Valley, where a midden analyzed by Wells and Woodcock contained macrofossils of this plant dated to 10,230 years ago at an elevation of 1,400′. Geoffrey Spaulding has white bursage from the Skeleton Hills at 9,200 years ago, but not in a series of earlier samples from here that go back to nearly 18,000 years ago. In Spaulding's Eureka View samples (see Chapter 6), white bursage appears at 6,795 years ago, even though he has samples from here that extend as far back as 14,700 years. In Lucerne Valley, Thomas King's midden samples first show the presence of white bursage at 7,900 years ago; his oldest samples are 12,100 years old. Nowhere has this plant been found in the Mojave Desert in a context older than 10,230 years. Today, it is one of the Mojave Desert's most abundant shrubs at elevations beneath 2,500′.

Creosote bush is also one of the Mojave Desert's most common shrubs; as I discussed in Chapter 2, the northern limit of this species sets the boundary between the Mojave Desert and the floristic Great Basin. The high abundance of creosote bush is not confined to the Mojave Desert, of course: this plant is extremely common throughout the Chihuahuan and Sonoran deserts as well (see Figure 2-9). "Oceans of creosote bush" is the appropriate phrase used by Julio Betancourt and his colleagues (1990:6) to describe the abundance of this plant in the warm deserts of North America.

Given this modern abundance, it came as a surprise when early analyses of North American packrat middens from the Chihuahuan, Sonoran, and Mojave deserts suggested that creosote bush was not in this vast region before 11,000 years ago. In 1976, the earliest midden-derived date for this species in North America fell at 10,580 years ago, obtained from one of Thomas Van Devender's middens in southwestern Arizona. Taking the lead from what appeared to be the very late arrival of creosote bush in this huge area, Philip Wells and Juan Hunziker observed that the closest relative of this species is South American in distribution, and argued that plants ancestral to North American creosote bush are South American—Argentinian—in origin. They speculated that, had creosote bush been in North America deep in the Pleistocene, it could not have survived full-glacial conditions, and must have been displaced far south. They also suggested that this shrub may not have arrived in North America until latest Pleistocene or earliest Holocene times.

We have far more midden dates available today, and, although Wells and Hunziker's argument for an ultimate

South American ancestry of North American creosote bush is very likely correct, the dates for the arrival of this plant in the north have been pushed back considerably since the time they published their analysis. In the Chihuahuan Desert of far southern Texas, those dates go as far back as 26,400 years ago, but the creosote bush fragments identified from this ancient midden were not dated directly, and Thomas Van Devender worries that they might be recent contaminants. This is surely not the case, however, for the directly dated creosote bush from the Chihuahuan Desert in south Texas that falls at 21,300 years ago. In the Sonoran Desert, James King and Van Devender have shown that creosote bush was present in the Artillery Mountains of west-central Arizona at 21,000 and 18,300 years ago, and Van Devender has shown that it was in the Tinajas Altas Mountains of southwestern Arizona at 18,700 years ago. Together, these records document that creosote bush was present during full-glacial, or close to full-glacial, times in the Chihuhuan Desert along the border between the United States and Mexico, and in the northern and central Sonoran Desert.

The situation is somewhat more complicated in the Mojave Desert. Most dates suggest an early Holocene or later arrival for creosote bush here. In the Amargosa Desert, for instance, the earliest date for creosote bush falls at 9,560 years ago, from one of Spaulding's Point of Rocks middens. A series of midden samples analyzed by Peter Wigand from Little Skull Mountain, some 20 miles north of Ash Meadows, first provided creosote bush at 8,480 years ago. Spaulding's Skeleton Hills samples first document this shrub at 8,200 years ago; his Penthouse midden samples, in the southern Sheep Range, first detect it in more than trace amounts at 8,100 years ago. In the Marble Mountains, east of Lucerne Valley, creosote bush is present in trace amounts at 9,515 years ago, but it is far more common at 7,900 years ago. To the east, in Lucerne Valley itself, it is not documented until 5,900 years ago. And Spaulding's Eureka View samples, on the very northern edge of the Mojave Desert, northwest of Death Valley, do not show creosote bush until 5,400 years ago (see Figure 6-4).

All this seems to provide a consistent picture. Creosote bush was in the Chihuahuan Desert, along the border between the United States and Mexico, and in the northern and central Sonoran Desert during full-glacial times. As the Pleistocene ended, it dispersed northward. Some parts of the Mojave Desert were occupied by this plant during the very early Holocene (Point of Rocks, for instance), but the more remote reaches of the Mojave Desert—for instance, Lucerne Valley and northern Eureka Valley—were not colonized until late in the middle Holocene.

Although this picture is consistent, it may not be correct. In 1961, Paul Martin and his colleagues analyzed the pollen content of Shasta ground sloth dung from Rampart Cave in Arizona's Grand Canyon. All of these dung samples are Pleistocene in age, and some contained creosote bush pollen; the oldest that held this pollen was over 35,500 years old. More recently, Richard Hansen's analysis of sloth dung samples from this cave showed the remains of this shrub in specimens that dated to 32,560 years ago, on the one hand, and between 12,000 and 13,100 years ago on the other. In addition, Spaulding has creosote bush that is 30,470 years old in his Eyrie midden samples, from the western Snake Range.

By themselves, the very early dates from creosote bush from Rampart Cave and the Sheep Range might simply imply that this shrub was in the region prior to the last glacial maximum, was eliminated during the full glacial, and then returned during the Holocene, just as Wells and Hunziker said might have happened. However, there is also a series of midden samples from the Mojave Desert that contain late Wisconsin creosote bush fossils. The Blue Diamond Road 3 midden in the southeastern Spring Range has creosote bush at 15,040 years ago. The Owl Canyon 1 midden sample, from the eastern edge of the Amargosa Desert, has creosote bush dated to 13,150 years ago. Spaulding's Penthouse samples first contain this shrub at 11,550 years ago.

Because creosote bush fossils are rare in all three of these middens and because these fossils have not been directly dated, it is possible that they represent modern contaminants. However, it is also possible that these specimens represent creosote bush growing in the heart of the Mojave Desert during the late Wisconsin. If so, the implication is that this species was present in the Mojave Desert during late Wisconsin times, but was so uncommon that it is difficult to find packrat middens that contain it. If that is correct, then the early Holocene dispersal of this plant across the Mojave Desert may have been in large part an internal affair, with the species dispersing widely from locally established populations. The only way to tell which of these options—an early Holocene arrival from the south (the accepted view) or dispersal from local populations—is correct is by dating the possible late Wisconsin–age creosote bush fragments from these middens directly. Until then, both possibilities will remain open.

Whichever possibility is correct, however, there is no doubt that creosote bush was spreading across the Mojave Desert during the early Holocene. As this was happening, it also appears that sagebrush was becoming less abundant here, although the early Holocene history of sagebrush in the Mojave Desert is not well understood.

That we do not have a good understanding of the history of this plant here may simply reflect the fact that sagebrush had become relatively uncommon in this area by 10,000 years ago. Spaulding's Point of Rocks midden samples from the Amargosa Desert, for instance, contain sagebrush macrofossils as late as 9,840 years ago, but not in two later samples that are 9,560 and 9,260 years old. His Last Chance Range samples not far to the south contain sage at 11,760 years ago, but not at 9,280 years ago. Other early Holocene middens do contain sagebrush macrofossils, but only in very small amounts—in the Basin Canyon series (central Sheep Range) at 9,365 years ago, for instance, and in the Penthouse (southeastern Sheep Range) series at 8,070 years ago. Perhaps this shrub was simply disappearing from the landscape as the early Holocene began.

On the other hand, there is superb evidence that, in at least parts of the Mojave Desert, sagebrush was present in some abundance through much of the early Holocene. Thomas King analyzed the pollen from the middens that he collected from the Lucerne Valley area, and found high levels of *Artemisia* pollen in samples dating to between 12,100 and 8,300 years ago, but not after that time. The sequence agrees quite well with independent data suggesting that Lake Mojave desiccated at around 8,700 years ago.

A similar phenomenon is known from the Tule Springs region in Las Vegas Valley. As I discussed in Chapter 6, Peter Mehringer's work here suggested that, at about 12,000 years ago, a juniper woodland with a sagebrush understory was replaced by desert shrub vegetation dominated by sagebrush and shadscale. In fact, sagebrush pollen is abundant in all of the samples he analyzed from Unit E_1, now dated to between 14,000 and 11,700 years ago. Sagebrush pollen is also common in his samples from Unit E_2, deposited between 11,000 and 7,200 years ago, with a fairly pronounced decline in abundance at about 7,500 years ago. Samples from above E_2 contain virtually no sagebrush pollen at all. The correlation between this vegetational sequence and the sequence derived by Haynes and Quade for the history of shallow lakes and marshes in Las Vegas Valley is striking.

Pollen evidence from two parts of the Mojave Desert—the Lucerne Valley region and Las Vegas Valley—thus suggests that, in at least some areas, sagebrush remained fairly common until about 8,000 years ago or so, after which it declined. The packrat middens, however, tend to contain significant numbers of sagebrush macrofossils only during the late Pleistocene.

Why might this be the case? One answer is suggested by King's samples from the Lucerne Valley region. Although these samples contain sagebrush pollen, documenting that sagebrush was present in the area, they provide no identifiable sagebrush macrofossils. Clearly, the pollen and the macrofossils in these middens are telling us different things.

Robert Thompson has shown that certain plants are routinely better represented in packrat middens by pollen than they are by macrofossils. Not only is sagebrush among those plants, but, of the nine groups of pollen that he analyzed, it was the one showing the greatest difference between pollen and macrofossil representation. Sagebrush macrofossils, it turns out, are often absent or rare in packrat middens that contain substantial amounts of sagebrush pollen. As Thompson notes, sagebrush is a wind-pollinated plant that most commonly grows on fine substrates; the plant might be common nearby, but not on the rocky outcrops that contain the middens. As a result, the middens may often contain sagebrush pollen, but not sagebrush macrofossils.

In short, the pollen records suggest that sagebrush was fairly common in at least some parts of the Mojave Desert during the early Holocene, whereas the packrat midden records suggest that it was rare to absent. The reason for this difference is likely to lie largely in the very different ways in which macrofossils and pollen become embedded in the deposits that paleobotanists analyze.

This cannot be the whole answer, however. Spaulding's Point of Rocks and Last Chance Range middens, for instance, may lack early Holocene sagebrush macrofossils, but they did provide late Pleistocene examples. In addition, some of his late Pleistocene middens—for instance, from the Eleana Range—contain them in impressive abundance. There is something more going on here than can be explained by the different ways in which pollen and macrofossils accumulate in packrat middens.

The rest of the answer is probably provided by the late Wisconsin and early Holocene history of sagebrush itself.

During the latest Wisconsin, this shrub was probably so abundant on many parts of the Mojave Desert landscape that it ended up, in the form of macrofossils, in many packrat middens. By the early Holocene, sage was sufficently reduced in abundance that the location of the middens, on rocky outcrops, had become critical. It was still present, and clearly common in some places, but no longer growing immediately adjacent to the middens. As a result, whereas the Las Vegas Valley pollen profiles show sagebrush on the floor of this valley through much of the early Holocene, middens from higher settings contain only small amounts of it. If this explanation is correct, then there is an excellent chance that the pollen from early Holocene midden samples that lack, or only contain very small amounts of, sagebrush would show that sagebrush was still common in many lower-elevation parts of the Mojave Desert through much of the early Holocene, just as the Lucerne Valley and Las Vegas Valley records imply.

THE MONTANE MAMMALS

During the early Holocene, shallow lakes and marshes existed at low elevations in many parts of the Great Basin. In the floristic Great Basin, sagebrush steppe covered areas that are now dominated by shadscale, and subalpine conifers, although generally moving upslope, persisted in favorable habitats at low elevations. In the Mojave Desert, junipers lasted at favorable low-elevation sites until at least 7,800 years ago, and the pollen evidence shows that, at least in some areas, sagebrush continued to exist at low elevations until about this time, even as such plants as white bursage and creosote bush spread across the landscape. Although some disagree, conditions cooler or moister than those of today are indicated. Given this situation, it would not be surprising to see that now-montane mammals also continued to exist at low elevations between 10,000 and 7,000 years ago or so.

In fact, that is the case, but our knowledge of the early Holocene history of these mammals is fairly ragged (see Tables 8-1 and 8-2, and Figure 8-2). The record for pikas, however, is reasonably clear, if sparse. Although there are no early Holocene records for pikas from the more southerly reaches of the Great Basin, the Connley Caves, in south-central Oregon, provided the remains of this animal from sediments that dated to as recently as about 7,200 years ago. Not far to the southwest, Hanging Rock Shelter, in northwestern Nevada, yielded pika specimens that are younger than 8,000 years old, though how much younger is not known. The equally sparse data available from the mountains are consistent. Pikas are now extinct in the Jarbidge Mountains and in the Snake Range, but they were still in the former range during earliest Holocene times, and in the latter as late as about 6,500 years ago.

The packrat midden sample from the southern Great Basin, and in particular from the Mojave Desert, seems sufficiently large that it is likely that, if pikas had been in lower-elevation settings here during the early Holocene, they would have been detected by now. Although it is fully possible that some lowland populations lingered into the early Holocene in favorable southern areas, it does seem that at least low-elevation populations of this small mammal were extirpated earlier in the south—and perhaps by the beginning of the Holocene—than they were in the north, where they continued to exist in some lowland settings until at least the end of the early Holocene. Such a history is consistent with the fact that such plants as creosote bush were spreading across Mojave Desert valleys at the same time as sagebrush was still occupying valleys to the north that are now dominated by shadscale. Not surprisingly, the latest low-elevation records we have for pikas are from sites that are not far removed from areas that still support these animals—a mere 20 miles in the case of the Connley Caves.

The other available Holocene records for montane mammals in areas where they no longer occur are not so easily interpreted. In most cases, that is because our understanding of the chronology of these records is so weak. The Humboldt and Lovelock cave yellow-bellied marmot and bushy-tailed packrat specimens are a case in point. The earliest excavations at Lovelock Cave were carried out at the beginning of this century, and continued sporadically through the 1960s. Humboldt Cave was excavated in the 1930s. None of these excavations paid much detailed attention to stratigraphy. In spite of intense efforts, for instance, archaeologist Stephanie Livingston, in her detailed analysis of the bird and mammal remains from Lovelock Cave, was unable to place the marmot specimens from this site (only two bones, but also a complete, desiccated individual) in their original stratigraphic context. All we know is that these remains are Holocene in age; only dating the specimens themselves can tell us any more.

Much the same is true for the marmots and bushy-tailed packrats from Hogup Cave, though for very different reasons. This site was excavated with great care by

Table 8-1. Holocene Extralimital Records for Great Basin Montane Mammals: Lowlands[a]

Location	Elevation (feet)	Species	Age (years ago)	Distance (miles)	Reference
Eetza Mountain, NV					
Hidden Cave (1)	4,105	*Marmota flaviventris*	21,000–<1,500	15 SW	5
		Neotoma cinerea		5 NW	
Fort Rock Basin, OR					
Connley Caves (2)	4,445	*Ochotona princeps*	11,200–7,200	20 NW	4
Hanging Rock Canyon, NV					
Hanging Rock Shelter (3)	5,660	*Ochotona princeps*	<8,000	30 NW	6
Hogup Mountain, Utah					
Hogup Cave (4)	4,700	*Marmota flaviventris*	8,350–1,500[b]	60 NW	3
		Neotoma cinerea		25 NNE	
Silver Island Mountains, UT					
Danger Cave (5)	4,310	*Neotoma cinerea*	11,000–9,000[c]	60 E	6
Snake Valley, NV					
Owl Cave One (6)	5,580	*Spermophilus lateralis*	Holocene	3 W	1
		Mustela erminea		3 NW	
West Humboldt Range, NV					
Humboldt Cave (7)	4,200	*Marmota flaviventris*	Holocene	40 S	2
Lovelock Cave (8)	4,240	*Marmota flaviventris*	Holocene	40 S	7

Notes: a, Numbers in parentheses indicate sites in Figure 8-2. The distance column provides the distance to the nearest known modern populations: see also Table 7-13; *b,* Stratigraphic mixing has affected the Hogup Cave deposits; *c,* There are a small number of *Neotoma cinerea* specimens from later deposits in this site; these may represent stratigraphic mixing.

References: 1, Birnie (1986), Turnmire (1987); 2, R. H. Brooks (1956); 3, Aikens (1970); Durrant (1970); 4, Grayson (1977a, 1979); 5, Grayson (1985); 6, Grayson (1988a); 7, Livingston (1988b).

archaeologist C. Melvin Aikens during the 1960s, but a variety of evidence, including radiocarbon dates out of proper stratigraphic order, shows that some of the deposits within Hogup had become mixed. As a result, we do not know exactly how old the now-montane mammals from this site are.

Danger Cave, at the base of the Silver Island Range in western Utah, does seem to document the persistence of bushy-tailed packrats at low elevations along the eastern edge of the Bonneville Basin into the early Holocene. Hidden Cave, on the other hand, clearly establishes the persistence of both bushy-tailed packrats and marmots in

Table 8-2. Holocene Extralimital Records for Great Basin Montane Mammals: Mountains[a]

Location	Elevation (feet)	Species	Age (years ago)	Distance (miles)	Reference
Jarbidge Mountains, NV					
Deer Creek Cave (9)	5,800	*Ochotona princeps*	10,085–9,670	60 S	2
Snake Range, NV					
Streamview Rockshelter SV3 (10)	6,100	*Ochotona princeps*	6,490–6,890	85 NW	1

Note: a, Numbers in parentheses indicate sites in Figure 8-2. The distance column provides the distance to the nearest known modern population.

References: 1, R. S. Thompson (1984); 2, Ziegler (1963).

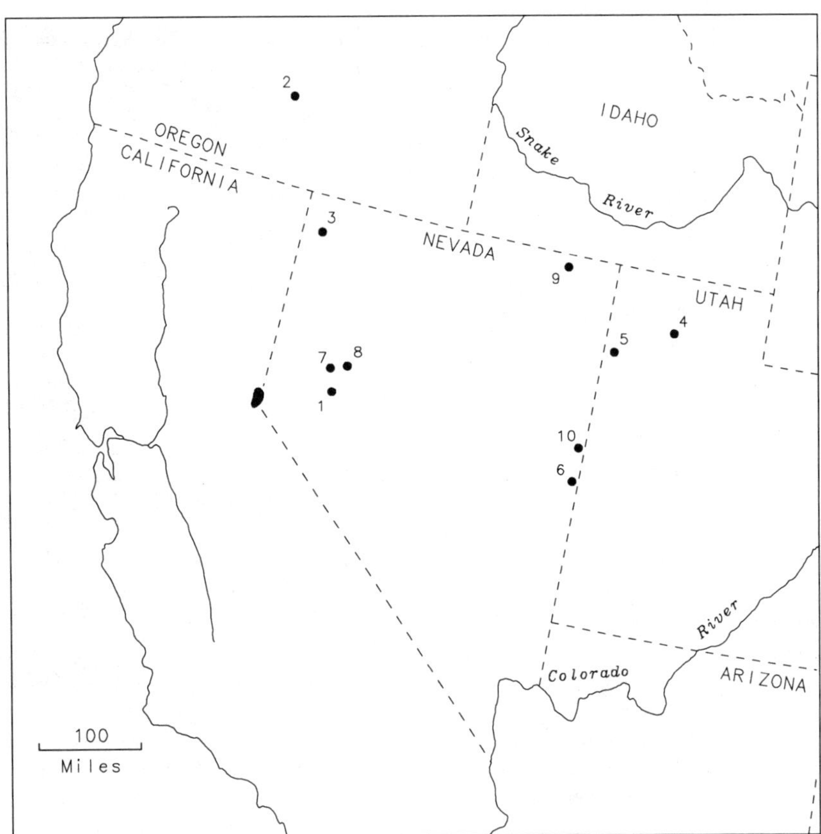

Figure 8-2. Sites providing Holocene extralimital records for montane mammals in the Great Basin. See Tables 8-1 and 8-2 for key to locations.

the southern Carson Desert from late Pleistocene times to nearly 1,500 years ago, as I discuss later in this chapter.

The general nature of lower-elevation habitats in at least the floristic Great Basin during the early Holocene suggests that a tremendous amount remains to be learned about the early Holocene history of montane mammals here. The scanty information that is available shows that at least pikas remained in lower-elevation settings until the end of this period, and strongly suggests that other mammals, in particular bushy-tailed packrats and marmots, did so as well.

That there is little evidence for the continued low-elevation existence of such mammals during the early Holocene almost undoubtedly reflects the fact that very few deposits of this age have been excavated. The packrat midden record for the Mojave Desert and the Snake Range area is strong, but packrats can be counted on only to provide us with information on pikas. The richest source of montane mammal fossils is provided by the sediments of caves and rockshelters, but very few such sites with early Holocene deposits have been excavated. Those that have been excavated—Danger Cave, Hidden Cave, and the Connley Caves, for instance—contain the mammals. Unfortunately, other sites that have been carefully excavated do not have early Holocene deposits. Gatecliff Shelter in the Toquima Range of central Nevada is an excellent example. This site provided some 13,000 bones and teeth of small mammals, all from well-controlled and well-dated stratigraphic contexts (see Figures 8-3 and 8-4). However, the oldest sediments in this site were deposited only shortly before 7,000 years ago. There is every reason to believe that, as more Great Basin sites of early Holocene age are excavated, more early Holocene, low-elevation populations of mammals that are now restricted to mountain settings in the Great Basin will be discovered.

There is also every reason to believe that we will learn that the history of montane mammals in the Great Basin is quite complex. It is reasonable to speculate that different species, and different populations of the same species, became extinct at different times and different places. The earliest losses likely occurred in the south, the latest in the north. Indeed, the latest securely dated low-elevation populations of marmots in the Mojave Desert are late Pleistocene in age; the latest such populations in the northern Great Basin are late Holocene in age. There is also every

Figure 8-3. Gatecliff Shelter from the south side of Mill Creek Canyon. Trees are singleleaf piñon and Utah juniper.

reason to believe that the differential extinction of these mammals on the mountains themselves was equally complex. Smaller, lower ranges likely lost their montane mammals first, with larger, higher ranges losing them later; southern ranges likely underwent extinctions before northern ones. The Sheep Range in southern Nevada, for instance, appears to have lost its pikas toward the end of the Pleistocene; the Snake Range far to the north and east supported them until at least about 6,500 years ago.

We can also speculate about the order in which montane mammals were lost from particular ranges. Biogeographers have begun to develop powerful methods for evaluating the "nestedness" of faunas on biogeographic islands. In a fully nested fauna, the same species that occur in smaller faunas on islands will also occur in all larger faunas in the same set of islands. There are statistical techniques, developed by Bruce Patterson and Wirt Atmar, for determining how "nested" a set of island faunas is, and for evaluating the odds that a given distribution could have come about as a result of chance alone.

A close look at Table 7-10, which displays the distribution of montane mammals across Brown's 19 ranges, suggests that these faunas are nested: the smaller faunas seem to form subsets of the larger ones. Statistical analysis shows that, although the nesting is not perfect (there are 21 deviations from perfect nestedness in this table), it is far greater than can be accounted for by chance. Indeed, many of the deviations from perfect nestedness that now exist may well reflect our inadequate knowledge of the modern distributions of these mammals.

The nested pattern shown by these faunas could reflect the differential colonization abilities of the mammals involved. However, it is far more likely, especially given the paleontological data that I have reviewed, that the nesting reflects the fact the smaller faunas have largely been produced by subtraction from a common set of species, and that these subtractions have been very predictable. Given the modern distributions, for instance, I would predict that white-tailed jack rabbits (found on only 2 of the 19 ranges) were lost from the Snake Range before pikas (on 5 of the ranges) were lost here. As

Figure 8-4. The stratigraphy of Gatecliff Shelter. Photo courtesy of David H. Thomas.

important, and as Patterson and others have pointed out, these patterns can also provide a powerful tool for conserving these faunas, guiding us both to species that are in particular need of protection and to the best ways of building preserves to ensure the well-being of those species.

EARLY HOLOCENE CLIMATES

The evidence from plants, mammals, marshes, and shallow lakes all suggests that the floristic Great Basin was cooler or moister, or both, during the early Holocene. Pikas, for instance, could not exist in low-elevation settings in this area were summer temperatures anything like what they are now. However, there have been relatively few attempts based on empirical data to measure exactly how much cooler or moister the floristic Great Basin was during this interval. This is, in part, because the data available are simply not as rich as they are for the late Wisconsin.

Robert Thompson, however, has pointed out that the optimal temperature for photosynthesis in limber pine seedlings is around 59°F. Coupling that fact with the abundance of limber pine macrofossils in lower-elevation packrat middens from the east-central Great Basin, he estimates that summer temperatures in this region were some 7°–9°F cooler than they are now. That figure is likely to be compatible with the existence of valley-bottom pikas.

In the last chapter, I noted that there are no Pleistocene records for singleleaf piñon pine (*Pinus monophylla*) in the floristic Great Basin. In fact, with one exception that I will soon discuss, the earliest records we have for piñon pine here postdate 7,000 years ago. Even the possible exception is only 7,410 years old.

Thompson observes that work by Dwight Billings, Neal West, and other botanists seems to have established four factors that are critical in limiting the distribution of singleleaf piñon in the Great Basin today: cold winters, cool summers, inadequate summer precipitation, and the absence of winter thermal inversions. Since there was no piñon in the floristic Great Basin during the early Holocene, and since source populations were available in the higher elevations of the Mojave Desert to the south, some combination of these negative factors must have kept it out.

Summer temperatures increased at the end of the early Holocene in the floristic Great Basin, and it is fully possible that it was cool summers that kept piñons out of the Great Basin until after about 7,000 years ago. Thompson, however, suggests that a change in the seasonality of precipitation may also have been involved.

In particular, he suggests that early Holocene precipitation in the floristic Great Basin may have fallen almost entirely in the winter, and that an increase in summer rainfall toward the end of this interval may have been involved in allowing the movement of piñons into the region. In this view, the continuing absence of piñon pine in the floristic Great Basin during the early Holocene would reflect summers that were cooler than those of today, as well as inadequate summer precipitation.

That summers here were cooler seems clear. That there was a shift toward increased summer rainfall in the floristic Great Basin toward the end of the early Holocene, however, may be debated. In fact, Thompson's position is at odds with a very different approach taken by Geoffrey Spaulding and Lisa Graumlich.

During the late Wisconsin and early Holocene, woodlands that consisted of various combinations of pine, oak, and juniper were widespread in the Sonoran Desert of the American Southwest. These woodlands were gone by 8,000 years ago; in fact, most of them were gone soon after 9,000 years ago. Spaulding and Graumlich observe that the elimination of woodland in the Sonoran Desert appears to have occurred later than it occurred in the Mojave Desert to the north. This appears to be the case even though many of the Sonoran Desert sites that document the existence of this woodland are not only further south than the Mojave Desert sites that seem to have lost their trees earlier, they are also lower in elevation.

Spaulding and Graumlich argue that this difference, as well as other aspects of the late Wisconsin and early Holocene vegetational record for this region (for instance, the distribution of succulent plants), is best explained by invoking strengthened monsoonal incursions between about 12,000 and 8,000 years ago. During this interval, they argue, summer temperatures were actually about 2°–4°F *warmer* than they are now, and winter temperatures about 2°F cooler. In addition, the strengthened monsoonal system brought greatly increased rainfall to the Sonoran Desert during the summer months. Since the source of that rainfall must have been either the Gulf of Mexico or the Gulf of California and Pacific Ocean, the Sonoran Desert received more of it than did the Mojave Desert. Because the Sonoran Desert was closer to the source of the moisture, low-elevation woodlands lasted longer here than in the Mojave Desert.

In this intriguing view, Mojave Desert precipitation during the early Holocene fell primarily during the summer months. This position is in sharp opposition to Thompson's. Thompson also derives his increased summer precipitation from strengthened monsoons, and thus from the south, but he argues that this shift occurred after 8,000 years ago, not between 12,000 and 8,000 years ago.

Thomas Van Devender, whose work has focused on the Sonoran Desert, disagrees strongly with Spaulding and Graumlich's view. Van Devender maintains that most of the Sonoran Desert lacked reliable summer rainfall during the early Holocene, receiving its moisture instead during the winter months. He also maintains that early Holocene temperatures in the Sonoran Desert were distinctly cooler, not warmer, than they are now.

Thompson's reconstruction is in strong agreement with Van Devender's. Together, the two are in almost perfect disagreement with Spaulding and Graumlich's. These latter authors note that their analysis is in accord with the reconstruction provided by a major climatic simulation model for this period of time. That model, however, also calls for early Holocene temperatures between 3.6° and 7.2°F warmer than those of today for the floristic Great Basin. Much of what we know about this region, from low-elevation limber pine to valley-dwelling pikas, suggests that these figures must be wrong.

If Spaulding and Graumlich's intensified monsoons between 12,000 and 8,000 years ago did extend into the Mojave Desert, they did not reach far into the floristic Great Basin: summer temperatures here were distinctly cooler than they are now, and cool summers are incompatible with strengthened monsoons. Indeed, it is also difficult to reconcile this hypothesis with the Tule Springs pollen record from the Mojave Desert itself. Spaulding and Graumlich's argument is based entirely on the packrat midden record, and calls for the reduction of such steppe shrubs as sagebrush during the early Holocene. As they note, steppe shrubs "are expected to be abundant when winter rains dominate" (Spaulding and Graumlich 1986:3). Exactly such shrubs, however, mark the early Holocene pollen record in Las Vegas Valley.

The Middle Holocene: 7,500 to 4,500 Years Ago

ERNST ANTEVS AND THE ALTITHERMAL

Scientists working on the late Pleistocene and Holocene history of the Great Basin today have a tremendous advantage over those who worked here fifty or sixty years ago. There are better roads and better vehicles, making it far easier to get around. There are more people working in any given discipline, so highly detailed information is being developed within multiple fields. As a result, not only is far more known about the history of, say, plants or animals, but the results from one set of investigations—on plant history, for instance—can be used to better our understanding of the results from a different set of investigations—on mammal history, for instance. In addition, we have access to an array of dating techniques that can be used to determine the absolute ages of a diverse set of materials, from seeds to fine-grained sediments.

These modern advantages make the accomplishments of Ernst Antevs all the more remarkable. Born in Sweden in 1888, Antevs studied under famed Swedish geologist Gerard de Geer, receiving his Ph.D. in geology from the University of Stockholm in 1917. De Geer had pioneered the study of varved deposits, and Antevs followed de Geer in his interest in such deposits.

Lakes that receive their water from streams issuing from melting glaciers are often marked by sediments that show alternating layers of coarse and fine material. These couplets are formed as a result of the seasonal influx of sediments into the lake. During the warm months of the year, when suspended sediment is being introduced into the lake, it is primarily the heavier fraction that is deposited. During the winter, when the lake freezes over, the finer particles settle. Each pair of coarse and fine layers produced in this way is a varve; each represents a single year of lake history. In addition, because of increased glacial melt during warm years, the varves that make up any given sequence of lake deposits have different thicknesses. As long as it can be assumed that the temperature changes driving varve thickness are not strictly local, the changing thicknesses allow varves from different lakes to be correlated, much as tree rings can be correlated on the basis of their changing thicknesses. It follows from all of this that counting varves, and patching together sequences from varved lakes, provides a means of extracting an absolute chronology for those lakes, and that is what de Geer did. Ultimately, he compiled a varve chronology for Sweden that extended back nearly 17,000 years. Independent dating has now shown that the Holocene portion of that chronology is extremely accurate.

If the age of each varve in a lake can be accurately determined, it follows that the age of anything incorporated in varved sediments, including pollen, can also be obtained. Pollen analysts in northern Europe were quick to take advantage of this fact. They were also quick to make use of the fact that the major changes they saw in the pollen content of these dated sediments could be correlated with similar, but undated, changes they were finding in the rich pollen and plant macrofossil sequences in Scandinavian peat bogs. By the early 1900s, it had been demonstrated that the Pleistocene had ended by 9,000 years ago or so, and that the Scandinavian middle Holocene had been warmer than both earlier and later Holocene times.

In 1920, de Geer came to North America to study varved deposits in New England. Antevs came with him, but, when de Geer returned, Antevs stayed, remaining here for the rest of his life.

During his early years in North America, Antevs studied varved deposits in New England and Canada, but he also started to work in the Great Basin; his first trip to this region came in 1922. By the mid-1930s, most of his publications began to deal not with varve chronologies and the northeast, but with the Pleistocene and Holocene history of the arid West.

Antevs, like de Geer, believed that major temperature changes are "simultaneous over the entire northern or southern hemisphere, and, perhaps, the entire world" (1931:1). From the very beginning of his work in North America, this belief led Antevs to assume that the broad outline of Holocene temperature history in North America was the same as it had been in Sweden. As early as 1925, he noted that the Holocene temperature maximum in Sweden appeared to fall between about 7,000 and 4,000 years ago, and that "the post-glacial maximum of temperature was fairly certainly contemporaneous in both continents" (1925:65).

Antevs was soon able to call on evidence from the arid West to support this argument. In 1914, the geologist Walton Van Winkle had measured the salt content of Abert and Summer lakes in south-central Oregon, and had found it to be lower than it should have been had these lakes been in continuous existence since the Pleistocene. Van Winkle calculated that the rebirth of these lakes had occurred about 4,000 years ago. Likewise, Hoyt S. Gale had measured the salt content of Owens Lake, publishing his results in 1915; that content, Gale argued, was also consistent with 4,000 years of accumulation. Gale did not think that Owens Lake was dry prior to 4,000 years ago, instead speculating that this was the time that Owens Lake stopped overflowing, and thus stopped flushing itself of salts. Antevs, however, argued that Gale's results were better interpreted as meaning that Owens Lake had dried up before this time, and had been reborn at about 4,000 years ago, just as Abert and Summer lakes had been argued to do. These dates, of course, were fully consistent with the varve-derived chronology for the end of the postglacial warm period in Sweden.

During the 1940s, other data on the Holocene climatic history of the West became available, including the results of Henry P. Hansen's pioneering pollen analyses in the region. In 1948, Antevs synthesized all of this information in an extremely powerful way.

What we now term the Holocene, Antevs called the "Neothermal," meaning the "new warm age." He argued that the Neothermal had begun, and the Pleistocene had ended, 9,000 years ago. He also divided the Neothermal into three "temperature ages." The first of these, the Anathermal, he characterized as having had temperatures that were at first like those of today, but that then became warmer; the Anathermal, he argued, dated to between 9,000 and 7,000 years ago. Although the focus of his subdivisions of the Holocene was on temperature, not on moisture, he also argued that the Anathermal was wetter than the Great Basin has been during historic times. His second temperature age was the Altithermal, which he characterized as having been distinctly warmer and drier than the present, and which he argued fell between 7,000 and 4,500 years ago. The last of his ages was the Medithermal, 4,500 years ago to the present, marked by conditions very much like those of the present (see Table 8-3).

Table 8-3. Ernst Antevs's Neothermal Sequence[a]

Temperature age	Dates (years ago)	Climates
Anathermal	9,000–7,000	Warm, moist
Altithermal	7,000–4,500	Hot, dry
Medithermal	4,500–Present	Cooler, moister

[a]From Antevs (1948).

As the years passed, Antevs made minor adjustments to the dates of his three-part Holocene. In 1955, for instance, he placed the end of the Pleistocene at 10,000 years ago, the beginning of the Altithermal at 7,500 years ago, and the end of this hot and dry interval at 4,500 years ago. The general nature of his Neothermal sequence, however, remained the same. A wetter early Holocene (the Anathermal) had been followed by a hot and dry middle Holocene (the Altithermal), which was in turn followed by a later Holocene (the Medithermal) marked by conditions that were, in general, very much like those of today.

Proposed in detail in 1948, Antevs's Neothermal model was widely accepted by archaeologists and geologists alike. Not only did the evidence that Antevs provided to support his climatic arguments appear convincing, but his three-part sequence was associated with real dates. An archaeologist working with Holocene deposits that were fairly old and that appeared to reflect moister conditions than those of today could assign them to the Anathermal, and then argue that they dated to between 10,000 and 7,000 years ago. Deposits that seemed to reflect hot and dry times could be assigned to the Altithermal and dated to between about 7,000 and 4,500 years ago. Until radiocarbon dating came into routine use, age assignments on this basis were standard in the arid West, especially in the Great Basin. As a result, the literature dealing with the Holocene of this area that appeared between about 1950 and the mid-1970s is often hard to follow without knowledge of Antevs's sequence.

It is important to recognize that this sequence was essentially based on two things. First, it was based on the assumption that major changes in temperature could be used to correlate depositional sequences in far-flung regions: in, for instance, Oregon and Sweden. Second, it was also based on the Scandinavian varve chronology.

Thus, when Antevs began to develop his Holocene climatic history of the Great Basin in some detail, he correctly pointed out that Van Winkle had estimated that Abert and Summer lakes had been reborn about 4,000 years ago. However, he dismissed Gale's suggestion that Owens Lake had decreased in size 4,000 years ago, substituting in its place the argument that it was dry prior to this time. And, although the 4,000-year dates were estimates made by Gale and Van Winkle, his conclusion was that "the warm Postpluvial age some 5500–2000 B.C. also was dry" (1938:191) in the Desert West. The 2000 B.C. date coincided with Van Winkle's estimate, but the 5500 B.C. date had no secure local basis: it was drawn entirely from the Scandinavian varve chronology.

The most famous part of Antevs's sequence is the Altithermal, the hot and dry middle Holocene. Indeed, this term is still in occasional use among Great Basin scholars, and is in common use in other parts of the West, with much the same meaning—both chronological and climatic—that Antevs gave it. Was his reconstruction of middle Holocene climatic history in the Great Basin correct?

ELEVATED TIMBERLINES IN THE WHITE MOUNTAINS

One of the most elegant and chronologically well-controlled analyses of the nature of middle Holocene climates in the Great Basin was performed by Valmore LaMarche, of the University of Arizona's famous Laboratory of Tree-Ring Research. LaMarche had become intrigued by his observation of dead trees well above timberline on both the White Mountains of eastern California and the Snake Range of eastern Nevada. He realized that at some time in the past, climatic conditions had to have been such as to allow trees to exist above where they can exist now. The problem was to know when this was, and what the climatic conditions responsible for it were.

LaMarche's detailed analysis of this situation was directed toward the dead bristlecone pines above timberline on Sheep and Campito mountains in the southern White Mountains. On Sheep Mountain, LaMarche found that dead trees extend as much as 500′ above the modern timberline (which falls here at about 11,500′). He also found that they extend nearly to the top of Campito Mountain, some 330′ above the current timberline (here at about 11,200′; see Figure 8-5).

Using a combination of radiocarbon and tree ring dating, LaMarche provided ages for nearly 140 dead, above-timberline trees on these two mountains. Because the innermost and outermost parts of these trees were not preserved, the dates he obtained did not tell him the precise times at which the trees had become established or had died. Because the remains of trees that had been higher might have decayed completely, he could not know that his uppermost dead trees also marked the uppermost limit of past timberlines. What he did establish, however, was that timberline was at or above the elevation of the dead trees during the years that his dates indicated the trees were alive.

On Sheep Mountain, LaMarche's oldest tree dated to about 6,500 years ago. From that time, until about 4,200 years ago, timberline remained nearly 500′ higher than it is now, after which it dropped sharply. On Campito Mountain, middle Holocene timberlines were also distinctly higher—from about 260′ to 360′ higher—than they are now, but these timberlines remained high until about 2,500 years ago. Putting both records together, and assuming that warmer summer temperatures are critical in allowing the upslope movement of the timberline, LaMarche concluded that the period of time between about 7,400 and 4,000 years ago was marked by relatively high summer temperatures. He also observed that the period from 5,000 to 4,000 years ago was especially favorable for bristlecone pine growth; this, he suggested, reflects both warm summer temperatures and fairly high precipitation.

Although LaMarche did not attempt to estimate precipitation values from his middle Holocene trees, he did use his Sheep Mountain data to estimate the difference between recent July temperatures and those 4,500 years ago, when timberline was at or above 11,975′. His calculations suggested that, 4,500 years ago, July temperatures were 3.5°F warmer than they have been during the past few

Figure 8-5. Campito Mountain in the White Mountains of California. Live bristlecone pines can be seen on the slopes, whereas dead trees extend nearly to the top of the mountain.

centuries. This, he observed, was strongly consistent with Antevs's notion of an Altithermal.

THE RUBY MARSHES DISAPPEAR

As I have discussed, Robert Thompson's analysis of sediment cores from the Ruby Marshes documents the fact that a freshwater lake, deeper than is found here today, existed in this basin from about 10,400 years ago to about 8,000 years ago. Thompson also found that sagebrush pollen declined dramatically, while that of the cheno-ams (including shadscale) increased, at about 7,700 years ago. This change Thompson interpreted as reflecting an expansion of shadscale vegetation at the expense of sagebrush.

More than that happened at about this time, however. Using the 11 radiocarbon dates he had obtained for the Holocene sections of his cores, plus the 6,800-year date provided by Mazama ash, Thompson was able to calculate the rate at which sediments accumulated in the Ruby Marshes during much of the Holocene. What he found was telling. Between 9,920 and 6,800 years ago, it took an average of 23 years for a centimeter (0.4″) of sediment to accumulate. Between 4,420 and 1,350 years ago, the same amount of material took 32 years to be deposited. But between 6,800 and 4,420 years ago, the same centimeter required 90 years to be laid down.

There are only two convincing ways to explain why it took nearly a century to accomplish during the middle Holocene what took only a few decades to accomplish during the early and late Holocene. Either deposition rates slowed to a crawl during this interval, or the deposits that were laid down during this time were eroded. No matter which of these situations pertains (and both may have happened), the implications are much the same. During the middle Holocene, the Ruby Marshes were extremely shallow, and may at times have dried up completely. The increased rate of sedimentation that begins at about 4,500 years ago suggests that the marshes deepened once again at about this time.

Thompson's careful work in Ruby Valley shows that the expansion of shadscale vegetation here was accompanied, or was perhaps soon followed, by a significant decline in water levels. For the next several thousand years, those levels were markedly low. Not until about 4,500 years ago did they deepen once again. As Thompson notes, his data on vegetation and marsh history are consistent. Together, they suggest a warm and/or dry middle Holocene. This again looks a lot like Antevs's Altithermal.

DESERT SHRUBS AND MARSH HISTORY IN THE STEENS MOUNTAIN REGION

Southeastern Oregon's Steens Mountain rises to an elevation of 9,733′, separating the Alvord Desert from Catlow Valley. Although there is a stand of grand fir on the west flank of this range, Steens Mountain is distinct from most other massive Great Basin ranges in that it lacks a zone of either montane or subalpine conifers. This fact makes Steens an excellent setting for studying the history of steppe vegetation at higher altitudes. Not only has Peter Mehringer pointed this out, but he has also taken advantage of the fact in an important way.

Mehringer cored two Steens Mountain lakes, Fish Lake, at an elevation of 7,380′, and Wildhorse Lake, at 8,480′ (see Figure 5-20). His analysis of the sediments he retrieved not only documents that the Fish Lake basin was free of glacial ice by 13,000 years ago, and the Wildhorse Lake cirque by 9,400 years ago, but also demonstrates that these sediments share six separate volcanic ashes that were deposited between about 7,000 and 1,000 years ago. Those ashes, coupled with the radiocarbon dates he obtained, allowed Mehringer to correlate the depositional records of these two lakes with exceptional precision.

Armed with these tightly correlated sequences, Mehringer took a close look at the changing ratios of sagebrush to grass pollen through time as recorded in the sediments of both lakes. What he found was both dramatic and convincing (Figure 8-6).

During the past 13,000 years, sagebrush pollen was, on the average, about six times more abundant than grass pollen in the Fish Lake sediments. By itself, of course, this figure has little meaning, and Mehringer calculated it simply to standardize the deviations around it through time. Doing that showed that, between 13,000 and about 8,500 years ago, the sagebrush/grass ratio remained below its Fish Lake average. By 8,700 years ago, however, it was on the rise. Shortly before 8,000 years ago, it climbed above its average value and remained there until about 5,500 years ago. For the next several hundred years, the ratio vacillated up and down; not until about 4,700 years ago did the ratio fall convincingly beneath its average value and remain there for any length of time.

Wildhorse Lake, some 1,100′ higher than Fish Lake, showed a very similar phenomenon, though not at exactly the same time. Here, the ratio of sagebrush to grass pollen exceeded its Wildhorse Lake average at about 7,200 years ago, and remained above that average until shortly after 4,000 years ago. Although the dates differ, the phenomenon is identical.

Mehringer argues that the middle Holocene episode of increased sagebrush abundance at Fish Lake indicates reduced effective moisture between about 8,700 and 4,700 years ago. The movement of sagebrush upslope, he suggests, was temperature controlled, and accounts for the temporal offset in the Fish Lake and Wildhorse Lake records. It is also worth noting that Wildhorse Lake is in a very deep, sheltered cirque, and winter snow accumulation in this

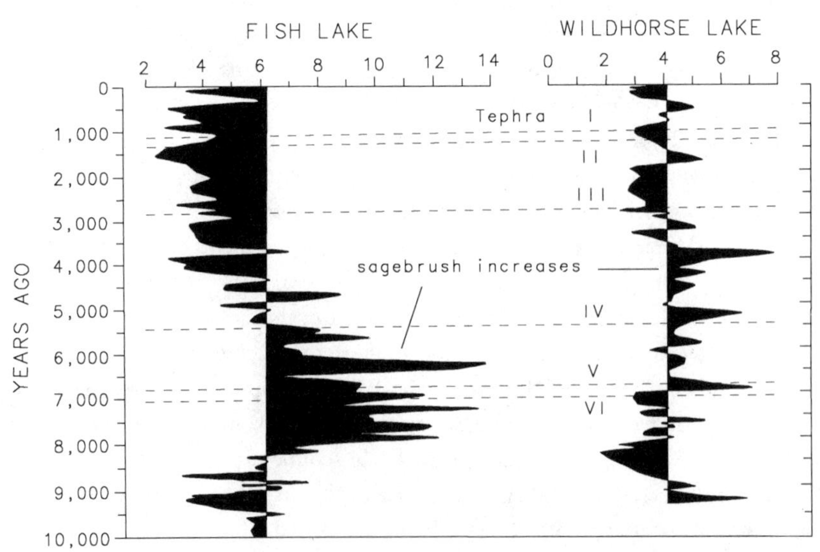

Figure 8-6. The ratio of sagebrush to grass pollen through time at Fish and Wildhorse lakes in Steens Mountain, Oregon. After Mehringer (1985).

setting may also have allowed sagebrush to remain dominant here longer than at the lower, less sheltered Fish Lake setting. Mehringer argues convincingly that both records together reflect a lengthy period of relatively higher temperature and reduced snowpack.

At the same time that Mehringer was focusing on Fish and Wildhorse lakes, his student, Peter Wigand, was focusing his work on Diamond Pond, just off the northwest slope of Steens Mountain. This small (300′ diameter) lake occupies a volcanic explosion crater in the southern Harney Basin's Diamond Crater volcanic complex. At an elevation of 4,150′, it also sits near the local boundary between the shadscale and sagebrush plant communities. Mehringer and Wigand cored this lake together, and retrieved a sequence of sediments that was nearly 50′ thick. Wigand identified 4 volcanic ashes in these sediments and obtained 11 radiocarbon dates, giving him precise chronological control over the last 5,500 years of deposition in the lake. Although he was unable to obtain absolute dates for earlier sediments in his sample, the tight control that he had over deposition rates throughout most of that sample allowed him to estimate that his entire record extended back about 6,000 years.

It would have been nice if the beginning of the middle Holocene had been represented in the Diamond Pond deposits, but it was not. When the pollen record begins, however, it is dominated by greasewood and other cheno-ams, these latter presumably consisting largely of *Atriplex*. From 6,000 to 5,400 years ago, greasewood pollen comprised up to 75% of the pollen samples as a whole. Wigand reasons that, during this time, greasewood and *Atriplex* covered the lower parts of Harney Basin, and that saline soils were widespread in the area.

Wigand also discovered that macrofossils from aquatic plants were virtually absent from sediments that accumulated between 6,000 and 4,500 years ago. This fact implies that, during those years, water within the crater was not deep enough to support such plants. Wigand suggests that the water table was likely so low during this interval that marshes in the Harney Basin as a whole were greatly reduced in size, and may even have been dry for much of the year. Those marshes, I note, include those that are now found at Harney Lake and at Malheur Lake, and that form the heart of the Malheur National Wildlife Refuge, just as the Ruby Marshes form the heart of Ruby Lake National Wildlife Refuge.

The middle Holocene drought so clearly indicated by Diamond Pond began to end by about 5,300 years ago, when the abundance of sagebrush increased sharply in Wigand's pollen record. By 5,000 years ago, the dominance of greasewood in these sediments had ended, and sagebrush, *Atriplex,* and grasses had taken over. By the same time, macrofossils from aquatic plants had become abundant in the lake's sediments. A permanent pond had formed, and, although that pond fluctuated in size through the next 5,000 years, no episode of drying comparable to that which occurred during the middle Holocene happened again.

The records extracted by Wigand and Mehringer from Steens Mountain and the Harney Basin are fully consistent with one another. They are also strikingly similar, as regards both lake and vegetation history, to the results obtained by Thompson in Ruby Valley, some 275 miles to the southeast. All bespeak a middle Holocene that was marked by relatively high temperatures and relatively low effective moisture.

A SAMPLER OF OTHER STUDIES

The analyses I have just described—LaMarche's in the White Mountains, Thompson's at Ruby Valley, Mehringer's at Steens Mountain, and Wigand's at Diamond Pond—provide the most detailed glimpses available of the nature of the middle Holocene in the floristic Great Basin. A number of other analyses that deal with this period of time say much the same thing, even if they do not necessarily say it as compellingly.

Thompson, for instance, has developed a pollen sequence from Mission Cross Bog, located in the Copper Basin just west of the Jarbidge Mountains at an elevation of 7,955′. His work shows that, from about 8,000 to at least 5,000 years ago, subalpine vegetation decreased, and shadscale steppe and juniper increased, in this area.

To the southwest, Roger Byrne, Colin Busby, and Robert F. Heizer developed a sequence with similar implications from Leonard Rockshelter. This site, at 4,175′, is on the northern slope of the West Humboldt Range, overlooking the Humboldt River and just east of the Humboldt Sink. Leonard Rockshelter was excavated for archaeological reasons by the University of California in 1950; sediment samples from the site had been saved, and it was these samples that Byrne, Busby, and Heizer analyzed in 1979. They found a three-part pollen sequence, with two episodes of pine-pollen dominance separated by an interval during which cheno-am, presumably *Atriplex,* pollen dominated. The period of cheno-am dominance occurred as wind-blown silts were being deposited in the rockshelter; in 1955, Antevs himself had assigned these silts to the Altithermal.

Byrne, Busby, and Heizer concluded that both the introduction of wind-blown silts, and the high frequencies of cheno-am pollen in those silts, reflect the middle Holocene desiccation of Humboldt Sink and the colonization of the dry lake bed by *Atriplex*. To the immediate south, ichthyologist Gerald Smith has shown that species of lake-dwelling fish in the deposits of Hidden Cave declined significantly in abundance at about 6,900 years ago. That decline, he suggested, reflects shrinking lakes in the Carson Desert.

Similar arguments have been made for sites on both the eastern and western fringes of the floristic Great Basin. David Madsen and Donald Currey's analysis of the pollen from Snowbird Bog, in the Wasatch Range just southeast of Salt Lake City at an elevation of 8,105′, suggested to them that the period from 8,000 to 6,000 years ago here was warm and dry, and that from 6,000 to 5,200 years ago, warm and moist. Indeed, Currey has suggested that Great Salt Lake may have dried up entirely, or nearly so, during the middle Holocene.

On the opposite side of the Great Basin, Jonathan Davis, Robert Elston, and Gail Townsend have argued that Lake Tahoe also shallowed significantly during the middle Holocene. They observed a series of phenomena along the south shore of Lake Tahoe, including valleys now submerged beneath water, that suggests that this lake was once significantly beneath its current level. They also noted that, during at least latest Pleistocene times, the lake was at a level roughly equivalent to its current level. The geological evidence strongly suggests that, sometime between the late Pleistocene and today, Lake Tahoe underwent a major episode of shallowing.

When did this lowered stand occur? Davis and his colleagues brought two kinds of data to bear on this question. First, they noted that archaeological sites found along the current Lake Tahoe shoreline date back to about 3,500 years ago. That in itself suggests that the lake has been at roughly its current level for at least this long.

A second and more compelling source of information on the apparent low stand is provided by a series of tree stumps that now emerge along the southern margin of the lake when water levels drop significantly. The existence of these stumps has been known for some time, but when they emerged in 1961, samples were taken for radiocarbon dating and showed the trees to be between 4,200 and 4,500 years old. More recently, Susan Lindstrom has obtained 14 radiocarbon dates for 10 of the drowned trees; these new dates range from 5,510 to 4,370 years ago. The stumps involved are substantial, up to about 3.5′ across; in 1934, the rings on some of these trees were counted, documenting that they had lived for at least 100 years. It is clear that, prior to about 4,300 years ago, the surface of Lake Tahoe was significantly beneath the level at which the trees were rooted, and that the trees were killed by rising water at about this time. It also seems likely that Lake Tahoe has not fallen significantly since about 4,300 years ago or so, or else the stumps would have rapidly decomposed. Davis and his colleagues estimate that the decrease in lake level involved is something on the order of 20′, and was enough to prevent Lake Tahoe from overflowing into the Truckee River. They also observe that the dates provided by the trees are consistent with the date provided by the archaeological sites: Lake Tahoe had reached something like modern levels soon after 4,500 years ago.

Although the date for the rise of Lake Tahoe to this level seems secure, the initial decline (if there was just one) is not. Davis, Elston, and Townsend estimate that the drop began at about 7,000 years ago, but this estimate is based on a single radiocarbon date from an archaeological site located several miles from the lake itself. As Davis and his colleagues explicitly recognize, this is not much to go on. At the moment, all that seems reasonably certain is that, during some part of the middle Holocene, Lake Tahoe was significantly lower than it is today, and that it had risen to something like modern levels by about 4,500 years ago. Although Larry Benson and Robert Thompson have suggested that tectonic activity may have lowered the drowned trees to the position they now occupy, Davis, Elston, and Townsend recognized this possibility when they conducted their work, and could find no evidence for it.

These studies, as well as a number of others that I have not mentioned, all suggest very much the same thing. An interval that began sometime between 8,000 and 7,000 years ago, and that ended sometime between 5,000 and 4,000 years ago, was warmer or drier, or both, than what came before or after.

THE MOJAVE DESERT

Most of the precipitation in the floristic Great Basin falls in the winter months, whereas summers are dry. In the Sonoran Desert to the south, the summers are wet, made so by monsoonal systems that derive their moisture from the Gulf of Mexico. The Mojave Desert lies in between.

In 1963, Paul Martin argued that increased temperatures during the middle Holocene could have led to strengthened monsoons, and thus to increased summer rainfall. In this view, the middle Holocene in the Sonoran Desert would have been warm and wet, not warm and dry. Indeed, Thomas Van Devender feels that his midden data indicate just such a phenomenon, though he does not think that these postulated middle Holocene monsoonal storms would have penetrated the Mojave Desert.

Nonetheless, if monsoonal circulation strengthened during the middle Holocene, it is possible that at least parts of the Mojave Desert would have been the recipient of increased summer rainfall. Until recently there has been little evidence that could be brought to bear on this issue. Very few middle Holocene–aged packrat middens had been described from this region, and Mehringer's superb pollen record from Tule Springs finally fails us here: this period of time might not even be represented in his samples. Recently, however, Geoffrey Spaulding has provided detailed information on a series of four middle Holocene midden samples from the McCullough Range, near the California border in far southern Nevada. This southern Mojave Desert location is some 60 miles north of the northern boundary of the Sonoran Desert.

Spaulding's four middle Holocene samples date to 6,800, 6,480, 5,510, and 5,060 years ago, and come from an elevation of 3,430′. To determine whether this region was arid between about 7,000 and 5,000 years ago, Spaulding compared the abundances of climatically sensitive plants in his middle Holocene middens with those in two late Holocene, and one modern, middens from the same location.

Each comparison he did suggested that the middle Holocene here was, in fact, arid. Creosote bush, for instance, was more abundant in his middle Holocene samples than in either the late Holocene or the modern ones. The same was true for desert spruce (*Peucephyllum schottii*), a shrub generally confined to low-elevation, dry settings. Spaulding also took a series of 12 species of plants represented in his middens and divided them into those that would be favored by aridity and higher winter temperatures ("thermophiles"), and those that would be favored by increased moisture availability ("mesophiles"). He then tracked the abundances of these two groups of plants through time. He found that the thermophiles peaked in abundance in his two earliest middle Holocene samples, and that the mesophiles were rare in all four middle Holocene samples, especially when compared to their abundances in the later samples. He concluded that conditions more arid than today characterized the McCullough Range between about 6,800 and 5,060 years ago, with the period between 5,500 and 5,060 years ago having been slightly less arid than what had come before.

Spaulding's analysis provides us with our first convincing, detailed look at the nature of middle Holocene vegetation in the Mojave Desert. It suggests that the middle Holocene here was warm and dry.

Analyses of middle Holocene packrat middens from the Mojave Desert have been a long time in coming. In fact, there is a scarcity of middle Holocene middens known from the arid West as a whole (see, for instance, Figure 6-14). Robert Webb and Julio Betancourt have argued that this scarcity might have resulted from collecting bias. Late Holocene middens, they suggest, are well known because they are well preserved. Late Pleistocene and early Holocene middens are well represented, on the other hand, because they contain plants that are no longer present in the region. Paleobotanists, seeing these plants on the surface of a packrat midden, collect it. As a result, they argue, these middens are better represented in our sample than they would otherwise be. My guess, however, is that the dearth of middle Holocene packrat middens also reflects the dearth of middle Holocene packrats, especially at lower elevations, and that the cause of this double dearth—of packrats and of their middens—is climatic in origin.

WAS ANTEVS RIGHT?

A diverse variety of studies show that the Great Basin during the middle Holocene was marked by high temperatures or low precipitation or, most likely, both. It is tempting, as a result, to conclude that Antevs was right.

It is fairly easy, decades after the fact, to provide a list of problems with Antev's Neothermal sequence for the Great Basin. The period of time he assigned to the Anathermal was not marked by temperatures that were at first like today's, and then growing warmer. Instead, both plants and mammals suggest that, within the Great Basin, this interval was distinctly cooler than it is now.

Recent studies do show that Anathermal-aged lakes and marshes existed in Great Basin valleys that no longer contain them, just as Antevs suggested. Antevs, however, supported his initial arguments on this score with an interpretation of Summer Lake history that was, for reasons not of his own making, wildly wrong. At the time he developed his model, Mazama ash was thought to be present deep within the Summer Lake stratigraphic sequence, implying a lake some 90′ deeper than modern Summer Lake at the time the ash fell. Antevs estimated that the climactic eruption of Mt. Mazama occurred between 8,500 and 9,000 years ago, well within the range of then-current estimates for this event. He then used this date to support his argument for a wetter Anathermal. Not until 1966 was it realized that the critical Summer Lake ash had been misidentified, and that it was Pleistocene in age. Antevs also depended very heavily on the salt chronologies derived from Abert, Summer, and Owens lakes to support his argument that the Altithermal had ended about 4,000 years ago. The extraction of time from the salt content of lakes, however, is now known to present virtually insurmountable difficulties.

The Altithermal, as Antevs painted it, did not really exist. He defined this interval rigidly, as a 3,000-year period during which the Great Basin was unrelentingly hot and dry: the "Long Drought," as he called it. That, in fact, was not the case. Dates for the onset of increased aridity vary from place to place; dates for the onset of less arid conditions likewise vary. Detailed studies of this interval do not show unrelenting aridity across 3,000 years, but instead suggest high variability within a more arid period of time. Mehringer's work at Fish and Wildhorse lakes is a case in point. His sagebrush/grass ratios exceed the average during the middle Holocene, and do so in an impressive way (see Figure 8-6). However, they are also tremendously variable, and some of the middle Holocene values are actually less than those of early and late Holocene times.

Antevs's rigidly defined Altithermal did not exist, even though something like it did. This is not a novel conclusion: Alan Bryan and Ruth Gruhn argued just this point almost 30 years ago, and many others have done so more recently.

It is, however, something of a cheap shot for me to observe that recent studies, assisted by technology developed after Antevs died in 1974, show him to have been wide of the mark. His Neothermal model for the Great Basin began to be developed in detail over 50 years ago, and it was not *that* far off. It also served to focus research on particular issues, places, and times that were then very poorly known. Had Antevs done only this, he would have accomplished a tremendous amount. In addition to doing this, however, he was also one of the pioneers in the use of geological approaches to analyze the contexts of North American archaeological sites: his contributions here were immense. Strange, then, that, although the Geological Society of America lauded his work in a lengthy obituary, the Society for American Archaeology never noticed his passing in the pages of its journal.

PIÑON PINE ARRIVES

Singleleaf piñon finally arrives in the floristic Great Basin during the middle Holocene. The evidence for this is almost, but not quite, indisputable, and is provided by both dated piñon pine macrofossils and by sharp increases in the abundance of pine pollen in areas that are today in or near piñon-juniper woodland.

Packrat middens from the floristic Great Basin that are older than 6,600 years lack any suggestion whatsoever of singleleaf piñon. With a single exception, the earliest secure record for singleleaf piñon in this region comes from its far southern edge, from Meadow Valley Wash in southeastern Nevada (see Figure 6-12). Here, David Madsen identified piñon pine macrofossils from a packrat midden sample dated to 6,590 years ago; earlier midden samples had no piñon. To the north, Robert Thompson's midden records from the Schell Creek and Snake ranges lack piñon older than 6,300 years old. In the Schell Creek Range, his earliest records come from midden samples that date to 6,250 years ago. In the Snake Range, his earliest piñon comes from a Smith Creek Valley midden that dates to 6,120 years ago. Today, all of these middens are in piñon-juniper woodland. With a single exception, these are the earliest dates for singleleaf piñon in the floristic Great Basin.

In the Toquima Range, in the heart of Nevada, the earliest evidence for piñon comes from Gatecliff Shelter, an archaeological site within the modern piñon-juniper zone at 7,610′, that was excavated by David Thomas (see Figures 8-3, 8-4, and 9-1). Two of the earliest hearths in this site, dated to about 5,350 years ago, contained piñon charcoal and burnt piñon needles, establishing that this tree was here by then. Packrat middens from Mill Canyon, in which Gatecliff sits, are in agreement. Robert Thompson and Eugene Hattori analyzed these middens, and found that the three earliest samples in their series, which date to between 9,500 and 9,000 years ago, lack piñon. The next youngest sample in the series, which dates to 4,790 years ago, contains it.

Thompson and Robert Kautz also analyzed the pollen from the Gatecliff sediments. They found that the earliest deposits in the site, which date to between about 7,300 and 6,000 years ago, were dominated by sagebrush and cheno-am pollen. Between 6,000 and 5,600 years ago, however, both piñon and juniper increased dramatically in abundance. A few hundred years later, the first hearths were built in Gatecliff, and they contained the remains of both piñon and juniper. The hearths, middens, and pollen provide a convincing picture: piñon pines arrived in the Gatecliff area soon after 6,000 years ago.

In all of these cases, from Meadow Valley Wash to the Toquima Range, there are packrat middens that predate 6,600 years ago and that lack piñon pine. The appearance of this tree in these areas after 6,600 years ago is not simply reflecting some preservational bias in our record. Even though the sample of middens is fairly small, the results are consistent. It appears that singleleaf piñon entered at least the central Great Basin, presumably from the south (where it was present during the late Pleistocene: see Chapter 6), at about 6,500 years ago.

Earlier in this chapter, I noted that botanists suspect that four factors now limit the distribution of singleleaf piñon in the Great Basin: cool summer temperatures, inadequate summer precipitation, cold winter temperatures, and the absence of winter thermal inversions. The seasonal distribution of rainfall in the Great Basin during the middle Holocene is essentially unknown, but there is little doubt that temperatures became warmer at the end of the early Holocene. Thompson calculated that growing season temperatures in east-central Nevada during the early Holocene were some 7°–9°F lower than they are now; LaMarche calculates that middle Holocene growing season temperatures were some 3°–4°F higher than they are now in the White Mountains of eastern California. This marked increase in growing season temperatures probably caused the extinction of low-elevation populations of pikas in the floristic Great Basin. It may also have have triggered the northward movement of singleleaf piñon into this region.

Although dates for the onset of middle Holocene aridity vary from place to place in the floristic Great Basin, nowhere are they as late as the 6,300-year date that Thompson has established for the arrival of piñon pine in east-central Nevada, or the 6,000-year date for the Toquima Range. If increased middle Holocene temperatures triggered the movement of piñon into the Great Basin, why did it take so long for these trees to arrive in the central Great Basin?

The movement of piñon pine across space depends on the movement of its seeds, and that movement took time. Piñon seeds lack the adaptations needed for wind-blown dispersal: they are far too large to be scattered by the wind, for instance, and they lack wings. As a result, some other vector is needed. Fortunately, that vector is well known. A group of birds belonging to the family Corvidae (the crows, jays, and magpies, and their close relatives) collect, eat, and cache piñon seeds, as well as the seeds of other pines. Throughout much of the Great Basin, the most important members of this group are Clark's Nutcracker (*Nucifraga columbiana*), Piñon Jay (*Gymnorhinus cyanocephalus*), and Scrub Jay (*Aphelocoma coerulescens*); on the eastern and western fringes of the Great Basin, Steller's Jay (*Cyanocitta stelleri*) also plays a role.

These birds are critical to the dispersal of piñon seeds. Stephen Vander Wall and Russell Balda of Northern Arizona University, for instance, calculated that a flock of 150 Clark's Nutcrackers cached approximately four million (!) Colorado piñon (*Pinus edulis*) seeds in a single autumn in an area they studied in north-central Arizona, moving those seeds as far as 14 miles to their final destination. Indeed, piñon pines have a variety of adaptations—from large seed size to cones that hold the seeds in such a way that they are easily visible to birds—that encourage bird-assisted dispersal.

Assuming that birds were the prime mechanism involved in the spread of piñon pine across the floristic Great Basin, the advent of environmental conditions conducive to the establishment of piñon populations would not translate to the rapid movement of these trees across the region. Instead, stands of piñon would have become established slowly, as birds introduced seeds into new areas, seedlings sprouted, trees grew and produced cones (a process that might take several decades), and the seeds they produced were then dispersed, a few miles at a time, by new generations of birds. Indeed, Ronald Lanner has calculated that piñon might move across Great Basin uplands at a rate of between 8 and 12 miles per century by this process. If birds were the major vector, then piñon pines would take several thousand years to spread across the Great Basin. If climatic change at the beginning of the middle Holocene, say 8,000 or 7,500 years ago, introduced conditions amenable to the establishment of piñon pine in the Great Basin, then those trees might well not appear in places like the Schell Creek Range until 6,300 years ago, or the Toquima Range until 6,000 years ago.

There are some unresolved complexities in this story. First, as Peter Mehringer has pointed out, birds are not the only mechanism that might have played an important role in moving piñon across the landscape: people may have done so as well. At the moment, however, there is no way of assessing this possibility. Second, nearly all of the records we have for the middle Holocene dispersal of piñon into the floristic Great Basin come from the central Great Basin. Robert Thompson has suggested that piñon pine might have migrated among lower-elevation corridors in the eastern and western Great Basin much earlier than it entered the higher elevations of the central Great Basin. Very recent work by Peter Wigand suggests that such movement did not occur along the western, Lahontan, trough, as I will discuss shortly. We still lack information, however, on possible movements through the eastern Great Basin.

The one exception to the post–6,600-year-old evidence that we have for the movement of piñon pine into the Great Basin is provided by Danger Cave (elevation 4,310′). This site is located in the Silver Island Range along the Utah-Nevada border (see Figure 7-8), some 100 miles north of Thompson's middle Holocene, piñon-bearing middens in the Snake Range. Justly famous in archaeological circles for the discoveries made here by Jesse D. Jennings of the University of Utah in the 1940s and 1950s, Danger Cave was recently reexcavated by David Madsen and his colleagues. Although the analysis of the material they retrieved from these deposits in 1986 is still underway, the pine fossils from this site have been identified and dated.

The sediments in Danger Cave began accumulating during the latest Pleistocene; the oldest deposits in this site were laid down about 11,000 years ago. The eight deepest Danger Cave strata defined by Madsen's recent work predate 8,000 years ago, and lack piñon. Stratum 9, however, contained 4 piñon hull fragments; stratum 10 contained 130 such fragments. Stratum 9 dates to 7,920 years ago; a piñon hull from stratum 10 was directly dated, by the accelerator method, to 7,410 years ago. The accelerator date shows that these surprisingly early piñon fragments do not simply represent the movement of later material into earlier deposits within the cave.

Madsen and his colleague David Rhode point out that these piñon hull fragments were not accompanied by needles or cone parts, and that they are not gnawed by rodents. Given this finding, and given that birds are not likely to have cached nuts inside a cave, it is extremely likely that people brought these seeds to the site. Even though this was probably the case, it is not likely that people carried piñon nuts from far enough away to make the dates any less surprising: except for Danger Cave, there is no evidence that piñon was in the floristic Great Basin at all at this time.

Piñon is in the higher elevations of the Silver Island Range today, but everything we knew of the history of this tree at the time Danger Cave was reexcavated suggested that it should not have been here 7,400 or more years ago. Given the Schell Creek and Snake range dates, and given the assumption that piñon moved north along major mountain masses, the Silver Island Range should have been colonized by piñon well after 6,300 years ago. How might this anomaly be explained?

There are a number of ways, but none is compelling. Perhaps the packrat midden record to the south is incomplete, and piñon actually arrived much earlier in the Schell Creek and Snake ranges than it now appears. The midden record, however, appears too strong for that to be likely, and the evidence from the Toquima Range, to the west, appears overwhelming. It is possible that the piñon pine remains from Danger Cave have been misidentified, but this also seems unlikely. As is often the case with critical fossils, Madsen and Rhode not only identified these specimens themselves, but they also sent them to other experts for confirmation. All agreed that these are piñon pine.

It is possible that piñon pine has been in the lower-elevation eastern Great Basin longer than it has been in the central part of this region. Indeed, perhaps piñon entered the Silver Island Range, and other nearby mountains, not from the south, but from the north. Perhaps there was a colonization route along the eastern margin of the Great Basin that carried them to the mountains of northern Utah, then west through the mountains along the Utah-Idaho border, ultimately reaching the Silver Island Range and other nearby mountain masses. The problem with this supposition is that, although singleleaf piñon is found in mountains to the west of the Wasatch Range, it is not found in the Wasatch Range itself. Dispersing northward from ranges within the Bonneville Basin would require crossing a formidable biogeographic barrier.

It is easy to think of other possibilities. Perhaps the history of the cattle egret should be evoked here (see Chapter 6), and we should wonder whether a flock of Clark's Nutcrackers was blown off course 8,000 years ago or so, and ended up seeding the Silver Island range with piñon. Perhaps piñon pine actually existed in isolated pockets in the Great Basin during the late Pleistocene, and then expanded outward when conditions more amenable to their existence returned. If so, then discordant arrival times across the Great Basin are to be expected, as different isolated populations expanded at different rates at different times. Perhaps piñon actually arrived in the Great Basin during the early part of the middle Holocene but along routes that are higher, not lower, than the elevations sampled by the middens. Perhaps it was confined to these higher elevations because lower ones were too warm for it, and the late dates from places like the Schell Creek, Snake, and Toquima ranges reflect the downslope movement of piñon as temperatures ameliorated.

All of these possibilities can be tested. If, for instance, piñon occurred at higher elevations earlier than, say, 6,500 years ago, higher-elevation packrat middens should show it. If piñon dispersed along the eastern margin of the Great Basin, then dates from mountain ranges in the eastern Bonneville Basin should show it. If errant, wind-blown birds introduced the Silver Island piñon, then additional dates should show this area as a separate center of piñon dispersal.

At the moment, however, all these possibilities are guesses. From the early 1980s, when it was realized that piñon pine did not seem to arrive in the floristic Great Basin until the middle Holocene, to 1990, when the Danger Cave dates came in, the history of piñon pine in the Great Basin seemed reasonably clear. Now, it seems less so, above and beyond the fact that there is absolutely no evidence for singleleaf piñon in the Great Basin prior to the middle Holocene.

HOW DID THE MAMMALS RESPOND?

It stands to reason that the relatively arid nature of the middle Holocene in the Great Basin should have been felt by mammal populations here. As far as we can tell now, however, that reasoning would only be half right.

Changes in the distribution and abundance of mammals at the end of the early Holocene are well known. For instance, pikas seem to have become extinct in low-elevation settings throughout the floristic Great Basin by about 7,000 years ago. Indeed, Gatecliff Shelter may show the extinction of low-elevation pikas in action.

Gatecliff sits at 7,610′, in the midst of a piñon-juniper woodland and more than 1,500′ above the floor of Monitor valley to the east. The careful excavations at this site provided a huge sample of identifiable small mammal bones and teeth—13,041 of them, nearly all of which come from extremely well-controlled and well-dated stratigraphic settings. The earliest deposits at Gatecliff do not extend much further back than 7,000 years; the latest sediments contain artifacts from latest prehistoric times.

Today, pikas are found in the upper reaches of the Toquima Range, the lowest known modern populations existing at an elevation of 8,700′, some 1,100′ above Gatecliff. Even though Gatecliff is now well beneath the lowermost Toquima Range pikas, there were 58 pika specimens in the sediments of the site. Of these, 55 were deposited prior to 5,100 years ago. During the last 5,100 years, while 9,500 bones and teeth of other small mammals were introduced into Gatecliff, only three pika specimens were incorporated into the deposits of this site. This decline probably records the passing of the lower elevational limits of pikas above the level of the site itself.

Gatecliff thus seems to show the movement of pikas upslope in the Toquima Range. Equally interesting, it also documents the fact that a small, montane mammal that no longer occurs in the Great Basin occupied the Toquima Range until nearly the end of the middle Holocene. In Chapter 7, I noted that heather voles, which are primarily animals of the coniferous forests, are today found only at high elevations on the far eastern and far western fringes of the Great Basin. I also noted that Smith Creek Cave shows that these animals were living in the heart of the Great Basin during the late Pleistocene. Gatecliff, however, provided heather vole specimens that are tightly dated to 5,300 years ago, documenting that this small rodent survived until at least that time in the Toquima Range.

There is no reason to think heather voles were living in the immediate vicinity of the site at this time. Instead, the Gatecliff specimens were probably transported here, as part of a complete vole, from much higher elevations by a raptor, probably an owl. There may also be nothing particularly meaningful about the fact that the Gatecliff specimens were deposited around 5,300 years ago. Heather voles may have lasted much longer than this on the Toquima Range, and, even if they did not, the last heather voles here may have succumbed to something as simple as random fluctuations in population numbers.

Pygmy cottontails (*Sylvilagus idahoensis*), however, did respond to middle Holocene climatic change. Throughout their range, these diminutive rabbits—they usually weigh less than 15 ounces—are typically found in dense stands of big sagebrush growing in deep, diggable substrates. Today, pygmy cottontails are characteristic, although declining, animals of the northern two-thirds of the Great Basin and the southern reaches of the Columbia Plateau to the north. Isolated populations also exist in south-central Washington. During the late Pleistocene, however, they were much more widespread, existing not only in the floristic Great Basin, but also at least as far south as central New Mexico.

Within the Great Basin, these rabbits appear to have undergone two major prehistoric decreases in abundance. At Danger Cave, 35 pygmy cottontail specimens were deposited between 11,000 and 10,000 years ago; during the ensuing 10,000 years, only 2 additional specimens of this mammal were deposited in the site. These numbers suggest that the abundance of pygmy cottontails was greatly reduced here at about the time that Lake Bonneville retreated from the Gilbert level. I would not be surprised if the abundance of pygmy cottontails declined throughout at least the central and northern, and perhaps the entire, Great Basin at the end of the Pleistocene, but there are no other faunal sequences from this period of time that can be used to examine this possibility.

It is, however, clear that pygmy cottontails declined in abundance throughout much of the Great Basin's sagebrush steppe at about 7,000 years ago. Archaeologist B. Robert Butler originally observed such a decline at the Wasden site on the Snake River plain in southern Idaho, and the same phenomenon is now reasonably well known from the floristic Great Basin. At the Connley Caves in south-central Oregon's Fort Rock Basin (see Figures 2-12, 8-1, and 9-1), pygmy cottontails were significantly more abundant in sediments that accumulated before 7,200 years ago than in those that accumulated after 4,400 years ago (deposits dating to the interval between these dates—the heart of the middle Holocene—are absent from these caves). At the higher-elevation Gatecliff Shelter, 7% or more of the small mammal specimens deposited prior to 5,000 years ago were contributed by the bones and teeth of pygmy cottontails; after this time, these animals contributed at most 4% of the small mammal specimens found in the various Gatecliff strata. These declines in pygmy cottontail abundance match evidence from places like the southern Carson Desert and Ruby Valley that shows that sagebrush underwent a significant decline at the end of the early Holocene.

There is scattered evidence that other mammals were also adversely affected by the climatic changes that marked the beginning of the middle Holocene. At the Connley Caves, for instance, 24 of the 25 specimens of elk found in these sites were deposited between 11,000 and 7,200 years ago; only one specimen was deposited after this time. These animals have never been reported from the Fort Rock Basin in historic times, although they are known from late Holocene, but prehistoric, contexts in northern Nevada. At the Connley Caves and at Danger Cave, jack rabbits decreased in abundance after 7,200 and 6,500 years ago, respectively; at Gatecliff Shelter, the stratum that contains the highest abundance of jack rabbits (16%) was also the oldest stratum at the site, deposited between about 7,300 and 6,900 years ago.

The early part of the middle Holocene thus saw the decline of a fairly diverse set of mammals. Interestingly, though, the end of the middle Holocene does not appear to have seen these animals increase in abundance. Pikas do not appear to have moved downslope; jack rabbits did not rebound; pygmy cottontails do not appear to have reoccupied lost habitat.

There are probably two reasons for that. First, the climatic changes that define the transition from the early to the middle Holocene were clearly far more significant than those that occurred at the end of the middle Holocene. Thus, the decline in sagebrush pollen detected by Wigand and Mehringer at Hidden Cave between about 7,000 and 6,500 years ago was not followed by a sagebrush resurgence as the middle Holocene came to an end. As they noted, shadscale vegetation has probably dominated the slopes surrounding Hidden Cave since the sagebrush decline. Areas that lost low-elevation conifers toward the end of the early Holocene did not regain them after the middle Holocene ended. The implications are obvious: the climatic changes that ushered in the middle Holocene were far more pronounced that those that ended it. As a result, changes in the ranges and abundances of mammals that occurred at the end of the middle Holocene were far less pronounced than those that occurred as the early Holocene drew to a close.

Nonetheless, middle Holocene climatic conditions in the Great Basin were different from those of the late Holocene, as I will discuss shortly. Mehringer's work at Steens Mountain shows a resurgence of grass pollen during the late Holocene; Thompson's work in Ruby Valley shows a resurgence of sagebrush at the same time; and so on. It is extremely likely that mammals, and other vertebrates, responded to these changes. That we have yet to detect this response in any convincing way probably reflects the fact that the mammal sequences now available for the period from about 5,500 to 3,500 years ago are not sensitive enough to tell us what the changes in mammalian distribution and abundance were at this time. Far more pronounced, changes at the end of the early Holocene have been far easier to detect.

The Late Holocene: The Last 4,500 Years

WHEN DID GREAT BASIN ENVIRONMENTS BECOME "MODERN"?

It is an obvious question to ask when the Great Basin came to look as it looks today. That question, however, has only one truly meaningful answer: "today." Geographer Garry Rogers of Columbia University, for instance, has carefully matched and analyzed a large series of photographs taken from the same camera location in a diverse set of areas within the Bonneville Basin. Most of the earliest photos in these matched pairs were taken between 1900 and 1915; the second set was taken during the late 1970s. Virtually all of these pairs show dramatic changes in vegetation across the six or so decades involved. Indeed, even matched photographs taken a decade apart show significant vegetational change. "Today" is the only meaningful answer to the question of when the Great Basin came to look as it now looks.

If we make the question more general, and simply ask when the Great Basin came to look pretty much as it has looked during the past few centuries, then a rough answer becomes possible. Certainly, the early Holocene cannot provide the answer: low-elevation conifers, the lack of piñon pine in the floristic Great Basin, expanded marshes, and valley-bottom "montane" mammals are not "modern." Climatic conditions during much of the middle Holocene were distinctly different from what they are now, so the answer cannot lie here either. If forced to pick a time, I would chose 4,500 years ago or so, when the middle Holocene came to an end. I would then hedge by noting that the answer to this question would differ in different parts of the Great Basin, and would depend on whether we had plants, vertebrates, bodies of water, or something else in mind, or all of these things together.

THE LATE EXPANSION OF PIÑON PINE

The late Holocene history of singleleaf piñon pine also shows why this question has no compelling answer. Recently, Peter Wigand has been focusing much of his work on the analysis of packrat middens from eastern California and western Nevada. Although this work is still underway, his results suggest that piñon was an extremely late arrival in this area. In Slinkard Valley, on the eastern flank of the Sierra Nevada and some 65 miles south of Reno, Wigand's middens first detect piñon at about 1,400 years ago. In the southern Virginia Range, near Silver City and some 20 miles south and east of Reno, piñon first shows up about 1,200 years ago. In the Hidden Valley area just east of Reno, piñon does not appear until about 400 years ago.

In this part of the Great Basin, the northern limits of piñon pine now lie in the southern end of the Pah Rah Range and in the Virginia Mountains just west of Pyramid Lake. As Wigand notes, this local northern limit appears to have been reached during the past 200 to 300 years. Why this is the case is not fully clear. Wigand hypothesizes that the movement of piñon into the northern part of its range here might have been sporadic, with its range expanding during episodes of favorable climatic conditions, and perhaps when fire had reduced its competitors. He also points out that the formidable barriers posed by the desiccated Lahontan Basin may also have slowed its arrival. It is Wigand's evidence that led me to say that piñon pine had not moved northward along the western margin of the Great Basin during the early Holocene.

The very late dates for the arrival of piñon in the Reno area also suggest that piñon may not have reached its northern limits yet. This is especially possible if, as Wigand speculates, the dispersal of this tree is episodic, depending on intervals of favorable climate or of fire-caused reduction in the abundance of its competitors. Given that the birds that play such a major role in dispersing this tree extend far to the north of the tree itself, the next few hundred years should tell.

EFFECTIVE MOISTURE INCREASES

The paleoenvironmental information available for the last 5,000 years or so of Great Basin history suggests that conditions cooler and moister than those of the middle Holocene, but not as cool and moist as those of the early Holocene, were established here at around 4,500 years ago. The onset of these conditions, presumably similar to Great Basin climates of the past few hundred years, defines the transition from the middle to the late Holocene.

Thompson's Ruby Valley sequence provides an excellent example. The aridity of the middle Holocene ended here by 4,700 years ago or so, when the Ruby Marshes were reborn. At the same time, cheno-am (probably *Atriplex*) pollen began to decline, and sagebrush pollen to increase, in the sediments that Thompson analyzed. The rebirth of the Ruby Marshes, coupled with the expansion of sagebrush steppe at the expense of shadscale vegetation, suggests, as Thompson notes, a return to cooler and/or moister conditions. In fact, the coolest and/or moistest conditions of the last 7,000 years seem to have been those of the last 500 years, when the marshes became even deeper and sagebrush pollen reached its highest frequencies since the early Holocene. It was, it appears, at about this time that the vegetation of Ruby Valley came to look much as it does now.

To the north and west, Mehringer's Fish and Wildhorse lake sequences carry similiar implications (see Figure 8-6). At lower-elevation Fish Lake, the sagebrush/grass ratios, which had become elevated shortly before 8,000 years ago, first fell beneath their average at around 5,500 years ago, then spiked upward, only to fall again at about 4,700 years ago. This time, however, they fell permanently. At higher-elevation Wildhorse Lake, the sequence is much the same, but the resurgence of grass in the pollen record occurs about 1,000 years later than at Fish Lake, perhaps because Wildhorse Lake is so much further upslope. As Mehringer notes, lower temperatures and increased snow accumulation would seem to account for the late Holocene grass resurgence here.

To the immediate north, Diamond Pond deepened by about 5,400 years ago; a few hundred years later, sagebrush, *Atriplex,* and grasses began to replace the greasewood-dominated vegetation that marked this area during the middle Holocene. By 4,400 years ago, Diamond Pond had risen significantly. As Wigand observes, the aridity of the middle Holocene had clearly given way to greater effective moisture by this time.

Although the greater effective moisture that marks the late Holocene became evident in Diamond Pond by about 4,400 years ago, Wigand's work also documents the kind of environmental variability through time that must have characterized much or all of the Great Basin during much or all of the Holocene, but that generally remains as yet undetected. He showed, for instance, that episodes of drought affected this area at about 2,900, 700, and 500 years ago, and that episodes of deeper water occurred four times during the past 4,000 years. These wetter episodes centered on 3,700, 2,500, 900, and 200 years ago, with Diamond Pond attaining its deepest late Holocene levels at about 3,700 years ago. Insofar as these droughts and periods of higher water levels reflect the regional water table, they probably reflect the state of the Malheur marshes as well.

Wigand also showed that the pollen of both juniper and grass increased between about 3,750 and 2,050 years ago, spreading into habitats that were then dominated by sagebrush and *Atriplex.* Although the species of juniper involved here could not be determined from the pollen itself, there is no doubt that it is western juniper, the same species that occurs here today. This is clear not only from western juniper macrofossils in the Diamond Pond sediments themselves, but also from macrofossils in 24 nearby packrat middens. Indeed, Mehringer and Wigand, in work of impressive precision, have shown that fluctuations in frequencies of juniper pollen in the sediments of Diamond Pond are matched closely by the frequencies of both juniper pollen and western juniper macrofossils in the packrat middens.

The rise in juniper and grass pollen between 3,800 and 2,100 years ago coincides closely with intervals of increased water levels within Diamond Pond (from 3,750 to 3,450, and from 2,800 to 2,050, years ago, interrupted by a brief episode of drought at about 2,900 years ago). The spread of juniper and grass into sagebrush and shadscale vegetation, Wigand suggests, reflects an increase in effective moisture during this interval. Work recently done by Mehringer and Wigand on the history of western juniper in this region strongly supports this suggestion: western juniper increases here as effective moisture increases, and retreats during times of drought. This, they note, has important implications for the management of modern Great Basin environments.

It is not surprising that Wigand found Diamond Pond to have undergone significant changes in depth during the late Holocene. Most studies of Great Basin lakes focused on this period of time have provided similar results, though not accompanied by the wealth of biotic detail supplied by Wigand's work. For instance, even though the late Holocene history of Great Salt Lake is not particularly well known, work by Donald Currey and his colleagues suggests that the highest Holocene stand reached by this lake occurred between 3,000 and 2,000 years ago. During this interval, Great Salt Lake rose to an elevation of 4,221′—21′ higher than its average historic level, 9′ higher than its historic highstand, and about 6′ higher than the thresholds that separate the Great Salt Lake Basin from the Great Salt Lake Desert to the west (see Chapter 5 and Figure 5-8). As a result, the lake overflowed into the Great Salt Lake Desert, covering some 4,200 square miles with water. How long this highstand lasted is not known, but it was long enough to create a highstand "trimline" that Currey and his colleagues have been able to map. The next known significant highstand reached by the lake—at 4,217′—also flooded the Great Salt Lake Desert, although to a lesser extent, and seems to have occurred at about A.D. 1700. Sevier Lake, to the south, seems to have undergone parallel fluctuations during the past few thousand years.

A PUZZLE FROM MONO AND WALKER LAKES

The late Holocene records available from Mono and Walker lakes, on the eastern edge of the Great Basin, are far more detailed. Geologist Scott Stine, of Columbia University, has documented that Mono Lake has had a series of at least six significant high, and intervening low, stands during the late Holocene. At the time his record begins, some 3,500 years ago, the surface of Mono Lake was at an elevation of about 6,499′, 121′ above its current level, and 75′ above the level it is estimated it would have were it not for the fact that so much of its water is diverted to southern California. The lake reached its lowest stand of the past 3,500 years between about 2,000 and 1,800 years ago. At that time, its surface stood at an elevation of about 6,368′, some 10′ lower than it is now. During the entire 3,500-year interval he studied, the level of Mono Lake has fluctuated 131′. Although it is now dangerously low as regards the welfare of the life it supports, it has been even lower during the fairly recent past.

The late Holocene history of Walker Lake has been developed by Larry Benson, P. A. Meyers, and Ronald Spencer on the one hand, and by Platt Bradbury, Richard Forester, and Robert Thompson on the other. These scientists have examined an impressive array of data drawn largely, though not entirely, from cored lake sediments. Most important here is that they have established that Walker Lake has also gone through a series of major increases and decreases in depth during the past 5,000 years.

I discussed Walker Lake in some detail in Chapter 5. There, I pointed out that the history of this lake is complicated by the fact that the Walker River, which today sustains it, can switch direction and flow not south into Walker Lake, but north into the Carson Desert. I also noted that there is little evidence that a lake actually existed in the Walker Lake Basin between about 14,000 and 4,700 years ago, a true conundrum given that Lake Lahontan was so high at 14,000 years ago that it must have flooded this area.

The late Holocene history of Walker Lake is less controversial, although open to several interpretations. As we now understand that history, the Walker Lake basin filled quickly at about 4,700 years ago. The speed of that filling suggests that the cause was not climatic, but instead reflected the fact that the Walker River now flowed south. From about 4,700 to 2,700 years ago, the lake was perhaps about as high as it would be now were its waters not drawn for other purposes (that is, with a lake surface elevation of about 4,111′). The lake then shallowed, and remained low—with a depth of less than 3′—until 2,100 years ago. It then deepened once again, peaking at about 1,250 years ago (with a surface elevation of about 4,085′), declined sharply to a minimum at about 1,000 years ago (to about 3,957′), then began a rise to its modern level.

Stine argues that the fluctuations of Mono Lake during the past few thousand years reflect climatic change; he even notes that increases in the levels of Mono Lake during this interval are correlated with fluctuations in sunspot activity during the past 2,000 years. Benson and his colleagues observe that there are general similarities in the histories of Mono and Walker lakes during the late Holocene: both were relatively high at 3,500 years ago and during the past few hundred years, and both were low at about 2,000 and 1,000 years ago. Benson and his co-workers suggest that the similarities between the histories of these lakes would be even greater if the Walker Lake record were better understood. Given these general correspondences, it is reasonable to suggest that the same climatic influences are driving the increases and decreases in the levels of both lakes. This, in fact, is exactly what Bradbury and his colleagues suggest.

Benson's team, however, does not think that this is the case at all. Instead, they argue that the late Holocene low levels of Walker Lake are due to the diversion of the Walker River into the Carson Desert. In that view, the Walker River flowed into the Carson Sink prior to 4,700 years ago, between 2,700 and 2,100 years ago, and at about 1,000 years ago.

The problem this argument raises is clear. If the major high and low stands of these two lakes during the past 4,000 years have corresponded in time, and if Mono Lake levels have been driven by climatic change (as Stine argues), whereas those of Walker Lake have been driven by the fickle nature of Walker River (as Benson and his colleagues argue), then what caused the similarities in lake histories here?

Clearly, if the similarities are real, some commonality probably underlies them. Since climate provides the obvious mechanism to account for the similarities in lake levels, perhaps the weakness lies in the reliance on shifts in the direction of flow of the Walker River.

If the Walker River flowed into the Carson Desert during the times suggested by Benson and his colleagues, the obvious place to look for evidence of this is in the Carson Desert itself. Although studies comparable to those on Mono and Walker lakes are not available for the Carson Desert, a good deal of archaeological work has been done here, much of which has focused on the environmental context of the prehistoric human occupants of the area. In addition, archaeological site locations themselves can provide information about water levels if they are in the right setting.

Between 1982 and 1985, water levels in the northern parts of the Great Basin were extremely high. In the Stillwater Marsh area of the Carson Sink, some 20 miles northeast of Hidden Cave (see Figure 6-5), erosion caused by high water revealed the presence of a large series of previously unkown archaeological sites. Stillwater Marsh forms the heart of the Stillwater National Wildlife Refuge; the U.S. Fish and Wildlife Service called on Robert Elston and his colleagues to preserve the information that was in danger of being lost from these highly significant sites, and to help formulate a plan to manage these archaeological resources. Elston's team conducted test excavations in five of the sites that had been revealed as a result of the flooding, all of which were in the midst of the marshes themselves. In addition, they surveyed the Stillwater Marsh area for other archaeological material.

By proceeding in this fashion, they established that significant human occupation of this area had begun soon after 5,000 years ago, that it had apparently intensified after about 1,400 years ago, and that it had then apparently declined after about 650 years ago. Although these general dates are of archaeological value, they do not help much in dealing with issues relating to the Walker River. In excavating the Stillwater sites, however, Elston and his colleagues obtained ten radiocarbon dates from the five sites they tested, and provided detailed information on the stratigraphic context of those dates (see Table 8-4; in this table, "cultural" simply means that the date is from material closely associated with the human occupation of a site).

We can be certain that, when people were living at these sites, there were marshes or shallow lakes nearby, since these sites were full of waterbirds, fish, and freshwater molluscs. We can also be sure that the human occupation of these places occurred when water levels were beneath the sites themselves.

The dates in Table 8-4 contain one very significant gap: none fall between about 2,700 and 1,900 years ago. This undated interval coincides almost perfectly with the shallowing of Walker Lake between 2,700 and 2,100 years ago. It might be that there are no Stillwater dates in this interval

Table 8-4. Radiocarbon Dates from Well-Controlled Archaeological Contexts in the Stillwater Marsh Area[a]

Site	Date (years ago)	Context
26Ch1052	3,290	Cultural?
26Ch1052	3,190	Cultural
26Ch1052	2,690	Cultural
26Ch1052	2,680	Cultural
26Ch1055	1,860	Marsh deposits
26Ch1173	1,350	Cultural
26Ch1068	1,320	Cultural
26Ch1052	1,040	Marsh deposits
26Ch1048	870	Cultural
26Ch1048	800	Cultural

[a]From Raven and Elston (1988).

because the area became so dry that human use of this area declined sharply, leaving no sites that date to this interval. However, that is not consistent with the date that terminates the gap in the Stillwater series. That date, of 1,860 years ago from site 26Ch1055 (this site name is explained in the Notes), is on marsh deposits; the sediments from beneath the dated material, and thus older than it, were also water laid. The indication is that, sometime shortly before 1,900 years ago or so, this area was wet, not dry.

It seems most likely that water levels here were high, not low, between about 2,700 and 1,900 years ago, and that they were high enough to flood this area and cause it to be abandoned by people. The 1,860-year date would thus be catching the very tail end of this wetter interval.

This, of course, is exactly what the argument advanced by Benson and his colleagues suggests should have happened. Mono Lake, however, reached its late Holocene low between 2,000 and 1,800 years ago, a level that Stine reasonably argues was climatically induced. If this were the case, then water levels in the Carson Desert should also have been low, since both Mono Lake and the Carson Desert derive the bulk of their waters from the eastern Sierra. The implication is that something other than climate was causing the higher water levels here, and the Walker River may well be it.

What of the Walker River diversion called for by Benson and his colleagues at 1,000 years ago? This shorter-lived event may be reflected in the 1,040-year date at site 26Ch1052. This date is on marsh deposits; sediments from both immediately above and below it were also water laid. The date also coincides with low levels in Mono Lake, with low levels in Walker Lake, and with another hypothesized diversion of the Walker River into the Carson Desert. Again, a wet Carson Desert during what appears to have been a dry climatic interval suggests that Walker River may have been involved.

These dates are nothing more than suggestive. The Carson River, which flowed through this area before historic diversions, moved around with remarkable frequency, and tectonic activity may also have played a role in altering the locations of lakes and marshes in the Carson Sink. As a result, the Stillwater sequence may simply be reflecting the very local consequence of these movements. It could be that the interval of high water that I suggest may have occurred between 2,700 and 1,900 years ago reflects the same climatic event that saw the flooding of the Great Salt Lake Desert at about this time, as well as deeper levels within Diamond Pond. It could even be that the gap in the Stillwater dates is just a function of a bad sample. But, read at face value, the dates obtained from the Stillwater Marsh area by Elston and his colleagues are remarkably consistent with the argument that Benson and his colleagues have made concerning the history of Walker River during the past 3,000 years.

Help in this area might also be expected from Hidden Cave, since it is located on the southern edge of the Carson Desert some 20 miles south and west of the Stillwater Marsh sites, and has deposits that span the Holocene. Unfortunately, although detailed analyses of the plants and animals from this site clarify the nature of the late Holocene here, they do not seem to provide much, if any, information on the late Holocene history of Walker River.

Wigand and Mehringer did discover two large spikes in the abundance of cattail pollen in Hidden Cave deposits laid down after 7,000 years ago. These spikes occurred in strata II and IV, which date to the intervals from 3,800 to 3,700, and from 3,680 to 3,600, years ago, respectively. Wigand and Mehringer attribute these elevated abundances of cattail pollen to human collecting activities.

There is no reason to doubt this interpretation. Not only do strata II and IV contain the major prehistoric occupations in the site, but cattail stalks themselves were abundant in these strata, and there is only one way they could have gotten there. Prehistorically, not only were cattails used as flooring and to line storage pits, but the roots, shoots, and flowering heads were also a significant food source. Wigand and Mehringer examined the pollen content of human coprolites—desiccated fecal material, to put it politely—and found them to contain huge quantities of cattail pollen.

They suggest that the higher abundances of cattail pollen in Hidden Cave at this time probably reflect the presence of nearby marshes, and may reflect deepening lakes in the Carson Sink. There are no dated sites from the Stillwater Marsh area that are contemporary with Hidden Cave strata II and IV, and, although it is fully possible that lakes did expand in this area as a whole at this time, it is also possible that the nearby marshes detected by Wigand and Mehringer reflect more local events, perhaps involving altered drainage patterns in this region.

Gerald Smith's analysis of the Hidden Cave fish remains documents, as I noted, shallowing lakes in the area during the middle Holocene. Fishes continue to be relatively well represented in the late Holocene deposits of the site, especially in stratum IV, but all of the species represented could have come from nearby sloughs.

The Hidden Cave mammals are also of little help in deciphering lake and marsh history in this area. Hidden Cave provided a large sample of mammal bones and teeth—nearly 6,900 of them—but there was little change in the kinds of species represented during the past 5,000 years, and little meaningful change in the abundances of those species.

In fact, the Hidden Cave mammal fauna was markedly uniform through time, at the same time as it contrasts strongly with the mammals found in the area today. Until sometime after 1,500 years ago, the Hidden Cave mammals are dominated by species that prefer cool or moist habitats—yellow-bellied marmots, bushy-tailed packrats, and Townsend's ground squirrels, for instance. Today, these species do not occur in the immediate area: there are no marmots here; the only packrat present is the desert packrat, and the common ground squirrel is the white-tailed antelope squirrel (*Ammospermophilus leucurus*), which is well adapted to hot and dry habitats. Sometime during the last 1,500 years, the nature of the mammal fauna of this part of the southern Carson Desert changed dramatically, becoming far more desert-like. Exactly when this happened is not clear, and there is a chance that this faunal turnover is very recent. However, none of this helps in understanding the deeper history of lakes and marshes in the area.

As it stands, Stine interprets the late Holocene fluctuations of Mono Lake in terms of climatic change; Bradbury, Forester, and Thompson also call on climatic change to explain the late Holocene fluctuations of Walker Lake. However, Benson and his colleagues interpret the history of Walker Lake during the past 4,700 years in terms of the wandering nature of Walker River, and the Stillwater Marsh data are consistent with those arguments. Since there is no reason to doubt Stine's explanation of the changing levels of Mono Lake during the past 3,500 years, that leaves an obvious question. Why should these lakes have fluctuated in concert for at least a significant part of this time but have done so for entirely different reasons? As of yet, there is no answer.

THE EXTINCTION OF THE NOBLE MARTEN

In Chapter 7, I mentioned that, until recently, the noble marten was thought to have become extinct at the end of the Pleistocene, but that several sites now suggest that it survived until at least 3,000 years ago or so in the arid West. Outside the Great Basin, Dry Creek Cave, in southwestern Idaho's Boise River valley, provided a noble marten specimen in deposits dated to about 3,300 years ago. Within the Great Basin, a single tooth was uncovered at Hidden Cave in deposits that are about 3,600 years old. And, at Bronco Charlie cave, on the western flank of the Ruby Mountains, yet another specimen came from deposits that were laid down between 3,500 and 1,200 years ago. All three sites together suggest that the noble marten may have existed in the Great Basin until some 3,000 years ago. If this is correct, then we are left with another obvious question: why was this animal able to survive the major environmental changes that occurred at the end of the Pleistocene and during the middle Holocene, only to become extinct as more modern conditions arrived? Again, there is, as of yet, no answer.

LATE HOLOCENE ENVIRONMENTAL VARIABILITY

The detailed records available for the late Holocene indicate impressive environmental variability through time and across space within the Great Basin. We do not have equally diverse records of fine-scale change for earlier Holocene times, a reflection of the fact that it is far easier to extract detailed paleoenvironmental records for more recent times than for more ancient ones. Where we do have sensitive records for the early and middle Holocene—as at Fish Lake and Diamond Pond, for instance—they, too, show marked variability. Earlier Holocene times were surely characterized by fine-scale change as much as the last few thousand years were so characterized. And, since these were the environments to which the prehistoric peoples of the Great Basin were adapted, we should expect to see significant spatial and temporal variability within the archaeological record as well.

Notes

The title of this part is borrowed from a book by the same name by Paul Martin (1963).

Details of the late Pleistocene and Holocene history of Las Vegas Valley may be found in Haynes (1967), Mehringer (1967), and Quade (1986); see also the notes to Chapters 6 and 7. Quade (1986) assigns Unit E_1 a beginning date of 11,200 years ago; Haynes (1967), however, questioned the validity of this date, and I have modified the age for the onset of E_1 accordingly. Quade and Pratt (1989) have documented a very similar late Pleistocene sequence from Indian Springs Valley, to the immediate northwest of Las Vegas Valley. Haynes (1991a) argues that an episode of drought may have coincided with the extinction of at least some Pleistocene mammmals. However, he tells me that he hesitates to place the erosional break between Las Vegas Valley units E_1 and E_2 in this context because it is possible that tectonic activity, not climatic change, may account for that break.

The evidence for a series of early Holocene lakes in the Lake Mojave basin is presented by W. J. Brown et al. (1990); later Holocene lakes in this basin are discussed by Enzel et al. (1989, 1992). The northern Alkali Lake Basin lake sequence is presented by Willig (1988, 1989); see also Haynes (1991a). Gehr (1978, 1980) discusses his work in the Harney Lake basin; the Connley Caves faunal data are discussed in Grayson (1979); on the Connley Caves themselves, see Bedwell (1973). On the Ruby Marshes, see R. S. Thompson (1992) and R. S. Thompson et al. (1990). Born (1972) provides a brief discussion of the early Holocene history of Pyramid Lake; the information I present on Mono Lake is drawn from Benson et al. (1990). For Walker Lake, see the references in Chapter 6.

References to the pollen work at Hidden Cave and the Ruby Marshes are provided in Chapter 6, as are references on the history of subalpine conifers in east-central Nevada and west-central Utah. For the latter, see especially R. S. Thompson (1984, 1990) and P. V. Wells (1983).

The best single discussion of the development of Mojave Desert vegetation is Spaulding (1990b). The Mercury Ridge record is provided by P. V. Wells and Jorgensen (1964), the Lucerne Valley sequence by T. J. King (1976). The Eureka View and Marble Mountains data are presented in Spaulding (1980), and, in briefer form, in Spaulding (1990b); this latter reference also discusses the Skeleton Hills data. The Little Skull Mountain analysis is found in Wigand (1990b). P. V. Wells and Woodcock (1985) present the results of their midden efforts in Death Valley. My comment on the modern distribution of creosote bush is taken from Benson and Darrow (1981). P. V. Wells and Hunziker (1976) present their views of the origin and history of North American creosote bush. Current early dates for this shrub in the Chihuahuan Desert are presented by Van Devender (1990a); for Sonoran Desert dates, see J. E. King and Van Devender (1977), Van Devender and Spaulding (1979), Van Devender et al. (1985), and Van Devender (1990b). The Point of Rocks data are given in Spaulding (1985), the Penthouse data, in Spaulding (1981). The Rampart Cave sloth dung analyses are provided in Martin et al. (1961) and R. M. Hansen (1978); on the Owl Canyon 1 and Blue Diamond Road 3 midden samples, see Spaulding (1981). Spaulding (1980) outlines much the same possibilities for the history of creosote bush in the Mojave Desert that I have given here, but argues for a Holocene arrival in Spaulding (1990b).

Spaulding (1980, 1981) provides the Basin Canyon midden data; on the Last Chance Range sequence, see Spaulding (1985). Other middens containing early, and in some cases middle, Holocene sagebrush specimens are also discussed in these references—Eureka Valley 4 (6,795 years old) and Marble Mountains 9(1) (at 8,925, 8,905, and 5,520 years ago), for instance. R. S. Thompson (1985a) analyzes differences between the pollen and macrofossil content of packrat middens; Van Devender (1988) emphasizes the importance of analyzing pollen from packrat middens.

References to the early Holocene mammalian sequence in the Great Basin are provided in Tables 8-1 and 8-2; for a more general, but somewhat dated, view, see Grayson (1987b). On nested faunas, see B. D. Patterson and Atmar (1986), B. D. Patterson (1987, 1990), Cutler (1991), and Grayson and Livingston (1993).

R. S. Thompson (1984, 1990) presents his reconstructions of early Holocene climates in the floristic Great Basin; on piñon pine, see also R. S. Thompson and Hattori (1983) and R. S. Thompson and Kautz (1983). Spaulding and Graumlich (1986) develop their arguments for strengthened monsoons in the Sonoran and Mojave deserts between 12,000 and 8,000 years ago; see also Spaulding (1985, 1990b) and R. S. Thompson et al. (1992). For strong opposition to this view, see Van Devender (1990a). The climatic model to which I (and Spaulding and Graumlich) refer is the Community Climate Model (CCM): see COHMAP Members (1988). The CCM is but one of a number of general circulation models (GCM); Street-Perrott (1991) provides an excellent, balanced critique of GCMs as a whole. For a very different view of early Holocene Great Basin climates, see R. S. Thompson et al. (1992).

My biographical discussion of Ernst Antevs has been drawn from Smiley (1977) and Haynes (1990). For brief introductions to varves, see Flint (1971) and Butzer (1971). Antevs (1925) provides the scientific results of his first foray into the Great Basin; his Neothermal climatic model is developed in Antevs (1938, 1948, 1952a,b, 1953a,b, 1955). A full list of Antevs's publications, many of which deal with the Neothermal model, is provided by Smiley (1977). The salt chronologies used by Antevs were provided by Van Winkle (1914) and Gale (1915). Recent discussions of the Swedish varve chronology are provided by Cato (1985) and Strömberg (1985).

LaMarche and Mooney (1967) discuss their work in the Snake Range, and their initial work on the ages of White Mountains timberlines. LaMarche (1973) presents his detailed analysis of those timberlines.

On Steens Mountain in general, see C. G. Hansen (1956), Lund and Bentley (1976), and McKenzie (1982). McKenzie (1982) assigns the Steens Mountain firs to white fir; I follow Critchfield and Allenbaugh (1969) and Lanner (1983b) in assigning them to grand fir. As Lanner (1983b) discusses, these trees appear to be hybrids between the two species, but are "more grand than white" (1983b:80). Mehringer (1985, 1986) discusses the results of his work at Fish and Wildhorse lakes. The Diamond Pond analysis is presented in Wigand (1985, 1987), and in Mehringer and Wigand (1990); see also Mehringer and Wigand (1987).

See R. S. Thompson (1984) on Mission Cross Bog, Byrne et al. (1979) and Antevs (1955) on Leonard Rockshelter, G. R. Smith (1983) on the Hidden Cave fishes, and D. B. Madsen and Currey (1979) on Snowbird Bog. Currey (1980) discusses the possibility that Great Salt Lake desiccated during the middle Holocene. See Harding (1965), J. O. Davis et al. (1976), Lindstrom (1990), and Benson and Thompson (1987a) on a mid-Holocene decline in Lake Tahoe. The archaeological site that provided the 7,000-year date in the Tahoe Basin is discussed in Elston (1971).

During times of low Lake Tahoe water levels, the drowned trees are easy to see. From South Lake Tahoe, take Highway 50 south, then Highway 89 north. The U.S. Forest Service's Lake Tahoe Visitor Center is 3.3 miles west of the Highway 50 junction, and one-half mile west of Camp Richardson. Park at the Visitor Center, then follow the trail to the lake itself. The "drowned" trees are south of the mouth of Taylor Creek. They can also be reached from the Kiva Picnic Area, between Camp Richardson and the Visitor Center. Lindstrom (1990) provides a general map showing the location of all known drowned trees in the southern Lake Tahoe area; Furgurson (1992) discusses Lindstrom's work briefly, and provides an excellent photo of drowned tree stumps.

Martin (1963) made the argument for a warm and moist middle Holocene in the Sonoran Desert. Van Devender (1990b) presents his arguments for strengthened monsoons in the Sonoran Desert during the middle Holocene; those who feel the Sonoran Desert middle Holocene was warm and/or dry include, among others, S. A. Hall (1985) and Spaulding (1991). Spaulding's McCullough Range arguments are found in Spaulding (1991); R. H. Webb and Betancourt (1990) provide data on, and a discussion of, the middle Holocene paucity of packrat midden records in the arid West.

Antevs's use of Summer Lake history can be seen in the references to his work provided earlier; I have taken his estimate of the age of Mazama ash from Antevs (1948). See I. S. Allison (1945, 1966b) on Summer Lake ashes and Feth (1959) on Great Basin salt chronologies. Bryan and Gruhn (1964) criticized the Altithermal notion many years ago, as did Aschmann (1958); for more recent critiques, see Mehringer (1977), Byrne et al. (1979), R. S. Thompson and Kautz (1983), and Spaulding (1991). See Haynes (1990) for a discussion of Antevs's geological analyses of archaeological sites, and Smiley (1977) for the Geological Society of America obituary of Antevs.

The Meadow Valley Wash piñon is discussed by D. B. Madsen (1986a) and R. S. Thompson and Hattori (1983). R. S. Thompson (1984) presents the Schell Creek and Snake range dates; on Gatecliff, see R. S. Thompson and Hattori (1983), R. S. Thompson and Kautz (1983), and Rhode and Thomas (1983). Information on the content of the Gatecliff hearths provided by Rhode and Thomas (1983) is not fully consistent with that presented elsewhere in the Gatecliff Shelter report; I have followed Thomas (1983:447) in my discussion. The role of corvids in dispersing piñon pine seeds has been analyzed in a number of papers; my discussion has depended on Vander Wall and Balda (1977) and Lanner (1983a); see also D. B. Madsen (1986a). For more general discussions, see Lanner (1981) and Ryser (1985). For the dispersal of bristlecone pine seeds by Clark's Nutcrackers, see Lanner (1988). Nearly two decades ago, D. B. Madsen and Berry (1975) discussed the possibility that piñon did not enter much of the Great Basin until well into the Holocene.

Mehringer (1986) suggested that people may have played a significant role in moving piñon seeds across the Great Basin. R. S. Thompson (1990) suggested the possibility of low-elevation piñon dispersal routes in the eastern and western Great Basin; Wigand (1990a) seems to eliminate the possibility of an early, Lahontan Trough dispersal. D. B. Madsen (1986a) discusses the migration of piñon pine into the floristic Great Basin, but this paper was written well before Danger Cave was reexcavated; see also D. B. Madsen (1985). The Danger Cave piñon data are presented in D. B. Madsen and Rhode (1990); on Danger Cave in general, see Jennings (1957) and Grayson (1988a). Data on the modern distribution of piñon pine in Utah are taken from Albee et al. (1988).

The Gatecliff small mammals are discussed by Grayson (1983). On pygmy cottontail habitats and distribution, see E. R. Hall (1946, 1981), Green and Flinders (1980), and Weiss and Verts (1984). Butler (1972) discusses the Wasden site sequence. For the Connley Caves data, see Grayson (1979). For the Danger Cave mammalian sequence, and a discussion of the history of elk (more properly called wapiti), see Grayson (1988a). A. H. Harris (1985) discusses pygmy cottontails in the Southwest; Lyman (1991) discusses the history of these animals in eastern Washington; see also Grayson (1987b).

Rogers (1982) analyzes matched photographs of central Great Basin landscapes. The Ruby Marshes, Fish Lake, Wildhorse Lake, and Diamond Pond references have already been presented. On the history of western juniper in the Diamond Pond area, see especially Mehringer and Wigand (1990). In recent years, Mehringer has focused his efforts on the fine-grained analysis of pollen and macrofossil sequences—on, for instance, the pollen contained *within* volcanic ashes (Mehringer et al., 1977; Blinman et al., 1979). Mehringer and Wigand (1990) show the benefits of this intensive approach.

Late Holocene highstands of Great Salt Lake are discussed by Currey and James (1982), Currey (1987), and Merola et al. (1989); comparable highstands in the Sevier Lake basin are discussed by Oviatt (1988). Stine (1984, 1990) presents his analysis of the late Holocene history of Mono Lake; Stine (1990) discusses his results in terms of calendar, not radiocarbon, years; as a result, his dates differ in a minor way from those I have used here. The Walker Lake sequence is developed by Benson et al. (1991). The results of the Stillwater Marsh excavations, including the radiocarbon dates, are presented in Raven and Elston (1988); the Stillwater archaeological survey is discussed in Raven and Elston (1989) and Raven (1990); data on the freshwater molluscs, fishes, and birds from these sites are provided by Drews (1988), Greenspan (1988), and Livingston (1988a, 1991). Raymond and Parks (1990) provide a valuable overview of the sites exposed as a result of flooding in the Stillwater area; they provide three radiocarbon dates (290, 1,140, and 2,265 years ago) in addition to those I have discussed here, but in the absence of detailed information on those dates—materials dated and stratigraphic context—they cannot be evaluated. As a result, I have not used them. Elston et al. (1988) note the possibility that a highstand contemporary with the late Holocene highstand of Great Salt Lake also occurred in the Carson Desert. Smith (1985) and Grayson (1985) discuss the fishes and mammals, respectively, of Hidden Cave.

In principle, every professionally recorded archaeological site in the United States receives its own number. These are composed of a state designation—for Nevada, 26—then a county abbreviation—Ch is Churchill County—and a sequential site number: 26Ch1055 is the 1,055th site to have been recorded in Churchill County, Nevada.

PART FIVE

○○○

Great Basin Archaeology

CHAPTER NINE

○○○

The Prehistoric Archaeology of the Great Basin

Pre-Clovis Sites in the Great Basin?

In 1932, Luther S. Cressman of the University of Oregon initiated a major program of archaeological research in the northern Great Basin. He began with a survey of the rich store of rock art that is found in this region, and then, in 1934, turned to an archaeological survey of Guano Valley. Between 1935 and 1938, he conducted the work I discuss here: the excavation of a series of caves and rockshelters in the Catlow, Fort Rock, and Summer Lake basins (see Figure 9-1 for the locations of sites discussed in this chapter). This work was to put Oregon prehistory on the map.

Luther Cressman is a remarkable scholar. Ordained as a priest in the Episcopal Church in 1923, he entered the graduate program in sociology at Columbia University in 1920, while still studying at General Theological Seminary. Receiving his Ph.D. in 1925, he accepted a position at the University of Oregon in 1929, where he spent the rest of his career. Along the way, he founded the Department of Anthropology and the museums of anthropology and natural history at this institution.

What made Cressman's archaeological work so outstanding was not that he was self-trained: that was common at the time. Instead, it was that he recognized that archaeology should be an interdisciplinary enterprise. Almost from the beginning, his projects included a wide range of scientists drawn from other disciplines. Ernst Antevs and Ira Allison helped analyze the geological contexts of his sites; geologist Howel Williams studied the volcanic ashes contained within the caves he excavated; Henry Hansen analyzed pollen taken from nearby deposits; paleontologists Chester Stock, Alexander Wetmore, and Ida deMay identified the animal bones he excavated, and so on. These were some of the earliest interdisciplinary archaeological investigations carried out in the New World; what Cressman began in the 1930s is now standard procedure.

When Cressman excavated Fort Rock Cave in 1938, he made an outstanding discovery. Not only did he find that this site contained a well-defined layer of volcanic ash, but he also found a large number of burned sagebrush-bark sandals and sandal fragments beneath that ash. Some 50 miles to the south and east, Cressman excavated two caves

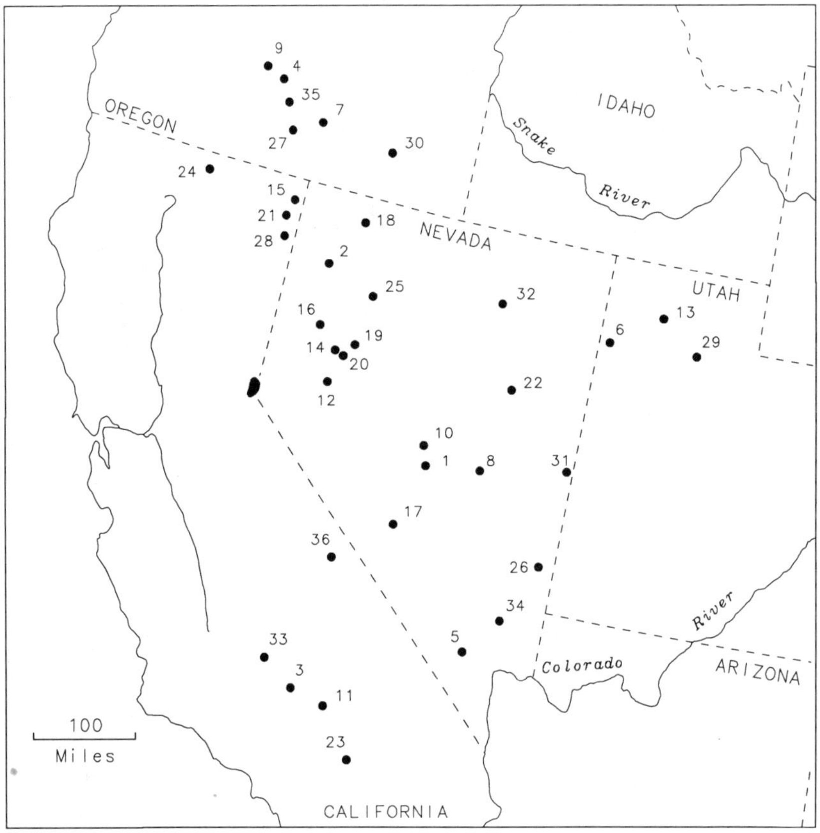

Figure 9-1. The location of archaeological sites and areas discussed in Chapter 9. *Key:* 1, Alta Toquima; 2, Black Rock Desert; 3, China Lake; 4, Connley Caves; 5, Corn Creek Dunes; 6, Danger Cave; 7, Dietz site; 8, Five Points site; 9, Fort Rock Cave; 10, Gatecliff Shelter; 11, Henwood; 12, Hidden Cave; 13, Hogup Cave; 14, Humboldt Lakebed site; 15, King's Dog; 16, Kramer Cave; 17, Lake Tonopah; 18, Last Supper Cave; 19, Leonard Rockshelter; 20, Lovelock; 21, Menlo Baths; 22, Newark Cave; 23, Newberry Cave; 24, Nightfire Island; 25, Old Humboldt site; 26, O'Malley Shelter; 27, Paisley Caves; 28, Rodriguez; 29, Sandwich Shelter; 30, Skull Creek Dunes; 31, Smith Creek Cave; 32, South Fork Shelter; 33, Stahl site; 34, Stuart Rockshelter; 35, Table Rock 1; 36, White Mountain villages.

at Five Mile Point, near the small town of Paisley. In one of these caves—Paisley Cave No. 1—he again found artifacts beneath volcanic ash.

There was no doubt in Cressman's mind that the artifacts lay beneath the ashes in these sites. This relationship raised two important questions in his mind: what ashes were these, and when had they been deposited? Howel Williams answered these questions for him: the ash in Paisley Cave No. 1 was from Mount Mazama; that in Fort Rock Cave, from Newberry Crater, to the north.

At the time, Williams estimated that the cataclysmic eruption from Mount Mazama had occurred between 4,000 and 10,000 years ago; he soon focused on 5,000 years as his best guess (Mount Mazama erupted a number of times between 6,700 and 7,000 years ago). Williams's estimate meant that Cressman's Paisley Cave artifacts were likely to be at least 5,000 years old. The Newberry Crater ash found within Fort Rock Cave was known to be younger, but how much younger was not known. Williams could estimate only that it might have been "several thousand years old" (Cressman and Williams 1940:78).

With help from Williams, Cressman would seem to have established considerable antiquity for the human occupation of the northern Great Basin. Such a fact had great significance, since at the time it was routinely argued that Great Basin cultural developments had depended heavily on late influences from the Southwest. Cressman's data clearly suggested otherwise.

Not all of Cressman's colleagues accepted his evidence at face value. The very first textbook of North American prehistory, published in 1947, ignored the careful work that Cressman had done. "The oldest culture" of the northern Great Basin, this influential book argued, "is probably not more than two thousand years old" (Martin et al. 1947: 228).

Cressman was justifiably annoyed that, while his work had not gone unnoticed, his well-argued conclusions had been ignored. Fortunately, he did not have to wait long to show that his assessment of the antiquity of southeastern Oregon's archaeological record was correct. One of the first dates to come out of Willard Libby's radiocarbon laboratory at the University of Chicago was on a Fort Rock Cave sandal. That sandal, Cressman triumphantly announced in 1951, was 9,053 years old. Indeed, Jesse Jennings was soon to provide even more support for Cressman: in 1951, Libby provided dates extending back nearly 11,000 years on organic materials associated with artifacts from Danger Cave, on the western edge of the Bonneville Basin. From that time on, there was little doubt that Great Basin peoples had had their own lengthy history, independent of that of the Southwest.

The documented great antiquity of Fort Rock Cave made this site famous. It was to become even more famous, however, as a result of work done in 1967 by Cressman's student, Stephen Bedwell. Bedwell's work made it fully clear that the Fort Rock Cave volcanic ash that Williams had identified as having come from Newberry Crater had actually come from Mt. Mazama. Bedwell also provided a series of radiocarbon dates documenting that the human use of Fort Rock Cave had begun by at least 10,200 years ago. These dates, of course, provided even more confirmation for the arguments that Cressman had made nearly 30 years earlier. By now, however, these arguments were not controversial.

What was controversial was Bedwell's claim that the first human occupation in Fort Rock Cave dated to 13,200 years ago. He based that claim on a single radiocarbon date from organic material lying on top of the gravels that are found at the base of the cave. Nearby, and apparently lying on the same surface, he discovered a series of 14 artifacts, including two projectile points and a fragmentary grinding stone. Bedwell argued that the 13,200-year date applied to these artifacts as well.

Some archaeologists accept Bedwell's argument that Fort Rock Cave provides evidence for pre-Clovis human occupation in the Great Basin, but most do not. The reason that most scientists reject Bedwell's claim is straightforward. As Vance Haynes pointed out in 1971, there is no detailed information available on the nature of the association between the dated material and the artifacts. Without that information, it is simply impossible to evaluate whether the dated organic material was likely to have been contemporaneous with the artifacts themselves. It is fully possible that materials of distinctly different ages were lying on the basal gravels at Fort Rock Cave, just as Coke cans and fluted points can now be found lying on the same surface in many parts of the Great Basin. Lacking the required contextual details, Fort Rock Cave must go down as just another site with inconclusive evidence for pre-Clovis peoples in the arid West.

In fact, there are no archaeological sites within the Great Basin that can be shown to predate 11,500 years ago. This is not to say that there are not a number of sites in addition to Fort Rock Cave and Calico (see Chapter 3) for which such claims have been made. In every case, however, the claims can be readily rejected.

In the 1950s, for instance, a series of sites in western Nevada, primarily from Lake Lahontan terraces, were argued to be 20,000 or more years old. That claim was based both on the presumed ages of the terraces involved and on the weathered nature of the artifacts themselves. More recent investigations of these sites by Donald Tuohy of the Nevada State Museum, however, strongly suggest them to be less than 11,000 years old. A second example comes from southern Nevada. Here, Tule Springs was at one time argued to contain archaeological materials older than 28,000 years. However, massive excavations, coupled with detailed attention paid to stratigraphy and chronology, have shown that the artifacts here date to no more than about 11,000 years ago.

More recently, a new dating technique, called cation-ratio dating, has been used to argue that a number of archaeological sites in the Manix Lake basin of southeastern California date to as old as 32,000 years ago, and that a series of petroglyph (rock art) sites in the Coso Range of southeastern California are as old as 18,200 years.

Cation-ratio dating is used to determine the age of the patina, often called desert varnish, that forms on rocks in a wide variety of environmental settings. The varnish is composed of clay minerals that are cemented to the underlying rock by manganese and iron oxides. The cation-ratio dating method attempts to determine the age of the varnish by examining time-dependent changes in the chemistry of that varnish. Once the age of the varnish has been determined, so has a minimum age for the exposure of the rock surface on which the varnish has formed.

If the cation-ratio dating method works, the possibilities are almost limitless: glacial deposits, volcanic rocks, chipped stone tools, and rock art could all have accurate ages assigned to them. Unfortunately, recent work suggests that cation-ratio dating, at least as it has been performed to date, does not provide trustworthy results. Therefore, the ancient dates given to Great Basin archaeological sites by this method cannot be trusted.

As it stands now, the earliest known archaeological sites in the Great Basin are no older than about 11,500 years. As yet, there are no Meadowcrofts or Monte Verdes to argue about here.

Great Basin Fluted Point Sites

To the east and south of the Great Basin, the earliest known archaeological sites are Clovis, marked by extremely distinctive fluted points and well dated to between 11,200 and 10,900 years ago (see Chapter 3 and Figure 4-1). In the Great Basin itself, fluted points are fairly common, and many, though by no means all, appear very similar to classic Clovis points from the Plains and Southwest. It would seem to follow from this fact that the earliest known archaeological sites in the Great Basin are those that are marked by fluted points. Although this may well be the case, it has proved surprisingly difficult to show it, and it is fully possible that a series of sites marked by a distinctly different set of artifacts are at least as old as Great Basin fluted point sites.

There are some Great Basin points that are fluted from base to tip, and that look very much like Folsom points from the Great Plains and Southwest, which date to between 10,900 and 10,200 years ago (see Chapter 3). However, most Great Basin fluted points do look more like classic Clovis points than they look like anything else. As a result, the term "Clovis" is routinely applied to both the points and the sites that contain them. Doing that, however, almost automatically implies that the Great Basin examples are the same age as those from elsewhere. This is a jump that many Great Basin archaeologists have made, but one that may well be wrong.

Calling the Great Basin forms "Clovis" also implies that the Great Basin versions are so similar to those from the Plains and Southwest that they are virtually indistinguishable. Great Basin fluted points, however, are extremely variable in form (see Figure 9-2); no one has ever studied all, or even a geographically diverse sample, of them, and no one has compared such a sample to classic Plains and Southwestern versions. Some of the variability in form shown by these points may be due to resharpening, a well-known Clovis phenomenon, but it does not appear that all can be explained in this way. Unfortunately, as

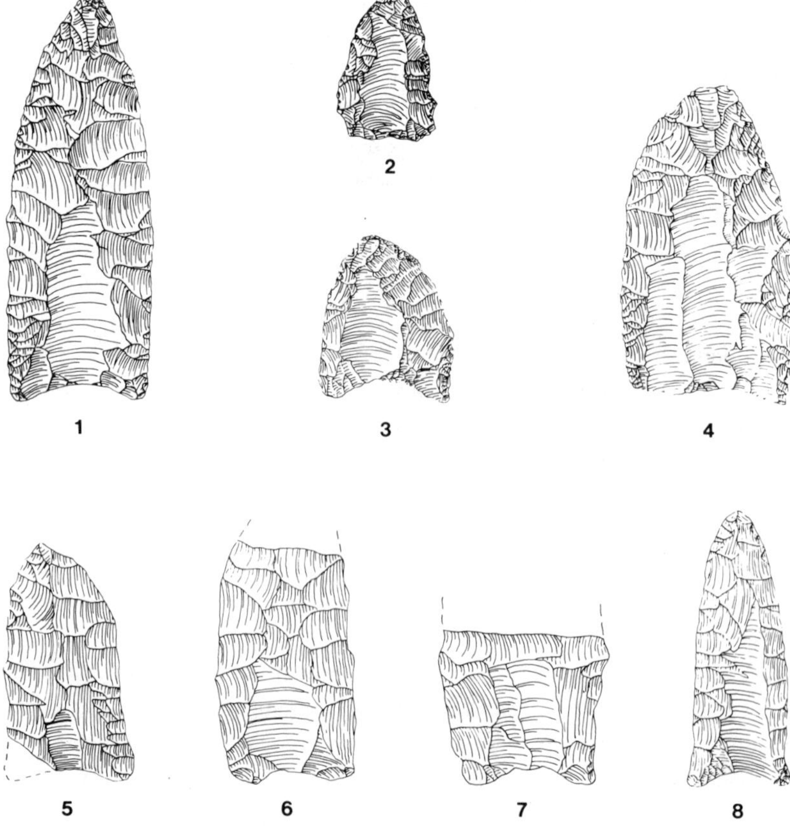

Figure 9-2. Fluted points from the Great Basin: 1–4, from the Dietz site, northern Alkali Lake Basin (after Willig 1989); 5–8, from Fort Irwin, central Mojave Desert (after Warren and Phagan 1988). Length of 1 is 3.4″; others to scale.

archaeologists Claude Warren and Carl Phagan have pointed out, there are no formulas or measurements that can be used to determine if a given fluted point belongs to the Clovis category: "one is simply supposed to be experienced or knowledgeable enough to know whether or not the item is or is not Clovis" (Warren and Phagan 1988: 121). Because of these ambiguities, I will simply call these objects Great Basin fluted points; to call them all "Clovis" implies too much.

Fluted points are known from most, but not all, parts of the Great Basin. In fact, it is easier to specify the major areas from which they are virtually unknown than to list the areas that have provided them in some number. Only a single fluted point is known from the high-elevation valleys of central Nevada, and, with the exception of two specimens found in Danger Cave, fluted points are unknown from the Bonneville Basin of northwestern Utah. It is possible that these absences reflect insufficient archaeological work in these areas, but that argument seems compelling only for the western Bonneville Basin. Central Nevada has been the focus of intensive archaeological surveys in environments seemingly comparable to those that have provided fluted points elsewhere.

Because fluted points represent one of the earliest known artifact styles from North America, discoveries of isolated examples often become widely known. As a result, most fluted point "sites" in the Great Basin consist of isolated points and nothing more. There are, however, a number of locations that have provided sizable numbers of these objects, along with other artifacts. Such concentrations are known, for instance, from China Lake in southeastern California, from the area of Pleistocene Lake Tonopah in the southern end of Big Smoky Valley in southern Nevada, from Long Valley in eastern Nevada, and from Alkali Lake Basin in south-central Oregon. When other artifacts are found so closely associated with these points that one can be fairly sure that they actually belong together, the associated items tend to be fairly nondescript stone tools that, if found on their own, would not be recognized as belonging to a fluted point toolkit. The exceptions to this statement generally involve debris from the manufacture of the points themselves: the channel flakes from producing the flutes are, for instance, distinctive. This situation parallels that for Clovis toolkits, as I discussed in Chapter 3.

Nearly all isolated finds of fluted points, and all true fluted point sites, from the Great Basin have been found on the surface. As a result, little progress has been made toward dating them. Indeed, not even the rare fluted points that have been found in a buried context in the Great Basin have been able to shed much light on their age.

In the early 1940s, Elmer Smith of the University of Utah recovered two fluted points from deep within Danger Cave. These points were misplaced, and were unavailable to Jesse Jennings when he discussed the results of his own work at this crucial site in 1957; not until 1986 was it reported that one of the missing points had been rediscovered. Although the earliest deposits at Danger Cave were laid down about 11,000 years ago, all we know about the Danger Cave fluted points is that they came from the "lower levels" of this site. This does not help in determining the age of these objects accurately.

In the Mojave Desert just south of the Granite Mountains (and not far northeast of the Calico site), Claude Warren and his colleagues excavated and analyzed the material from the Henwood site as part of their archaeological work on the Fort Irwin Military Reservation. Here they found two fluted points, one on the surface, one buried. They found these points to be indistinguishable from a series of classic Clovis points from the Plains and elsewhere. They also obtained a radiocarbon date of 8,470 years from material associated with the buried point. This, of course, is far younger than the known time range for classic Clovis points.

There are three obvious ways of accounting for this young date, none of which can be eliminated at the moment. First, it is possible that Great Basin fluted points were in use well into the early Holocene. Second, it is possible that this point had been picked up and transported here by later peoples; indeed, the Henwood site also provided a series of artifacts that we know to have been in use at about 8,500 years ago, as I will discuss shortly. Third, it may also be that the date is incorrect. A second date from the same context provided an age of 4,360 years, and was rejected by Warren and his team as clearly in error. Perhaps, then, the 8,470-year date is in error as well.

Thus, although there are a few Great Basin sites that have provided fluted points in a buried context, they provide little help in determining exactly when these artifacts were in use. Because nearly all other Great Basin fluted point sites have been found on the surface and so cannot be accurately dated, we simply do not know when these sites were occupied. They might be latest Pleistocene in age, as I suspect is the case, but they might also be early Holocene, and they might well be both.

Although we do not know much about fluted point sites in the Great Basin, we at least know that nearly all of these sites are located along the edges of the now-extinct lakes and marshes that existed in the Great Basin during the late Pleistocene and early Holocene. Because no buried fluted point sites are known from the Great Basin, we have no direct evidence on what these people were doing for a living. It is, however, clear that, whatever they were doing, they were doing a lot of it near shallow water.

At one time, some Great Basin archaeologists argued that the makers of fluted points in this region were big-game hunters. That interpretation was derived directly from the spectacular Clovis sites in the Plains and Southwest, sites that contain fluted points tightly associated with mammoths. This view is no longer common among Great Basin archaeologists; even some of its strongest adherents have abandoned it.

There are no convincing associations between fluted points and the remains of extinct Pleistocene mammals in the Great Basin. However, although the lack of such associations may have led some to discard the notion that the makers of Great Basin fluted points were big-game hunters, the lack of such sites may mean very little. Since virtually all of our fluted point sites come from the surface, convincing associations with mammals, large or small, are hardly to be expected. As I mentioned in Chapter 7, it would be exciting, but not all that surprising, if an association of this sort were to be discovered. Given the general North American pattern, one would predict that, if fluted points are found tightly associated with an extinct mammal in the Great Basin, that mammal will be a mammoth.

Instead, the demise of the big-game hunting interpretation for the makers of Great Basin fluted points follows in the wake of similar conclusions that have been reached for other parts of North America. It also follows from the fact that the distribution of fluted points in the Great Basin is so tightly tied to what would have been highly productive shallow-water environments and immediately adjacent settings. If fluted point makers had been heavily involved in the pursuit of such mammals as mammoth and horse, the distribution of the artifacts they produced would not be this restricted.

If Great Basin fluted points are latest Pleistocene in age, then the concentration of these sites adjacent to productive shallow-water settings makes good ecological sense. As I have discussed, our knowledge of the vegetational history of the Great Basin strongly suggests that subalpine conifers extended well down along mountain flanks until after 11,000 years ago or so. Although such subalpine conifers as limber pine do produce edible nuts, they are expensive to procure and process, whereas the productivity of subalpine woodlands is, in general, low. The most productive environments in the latest Pleistocene Great Basin would have been provided by the plants and animals associated with shallow-water settings and in the steppe vegetation immediately above those settings, and this is precisely where fluted points are found.

Great Basin Stemmed Point Sites

In the 1930s, Elizabeth and William Campbell conducted a detailed archaeological survey of the shores of Pleistocene Lake Mojave in southeastern California (see Figure 6-2). Deeply interested in the early peoples of arid western North America, they had come to Lake Mojave for two specific reasons. First, they felt that, in order to demonstrate that a site was of truly great antiquity, they would have to show that it did not, or at least was not likely to, contain artifacts representing a jumble of different occupations that had occurred through the ages—that it was, in their words, "pure" (E. W. C. Campbell et al. 1937:9). That logic dictated that they look in areas that appeared to have been inhabitable only during remote times.

Second, they also recognized that the best case they could make for the antiquity of their material would stem from its geological context. If it could be shown that the context was ancient, and that the area had not been suitable for human occupation since that time, then it would follow that the site must be ancient as well.

Their reasoning was sound and they were successful. Scattered along the shorelines of Lake Mojave, the Campbells and their colleagues found a series of sites that contained artifacts so weathered that they often had to be turned over to be identified as such. Although those artifacts included a diverse variety of fairly large core and flake tools, most distinctive among them were projectile points and a series of objects they called "crescentic stones" and that are now simply referred to as crescents.

Nearly all of the projectile points found at these sites fell into two groups, which they called Lake Mojave and Silver Lake points. Both of these point styles have distinct stems with bases that are generally, but not always, rounded. In

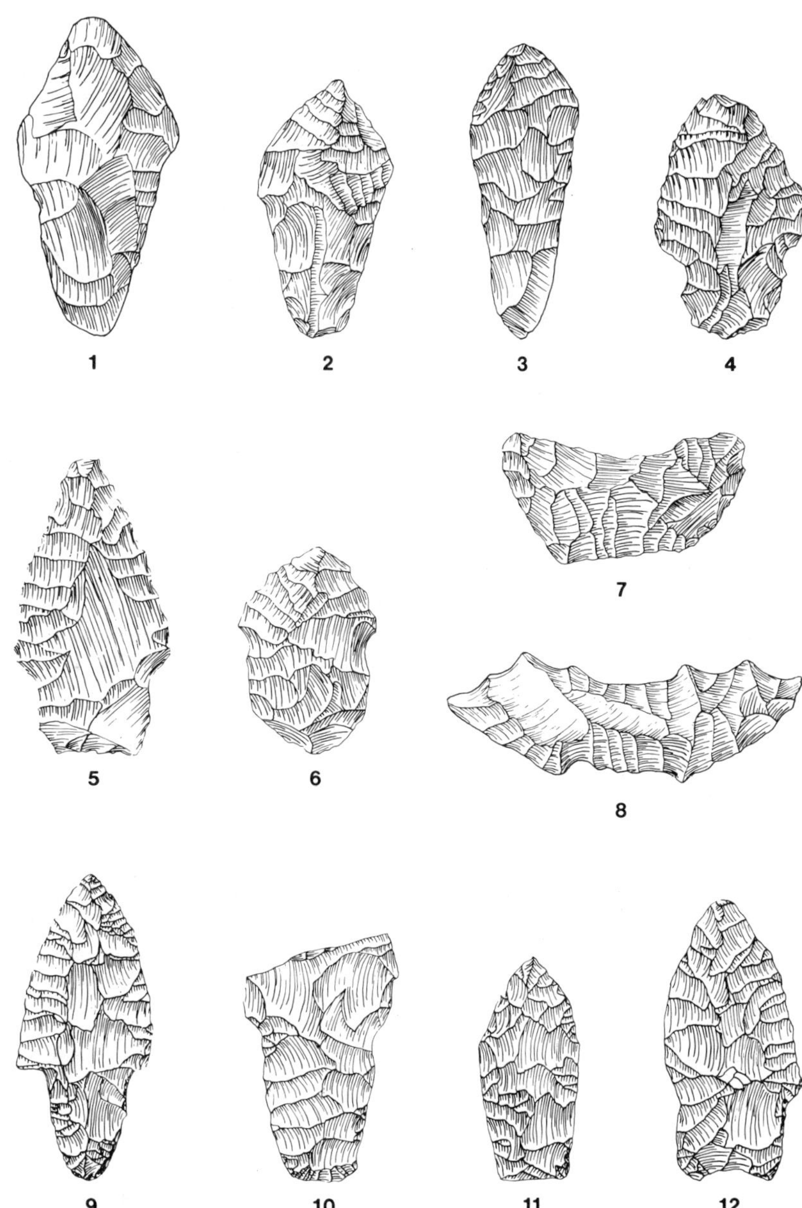

Figure 9-3. Great Basin stemmed points and crescents. 1–3, Lake Mojave points; 4–6, Silver Lake points; 7–8, crescents (1–8 from the Mojave Desert, after Warren and Crabtree 1986); 9, Parman point; 10, Cougar Mountain point; 11, Haskett point; 12, Windust point (9–11 from the northern Alkali Lake Basin, after Willig 1989). Length of 1 is 2.2″; length of 9 is 2.4″; the rest are to scale.

Lake Mojave points, however, the stems—the part of the point that was hafted—are distinctly longer than they are in Silver Lake points. Indeed, Silver Lake points generally have stems that are less than half the length of the point, while Lake Mojave points have stems that take up half or more of the whole object (see Figure 9-3).

The crescents that the Campbells found are as distinctive as the projectile points. These crescent-shaped stone objects are generally one to two inches from tip to tip, and up to about one-half inch wide at their center (see Figure 9-3). Often carefully flaked, the front and back edges of the central portion of crescents are frequently rendered dull by grinding or very steep retouching. To many, the fact that the edges of the midsections of these implements are dulled suggests that they were hafted at this spot. In this view, the dulling was performed to prevent the hafting material, presumably sinew, from being damaged.

Since the geological context of their sites was critical to the Campbells, they relied on experts to interpret that context. Ernst Antevs spent several weeks with the Campbells at Lake Mojave, and, in 1937, was convinced that the location of these sites, on terraces of Pleistocene Lake Mojave, implied that they were at least 15,000 years old.

The Campbells assigned the material they had found to what they called the "Lake Mojave Culture." With 60 years of additional research, and 40 years of radiocarbon dating, behind us, we now have a deeper understanding of the age of what they found, and of how it relates to other aspects of Great Basin prehistory.

In Chapter 8, I discussed the fact that Lake Mohave seems to have reached high levels between 18,000 and 16,000 years ago (Lake Mojave I) and between 13,700 and 11,400 years ago (Lake Mojave II). I also noted that a series of shallow lakes formed in this basin between 11,400 and 8,700 years ago (Intermittent Lake III). It now appears fairly certain that the occupation of the sites collected and analyzed by the Campbells was contemporary with Intermittent Lake III. That this was so follows not so much from the placement of the sites on various Lake Mojave terraces, though the lowest of the artifact-bearing terraces is beneath the Lake Mojave II highstand. Instead, this conclusion follows more securely from the fact that the distinctive artifacts that mark the "Lake Mojave Culture"—the projectile points and crescents—are now fairly well dated in various parts of the Great Basin. Those dates fall between about 11,200 and 7,500 years ago.

The Lake Mojave and Silver Lake points that characterize the Campbells' "Lake Mojave Culture" are not the only large, stemmed points known from the Great Basin and immediately adjacent areas during the latest Pleistocene and early Holocene. There is, in fact, an almost bewildering variety of them, archaeologists having named about a dozen kinds. In addition to Lake Mojave and Silver Lake points, there are Cougar Mountain points, Haskett points, Lind Coulee Points, Mount Moriah points, Parman points, and Windust points (see Figure 9-3). There are even named varieties within some of these groups.

All of them have in common fairly thick stems that usually contract to a base that is rounded to square in outline; many also have a distinct shoulder that separates the stem from the blade portion of the point. It is also fully typical of these points that the edges of the stems have been dulled by grinding, an attribute they share with fluted points. As with fluted points, the grinding was probably done either to prevent damage to the sinew that was used to haft them or to remove irregularities that would have increased the chances of breakage.

Great Basin archaeologists recognize both the variability displayed by these early stemmed forms and the fact that they are similar in many significant ways. As a result, these named types are routinely grouped together and referred to as the "Great Basin Stemmed" projectile point series.

Sites that contain Great Basin Stemmed points also often contain lanceolate points with concave bases. These points are not stemmed, but they are usually edge ground, and often have the basal portion carefully thinned. There are several named styles of these, but as a group they are routinely referred to as "Great Basin Concave-based" points. Many of them are quite similar to fluted points that simply have not been fluted. Indeed, some archaeologists stress this similarity and include Great Basin fluted points with the Great Basin Concave-based group.

These two sets of points—stemmed and concave-based—are distinctly different, even though many of them seem to have been in use at about the same time. Why should this have been the case? In 1980, Alan Bryan suggested that the difference between the stemmed and basally thinned points simply reflects hafting technology.

That argument has now been elaborated by both Bryan and Robert Musil. They suggest that the basally thinned lanceolate points were hafted onto a split or beveled shaft. The basal thinning was done to fit the point into the shaft, and the point was kept firmly in place by binding it with sinew. Thick-stemmed points, on the other hand, were hafted in an entirely different manner. A socket was carved into the shaft, and the base of the point was inserted into it and then bound. Because the stems of these points generally contracted, the binding would contact less of the edge than with the lanceolate points, whereas the thick base would diffuse the force of the blow sustained by the shaft on impact. In both of these ways, the socketed hafting of stemmed points would represent a technological improvement over the split-shaft hafting of the lanceolate ones.

In addition to the points, stemmed point sites have provided a diverse set of associated artifacts. Most distinctive among these are the crescents. The function of these objects, unfortunately, remains unknown. Even if they were hafted at the midsection, as is widely assumed, that fact would not shed much light on what they were hafted for. Suggestions as to their use vary widely: as cutting and scraping tools, as sickle blades, as drill bits, and even as blades mounted on throwing sticks. The proposal that has captured the most attention, however, is that crescents were transversely mounted projectile points, perhaps used to stun birds. As a result, they are at times called "Great Basin Transverse" points, though most archaeologists prefer the more neutral, descriptive term "crescents."

Crescents also tend to be made from a particular kind of raw material. Archaeologists Charlotte Beck and George T. Jones recently examined a sample of 95 Great Basin Stemmed points and 174 crescents from seven sites in Oregon and Nevada, and discovered that distinctly different kinds of stones were used to manufacture these categories of tools. Obsidian was used to make 85% of the stemmed points, but only 6% of the crescents. Chert, on the other hand, was used for 94% of the crescents, but only 6% of the points. Chert is a far tougher material than obsidian, and, although Beck and Jones make no guesses as to what crescents were used for, they do note that, whatever those uses were, they required a durable stone.

An equally valuable attempt to address the function of these artifacts was made by Eugene Hattori, Margaret Nelson, and Donald Tuohy. These investigators analyzed the protein residues adhering to a sample of 30 crescents, and discovered that those proteins had come from a wide variety of animals, from fish and waterfowl to rabbits or hares. Most abundant were those from rabbits or hares, found on 10 of the 17 crescents that held identifiable residues. Unfortunately, although the proteins are real enough, Hattori and his colleagues also recognized that the residues could represent either the kinds of animals the tools were used to procure or the animal products that had been used to haft the objects.

The stemmed point sites also provide a series of less distinctive artifact types. These include a variety of stone flake and core tools commonly referred to as scrapers, knives, and gravers, although their functions are not well known. These sites also often contain small numbers of ground stone implements, presumably manos and metates.

Manos and metates are the classic seed-grinding implements used by the native peoples of the Great Basin in historic times. The material to be ground—often, but by no means always, seeds—was placed on the larger metate, then ground with the smaller hand stone, or mano (not coincidentally, the Spanish word for hand). There is no direct evidence that ground stone tools from stemmed point sites were used for plant processing—evidence that might be provided, for instance, by residue analysis—and it is well known that such tools were used historically for a wide variety of purposes. Nonetheless, they are absent from the toolkits of Great Basin sites that contain only fluted points.

Great Basin fluted point sites remain undated because they have never been found in a buried context. Fortunately, that is not the case for the stemmed point sites. A number of these sites have been excavated, both within the Great Basin and in nearby areas, and many of them have been provided with radiocarbon dates. The early occupations at Fort Rock Cave and at the Connley Caves provide examples, as do the early occupations at Danger Cave and Hogup Cave in Utah, and at Last Supper and Smith Creek caves in Nevada. The dates from these sites are consistent, and show that the stemmed point occupations date from about 11,200 years ago to about 7,500 years ago. In fact, these occupations provide the earliest well-dated archaeological sites now known from the Great Basin. At both the Connley Caves and Smith Creek Cave, for example, the earliest secure dates for the stemmed point occupations fall at about 11,200 years ago. Indeed, Alan Bryan has argued that the Smith Creek Cave stemmed point occupation may have begun as much as a thousand years earlier, but these early dates are controversial.

The fact that stemmed point sites were being deposited for some 4,000 years or more might account for some of the tremendous variability shown by the stemmed points themselves: that variability might reflect change through time. However, it is also true that many of the named kinds of stemmed points can be found at the same site. Judy Willig, for instance, identified seven different kinds of stemmed and shouldered points at the Dietz site in south-central Oregon, including a peculiar square-based form that is very similar to early points from the Great Plains (similar square-based points have been found in number from the Black Rock Desert of northwestern Nevada). Amazingly enough, she identified these seven kinds of points from a sample of only 17 that she was able to classify! The situation at Dietz is not at all uncommon: a single stemmed point site often contains a remarkable variety of these artifacts.

Charlotte Beck and George T. Jones, who, along with Willig, have done some of the most exacting work on stemmed point sites, suggest that much of the variability shown by these points may not reflect time at all. They observe that many of the named forms of these points are actually quite similar to one another, and that they were frequently resharpened. As a result, Beck and Jones suggest that much of the variability shown by these artifacts may simply reflect the degree to which they have been reworked.

Much more work will be needed before we will know whether the tremendous variability of these points reflects change through time or across space, or the fact that they were often resharpened, or, as seems most likely, a combination of all of these explanations. One thing we do know, however, is the kind of settings in which these sites are found. Most have been found in valley bottoms, in locations that would have been adjacent to lakes or marshes, or to streams that fed those lakes and marshes. Such settings are extremely similar to those in which fluted point sites are found.

There is, however, a major difference between the locations of stemmed and fluted point sites. Whereas the latter seem confined to valley bottoms, many stemmed point sites are known from very different contexts as well. Northwestern Nevada's Last Supper Cave, for instance, held a significant stemmed point occupation dated to between about 9,000 and 8,500 years ago, yet is located adjacent to a small stream in rugged country, some 25 miles from, and some 1,200′ higher than, the nearest valley setting that would have supported a significant lake or marsh. To the south, the Old Humboldt site is adjacent to the Humboldt River, at Rye Patch Reservoir, and contains a variety of Great Basin stemmed points that were deposited prior to the eruption of Mt. Mazama at about 6,800 years ago. In central Nevada, the Five Points site sits at an elevation of 8,520′, just beneath the summit of Park Mountain and overlooking a series of small meadows. This site is undated, but contains Silver Lake and other point styles that show its affinities clearly.

Many other sites lead to the same conclusion. Although virtually all fluted point sites are located in valley bottoms, stemmed point sites are found not only here, but also in a wide range of other environments, from mountain meadows to riversides. Insofar as we can judge from artifact distributions, the makers of stemmed points were utilizing a far wider range of environments than were the makers of fluted points.

I suggested that fluted point occupations may have been confined to valley bottoms because these marsh-rich settings provided environments that were not only highly productive, but were also separated from one another by mountains whose lower elevations, at least, were covered by relatively unproductive subalpine woodlands. Since the makers of fluted points occupied a region whose human population density was surely low, the adaptations of these people focused on the rich resources provided by the valleys themselves, and they seem to have made little use of the much less productive settings that lay above them.

As the Pleistocene ended, however, the subalpine woodlands began to thin, and the elevation of the lower timberline began to move upward. It appears that as this happened, and perhaps as human population densities increased, the range of environments utilized by people in the Great Basin expanded to include the increasingly productive uplands.

In this view, the earliest stemmed point occupations would have been largely confined to lower-elevation settings, just as the fluted point occupations were. The utilization of higher elevations would have come first in those areas that saw the early upslope movement of subalpine conifers. Throughout the Great Basin, the range of environments utilized by these people would have increased as the early Holocene wore on. Whether or not this actually occurred will not be known until we have secure dates for higher-elevation stemmed point sites. If this view is correct, however, it does imply that such sites as Five Points were not occupied until after the upslope movement of the subalpine conifers was well under way.

The known distribution of stemmed point sites also implies that the name often given to these occupations is misleading. In the early 1970s, Stephen Bedwell defined what he called the Western Pluvial Lakes Tradition to encompass the late Pleistocene and early Holocene human occupations of the western and northern Great Basin, occupations that he saw as "directed toward the exploitation of a lake environment" (1973:171). The use of this term was soon expanded to include the entire Great Basin and adjacent areas, and it is now in very common use to refer to the stemmed point sites that I have been discussing. Some archaeologists also define it in such a way as to include Great Basin fluted point sites as well.

The more we learn of the stemmed point occupations, however, the more we realize how diverse they were, and the more we realize that these people utilized a wide range of environments. There is no reason to doubt that lakes and marshes were key to the adaptations of these people. When these bodies of shallow water largely disappeared from the Great Basin, at about 7,500 years ago, so did the stemmed point sites.

However, the Western Pluvial Lakes Tradition was not only defined as a way of life "directed toward the exploitation of a lake environment," it was also perceived as one in which "groups could travel north and south . . . and never leave the lacustrine environment" (Bedwell 1973:170). Insofar as the range of environments used by these people went far beyond lake- and marshside settings, and insofar as the notion of a Western Pluvial Lakes Tradition implies similar adaptations across thousands of years, it seems clear that the time has come to abandon the term. This is no criticism of Bedwell's work. For over twenty years, his definition gave real focus to the research that has occurred on this aspect of Great Basin prehistory. But if the term can be said to apply well to anything, what it applies best to are not the stemmed point occupations, but the fluted point ones.

Information on subsistence that is more direct than that provided by site location alone is available from a few stemmed point sites. At Last Supper Cave, for instance, the stemmed point occupation was associated with large numbers of the freshwater mollusc *Margaritifera falcata,* suggesting that the early occupants of this site were here at least in part to collect these bivalves. At the Old Humboldt site, Amy Dansie found that the fauna associated with the stemmed point occupation was dominated by jack rabbits, but also included fragments of mollusc shells, the bones of small artiodactyls (probably from deer, mountain sheep, or antelope), and even a few bison bones. In the Mojave Desert, Charles Douglas and his colleagues found that the stemmed point occupations at Henwood and nearby sites provided faunas that were dominated by the bones of small artiodactyls, rabbits, and jack rabbits; the presence of burned bones from small rodents and lizards suggests that these animals may have been taken as well. In addition, although we do not know what the ground stone implements that are generally found in small numbers at some stemmed point sites were used for, the chances seem good that they were used for plant processing. All indications are that these people utilized a diverse variety of resources from a set of environments that may well have broadened through time. This is no surprise, but it would be helpful if we had comparable information from fluted point sites.

Given that many stemmed point sites are found in exactly the same kinds of environmental settings as many of the fluted point sites—valley bottoms adjacent to what would have been shallow lakes or marshes—it may come as no surprise that many sites contain both fluted and stemmed points. Such sites have been found in the China Lake basin, in Jakes Valley, in Railroad Valley, in Long Valley, in the southern Big Smoky Valley, in the Sevier Desert, and elsewhere. At one time, the fact that these distinctive artifact types are so often found together led some to argue that they were different parts of the same toolkit. However, detailed analyses of the steps taken to manufacture fluted and stemmed points, analyses conducted by John Fagan, Lorann Pendleton, and others, have shown that the two groups of artifacts were made in distinctly different ways. That fact strongly suggests that they were deposited as a result of two different sets of occupations, and have become mixed simply because the surfaces on which they were left either have been exposed for so long, or have been deflated.

That, of course, leaves open the question as to the temporal relationship between the two. I have noted several times that we do not know what this relationship was. Fluted and stemmed points may have been in use at the same time during the late Pleistocene, with only the stemmed point sites continuing to be deposited through the early Holocene. It is also possible that fluted points continued to be used well into the early Holocene, as sites like Henwood might seem to suggest.

I suspect, however, that the fluted point occupations were the earlier of the two. It seems telling that Great Basin sites with deposits that immediately postdate 11,000 years ago have not provided fluted points: Fort Rock Cave, the Connley Caves, Last Supper Cave, even the deposits of Danger Cave so well-excavated by Jennings: all lack these points. The implication is that fluted points were out of use soon after 11,000 years ago.

There is, in fact, excellent evidence that, in at least one area, fluted point occupations did precede the formation of stemmed point sites. In Chapter 8, I discussed the fact that Judy Willig's work in south-central Oregon's northern Alkali Lake Basin has established that this area held a shallow, marsh-fringed lake (Lake Koko) toward the end of the Pleistocene. This lake dried up, perhaps at about 11,000 years ago, only to see a larger lake take its place. A single radiocarbon date places this lake at about 9,610 years ago. It, in turn, was replaced by a third, shallower lake, but by the time Mazama ash fell in this basin, at about 6,800 years ago, the lakes were gone.

Willig also established that the shores of these lakes attracted distinctly different kinds of human occupation. The margins of Lake Koko attracted the makers of fluted points; the Dietz site sits here. The edges of the two early

Holocene lakes also have archaeological sites, but these are all stemmed point occupations. Willig's work, coupling the analysis of local geomorphology with the precise mapping of artifacts, has clearly shown that the fluted point occupation in this basin occurred before the stemmed point occupations, even though both sets of occupations were focused on the margins of the lakes that formed in this basin.

Alkali Lake Basin is just one place, of course, and it is fully possible that similar work in other basins will show that fluted point occupations did not always predate the stemmed point ones. However, coupled with the fact that fluted points have yet to be found in a secure context in Great Basin sites containing deposits that date to, or nearly to, 11,000 years ago, Willig's results suggests that the makers of fluted points in the Great Basin were at the latest contemporaneous with the earliest makers of stemmed points here, and that they may have preceded them entirely.

The end of the early Holocene in the Great Basin was marked by the desiccation of many low-elevation valleys, as I discussed in Chapter 8. Although this desiccation happened at different times in different places, the early Holocene era of shallow lakes and marshes, and the biological productivity that they imply, was over by about 7,500 years ago. As the lakes and marshes disappeared, so did the distinctive artifacts, and the distinctive distribution of the artifacts, that mark the stemmed point tradition. As Robert Elston has said, "Whatever it was that [these] people were doing, they seem to have stopped doing it by about 7000 years ago" (1982:193). The correlation between climatic change and cultural change at this time is stark.

Adapting to a Poorer World: The Middle Holocene

From the point of view of its human occupants, the Great Basin may never have been more productive than it was during the early Holocene. These were, as Elston has also put it, the good times. What followed was quite different.

Although the Great Basin did not undergo Ernst Antevs's rigidly defined Altithermal, the middle Holocene (about 7,500 to 4,500 years ago) was certainly far more arid than what came before, and seems to have been generally more arid than what has come since. From a human perspective, the rich resources supported by widespread shallow-water systems were largely gone; indeed, even the Ruby Marshes dried up. Piñon pine did not reach the central latitudes of the Great Basin until after 6,500 years ago or so, and did not reach further north until later still. Obviously, this food source, so critical in so many parts of the Great Basin during late prehistoric and early historic times, was not immediately available to help take the place of what was lost to regional drying at the end of the early Holocene.

A few decades ago, some archaeologists, adhering closely to Antevs's vision of an Altithermal, pictured the Great Basin as having been markedly inhospitable to people during the middle Holocene. Although later archaeologists have questioned this view, a strong case can be made that these earlier arguments were correct, even though the modern view of middle Holocene climates sees far more variability through time and across space than earlier archaeologists granted.

The broad picture I drew of the nature of human adaptation in the Great Basin during the early Holocene gave a critical role to abundant shallow-water resources, with upland resources becoming increasingly important as the lower limits of subalpine coniferous woodland moved upward. If this picture is correct, then we would expect to see some major changes in the nature and distribution of artifacts and sites as we move into the middle Holocene. In fact, we do.

GRINDING STONES AND SEED PROCESSING

Although grinding stones are usually rare, and are often absent, in early Holocene stemmed point sites, that is not the case for the sites that immediately follow them. These implements—primarily manos and metates—are common in the middle Holocene deposits of O'Malley Shelter in southern Nevada, Hogup Cave in the Great Salt Lake Desert, Corn Creek Dunes in Las Vegas Valley, and other middle Holocene sites as well.

Once grinding stones become common in Great Basin archaeological sites, they remain so throughout the rest of prehistory, emerging as key plant processing tools during early historic times.

Given that these tools were widespread and abundant for some 7,500 years, it might appear odd that they were anything but that before the middle Holocene began. Danger Cave stands out as the only major exception. Danger Cave Stratum II, which dates to between about

10,000 and 9,000 years ago, contained some 160 of them, making it clear that the technology was well known during the early Holocene. That technology, however, was not widely used, and Robert Elston has pointed out to me that the grinding stones on many stemmed point sites do not appear to be heavily worn. Why might this have been the case, and why is Danger Cave such an exception? Ecological economics and Australian ethnography suggest the answer.

James O'Connell spent nearly a year living among the Alyawara in the central Australian desert. Interested in why these hunting and gathering people utilized only some of the food resources available to them, and those in very different abundances, O'Connell collected detailed information on the amount of effort needed to acquire and process the plants and animals on which the Alyawara depend for their subsistence. He also collected data on the number of calories they gained in return for these efforts. When O'Connell and his colleague Kristen Hawkes analyzed this information, they found that the decisions the Alyawara make regarding what plants to collect and what animals to hunt were well explained by the costs and benefits involved in taking the species involved. They also discovered that seeds were among the most costly of Alyawara foods.

Seeds were costly not so much because they tend to be time consuming to collect, but because they require so much effort to process with stone tools. O'Connell found that processing one kilogram (2.2 pounds) of seeds routinely took about five hours, and that they returned some 500–750 kilocalories per hour. That caloric return is very low: some roots and fruits, for instance, routinely returned ten times the calories that seeds returned in a given amount of time. No wonder, then, that seeds are among the first foods to be dropped from the Alyawara diet when other foods become available, and that they are dropped before such things as lizards and insect grubs. Seeds simply rank so low in terms of their costs and benefits that they are quickly replaced when higher-ranked foods can be utilized.

What O'Connell and his colleagues found for the Alyawara, Scott Cane also found for the Gugadja, hunter-gatherers of the Great Sandy Desert in north Western Australia. Here, too, seeds were costly, taking an average of five hours to be turned into a kilogram of food, and providing an average return of only 340 kilocalories an hour. As Cane noted, one woman—and women are the seed collectors and processors here, as they are among virtually all hunters and gatherers—would have to work some 10 to 15 hours a day to provide a family of five with at most half their daily caloric intake. Experimental work done by Steven Simms of Utah State University on a wide variety of Great Basin seed plants carries the same message: seeds are expensive.

If seeds are dropped from hunter-gatherer diets as resources with more favorable cost/benefit ratios become available, it follows that they will be added to the diet as foods with more favorable ratios become unavailable. It is this fact that most likely explains the sharp rise in abundance of grinding stones in Great Basin archaeological sites between about 7,500 and 7,000 years ago. The loss of shallow-water habitats, and the associated decline in biological productivity, led not only to the demise of the stemmed point tradition, but also to the widespread incorporation of seeds into the diets of Great Basin peoples. The grinding stones are the artifactual correlate of that dietary addition.

How then do we account for the fact that Danger Cave had grinding stones in abundance between 10,000 and 9,000 years ago? The reason for that also seems clear. After Lake Bonneville declined from the Gilbert level, shortly before 10,000 years ago, Danger Cave found itself fronting a featureless, saline lakebed in an environment far less productive than that which characterized many Great Basin low-elevation settings during the early Holocene. Indeed, with the decline of Lake Bonneville and the exposure of its bed, much of the northern Bonneville Basin may have been resource poor. Danger Cave was routinely occupied throughout the Holocene because there was a spring nearby, but seeds became incorporated into the diet of the people who occupied this site during the early Holocene because sufficient higher-ranking foods simply were not available.

There is no need to guess that seeds were utilized by the people who occupied Danger Cave during the early Holocene. Pickleweed, a salt-tolerant shrub common in the Great Basin, bears tiny seeds that were collected and eaten by people during historic times. Botanists K. T. Harper and G. M. Alder have shown that the chaff of these seeds is abundant in Danger Cave stratum II, and Gary Fry has shown that the human coprolites from those deposits contain pickleweed seeds. In 1957, Jesse Jennings argued that people were processing pickleweed seeds at Danger Cave, and he was surely correct.

In short, grinding stones are routinely rare in early Holocene archaeological sites because the prime function they performed—seed processing—was rarely needed. They appear in number at the beginning of the middle Holocene, in response to the loss of foods with cost/benefit ratios far more favorable than those associated with seeds. In areas that saw the earlier loss of these more favorable foods, as at Danger Cave, people responded by incorporating significant amounts of seeds into their diet.

WHERE DID THE PEOPLE GO?

Archaeologists do not talk as much as they used to about a middle Holocene human population decline in the Great Basin. For one thing, the arguments that were once made along these lines, primarily between the 1940s and the 1970s, were tightly linked to the notion of an Altithermal; indeed, Antevs himself was one of the first to make the population decrease argument, in 1948. Given that the Altithermal concept is now dated, arguments for population decreases during this interval almost automatically make an archaeologist seem dated, and that is something most of us strive to avoid. In this context it is telling to look at the Great Basin volume of the authoritative *Handbook of North American Indians,* published by the Smithsonian Institution in 1986. Of the five papers in this volume that deal with the middle Holocene archaeology of the Great Basin, only one calls boldly on Altithermal desiccation to account for regional abandonment. That paper is by Luther Cressman, who, many years ago, worked so closely with Antevs.

Although archaeologists can and do address the question of abandonment on many scales, from sites to regions, it is far harder to address issues of population decline. In recent decades, a great deal of effort has been spent attempting to devise ways of measuring population density from the archaeological record. There have been gains in this area, but they are largely for the prehistory of agricultural peoples who lived in substantial villages that can be precisely dated, and not for the record left by hunters and gatherers. The stemmed point sites provide a good example of the difficulties here. These sites are not uncommon, but they cannot be translated into estimates of population density, since they may have been created by a small number of highly mobile people, or by a large number of relatively sedentary ones. Either one or both is possible, and both alternatives have been considered by archaeologists.

The fact that the Altithermal notion is dated does not change the fact that the middle Holocene was relatively arid, and that shallow-water resources played a key role in the lives of hunter-gatherers in the Great Basin whenever they were available. In historic times, Great Basin population densities were highest in areas that were well watered, lowest in areas that were not. There is every reason to believe that the disappearance of the Ruby Marshes had a dramatic impact on the people who occupied Ruby Valley, and Cressman's argument that Paulina Marsh, fronting the Connley Caves, dried up during the middle Holocene is very likely correct. His argument that people were affected thereby follows almost automatically.

Indeed, there is something very curious about the number, location, and dates of middle Holocene sites in the Great Basin. In the Bonneville Basin, such sites as Danger Cave, Hogup Cave, and Sandwich Shelter appear to have been utilized throughout this period. As a result, such archaeologists as Jesse Jennings and C. Melvin Aikens have long contended that middle Holocene climatic change did not have major impacts on the peoples of this region.

On the other hand, archaeologists working in other parts of the Great Basin routinely note how hard it is to find sites that can actually be radiocarbon dated to this time period. "Sites are rare and dates scarce" in the western Great Basin, Robert Elston (1986:138) has observed. The period between 7,000 and 4,000 years ago, Claude Warren and Robert Crabtree (1986:138) note, "is not represented in the dated archaeological remains" of the southwestern Great Basin. In the central Great Basin, David Thomas (1982a:165) observes, very few middle Holocene sites have been found, those that are known do not predate 5,500 years ago, and "site density data suggest that human populations increased markedly" beginning at about 4,500 years ago.

Table 9-1 provides a list of dated archaeological sites of middle Holocene age from the Great Basin, exclusive of the Bonneville Basin. These dates represent several different kinds of events. For O'Malley Shelter and the Connley Caves, I give both the latest date that precedes what the investigators felt was a gap in the utilization of the site (6,520 years ago at O'Malley, for instance), and the earliest date that follows this apparent gap (4,630 years ago at O'Malley). For other sites, the date marks the onset of what appears to have been fairly continuous occupation thereafter—6,080 years ago at Nightfire Island, for instance, and 5,640 years ago at King's Dog. For still others,

Table 9-1. Great Basin Archaeological Sites with Middle Holocene Dates, Exclusive of Those from the Bonneville Basin

Site	Date (years ago)	References
California		
King's Dog, Surprise Valley	5,640	O'Connell (1975)
Menlo Baths, Surprise Valley	5,250	O'Connell (1975)
Nightfire Island	6,080	Sampson (1985)
Nevada		
Amy's Shelter, Snake Range	4,950	Gruhn (1979)
Corn Creek Dunes, Las Vegas Valley	5,200	P. A. Williams and Orlins (1963)
Cowbone Cave, Winnemucca Lake	5,670	Orr (1974), Hattori (1982)
Gatecliff Shelter, Toquima Range	5,370	Thomas (1983)
Guano Cave, Winnemucca Lake	6,500	Orr (1974); Hattori (1982)
Hidden Cave, Carson Desert	5,365	Thomas (1985)
Leonard Rockshelter	5,740	Heizer (1951)
	7,040	
Lovelock Cave, West Humboldt Range	4,690	Heizer and Napton (1970), Livingston (1988b)
Newark Cave, Newark Valley	5,470	D. D. Fowler (1968)
O'Malley Shelter, Clover Valley	6,520	D. D. Fowler et al. (1973)
	4,630	
Shinner Site D, Winnemucca Lake	5,100	Hattori (1982)
Shinner Site I, Winnemucca Lake	6,730	Hattori (1982)
Silent Snake Springs, Division Peak	5,250	Layton and Thomas (1979)
Triple T Shelter, Toquima Range	5,430	Thomas (1988)
Oregon		
Connley Cave 4B, Fort Rock Basin	7,240	Bedwell (1973)
Connley Cave 5B, Fort Rock Basin	7,430	Bedwell (1973)
Connley Cave 6, Fort Rock Basin	4,720	Bedwell (1973)
Table Rock 1, Fort Rock Basin	5,220	Bedwell (1973)
Utah		
Swallow Shelter, Goose Creek Mountains	5,410	Dalley (1976)
Remnant Cave, Grouse Creek Mountains	4,990	Berry (1976)

the dates represent what appears to have been very short-term use of the site. At Leonard Rockshelter, for instance, the 5,740-year date is for a human burial, the 7,040-year date for what seems to have been an artifact cache; at Table Rock 1, the date is for a cache pit. All, however, reflect the presence of people in the area at the times indicated. I have also included sites that date to just beyond the middle Holocene.

Figure 9-4 shows how these dates stack up through time. Clearly, outside the Bonneville Basin, sites that we can actually demonstrate to have been occupied during the middle Holocene are fairly rare. Not until we reach the end of this period does this situation change. This rarity is not a reflection of the scarcity of radiocarbon-dated sites from the Great Basin in general, nor is it a result of the fact that we are looking for things that are quite old. Indeed, there are as many Great Basin stemmed point sites that have been dated to the 500-year period between 8,500 and 9,000 years ago as there are middle Holocene sites that fall in the 1,500-year interval between 5,500 and 7,000 years ago (seven).

These dates only allow us to say one thing with certainty: not many sites can be securely assigned to the middle Holocene in these areas. The lack of dated sites might simply reflect some oddity in the sample of sites that we happen to have, or some quirk in the sample of dates that we have obtained for those sites.

It seems far more likely, however, that this pattern of dates is telling us something about the use of caves during

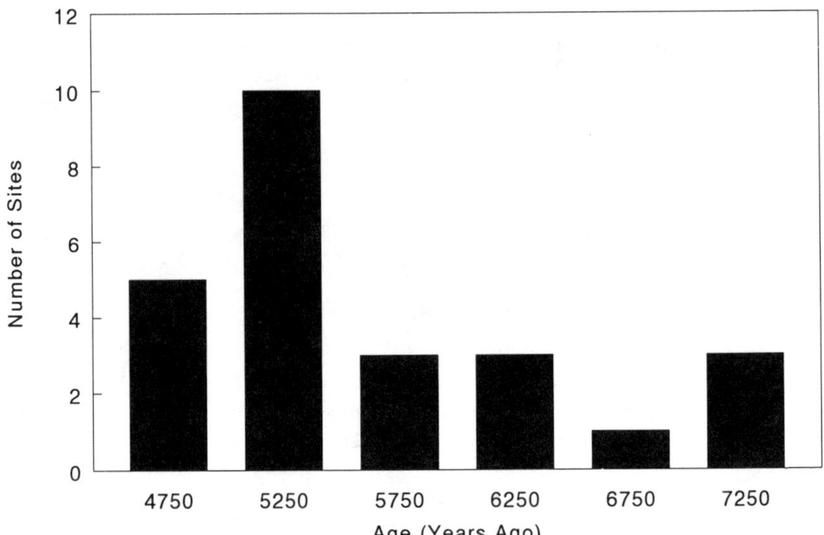

Figure 9-4. The temporal distribution of dated middle Holocene archaeological sites in the Great Basin.

this time period. Of the 23 dated sites, 18 are caves, and the most evident conclusion to draw from these dates is that, for some reason, people made less use of caves during the middle Holocene than they did before and, especially, after this time.

It is likely that the decreased use of caves follows from the fact that most of these sites are near shallow water: five near Winnemucca Lake, four near Paulina Marsh, Lovelock Cave near Humboldt Sink, Newark Cave near Newark Lake, and so on. There is strong evidence that Lake Tahoe retreated substantially during the middle Holocene, thus reducing or perhaps even eliminating flow in the Truckee River, the prime source of water for Winnemucca Lake. Pollen work at Leonard Rockshelter strongly suggests desiccation of the Humboldt Sink at this time; Newark Valley is just southwest of the Ruby Marshes, which dried up during this interval. Middle Holocene aridity might well explain the fact that nearby caves were not used during this period. People were utilizing other, and presumably better watered, locations.

In this light, the location of the Bonneville Basin sites that were used throughout this period becomes significant: they were near sources of water that continued to exist. Danger Cave, for instance, is adjacent to a spring, as is Hogup Cave; Sandwich Shelter is about a mile from the nearest active spring, but is adjacent to Great Salt Lake itself.

With the exception of Leonard Rockshelter, which held a 5,740-year-old burial and a 7,040-year-old cache, occupation sites outside the Bonneville Basin that date to the heart of the middle Holocene are open sites, not caves: Nightfire Island adjacent to Lower Klamath Lake, and King's Dog, adjacent to a spring in Surprise Valley. Such sites suggest that the scarcity of Great Basin middle Holocene sites outside the Bonneville Basin reflects the fact that caves that were used when there was water nearby were not used when the water was not there. This is exactly what Luther Cressman was saying for the northern Great Basin.

MIDDLE HOLOCENE HOUSES

We have virtually no secure information on the kinds of dwellings constructed by the late Pleistocene and early Holocene peoples of the Great Basin; this absence is perhaps a reflection of the fact that most known sites that date to this time are either from caves or from surface settings. Fortunately, one of the middle Holocene open sites that has been excavated provides excellent information on the kinds of houses that were constructed in one part of the Great Basin at this time.

That site is King's Dog, located just west of Middle Alkali Lake in Surprise Valley. Excavated during the late 1960s by James O'Connell, King's Dog is adjacent to a hot spring (the site takes its name from Danny King's dog, which died after jumping into this spring). The spring now provides potable water and feeds a substantial marsh, and was likely to have been key to the occupation of the site itself.

O'Connell's work in the earliest, middle Holocene, deposits of this site yielded a wide variety of artifacts: side-notched projectile points, chipped stone drills and a diverse set of other kinds of stone tools; antler wedges, bone awls, and other bone tools; and large cylindrical mortars and carefully fashioned pestles.

O'Connell also found, and carefully excavated, a series of five superimposed house floors in the deeper parts of King's Dog, the second oldest of which provided the 5,640-year date given in Table 9-1. These early houses were substantial: 22′ to 25′ across and about 2.5′ deep, with a central fireplace and a sloping ramp entryway. From the pattern of postholes that was preserved on these floors, O'Connell observed that there must have been a ring of from 5 to 7 posts arranged around the central hearth within the house pits. He speculated that horizontal stringers had been attached to the tops of these, and that rafters sloped down from the stringers to just beyond the edge of the house pit itself. Presumably, the rafters were covered by mats, and then by earth.

Much of this reconstruction stems directly from what O'Connell discovered from his excavations here: substantial house pits, central fireplaces, and postholes arrayed around those fireplaces. He found no timbers and no mats, so the rest of his reconstruction is speculative. That he did not find these items, however, is not surprising. Had they once been there, they might easily have decayed during the past 5,000 years or so. It is at least equally likely, however, that they were not left behind to begin with. People like the Modoc and Klamath made very similar houses during historic times; when they were about to leave them for substantial periods, they removed the timbers and mats and carefully stored them.

In fact, the middle Holocene houses unearthed by O'Connell at King's Dog are extremely similar to early historic Modoc and Klamath winter houses. For instance, the Modoc, who lived some 80 miles to the northwest of Surprise Valley, built earth-covered winter lodges above a circular pit that averaged about 22′ across and 4′ deep (the Klamath, to the immediate north, built similar winter houses but with pits that were about 2.5′ deep: the difference in depth may reflect differences in winter temperatures). The superstructure of these dwellings was supported by four main posts placed around the central fire. Horizontal stringers were placed at the top of these posts, and rafters angled down from the stringers to just beyond the edges of the house pit; the rafters were then covered by mats and earth. These houses were costly to construct: a typical one would take the one or more families who were to occupy it about a month to build. They repaid the expense, however, since they were spacious, warm, and durable.

Those parts of the King's Dog structures that were well represented archaeologically—the large pits, central fireplaces, and central support posts—are nearly identical to the Modoc earth lodges. There is one exception: most Modoc structures were entered through an opening in the roof, whereas the King's Dog houses were entered by a rampway that exited to the east. However, some Modoc houses did have ramp entrances, and, although the similarity may be entirely coincidental, the Modoc ramp entries would have faced east: the land of the dead lay to the west, and most Modoc houses that had steps or doorways had them facing east.

Not far from King's Dog, the Menlo Baths site provided the remains of a middle Holocene structure much like those at King's Dog. Also located next to a hot spring (hence the name), Menlo Baths had been the focus of uncontrolled digging by artifact collectors. As a result, much of the site had been destroyed by the time O'Connell arrived, and he was able to excavate only a small portion of the house he encountered here.

O'Connell thought that both of these sites were occupied year-round. More recently, however, Steven James has analyzed the faunal remains recovered from both locations, and has argued convincingly that both are likely to represent winter occupations. The Modoc houses so similar to those at King's Dog and Menlo Baths were also winter dwellings.

Nightfire Island, on the shores of Lower Klamath Lake, provided the remains of houses that were constructed at the very end of middle Holocene times (at about 4,500 years ago), but these were not excavated in their entirety, and there is little that can be said about them. Otherwise, little convincing evidence of middle Holocene structures exists in the Great Basin. In fact, it is fair to say that there is relatively little evidence of human occupation in the Great Basin at all during the middle Holocene. To explore that issue further, however, requires a discussion of how Great Basin archaeologists routinely assign ages to sites that cannot be directly dated.

PROJECTILE POINT CHRONOLOGIES

Most Great Basin archaeological sites are surface sites, found there either because the surface has never been buried or because the sediments that once covered it have been eroded. Unfortunately, there are no dating techniques known that can be used to assign precise ages to the vast majority of these surface sites. As a result, to date these sites, archaeologists rely on the presence of artifact types whose forms are known to change through time.

Throughout North America, two major kinds of artifacts—pottery and projectile points—are routinely used for this purpose. In general, ceramics tend to provide North American archaeologists with their best artifactual time markers because they were often decorated in ways that changed sensitively as time passed. The highly mobile life-style of most Great Basin peoples, however, did not lend itself readily to the routine use of items that are cumbersome and difficult to transport securely. In addition, many of the functions for which ceramics were used elsewhere—food storage and cooking, for instance—were taken over by basketry in the Great Basin. Pottery did not become truly widespread here until after about 1,000 years ago, and even then did not become very common in most areas.

As a result, archaeologists use projectile points as the major artifactual time-telling device for Great Basin sites. These tend to be far less sensitive temporal indicators than ceramics, but they are found throughout the area and, as far as we know, were in use during the entire span of human occupation in the Great Basin.

I have, of course, already used projectile points in just this way. Great Basin stemmed point sites from buried contexts routinely date to between about 11,200 and 7,500 years ago. It follows that surface sites that contain these points were also occupied during this period. Although this is a substantial timespan, it is far better than nothing, and it is fully possible that future work in well-stratified sites will allow finer temporal distinctions to be made within this large and variable complex of points. In that case, we will be able to assign finer dates to the surface sites that contain them.

My concern here, however, is not with late Pleistocene and early Holocene projectile points, but instead with the forms that follow them. Much of what we know about changing human use of Great Basin landscapes during the past 7,500 years has come from using these later points to date surface sites, and to assign ages to buried sites that could be dated in no other way.

GREAT BASIN PROJECTILE POINTS: THE LAST 7,500 YEARS

Following a system devised by Robert F. Heizer and his students, most Great Basin projectile point types that occurred during the past 7,500 years are given a two-part name, in which the first term refers to a site or to an area from which the type was first defined, and the second refers to some aspect of the shape of the point involved. "Cottonwood Triangular," for instance, refers to a triangular point first defined from a site along Cottonwood Creek in Owens Valley. In addition to being named in this fashion, points that are similar to one another are routinely grouped into "series;" the various types within each series are generally distinguished from one another on the basis of the morphology of the hafted end of the point.

Heizer and his students began the difficult process of making sense of the morphological and temporal variation shown by middle and late Holocene Great Basin projectile points; in recent years, it has been David Thomas who has done the most to codify the description of these points. The result of the work of these and other scholars has been the definition of four major series of chronologically sensitive Great Basin projecile point types that were in use during the past 7,500 years:

Gatecliff Series points have triangular blades and medium to large stems (the hafted part of the point); the stems contract toward the base and are set off from the blade by angles that exceed 60°. There are two types in the series: Gatecliff Split Stem, and Gatecliff Contracting Stem (see Figure 9-5).

Elko Series points are large and corner-notched; the angles at the notches are less than 60°, the width at the base greater than one centimeter (0.40″), and the weight generally greater than 1.5 grams (0.05 ounce). There are two named types: Elko Corner-notched and Elko Eared (see Figure 9-5).

Rosegate Series points are small and corner-notched with triangular blades and expanding stems; the base is generally less than one centimeter wide, the weight generally less than 1.5 grams. Many archaeologists recognize two major types within the series (Rose Spring and Eastgate points), but others feel that the two are so similar to one another than there are best treated as a single type, called Rosegate (see Figure 9-6).

Desert Series points include three named forms: Desert Side-notched, Cottonwood Triangular, and Cottonwood

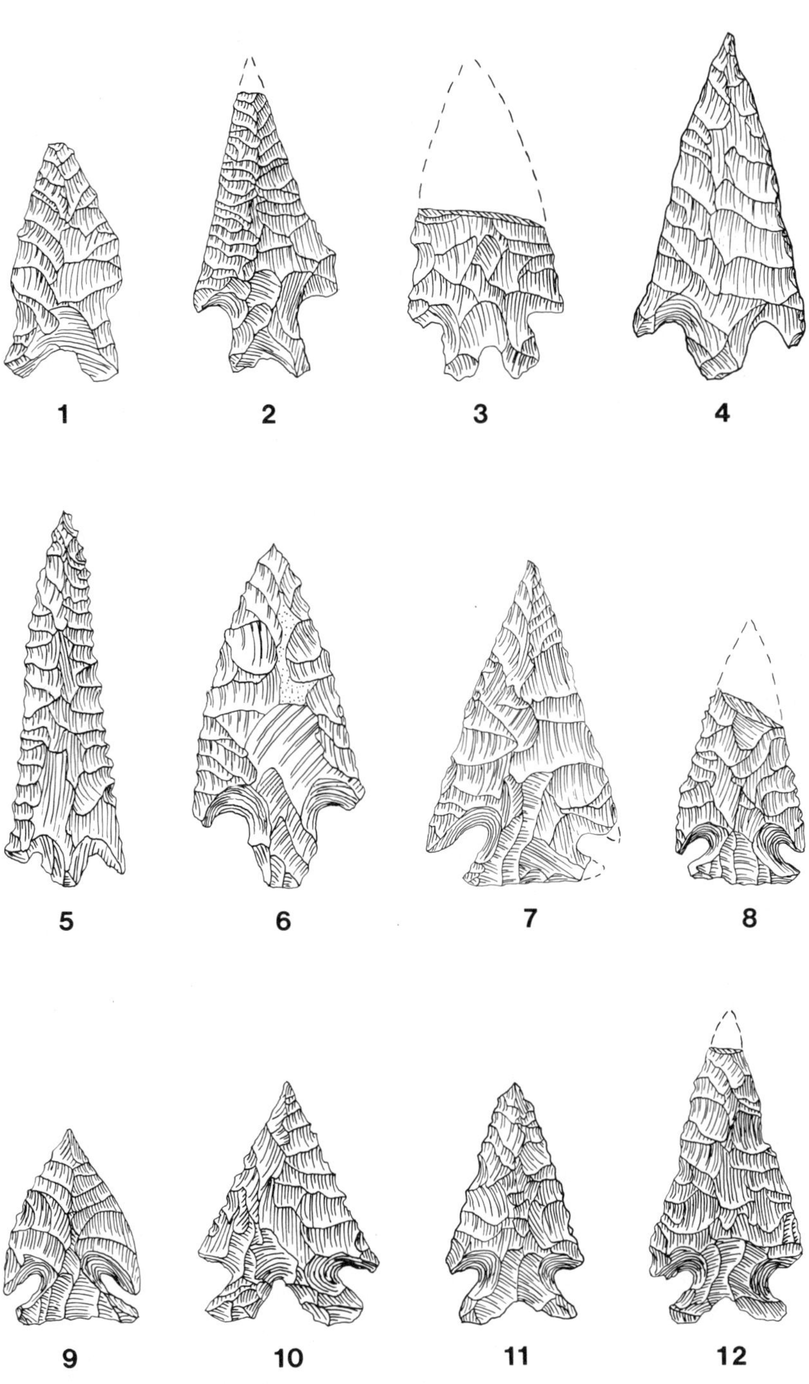

Figure 9-5. Gatecliff and Elko series points. 1–3, Gatecliff Split Stem points from the Steens Mountain area; 4–6, Gatecliff Contracting Stem points from Hidden Cave (after Thomas 1985); 7–9, Elko Corner-notched points from the Steens Mountain area; 10–12, Elko Eared points from the Steens Mountain area. Length of 1 is 1.4″; others to scale.

Leaf-shaped (see Figure 9-6). Desert Side-notched points are small and triangular, with notches fairly high on the sides and weights of no more than 1.5 grams. Cottonwood Triangular points are unnotched, thin, triangular points with straight to convex bases; they also weigh no more than 1.5 grams. Cottonwood Leaf-shaped points are identical to Cottonwood Triangular points except that they have rounded bases.

Gatecliff and Elko series points are broader at the base and heavier than Rosegate and Desert series points. They were used to tip atlatl darts, which were then propelled

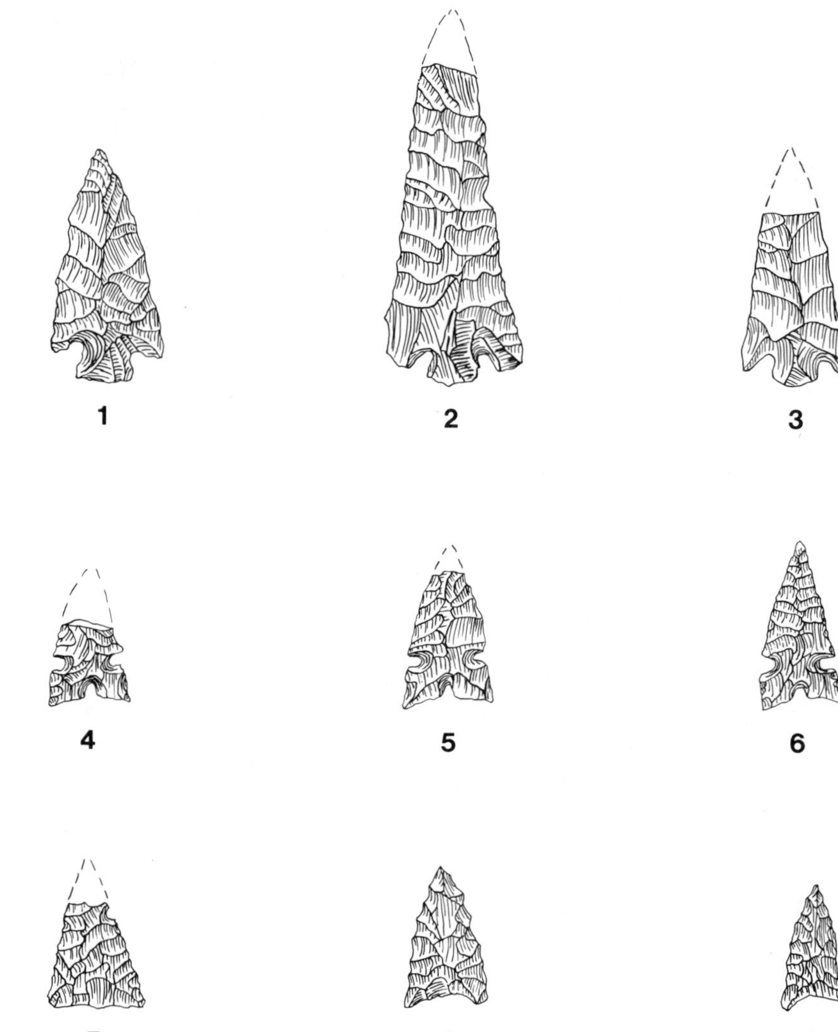

Figure 9-6. Rosegate and Desert series points. 1–3, Rosegate points from the Steens Mountain area; 4–6, Desert Side-Notched points from Gatecliff Shelter (after Thomas 1985); 7–9, Cottonwood Triangular points from Gatecliff Shelter (after Thomas 1985). Length of 1 is 1.4″; others to scale.

with an atlatl or spear-thrower (see Figure 9-7). The atlatl was not in use in the Great Basin or any nearby area during historic times, though it was used in the Arctic, along the Northwest Coast, near the mouth of the Mississippi, and in northern Mexico, including parts of Baja California. When Europeans entered the Great Basin, the native peoples of this area were armed with bows and arrows, and the more gracile Rosegate and Desert series points were used as arrowpoints.

A good case for these different uses can be made from the points themselves. David Thomas, for instance, has shown that historic period atlatl points tend to be more robust than historic arrowpoints. However, the best case can be made from the archaeological record itself. Atlatls, atlatl darts, bows, and arrows (and, even more commonly, fragments of these weapons) have been found in some number in Great Basin archaeological sites. Most of the darts and arrows do not have points attached, but, when they do, Gatecliff and Elko series points tip darts, whereas Desert series points tip arrows. In fact, Desert series points are also found on historic Great Basin arrows. To my knowledge, Rosegate points have not been found attached to arrows, but they have been found in deposits that have yielded arrow fragments.

If atlatls were not in use during historic times in the Great Basin but bows were, it follows that the atlatl dart points must be earlier than the arrow points. If the known historic arrows of the Great Basin were tipped with Desert series points, it follows that Rosegate points, which were also used to tip arrows, must have gone out of use before then.

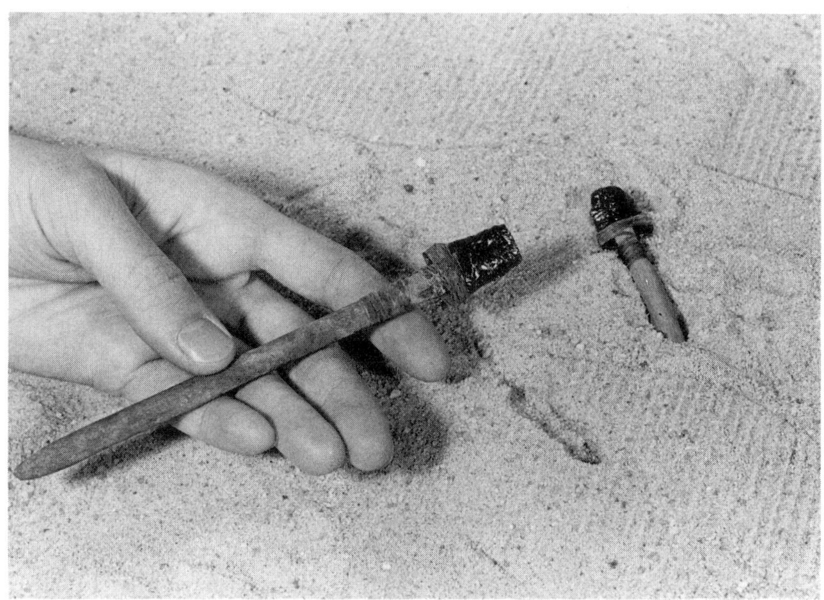

Figure 9-7. Projectile points hafted to atlatl foreshafts, from Hidden Cave, Nevada. Photograph by Judith Silverstein, courtesy of the American Museum of Natural History and Silverstein, Roe Photographics.

In fact, the introduction of the bow and arrow into the Great Basin is marked by the advent of Rosegate points. These seem to appear first in the eastern Great Basin, about 1,700 years ago (A.D. 300), and then slightly later in the central and western Great Basin (A.D. 700). These dates suggest, as Richard Holmer has pointed out, that the bow and arrow entered the Great Basin about 1,700 years ago, and had replaced the atlatl by about 1,300 years ago.

Rosegate points remained in common use in the eastern Great Basin until about 1,000 years ago, and until about 700 years ago in the central and western parts of the region. They were then replaced by Desert series points (and a few other, less common forms), which continued in use into historic times (Table 9-2).

The chronology of arrowpoints in the Great Basin is fairly straightforward. The chronology of atlatl dart points, however, is far more complicated. The complications come from the fact that there are some major differences in the dates available for the western and central Great Basin on the one hand, and from the eastern and northern Great Basin on the other. Table 9-2 provides these dates.

The Gatecliff series points present little problem. Gatecliff Split Stem points have identical dates from east to west. Although Gatecliff Contracting Stem points seem to have lasted considerably longer in the east than in the west, they appear to have come into use at about the same time throughout this area.

The problem is created by Elko points. Thomas's analysis supports the conclusion that these points were in use from about 3,500 to 1,300 years ago in the central and western Great Basin. In the eastern Great Basin, however, Holmer's work suggests that they were in use far earlier (by 7,500 years ago), and lasted later (to 1,000 years ago). An early use of Elko points is also clear in the northern Great Basin. James Wilde, for instance, found Elko points beneath Mazama Ash at the Skull Creek Dunes site in Catlow Valley, just west of Steens Mountain. Although no radiocarbon dates are available for this level of the site, the points must predate the deposition of the ash at about 6,800 years ago.

It is not known why Elko points make such a late appearance in the central and western Great Basin. Indeed, when C. Melvin Aikens first argued from his Hogup Cave data that Elko points occurred far earlier in the eastern

Table 9-2. Dates for Some Major Great Basin Projectile Point Series and Types

	Date (years ago)	
Series or type	**Central/western Great Basin**	**Eastern Great Basin**
Gatecliff Split Stem	5,000–3,200	5,000–3,200
Gatecliff Contracting Stem	5,000–3,200	5,000–1,500
Elko Series	3,500–1,300	7,500–3,500 (Gap?) 2,000–1,000
Rosegate Series	1,300–700	1,700–1,000
Desert Series	700–Historic	1,000–Historic

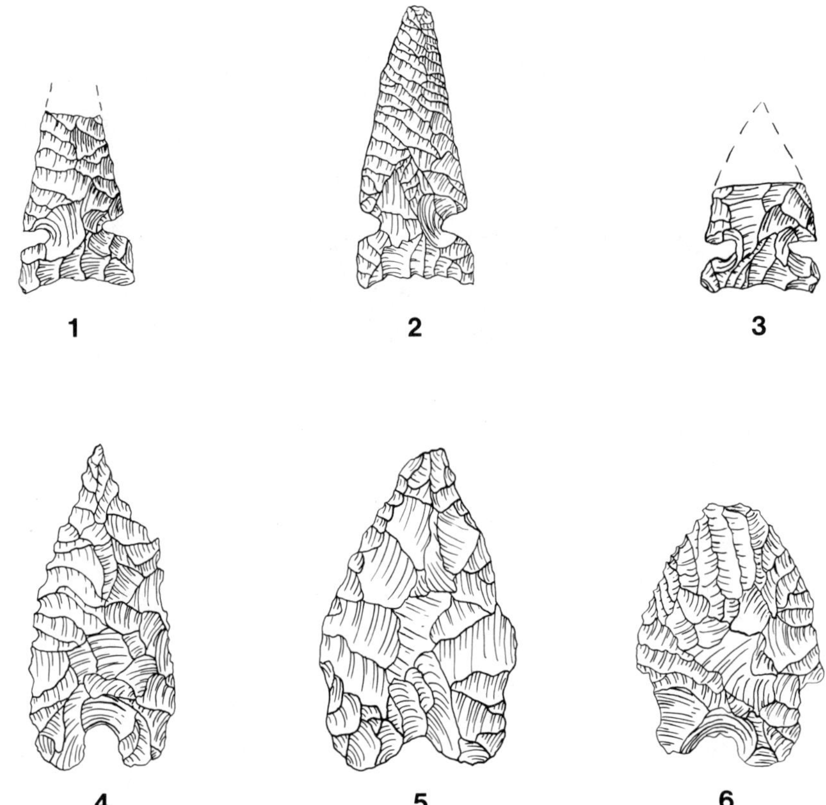

Figure 9-8. Northern Side-Notched and Pinto points. 1–3, Northern Side-Notched points from the Nightfire Island site (after Sampson 1985); 4–6 Pinto points from the Stahl site (after Warren and Crabtree 1986). Length of 2 is 1.6″; others to scale.

than in the western Great Basin, many archaeologists were reluctant to believe it. A number of sites, however, now show that he was right, and the problem becomes understanding why this temporal difference exists.

There is some chance that Gatecliff series points were in use during the middle Holocene in the western parts of the Great Basin, but that we are unaware of that fact because we have so few sites from this region that date to that period of time. In this view, Gatecliff points in the west would have been the middle Holocene counterparts of Elko points to the east. Although that might be the case, it is a hard argument to make, since Elko and Gatecliff points formed part of the same toolkit for several thousand years in the eastern Great Basin.

There are many other named projectile point types for the Great Basin, but only two of them need concern us here. Northern Side-notched points (see Figure 9-8) are best known from areas north of the Great Basin, particularly Idaho, but they were also used in parts of the Great Basin, especially in its northern reaches and in areas adjacent to the Rockies. In general, they date to between about 7,200 and 4,500 years ago, and thus seem to be good markers of the middle Holocene where they occur. The middle Holocene Surprise Valley houses that I discussed are characterized by these points.

Pinto points, first defined during the 1930s, are more problematic. These points look superficially like Gatecliff Split Stem points, but tend to be cruder, and differ from them in details of the form of the stem (see Figure 9-8). Found primarily in the Mojave Desert and in the eastern Great Basin, they have been directly dated in the latter area to between about 8,300 and 6,300 years ago.

Their age in the Mojave Desert is quite a different matter. Here, they are often thought to mark the middle Holocene, largely on the basis of the fact that they seem to postdate such stemmed forms as Lake Mojave and Silver Lake points, and to predate Gatecliff Split Stem points. However, in the central Mojave Desert, Pinto points have been recovered in sites dated to between 7,000 and 9,000 years ago, and they may have been in use after 4,000 years ago. As a result, their presence cannot be taken as diagnostic of middle Holocene occupation in this area.

ELUSIVE SITES AND LOW POPULATION DENSITIES

These are the prime artifactual time markers available for the last 7,500 years ago or so in the Great Basin. If our concern is with understanding the nature of middle Holocene human occupation in this region, then there is an obvious problem. Surface sites, and buried sites that cannot be directly dated, make up the bulk of the known archaeological record in the Great Basin. These sites are routinely assigned ages on the basis of the time-sensitive artifacts they contain. Unfortunately, there are precious few of these known for the middle Holocene.

In the central and western Great Basin, only Northern Side-notched points fill the bill, but these are common only toward the northern reaches of the area. Here, however, they are found both in surface sites, as in the Black Rock Desert, and in buried sites, as I will discuss shortly.

In the eastern Great Basin, Northern Side-notched points are common toward the the northern edge of the area, and also in sites near the Rocky Mountains. They are, however, rarely found in abundance on surface sites. Pinto points may do the job here but they do not show up very often in surface assemblages either. Even when they do, they may be early Holocene in age. In the Mojave Desert, Pinto points may date to the middle Holocene, but they also date to before and, perhaps, after this time. As a result, they are of little help.

The pattern is fairly consistent. We do not have good middle Holocene time markers from the central and western Great Basin because sites that can be dated to this interval have proved so hard to find. When we do have a widespread time marker—Pinto points in the eastern Great Basin—we do not find them in abundance in many settings. The most obvious inference to draw from all this is that middle Holocene human population densities were not very high in the Great Basin. The sites are scarce because people were scarce.

Some apparent exceptions to this situation do exist. Some years ago, John Fagan, following arguments that had been made by Bedwell and Cressman, reasoned that, if aridity had caused places like the Fort Rock Basin to be less intensively used during the middle Holocene, people might have focused their activities on higher-elevation springs. Accordingly, Fagan examined 12 springside archaeological sites scattered across a broad swath of southeastern Oregon, from just west of Warner Valley to just east of Steens Mountain. He found that ten of these 12 sites contained Northern Side-notched points, and concluded that these were middle Holocene occupations. Given that Northern Side-notched points were in use between 7,200 and 4,500 years ago, there is no reason to doubt him.

Fagan's northern Great Basin sites are similar to middle Holocene sites elsewhere in the Great Basin in an important way. They are near dependable supplies of water, just like such sites as Danger Cave, Hogup Cave, King's Dog, Menlo Baths, and Nightfire Island. Great Basin sites of this age that are not directly adjacent to water reflect extremely ephemeral use—the caches and burials at Table Rock No. 1 and Leonard Rockshelter, for instance. It is easy to observe that most substantial Great Basin sites are near water, no matter what their age. This is, after all, a desert. But there is a big difference between most substantial sites being near dependable water sources and all of them being in such a setting. Certainly, this was not the case immediately before or after the middle Holocene.

Although it is somewhat out of fashion to say so, it does appear that middle Holocene aridity had a fairly dramatic impact on the human occupants of the Great Basin. Grinding stones became common as this interval began, rather clearly reflecting the intensified use of seeds. Sites that had once been occupied were abandoned, and human use of the landscape seems to have been heavily focused on dependable sources of water.

With the exception of the arguments concerning grinding stones, similar statements were being made 30 years ago and more. Back then, those who disagreed could reasonably observe that not enough archaeology had been done in the Great Basin to make this argument securely. Today, this is still true for some areas: the central Bonneville Basin comes immediately to mind. It is, however, far harder to take this position for the Great Basin as a whole. It does, indeed, look as if the Great Basin during the middle Holocene was marked by relatively low human population densities, and it is very likely that those low densities were caused by increased aridity. Ernst Antevs, Luther Cressman, Robert Heizer, and other scholars of earlier decades who took this position appear to have been right.

Human Adaptations during the Late Holocene

In Chapter 8, I noted that, if I had to pick a time when the Great Basin began to look very much as it did when

Europeans first arrived, I would pick 4,500 years ago, the beginning, more or less, of the late Holocene. That conclusion would also seem to apply to the adaptations of the people who occupied this region. As with Great Basin environments, the exact date differs from place to place, but, between about 5,000 and 4,000 years ago, the archaeological record begins to look very much as if it could have been created by people living much the way Great Basin native peoples lived when Europeans first encountered them.

The beginning of the late Holocene is marked by a tremendous increase in the numbers of known archaeological sites, both those dated directly and those dated by associated projectile points. It is also marked by a tremendous increase in the diversity of habitats in which sites are found.

The caves alone suggest that something significant has happened. At O'Malley Rockshelter, the occupational hiatus ended at about 4,600 years ago; at the Connley Caves, far to the north, the hiatus ended at about 4,700 years ago. The first human occupation of Newberry Cave, in the western Mojave Desert, is marked by Gatecliff Contracting Stem points; the earliest radiocarbon date here falls at 3,765 years ago. At Stuart Rockshelter, in the eastern Mojave Desert, the earliest occupation occurred at 4,050 years ago. The earliest intense use of Hidden Cave, again marked by Gatecliff series points, began at about 3,900 years ago. At Kramer Cave, the earliest intense use also began at about 3,900 years ago, and is marked by Gatecliff series points. Indeed, as Dave Thomas has noted, the averages of the radiocarbon dates for the early occupations of Hidden and Kramer caves differ by only 38 years. Lovelock Cave seems to have been utilized soon after 4,700 years ago; South Fork Shelter, at about 4,360 years ago, and so on. These dates are impressively consistent.

Open sites, often associated with the remains of dwellings, become fairly common as well. The first occupation at the Humboldt Lakebed site, in the Humboldt Sink not far from Hidden Cave, is marked by Gatecliff series points. At the Stillwater Marshes, in the Carson Sink to the immediate south, there is virtually no evidence of middle Holocene occupation, but people had begun to use the area shortly after 5,000 years ago, and were utilizing it intensely by 3,300 years ago. To the north, substantial sites with structures appear along the shores of Abert Lake soon after 4,000 years ago.

This situation is completely different from that encountered with the middle Holocene, when it is difficult to find any sites at all. Once the late Holocene begins, sites become abundant. They are also found almost everywhere. In the eastern Great Basin, where sites such as Danger Cave and Hogup Cave appear to have been utilized throughout the middle Holocene, the onset of the late Holocene sees not only a tremendous increase in the number of known sites, but also, as C. Melvin Aikens and David Madsen have pointed out, the first truly significant use of upland settings. Indeed, Gatecliff series points are frequently found in the alpine zone of the mountains of the central Great Basin. Here, they are commonly associated with rock walls, cairns, and rings, features that appear to have been used in conjunction with hunting.

The intensive use of a broad variety of environments was fully characteristic of the native peoples of the Great Basin at the time of European contact. The archaeological record suggests that such use began as the late Holocene began. Indeed, even the houses that date to early in the late Holocene are much like those known from the region historically.

In Surprise Valley, for instance, the large housepit structures that marked the middle Holocene occupation at King's Dog and Menlo Baths gave way to far less substantial structures, associated with Gatecliff series points, after 5,000 years ago. James O'Connell excavated 46 of these structures at two Surprise Valley sites, King's Dog (where they are stratigraphically above the large middle Holocene houses) and Rodriguez. All of these houses were preserved as saucer-shaped depressions from 10′ to 18′ in diameter and up to about 20″ deep, with postholes ringing the inner edge of the depression and hearths located in the center.

Unlike the situation with the larger, earlier houses, the superstructures of many of these later forms had burned, and were preserved as charred remains. As a result, O'Connell was able discover that two different kinds of structures were involved. The most abundant of these was a dome-shaped wickiup whose superstructure was formed by light willow or aspen poles, which were then covered by grasses, brush, and tule mats. The other form was a simple brush windscreen—a circular, unroofed frame of poles that had brush and mats tied to it. Both kinds of structures were widely used in the Great Basin during historic times.

The 46 structures at these two sites were by no means contemporaneous. King's Dog, for instance, had 15 of the saucer-shaped depressions stacked one on top of the other, and the radiocarbon dates indicate that these structures had been built across several thousand years. Whereas the earliest projectile points associated with these structures are Gatecliff series, the latest are Rosegate.

It is not clear why there was such a dramatic shift in house types from middle to late Holocene times here. Perhaps the answer is simple: the substantial middle Holocene houses may represent winter occupations, and the more lightly built late Holocene structures were for summer use. Perhaps, however, the reason for this shift is far more complex, as I discuss subsequently.

A number of other Great Basin sites dating to early in the late Holocene have houses not dissimilar to those that were in use during early historic times: the Humboldt Lakebed site provides an excellent example. At the same time, archaeological sites begin to be found in number across a full range of Great Basin environments, from valley bottoms to mountaintops.

This represents a dramatic change from anything that appears to have gone on before. Fluted point sites are confined to valley bottom settings. Although some stemmed point sites are found in the uplands, most are also in valley bottoms. Middle Holocene sites are simply scarce, and most of those that we can date securely to this period are located near lakes and springs. The scarcity of such sites suggests that human population densities in the Great Basin were low during this period, just as they were low in water-poor areas during early historic times. Once the middle Holocene ends, however, sites become common, and they become so in diverse environmental settings. The difference is pronounced and makes it appear as if we are seeing, for the first time, human adaptations, and human population densities, much like those of early historic times.

It is tempting to argue that this pronounced shift was related to the arrival of piñon pine through much of the Great Basin. Historically, piñon was an extremely important food source throughout those areas of the Great Basin that contained it, providing a resource that was often critical for winter survival. Piñon, however, did not arrive in the central latitudes of the Great Basin until after about 6,500 years ago, and was probably not abundant here until well after that. Much of the middle Holocene had neither the rich valley-bottom resources that were critical to people during the late Pleistocene and early Holocene, nor the piñon that was critical in many areas during early historic times. Scarce resources lead to scarce people.

Once piñon arrived, we would expect human populations to respond, and perhaps to respond quickly. Gatecliff Shelter, in fact, shows the kind of correlation between the arrival of this productive resource and the arrival of people that would be expected in a relatively resource-poor environment. Piñon arrived in this part of the Toquima Range at or soon after 6,000 years ago. The first human occupation at Gatecliff occurred at about 5,300 years ago, and the first hearths in this site, which date to about the same time, contain the remains of piñon pine.

Other sites make the same point. The earliest intense use of Hidden Cave, for instance, began shortly after 3,900 years ago. We know that the people who visited the site at this time were utilizing piñon because a human coprolite from these deposits contained a piñon nut hull. Today, the closest piñon to Hidden Cave is in the Stillwater Range, some 20 miles to the northeast. We do not know when piñon first arrived here, but we can be fairly certain that it was after, and probably long after, it arrived in the central Toquima Range, some 100 miles to the south and east.

Once piñon arrived, it appears to have been used, and Gatecliff itself was not used until it was there. Piñon, however, cannot account for the changes that occur in the archaeological record at the same time in south-central Oregon. Piñon never reached this area, yet the occupational hiatus at the Connley Caves ends at about 4,700 years ago, and substantial sites appear along the shores of Abert Lake soon after 4,000 years ago. The phenomenon appears to match what was happening to the south, but it happened in the absence of piñon.

Although the arrival of piñon certainly made a difference, the end of middle Holocene aridity appears to have been far more important. The Ruby Marshes were reborn at about 4,700 years ago, about the same time that the sagebrush/grass ratios at Fish Lake, in Steens Mountain, fell, and the Connley Caves were reoccupied. The pollen from Leonard Rockshelter strongly suggests desiccation of the Humboldt Sink during the middle Holocene, but when nearby Lovelock Cave was first utilized, at or soon after 4,600 years ago, the coprolite evidence shows that people were making heavy use of sedges and cattails. The same is true for Hidden Cave: coprolites from the earliest human use of this site are full of the remains of these two plants.

During historic times in the Great Basin, human population densities were highly correlated with the abundance of shallow water. Where shallow water was abundant, population densities were high. Where water was scarce, population densities were low. Prehistorically, when middle

Holocene aridity ended, human population densities appear to have increased. In some cases, piñon was important, but in others it was not. What counted everywhere was that it was no longer as arid as it had been.

THE "NUMIC EXPANSION"

The foodstuffs utilized by the native peoples of the Great Basin during early historic times often presented significant incongruities in both time and space. Piñon nuts, for instance, are to be found only in the middle elevations of the mountains, and only during the fall. Sedge fruits are also available only in the fall, but are most abundant in low-elevation marshes. The flowering heads of cattails are found in these marshes as well, but only during the summer. Yellow-bellied marmots are generally active from late spring to early fall, but they are found above the upper timberline. Townsend's ground squirrels can be taken during spring and summer, but only beneath the lower timberline.

Such spatial and temporal incongruities presented significant challenges to Great Basin native peoples. To be sure, the severity of the challenge varied from place to place. Where resources were densely packed, generally because the area was well watered, as in Owens Valley, the challenges were lessened, and population densities were higher. Where resources were widely scattered, generally because the area was poorly watered, as in much of the Bonneville Basin, the challenges were more severe, and population densities were lower. But whether we look at the Owens Valley Paiute or the Gosiute, the solution was the same. People dispersed across the landscape to gain access to far-flung resources that were only seasonally available, and they stored many of these resources to level the temporal differences in resource availability.

This pattern was also in existence in the Great Basin early in the late Holocene. Although there are a number of ways to document this fact, the coprolites alone are compelling. For instance, one of the coprolites from the deeper deposits at Hidden Cave, dated to about 3,800 years ago, contained both cattail pollen and sedge seeds. As Peter Wigand and Peter Mehringer have pointed out, either the pollen or the seeds, or both, had to have been stored, because, although they may be available in the same environment, they do not become available at the same time. Another Hidden Cave coprolite, of about the same age, contained sedge seeds and a piñon nut hull, incorporating resources that are available at the same time of year, but from environments that are now at least 20 miles apart in this area.

What we know of the adaptations of Great Basin peoples some 4,000 years ago makes them sound very similar to the adaptations of the peoples encountered by Europeans in early historic times. There were, of course, some substantial differences: to take but one example, the earlier peoples did not have the bow and arrow. But the general use of the landscape seems to have been quite similar.

That the use of the landscape at 4,000 years ago and at the time of European contact was similar, however, does not necessarily mean that we are dealing with people who are lineally related. Because language, race, and culture are totally independent phenomena—any person has the capability of speaking any language and belonging to any culture—it is usually impossible to tell from the prehistoric archaeological record what language a given set of people spoke. As a result, the general similarities between human adaptations during early historic times and those 4,000 years ago in the Great Basin can not be taken to mean that these earlier peoples spoke languages that were closely related to those spoken by the native peoples of the Great Basin during historic times.

In fact, many archaeologists and anthropologists think that they were not closely related at all. Many scholars believe that the Numic speakers who occupied much of the Great Basin at the time of European contact (see Chapter 2 and Figure 2-16) spread across this region only about 1,000 years ago. This postulated late prehistoric population movement is referred to as the "Numic expansion."

Similar movements are documented to have occurred at other times and in other places. Bantu speakers, for instance, spread across vast expanses of central and southern Africa beginning shortly after 2,000 years ago; Athapaskan speakers moved into the Southwest a few hundred years ago. Even though such expansions do occur, however, and even though there is no reason that a Numic expansion could not have happened at about 1,000 years ago, there is no compelling reason to think that it did. To see why this is the case requires a brief tour of a particular approach to historical linguistics.

GLOTTOCHRONOLOGY

French, Italian, Spanish, and Portuguese are all descended from Latin, a fact that is abundantly clear from the similarities these languages show in their structure and content.

For instance, a significant amount of the vocabulary in all four of these modern languages is derived from Latin. *Milk* in Spanish is *leche;* in French, *lait;* in Italian, *latte,* and in Portuguese, *leite.* In the ancestral Latin, it was *lactem.* Words possessing a common origin of this sort are called "cognates."

The differences between cognates, as between *lait* and *leche,* are due to the slow changes that languages undergo as time passes. In addition to these kinds of changes, however, words used to convey a given concept can also be replaced by new terms borrowed from a different language or by ones created anew. Where the Spanish say *fin de semana,* the Italians *fine settimana,* and the Portuguese *fim de semana* for *weekend,* many French speakers now say *week-end,* a loan word from English that is replacing the French *fin de semaine.*

Given that related languages become increasingly different from one another as time passes, it follows that the number of cognates they share will decrease through time. This in turn suggests that the percentage of cognates in a pair of related languages might be used as a linguistic clock: the fewer the number of remaining cognates in a pair of related languages, the longer those languages have been separated. Further, if the rate of "decay" or loss in the number of cognates were known, then perhaps the actual time of divergence of a language pair could be calculated.

Beginning late in the 1940s, the linguist Morris Swadesh began to develop these thoughts in detail. Ultimately, he and others produced a method for calculating the time of divergence of language pairs. That method soon became referred to as glottochronology. Glottochronological methods other than the one developed by Swadesh exist, but only Swadesh's approach has been applied to Great Basin languages, and it is this approach to which I refer in the text that follows.

In Swadesh's method, languages were not compared on the basis of their entire vocabulary, but instead on the basis of a core vocabulary containing items felt to be universal and noncultural, words referring to "things found anywhere in the world and familiar to every member of a society" (Swadesh 1952:457). At first, the core vocabulary used by Swadesh contained 200 words; later, it was shortened to 100. Both lists contained such words as (in English) *see, woman, tongue, hair,* and *hand.*

In 1950, Swadesh determined that, during the past 1,000 years, English had retained about 85% of a set of its core vocabulary words. Soon after, linguist Robert Lees examined the histories of 13 languages and determined that the average core vocabulary retention rate in these languages for the 200-word list was 81% per thousand years. If it is assumed that this retention rate is both accurate and truly constant through time, it can be used to estimate the time of divergence of two languages from a common parent. For instance, two languages that have 66% cognate items in their core vocabulary can be calculated to have been separated for 1,000 years. The calculation is simple: each language will retain 81% of core vocabulary items after 1,000 years; 81% × 81% = 66%.

For a variety of reasons, the estimates of the length of linguistic divergence provided by Swadesh's glottochronology are minimum estimates only. As a result, they are often referred to as "minimum centuries of divergence." If glottochronology works, it would provide a minimum estimate of the amount of time that has passed since two languages diverged from a common parent.

Unfortunately, there is every reason to think that glottochronology does not work. For starters, linguists strongly question the assumption that there really is a culture-free vocabulary. In addition, serious difficulties are associated with both the idea and the calculation of constant retention rates. When Swadesh, Lees, and others calculated their retention rates, they did it in the only way they could: by using written languages. Writing, however, stabilizes a language, and there is absolutely no reason to think that retention rates drawn from written languages have anything to do with retention rates drawn from those that are not written. Worse, there is not even any way to find out, since we cannot talk to people who lived 1,000 or 2,000 years ago.

It is also true that retention rates should not be constant, but should instead reflect the contexts in which people live. Such things as population densities, degrees of mobility, environmental complexity, and external contacts should play a significant role in determining the length of time items are retained in a vocabulary. As anthropologist Joseph Jorgensen has discussed in some detail, people who live in areas that are resource rich tend to develop private ownership of those resources and to reside in relatively restricted areas. Contacts among local communities are reduced, and linguistic diversification hastened, as a result. In contrast, people who live in areas that are only modestly endowed with resources do not develop concepts of private ownership of those resources and tend to be highly mobile. Contacts among groups in this setting are higher, and the speed of linguistic diversification is reduced.

Even if glottochronology did work for unwritten languages, we would have no way of knowing it. But if these arguments are not enough, there is also the fact that applications of glottochronology to languages whose history is known provide horrendous results. To take but one example, John Rea's glottochronological analysis of Italian and French determined that these languages had split by A.D. 1586. As Rea observed, however, French and Italian were well differentiated by that time. The first *written* record of French dates to A.D 842. and of Italian, to A.D. 960, but these written records postdate the divergence of the languages themselves. At the Council of Tours, in A.D. 813, French bishops decided that priests were to speak in the vernacular, not in Latin, "so that all may understand what is said" (Rickard 1989:18).

Many scholars have obtained similar incorrect results for a diverse variety of other languages. Theresa Bynon has pointed out that, where they can be tested, many results of the results of glottochronological analyses are, simply put, "absurd" (Bynon 1977:270). Although more sophisticated methods of extracting time from linguistic data may someday be derived, we are not there yet.

Linguists routinely reject Swadesh's glottochronology as a means of extracting absolute time. It is something of a surprise, then, to find that many archaeologists have fully accepted the results of glottochronological analyses of Great Basin languages.

SYDNEY LAMB AND NUMIC TIME DEPTH

In 1954, Swadesh applied his glottochronological methods to Uto-Aztecan languages, hoping thereby to clarify the position of Nahuatl, the language of the Aztecs (see Chapter 2). As part of this work, Swadesh calculated that Numic and its closest relative, Tubatulabal, had diverged a minimum of 3,500 years ago, that Ute and Tubatulabal had split at least 2,900 years ago, and that Mono and Ute had diverged at least 1,900 years ago.

Swadesh's paper, published in Spanish in a Mexican journal and dealing primarily with Mexican languages, might have gone unnoticed by Great Basin archaeologists were it not for the linguist Sydney Lamb.

In a tremendously influential paper on Numic languages, Lamb set down many of the observations that I recounted in Chapter 2: that there are six closely related Numic languages in the Great Basin (see Figure 2-16); that these fall into three groups of two languages each; that one member of each pair occupied a very small part of the southwestern Great Basin while the second member of each pair spread over tremendous distances to the north and east; and that dialectical variation within languages seemed greater in the southwestern Great Basin than in other areas occupied by Numic speakers.

These geographic considerations led Lamb (1958:98) to suggest an original homeland for Numic speakers:

> We have six languages in the Numic family, two belonging to each subdivision. Three of these languages are in a small cluster near the southwestern part of the Great Basin, while the other three occupy a vast area to the north and east. Remembering that the split into the three subfamilies preceded the separation of each of them into a pair of languages, one must place the linguistic center of gravity of the Numic family somewhere around Death Valley.

This conclusion, Lamb noted, is supported by the fact that Tubatulabal, Numic's closest relative, was spoken directly across the Sierra Nevada from the area he had targeted as the Numic homeland.

Having inferred the location of this homeland, Lamb attempted to determine when Numic peoples had begun to disperse across the Great Basin. Here, he turned to Swadesh's glottochronological work. He followed Swadesh in suggesting that Numic and Tubatulabal were becoming distinct between 3,000 and 4,000 years ago, and that the division of Numic into three separate languages, all then located in the southwestern Great Basin, occurred at about 2,000 years ago or shortly thereafter.

From this point, Lamb was on his own, since Swadesh had not calculated separation times within the three pairs of languages that comprise Numic. Lamb speculated that Numic speakers remained confined to the southwestern Great Basin until about 1,000 years ago, at which time "there began a great movement northward and eastward, which was to extend the domain of Numic far beyond its earlier limits" (Lamb 1958:99). This movement—the Numic expansion—saw the replacement of the people who had lived here earlier. The linguistic affiliation of these earlier people, Lamb observed, is simply unknown.

In Lamb's view the Numic speakers encountered by Europeans in the Great Basin had been there for a very short period of time indeed—no longer than 1,000 years and perhaps, toward the northern and eastern edges of the region, far less. Although Lamb's estimated 1,000-year date for the Numic expansion was speculative, glottochronological data that appeared after Lamb wrote his essay supported that estimate. In 1958, linguist Kenneth Hale calculated minimum dates of under 1,000 years for the development of Paviotso, Shoshone, and Ute; in 1968, James Goss estimated a minimum of 900 years for the division of Kawaiisu-Ute into its component languages; in 1971, Wick Miller and his colleagues calculated a minimum of 700 years for the split between Panamint and Shoshone. The consistency is impressive.

Many Great Basin archaeologists and anthropologists have accepted this view. There have been detailed attempts to explain why such a population replacement occurred, and even a computer simulation to show how it could have occurred. But caution is clearly required here. After all, we know that the key assumptions required by glottochronology cannot be safely made, and that glottochronology does not provide valid dates of linguistic divergence. Indeed, Lamb noted that the results of glottochronology are merely "very rough approximations" that are "better than nothing at all" and that must be used "only with great caution" (1958:98).

All this work has made it abundantly clear that Numic languages are very closely related. That the center of diversity of these languages occurs in the far southwestern Great Basin strongly suggests that this region incorporates the homeland of Numic peoples, a view that is supported by a variety of other linguistic data. What is anything but clear, however, is that the linguistic splits within the branches of Numic occurred only 1,000 years ago, and that Numic peoples began to move across the Great Basin from southeastern California at about that time. That glottochronology provides consistent results does not necessarily mean that it provides correct ones.

THE ARCHAEOLOGICAL EVIDENCE

There can be no doubt that Numic peoples really did expand across the Great Basin. After all, they are there now, and they were not there 20,000 years ago. It is also true, however, that archaeological data created by people without writing can rarely speak to linguistic issues. As a result, it is very tempting to simply conclude, with Robert Heizer and Lewis Napton, that "the linguists have formulated a very interesting problem, and they must shoulder the burden of devising tests for its solution" (1970:11). Given that linguists have thoroughly rejected glottochronology, it might be said that the linguists actually have solved the problem, and that there is no linguistic reason to think that Numic peoples expanded across the Great Basin about 1,000 years ago. They might, in fact, have been here "from time immemorial," as the great anthropologist Alfred Kroeber (1953:580) once said. Indeed, linguist James Goss, who at one time accepted Lamb's account, later rejected it, observing that the diversity of Numic languages appears highly correlated with the degree of isolation in which the speakers of these varied languages lived.

However, this issue is very much alive in Great Basin archaeology, and it is certainly true that some intriguing things did happen in the Great Basin about 1,000 years ago, plus or minus a few centuries. I begin my discussion of it with one of the most remarkable discoveries to have been made in this region during the past few decades: the existence of small villages in the alpine tundra zone of several Great Basin mountain ranges.

THE ALPINE VILLAGES: ALTA TOQUIMA. In 1978, David Thomas led a small archaeological crew to Mt. Jefferson, the summit of the Toquima Range, above and south of Gatecliff Shelter. They came here because the U.S. Forest Service had reported the existence of stone structures in this area, and Thomas wanted to see exactly what they were. He was expecting to discover hunting features of the sort that I have already discussed. Such features were there, but, at an elevation of 11,000′, Thomas also found something distinctly different: a complex of some three dozen stone structures spread across an area about 300′ by 600′ that were not hunting features at all.

These structures included storage facilities, windbreaks, and the remains of a substantial number of houses, all adjacent to the headwaters of a small creek and to a small stand of limber pine (see Figure 2-13). Above and beyond the limber pine stretched a large expanse of alpine tundra vegetation. The site soon became known as Alta Toquima Village; at the time of its discovery, it was the highest village site known from North America.

Thomas later discovered a series of smaller sites that also contain houses in the Alta Toquima area. These have not been studied in any detail, but do establish that there was more than one village in the alpine tundra zone of the Toquima Range.

In 1981 and 1983, Thomas excavated portions of Alta Toquima. This work, coupled with careful mapping of the associated surface features, has gone far toward revealing the nature of this site. The most obvious feature of Alta

Figure 9-9. House structure at Alta Toquima, Toquima Range.

Toquima is the houses, which are marked by carefully constructed circles consisting of several courses of flat rocks stacked on top of one another to heights of about three feet (see Figure 9-9). These circles formed the foundation for a superstructure that has not been preserved, and whose nature is not known. As at King's Dog, the superstructure may have been removed after use, and stored for the future. However the superstucture might have been built, the houses were substantial. From wall to wall, the interiors measured about ten feet across. There were also quite a few of them: Thomas counted 27, and it is fully possible that some went unrecognized.

Because the structures sit on the surface, their existence and size were known before the excavations began. However, by excavating over a dozen of the houses, as well as part of the rich midden deposits associated with them, Thomas recovered a diverse set of artifacts and a smaller sample of faunal and floral remains. He also discovered that most of the houses had one or more hearths inside. Because these hearths held well-preserved charcoal, Thomas was able to obtain 23 radiocarbon dates for 12 of the structures. Of these 12 houses, 7 had been in use at different times between A.D. 900 and early historic times. Five had earlier occupations, the earliest of which fell at about A.D. 200. The abundant projectile points associated with the houses say much the same thing: they are primarily Desert series and, to a lesser extent, Rosegate forms, although Elko points were also present.

In addition to the points, Alta Toquima provided a wide variety of other artifacts, including large numbers of grinding stones and a surprising number of broken ceramic vessels. The Alta Toquima sherds—some 420 of them—are fairly thick, with coarse temper (the inclusions that are added to prevent the vessel from cracking when fired), and are very variable in both the paste that was used to make them and the hardness of the end product.

The unimpressive nature of the Alta Toquima ceramics is fully characteristic of the pottery that appears across much

Figure 9-10. Panamint Shoshone ceramic vessel from Death Valley.

of the Great Basin late in prehistory, and that was used in this area during early historic times (see Figure 9-10). Great Basin native Americans, like many native Californians, excelled in basketry; pottery was a secondary enterprise, as befits highly mobile peoples.

Archaeologists have named three different, major types of this pottery: Shoshone Ware (as at Alta Toquima), Southern Paiute Utility Ware, and Owens Valley Brown Ware. All of these ceramics, however, are highly variable, and archaeologist Lonnie Pippin has suggested that they all be referred to as "Intermountain Brown Wares" until they are better understood.

Although it is clear that these ceramics did not appear in the Great Basin until quite late, exactly when this happened is not clear. The earliest dates for Intermountain Brown Wares have been interpreted in a number of different ways. David Madsen, for instance, has argued that these wares appear earliest in southern Nevada and east-central California, at about A.D. 1000, and that the dates become later as one moves to the north and east. Madsen also argues that these ceramics were carried by Numic peoples as they expanded out of the southwestern Great Basin. Pippin, on the other hand, feels that many of the early dates for Intermountain Brown Wares are misleading, reflecting stratigraphic mixture in many of the sites that have been used to date them. He feels that the earliest secure dates fall no earlier than about A.D. 1400.

Alta Toquima does not help here. In the Alta Toquima midden, sherds are fairly common in deposits laid down as early as A.D. 500, but this may simply reflect the downward movement of these small objects from their original, later contexts. In the more secure stratigraphic situation provided by the houses, ceramics do not appear until after A.D. 1400. As a result, the positions taken by both Madsen and Pippin could find support here. Until the timing of the appearance of Intermountain Brown Wares is better understood, it is not likely that they will be able to play a convincing role in any arguments concerning the history of Numic speakers in the Great Basin.

Alta Toquima provided more than just structures and artifacts. Thomas's excavations also provided small samples of the remains of both plants and mammals, remains that provide direct information on the food resources that were utilized by the people who occupied this site. Two species of mammals—yellow-bellied marmots and mountain sheep—provided the bulk of the animal remains; both species may be seen in the immediate vicinity of the site today. Marmots remain above ground only during the late spring and summer at this elevation; their presence in the deposits of Alta Toquima demonstrates that this site was occupied during those months.

The very small assemblage of plant remains from the site was analyzed by David Rhode. He found that the fuel requirements of these people were met by using locally available limber pine and sagebrush, but that plant foods apparently came from both local and valley bottom settings. Limber pine nuts may have been utilized, and Simpson's pediocactus (*Pediocactus simpsonii*), which grows near the site today, certainly was. On the other hand, seeds from alkali bulrush (*Scirpus maritimus*) must have been transported to this setting from marshes that lie at least 4,300′ beneath the site. Although all the mammals that were taken by the residents of Alta Toquima were local, the plants that were utilized came from both local and far-removed settings.

Alta Toquima is a remarkable site. A good deal of labor was invested in building the houses here; this fact, along with the storage facilities, suggests that more than a single brief stay was involved. The artifacts suggest that a variety of activities were conducted: the projectile points suggest hunting; the grinding tools, plant processing. The direct evidence from the animal and plant remains shows that, although local resources were utilized, some plant foods were transported here from the valley bottom. It would appear that entire family groups moved to this alpine location to utilize a diverse set of local resources, and that this movement occurred during the late spring or summer. It also appears that, whereas such use may have begun as early as A.D. 200, it intensified substantially at about A.D. 900, and then continued until early historic times. It is also fairly likely that these same people used Gatecliff Shelter, located some 18 miles to the north and 3,400′ lower.

In addition to the sites with house structures, Thomas found that the Toquima Range highlands hold a diverse set of hunting features: rock walls that appear to have served as parts of game drives, for instance, and stone circles that seem to have functioned as hunting blinds. It is difficult to date such features, but it is certainly meaningful that, although the projectile point assemblage at Alta Toquima is dominated by arrowpoints, the hunting features are associated mainly with the earlier Elko and Gatecliff atlatl dart points.

From these findings it appears, as Thomas has speculated, that the "previllage" use of the Toquima Range was distinctly different from that which occurred here during village times. In particular, he has suggested that, although Alta Toquima was occupied by family groups whose diverse activities were based at the village itself, the earlier use of the area was marked by the activities of small groups of male hunters. Given the projectile points, this earlier use occurred between about 5,000 and 1,300 years ago. Intense use of Alta Toquima followed soon therafter.

THE ALPINE VILLAGES: WHITE MOUNTAINS. No sooner had Great Basin archaeologists taken in the surprise provided by Alta Toquima than Robert Bettinger, of the University of California (Davis), presented them with another. In 1982, Bettinger discovered a near duplicate of Alta Toquima at an elevation of 10,400′ in the southern White Mountains of eastern California, again above the timberline. This discovery spurred Bettinger to launch a detailed archaeological survey of this area. By the time he was done, he had discovered 12 village sites that contained from one to about a dozen circular houses, and that fell between 10,400′ and 12,640′ in elevation (see Figures 9-11 and 9-12).

Although it stretches the concept to call a site with one house a "village," these sites are, as a whole, very similar to Alta Toquima and to the smaller settlements associated with it. The White Mountains sites have circular stone house foundations with internal hearths, storage facilities, occasional ceramics, abundant grinding tools, and hunting equipment. As at Alta Toquima, the faunas from these sites are dominated by the remains of marmots and mountain sheep, both of which are locally available. And, as at Alta Toquima, the plant remains from at least one of these sites—Midway, at an elevation of 11,290′—show the use of both local species (for instance, alpine chickweed, *Cerastium berringianum*), and those transported from below (for instance, piñon pine, today available only some 1,800′ downslope). In many ways, the White Mountains and Alta Toquima sites are peas in a pod, even though Alta Toquima is 130 miles northeast of the White Mountains villages.

The earliest radiocarbon date for the White Mountains villages falls at A.D. 240, very close to the earliest house date at Alta Toquima. Most radiocarbon dates, however, are fairly late, falling after about A.D. 1200. On the other hand the projectile points—and, in particular, the abundance of Rosegate points in the villages—suggests that intense use of these sites began prior to A.D. 1200, and Bettinger estimates that intense use of these villages began at about A.D. 660. This, of course, is slightly earlier than the intense use of Alta Toquima seems to have begun, even though the earliest houses at both places may have come into use at about the same time (A.D. 200).

I noted that the uppermost elevations of the Toquima Range are marked by the presence of both small villages, which were primarily in use during later prehistoric times, and hunting features, which seem to have been the focus of earlier use. The same pattern appears in the White Mountains, but here it is somewhat better understood because many of the sites that were occupied during village times also hold earlier ("previllage") occupations. Bettinger has excavated several sites that were in use only during "previllage" times, and has analyzed the artifacts associated with the hunting features that are scattered across the White Mountains alpine tundra zone.

As on the Toquima Range, the high-elevation hunting features in the White Mountains are associated with Elko and Gatecliff series atlatl dart points. At the excavated village sites, the occupations of the houses are dominated by Desert and Rosegate series points. The occupations that predate the houses are associated with Elko and Gatecliff points, suggesting that these earlier occupants were also the people who used the hunting features.

Figure 9-11. The setting of site 12640, White Mountains; house structures can be seen as rings in the snow.

Figure 9-12. House structures emerging from the snow at site 12640.

Bettinger has documented a series of other differences between the earlier, previllage, and later, village, occupations of these sites. Compared to the previllage occupations, the villages have significantly more plant-processing equipment, tools to make other tools (for instance, drills), and projectile points. The previllage occupations, on the other hand, are loaded with artifacts that appear to reflect the repair of hunting tools, and also have large numbers of implements that could have been used to process hunted animals.

Bettinger argues that the previllage occupations of these sites were focused on hunting, probably by small groups of males. The villages, he argues, were used by family groups performing a diverse set of activities. Since the faunal remains from both village and previllage occupations contain marmots, these sites were likely used between the late spring and late summer months. With the exception of the apparent several-hundred-year difference in the timing of the onset of the intense occupation of the village sites, this is the same pattern that Thomas found in the Toquima Range.

An argument can, and has, been made not only that the distinctive alpine villages on the Toquima Range and the White Mountains were occupied by Numic speakers (which must be the case), but that they also reflect the process of Numic expansion across Great Basin landscapes at about 1,000 years ago. Before examining this argument, however, I will take a brief look at another phenomenon that many archaeologists feel is related to Numic expansion. This phenomenon is the demise, in the eastern Great Basin, of the people archaeologists refer to as the Fremont.

THE FREMONT. Between about A..D. 400 and 1350, much of the eastern Great Basin and northern Colorado Plateau supported people whose lifeways clearly differed from those of the people who were there before and after (see Figure 9-13). Not only did these people manufacture well-made, thin-walled gray pottery, but they also grew corn, beans, and squash, and frequently lived in sizable villages. The villages were routinely located along perennial streams near arable land, and include a wide variety of substantial structures: pithouses, above-ground adobe dwellings and storage facilities of either adobe or stone, and carefully made storage pits. Because sites of this sort were first described from along south-central Utah's Fremont River, the people who made them are referred to as the "Fremont."

In addition to well-made ceramics, domesticated plants, and substantial villages, the Fremont possessed distinctive styles of basketry, moccasins, and clay figurines. The figurines, however, are rare, and the basketry and moccasins do not preserve in many settings. As a result, most Fremont sites are identified as such on the basis of the pottery, domesticated plants, and villages, and many smaller sites are identified from the pottery alone.

Those familiar with the archaeology of the Southwest might be struck by the fact that the use of corn, beans, and squash, of well-made gray ceramics, and of above-ground adobe structures sounds very southwestern. In fact, the similarities go even further. Duncan Metcalfe and Lisa Larrabee, for instance, have shown that at least some Fremont peoples constructed irrigation ditches, much as was done in some parts of the Southwest. In addition, many of the pithouses on Fremont sites have constructional features that clearly tie them to the Southwest. As a result of all this, there is no doubt that the source of some of the traits that make the Fremont distinctive lies to the immediate south.

It does not follow, however, that Fremont peoples themselves came from that area. Everything we know about these people suggests that their way of life developed locally, even if some of the items they incorporated into that way of life came from elsewhere. Many of the characteristics that came together to define what we call the Fremont were present in this area well before the Fremont lifeway came into being. James Wilde and Deborah Newman, for instance, have shown that corn was being grown in the Sevier River Valley of central Utah by 200 B.C., long before Fremont existed. C. Melvin Aikens's work at Hogup Cave suggests that the distinctive Fremont basketry and moccasins were in use before the equally distinctive ceramics began to be employed. Detailed studies of eastern Great Basin basketry by James Adovasio also document the local origins of Fremont basketry.

Fremont sites are remarkably variable, ranging from large villages with substantial structures to small, isolated locations that contain one or two wickiups and associated living debris. There are occupations in caves, as at Hogup, and large numbers of open-air sites that consist of little more than scattered lithics and sherds. The architecture in the villages varies from north to south, from east to west, and through time. Some Fremont sites contain substantial amounts of domesticated plants; others provide none at all.

For many years, archaeologists attempted to deal with all of this variability by dividing the Fremont into regional

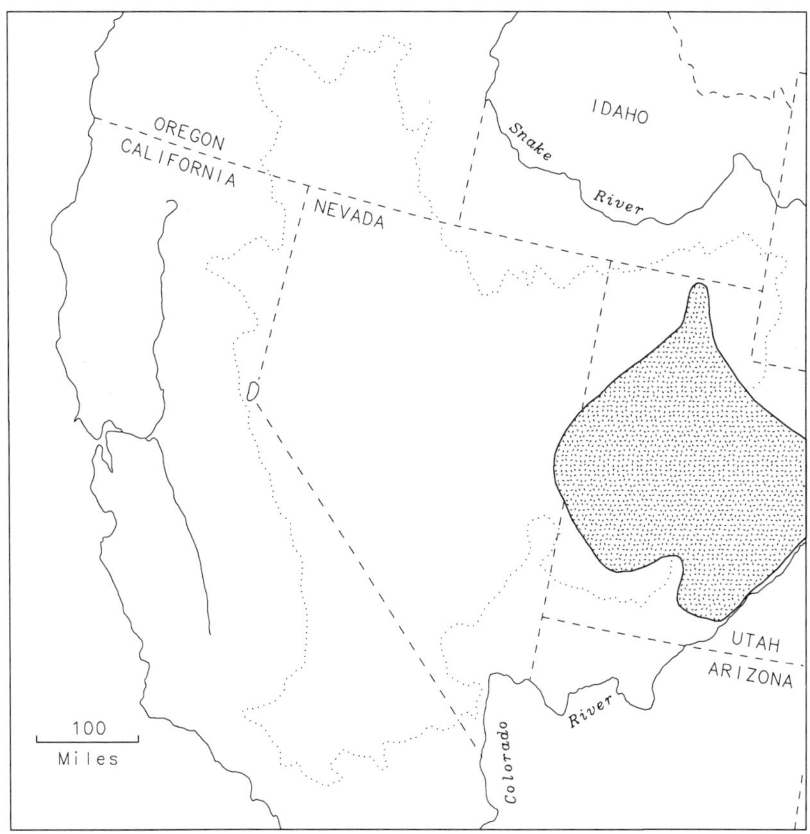

Figure 9-13. The maximum distribution of Fremont (stippled), A.D. 1040–1190. After Talbot and Wilde (1989).

variants and chronological phases, much as they divide projectile points into regional and temporal types. As time has gone on, however, archaeologists have come to realize that one of the most characteristic attributes of Fremont is its variability, and that, if Fremont is to be understood, we should spend more time studying that variability and less time trying to divide it into regional and temporal chunks. "The key to understanding the Fremont," as David Madsen (1989:63) has said, "is variation."

Steven Simms has suggested that at least some of the variability shown by Fremont sites may reflect the fact that Fremont peoples may have practiced three very different adaptive strategies. Some may have lived year-round in large horticultural villages while making short-term forays for particular kinds of resources into the surrounding environment. Some may have been far more mobile, moving widely across the landscape during certain times of the year when not tied down by the demands of their crops, or during times when plant crops were not productive. Some, he thinks, may even have been full-time hunter-gatherers, utilizing the same areas as people more dependent on domesticated plants. Any or all of these strategies may have operated through time and across space within the Fremont area.

Richard Talbot and James Wilde have recently shown that the "Fremont area" itself changed through time. From beginning (about A.D. 400) to end (about A.D. 1350), Fremont sites are found in a core area centering on the Wasatch Mountains, an area that is well watered, contains abundant marshes and productive lands for agriculture, and supports a diverse variety of wild resources within fairly short distances. Through time, they show, the distribution of Fremont expanded and contracted, reaching its greatest extent between about A.D. 1040 and 1190, when sites were distributed from eastern Nevada to northwestern Colorado, and from northern to southern Utah. During the next 60 years or so, Fremont sites seem to have been largely confined to the core area, but they increased in number once again between A.D. 1250 and 1350. After that, however, the sites largely disappear. Fremont, whatever it was, was gone.

There is some consensus that the use of corn, beans, and squash by Fremont peoples was made possible by deeper northward incursions of warm and moist Gulf air masses during these centuries, and that, when those incursions ceased, the Fremont adaptation was doomed. Deborah Newman's pollen work in central Utah's Clear Creek Canyon has shown that conditions marked by both warmth and abundant summer precipitation ended here at about A.D. 1350. Although more fine-scale pollen work is needed to show how widespread this phenomenon was, it seems unlikely to be coincidental that the Fremont demise occurred at the same time as warm, summer-wet conditions ended in this part of central Utah.

Changes in the length of the growing season and in the abundance of summer precipitation very likely account for both the rise and the fall of the Fremont. But was that all there was to it? And even if these apparent climatic fluctuations explain the demise of the Fremont as a way of life, what happened to the people themselves? After all, when Europeans arrived in what was once Fremont territory, they encountered Numic peoples who did not grow corn, beans, and squash (explained by the altered climatic conditions), but who also used basketry that was distinctly different from that which had marked the Fremont, used ceramics that were not particularly similar to the bulk of Fremont wares, and even used footwear that had little in common with Fremont moccasins. Did Fremont peoples change their life-styles this sharply, or did Numic peoples, in one way or another, replace them?

HIGH-ELEVATION VILLAGES, THE FREMONT, AND NUMIC EXPANSION

Bettinger estimates that intense use of high-elevation villages in the White Mountains began about A.D. 660. In the Toquima Range, Thomas's work suggests that intense occupation at Alta Toquima began at about A.D. 900. To the east, the demise of the Fremont occurred at about A.D. 1350. Could it be that the onset of heavy use of the high-elevation villages in the White Mountains some 1,300 years ago reflects the origin of the highly effective adaptive strategies that mark Numic peoples? Could it also be that the intense use of Alta Toquima some 300 years later marks the arrival of Numic speakers here, and that the replacement of Fremont horticulturalists by hunters and gatherers in the eastern Great Basin likewise reflects the Numic arrival? Certainly, the direction and timing of these changes match Lamb's hypothesis—earliest in the west, latest in the east, and, outside southeastern California, all within the last 1,000 years.

A number of archaeologists have argued that Fremont basketry, ceramics, and other items of material culture differ so starkly from what comes later that the arrival of peoples from elsewhere is clearly implied. James Adovasio, for instance, insists that the basketry made by Fremont and later peoples differs so greatly that "the dispersion of Numic-speaking peoples" (1986b:204) must be involved. Madsen finds the artifact dissimilarities between Fremont and later peoples to be so marked as to imply that Fremont peoples were "pushed out of the region and were replaced rather than integrated into Numic-speaking groups" (1989:15).

It is Bettinger, however, who has argued most forcefully that both the alpine villages and the Fremont are tightly related to Numic expansion. Bettinger believes that Numic speakers were able to replace "pre-Numic" peoples in the Great Basin because their adaptations allowed them to extract larger numbers of calories from a given unit of territory. In particular, he argues that pre-Numic peoples traveled widely in search of such high-quality resources as mountain sheep. Numic peoples, on the other hand, he sees as having been far more dependent on lower-quality resources, including small mammals and seeds, that demanded less time to reach but more time and effort to process. Though Numic peoples would take high-quality resources when they encountered them, pre-Numic peoples simply did not utilize lower-quality foods. This adaptive difference, he argues, provided Numic peoples with more calories per unit of territory, and thus allowed higher population densities than those that characterized pre-Numic peoples. As a result, "pre-Numic peoples were powerless to stay the invasive spread of the more costly, but less spatially demanding, Numic adaptation" (1991a:674).

Bettinger argues that regional population growth in eastern California led to increased pressure on lower-elevation resources, and to the more intense use of costly resources, including alpine plants and animals. He sees this shift as part of the development of a distinctive Numic adaptation, an adaptation that is reflected in the heavy use of the White Mountains villages soon after A.D. 600. Once this adaptation had evolved, he argues, Numic peoples spread across the Great Basin. They are detected at Alta Toquima at about A.D. 900, and in the eastern Great Basin by about A.D. 1350. Bettinger does not argue that Numic peoples outcompeted Fremont horticulturalists, but instead suggests that the Fremont were already on the decline, and had perhaps even reverted to hunting and gathering, by the time Numic speakers arrived and, ultimately, replaced them.

To those who see no linguistic reason to accept Lamb's hypothesis that Numic peoples expanded across the Great Basin at about 1,000 years ago, Bettinger's arguments seem somewhat odd, since they attempt to explain something that we do not know to have occurred. But, even if we assume that that expansion did occur, there are many reasons to think that Bettinger's explanation cannot account for it.

For instance, he argues that such costly resources as piñon and small seeds were used "casually or ignored altogether" (1991a:675) by the people who preceded Numic speakers. As must be clear from what I have already discussed in this chapter, and as Steven Simms observed a number of years ago, Bettinger's arguments do not take into account the deep history of small seed use in the Great Basin. The human coprolites from such sites as Danger, Hidden, Hogup, and Lovelock caves show clearly that high-cost resources were being utilized long before Bettinger's account would have the Numic arrive.

There are other severe problems with Bettinger's arguments as well. The "pre-Numic" peoples were, in his view, travelers who wandered far and wide in search of high-quality resources. However, there is ample evidence that the human occupants of the Great Basin prior to the time of the supposed Numic expansion spent significant amounts of time in one spot—substantial settlements in Surprise Valley, the Humboldt Sink, the Lake Abert basin and elsewhere predate the hypothesized Numic expansion by several thousand years.

It is true that intense use of the White Mountains alpine villages does seem to have begun a few hundred years earlier than such use began at Alta Toquima. However, the earliest known houses at both places were in use long before intense occupation began, and those earliest houses came into use at about the same time, around A.D. 200. In Bettinger's view, the "pre-Numic" peoples on these ranges should have focused their hunting efforts on such high-quality resources as mountain sheep. However, the faunal assemblage from Alta Toquima is more heavily dominated by mountain sheep than are the faunal assemblages from the previllage sites in the White Mountains, providing little support for Bettinger's arguments.

I suspect that the utilization of the high-elevation villages has nothing to do with Numic expansion. Instead, it seems more likely that the intense, village-based use of the alpine zone of both the White Mountains and the Toquima Range relates to population growth in the lowlands, and to the pressure this put on low-elevation resources. It is unlikely to be coincidental that the two sets of high-elevation villages currently known from the Great Basin are in close proximity to low-elevation areas that supported some of the highest early historic human population densities reported from the Great Basin: the Owens and Reese River valleys. To me, this fact suggests that high-elevation village occupation may have occurred in response to increasing low-elevation population densities and attendant pressures on at least lowland resources.

If the high-elevation villages can be explained without recourse to a late prehistoric Numic expansion, how about the Fremont? It is certainly true that, on the whole, Fremont basketry, ceramics, and even projectile points are distinctly different from those that were in use in this area during early historic times. Steven Simms's work in the Great Salt Lake area, however, is beginning to suggest that there may be more similarities between Fremont and later occupations than we had realized. He has found a high degree of variability in ceramics and projectile points in both Fremont and post-Fremont sites in this area, and he has also found that the Fremont made some pottery that is very similar to that made in the same area after the Fremont demise. Simms suggests that there may be significant continuity in material culture across the "Fremont transition." He attributes our failure to detect this continuity to the fact that archaeologists have placed too little emphasis on studying Fremont variability, and have spent too little time studying what came after.

Nonetheless, as far as we can tell now, the differences in the material cultures possessed by Fremont and later peoples are pronounced. Insofar as one can judge from artifacts, the eastern Great Basin is one place where population replacement may have occurred, although the artifacts tell us nothing about the language or languages spoken by the people who made them. Simms has suggested that the only way to resolve the question of population replacement in the Fremont area is by analyzing the genetic material from the bones of the people who made the artifacts about which archaeologists argue. The technology to do that is available, and it seems unlikely that convincing answers to this question—either here or elsewhere in the Great Basin—will be arrived at in any other way.

OTHER POSSIBILITIES

C. Melvin Aikens and Y. T. Witherspoon have suggested a distinctly different view of Numic prehistory. They reject the glottochronological dates for the expansion, observe that the archaeological record for central Nevada suggests very little significant change during the past 5,000 years or so, posit that the Numic homeland is to be found in the central Great Basin, and suggest that, over time, desert-adapted Numic peoples expanded outward and contracted inward as environmental conditions allowed. In this view, the shift from Modoc-like houses to Numic-like houses in Surprise Valley soon after 5,000 years ago could be related to Numic expansion, as could the shifts in material culture that occurred as the Fremont adaptation disintegrated.

Aikens and Witherspoon thus argue that Numic peoples have a lengthy history within the Great Basin, and that the effects of any Numic expansion would have been felt on the periphery of the region. Long ago, Alfred Kroeber pointed out that Numic languages contain "no foreign element or anything else to indicate that they ever had any antecessors on the spot" (1953:580). Aikens and Witherspoon's position is fully consistent with this observation.

In an attempt to discover linguistic clues to the Numic homeland, Kay Fowler has examined the words used by Numic peoples for a diverse set of plants and animals. She found that many of these words were cognates, implying that the species involved were likely to have been present in the area occupied by the speakers of the language ancestral to modern Numic tongues. Although some of these species are so widely distributed as to be of little assistance—"badger," for instance, and "woodrat"—others are found only in geographically restricted areas. Those restricted forms include oak, piñon, and chia (*Salvia columbariae,* a member of the mint family). According to her reconstruction, the ancestors of modern Numic peoples probably came from an area where all three of these plants would have been encountered. Those areas range from southwestern Utah across the southern Great Basin and north into eastern California.

As a result, if Aikens and Witherspoon are correct, the "central Great Basin" Numic homeland must have included parts of the southern fringes of this area. Oaks, for instance, are not to be found in central Nevada today, and there is no evidence that they were ever here during the Holocene. With this in mind, Aikens and Witherspoon included Owens Valley in their "central Great Basin" (oaks occur in the Sierra Nevada, chia in the White Mountains). However, the evidence they present for cultural continuity is from central Nevada, not from eastern California.

Because of this, Aikens and Witherspoon's view of Numic prehistory might seem to stumble on Fowler's linguistic reconstruction. However, recent archaeological data from central and southern Idaho, an area occupied historically by Numic-speaking peoples, show strong continuities in artifact assemblages from 3,500 years ago to early historic times. Because of this continuity, Richard Holmer suggests that the ancestors of modern Shoshonean peoples arrived here between 3,500 and 4,000 years ago. That conclusion, as Holmer notes, is fully consistent with Aikens and Witherspoon's arguments.

Aikens and Witherspoon are likely correct in seeing Numic peoples as having resided within large parts of the Great Basin for thousands of years. James Goss estimated that Numic speakers had arrived in the Great Basin some 4,000 years ago, and also argued that the diversity of Numic languages in the southwestern Great Basin might simply reflect the relative degree of isolation in which the Mono, Panamint, and Kawaiisu lived. Likewise, Joseph Jorgensen observes that the linguistic homogeneity found in vast parts of the Great Basin surely reflects the fact that the resources of this region were so diffuse that the people who depended on them were highly mobile, and that close contacts between far-flung peoples were routine. In such a setting, intuitive estimates of times of linguistic divergence may be wildly misleading.

WHEN DID NUMIC SPEAKERS ARRIVE?

There are only a few things that can be said with any certainty about Lamb's Numic expansion hypothesis. First, glottochronology cannot be relied upon to provide accurate times of linguistic divergence. That in itself strongly suggests that detailed explanations as to why the expansion might have occurred at 1,000 years ago, and computer simulations meant to show exactly how it could have occurred, may well be directed toward accounting for something that never happened.

As a result, the first order of business for archaeologists working on this issue should be to discover whether or not there is something going on here. Indeed, the second thing we can be certain of as regards the large-scale movement of Numic speakers across the Great Basin is that we do not know exactly when, where, or how these people entered this region. Linguistic problems, as Heizer and Napton observed years ago, are not easily solved using archaeological data.

The Immediate Effects of European Contact

We also know that, when Europeans first entered the Great Basin, most of this region was occupied by Numic-speaking peoples. As I discussed in Chapter 2, the basic description of the lifeways of these people was provided by Julian Steward, based on fieldwork he conducted during the 1920s and 1930s. As I also discussed, that description was strongly questioned by Elman Service, who argued that what Steward had recorded were the lifeways of people whose cultures were in disarray as a result of the European arrival.

David Thomas attempted to resolve the debate between Steward and Service using archaeological data. To do that, Thomas asked a simple question. If Steward's description applied to the period before European contact, how would the artifacts have fallen on the ground? Steward's descriptions were so detailed that Thomas was able to make fairly precise predictions about the kinds, abundances, and distributions of artifacts that would have occurred had Steward been right.

Armed with these predictions, Thomas asked the next question: had the artifacts actually fallen that way? He chose to address this issue in central Nevada's Reese River Valley, an area in which Steward himself had worked. During the course of two summers, Thomas conducted an intensive archaeological survey here, focusing his labor on the past 4,500 years of human occupation.

What Thomas found led him to side squarely with Steward: 86% of the predictions he derived from Steward's descriptions were met by the archaeological data. The small number of predictions that were not met, he suggested, were due not to failures on Steward's end, but instead to the shortcomings inherent in making precise predictions about artifact distributions from ethnographic accounts. Thomas concluded that the system Steward described had operated in the Reese River Valley for the past 4,500 years. Indeed, although Thomas refrained from equating the continuity he found in landscape use with continuity in language, his results led Aikens and Witherspoon to argue that Numic peoples have been in the central Great Basin throughout the late Holocene.

Thomas's work suggests that Steward's descriptions do apply to late prehistoric lifeways, and most Great Basin anthropologists continue to accept them as such. However, it is important to recognize that, although Thomas asked whether the artifact distributions that he found were consistent with Steward's description, he did not ask whether they might be consistent with other descriptions as well. In fact, a strong case can be made that Steward *was* describing cultural systems in disarray, just as Service said.

That case comes from the alpine villages. In 1938, Steward noted the presence of "house remains . . . near and above timber line" (1938:58) in the White Mountains, and there can be little doubt that he was referring to one or more of the sites later excavated by Bettinger, or to something just like them.

Steward, however, spent four months with the Owens Valley Paiute in 1927 and 1928 without anyone mentioning that they had ever resided in such small, high-elevation villages. Although Steward spent less time in central Nevada, no one mentioned high-elevation villages to him here either.

Yet both the White Mountains villages and Alta Toquima were occupied into early historic times. That these sites were occupied so late, but were unknown to the people who provided Steward with his information, must mean that this part of their settlement pattern was lost almost immediately after contact. Direct economic disruption could have caused this, but it seems far more likely that population collapse in the lowlands, caused by infectious diseases introduced by Europeans, was to blame.

It is sometimes suggested that Great Basin population densities were too low to allow the rapid spread of such diseases as smallpox and measles, to which native Americans had virtually no immunity. However, it is in precisely such places as the Owens and Reese River valleys, with relatively dense human populations, that infectious diseases can be expected to have taken a significant toll. In fact, there is evidence that the Indians living adjacent to Upper Klamath and Pyramid lakes suffered significant losses to infectious disease in 1833. Just as I suspect that the establishment of the high-elevation villages was a response to population growth in the lowlands, I also suspect that the abandonment of these sites resulted from population loss in the lowlands, loss that resulted from infectious diseases transmitted during early historic times.

The general nature of Great Basin lifeways immediately prior to European contact may well have been just as

Steward said it was. On the other hand, the alpine villages suggest that Service was correct. Part of the lifeway so carefully described by Steward had been extinguished long before he arrived on the scene, and so early on that not even his oldest informants remembered it. I suspect that introduced diseases help account for these changes. Although the effects that those diseases had on the native occupants of the Great Basin remain largely unknown, it would not be surprising to find that, in the more densely occupied parts of this region, they were as significant as they were in other parts of the New World.

Notes

For overviews of Great Basin prehistory, see Aikens (1978), Jennings (1989), and the articles on Great Basin prehistory in D. B. Madsen and O'Connell (1982) and in d'Azevedo (1986). Analyses of the prehistory of particular states also include discussions of the Great Basin: for California, see Moratto (1984); for Oregon, Aikens (1986); for Utah, Jennings (1978).

On the Paisley Caves and Fort Rock Cave, see Cressman et al. (1940), and Cressman (1942, 1977); Cressman (1951) announced the 9,053-year radiocarbon date for a Fort Rock sandal. Bedwell (1973) discusses the results of his excavations in Fort Rock Cave; see also Bedwell and Cressman (1971). Cressman (1937) presents his early survey of Oregon petroglyphs; his Guano Valley work is discussed in Cressman (1936a,b). Cressman (1988) is a fascinating autobiography; I have depended on it heavily here. Haynes (1971) was the first to question the 13,200-year date from Fort Rock Cave.

Jennings (1957:285) discusses the support provided by the early Danger Cave dates for Cressman's arguments. In 1951, Libby visited Danger Cave and told Jennings the dates during that trip. Jack Rudy, who was involved in excavating the site, recorded Jennings's reaction on June 19 of that year:

> The AM part of this day proved to be worth getting up for . . . we were informed that Dr. Jennings, who had returned to Salt Lake the night before, would be out this morning with Dr. Lybie [*sic*] . . . of C14 fame. We were also informed . . . that Dr. Lybie had dated some sheep dung from F18 and a piece of sage brush from the same F number (I believe) at roughly 11,000 years ago . . . I must say that Dr. Jennings was really elated over the news. You could see it in every one of his actions. (Danger Cave field notes, Utah Museum of Natural History, for June 19, 1951)

F18 (for Feature 18), which provided these early dates, also contained artifacts. It was not long before every archaeologist knew how to spell Willard Libby's name.

Carter (1958) argued that the Lahontan terrace sites were 20,000 years old or older; Tuohy (1970) established otherwise. Hattori (1985) examines and rejects not only Carter's arguments, but also claims of great antiquity made for other Nevada sites. Harrington and Simpson (1961) argued that the Tule Springs site was pre-Clovis in age; for the refutation, see Wormington and Ellis (1967). Much of what we know of the late Pleistocene and Holocene geology (Vance Haynes), paleobotany (Peter Mehringer), and vertebrate paleontology (John Mawby) of Las Vegas Valley, discussed in many places in this book, resulted from the Tule Springs project.

The cation-ratio dates for the Manix Lake Industry sites are provided by Bamforth and Dorn (1988); for the Coso Range petroglyph sites, by Whitley and Dorn (1988). On cation-ratio dating, see Dorn (1983), and Dorn and Krinsley (1991). Bierman and Gillespie (1991) and Bierman et al. (1991) provide compelling critiques of this approach; Reneau and Raymond (1991) question the time dependency of the chemical changes that form the heart of cation-ratio dating.

Those hesitating to assign Great Basin fluted points to Clovis without deeper analysis include Warren and Phagan (1988), Pendleton (1979), and Tuohy (1988). There are a number of published surveys of Great Basin fluted point finds: for Utah, see Copeland and Fike (1988) and, for a very general review, Schroedl (1991); for California, see E. L. Davis and Shutler (1969) and, on the Mojave Desert in particular, Warren and Phagan (1988); for Oregon, Willig and Aikens (1988); for Nevada, E. L. Davis and Shutler (1969) and Tuohy (1985, 1986). For a more general review, see Willig (1991).

On Lake Tonopah, see Campbell and Campbell (1940) and, especially, Pendleton (1979); this latter reference includes an excellent analysis of a sample of the Tonopah fluted points, as well as Elizabeth Campbell's field notes on the early work in this locale. On Long Valley, see Hutchinson (1988); on China Lake, E. L. Davis (1978a,b); on Alkali Lake, and on artifacts found associated with the fluted points themselves, see J. L. Fagan (1988) and Willig (1988, 1989). Jennings (1957) and Holmer (1986) discuss the fluted points from Danger Cave; the Henwood site is discussed by Warren and Phagan (1988) and Douglas et al. (1988). A fragment of a fluted point was also found in a buried context at the Old Humboldt site in Rye Patch Reservoir, northern Nevada, in a cultural context similar to that provided by the Henwood site; no radiocarbon dates are available for the Old Humboldt site, but it is clearly more than 7,000 years old (J. O. Davis and Rusco, 1987).

Many of the general points I advance here about Great Basin fluted points and their makers were made a number of years ago by Heizer and Baumhoff (1970) and by Wilke et al. (1974).

E. W. C. Campbell et al. (1937) presents the results of the work of the Campbells and their colleagues at Pleistocene Lake Mojave; Antevs's 15,000-year estimate appears in his contribution to this volume. Warren and De Costa (1964) and Ore and Warren (1971) discuss the dating of the Lake Mojave artifacts within the constraints provided by what was then known of the history of the lake; Warren and Ore (1978) discovered buried artifacts at Lake Mohave, obtained a single radiocarbon date on mollusc shell, and argued that these materials had been deposited from at least 10,270 years ago to about 8,000 years ago. W. J. Brown et al. (1990) present what is now known of the history of Pleistocene Lake Mojave, incorporating the work done by Ore and Warren (1971); see also Chapter 8. Warren (1967) clarified the nature of earlier work done on Lake Mojave materials.

My comment that the lowest artifact-bearing terrace at Lake Mojave is beneath the Lake Mojave II highstand is based on the fact that, with the exception of eroded sites, the lowest artifacts found by the Campbells were at an elevation of 937′ (285.6 m). The A shoreline of W. J. Brown et al. (1990), formed during Lake Mojave II times, is higher, sitting at 944.5′ (287.9 m).

Tuohy and Layton (1977) suggested the name "Great Basin Stemmed" for these projectile points. See Bryan (1980, 1988) and Musil (1988) for the hafting arguments I have reviewed here; Titmus and Woods (1991) suggest that edge grinding was done to control projectile point breakage, not to prevent sinew damage. Frison (1973, 1991) addresses very similar issues for early projectile points from the Great Plains. On crescents, see Tadlock (1966), Clewlow (1968), Butler (1970), and E. L. Davis (1978a:57–60). Beck and Jones (1990b) present their analysis of toolstone selection in Great Basin Stemmed point sites. I have also relied heavily on two unpublished papers in my discussion of these objects: Hattori et al. (1976) and Hattori et al. (1990). Schroedl (1991) provides a general review of stemmed point sites in Utah.

Grinding stones have been found in a variety of stemmed point sites, including Dietz (J. L. Fagan 1988; Willig 1988, 1989), Fort Rock Cave (Bedwell 1973), Danger Cave (Jennings 1957), 42MD743 in the Sevier Desert (Simms and Isgreen 1984), and Lake Mohave itself (E. W. C. Campbell et al. 1937). On the varied uses to which these artifacts may be put, see Adams (1988) and Yohe et al. (1991). For dates associated with stemmed point occupations, see Willig and Aikens (1988), Beck and Jones (1988, 1990a), and G. T. Jones and Beck (1990); on Hogup Cave, see Aikens (1970); on Last Supper Cave, Layton (1970) and Grayson (1988a). For Smith Creek Cave, and the debate over the earliest dates from this site, see Bryan (1979, 1988) and R. S. Thompson (1985b).

Among others, J. L. Fagan (1988) and Price and Johnston (1988) attribute the variability in stemmed points to change through time; Beck and Jones (1988) argue that much of this variability is due to resharpening (see also Beck and Jones 1990a); Basgall and Hall (1991) suggest that these artifacts served a wide variety of functions. On the square-based stemmed points from the Black Rock Desert, see Wallman and Amick (1992), Dansie et al. (1988), and Livingston (1992); similar points in the Great Basin and immediately adjacent areas have been reported not only from the Dietz site, but also from Dirty Shame Rockshelter in southeastern Oregon (Hanes 1988a,b). As Wallman and Amick (1992) discuss, these artifacts are strikingly similar to points assigned to the Cody complex on the Great Plains, and dated there to about 9,000 years ago (see Frison 1991). Earlier work on the surface archaeology of the Black Rock Desert is discussed by Clewlow (1968). Simms and Lindsay (1989) discuss an association of Plains-like lanceolate points with Great Basin stemmed points in the Sevier Desert.

The Old Humboldt site is discussed by J. O. Davis and Rusco (1987); the Five Points site, by Price and Johnston (1988). See Bedwell and Cressman (1971) and Bedwell (1973) for the definition of the Western Pluvial Lakes Tradition, and T. R. Hester (1973) for the expanded version of this concept. Price and Johnston (1988) and Beck and Jones (1990a), among others, have also observed that this concept is losing its value. For the faunas from stemmed point sites, see Layton (1970) and Grayson (1988a) on Last Supper Cave; Dansie (1987) on the Old Humboldt Site; and, Douglas et al. (1988) on Henwood and nearby sites.

For sites that contain both fluted and stemmed points, see E. L. Davis (1978b) on China Lake, Price and Johnston

(1988) on Jakes Valley, Zancanella (1988) on Railroad Valley, Hutchinson (1988) on Long Valley, and Pendleton (1979) and Tuohy (1988) on southern Big Smoky Valley. Comparative analyses of the production of stemmed and fluted points have been conducted by J. L. Fagan (1988), Pendleton (1979), and Warren and Phagan (1988). For references to Willig's work in the northern Alkali Lake Basin, see references cited earlier and the Notes to Chapter 8.

Baumhoff and Heizer (1965), among many others, saw the Great Basin during the middle Holocene as markedly inhospitable; they were, of course, working long before the detailed paleoclimatic records I have discussed in Chapter 8 became available. Jennings (1957) and Aikens (1970) disagreed strongly with that argument; not coincidentally, Jennings and Aikens worked in the Bonneville Basin, whereas Baumhoff and Heizer worked in the western Great Basin and California.

References to most of the sites I discuss in this section appear in Table 9-1. On Sandwich Shelter, see Marwitt et al. (1970). On the costs of seeds, see O'Connell and Hawkes (1981, 1984), O'Connell et al. (1983), Cane (1987), and Simms (1984). For the theoretical basis of this work, see the excellent book by E. A. Smith and Winterhalder (1992). O'Connell et al. (1982) were the first to suggest that the middle Holocene increase in grinding stones could be explained by a cost/benefit analysis; I have simply followed their lead here. See also the related discussion by Tucker et al. (1992). Harper and Alder (1972) present the botanical results of their resampling of Danger Cave; Fry (1976) presents the results of his analysis of the human coprolites from this site.

The five Handbook papers to which I refer are Cressman (1986), Elston (1986), Aikens and Madsen (1986), D. D. Fowler and Madsen (1986), and Warren and Crabtree (1986). See Ramenofsky (1987) for a discussion of converting archaeological sites into estimates of changing population densities, and D. B. Madsen (1982) for a discussion of the mobility of early Holocene Great Basin hunter-gatherers. The relationship between shallow-water resources and human population densities may be seen in Steward (1938); see Thomas (1972b) for a discussion of this issue, C. S. Fowler (1990) and Janetksi (1991) for discussions of marsh- and lake-oriented adaptations in the western and eastern Great Basin, respectively, and Kelly (1990) for a more general approach to the relationship between marsh resources and human mobility in this region.

In addition to O'Connell (1975), see O'Connell and Hayward (1972), O'Connell and Ericson (1974), and James (1983) on the King's Dog and Menlo Baths sites. Descriptions of Modoc and Klamath winter earth lodges are provided by Ray (1963) and Stern (1966). Sampson (1985) provides a detailed analysis of the Nightfire Island site. Two Great Basin sites with structures are routinely discussed as being middle Holocene in age: the Stahl (Harrington 1957), and Cocanour (Stanley et al. 1970) sites. However, Cocanour, a surface site, has not been radiocarbon dated, and dates now available for the Stahl site (Schroth 1992) suggest that is about 8,500 years old.

There is a huge literature on Great Basin projectile points: the best places to start are Hester (1973), Holmer (1986), and Thomas (1981). I have depended heavily on these last two references in my discussion. On the distribution of the atlatl during historic times in North America, see Driver and Massey (1957). For discussions of archaeological atlatls and darts, see Hester et al. (1974), Tuohy (1982), and Hattori (1982). Among other places, Gatecliff and Elko series points hafted to atlatl darts are known from Kramer Cave (Hattori 1982) and the NC site in southern Nevada (Tuohy 1982), respectively; Desert series points hafted on arrows are known from Tommy Tucker Cave (Fenenga and Riddell 1949) and Gypsum Cave (Harrington 1933); Desert series points on historic Great Basin arrows are illustrated in the important volume by D. D. Fowler and Matley (1979). Rosegate points have been found associated with arrow fragments at James Creek Shelter (Elston and Budy 1990). Thomas (1978) discusses the morphological differences between atlatl and dart points (but see also Tuohy 1982). For an excellent discussion of atlatls and their use, see Raymond (1986). On the Skull Creek Dunes, see Wilde (1985). On Northern Side-notched points, see Gruhn (1961), Warren (1968), Butler (1978), Sampson (1985), and Holmer (1986).

Understanding the literature on Pinto points is complicated by the fact that points in the central and western Great Basin that were until recently assigned to Pinto are now routinely assigned to Gatecliff Split Stem (see Thomas 1981 and Holmer 1986). Other critical sources on Pinto points include Amsden (1935), Bettinger and Taylor (1974), Warren (1980), Jenkins and Warren (1984), S. J. Vaughan and Warren (1987), and Meighan (1989). Radiocarbon dates for Pinto points in the Mojave Desert are provided by Jenkins (1987) and Schroth (1992); Jenkins and Warren (1984) discuss the possibility that Pinto points were in use well after the end of the middle Holocene.

Flenniken and Wilke (1989) have argued that the variability in Great Basin atlatl dart points does not reflect time at all, but instead reflects different stages in the rejuvenation of broken points. Their argument may account for much of the variability in stemmed and fluted points in the Great Basin, but does not account for such variability among dart points. Among other things, it cannot explain the fact that dart points at such sites as Gatecliff Shelter (Thomas 1983:177) are distributed through time in the same unimodal form shown by such temporally sensitive stylistic markers as ceramics in the southeastern United States. It also cannot explain Richard Hughes's discovery that different projectile point types in O'Connell's Surprise Valley sequence tended to be made from different raw materials (Hughes 1986; see also Bettinger et al. 1991).

Clewlow (1968) describes a number of Black Rock Desert sites that contained Northern Side-notched points; J. L. Fagan (1974) discusses the results of his work at spring sites in southeastern Oregon. See Janetski (1981) for an example in which Pinto points appear in eastern Great Basin (Escalante Desert) surface sites, but in low numbers.

On Newberry Cave, see C. A. Davis and Smith (1981) and C. A. Davis et al. (1981); on Stuart Rockshelter, Shutler et al. (1960); on South Fork Shelter, Heizer et al. (1968); on the Humboldt Lakebed site, Livingston (1986); on the Stillwater Marshes, Raven and Elston (1988); on the increased use of upland settings, Aikens and Madsen (1986) and Madsen (1982); on Gatecliff series points at high elevation, Thomas (1988). The Hidden Cave coprolites are discussed by Roust (1967), Wigand and Mehringer (1985), and Thomas (1985, Chapter 27); the Lovelock Cave coprolites by Ambro (1967), Cowan (1967), and Napton and Heizer (1970).

My discussion of glottochronology is based on Swadesh (1950, 1952, 1959), Lees (1953), Gudschinsky (1956), Hockett (1958), Hymes (1960), and Chrétien (1962); Bynon (1977) discusses the current status of Swadesh's glottochronology; Eastman (1990) provides a succinct discussion of this technique. Rea (1958, 1973) provides his telling analyses of the validity of glottochronology. My discussion of the history of French is based on Rickard (1989); the A.D. 960 date for written Italian comes from Embleton (1991). This latter reference reviews glottochronological methods in general, including a revision of Swadesh's approach that takes into account borrowing rates. It, too, severely underestimates divergence times for Romance languages. Jorgensen (1980, 1987) presents an insightful discussion of linguistic diversification in the western North American setting. Swadesh (1955) presented his glottochronological analysis of Uto-Aztecan; Lamb (1958) placed this work in the Numic context. The other glottochronological assessments I discuss were provided by Hale (1958), Goss (1968), and W. R. Miller et al. (1971). Goss (1977) rejected Lamb's Numic expansion hypothesis. W. R. Miller (1983) discusses linguistic evidence that suggests a southwestern Great Basin homeland for Numic peoples.

Thomas (1993) provides a detailed analysis of Alta Toquima. The plant and animal remains from this site are discussed by Rhode (1993) and Grayson (1993), respectively. See Pippin (1986), D. B. Madsen (1975, 1986b), and the papers in Griset (1986) and J. M. Mack (1990) for recent discussions of Great Basin ceramics. Thomas (1982b, 1993) discusses the early and late occupations in the Toquima Range.

The analysis of the material recovered from the White Mountains sites is still underway. Key references include Bettinger and Oglesby (1985), Bettinger (1991a,b), and Grayson (1991a); additional information on the faunas from these sites is provided by Grayson (1989a). Scharf (1992) provides information on the plant remains from Midway; my comments on the modern distribution of plants in the White Mountains are based on DeDecker (1991) and Elliot-Fisk and Peterson (1991).

Excellent summaries of Fremont have been provided by Jennings (1978), Marwitt (1986), and D. B. Madsen (1989); this last citation is a superb introduction to the issues I discuss here. Fremont basketry is discussed by Adovasio (1975, 1980, 1986a,b). Wilde and Newman (1989) discuss the early Sevier River Valley corn; see also Jett (1991). On Hogup Cave, see Aikens (1970). Metcalfe and Larrabee (1985) provide evidence for Fremont irrigation. Marwitt (1970, 1980) defined, and then questioned, the most widely accepted scheme for subdividing Fremont regional variability. That variability is assessed in the papers in D. B. Madsen (1980), by D. B. Madsen (1989), and by Simms (1986, 1990). Talbot and Wilde (1989) analyze temporal variability in the distribution of Fremont sites; Newman (1988) discusses the results of her pollen work in the Clear Creek drainage.

Bettinger's views on Numic expansion are developed in Bettinger and Baumhoff (1982, 1983), Bettinger (1991a), and Young and Bettinger (1992); see also Richerson and Boyd (1992). Criticisms of that view are presented in Simms (1983), Aikens and Witherspoon (1986), Shaul (1986), Grayson (1991a), and Musil (1992). The faunas from the high-elevation villages, and their implications for Bettinger's views, are discussed in Grayson (1991a, 1993); see also D. B. Madsen (1993) and Broughton and Grayson (1993). Simms (1990) discusses continuities from Fremont to late prehistoric times; on human skeletal remains from this period of time, see Simms (1990) and Simms et al. (1991). M. Q. Sutton (1986) suggests that Numic peoples were more militant than their neighbors, and that their warlike nature accounts for their expansion. In general, however, Numic peoples lacked military organizations, and it seems likely that the historic-period aggression Sutton describes applies only to the postcontact period.

Aikens and Witherspoon (1986) argue for a central Great Basin Numic homeland; C. S. Fowler (1972) presents her reconstruction of selected terms in proto-Numic; Holmer (1990) discusses the relevance of his data from central and southern Idaho to the debate. References to the Surprise Valley, Humboldt Sink, and Lake Abert sites are provided in the notes to Chapter 2; see Musil (1992) for a recent review.

Thomas (1971, 1972a, 1973, 1974) discusses his archaeological evaluation of the ethnographic accounts provided by Steward (1938). Arkush (1990) discusses possible effects of infectious diseases on Great Basin native Americans during earliest historic times, an important topic that has received little attention in the Great Basin. Cook (1955) presents evidence for disease-driven population losses in the Upper Klamath and Pyramid lakes area in 1833.

CHAPTER TEN

○○○

Historic Archaeology and the Donner Party

Abraham Lincoln was the second Republican candidate for President of the United States, and the first one to win, four years after Frémont tried and failed. Lincoln fought Indians in the Black Hawk War, then led his country into the Civil War and freed the slaves, a powerful combination for building an American legend. Lincoln went east from Illinois to become a legend; others went west. Some of their names meet on a simple sign in Springfield, Illinois:

> Lincoln Square marks the departure point of the Donner Party on April 15, 1846 for their ill-fated trip to California.

You can see the sign from the Lincoln Square McDonald's.

I discussed the Donner Party's route across the Great Salt Lake Desert in Chapter 5 (see Figure 5-7). Here I take a closer look at this remarkable episode in American history, not simply because this is one aspect of Great Basin history that many Americans learn about during their childhood, but also because some of the debris left behind by the Donner Party became incorporated into archaeological sites that have now been professionally excavated. That work sheds new light on the Donner Party, and exemplifies the fact that even the recent past can be successfully investigated using archaeological techniques.

The Donner Party Journey

There were far more people in the Donner group than just the Donners themselves. In all, 87 people made the multiple bad decisions that headed them straight into the early winter snows that fell in the Sierra Nevada in 1846 (Table 10-1). Only 16 of them were actually Donners. The other family to play a leading role was the Reeds: James Frazier and his wife Margaret, and their four children. In the Black Hawk War, Lincoln mustered number four in his company; Reed mustered fifth in the same company.

Historians often refer to this group of 87 people as the Donner-Reed Party, but I will use the more common "Donner Party." To avoid confusion, I will simply refer to the families of George and Jacob Donner as the "Donners." Brothers and prosperous Illinois farmers, George and Jacob Donner decided, late in life, to move west. Of the many reasons that have been given for that decision, the most accurate assessment was surely provided by James Clyman.

Table 10-1. Donner Party Statistics[a]

Name	Sex	Survived?	Age	Family size
Antoine	Male	No	23	1
Breen, Edward	Male	Yes	13	9
Breen, Isabella	Female	Yes	1	9
Breen, James	Male	Yes	4	9
Breen, John	Male	Yes	14	9
Breen, Mary	Female	Yes	40	9
Breen, Patrick	Male	Yes	40	9
Breen, Patrick, Jr.	Male	Yes	11	9
Breen, Peter	Male	Yes	7	9
Breen, Simon	Male	Yes	9	9
Burger, Charles	Male	No	30	1
Denton, John	Male	No	28	1
Dolan, Patrick	Male	No	40	1
Donner, Elitha	Female	Yes	14	16
Donner, Eliza	Female	Yes	3	16
Donner, Elizabeth	Female	No	45	16
Donner, Frances	Female	Yes	6	16
Donner, George	Male	No	62	16
Donner, George	Male	Yes	9	16
Donner, Georgia	Female	Yes	4	16
Donner, Isaac	Male	No	5	16
Donner, Jacob	Male	No	65	16
Donner, Leanna	Female	Yes	12	16
Donner, Lewis	Male	No	3	16
Donner, Mary	Female	Yes	7	16
Donner, Samuel	Male	No	4	16
Donner, Tamsen	Female	No	45	16
Eddy, Eleanor	Female	No	25	4
Eddy, James	Male	No	3	4
Eddy, Margaret	Female	No	1	4
Eddy, William	Male	Yes	28	4
Elliot, Milton	Male	No	28	1
Fosdick, Jay	Male	No	23	12
Fosdick, Sarah	Female	Yes	22	12
Foster, George	Male	No	4	13
Foster, Sarah	Female	Yes	23	13
Foster, William	Male	Yes	28	13
Graves, Eleanor	Female	Yes	15	12
Graves, Elizabeth	Female	No	47	12
Graves, Elizabeth	Female	No	1	12
Graves, Franklin	Male	No	57	12
Graves, Franklin, Jr.	Male	No	5	12
Graves, Jonathan	Male	Yes	7	12
Graves, Lavina	Female	Yes	13	12
Graves, Mary	Female	Yes	20	12
Graves, Nancy	Female	Yes	9	12
Graves, William	Male	Yes	18	12
Halloran, Luke	Male	No	25	1
Hardkoop, Mr.	Male	No	60	1

Table 10-1 ***(continued)***

Name	Sex	Survived?	Age	Family size
Herron, William	Male	Yes	25	1
Hook, Solomon	Male	Yes	14	16
Hook, William	Male	No	12	16
James, Noah	Male	Yes	20	1
Keseberg, Ada	Female	No	3	4
Keseberg, Lewis	Male	Yes	32	4
Keseberg, Lewis, Jr.	Male	No	1	4
Keseberg, Phillipine	Female	Yes	32	4
McCutcheon, Amanda	Female	Yes	24	3
McCutcheon, Harriet	Female	No	1	3
McCutcheon, William	Male	Yes	30	3
Murphy, John	Male	No	15	13
Murphy, Lavina	Female	No	50	13
Murphy, Lemuel	Male	No	12	13
Murphy, Mary	Female	Yes	13	13
Murphy, Simon	Male	Yes	10	13
Murphy, William	Male	Yes	11	13
Pike, Catherine	Female	No	1	13
Pike, Harriet	Female	Yes	21	13
Pike, Naomi	Female	Yes	3	13
Pike, William	Male	No	25	13
Reed, James	Male	Yes	46	6
Reed, James, Jr.	Male	Yes	5	6
Reed, Margaret	Female	Yes	32	6
Reed, Patty	Female	Yes	8	6
Reed, Thomas	Male	Yes	3	6
Reed, Virginia	Female	Yes	12	6
Reinhardt, Joseph	Male	No	30	1
Shoemaker, Samuel	Male	No	25	1
Smith, James	Male	No	25	1
Snyder, John	Male	No	25	1
Spitzer, Augustus	Male	No	30	1
Stanton, Charles	Male	No	35	1
Trubode, J. B.	Male	Yes	23	1
Williams, Baylis	Male	No	24	2
Williams, Eliza	Female	Yes	25	2
Wolfinger, Mr.	Male	No	?	2
Wolfinger, Mrs.	Female	Yes	?	2

[a]From Stewart (1960).

Heading east from California in 1846, Clyman was amazed at the number of people he met who were going in the other direction ("117 teams in six different squads all bound for oregon and california"). On June 24, 1846, riding the trail west of Fort Laramie, Clyman found it "strange that so many of all kinds and classes of People should sell out comfortable homes in Missouri and Elsewhare pack up and start across such an emmence Barren waste to settle in some new Place of which they have at most so uncertain information." Why would they do this? To Clyman, the answer was simple: "this is the character of my countrymen" (Clyman 1984:260).

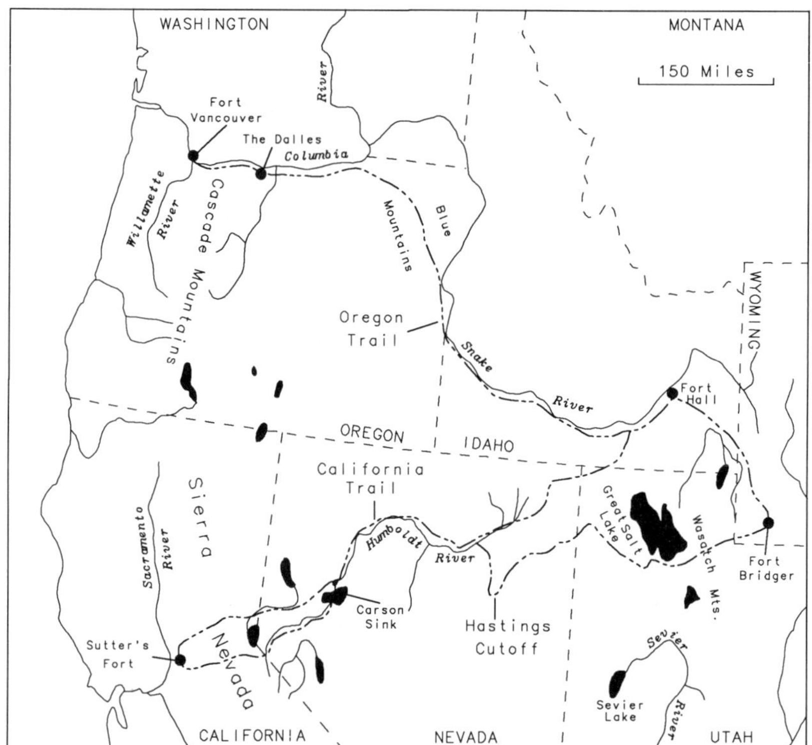

Figure 10-1. The locations of the California and Oregon trails and Hastings Cutoff.

To some extent, the "Donner Party" is often called that because George Donner was elected captain of the group on June 20, 1846. To a larger extent, though, it is credit in death. Of the 16 Donners, half died. Sierran place names mark the tragedy of the Donners, not the survival of the Reeds—Donner Pass, Donner Park, Donner Lake. Of the 40 who died after the decision to come this way was made, 8 were Donners. Of the four other families with more than five members, only the Murphys suffered as much, losing half of their six members. Eight of the 12 Graveses made it (the two Fosters were part of this family), as did all of the Breens, and all of the Reeds.

Bad luck? Only in part. Bad luck was hitting massive October snows in the Sierra Nevada when, in other years, crossing at this time would have been difficult but possible. But if, as Branch Rickey once said, luck is the residue of design, then bad luck is the residue of bad design, and the Donner Party had plenty of that, in the form of bad decisions made, bad advice accepted, good advice rejected, and the inability to get along.

The bad decisions were, ultimately, their own fault, but they would not have happened without Lansford W. Hastings. By 1846, the wagon routes to Oregon and California were established, if not, in California's case, well traveled (see Figure 10-1). After crossing the Plains into Wyoming, travelers followed South Pass to reach the Green River in southwestern Wyoming, then turned north and west along the Bear River, crossed the Snake River Plains, and reached Fort Hall. Run by the Hudson's Bay Company from 1837 to 1856, and located near modern Pocatello, Fort Hall became the junction between two separate routes west. The Oregon Trail ran west along the Snake River to Fort Boise and then to the Columbia River. The second trail also followed west along the Snake River from Fort Hall, but soon cut south, at the Raft River, to follow Goose Creek and Thousand Springs Valley in far northeastern Nevada to Humboldt Wells (near modern Wells, Nevada) and the Humboldt River. The Humboldt then became, in historian Dale Morgan's phrase, the "highroad of the west"—the conduit to California.

Although professional opinion of Hastings is now higher than it was a few decades ago, there can be no doubt that he was a schemer of the first order. Born in Ohio, Hastings went to Oregon in 1842, then to California, where he remained until 1844. Hastings spent his life in schemes, the last of which killed him. In 1867, at the age of 47, he decided to found a colony of ex-Confederates in Brazil; he died shipboard, bound for South America with his second group of colonists. But the scheme for which he is best remembered was his successful attempt to bring Americans to California.

Why he did this is not clear. That he wished fame is evident; those who knew him well claimed he also wished to be governor of an American California. What he did during the mid-1840s is consistent with that claim, though it certainly does not prove it true.

What better way to both gain fame and lure potential supporters to California, however, than by publishing an emigrant's guide to the region, one that extolled the virtues of the place, and that extolled the ease with which it could be reached? When he returned east from California in 1844, that book became Hastings's top priority. *The Emigrant's Guide to Oregon and California* appeared in 1845.

It might seem odd that someone who wanted to lure people to California would publish a guide that could be used to bring them to Oregon as well, but there were two tightly related reasons that led Hastings to include both places. First was the fact that, in 1845, the interest was in Oregon, then peacefully shared with the British, and not in California, then thoroughly Mexican. In that year, the ratio of immigrants going overland to Oregon, as opposed to California, was 10:1; in previous years, it was nearly 30:1 (in 1845, the actual numbers were 2,500 to Oregon and 260 to California; in 1844, 1,475 to Oregon and 53 to California). People had first to be compelled to come west, and Oregon was the real draw. Once compelled westward, they then had to be compelled to chose California instead.

Second, then, was the fact that Hastings's *Guide* was a piece of double propaganda, extolling the virtues of California to the detriment of Oregon, and extolling the virtues of the route to California to the detriment of the route to Oregon:

> From Fort Hall to the Pacific, by the Oregon Route, a distance of about eight hundred miles, there is but one continued succession of high mountains, stupendous cliffs, and deep, frightful caverns, with an occasional limited valley. . . . there are many places below Fort Boisia, where wood, for fuel, can not be obtained, only as it is purchased of the Indians, who always take immediate possession of every stick, which they find, either upon the shores, or floating down the streams. Although the Indians appear inclined to monopolize the entire wood trade, yet the course, which they pursue, is highly serviceable to the emigrants; for if they were here left to their own resources entirely, they would be unable to procure, either wood, or the excrement of the buffalo. From the dalles to the Pacific, there is ample timber, as much of the country is covered with dense forests. This portion of the Oregon route, from Fort Hall to the Pacific, has always been considered, wholly impassable for wagons, or any other vehicles; yet it is said, that the emigrants of 1843, succeeded in getting their wagons entirely down to the Willammette settlement. This they may have done, but I am confident, from my own experience, that each wagon must have cost the owner of it, more time and labor, than five wagons are worth, even in Oregon. (Hastings 1845:137)

How stupid it would be to take a route composed of nothing but "high mountains, stupendous cliffs, and deep, frightful caverns" when a far easier route, albeit to California, existed:

> By recent explorations, however, a very good, and much more direct wagon way, has been found, about one hundred miles, southward from the great southern pass, which, it will be observed, lies principally through the northern part of California. The California route, from Fort Hall to the Sacramento River, lies through alternate plains, prairies, and valleys, and over hills, amid lofy mountains; thence down the great valley of the Sacramento, to the bay of St. Francisco, a distance from Fort Hall, of nine hundred miles. The Indians are, in many places, very numerous; yet they are extremely timid, and entirely inoffensive. Wagons can be as readily taken from Fort Hall to the bay of St. Francisco, as they can from the States to Fort Hall; and, in fact, the latter part of the route, is found much more eligible for a wagon way, than the former.

Hastings also had a suggestion as to how to improve on the California route:

> The most direct route, for the California emigrants, would be to leave the Oregon route, about two hundred miles east from Fort Hall; thence bearing southwest, to the Salt Lake; and thence continuing down to the bay of St. Francisco.

In truth, the first attempt to bring wagons the way Hastings suggested, the 1841 Bidwell-Bartleson Party, began abandoning their wagons soon after they had reached Great Salt Lake. Although the 34 members of this group made it—in fact, they were the first emigrants to follow the Humboldt across—they did so by leaving their wagons, and most of their belongings, behind. Not a single wagon from this group made it more than 25 or so miles into Nevada.

The second attempt was made in 1843, led by Joseph Chiles, who had been a member of the Bidwell-Bartleson group. Chiles had been fortunate enough to engage Joseph Walker as a guide, and Walker brought his party from Fort Hall to the Humboldt via Raft River and Goose Creek, thus opening what became the standard wagon route. When food ran low along the Humboldt, a small group, including Chiles, crossed the Sierra Nevada on horseback to resupply the party, but snow prevented their return. Walker then went the way he knew best: south through Owens Valley, and west across Walker Pass. But even then, the wagons did not make it.

The first wagons to follow anything like the route Hastings suggested and to actually make it across the Sierra Nevada did so in 1844. The Stevens party avoided the Great Salt Lake Desert and followed Walker's Raft River–Goose Creek route to the Humboldt. In the end, they actually got wagons into the Sacramento Valley, but the effort required was enormous. Wagons and people ended up spread from Donner Lake on the east side of the summit to the upper Yuba River on the west side. They arrived at what is now Donner Lake on November 15; the last of the party did not make it across until March 1, 1845.

Indeed, when Hastings extolled the ease of what came to be known as the Central Overland Trail, he had not even been there. He had reached Oregon by the Oregon Trail, and California from Oregon. He had never been in Nevada east of the Sierra Nevada, much less seen the Humboldt River, or, further afield, Great Salt Lake. He had left California before the Stevens party had made it across. Yet here he was, in his 1845 *Emigrant's Guide,* telling people not only to swing south from Fort Hall to the Humboldt, and not only that the going was easy for wagons, but also that they could save time and effort by swinging south long before they got to Fort Hall, in order to reach Great Salt Lake "and thence continuing down to the bay of St. Francisco."

Hastings's *Emigrant Guide* sold well, subsequent editions appearing in 1847, 1848, and 1857 (his later *Emigrant's Guide to Brazil* did not do nearly as well). However, only in the first, 1845, edition was the possibility of a Great Salt Lake route a guess based on what he had learned from others. In January 1846 he heard from Frémont himself that the desert west of Great Salt Lake could be crossed. Hastings decided that he, too, would make that crossing.

Frémont had returned to the Great Basin in 1845, on his way to California, to participation in the Bear Flag rebellion, and, ultimately, to a court-martial. In October of that year, his expedition reached the shores of Great Salt Lake; by the end of the month, they were camped in Skull Valley, between the Cedar and Stansbury mountains and just south of the main body of the lake. From the Cedar Range, Frémont could look west across a desert about which neither he nor his men knew anything; Indians he met told him that none of them knew what they might face in the crossing, except for the fact that, as far as any of them had gone, there was no water to be found. In the distance, "at the farther edge of the desert, apparently fifty to sixty miles away, was a peak-shaped mountain" (Frémont 1887:432). After several days spent pondering the direction to take, the decision was made to head straight across the desert for that distant landmark. A group of four, including Kit Carson, took a pack mule and horses, and, at night, headed for what Frémont was to name Pilot Peak. If they found water, they were to signal the main camp by lighting a fire. That fire was lit late the next day, and Frémont and the rest of the crew then made the crossing themselves.

Shortly after, the party split up, Frémont himself heading south and west and thus assuring that he would once again miss the Humboldt River. By December, Frémont was in the Sacramento Valley, and it was in mid-January 1846 that Hastings and Frémont met at Sutter's Fort. Here Hastings learned of Frémont's successful crossing.

After completing his publishing venture in the east, Hastings had returned to California, coming down the Humboldt, but reaching it by the Fort Hall route, and traveling not by wagon but by horse. Now, however, he had Frémont's direct account of the Great Salt Lake Desert crossing. In April 1846, Hastings headed east again, determined to follow his suggested cutoff in reverse—Humboldt River to Great Salt Lake Desert to Fort Bridger.

In addition to wanting to try his own route, Hastings had a second goal in mind. It was his plan to intercept emigrants coming west in order to convince them that it was California, not Oregon, that should be their goal, and that it was his cutoff, not the standard route, that they should follow. Indeed, Hastings's plans were well known, and the threat to Oregon significant enough, that, in June of that year, settlers in Oregon City, Oregon, decided to "meet the emigration from the United States—to prevent their being deceived and led astray by the misrepresentation of L. W. Hastings, who is now on his way from California for that object" (C. H. Carey 1932:xvii). By June, however, it was too late: Hastings was already at Fort Bridger.

Hastings did not make the journey east unaccompanied. He left with 23 others, including James Clyman, a mountain man of the Jed Smith and Joseph Walker school (in 1823, Clyman had sewn Smith's ear back on after it had been nearly ripped off, along with much of the rest of his head, by a grizzly). Not only was Clyman experienced in the wilderness, but he, too, had served in the Black Hawk War in the same company as both Lincoln and Reed. Now, in the spring of 1846, he was heading east with Hastings as the Reeds and Donners were heading west.

The passage over the Sierra Nevada and up the Humboldt was relatively uneventful for Clyman and Hastings. On May 21, they reached the North Fork of the Humboldt, and the "point whare Mr Freemant intersected the wagon Trail last fall on his way to california" (Clyman 1984:246). Hastings was adamant that the party should follow Frémont's trail across the desert, but Clyman thought the distances to Fort Bridger about equal, and the Fort Hall road far better. Hastings held out, and "after long consultation and many arguments for and against the two different routs one leading Northward by fort Hall and the other by the Salt Lake we all finally tooke Fremonts Trail by way of the Salt Lake" (Clyman 1984:247). Clyman had been by Great Salt Lake before—in fact, he and three companions had actually circumnavigated the lake in skin boats in 1826—but this was to be his first encounter with the desert to the west of that lake.

He was impressed:

> This is the [most] desolate country perhaps on the whole globe there not being one spear of vegitation and of course no kind of animal can subsist and it is not yet assertained to what extent this immince salt and sand plain can be south of whare we [are now]. (Clyman 1984:249)

As desolate as the terrain was, the party made it across safely, spending the last four days of May in the journey from the eastern flank of the Pilot Range to the Oquirrh Mountains at the southern end of Great Salt Lake. Once again in familiar country, the group moved up and over the Wasatch Range to the Bear River, and, on June 7, to Fort Bridger.

Hastings and his companion, James Hudspeth, soon left Clyman to begin the task of intercepting westbound emigrants to guide them along his own route to California. After a delay of several days, Clyman headed east, on his way back to Independence, Missouri.

Three groups were immediately affected by Hastings and Hudspeth. The first was the nine-man Bryant-Russell Party, mounted on horses and mules. Although Bryant met Joseph Walker at Fort Bridger, and noted that Walker "spoke discouragingly of the new route via the south end of the Salt Lake" (Bryant 1848:143), all nine followed Hudspeth over the Wasatch Range, down through Weber Canyon, into Great Salt Lake Valley, and as far west as the Cedar Range. Here, Hudspeth left them, as had been agreed he would. The nine men then crossed the 80 miles of salt flats in a single day, the slowest of them taking 17 hours for the trip. Forty-three days after leaving Fort Bridger, they all arrived safely at Sutter's Fort in the Sacramento Valley.

Hastings had stayed behind in order to take his turn with emigrants coming across by wagon. The Harlan-Young Party, including some 60 wagons in separate bunches, was the second to take his route. When Hastings fell behind to assist stragglers, the leading members of the party encountered Hudspeth, who had returned to recommend that they take their wagons down Weber Canyon into Salt Lake Valley. This they did, only to find that the lower part of the canyon had barely enough room for a river, let alone wagons. Seven days of hard work, cutting a road and winching wagons, brought them to the valley. Crossing the Great Salt Lake Desert came next. This took them three days and cost an unknown number of animals, but, even though they abandoned 24 wagons in their initial attempt to cross, these were retrieved and the group, along with Hastings, continued on to California.

The Donner Party was still further behind. They did not reach Fort Bridger until July 27 and did not leave until July 31, waiting at the fort while their animals regained their strength. The leading wagons in the Harlan-Young Party had left eleven days earlier.

The final decision to take Hastings's route was made here, but they had run this decision through their minds well before their arrival at this spot. Indeed, on June 24, the Donners and the Reeds had met Clyman at Fort Laramie. Clyman had just followed Hastings's trail in the opposite direction, and he now told James Reed, his Black Hawk War fighting companion, that he thought this route might be impossible for them to negotiate. Coming through South Pass, however, the Donner Party received an open letter from Hastings recommending his route and offering to meet them at Fort Bridger. It was this latter offer, and not Clyman's advice, that the group accepted.

By the time they arrived at Fort Bridger, however, Hastings was long gone. They could have continued via Fort Hall, but their minds were made up. Bridger himself urged the party to follow Hastings's trail, telling them, according to Reed, that, except for a 40-mile waterless stretch, "the route we design to take, is a fine level road, with a plenty of water and grass" (Korns 1951:193). Bridger had much to gain from such advice, since a shortcut to the north threatened to deny him business along the trail to Oregon, and his fort stood to profit from all who followed the new route.

On July 31, the Donner Party set out on their own, following the trail to Weber Canyon. By then, Hastings knew that this canyon was a mistake. To his credit, he had left a note that advised against this route and that suggested he would return to guide the way if members of any later party would but come for him.

Reed, William McCutcheon, and Charles Stanton did just that, finding Hastings in the Tooele Valley just south of Great Salt Lake. Hastings, now committed to the Harlan-Young group, could not live up to his promise to guide later arrivals, but he did ride back with Reed as far as Big Mountain, on the west flank of the Wasatch Range, and pointed out the route he would take were he going to do it again.

By the time Reed returned to the group, another four days had passed. Nor did Hastings's alternative prove easy. It took 16 days, marked by extraordinary effort and much bickering, for the Donner Party to fight its way through the Wasatch Range and ultimately down Emigration Canyon (just east of Salt Lake City) to reach Great Salt Lake Valley. The Donner Party had left Fort Bridger on July 31; they emerged from the Wasatch Range on August 22, a full 26 days spent in doing what the Harlan-Young party had done in 18. On August 22, the Donners and Reeds had just reached the valley of Great Salt Lake; on the same day, the Harlan-Young Party was at the Pilot Range, on the other side of the Bonneville Basin.

The great challenge after the Wasatch Range was the desert west of Great Salt Lake, some 80 waterless miles lying between the Cedar Mountains and the Pilot Range. According to Reed, the quickest members of the Donner Party made it across in three days, leaving the Cedar Mountains on August 31 and reaching Pilot Springs on September 3; the rest made it the next day. But getting yourself across the desert was not the same as getting your livestock and wagons across, and the Donner Party had to abandon some of both as they approached Floating Island on the western edge of the salt flats. How many animals were lost is not clear; one member of the party put it at 36. Reed himself lost 18 of his 20 cattle here—"the first of my sad misfortunes" (Korns 1951:211) he was later to say. In fact, the Reeds reached Pilot Springs with all three of their wagons stuck in the wet muck that lay beneath the salt crust east of Floating Island.

In the end, Reed retrieved only one of his wagons from the salt flats. The two remaining vehicles were left in the desert, not far from two other abandoned wagons, one belonging to the Donners, the other to the Kesebergs. A week was to pass before the strays had been rounded up, retrievable wagons had been retrieved, and the animals were in condition to resume the march. Only then did the party get underway again. The toll of the desert: some three dozen animals, four wagons, and, most importantly, another eleven days.

The fatal significance of these twin delays—one in the Wasatch, one as a result of the salt flats—need not be guessed at. Heinrich Lienhard's section of the Harlan-Young Party had left Fort Bridger later than the rest, on July 26. They reached Pilot Springs on August 19, rested, then continued west on August 24. The Donner Party left the fort only five days after Lienhard's departure, and headed west from Pilot Springs on September 10, eleven days behind Lienhard. Lienhard's group made it to California safely. The Donner Party hit late October snows in the Sierra Nevada, where they were forced to camp, spending the winter not far from today's Donner Lake. The last survivor was not rescued until April 21, 1847.

It is easy to blame Hastings for what happened to the Donner party. After all, it was his route that cost the lives of so many in that party. Had they gone to Oregon the established way, or to California by the Fort Hall-Humboldt River trail, all would likely have arrived safely.

Although Hastings was a schemer of the first degree, it might be better to consider what the Donner Party did to him than to focus on what he did to them. The Bryant-Russell Party had no serious problems in taking Hastings's route, but they had not taken wagons. However, the Harlan-Young group did have wagons, and, although many of those were abandoned, the group as a whole made it, and they made it under Hastings's leadership. Hudspeth returned from his duties with the Bryant-Russell Party to assist the lead members of the Harlan-Young group. Hastings returned with Reed to point out the way their party should take. Nothing in his behavior suggests that he would have not have accompanied the Donner Party had he not already been committed to an earlier group. Lienhard and his companions left Fort Bridger only five days before the Donner Party; trailing behind the main body of the Harlan-Young Party, Lienhard's group got their wagons across safely. Even if they had not done so, wagons were routinely abandoned along the Central Overland Trail, particularly between the Humboldt Sink and the Truckee or Carson rivers, depending on which trail was taken from the end of the Humboldt.

Had Hastings simply published his book and left emigrants to read it and die, then he would, indeed, have been a villain. In publishing that book without ever having traveled the routes he recommended, he left himself open to charges of villainy. But the fact is that, by the time people had been influenced by his book and were responding to it, Hastings had taken both Walker's Fort Hall–Raft River–Humboldt River route and Frémont's Great Salt Lake Desert route, albeit on horse. More to the point, he met emigrants coming through, and either he or Hudspeth was there to assist them to one degree or another. Two years earlier, the Stevens party had also gotten stuck in the Sierran snows, but they had all managed to survive, so there is no discussion of blame here.

The suffering of the Donner Party cannot fairly be laid at Hastings's feet. Whenever they had a crucial decision to make, they made the wrong one. Whenever they had to cooperate to survive, they bickered. Their tragedy occurred because of themselves, not because of Hastings. Hastings was not blameless: he wrote the book with only hearsay knowledge of the California routes, and wrote it in such a way as to strongly encourage people to go to California, not Oregon. Hastings's cutoff included not only the Great Salt Lake Desert, but also a lengthy diversion down Ruby Valley, then up Huntington Valley, which the Donner Party faithfully followed. Hastings was not blameless, and thus got himself into the position in which he would be considered the villain if anything were to go seriously wrong; the revisionist histories should not be carried too far. Nonetheless, the Donner Party went as seriously wrong as was possible, and Hastings's reputation has paid for it ever since.

But all 87 shared in the bad design, and only 40 died. Of those 40, 8 were members of the Donner family. As I mentioned, only one other family with more than five members suffered as much. Why they lost so many members is clear: sex and age were against them.

Donner Party Deaths and Demographics

Modern studies of human mortality have established that three factors are critical in determining human longevity: age, sex, and social networks. Each of these played a major role in determining which members of the Donner Party lived and which died.

Analyses of the ages of death within human populations ("age-specific mortality rates") have long shown that high death rates characterize both the oldest and the youngest members of human societies. Mortality is generally very high between the ages of 1 and 5, after which it decreases. By the age of 35, mortality begins to increase again, becoming ever higher in older age classes. Older individuals are also more vulnerable to famine, and both infants and the old suffer higher mortality rates due to hypothermia. Death among the members of the Donner Party, then, should have struck the old and the young more than it struck those in between.

Studies of the relationship between sex and mortality routinely show that, for most human populations, male mortality is greater than female mortality. Scientists argue over whether these differences are due to biological or cultural factors, but it is clear that biology plays a major role.

That the cause is essentially biological is shown by the fact that other organisms besides humans show this pattern. As biologist Wirt Atmar has discussed, the pattern is characteristic of vertebrates as a whole: males generally die more readily in response to disease, injury, starvation, and exhaustion; they die in greater numbers as a result of accidents and violence, and they show higher embryonic mortality rates. Indeed, males in human populations even tend to have higher loads of parasitic worms. In some mammals, Atmar observes, the differences are likely caused by hormones, and in particular by testosterone levels: castrated human males live an average of 13.6 years longer than normal males, and similar patterns exist in sheep. Males, in other words, are physiologically more fragile than females.

That men are physiologically more fragile than women might seem to fly in the face of common sense. After all, men are bigger than women and have greater muscle mass. In a fair fight between a man and a woman, the outcome is rarely in doubt. Yet many of the differences between male and female human anatomy that do not relate directly to reproduction are tied to what physical anthropologist Sherwood Washburn once called the anatomy of aggression. Males are more aggressive than females, and male body size, muscle mass, and the like relate to this fact. So does the fact that, in the United States, male deaths from suicide and homicide are three times higher than they are for females. In the longer term, the "weaker sex" is not female, but male.

Under conditions of stress caused by famine and cold, the relationship between sex and mortality in human populations is not quite so clear. J. P. W. Rivers has argued convincingly that, on purely biological grounds, women should fare better here as well. On the average, women are smaller than men, have a greater proportion of subcutaneous fat, and have a lower basal metabolic rate (indeed, female basal metabolic rates tend to become lower than those of males above the age of five). In addition, inactive adult males also suffer greater core temperature reduction than inactive adult females. For these and other reasons, adult and subadult females should do better under conditions of famine and extreme cold than their male counterparts.

That they may or may not actually do so, Rivers and others have observed, is due to cultural factors: men, who excel at short-term aggression, can gain control of resources critical to survival, and can do so at the expense of women.

For all these reasons, survivorship in the Donner Party should have been heavily weighted toward the female members of the group, as long as resources were not being differentially taken by the males, and as long as the influence of sex on survivorship was not outweighed by other matters, including age.

A third critical factor in longevity is provided by participation in social networks. Many studies have shown that, the greater the participation in such networks, the lower the mortality. Those who are married live longer than those who are not; those who maintain routine contact with friends and relatives live longer than those who do not; those who become actively involved in such things as church groups and social clubs live longer than those who do not.

It is hard to know exactly why this is the case, though, in normal living conditions, a sense of belonging, access to information, and the availability of timely assistance all seem to play a role. These factors are also in effect in stressful situations produced by natural hazards. Here, physical assistance and the increased availability of information clearly play an important role.

This third important variable in mediating longevity suggests that, in addition to age and sex, the size of the kin (family) group with which a person traveled in the Donner Party should also have played a significant role in determining whether that person lived or died.

The members of the Donner Party with the best chances of survival should have been women traveling in large family groups, and that is exactly what happened.

DEATHS IN THE DONNER PARTY

Although Margaret Reed's elderly mother, Sarah Keyes, died shortly after the journey had begun, the first death in the Donner Party after they had departed from Fort Bridger occurred just south of Great Salt Lake. Here, Luke Halloran (25 years old), who had been ill from the outset of the trip, died of "consumption." By the time the party had reached the foothills of the Sierra Nevada, four additional males had died, all as a result of active or passive violence. John Snyder (25) was killed along the Humboldt River by James Reed, leading to Reed's expulsion from the group. A Mr. Hardkoop (60) lacked a wagon or draft animal of his own; when forcefully denied access to transportation, he also succumbed along the Humboldt. A Mr. Wolfinger (age unknown) died in the Humboldt Sink, apparently murdered by Joseph Reinhardt and Augustus Spitzer. Further along the trail, in the Truckee Meadows, William Pike (25) was accidentally shot and killed while passing a weapon to his brother-in-law, William Foster. All four of these deaths involved males, a typically human pattern.

The remaining 35 deaths occurred after the winter encampment was established near Donner Lake. Of these deaths, 22 happened in the winter encampment itself, as members of the group awaited rescue. The remaining 13 deaths took place either while members of the party attempted to escape on their own or during a series of rescue attempts that were mounted from the Sacramento Valley. Of these 13 losses, 12 occurred in the Sierra Nevada or on its western flank, and one infant (Elizabeth Graves) succumbed at Sutter's Fort soon after she had been rescued. The exact causes of these deaths are unknown, but the general cause is quite clear. Even though it is possible that one member of the party, Lewis Keseberg, hastened the demise of one or more people during the spring of 1847, and the young William Hook is said to have died after gorging himself when rescuers made food available, all or

Table 10-2. Sex and Survivorship among the Members of the Donner Party

	Sex							
	Male			Female				
	Survived?			Survived?				
Age class	**Yes**	**No**	**Percent no**	**Yes**	**No**	**Percent no**	**Totals**	**Percent no**
1–4	2	5	71.4	4	5	55.6	16	62.5
5–9	5	2	28.6	4		0.0	11	18.2
10–14	6	2	25.0	5		0.0	13	15.4
15–19	1	1	50.0	1		0.0	3	33.3
20–29	5	10	66.6	6	1	14.3	22	50.0
30–39	2	4	66.6	2		0.0	8	50.0
40–49	2	1	33.3	1	3	75.0	7	57.1
50–59		1	100.0		1	100.0	2	100.0
60–69		3	100.0				3	100.0
?		1		1			2	
Totals	23	30	56.6	24	10	29.4	87	45.0

virtually all of the 35 died of some combination of starvation and exposure.

Modern studies of human mortality lead to the expectation that male mortality among the Donner Party should have been much higher than female mortality. This was, in fact, very much the case. Males succumbed at approximately twice the rate of females (56.6% for males versus 29.4% for females: see Table 10-2). Of the male deaths, five occurred prior to the Sierran encampment, and four of these were due either directly or indirectly to male aggression (Hardkoop, Pike, Snyder, Wolfinger). Thus, of the 30 males who died, 13.3% died as a result of violence; there is no convincing evidence that any female member of the Donner Party died violently. Eliminating those deaths known to have been due to violence, the male death rate (53.1%) remains far higher than that for females.

Not only did males succumb at a higher rate than females, but they also died sooner. Table 10-3 shows the number of deaths, by months and by sex, that occurred among those who reached the Sierran encampment. Of the 25 males who died after reaching the Sierra Nevada, 14 had died by the end of January, the remaining 11 dying between February and April. Of the 10 female deaths, all occurred during those latter months. That is, even excluding those who died from violence, 14 males died before a single female lost her life.

Table 10-3. The Chronology of Deaths by Sex after Establishment of the Sierran Encampment

Months	Number of Males	Number of Females
December–January[a]	14	0
February–April[b]	11	10

Notes: a, Names and ages of individuals involved: Antoine (23), C. Burger (30), P. Dolan (40), J. Donner (65), J. Fosdick (23), F. Graves (57), L. Keseberg (1), J. Murphy (15), L. Murphy (12), J. Reinhardt (30), S. Shoemaker (25), J. Smith (25), C. Stanton (35), B. Williams (24).

b, Names and ages of individuals involved: (a) Male—J. Denton (28), G. Donner (62), I. Donner (5), L. Donner (3), S. Donner (4), J. Eddy (3), M. Elliot (28), G. Foster (4), F. Graves, Jr. (5), W. Hook (12), A. Spitzer (30). (b) Female—E. Donner (45), T. Donner (45), M. Eddy (1), E. Eddy (25), E. Graves (1), E. Graves (47), A. Keseberg (3), H. McCutcheon (1), L. Murphy (50), C. Pike (1).

Table 10-4. Average Ages of Donner Party Members: Males and Females, Survivors and Nonsurvivors[a]

	Total group	Survivors	Nonsurvivors
Females	17.5 (33)	15.6 (23)	21.9 (10)
Males	21.8 (52)	17.7 (23)	25.0 (29)
All members combined	20.1 (85)	16.7 (46)	24.2 (39)

[a] Ages are in years. The total number of people involved is given in parentheses. The two members of the party whose ages are unknown are not included in this table.

Given that the combination of famine and exposure caused these deaths, and given that there is no evidence that males and females within family groups had differential access to resources, it would appear that the higher mortality of males than females in the Sierras is in part a result of the greater female endurance of cold stress and famine.

Modern studies also suggest that the greatest losses should have been in the oldest and youngest age classes. This was also the case. Children beneath the age of five (62.5% mortality) and adults above the age of 49 (100% mortality) suffered the heaviest losses. In general, it was better to be a younger member of the Donner Party than an older one. For females, males, and the group as a whole, those who survived were younger on the average that those who did not. The males who survived were an average of 7.3 years younger than those who died; the females who survived averaged 6.3 years younger than those who died. For the group as a whole, survivors were on the average 7.5 years younger than nonsurvivors (see Table 10-4).

There are, however, some apparent oddities in the death rates for males. In particular, the death rates for males between 20 and 39 years of age are extremely high: 66.6% of the males of this age failed to survive. Indeed, most had died well before mortality had begun to strike any female members of the party (Table 10-3). Whereas higher male than female mortality across all age categories is to be expected, male mortality in these particular age classes, at rates higher than those for immediately younger and older males, needs to be explained.

It is possible that these men died quickly because they had exhausted themselves both en route and in camp, cutting their way through the Wasatch, hunting in deep snows, and, in general, doing those aggressive tasks at which males excel. There is no way to measure these likely effects of short-term male aggression. However, it is equally likely that another factor played a role: many of these men traveled alone or nearly so.

Table 10-5 presents the sex, family group size, and fate of Donner Party members between 20 and 39 years of age who were in the Sierran encampment (excluded are William Herron [25] and William McCutcheon [30], both of whom crossed the Sierra Nevada well in advance of the main party). Those who are listed as "rescue" in this table left the Sierran encampment with rescue parties sent from the Sacramento Valley. Of all those leaving with rescue groups, 86% (38 of 45) survived, five of the seven nonsurvivors being children 12 years old or younger.

Those listed as "snowshoe" in Table 10-5 were among 15 people who attempted to walk from the Sierran encampment to the Sacramento Valley in late December. This torturous trip up and over the crest of the Sierra Nevada in full winter conditions, using snowshoes made from materials that happened to be at hand, took the survivors 33 days. Of the 15 who made the attempt, 8 died. As in the Donner Party as a whole, losses among the snowshoers were differentially distributed across the sexes: 8 of 10 males died but all 5 females survived. The eight males who died included two Indians from the Sacramento Valley who had joined the party as part of a relief attempt, and who were murdered by William Foster (indeed, if these Sacramento Valley natives are counted as full members of the Donner Party, then 18.8% of all male deaths in that party were due to violence). The remaining males ranged from 12 to 57 years in age; the males who survived averaged 28 years of age, whereas those who died averaged 31.7 years. The females averaged 22 years. Once again, it paid to be younger, and it paid to be female.

Why was there such high mortality among males between 20 and 39 years of age? Age-related differences in male basal metabolic rates cannot account for this pattern. Although males between 20 and 39 years old have slightly

Table 10-5. Sex, Family Group Size, and Fate of Donner Party Members between 20 and 39 Years Old Who Reached the Sierran Encampment

Name	Sex	Family group size	Fate
Antoine	Male	1	Died walking out (snowshoe)
C. Burger	Male	1	Died in Sierra camp
J. Denton	Male	1	Died walking out (rescue)
E. Eddy	Female	4	Died in Sierra camp
M. Elliot	Male	1	Died in Sierra camp
J. Fosdick	Male	12	Died walking out (snowshoe)
J. Reinhardt	Male	1	Died in Sierra camp
S. Shoemaker	Male	1	Died in Sierra camp
J. Smith	Male	1	Died in Sierra camp
A. Spitzer	Male	1	Died in Sierra camp
C. Stanton	Male	1	Died walking out (snowshoe)
B. Williams	Male	2	Died in Sierra camp
W. Eddy	Male	4	Walked out (snowshoe)
S. Fosdick	Female	12	Walked out (snowshoe)
S. Foster	Female	13	Walked out (snowshoe)
W. Foster	Male	13	Walked out (snowshoe)
M. Graves	Female	12	Walked out (snowshoe)
N. James	Male	1	Walked out (rescue)
L. Keseberg	Male	4	Walked out (rescue)
P. Keseberg	Female	4	Walked out (rescue)
A. McCutcheon	Female	3	Walked out (snowshoe)
H. Pike	Female	13	Walked out (snowshoe)
M. Reed	Female	6	Walked out (rescue)
J. B. Trubode	Male	1	Walked out (rescue)
E. Williams	Female	2	Walked out (rescue)

higher basal metabolic rates than those between the ages of 40 and 64, the differences are not significant. However, as I have noted, studies of modern mortality have shown that, the greater the kin group size, the lower the mortality rate. In addition, studies of behavior during natural disasters have shown that kin groups—individuals related by descent or by marriage—provide key support in those situations. Perhaps the extremely high mortality among Donner males between 20 and 39 years old is to be accounted for at least in part by the number of related individuals with whom they traveled.

Of the 25 individuals in the Sierran encampment between 20 and 39 years old, the average kin group size of the survivors was 6.8 individuals, whereas the average kin group size of the nonsurvivors was only 2.3 individuals. That is, individuals of this age who survived had kin groups approximately three times larger than those who did not. Importantly, and as Table 10-6 shows, this difference characterizes losses within sexes as well. Surviving females between 20 and 39 years old had kin groups averaging 12.3 members, whereas the single female of this age who died had a kin group of only 4 members. Among males of this age, the survivors had kin groups averaging 4.6 members, whereas nonsurvivors had kin groups averaging 2.1 individuals. If males between 20 and 39 who did not reach the Sierran encampment are included, the values change, but the conclusion does not. The average kin group size for all males between 20 and 39 who died was 2.7 individuals; for male survivors, the average kin group size was 4.6 individuals.

It seems likely, then, that kin group size played a major role in mediating deaths among Donner Party members between 20 and 39 years of age, just as it does in modern populations. If so, the extremely high mortality of Donner males of this age relates to the fact that their support group was, on the average, so small.

Table 10-6. Kin Group Sizes of Donner Party Survivors and Nonsurvivors between the Ages of 20 and 39 Who Reached the Sierran Encampment

Survived?	Males	Females	Total
Yes	4.6 (*N* = 5)	12.3 (*N* = 8)	6.8 (*N* = 13)
No	2.1 (*N* = 11)	4.0 (*N* = 1)	2.3 (*N* = 12)

The kin group effect seems to have applied to the group as a whole. Age was clearly the critical factor leading to mortality in Donner Party members over 50 or under 5 years in age. If those people are excluded, then the average kin group size of those who survived was 9.4 people, whereas the average kin group size of those who died was 6.5 people.

In short, bad luck (the snows of October) and bad decisions (following Hastings's route) led the Donner Party into the tragedy that befell them. After that, however, human biology and small group dynamics took over. Age, sex, and social network then played a major role in determining who lived and who died. The Donner Party disaster teaches us that women are the physiologically stronger sex, and that the strength of one's social network can be critical in determining longevity.

The Archaeology of the Donner Party

THE SIERRA NEVADA

When the Donner Party realized they could go no further, they stopped and began the task of digging in for the winter. Two distinct, but nearby, camps resulted. One complex of cabins was built just south of Donner Lake, including what has come to be called Murphy's Cabin (see Figure 10-2; the Donner Lake locations are referred to as the "Southern Donner camps" in this figure). This log structure housed the Murphy, Foster, and Eddy families, 16 people in all. Not far from here, the Breens moved into a cabin that was there when they arrived. That cabin had been built two years earlier by Moses Schallenberger, a member of the Stevens party who became caught in the snow, and survived the winter by eating Sierran foxes. The Kesebergs lived in a lean-to that they attached to the Breen-Schallenberger cabin. A third cabin was built nearly a half mile away; this housed the Graveses and Reeds, and completed the Donner Lake encampment. The Donners never made it this far; they, and others who were with them, built three less substantial structures along Alder Creek, some five miles to the northeast.

After it was all over, and the members of the party were either dead or safe in California, the Donner Party winter camps were found by others. The first significant encounter was by General Stephen Watts Kearny, who was moving east from California following his involvement in seizing California from Mexico. Following closely behind, under orders but not yet under arrest, was Frémont with his contingent. And traveling with Kearny was Edwin Bryant, of the Bryant-Russell party of two years earlier. Bryant's description of what they found could not have been much more graphic:

> On the 22nd of June, 1847, a halt was ordered, for the purpose of collecting and interring the remains. Near the principal cabins, I saw two bodies, entire with the exception that the abdomens had been cut open and the entrails extracted. Their flesh had been either wasted by famine or evaporated by exposure to the dry atmosphere, and they presented the appearance of mummies. Strewn around the cabins were dislocated and broken bones—skulls, (in some instances sawed asunder with care for the purpose of extracting the brains,)—human skeletons, in short, in every variety of mutilation. A more revolting and appalling spectacle I never witnessed. The remains were, by an order of Gen. Kearny, collected and buried under the superintendence of Major Swords. They were interred in a pit which had been dug in the centre of one of the cabins for a *cache*. These melancholy duties to the dead being performed, the cabins, by order of Major Swords, were fired, and with every thing surrounding them connected with this horrid and melancholy tragedy, were consumed. The body of George Donner was found at his camp, about eight or ten miles distant, wrapped in a sheet. He was buried by a party of men detailed for that purpose. (Bryant 1848:263)

Kearny and his men did not do a complete job, and later visitors found goods, cabins, and human remains. By 1872, however, the standing structures were gone, although relic hunters continued their searches long thereafter.

Members of the Donner Party indicated that a huge rock helped form one of the walls of Murphy's Cabin. The exact site of that cabin was identified by Charles F. McGlashan, whose *History of the Donner Party* (1880) is one of the classic accounts of the journey. It was in Murphy's cabin that Kearny's men were thought to have buried the remains they discovered at the southern Donner camps.

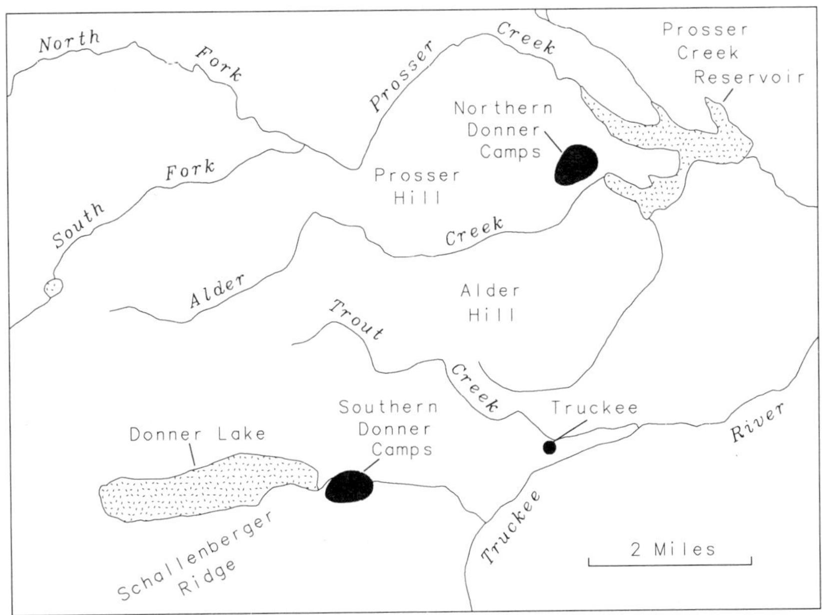

Figure 10-2. The location of the Donner Party camps in the Sierra Nevada.

In 1984, archaeologist Donald Hardesty of the University of Nevada returned to excavate at the presumed site of Murphy's Cabin, now in Donner Memorial State Park. He had four goals in mind in conducting this work. Most basically, he wanted to confirm that this was the correct site. He also wished to provide further details on the construction of the cabin and to recover material remains of the occupation there, to flesh out, as it were, what had happened within. Finally, he wanted to pursue what Bryant had observed: that a mass burial had been made within one of the cabins. Bryant had not indicated which cabin had been the scene of the burial, but McGlashan had dug in the two others, and had found no such thing. Murphy's Cabin remained as the obvious location.

With support from the National Geographic Society, Hardesty's work took place in 1984 and 1985. Over a century of relic collecting had taken its toll, and the artifactual rewards from his work were not high. In all other ways, however, he was successful, even if some of his successes were not what he had been after. He showed that this was the site of Murphy's Cabin, and that the building was slightly more than 18′ by 25′ in dimension. Several hearths had been built adjacent to the rock wall, and the door to the structure seems to have been placed opposite that wall. Just as the documentary evidence indicates, the whole had been burned. There was, however, no mass burial of human remains in the site: only a few scraps of bone that may be human were identified, even though bone as a whole was relatively well preserved. The location of Kearny's mass burial remains unknown.

Amy Dansie of the Nevada State Museum found that the bone Hardesty recovered came primarily from domestic cattle. This is no surprise, given that the stranded party ate their cattle, and then the skin of their cattle, as the winter progressed. Dansie also identified grizzly bear specimens from the cabin, matching the fact that William Eddy shot and killed a grizzly on November 12, 1846. The bear was shared with the Reeds, Graveses, and Fosters, Foster getting half since it was his gun that Eddy had used. Given that Foster shared Murphy's Cabin with Eddy, it seems odd that the only grizzly remains recovered from the cabin site were teeth and foot bones, parts of the body that have little meat attached, but there is some possibility that the rest of the skeleton had long since disappeared.

Although Hardesty's work recovered some 560 artifacts, many of these were small bits of glass and metal. Firearms were well represented in the collection—64 musket balls and 50 pieces of shot, for instance, along with three gunflints. The gunflints are of particular interest. The historical literature indicates that the Donner Party was largely equipped with percussion, not flintlock, weapons, but there was no indication of percussion weapons in the cabin. Hardesty also uncovered a variety of household gear—utensils, containers, and a cooking pot—as well as tobacco pipe fragments and ornaments. The ornaments included 12 glass beads and a small religious medal depicting Jesus on one side and the Virgin Mary on the other, a medal of the sort used by American Roman Catholics between 1825 and 1875.

Although Hardesty might not have learned all that he wanted to learn from his work at Murphy's Cabin, and in particular did not discover the location of the mass burial, he was able to establish securely the location of the cabin and to provide detailed information on the materials the Donner Party had carried with them.

After this success, Hardesty tackled an even more difficult issue. Whereas the location of Murphy's Cabin had been well described, the location of the Donner camp had not. The descriptions that are available suggest that three structures were built by the Donners and the four men who traveled with them. The families of George and Jacob Donner occupied tents covered with quilts, buffalo robes, and other material, with pine branch lean-tos built adjacent to the tents. The men traveling with the Donners built a third structure across the stream from the Donner encampment. It has long been thought that all three facilities were along Alder Creek (see Figure 10-2; this location is labeled "Northern Donner Camps" in this figure). However, not only has the precise location of these structures been unknown, but it has even been questioned whether Alder Creek was the stream involved.

During the summer of 1990, Hardesty and Susan Lindstrom began the process of solving these problems. Relying heavily on a combination of metal detectors and test excavations, they canvased the Alder Creek area in hopes of locating the Donner family camps. They soon discovered that the "George Donner Tree," felt by some to have been the tree against which the George Donner family built its lean-to, did not mark a camp location: they found no mid-nineteenth-century artifacts here at all. Elsewhere in the Alder Creek area, however, their results were quite different.

In what Hardesty and Lindstom call the Jacob Donner Meadow, they discovered musket balls, fragments of glass bottles, burned bone, charcoal, and other items. Among those other items were 33 fragments of decorated and plain ceramic dishes, including the base of a cup with a red and green flower painted on the inside. The material that came from this site is consistent with an 1846 date, and, as Hardesty and Lindstrom note, the amount of material they found is consistent with a fairly prolonged stay. Alder Creek, they concluded, is the correct location of the Donner family camps.

But is the Jacob Donner Meadow site the location of one of the Donner family structures? It is, at the moment, impossible to know: the items found here may represent the remains of the two structures built by the Donners, or the structure built by the four men who traveled with them. Only more work can answer this question. However, Hardesty and Lindstrom located a second concentration of material that also appears to have been left by the Donner group. At an area called Ant Hill Stump, they found six percussion caps and two coins. One of those coins is an 1830 U.S. Liberty penny. The other is an 1839 copper farthing from the Isle of Man. The only person in the Donner Party known to have come from England was John Denton, who passed part of the winter with the Donners at Alder Creek. Hardesty and Lindstrom are not convinced that the Ant Hill Stump site represents a dwelling, since there are no domestic artifacts here. They do, however, speculate that, if this is not the site of the structure built by the four men who traveled with the Donners, it may well mark the location of a Donner wagon or material dumped or lost from the Donner encampment.

Hardesty and Lindstrom spent only some five weeks at Alder Creek, but accomplished a tremendous amount in that time. They hope to return here; if they are able to, then some of the questions they have raised may well be answered in the near future. Answered already, however, were the questions that have lingered about the exact location of the Donner family encampment. Although the precise locations of the three dwellings remains in doubt, that Alder Creek was the spot now seems clear.

THE BONNEVILLE BASIN

Shortly after Hardesty began his work at the Murphy's Cabin site, archaeologists Bruce Hawkins and David Madsen began excavations some 325 miles to the northeast, in the Great Salt Lake Desert. Their focus was on the wagons left behind by the Donner Party east of Floating Island as they made their way toward Pilot Peak (Figure 5-7).

In working at Murphy's Cabin, Hardesty was simply pursuing research questions that intrigued him. Although Hawkins and Madsen were also pursuing their own set of research interests, their work was required by a scheme devised by the State of Utah in response to the extremely high levels reached by Great Salt Lake during the mid-1980s. To attempt to reduce the level of that lake, the state decided to pump water from it into the Great Salt Lake

Desert, where it would then evaporate. As part of the West Desert Pumping Project, as this enterprise was called, dikes were built to impound the pumped water between the Newfoundland Mountains on the east and Floating Island on the west. The impounded water would flood parts of Hastings Cutoff, including the area where the Donner Party abandoned four of their wagons. Hawkins and Madsen did their work in order to salvage what otherwise might have been destroyed by the rising waters.

Their preliminary efforts established the existence of five archaeological sites in this area, located between 3.7 and 5.4 miles east-southeast of Floating Island, and scattered along a 1.7-mile stretch of Hastings Cutoff. Each site had the potential of containing wagon remains, since not only had the Donner party left four wagons here, but a fifth had been abandoned in this area in 1850.

How much might be left at these sites, however, was not at all clear. Other emigrants might have salvaged items left behind by the Donner-Reed party, and two later expeditions were known to have used the sites.

In the fall of 1847, a detachment of the Mormon Battalion returned from California to Salt Lake City. They began their trip with Kearny, and thus were in the group that came across the Donner Party encampment in the Sierra Nevada. They took the Great Salt Lake Desert route to Salt Lake City, and, on their way, camped by wagons that had been abandoned east of Floating Island. While there, they used parts of those wagons for firewood.

Two years later, on November 2, 1849, Howard Stansbury passed this way during his survey of the Great Salt Lake region. As Stansbury said, "We passed during the night 4 wagons & one cart, with innumerable articles of clothing, tools chests trunks books &c yokes, chains, & some half dozen dead oxen. Encamped on the wet sand & had for wood part of an ox yoke & the remains of a barrel & part of an old wagon bed. The whole plain is as desolate barren & dreary as can well be imagined" (Madsen 1990a: 185).

In addition to these early impacts, Hawkins and Madsen documented 15 separate collecting expeditions to the area since the 1870s, expeditions that scattered some artifacts to museums but most to oblivion (see Figure 10-3). A 1929 collecting expedition visited a site called the "birds nests," some 19 miles southeast of Floating Island (see Figure 10-4). From here, the expedition retrieved wagon parts, wooden-pegged leather boot soles, the remains of a tar bucket, and broken ceramics. Among those ceramics is the decorated base of a teacup so similar to that which Hardesty and Lindstrom found at the Jacob Donner Meadow site at Alder Creek that they suggested it probably came from the same set.

Three of the sites excavated by Hawkins and Madsen still preserved the ruts made by the wagons as they passed through; bearings taken on these ruts showed them to be aligned with one another. The ruts at two locations measured 58″ and 59″ across, a standard size for emigrant wagons of this period.

The ruts in the third site, however, were 86″ across. The Reeds had brought an immense, double-decker wagon with them, named the "Pioneer Palace" by Virginia Reed. Although no detailed description of this huge wagon exists, it was one of the three wagons belonging to Reed that got stuck near Floating Island. It was also the only one Reed was able to retrieve. The 86″ ruts appear to have been made by the Pioneer Palace, and Hawkins and Madsen appear to have discovered the exact spot at which this luxury vehicle—the Pioneer Winnebago, as Madsen calls it—had been temporarily abandoned. They found no wagon parts at this spot, but they did find a variety of artifacts, including medicine bottles and a shaving brush. The latter appears to have belonged to James Reed himself.

Four of the sites provided wagon parts, either to Hawkins and Madsen or to earlier collecting parties. These sites contained the remains of at least three wagons (two of the sites are so close together that the same wagon may be represented), and perhaps more.

It even appears that they discovered where Stansbury camped on that November night. This, Hawkins and Madsen infer, was at site 42To469 (see Figures 10-4 and 10-5). In addition to wagon parts and ruts spaced 59″ apart, 42To469 provided two large areas of charcoal and ash, as well as buttons from a military uniform, percussion caps, and seven geological specimens that could only have come from mountains to the west or north of the site itself. Although the percussion caps could have belonged to members of the Donner party, the military buttons and geological specimens, along with the charcoal deposits, suggest that this is the spot where Stansbury "encamped on the wet sand" and burned wagon parts for comfort.

What the ground provided to Hawkins and Madsen contrasts in a number of ways with what it provided to Hardesty. The ornaments that were relatively common at Murphy's Cabin have no counterpart at the abandoned

Figure 10-3. Photograph taken during a 1929 excavation of what is now thought to be site 42To469. Floating Island is in the left distance; the Silver Island Range is in the far distance. Photo courtesy of David B. Madsen and the Utah State Historical Society.

wagon sites, nor do the tobacco pipes. Although the domestic items—the kinds of china and stoneware, for instance—from the two collections are very similar, they are far more common at the wagon sites. Inexpensive jewelry and pipes do not appear to have been abandoned in the desert, perhaps because what was abandoned early on was heavy or bulky or both, although jewelry and tobacco have associated symbolic and physical values that make them

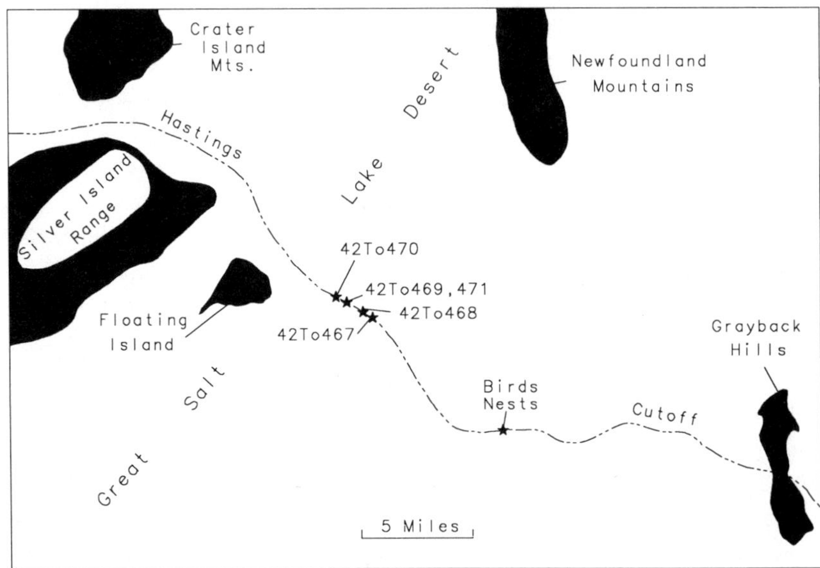

Figure 10-4. Wagon sites along Hastings Cutoff. After Hawkins and Madsen (1990).

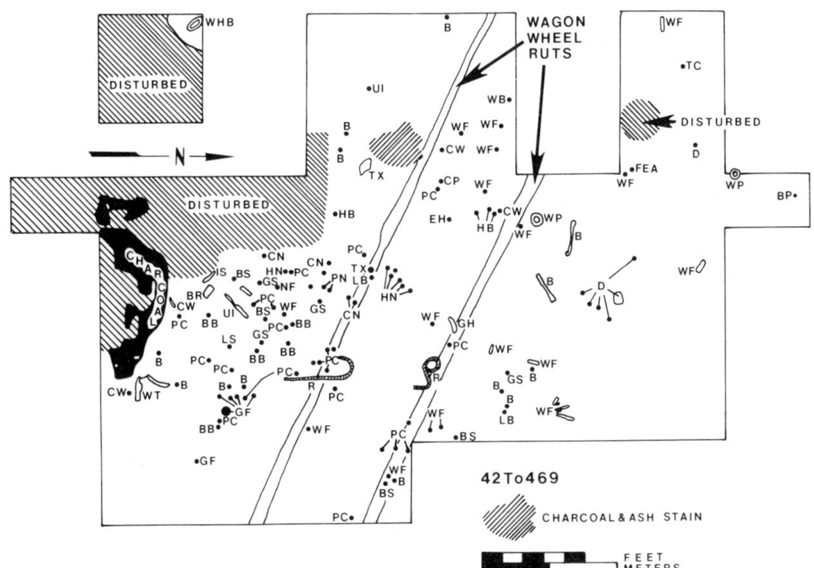

Figure 10-5. Site 42To469. B, bone; BB, button; BR, brush; BP, barrel plug; BS, botanical specimen; CN, cut nail; CP, canteen plug; CW, charred wood; D, dung; EH, earthenware handle; FEA, feathers; GF, glass fragments; GH, grass hook blade; GS, geological specimen; HB, harness buckle; HN, horse or ox shoe nail; IS, iron strap; LB, lead ball; LS, lead shot; PC, percussion cap; PN, pin; R, rope; TC, tack part (?); TX, textile; UI, unidentified iron object; WB, wagon axle brace; WF, wood fragment WHB, wagon hub band; WP, wagon part; WT, wagon tire. Drawing courtesy of David B. Madsen.

more valuable than extra plates. Certainly, a religious medal depicting Jesus and the Virgin Mary is not to be purposely left behind during hard times. Artifacts relating to weapons were common at the wagon sites, as they were at Murphy's Cabin: this was a well-armed group. Hawkins and Madsen found both gunflints and percussion caps; Hardesty and Lindstrom found the latter at Alder Creek, but not at Murphy's Cabin.

It is hard to know whether the percussion caps found east of Floating Island were left by the Donner Party or by later peoples. In fact, it is not even possible to be certain that all five of these sites relate to the Donner Party, since others abandoned, or might have abandoned, wagons here as well. The position and spacing of the ruts, however, is convincing, and it is hard to see that there can be much doubt about the ruts from the Pioneer Palace, or about the location of Stansbury's camp on November 2, 1849.

Assuming that more extensive excavations in the Sierran encampment will provide larger samples of material remains left behind by the Donner Party, the potential of such work to shed light on the Donner Party experience has just begun to be tapped. For instance, the diaries indicate that food was shared not just within families, but also between them. To give one example, the bear shot by William Eddy in mid-November was shared by the Eddy, Foster, Graves, and Reed families. If the bone preservation in the separate Donner Party structures is good enough, then careful work could document how much food sharing of this sort went on, and whether there is a relationship between such sharing and survivorship rates. Given adequate preservation, a continuation of the archaeological studies that have already been started here not only might determine the exact location of each of the Donner Party structures, and add the humanizing touches provided by such things as James Reed's shaving brush and the Isle of Man farthing, but could also help us better understand exactly why the various members of the Donner Party suffered the fates they did. Much could be learned about human biology as a result.

Notes

On the Bidwell-Bartleson group, see Nunis (1991). Basic references on the Donner-Reed party include C. G. McGlashan (1800) and Stewart (1960), the latter the source of my information on the members of the Donner Party. In some cases, ages provided by J. A. King (1992) differ from those provided by Stewart, but I have not redone my analysis of the Donner Party to take King's work into account. Any differences in the results would be minor. For McGlashan's letters to Eliza Donner, the youngest Donner daughter, see M. N. McGlashan and McGlashan (1986); on McGlashan himself, see M. N. McGlashan (1977). Table 10-1 lists only 14 people as Donners, but the two Hook children were Elizabeth Donner's sons by a previous marriage.

Many other accounts of the Donner Party ordeal exist: see, for instance, Murphy (1980), which provides Virginia

Reed's story. Smart (1988) contains a well-illustrated discussion of the Utah section of Hastings's cutoff. Stewart (1953) provides Moses Schallenberger's "Overland in 1844," a narrative of the Stevens party journey, along with an analysis of that document. For an important study of overland travel during the 1840s and 1850s, see Unruh (1979); this is my source for the numbers of emigrants going overland to Oregon and California during the 1840s. The journals of Edwin Bryant, Heinrich Lienhard, and James Reed are published in Korns (1951); see also Bryant's classic book on his 1846 trip (Bryant 1848). Clyman's journals are in Camp (1960) and Clyman (1984). Curran (1982) is the best source on the details of the Central Overland Trail in Nevada. My discussion of Frémont's passage across the Great Salt Lake desert is taken from Frémont (1887) and Quaife (1966). My comments on Hastings's life are taken from C. H. Carey (1932). Revisionist views of Hastings's role in the Donner-Reed tragedy are found in Andrews (1973) and Topping (1990).

For a more detailed analysis of Donner Party deaths and demographics, see Grayson (1990), from which my discussion is drawn. On human age-specific mortality rates, see Bogue (1969); for age-related mortality due to starvation and cold, see Rivers (1988), Harrison et al. (1988), and Seaman et al. (1984). Bogue (1969) and de Jong (1972) discuss the relationship between sex and mortality; whether the differences in longevity between males and females are cultural or biological in origin is discussed by Nathanson (1984), Stinson (1985), Verbrugge (1985, 1989), and Waldron (1983). That cultural factors may tip the scales is clear; that women are the physiologically stronger sex is a biological fact. See Atmar (1991) for a discussion of the fragility of males in general and for an intriguing account of why this may be the case. Rivers (1982, 1988) develops the argument that women should fare better than men under conditions marked by cold and/or famine; see also Harrison et al. (1988) and Widdowson (1976). On male deaths due to violence see Wingard (1984) and Nathanson (1984). The relationship between participation in social networks and longevity has been developed in many places: see Berkman and Syme (1979), Berkman (1984), Blazer (1982), House et al. (1982), and the discussion in Verbrugge (1985). On social networks in times of stress, see Neal et al. (1988). My comments on age and sex differences in basal metabolic rate are based largely on Durnin and Passmore (1967).

See Hardesty (1987) for his Murphy's Cabin results, including Dansie's work, and Hardesty and Lindstrom (1990) for the Alder Creek work. Hawkins and Madsen (1990) discuss their work east of Floating Island, and summarize what is known of the results of earlier collecting at the wagon sites. On the Mormon Battalion, see Bancroft (1982) and Stegner (1981); on this battalion and the abandoned Donner Party wagons, see Topping (1990). B. D. Madsen (1990a,b) discusses the relationship between those wagons and Stansbury's November campsite.

The Donner Party wagon sites are on Hill Air Force Base and are not accessible to the public. The Murphy's Cabin site, however, is part of Donner Memorial State Park. This park is just south of I-80 a short distance west of Truckee, California; in addition to the well-marked cabin site, it includes an interpretive center and trail. The Alder Creek location is only a few miles from Donner Memorial State Park, and is on land administered by the U.S. Forest Service. To visit, take the Highway 89 exit from I-80 and travel north for three miles; turn right at the "Tahoe National Forest–Donner Campground" sign. There is an interpretive trail here, but Hardesty and Lindstrom (1990) have shown that some of the signs will have to be redone.

Sutter's Fort has been reconstructed, and is now part of the California State Park System. Located in Sacramento (27th and L Streets), Sutter's Fort State Historic Park has a Donner Party display that includes Virginia Reed's doll. There is a small admission fee; for information, call (916) 445-4422.

On the eastern edge of the Great Basin, Grantsville, Utah, is home to the Donner-Reed Pioneer Museum. This museum, in an 1861 schoolhouse, contains a diverse variety of pioneer artifacts collected from Hastings Cutoff, including many from the Donner Party sites themselves; a number of these are illustrated in Hawkins and Madsen (1990). Grantsville is just south of I-80, some 40 miles southwest of Salt Lake City. Visiting the museum usually requires a stop at the Grantsville City Hall (at the corner of Park and Main streets) to obtain a guide; those on a tight schedule might wish to call ahead.

PART SIX

○○○

Conclusions

CHAPTER ELEVEN

○○○

Cougars, Cheatgrass, and the Natural Landscape

It has become almost routine to close regional natural histories of the New World with discussions of all the disastrous things that have happened since the arrival of Europeans, and of the dire consequences that will emerge if we do not change our ways. The warnings are warranted. The nature of the human world is driven, for good and bad, by population increase, and both technological advances and environmental degradation follow as a result.

The technological advances follow in part from the greater number of innovators found in larger populations. They also follow from the increasing specialization that is made possible by greater numbers of people working in a context in which knowledge has been made cumulative by the printing press. Environmental degradation follows from the sheer impact that so many people have on the "natural" landscape.

It is also true, however, that many of the concerns expressed by those worried about the fate of natural landscapes in the New World tend to lose track of the fact that it is not always easy to know what a "natural" landscape really is. Many Americans—natural history writers included—have a highly romanticized view of native Americans, one in which Indians are presumed to have lived in peace and harmony with the natural world, as if they were intellectually akin to deer, bears, or fish. In this view, North America prior to the arrival of Europeans was pristine; North America after that arrival, despoiled.

That view is wrong in many ways. The prehistoric peoples of the New World were, after all, people, and had significant impacts on their environment. The hunters and gatherers of the Great Basin were no exception. As I mentioned in Chapter 2, a communal pronghorn hunt in a Great Basin valley might not be repeated for a decade, since it took that long for the animals to recover. In the White Mountains, mountain sheep are far less common in the village than in the previllage occupations, perhaps reflecting the decimation of mountain sheep populations as a result of human predation (see Chapter 9). The landscape that Europeans encountered when they first arrived in the Great Basin was not "pristine," if by pristine we mean "devoid of significant human influence."

Nonetheless, the magnitude of European impacts on Great Basin environments has been far greater than anything wrought by native Americans, a function of the vast technological differences between the two sets of people.

Some of the impacts are obvious: Reno, Las Vegas, and Salt Lake City provide examples; the Newlands Project in the Truckee and Carson river basins and the diversion of the waters of Mono Lake and Owens Valley are others.

There are changes that have occurred in Great Basin ecosystems as a result of the European arrival that are far less immediately evident than these. I close this volume by discussing two of them.

Deer, Cougars, Cattle, and Native Americans

European explorers and early settlers routinely noted the scarcity of deer in the Great Basin. Today, however, deer are abundant here. As James Moffit (1934:53) noted for the area surrounding Lower Klamath Lake, in the late nineteenth century "one could ride for a day without seeing a deer in regions where similar excursions would today reveal many of these animals."

That deer have undergone a tremendous increase in abundance in the Great Basin during the past century or so has been known for many years. Archaeological and paleontological work undertaken during the past few decades has now expanded this picture by showing that deer were also uncommon during later prehistoric times. The faunas from the White Mountains sites, for instance, held but 4 specimens of deer, compared to over 500 of mountain sheep. In fact, there were even more specimens of pronghorn here (seven) than of deer, even though pronghorn are hardly animals of the alpine tundra. Many other sites tell the same story: deer are probably now far more abundant in the Great Basin then they were during the preceding 10,000 years.

Zoologists Joel Berger and John Wehausen have recently observed one of the apparent side effects of this population explosion. To judge from archaeological and paleontological faunas, mountain lions or cougars (*Felis concolor*) were also rare in the Great Basin during late prehistoric times. That cougars are virtually absent from late prehistoric faunas does not reflect a general scarcity of carnivores from these sites: bobcats (*Lynx rufus*), coyotes (*Canis latrans*), and badgers (*Taxidea taxus*) are routinely found in Holocene faunas, and even such historically rare carnivores as bears (*Ursus americanus*) and wolves (*Canis lupus*) are known from these sites.

Although the remains of cougars are extremely rare in prehistoric sites, they are sighted with some frequency in the Great Basin today. It appears that cougars are now far more abundant in this region than they were during late prehistoric times, and perhaps even far more abundant than they have been since at least the end of the early Holocene, some 7,500 years ago.

That deer were rare prehistorically eliminates one possible explanation for their increase in historic times. It might be argued that the increased abundance of deer during the last century simply reflects the removal of native American hunting pressure on these animals. Deer were scarce in early historic times, this argument would go, because Indian hunting kept their numbers down; deer populations rebounded when that hunting declined.

There is nothing conceptually wrong with that argument. Some years ago, anthropologist Harold Hickerson showed that adjacent but hostile groups of Chippewa and Sioux in western Wisconsin and central Minnesota had virtually eliminated deer from their respective territories. Those territories, however, were separated by a buffer zone that was controlled by neither group but coveted by both. If either Sioux or Chippewa entered that zone, they risked armed confrontation with their enemies. Freed from hunting pressure, deer abounded here.

Although conceptually sound, the hunting pressure argument will not work in the Great Basin. Archaeological faunas show that deer were rarely taken in any number prehistorically. The implication is that these animals were rare long before the European arrival, and that their rarity has little or nothing to do with native American hunting. As a result, their increase in historic times can have nothing to do with the removal of native American hunting pressure.

It is far more likely that the modern abundance of these animals in the Great Basin has resulted from complex interactions among plants, domestic livestock, and the deer themselves. Berger and Wehausen, among others, note that the introduction of cattle, sheep, and horses into the Great Basin led to the removal of grasses and to the spread of plant species favorable to deer (see the next section). In response to this massive habitat alteration, deer expanded tremendously in number.

Berger and Wehausen also observe that it is not likely to be coincidental that cougars have increased in number at the same time as deer have increased. Deer provide prime prey for these large carnivores, and Berger and Wehausen argue that cougars have become more abundant because their prey has become so.

That this is likely to be the case raises an intriguing question, as Berger and Wehausen point out. The increased abundance of cougars in the Great Basin would seem to follow from the increased abundance of deer. The increased abundance of deer follows from the introduction of exotic livestock. If one of the goals of modern conservation biology is to foster the maintenance of environments that are as close to "natural" as possible, then what does one do about the cougars? Should conservation biologists applaud the healthy Great Basin populations of this magnificent and relatively uncommon carnivore, or should they instead bemoan the fact that the current abundance of cougars here is a direct result of the introduction of exotic herbivores?

Native Plants, Livestock, Cheatgrass, and Fire

The native grasses of the floristic Great Basin are not adapted to heavy grazing by large mammals. Richard Mack has observed that native Great Basin grasses often fail to reproduce if heavily trampled, and that they have difficulty replacing leaf area lost to grazers. In addition, the floristic Great Basin lacks annual grasses and herbs that aggressively colonize heavily grazed sagebrush steppe, and the native perennial grasses that reproduce from seed are unable to store sufficient carbohydrates to flower and set seed under conditions of heavy grazing. Big sage (*Artemisia tridentata*), on the other hand, contains volatile oils that retard digestion by cattle if taken in large amounts, greasewood (*Sarcobatus*) is toxic to larger herbivores, and rabbitbrush (*Chrysothamnus*) is not preferred browse for livestock.

As a result, the introduction of exotic livestock—cattle, sheep, and horses—into the sagebrush steppe quickly led to the loss of native grasses and to the increase of shrubby vegetation. The speed with which that transition occurred is impressive. James A. Young and B. Abbott Sparks point out that the first cattle were wintered in Nevada in 1851. By the 1880s, many who lived in the Great Basin felt that the countryside was already overgrazed: the sagebrush steppe of the intermountain area had been "destroyed in forty years of domestic livestock grazing" (Young and Sparks 1985:234).

The introduction of domestic livestock, as well as the advent of farming, in the Great Basin created disturbed environments that provided superb habitat for weedy species. Prime among these was downy brome or cheatgrass (*Bromus tectorum*), an aggressive annual grass that produces seed between fall and spring and then dies, leaving its seed behind.

Cheatgrass is native not to North America, but to the arid steppes of central Eurasia, where it evolved in the presence of large herds of grazing ungulates in an environment characterized by wet, cold winters and hot, dry summers. That is, it evolved in conditions much like those found in the sagebrush steppe of the floristic Great Basin once the introduction of livestock had taken its toll.

It is not clear exactly when cheatgrass was first introduced into the Great Basin, but Mack has established that it had been introduced to interior British Columbia by 1889, to eastern Washington by 1893, and to Provo, Utah, by 1894. The fact that all of these areas were then producing wheat suggests to Mack that seeds of this plant were introduced as a contaminant in shipments of wheat seed. As he notes, however, it was probably introduced in other ways as well. Cheatgrass was purposely grown at Pullman, Washington, in 1897, and could have spread from there. It could also have spread in the dung of cattle brought from outside the region, and even in straw used for packing.

However it arrived in the Great Basin, it was here by the 1890s. By 1930, it had reached its current distribution, found across more than 160,000 square miles of the intermountain west, from southern British Columbia through southern Nevada and Utah.

Chatgrass obtained its common name from the fact that it readily invaded areas that had been plowed for wheat on the Columbia Plateau, and often cheated farmers of their crops. Both on the Columbia Plateau and in the floristic Great Basin to the south, cheatgrass also outcompetes native grasses, both perennial and annual, on disturbed sites. In addition, it thrives on fire.

In wet years, cheatgrass fills in the voids that would otherwise appear between shrubs, and produces heavy loads of easily ignited debris. Young and Sparks noted that, in response to late spring rains, cheatgrass productivity was high in northeastern Nevada's Elko County in 1964, experimental plots providing range scientists with 4,000 pounds of this plant per acre. Not coincidentally, some 300,000 acres of Elko County went up in flames in the summer of that year.

Because of the spread of cheatgrass, it is very likely that fires are now far more frequent in the sagebrush steppe than they were in the past. Unfortunately, the very fires that cheatgrass fosters in turn foster cheatgrass. The cycle, elaborated in detail by Young and his colleagues, is fairly simple. Cheatgrass tends to mature and drop its seeds before the native perennial grasses and herbs have done so. As a result, the fires that cheatgrass helps create tend to destroy any native perennial grasses that might have been present. Since some cheatgrass seeds survive all but the heaviest fires, it returns in abundance. Even if perennial grasses manage to seed themselves—problematic, since they have been so reduced by overgrazing—they are at a strong competitive disadvantage. Grant Harris has shown that, compared to bluebunch wheatgrass (*Agropyron spicatum*), a native perennial, cheatgrass germinates earlier in the fall and has roots that grow faster in the winter. As a result, cheatgrass exhausts the soil moisture that would otherwise be available to bluebunch wheatgrass, which thus succumbs to drought. As Young and his colleague Raymond Evans put it, "the dominance of downy brome after wildfires in sagebrush grasslands resembles the phoenix of an alien life form rising from the ashes to haunt the post-burn environment" (Young and Evans 1978:288).

There is every reason to believe that the floristic Great Basin has been unalterably changed as a result of these relationships. Even a decrease in grazing pressure will not bring back the native grasses, since the immediate effects of such a decrease would likely be an increase in the amount of fuel on the Great Basin landscape. Increased fuel means more fires, and that plays into the hands, or more appropriately, the seeds, of cheatgrass.

Conclusions

Human history in the Great Basin cannot be separated from the history of Great Basin environments. During most of the last 11,500 years or so, it was the people who reacted to major environmental change. The correlation between human prehistory and environmental history in the Great Basin is striking, as the human responses to the desiccation of shallow lakes and marshes at the end of the early Holocene and to the aridity of the middle Holocene show.

During the last century, the situation has been reversed, and it is now primarily the environment that reacts to human influence. The future for the Great Basin will almost certainly be the same. The only question regards the magnitude and direction of change, and how much we will do to influence the outcome in a purposeful way.

Those who simply drive through the Great Basin may come away with the impression that much of what they have seen is sheer wilderness. In fact, much of what they have seen has been heavily modified by human activities. Even the deer that many find so exciting reflect the presence of exotic livestock as much as they reflect anything else.

Many, though not all, of the substantial areas within the Great Basin that can be considered to be in a generally natural condition are to be found toward the tops of the higher mountains. Many of these remote areas have been significantly modified during the past century, but they are under increasing pressure today. That pressure comes not just from obvious sources, like mining, but also from almost unpredictable ones. When the University of Arizona was reviewing mountains on which to place the new and highly controversial telescope facility it hoped to build, it included Mount Wheeler (Snake Range), Mount Jefferson (Toquima Range), and Arc Dome (Toiyabe Range) on its list. That it did so was astounding. The southern Snake Range had long been discussed for national park status, and the summit of the Toquima Range had already been set aside as a Research Natural Area. The university chose Mount Graham, on Arizona's Pinaleño Mountains, for the facility, and immediately became involved in a legal and ethical battle over its plans. Today, on the other hand, Mount Wheeler is the heart of Great Basin National Park, Mount Jefferson the heart of the Alta Toquima Wilderness, and Arc Dome the heart of the Arc Dome Wilderness.

Indeed, the passage of the Nevada Wilderness Protection Act (Public Law 101-195) in 1989 set aside some 733,000 acres on 14 mountain ranges, including the Alta Toquima and Arc Dome wilderness areas. That act was the product of substantial compromise, protecting only half of the area initially proposed. But at least these wilderness areas now exist, providing some protection for long-isolated populations of montane mammals and for significant areas of fragile alpine tundra. The floras and faunas of other Great Basin states are not so fortunate. The Great Basin sections of Utah and Oregon have only one wilderness area each: in Utah, the Deseret Peak Wilderness protects 25,500 acres of the Stansbury Mountains; in Oregon, the Gearhart Wilderness protects 22,800 acres astride the Klamath and Lake Abert drainages. Decisions are still to be rendered on vast areas currently under study for possible protection in one form or another, including parts of the Black Rock Desert, Steens Mountain, the Deep Creek Range, and the

Wah Wah Mountains. It remains to be seen how proficient Great Basin states and the federal government will prove to be at balancing economic goals with the preservation of what remains of those areas that might still be defined as parts of the natural landscape.

Notes

Eisenstein (1979) evaluates the profound impact of the printing press on western history. The story of the Newlands Project is provided by Townley (1977). Berger and Wehausen (1991) discuss the recent history of deer and cougars in the Great Basin; see also Berger (1986) on the relationship among horses, cattle, and deer. Hickerson (1965) analyzed the role of boundary zones in maintaining mammalian populations. My discussion of cheatgrass, native plants, and livestock is drawn from Harris (1977), Mack (1981, 1984, 1986), Mack and Thompson (1982), Young et al. (1972, 1976, 1979), Young and Evans (1973, 1978), Young and Sparks (1985), and West (1988). On sagebrush as food for herbivores, see Nagy (1979); for a general discussion of cheatgrass, see Klemmedson and Smith (1964). The history of the establishment of Great Basin National Park is reviewed in Lambert (1991). My comments on the ranges included on the list of possible settings for the University of Arizona's proposed telescope facility are based on an unpublished talk given by Peter Strittmatter on October 21, 1989, at the Workshop on the Biology of Mount Graham, sponsored by the University of Arizona and the Smithsonian Institution. On Utah wilderness, see the important book by the Utah Wilderness Coalition (1990); on Nevada mountains, see Wuethner (1992).

APPENDIX

○○○

Concordance of Common and Scientific Plant Names

By Common Name

Alkali bulrush	*Scirpus maritimus*
Alkali sacaton grass	*Sporobulus airoides*
Alpine chickweed	*Cerastium berringianum*
Arrow weed	*Pluchea sericea*
Bailey's greasewood	*Sarcobatus baileyi*
Baltic rush	*Juncus balticus*
Beaked sedge	*Carex rostrata*
Beavertail cactus	*Opuntia basilaris*
Big greasewood	*Sarcobatus vermiculatus*
Big sagebrush	*Artemisia tridentata*
Bigtooth maple	*Acer grandidentatum*
Black sagebrush	*Artemisia arbuscula*
Blue spruce	*Picea pungens*
Bristlecone pine	*Pinus longaeva*
Brittle bush	*Encelia farinosa*
Bud sage	*Artemisia spinescens*
Bulrush	*Scirpus* spp.
Cattail	*Typha* spp.
Cheatgrass (downy brome)	*Bromus tectorum*
Chia	*Salvia columbariae*
Cliffrose	*Cowania mexicana*
Colorado piñon	*Pinus edulis*
Common cattail	*Typha latifolia*
Common juniper	*Juniperus communis*
Creosote bush	*Larrea tridentata*
Curlleaf mountain mahogany	*Cercocarpus ledifolius*
Desert almond	*Prunus fasciculata*
Desert holly	*Atriplex hymenelytra*
Desert peach	*Prunus andersonii*
Desert saltbush	*Atriplex polycarpa*
Desert spruce	*Peucephyllum schottii*
Ditchgrass	*Ruppia* spp.
Douglas-fir	*Pseudotsuga menziesii*
Englemann spruce	*Picea englemannii*
Fern bush	*Chamaebatiara millifolium*
Four-winged saltbush	*Atriplex canescens*
Fremont cottonwood	*Populus fremontii*
Gambel oak	*Quercus gambelii*
Grand fir	*Abies grandis*
Great Basin wildrye	*Elymus cinereus*
Green rabbitbrush	*Chrysothamnus viscidiflorus*
Hardstem bulrush	*Scirpus acutus*
Honey mesquite	*Prosopis juliflora*
Horsebrush	*Tetradymia* spp.

Incense-cedar	*Calocedrus decurrens*
Indian ricegrass	*Oryzopsis hymenoides*
Jeffrey pine	*Pinus jeffreyi*
Joshua tree	*Yucca brevifolia*
Limber pine	*Pinus flexilis*
Lodgepole pine	*Pinus contorta*
Mormon tea	*Ephedra viridis*
Mountain avens	*Dryas* spp.
Mountain hemlock	*Tsuga mertensiana*
Mountain mahogany	*Cercocarpus* spp.
Nevada Mormon tea	*Ephedra nevadensis*
Nuttall's saltbush	*Atriplex nuttallii*
Ocean spray	*Holodiscus* spp.
Pickleweed	*Allenrolfea occidentalis*
Ponderosa pine	*Pinus ponderosa*
Quaking aspen	*Populus tremuloides*
Rabbitbrush	*Chrysothamnus* spp.
Red fir	*Abies magnifica*
Rocky Mountain juniper	*Juniperus scopulorum*
Rubber rabbitbrush	*Chrysothamnus nauseosus*
Sagebrush	*Artemisia* spp.
Saltbush	*Atriplex* spp.
Saltgrass	*Distichlis spicata*
Screw bean mesquite	*Prosopis pubescens*
Shadscale	*Atriplex confertifolia*
Shrubby cinquefoil	*Potentilla fruticosa*
Silver buffaloberry	*Shepherdia argentea*
Silverweed	*Potentilla anserina*
Simpson's pediocactus	*Pediocactus simpsonii*
Singleleaf piñon pine	*Pinus monophylla*
Smokebush	*Psorothamnus polydenius*
Snowberry	*Symphoricarpos* spp.
Subalpine fir	*Abies lasiocarpa*
Sugar pine	*Pinus lambertiana*
Tamarisk	*Tamarix* spp.
Torrey inkweed	*Suaeda torreyana*
Torrey saltbush	*Atriplex torreyi*
Utah juniper	*Juniperus osteosperma*
Washoe pine	*Pinus washoensis*
Western juniper	*Juniperus occidentalis*
Western white pine	*Pinus monticola*
Whipple yucca	*Yucca whipplei*
White bursage	*Ambrosia dumosa*
White fir	*Abies concolor*
Whitebark pine	*Pinus albicaulis*
Winterfat	*Ceratoides lanata*

By Scientific Name

Abies concolor	White fir
Abies grandis	Grand fir
Abies lasiocarpa	Subalpine fir
Abies magnifica	Red fir
Acer grandidentatum	Bigtooth maple
Allenrolfea occidentalis	Pickleweed
Ambrosia dumosa	White bursage
Artemisia spp.	Sagebrush
Artemisia arbuscula	Black sagebrush
Artemisia spinescens	Bud sage
Artemisia tridentata	Big sagebrush
Atriplex spp.	Saltbush
Atriplex canescens	Four-winged saltbush
Atriplex confertifolia	Shadscale
Atriplex hymenelytra	Desert holly
Atriplex nuttalli	Nuttall's saltbush
Atriplex polycarpa	Desert saltbush
Atriplex torreyi	Torrey saltbush
Bromus tectorum	Cheatgrass (downy brome)
Calocedrus decurrens	Incense-cedar
Carex rostrata	Beaked sedge
Cerastium berringianum	Alpine chickweed
Ceratoides lanata	Winterfat
Cercocarpus spp.	Mountain mahogany
Cercocarpus ledifolius	Curlleaf mountain mahogany
Chamaebatiara millifolium	Fern bush
Chrysothamnus spp.	Rabbitbrush
Chrysothamnus nauseosus	Rubber rabbitbrush
Chrysothamnus viscidiflorus	Green rabbitbrush
Cowania mexicana	Cliffrose
Distichlis spicata	Saltgrass
Dryas spp.	Mountain avens
Elymus cinereus	Great Basin wildrye
Encelia farinosa	Brittle bush
Ephedra nevadensis	Nevada Mormon tea
Ephedra viridis	Mormon tea
Holodiscus spp.	Ocean spray
Juncus balticus	Baltic rush
Juniperus communis	Common juniper
Juniperus occidentalis	Western juniper
Juniperus osteosperma	Utah juniper
Juniperus scopulorum	Rocky Mountain juniper
Larrea tridentata	Creosote bush
Opuntia basilaris	Beavertail cactus

Oryzopsis hymenoides	Indian ricegrass
Pediocactus simpsonii	Simpson's pediocactus
Peucephyllum schottii	Desert spruce
Picea englemannii	Englemann spruce
Picea pungens	Blue spruce
Pinus albicaulis	Whitebark pine
Pinus contorta	Lodgepole pine
Pinus edulis	Colorado piñon
Pinus flexilis	Limber pine
Pinus jeffreyi	Jeffrey pine
Pinus lambertiana	Sugar pine
Pinus longaeva	Bristlecone pine
Pinus monophylla	Singleleaf piñon pine
Pinus monticola	Western white pine
Pinus ponderosa	Ponderosa pine
Pinus washoensis	Washoe pine
Pluchea sericea	Arrow weed
Populus fremontii	Fremont cottonwood
Populus tremuloides	Quaking aspen
Potentilla anserina	Silverweed
Potentilla fruticosa	Shrubby cinquefoil
Prosopis juliflora	Honey mesquite
Prosopis pubescens	Screw bean mesquite
Prunus andersonii	Desert peach
Prunus fasciculata	Desert almond
Pseudotsuga menziesii	Douglas-fir
Psorothamnus polydenius	Smokebush
Quercus gambelii	Gambel oak
Ruppia spp.	Ditchgrass
Salvia columbariae	Chia
Sarcobatus baileyi	Bailey's greasewood
Sarcobatus vermiculatus	Big greasewood
Scirpus spp.	Bulrush
Scirpus acutus	Hardstem bulrush
Scirpus maritimus	Alkali bulrush
Shepherdia argentea	Silver buffaloberry
Sporobulus airoides	Alkali sacaton grass
Suaeda torreyana	Torrey inkweed
Symphoricarpos spp.	Snowberry
Tamarix spp.	Tamarisk
Tetradymia spp.	Horsebrush
Tsuga mertensiana	Mountain hemlock
Typha spp.	Cattail
Typha latifolia	Common cattail
Yucca brevifolia	Joshua tree
Yucca whipplei	Whipple yucca

○○○

Literature Cited

Adam, D. P. 1967. Late-Pleistocene and recent palynology in the central Sierra Nevada, California. In *Quaternary Paleoecology,* edited by E. J. Cushing and H. E. Wright, Jr., pp. 275–302. Yale University Press, New Haven, Connecticut.

Adam, D. P. 1985. Quaternary pollen records from California. In *Pollen Records of Late-Quaternary North American Sediments,* edited by V. M. Bryant, Jr., and R. G. Holloway, pp. 125–140. American Association of Stratigraphic Palynologists, Dallas.

Adam, D. P., A. M. Sarna-Wojcicki, H. J. Rieck, J. P. Bradbury, W. E. Dean, and R. M. Forester. 1989. Tulelake, California: The last 3 million years. *Palaeogeography, Palaeoclimatology, Palaeoecology* 72:89–103.

Adams, J. L. 1988. Use-wear analyses on manos and hide-processing stones. *Journal of Field Archaeology* 15:307–315.

Adovasio, J. M. 1975. Fremont basketry. *Tebiwa* 17(2):67–76.

Adovasio, J. M. 1980. Fremont: An artifactual perspective. In *Fremont Perspectives,* edited by D. B. Madsen, pp. 35–40. Selected Papers 7(16). State of Utah Division of State History Antiquities Section.

Adovasio, J. M. 1986a. Artifacts and ethnicity: Basketry as an indicator of territoriality and population movements in the prehistoric Great Basin. In *Anthropology of the Desert West: Essays in Honor of Jesse D. Jennings,* edited by C. J. Condie and D. D. Fowler, pp. 43–88. University of Utah Anthropological Papers 110.

Adovasio, J. M. 1986b. Prehistoric basketry. In *Handbook of North American Indians,* Volume 11: *Great Basin,* edited by W. L. d'Azevedo, pp. 194–205. Smithsonian Institution Press, Washington, D.C.

Adovasio, J. M., and R. C. Carlisle. 1988. The Meadowcroft Rockshelter. *Science* 239:713–714.

Adovasio, J. M., J. D. Gunn, J. Donahue, R. Stuckenrath, J. E. Guilday, and K. Volman. 1980. Yes, Virginia, it really is that old: A reply to Haynes and Mead. *American Antiquity* 45:588–595.

Adovasio, J. M., A. T. Boldurian, and R. C. Carlisle. 1988. Who are those guys? Some biased thoughts on the initial peopling of the New World. In *Americans before Columbus: Ice-Age Origins,* edited by R. C. Carlisle, pp. 45–61. Ethnology Monographs 12.

Adovasio, J. M., J. Donahue, and R. Stuckenrath. 1992. Never say never again: Some thoughts on could haves and might have beens. *American Antiquity* 57:327–331.

Ager, T. A., and L. Brubaker. 1985. Quaternary palynology and vegetational history of Alaska. In *Pollen Records of Late-Quaternary North American Sediments,* edited by V. M. Bryant, Jr., and R. G. Holloway, pp. 353–384. American Association of Stratigraphic Palynologists, Dallas.

Aikens, C. M. 1970. *Hogup Cave.* University of Utah Anthropological Papers 93.

Aikens, C. M. 1978. The far west. In *Ancient Native Americans,* edited by J. D. Jennings, pp. 131–181. W. H. Freeman, San Francisco.

Aikens, C. M. 1986. *Archaeology of Oregon.* Second edition. U.S. Department of the Interior, Bureau of Land Management, Portland, Oregon.

Aikens, C. M., and D. B. Madsen. 1986. Prehistory of the eastern area. In *Handbook of North American Indians,* Volume 11: *Great Basin,* edited by W. L. d'Azevedo, pp. 149–160. Smithsonian Institution Press, Washington, D.C.

Aikens, C. M., and Y. T. Witherspoon. 1986. Great Basin Numic prehistory: Linguistics, archaeology, and environment. In *Anthropology of the Desert West: Essays in Honor of Jesse D. Jennings,* edited by C. J. Condie and D. D. Fowler, pp. 7–20. University of Utah Anthropological Papers 110.

Aitken, M. J. 1989. Luminescence dating: A guide for non-specialists. *Archaeometry* 31:147–159.

Albee, B. J., L. M. Shultz, and S. Goodrich. 1988. *Atlas of the Vascular Plants of Utah.* Utah Museum of Natural History Occasional Paper 7.

Alcorn, G. 1988. *The Birds of Nevada.* Fairview Press, Fallon, Nevada.

Allen, J. E., M. Burns, and S. C. Sargent. 1986. *Cataclysms on the Columbia.* Timber Press, Portland, Oregon.

Allison, I. S. 1945. Pumice beds at Summer Lake, Oregon. *Geological Society of America Bulletin* 56:789–807.

Allison, I. S. 1966a. *Fossil Lake, Oregon: Its Geology and Fossil Faunas.* Oregon State Monographs, Studies in Geology 9.

Allison, I. S. 1966b. Pumice at Summer Lake, Oregon—A correction. *Geological Society of America Bulletin* 77:329–330.

Allison, I. S. 1982. *Geology of Pluvial Lake Chewaucan, Lake County, Oregon.* Oregon State Monographs, Studies in Geology 11.

Allison, I. S., and C. E. Bond. 1983. Identity and probable age of salmonids from surface deposits at Fossil Lake, Oregon. *Copeia* 1983:563–564.

Allison, N. 1988. Lehner Ranch Site: Officially on the map. *Mammoth Trumpet* 4(4):3.

Ambro, R. D. 1967. Dietary–technological–ecological aspects of Lovelock Cave coprolites. *University of California Archaeological Survey Reports* 70:37–48.

Amsden, C. A. 1935. The Pinto Basin artifacts. In *The Pinto Basin Site,* by E. W. C. Campbell and W. H. Campbell, pp. 33–51. Southwest Museum Papers 9.

Anderson, E. 1970. Quaternary evolution of the genus *Martes* (Carnivora, Mustelidae). *Acta Zoologica Fennica* 130.

Anderson, P. 1985. Late Quaternary vegetational change in the Kotzebue Sound area, northwestern Alaska. *Quaternary Research* 24:307–321.

Andrews, T. F. 1973. Lansford W. Hastings and the promotion of the Salt Lake Desert Cutoff: A reappraisal. *Western Historical Quarterly* 4:133–150.

Antevs, E. 1925. On the Pleistocene history of the Great Basin. *Carnegie Institute of Washington Publications* 352:51–114.

Antevs, E. 1931. *Late-Glacial Correlations and Ice Recession in Manitoba.* Canada Geological Survey Memoir 168.

Antevs, E. 1938. Postpluvial climatic variations in the southwest. *Bulletin of the American Meteorological Society* 19:190–193.

Antevs, E. 1948. Climatic changes and pre-white man. *University of Utah Bulletin* 38(20):167–191.

Antevs, E. 1952a. Cenozoic climates of the Great Basin. *Geologische Rundschau* 40:96–109.

Antevs, E. 1952b. Climatic history and the antiquity of man in California. *University of California Archaeological Survey Reports* 16:23–31.

Antevs, E. 1953a. Geochronology of the deglacial and Neothermal ages. *Journal of Geology* 61:195–230.

Antevs, E. 1953b. The postpluvial or Neothermal. *University of California Archaeological Survey Reports* 22:9–23.

Antevs, E. 1955. Geologic-climatic dating in the west. *American Antiquity* 20:317–335.

Arkush, B. S. 1990. The protohistoric period in the western Great Basin. *Journal of California and Great Basin Anthropology* 12:28–36.

Arno, S. F., and R. P. Hammersly. 1984. *Timberlines: Mountain and Arctic Forest Frontiers.* The Mountaineers, Seattle.

Arnold, J. R., and W. F. Libby. 1951. Radiocarbon dates. *Science* 113:111–120.

Arnow, T. 1980. Water budget and water surface fluctuations of Great Salt Lake. In *Great Salt Lake: A Scientific, Historical, and Economic Overview,* edited by J. W. Gwynn, pp. 255–261. Utah Geological and Mineral Survey Bulletin 116.

Arnow, T. 1984. *Water-Level and Water-Quality Changes in Great Salt Lake, Utah, 1847–1983.* U.S. Geological Survey Circular 913.

Arnow, T., and D. Stephens. 1990. *Hydrologic Characteristics of the Great Salt Lake, Utah: 1847–1986.* U.S. Geological Survey Water-Supply Paper 2332.

Aschmann, H. H. 1958. Great Basin climates in relation to human occupance. *University of California Archaeological Survey Reports* 42:23–40.

Atmar, W. 1991. On the role of males. *Animal Behaviour* 41:195–205.

Atwater, B. F. 1987. Status of glacial Lake Columbia during the last floods from glacial Lake Missoula. *Quaternary Research* 27:182–201.

Axelrod, D. A. 1990. Age and origin of the subalpine forest zone. *Paleobiology* 16:360–369.

Axelrod, D. A., and P. H. Raven. 1985. Origins of the Cordilleran flora. *Journal of Biogeography* 12:21–47.

Bada, J. L. 1985. Aspartic acid racemization of California Paleoindian skeletons. *American Antiquity* 50:645–647.

Bada, J. L., and P. M. Helfman. 1975. Amino acid racemization dating of fossil bone. *World Archaeology* 7:160–173.

Bada, J. L., R. Gillespie, J. A. J. Gowlett, and R. E. M. Hedges. 1984. Accelerator mass spectrometry radiocarbon ages of amino acid extracts from California Paleo-Indian skeletons. *Nature* 312:442–444.

Bagley, M. 1988. A sensitive-plant monitoring study on the Eureka Dunes, Inyo County, California. In *Plant Biology of Eastern California,* edited by C. A. Hall, Jr., and V. Doyle-Jones, pp. 223–243. Natural History of the White-Inyo Range Symposium Volume 2. White Mountain Research Station, University of California, Los Angeles.

Bailey, V. 1936. *The Mammals and Life Zones of Oregon.* North American Fauna 55.

Baker, V. R. 1973. Paleohydrology and sedimentology of Lake Missoula flooding in eastern Washington. *Geological Society of America Bulletin* 144.

Baker, V. R. 1983. Late-Pleistocene fluvial systems. In *Late-Quaternary Environments of the United States,* Volume 1: *The Late Pleistocene,* edited by S. C. Porter, pp. 115–129. University of Minnesota Press, Minneapolis.

Baldwin, E. 1981. *Geology of Oregon.* Third edition. Kendall/Hunt, Dubuque, Iowa.

Bamforth, D. B., and R. I. Dorn. 1988. On the nature and antiquity of the Manix Lake Industry. *Journal of California and Great Basin Anthropology* 10:209–226.

Bancroft, H. H. 1982. *History of Utah 1540–1886.* Nevada Publications, Las Vegas.

Barbour, M. G. 1988. Mojave Desert scrub vegetation. In *Terrestrial Vegetation of California,* edited by M. G. Barbour and J. Major, pp. 835–867. Publication 9. California Native Plant Society.

Bard, E., B. Hamelin, R. G. Fairbanks, and A. Zindler. 1990. Calibration of the ^{14}C timescale over the past 30,000 years using mass spectrometric U-Th ages from Barbados corals. *Nature* 345:405–410.

Basgall, M. E., and M. C. Hall. 1991. Relationships between fluted and stemmed points in the Mojave Desert. *Current Research in the Pleistocene* 8:61–64.

Baugh, T. M., and J. E. Deacon. 1983. The most endangered pupfish. *Freshwater and Marine Aquarium* 6(6):22–26, 78–79.

Baumhoff, M. A., and R. F. Heizer. 1965. Postglacial climate and archaeology in the desert west. In *The Quaternary of the United States,* edited by H. E. Wright, Jr., and D. G. Frey, pp. 697–708. Princeton University Press, Princeton, New Jersey.

Beck, C., and G. T. Jones. 1988. Western Pluvial Lakes Tradition occupation in Butte Valley, eastern Nevada. In *Early Human Occupation in Far Western North America: The Clovis-Archaic Interface,* edited by J. A. Willig, C. M. Aikens, and J. L. Fagan, pp. 273–301. Anthropological Papers 21. Nevada State Museum.

Beck, C., and G. T. Jones. 1990a. The late Pleistocene/early Holocene archaeology of Butte Valley, Nevada: Three seasons' work. *Journal of California and Great Basin Anthropology* 12:231–261.

Beck, C., and G. T. Jones. 1990b. Toolstone selection and lithic technology in early Great Basin prehistory. *Journal of Field Archaeology* 17:283–299.

Bedinger, M. S., J. R. Harril, and J. M. Thomas. 1984. *Maps Showing Ground-Water Units and Withdrawal, Basin and Range Province, Nevada.* U.S. Geological Survey Water-Resources Investigations Report 83-4119-A.

Bedwell, S. F. 1973. *Fort Rock Basin: Prehistory and Environment.* University of Oregon Books, Eugene.

Bedwell, S. F., and L. S. Cressman. 1971. Fort Rock report: Prehistory and environment of the pluvial Fort Rock Lake area of south-central Oregon. In *Great Basin Anthropological Conference 1970: Selected Papers,* edited by C. M. Aikens, pp. 1–26. University of Oregon Anthropological Papers 1.

Behle, W. H. 1978. Avian biogeography of the Great Basin and intermountain region. In *Intermountain Biogeography: A Symposium,* edited by K. T. Harper and J. L. Reveal, pp. 55–80. Great Basin Naturalist Memoirs 2.

Beiswenger, J. M. 1991. Late Quaternary vegetational history of Grays Lake, Idaho. *Ecological Monographs* 61:165–182.

Bell, J. W., and T. Katzer. 1987. *Surficial Geology, Hydrology, and Late Quaternary Tectonics of the IXL Canyon Area, Nevada.* Nevada Bureau of Mines and Geology Bulletin 102.

Benson, L., and R. A. Darrow. 1981. *Trees and Shrubs of the Southwestern Deserts.* University of Arizona Press, Tucson.

Benson, L. V. 1978. Fluctuation in the level of Pluvial Lake Lahontan during the last 40,000 Years. *Quaternary Research* 9:300–318.

Benson, L. V. 1988. *Preliminary Paleolimnologic Data for the Walker Lake Subbasin, California and Nevada.* U.S. Geological Survey Water-Resources Investigations Report 87-4258.

Benson, L. V. 1991. Timing of the last highstand of Lake Lahontan. *Journal of Paleolimnology* 5:115–126.

Benson, L. V. 1993. Factors affecting ^{14}C ages of lacustrine carbonates: Timing and duration of the last highstand lake in the Lahontan Basin. *Quaternary Research* (in press).

Benson, L. V., and F. L. Paillet. 1989. The use of total lake-surface area as an indicator of climatic change. *Quaternary Research* 32:262–275.

Benson, L. V., and R. S. Thompson. 1987a. Lake-level variation in the Lahontan Basin for the past 50,000 years. *Quaternary Research* 28:69–85.

Benson, L. V., and R. S. Thompson. 1987b. The physical record of lakes in the Great Basin. In *The Geology of North America,* Volume K-3: *North America and Adjacent Oceans during the Last Deglaciation,* edited by W. F. Ruddiman and H. E. Wright, Jr., pp. 241–260. Geological Society of America, Boulder, Colorado.

Benson, L. V., D. R. Currey, R. I. Dorn, K. R. Lajoie, C. G. Oviatt, S. W. Robinson, G. I. Smith, and S. Stine. 1990. Chronology of expansion and contraction of four Great Basin lake systems during the past 35,000 years. *Palaeogeography, Palaeoclimatology, Palaeoecology* 78:241–286.

Benson, L. V., P. A. Meyers, and R. J. Spencer. 1991. Change in the size of Walker Lake during the past 5000 years. *Palaeogeography, Palaeoclimatology, Palaeoecology* 81:189–214.

Berger, G. W. 1988. Dating Quaternary events by luminescence. *Geological Society of America Special Paper* 227:13–50.

Berger, G. W. 1991. The use of glass for dating volcanic ash by thermoluminescence. *Journal of Geophysical Research* 96: 19,705–19,720.

Berger, G. W., and J. O. Davis. 1992. Dating volcanic ash by thermoluminescence: Test and application. *Quaternary International* 13/14:127–130.

Berger, J. 1986. *Wild Horses of the Great Basin.* University of Chicago Press, Chicago.

Berger, J., and J. D. Wehausen. 1991. Consequences of a mammalian predator-prey disequilibrium in the Great Basin desert. *Conservation Biology* 5:244–248.

Berkman, L. F. 1984. Assessing the physical health effects of social networks and social support. *Annual Review of Public Health* 5:413–432.

Berkman, L. F., and S. L. Syme. 1979. Social networks, host resistance, and mortality: A nine-year follow-up study of Alameda County residents. *American Journal of Epidemiology* 109: 186–204.

Berry, M. S. 1976. Remnant Cave. In *Swallow Shelter and Associated Sites,* by G. F. Dalley, pp. 115–128. University of Utah Anthropological Papers 96.

Betancourt, J. L., T. R. Van Devender, and P. S. Martin. 1990a. Introduction. In *Packrat Middens: The Last 40,000 Years of Biotic Change,* edited by J. L. Betancourt, T. R. Van Devender, and P. S. Martin, pp. 2–11. University of Arizona Press, Tucson.

Betancourt, J. L., T. R. Van Devender, and P. S. Martin, eds. 1990b. *Packrat Middens: The Last 40,000 Years of Biotic Change.* University of Arizona Press, Tucson.

Bettinger, R. L. 1991a. Aboriginal occupation at high altitude: Alpine villages in the White Mountains of eastern California. *American Anthropologist* 93:656–679.

Bettinger, R. L. 1991b. Native land use: Archaeology and anthropology. In *Natural History of the White-Inyo Range,* edited by C. A. Hall, Jr., pp. 463–486. University of California Press, Berkeley and Los Angeles.

Bettinger, R. L., and M. A. Baumhoff. 1982. The Numic spread: Great Basin cultures in competition. *American Antiquity* 47: 485–503.

Bettinger, R. L., and M. A. Baumhoff. 1983. Return rates and intensity of resource use in Numic and Prenumic adaptive strategies. *American Antiquity* 48:830–834.

Bettinger, R. L., and R. Oglesby. 1985. Lichen dating of alpine villages in the White Mountains, California. *Journal of California and Great Basin Anthropology* 7:202–224.

Bettinger, R. L., and R. E. Taylor. 1974. Suggested revisions in the archaeological sequences of the Great Basin in interior southern California. *Nevada Archaeological Survey Research Papers* 5:1–26.

Bettinger, R. L., J. F. O'Connell, and D. H. Thomas. 1991. Projectile points as time markers in the Great Basin. *American Anthropologist* 93:166–173.

Bierman, P. R., and A. R. Gillespie. 1991. Accuracy of rock-varnish chemical analysis: Implications for cation-ratio dating. *Geology* 19:196–199.

Bierman, P. R., A. R. Gillespie, and S. Kuehner. 1991. Precision of rock-varnish chemical analyses and cation-ratio ages. *Geology* 19:135–138.

Billings, W. D. 1945. The plant associations of the Carson Desert region. *Butler University Botanical Studies* 7:89–123.

Billings, W. D. 1950. Vegetation and plant growth as affected by chemically altered rocks in the western Great Basin. *Ecology* 31:62–74.

Billings, W. D. 1951. Vegetational zonation in the Great Basin of western North America. In *Les Bases écologiques de la Régénération de la Végétation des Zones arides,* pp. 101–122. International Union of Biological Sciences, Series B, No. 9.

Billings, W. D. 1954. Temperature inversions in the Piñon-Juniper Zone of a Nevada mountain range. *Butler University Botanical Studies* 11:112–118.

Billings, W. D. 1978. Alpine phytogeography across the Great Basin. In *Intermountain Biogeography: A Symposium,* edited by K. T. Harper and J. L. Reveal, pp. 105–117. Great Basin Naturalist Memoirs 2.

Billings, W. D. 1988. Alpine vegetation. In *North American Terrestrial Vegetation,* edited by M. G. Barbour and W. D. Billings, pp. 391–420. California Native Plant Society Publication 9.

Billings, W. D. 1990. The mountain forests of North America and their environments. In *Plant Biology of the Basin and Range,* edited by C. B. Osmond, L. F. Pitelka, and G. M. Hidy, pp. 47–86. Springer-Verlag, Berlin.

Birnie, R. I. 1986. Late Quaternary Environments and Archaeology of the Snake Range, East Central Nevada. M.S. thesis, Quaternary Studies, University of Maine, Orono.

Bischoff, J. L., R. J. Shlemon, T. L. Ku, R. J. Rosenbaum, and F. E. Budinger, Jr. 1981. Uranium-series and soil-geomorphic dating of the Calico archaeological site, California. *Geology* 9:576–582.

Blackwelder, E. 1931. Pleistocene glaciation in the Sierra Nevada and Basin ranges. *Geological Society of America Bulletin* 42:865–922.

Blackwelder, E. 1934. Supplementary notes on Pleistocene glaciation in the Great Basin. *Journal of the Washington Academy of Sciences* 24:212–222.

Blackwelder, E. 1954. Pleistocene lakes and drainage in the Mojave region, southern California. In *Geology of Southern California,* edited by R. H. Jahns, pp. 35–40. *California Division of Mines and Geology Bulletin* 170(5).

Blake, E. R. 1977. *Manual of Neotropical Birds,* Volume 1: *Spheniscidae (Penguins) to Laridae (Gulls and Allies).* University of Chicago Press, Chicago.

Blazer, D. G. 1982. Social support and mortality in an elderly community population. *American Journal of Epidemiology* 115: 684–694.

Blinman, E., P. J. Mehringer, Jr., and J. C. Sheppard. 1979. Pollen influx and the deposition of Mazama and Glacier Peak tephra. In *Volcanic Activity and Human Ecology,* edited by P. D. Sheets and D. K. Grayson, pp. 393–426. Academic Press, New York.

Bogue, D. J. 1969. *Principles of Demography.* Wiley, New York.

Born, S. M. 1972. *Late Quaternary History, Deltaic Sedimentation, and Mudlump Formation at Pyramid Lake, Nevada.* Center for Water Resources Research, Desert Research Institute, Reno, Nevada.

Botkin, D., W. S. Broecker, L. G. Everett, J. Shapiro, and J. A. Wiens. 1988. The Future of Mono Lake. Report 68. University of California Water Resources Center, Riverside.

Bradbury, J. P. 1987. Late Holocene diatom paleolimnology of Walker Lake, Nevada. *Archiv für Hydrobiologie, Supplement 79, Monographische Beiträge* 1:1–27.

Bradbury, J. P., R. M. Forester, and R. S. Thompson. 1989. Late Quaternary paleolimnology of Walker Lake, Nevada. *Journal of Paleolimnology* 1:249–267.

Brattstrom, B. H. 1958. New records of Cenozoic amphibians and reptiles from California. *Bulletin of the Southern California Academy of Sciences* 57:5–12.

Bright, R. C. 1966. Pollen and seed stratigraphy of Swan Lake, southeastern Idaho. *Tebiwa* 9(2):1–47.

Brodkorb, P. 1963. Catalogue of Fossil Birds, Part 1: Archaeopterygiformes through Ardeiformes. *Bulletin of the Florida State Museum* 7(4).

Brodkorb, P. 1964. Catalogue of Fossil Birds, Part 2: Anseriformes through Galliformes. *Bulletin of the Florida State Museum* 8(3).

Broecker, W. S., and G. H. Denton. 1990. What drives glacial cycles? *Scientific American* 250(1):49–56.

Broecker, W. S., and J. L. Kulp. 1957. Lamont natural radiocarbon measurements IV. *Science* 126:1324–1334.

Brooks, G. R. 1989. *The Southwest Expedition of Jedediah S. Smith: His Personal Account of the Journey to California, 1826–1827.* University of Nebraska Press, Lincoln.

Brooks, J. 1962. *The Mountains Meadows Massacre.* University of Oklahoma Press, Norman.

Brooks, R. H. 1956. Faunal remains. In *The Archaeology of Humboldt Cave, Churchill County, Nevada,* by R. F. Heizer and A. D. Krieger, pp. 106–112. University of California Publications in American Archaeology and Ethnology 47.

Brooks, S. T., M. B. Haldeman, and R. H. Brooks. 1988. *Osteological Analyses of the Stillwater Skeletal Series, Stilwater Marsh, Churchill Count, Nevada.* U.S. Department of the Interior, U.S. Fish and Wildlife Service, Region 1, Cultural Resource Series 2.

Broughton, J. M., and D. K. Grayson. 1993. Diet breadth, Numic expansion, and White Mountains faunas. *Journal of Archaeological Science* (in press).

Brown, J. H. 1971. Mammals on mountaintops: Nonequilibrium insular biogeography. *American Naturalist* 105:467–478.

Brown, J. H. 1978. The theory of insular biogeography and the distribution of boreal birds and mammals. In *Intermountain Biogeography: A Symposium,* edited by K. T. Harper and J. L. Reveal, pp. 209–227. Great Basin Naturalist Memoirs 2.

Brown, J. H., and A. C. Gibson. 1983. *Biogeography.* C. V. Mosby, St. Louis.

Brown, L. 1971. *African Birds of Prey.* Houghton Mifflin, Boston.

Brown, T. A., D. E. Nelson, R. W. Mathewes, J. S Vogel, and J. R. Southern. 1989. Radiocarbon dating of pollen by accelerator mass spectrometry. *Quaternary Research* 32:205–212.

Brown, W. J., S. G. Wells, Y. Enzel, R. Y. Anderson, and L. D. McFadden. 1990. The late Quaternary history of pluvial Lake Mojave–Silver Lake and Soda Lake basins, California. In *At the End of the Mojave: Quaternary Studies in the Eastern Mojave Desert,* edited by R. E. Reynolds, S. G. Wells, and R. H. Brady III, pp. 55–72. San Bernardino County Museum Association, Redlands, California.

Bryan, A. L. 1979. Smith Creek Cave. In *The Archaeology of Smith Creek Canyon, Eastern Nevada,* edited by D. R. Tuohy and D. L. Rendall, pp. 162–251, Nevada State Museum Anthropological Papers 17.

Bryan, A. L. 1980. The stemmed point tradition: An early technological tradition in western North America. In *Anthropological Papers in Memory of Earl H. Swanson, Jr.,* edited by L. B. Harten, C. N. Warren, and D. R. Tuohy, pp. 77–107. Idaho Museum of Natural History, Pocatello.

Bryan, A. L. 1988. The relationship of the stemmed point and the fluted point traditions in the Great Basin. In *Early Human Occupation in Far Western North America: The Clovis-Archaic Interface,* edited by J. A. Willig, C. M. Aikens, and J. L. Fagan, pp. 53–74. Nevada State Museum Anthropological Papers 21.

Bryan, A. L., and R. Gruhn. 1964. Problems relating to the Neothermal climate sequence. *American Antiquity* 29:307–315.

Bryant, E. 1848. What I Saw in California. Appleton, New York (reprinted by the University of Nebraska Press, Lincoln, 1985).

Budinger, F. E., Jr. 1983. The Calico Early Man Site, San Bernardino, California. *California Geology* 36:75–82.

Burns, J. A. 1990. Paleontological perspectives on the ice-free corridor. In *Megafauna and Man: Discovery of America's Heartland,* edited by L. D. Agenbroad, J. I. Mead, and L. W. Nelson, pp. 61–66. The Mammoth Site of Hot Springs, South Dakota, Inc., Scientific Papers 1.

Burr, T. N., and D. R. Currey. 1988. The Stockton Bar. In *In the Footsteps of G. K. Gilbert—Lake Bonneville and Neotectonics of the Eastern Basin and Range Province,* edited by M. N. Machette, pp. 66–73. Utah Geological and Mineral Survey Miscellaneous Publication 88-1.

Butler, B. R. 1970. A surface collection from Coyote Flat, southeastern Oregon. *Tebiwa* 13(1):34–57.

Butler, B. R. 1972. The Holocene or postglacial ecological crisis on the eastern Snake River Plain. *Tebiwa* 15(1):49–63.

Butler, B. R. 1978. *A Guide to Understanding Idaho Archaeology.* Third edition. Idaho State Museum of Natural History, Pocatello.

Butzer, K. W. 1971. *Environment and Archaeology: An Ecological Approach to Prehistory.* Second edition. University of Chicago Press, Chicago.

Bynon, T. 1977. *Historical Linguistics.* Cambridge University Press, London.

Byrne, R., C. Busby, and R. F. Heizer. 1979. The Altithermal revisited: Pollen evidence from the Leonard Rockshelter. *Journal of California and Great Basin Anthropology* 1:280–294.

Camp, C. L., ed. 1960. *James Clyman, Frontiersman.* Champoeg Press, Portland, Oregon.

Campbell, E. W. C., and W. H. Campbell. 1940. A Folsom complex in the Great Basin. *The Masterkey* 14(1):7–11.

Campbell, E. W. C., W. H. Campbell, E. Antevs, C. A. Amsden, J. A. Barbieri, and F. D. Bode. 1937. *The Archaeology of Pleistocene Lake Mohave: A Symposium.* Southwest Museum Papers 11.

Campbell, K. E., Jr., and E. P. Tonni. 1980. A new genus of teratorn from the Huayquerian of Argentina (Aves: Teratornithidae). *Natural History Museum of Los Angeles County Contributions in Science* 330:59–68.

Cane, S. 1987. Australian Aboriginal subsistence in the Western Desert. *Human Ecology* 15:391–434.

Carey, C. H. 1932. Historical notes. In *The Emigrants Guide to Oregon and California,* by L. W. Hastings, pp. vii–xxii. Princeton University Press, Princeton, New Jersey (reprint).

Carey, H. V., and J. D. Wehausen. 1991. Mammals. In *Natural History of the White-Inyo Range,* edited by C. A. Hall, Jr., pp. 437–560. University of California Press, Berkeley and Los Angeles.

Carlisle, R. C., and J. M. Adovasio, eds. 1982. *Collected Papers on the Archaeology of Meadowcroft Rockshelter and the Cross Creek Drainage.* Department of Anthropology, University of Pittsburgh, Pittsburgh.

Carter, G. F. 1958. Archaeology in the Reno area in relation to age of man and the culture sequence in America. *Proceedings of the American Philosophical Society* 102:174–192.

Casjens, L. A. 1974. The Prehistoric Human Ecology of Southern Ruby Valley, Nevada. Ph.D. dissertation, Department of Anthropology, Harvard University, Cambridge, Massachusetts.

Cato, I. 1985. The definitive connection of the Swedish geochronological time scale with the present, and the new date of the zero year in Döviken, northern Sweden. *Boreas* 14: 117–122.

Catto, N., and C. A. Mandryk. 1990. Geology of the postulated ice-free corridor. In *Megafauna and Man: Discovery of America's Heartland,* edited by L. D. Agenbroad, J. I. Mead, and L. W. Nelson, pp. 80–85. The Mammoth Site of Hot Springs, South Dakota, Inc., Scientific Papers 1.

Chalfant, W. A. 1975. *The Story of Inyo.* Chalfant Press, Bishop, California.

Charlet, D. A. 1991. Relationships of the Great Basin Alpine Flora: A Quantitative Analysis. M.A. thesis, Department of Biology, University of Nevada, Reno.

Charlet, D. A. 1993. Floristics of the Mt. Jefferson alpine florula. In *The Archaeology of Monitor Valley. 4. Alta Toquima and the Mt. Jefferson Complex,* by D. H. Thomas. American Museum of Natural History Anthropological Papers (in press).

Chrétien, C. D. 1962. The mathematical models of glottochronology. *Language* 38:11–37.

Clark, T. W., E. Anderson, C. Douglas, and M. Strickland. 1987. *Martes americana. Mammalian Species* 289.

Clarke, G. K. C., W. H. Mathews, and R. T. Pack. 1984. Outburst floods from glacial Lake Missoula. *Quaternary Research* 22: 289–299.

Clewlow, C. W., Jr. 1968. Surface archaeology of the Black Rock Desert, Nevada. *University of California Archaeological Survey Reports* 73:1–94.

Cline, G. G. 1988. *Exploring the Great Basin.* University of Nevada Press, Reno.

Clyman, J. 1984. *Journal of a Mountain Man,* edited by L. M. Hasselstrom. Mountain Press, Missoula, Montana.

Coats, R. R. 1964. Geology of the Jarbidge Quadrangle, Nevada-Idaho. U.S. Geological Survey Bulletin 1141-M.

Coats, R. R., R. C. Green, and L. D. Cress. 1977. *Mineral Resources of the Jarbidge Wilderness and Adjacent Areas, Elko County, Nevada.* U.S. Geological Survey Bulletin 1439.

COHMAP Members. 1988. Climatic changes of the last 18,000 years: Observations and model simulations. *Science* 241:1043–1052.

Colinvaux, P. A. 1986. Plain thinking on Bering Land Bridge vegetation and mammoth populations. *Quarterly Review of Archaeology* 7(1):8–9.

Connor, E. F., and E. D. McCoy. 1979. The statistics and biology of the species-area relationship. *American Naturalist* 113:791–833.

Constantz, G. D. 1981. Life history patterns of desert fishes. In *Fishes in North American Deserts,* edited by R. J. Naiman and D. L. Soltz, pp. 237–290. Wiley, New York.

Cook, S. F. 1955. The epidemic of 1830–1833 in California and Oregon. *University of California Publications in American Archaeology and Ethnology* 43:303–326.

Cope, E. D. 1889. The Silver Lake of Oregon and its region. *American Naturalist* 23:970–982.

Copeland, J. M., and R. E. Fike. 1988. Fluted projectile points in Utah. *Utah Archaeology* 1(1):5–28.

Cowan, R. A. 1967. Lake-margin ecologic exploitation in the Great Basin as demonstrated by an analysis of coprolites from Lovelock Cave, Nevada. *University of California Archaeological Survey Reports* 70:21–36.

Cressman, L. S. 1936a. *Archaeological Survey of the Guano Valley Region in Southeastern Oregon.* University of Oregon Monographs, Studies in Anthropology 1.

Cressman, L. S. 1937. *Petroglyphs of Oregon.* University of Oregon Monographs, Studies in Anthropology 2.

Cressman, L. S. 1942. Archaeological researches in the northern Great Basin. *Carnegie Institute of Washington Publications* 538.

Cressman, L. S. 1951. Western prehistory in the light of carbon 14 dating. *Southwestern Journal of Anthropology* 7:289–313.

Cressman, L. S. 1977. *Prehistory of the Far West: Homes of Vanished Peoples.* University of Utah Press, Salt Lake City.

Cressman, L. S. 1986. Prehistory of the northern area. In *Handbook of North American Indians,* Volume 11: *Great Basin,* edited by W. L. d'Azevedo, pp. 120–126. Smithsonian Institution Press, Washington, D.C.

Cressman, L. S. 1988. *A Golden Journey: Memoirs of an Archaeologist.* University of Utah Press, Salt Lake City.

Cressman, L. S., and H. Williams. 1940. Early man in Oregon: Evidence from stratified sites. In *Early man in Oregon: Archaeological Studies in the Northern Great Basin,* by L. S. Cressman, H. Williams, and A. Krieger, pp. 53–78. University of Oregon Monographs, Studies in Anthropology 2.

Cressman, L. S., H. Williams, and A. Krieger. 1940. *Early Man in Oregon: Archaeological Studies in the Northern Great Basin.* University of Oregon Monographs, Studies in Anthropology 2.

Critchfield, W. B. 1984. Impact of the Pleistocene on the genetic structure of North American conifers. In *Proceedings of the Eighth North American Forest Biology Workshop,* edited by R. M. Lanner, pp. 70–118. Department of Forest Resources, Utah State University, Logan, Utah.

Critchfield, W. B., and G. L. Allenbaugh. 1969. The distribution of Pinaceae in and near northern Nevada. *Madroño* 19:12–26.

Cronquist, A., A. H. Holmgren, N. H. Holmgren, and J. L. Reveal. 1972. *Intermountain Flora: Vascular Plants of the Intermountain West, U.S.A.,* Volume 1. Hafner, New York.

Curran, H. 1982. *Fearful Crossing: The Central Overland Trail through Nevada.* Great Basin Press, Reno, Nevada.

Currey, D. R. 1980. Coastal geomorphology of Great Salt Lake and vicinity. In *Great Salt Lake: A Scientific, Historical, and Economic Overview,* edited by J. W. Gwynn, pp. 69–82. Utah Geological and Mineral Survey Bulletin 116.

Currey, D. R. 1987. Great Salt Lake levels: Holocene geomorphic development and hydrographic history. In *Third Annual Landsat Workshop,* pp. 127–132. Laboratory for Terrestrial Physics, National Aeronautics and Space Adminstration.

Currey, D. R. 1988. Isochronism of final Pleistocene lakes in the Great Salt Lake and Carson Desert region of the Great Basin. In *Programs and Abstracts of the Tenth Biennial Meeting of the American Quaternary Association,* p. 117. Amherst, Massachusetts.

Currey, D. R., and T. N. Burr. 1988. Linear model of threshold-controlled shorelines of Lake Bonneville. In *In the Footsteps of G. K. Gilbert—Lake Bonneville and Neotectonics of the Eastern Basin and Range Province,* edited by M. N. Machette, pp. 104–110. Utah Geological and Mineral Survey Miscellaneous Publication 88-1.

Currey, D. R., and S. R. James. 1982. Paleoenvironments of the northeastern Great Basin and northeastern Basin rim region: A review of geological and biological evidence. In *Man and Environment in the Great Basin,* edited by D. B. Madsen and J. F. O'Connell, pp. 27–52. Society for American Archaeology Papers 2.

Currey, D. R., and C. G. Oviatt. 1985. Durations, average rates, and probable causes of Bonneville expansion, stillstands, and contractions during the last deep-lake cycle, 32,000 to 10,000 years ago. In *Problems of and Prospects for Predicting Great Salt Lake Levels,* edited by P. A. Kay and H. F. Diaz, pp. 9–24. Center for Public Affairs and Administration, University of Utah, Salt Lake City.

Currey, D. R., C. G. Oviatt, and J. E. Czarnomski. 1984a. Late Quaternary geology of Lake Bonneville and Lake Waring. *Utah Geological Association Publications* 13:227–238.

Currey, D. R., G. Atwood, and D. R. Mabey. 1984b. *Major Levels of Great Salt Lake and Lake Bonneville.* Utah Geological and Mineral Survey Map 73.

Cutler, A. 1991. Nested faunas and extinction in fragmented habitats. *Conservation Biology* 5:496–505.

Dalley, G. F. 1976. *Swallow Shelter and Associated Sites.* University of Utah Anthropological Papers 96.

Dansie, A. J. 1987. Archaeofauna from 26PE670. In *Studies in Archaeology, Geology and Paleontology at Rye Patch Reservoir, Pershing County, Nevada,* by M. K. Rusco and J. O.Davis, pp. 69–73. Nevada State Museum Anthropological Papers 20.

Dansie, A. J., J. O., Davis, and T. W. Stafford, Jr. 1988. The Wizards Beach Recession: Farmdalian (25,500 yr B.P.) vertebrate fossils co-occur with early Holocene artifacts. In *Early Human Occupation in Far Western North America: The Clovis-Archaic Interface,* edited by J. A. Willig, C. M. Aikens, and J. L. Fagan, pp. 153–200. Nevada State Museum Anthropological Papers 21.

Davis, C. A., and G. A. Smith. 1981. *Newberry Cave.* San Bernardino County Museum Association, Redlands, California.

Davis, C. A., R. E. Taylor, and G. A. Smith. 1981. New radiocarbon determinations from Newberry Cave. *Journal of California and Great Basin Anthropology* 3:144–147.

Davis, E. L. 1978a. Associations of people and a Rancholabrean fauna at China Lake, California. In *Early Man in America from a Circum-Pacific Perspective,* edited by A. L. Bryan, pp. 183–217.

Occasional Papers 1. Department of Anthropology, University of Alberta.

Davis, E. L., ed. 1978b. *The Ancient Californians: Rancholabrean Hunters of the Mojave Lakes Country.* Natural History Museum of Los Angeles County Science Series 29.

Davis, E. L., and R. Shutler, Jr. 1969. Recent discoveries of fluted points in California and Nevada. *Nevada State Museum Anthropological Papers* 14:154–179.

Davis, J. O. 1982. Bits and pieces: The last 35,000 years in the Lahontan area. In *Man and Environment in the Great Basin,* edited by D. B. Madsen and J. F. O'Connell, pp. 53–75. Society for American Archaeology Papers 2.

Davis, J. O. 1983. Level of Lake Lahontan during deposition of the Trego Hot Springs tephra about 22,400 years ago. *Quaternary Research* 19:312–324.

Davis, J. O. 1985a. Correlation of Late Quaternary tephra layers in a long pluvial sequence near Summer Lake, Oregon. *Quaternary Research* 23:38–53.

Davis, J. O. 1985b. Sediments and geological setting of Hidden Cave. In *The Archaeology of Hidden Cave, Nevada,* edited by D. H. Thomas, pp. 80–103. Anthropological Papers of the American Museum of Natural History 61(1).

Davis, J. O. 1987. Geology at Rye Patch. In *Studies in Archaeology, Geology and Paleontology at Rye Patch Reservoir, Pershing County, Nevada,* by M. K. Rusco and J. O. Davis, pp. 9–22. Nevada State Museum Anthropological Papers 20.

Davis, J. O., and M. K. Rusco. 1987. The Old Humboldt Site—26Pe670. In *Studies in Archaeology, Geology and Paleontology at Rye Patch Reservoir, Pershing County, Nevada,* by M. K. Rusco and J. O. Davis, pp. 41–73. Nevada State Museum Anthropological Papers 20.

Davis, J. O., R. Elston, and G. Townsend. 1976. Coastal geomorphology of the south shore of Lake Tahoe. In *Holocene Environmental Change in the Great Basin,* edited by R. Elston, pp. 40–65. Nevada Archaeological Survey Research Paper 6.

d'Azevedo, W. L., ed. 1986. *Handbook of North American Indians,* Volume 11: *Great Basin.* Smithsonian Institution Press, Washington, D.C.

Deacon, J. E., and M. S. Deacon. 1979. Research on endangered fishes in the National Parks with special emphasis on the Devils Hole pupfish. In *First Conference on Scientific Research in National Parks,* edited by R. M. Linn, pp. 9–19. National Park Service Transactions and Proceeding Series 5.

Deacon, J. E., and C. D. Williams. 1991. Ash Meadows and the legacy of the Devils Hole pupfish. In *Battle Against Extinction: Native Fish Management in the American West,* edited by W. L. Minckley and J. E. Deacon, pp. 69–91. University of Arizona Press, Tucson.

DeDecker, M. 1984. *Flora of the Northern Mojave Desert, California.* California Native Plant Society Special Publication 7.

DeDecker, M. 1991. Shrubs and flowering plants. In *Natural History of the White-Inyo Range,* edited by C. A. Hall, Jr., pp. 108–241. University of California Press, Berkeley and Los Angeles.

de Jong, G. F. 1972. Patterns of human fertility and mortality. In *The Structure of Human Populations,* edited by G. A. Harrison and A. J. Boyce, pp. 32–56. Clarendon Press, Oxford.

Delacour, J. 1954. *The Waterfowl of the World,* Volume 1. Country Life, London.

Delorme, L. D. 1969. Ostracodes as Quaternary paleoenvironmental indicators. *Canadian Journal of Earth Sciences* 6:1471–1476.

Delorme, L. D., and S. C. Zoltai. 1984. Distribution of an Arctic ostracod fauna in space and time. *Quaternary Research* 21:65–74.

DeLucia, E. H., and W. H. Schlesinger. 1990. Ecophysiology of Great Basin and Sierra Nevada vegetation on contrasting soils. In *Plant Biology of the Basin and Range,* edited by C. B. Osmond, L. F. Pitelka, and G. M. Hidy, pp. 143–178. Springer-Verlag, Berlin.

DeLucia, E. H., and W. H. Schlesinger. 1991. Resource-use efficiency and drought tolerance in adjacent Great Basin and Sierran plants. *Ecology* 72:51–58.

DeLucia, E. H., W. H. Schlesinger, and D. W. Billings. 1988. Water relations and the maintenance of Sierran conifers on hydrothermally altered rock. *Ecology* 69:303–311.

DeLucia, E. H., W. H. Schlesinger, and D. W. Billings. 1989. Edaphic limitations to growth and photosynthesis in Sierran and Great Basin vegetation. *Oecologia* 78:184–190.

DeMay, I. S. 1941a. Pleistocene bird life of the Carpinteria asphalt, California. *Carnegie Institute of Washington Publications* 530:61–66.

DeMay, I. S. 1941b. Quaternary bird life of the McKittrick asphalt, California. *Carnegie Institute of Washington Publications* 530:35–60.

Dicken, S. N. 1980. Pluvial Lake Modoc, Klamath County, Oregon, and Modoc and Siskyou counties, California. *Oregon Geology* 42:179–187.

Dial, K. P., and N. J. Czaplewski. 1990. Do woodrat middens accurately represent the animals' environments and diets? The Woodhouse Mesa Study. In *Packrat Middens: The Last 40,000 Years of Biotic Change,* edited by J. L. Betancourt, T. R. Van Devender, and P. S. Martin, pp. 43–58. University of Arizona Press, Tucson.

Dikov, N. N. 1978. Ancestors of Paleo-Indians and Proto-Eskimo Aleuts in the Paleolithic of Kamchatka. In *Early Man in America from a Circum-Pacific Perspective,* edited by A. L. Bryan, pp. 68–69. Department of Anthropology, University of Alberta Occasional Papers 1.

Dikov, N. N. 1990. Major results of archaeological research on the eastern Chukchi Peninsula. In *Prehistoric Monuments of the*

Northern Soviet Far East, pp. 7–35. Northeastern Interdisciplinary Research Institute, Far Eastern Branch, USSR Academy of Sciences, Magadan (in Russian).

Dillehay, T. D. 1989. *Monte Verde: A Late Pleistocene Settlement in Chile,* Volume 1: *Paleoenviroment and Site Context.* Smithsonian Institution Press, Washington, D.C.

Division of Water Resources, State of Nevada. 1972. Water resources and inter-basin flows. In *Water for Nevada: Hydrologic Atlas, Map S-13.* Department of Water Resources, State of Nevada, Carson City.

Dohrenwend, J. C. 1984. Nivation landforms in the western Great Basin and their paleoclimatic significance. *Quaternary Research* 22:275–288.

Dorn, R. I. 1983. Cation-ratio dating: A new rock varnish age-determination. *Quaternary Research* 20:49–73.

Dorn, R. I., and D. H. Krinsley. 1991. Cation-leaching sites in rock varnish. *Geology* 19:1077–1080.

Dorn, R. I., A. J. T. Jull, D. J. Donahue, T. W. Linick, and L. J. Toolin. 1989. Accelerator mass spectrometry radiocarbon dating of rock varnish. *Geological Society of America Bulletin* 101:1363–1372.

Dorn, R. I., A. J. T. Jull, D. J. Donahue, T. W. Linick, and L. J. Toolin. 1990. Latest Pleistocene shorelines and glacial chronology in the Western Basin and Range Province, U.S.A.: Insights from AMS radiocarbon dating of rock varnish and paleoclimatic implications. *Palaeogeography, Palaeoclimatology, Palaeoecology* 78: 315–331.

Douglas, C. L., D. L. Jenkins, and C. N. Warren. 1988. Spatial and temporal variability in faunal remains from four Lake Mojave–Pinto period sites in the Mojave Desert. In *Early Human Occupation in Far Western North America: The Clovis-Archaic Interface,* edited by J. A. Willig, C. M. Aikens, and J. L. Fagan, pp. 131–144. Nevada State Museum Anthropological Papers 21.

Downs, T., H. Howard, T. Clements, and G. A. Smith. 1959. *Quaternary Animals from Schuiling Cave in the Mojave Desert, California.* Los Angeles City Museum Contributions in Science 29.

Drews, M. P. 1988. Freshwater molluscs. In *Preliminary Investigations in Stillwater Marsh: Human Prehistory and Geoarchaeology,* edited by C. Raven and R. G. Elston, pp. 328–339. U.S. Department of the Interior, U.S. Fish and Wildlife Service, Region 1, Cultural Resource Series 1.

Driver, H. E., and W. C. Massey. 1957. Comparative studies of North American Indians. *Transactions of the American Philosophical Society* 47(2).

Durnin, J. V. G. A., and R. Passmore. 1967. *Energy, Work, and Leisure.* Heinemann, London.

Durrant, S. D. 1952. *Mammals of Utah: Taxonomy and Distribution.* University of Kansas Publications, Museum of Natural History 6.

Durrant, S. D. 1970. Faunal remains as indicators of Neothermal climates at Hogup Cave. In *Hogup Cave,* by C. M. Aikens, pp. 241–245. University of Utah Anthropological Papers 93.

Eastman, C. W. 1990. *Aspects of Language and Culture.* Second edition. Chandler and Sharp, Novato, California.

Egan, F. 1985. *Frémont: Explorer for a Restless Nation.* University of Nevada Press, Reno.

Eisenstein, E. L. 1979. *The Printing Press as an Agent of Change.* Cambridge University Press, Cambridge.

Elias, S. A., S. K. Short, and R. L. Phillips. 1992. Paleoecology of late-glacial peats from the Bering Land Bridge, Chukchi Sea shelf region, northwestern Alaska. *Quaternary Research* 38:371–378.

Elliot-Fisk, D. L. 1987. Glacial geomorphology of the White Mountains, California and Nevada: Establishment of a glacial chronology. *Physical Geography* 8:299–323.

Elliot-Fisk, D. L., and A. M. Peterson. 1991. Trees. In *Natural History of the White-Inyo Range,* edited by C. A. Hall, Jr., pp. 87–107. University of California Press, Berkeley and Los Angeles.

Elston, R. G. 1971. *A Contribution to Washo Archaeology.* Nevada Archaeological Survey Research Paper 2.

Elston, R. G. 1982. Good times, hard times: Prehistoric culture change in the western Great Basin. In *Man and Environment in the Great Basin,* edited by D. B. Madsen and J. F. O'Connell, pp. 186–206. Society for American Archaeology Papers 2.

Elston, R. G. 1986. Prehistory of the western area. In *Handbook of North American Indians,* Volume 11: *Great Basin,* edited by W. L. d'Azevedo, pp. 135–148. Smithsonian Institution Press, Washington, D.C.

Elston, R. G., and E. E. Budy, eds. 1990. *The Archaeology of James Creek Shelter.* University of Utah Anthropological Papers 115.

Elston, R. G., K. L. Katzer, and D. R. Currey. 1988. Chronological summary. In *Preliminary Investigations in Stillwater Marsh: Human Prehistory and Geoarchaeology,* edited by C. Raven and R. G. Elston, pp. 373–384. U.S. Department of the Interior, U.S. Fish and Wildlife Service, Region 1, Cultural Resource Series 1.

Embleton, S. 1991. Mathematical methods of genetic classification. In *Sprung from Some Common Source,* edited by S. M. Lamb and E. D. Mitchell, pp. 365–388. Stanford University Press, Stanford, California.

Emslie, S. D. 1990. Additional ^{14}C dates on fossil California condors. *National Geographic Research* 6:134–135.

Emslie, S. D., and N. J. Czaplewski. 1985. A new record of giant short-faced bear, *Arctodus simus,* from western North America with a re-evaluation of its paleobiology. *Natural History Museum of Los Angeles County Contributions in Science* 731:1–12.

Enzel, Y., D. R. Cayan, R. Y. Anderson, and S. G. Wells. 1989. Atmospheric circulation during Holocene lake stands in the Mojave Desert: Evidence of regional climatic change. *Nature* 341:44–47.

Enzel, Y., W. J. Brown, R. Y. Anderson, L. D. McFadden, and S. G. Wells. 1992. Short-duration Holocene lakes in the Mojave River drainage basin, southern California. *Quaternary Research* 38:60–73.

Everett, D. E., and F. E. Rush. 1967. *A Brief Appraisal of the Water Resources of the Walker Lake Area, Mineral, Lyon, and Churchill Counties, Nevada.* Nevada Department of Conservation and Natural Resources Water Resources–Reconnaissance Series Report 40.

Fagan, B. M. 1987. *The Great Journey: The Peopling of Ancient America.* Thames and Hudson, New York.

Fagan, J. L. 1974. *Altithermal Occupation of Spring Sites in the Northern Great Basin.* University of Oregon Anthropological Papers 6.

Fagan, J. L. 1988. Clovis and western Pluvial Lakes Tradition lithic technologies at the Dietz site in south-central Oregon. In *Early Human Occupation in Far Western North America: The Clovis-Archaic Interface,* edited by J. A. Willig, C. M. Aikens, and J. L. Fagan, pp. 389–416. Nevada State Museum Anthropological Papers 21.

Fenenga, F., and F. A. Riddell. 1949. Excavation of Tommy Tucker Cave, Lassen County, California. *American Antiquity* 14:203–214.

Ferguson, S. A. 1992. *Glaciers of North America: A Field Guide.* Fulcrum Publishing, Golden, Colorado.

Feth, J. H. 1959. Re-evaluation of the salt chronology of several Great Basin lakes: A discussion. *Geological Society of America Bulletin* 70:637–640.

Finley, R. B., Jr. 1990. Woodrat ecology and behavior and the interpretation of Paleomiddens. In *Packrat Middens: The Last 40,000 Years of Biotic Change,* edited by J. L. Betancourt, T. R. Van Devender, and P. S. Martin, pp. 28–42. University of Arizona Press, Tucson.

Firby, J. R., J. E. Mawby, and J. O. Davis. 1987. Vertebrate paleontology and geology of the Rye Patch paleontological locality. In *Studies in Archaeology, Geology, and Paleontology at Rye Patch Reservoir, Pershing County, Nevada,* by M. K. Rusco and J. O. Davis, pp. 23–40. Nevada State Museum Anthropological Papers 20.

Fisher, F. I. 1945. Locomotion in the fossil vulture *Teratornis. American Midland Naturalist* 33:725–742.

Fladmark, K. R. 1979. Routes: Alternative migration corridors for early man in North America. *American Antiquity* 44:55–69.

Flaschka, I., C. W. Stockton, and W. R. Boggess. 1987. Climatic variation and surface water resources in the Great Basin region. *Water Resources Bulletin* 23:47–57.

Flenniken, J. J., and P. J. Wilke. 1989. Typology, technology, and chronology of Great Basin dart points. *American Anthropologist* 91:149–158.

Flint, R. F. 1971. *Glacial and Quaternary Geology.* Wiley, New York.

Force, C. 1991. Late Pleistocene–early Holocene woodrat (*Neotoma* sp.) dental remains from Kokoweef Cave, San Bernardino, California. In *Crossing the Borders: Quaternary Studies in Eastern California and Southwestern Nevada,* edited by R. E. Reynolds, pp. 104–106. San Bernardino County Museum Association, Redlands, California.

Forester, R. M. 1987. Late Quaternary paleoclimatic records from lacustrine ostracodes. In *The Geology of North America,* Volume K-3: *North America and Adjacent Oceans during the Last Deglaciation,* edited by W. F. Ruddiman and H. E. Wright, Jr., pp. 261–276. Geological Society of America, Boulder, Colorado.

Fortsch, D. E. 1978. The Lake China Rancholabrean Faunule. In *The Ancient Californians: Rancholabrean Hunters of the Mojave Lakes Country,* edited by E. L. Davis, pp. 173–176. Natural History Museum of Los Angeles County Science Series 26.

Foster, L. 1987. *Adventuring in the California Desert.* Sierra Club Books, San Francisco.

Fowler, C. S. 1972. Some ecological clues to proto-Numic homelands. In *Great Basin Cultural Ecology: A Symposium,* edited by D. D. Fowler, pp. 105–122. Desert Research Institute Publications in the Social Sciences 8.

Fowler, C. S. 1982. Settlement patterns and subsistence systems in the Great Basin: The ethnographic record. In *Man and Environment in the Great Basin,* edited by D. B. Madsen and J. F. O'Connell, pp. 121–138. Society for American Archaeology Papers 2.

Fowler, C. S. 1986. Subsistence. In *Handbook of North American Indians,* Volume 11: *Great Basin,* edited by W. L. d'Azevedo, pp. 64–97. Smithsonian Institution Press, Washington, D.C.

Fowler, C. S., ed. 1989. *Willard Z. Park's Ethnographic Notes on the Northern Paiute of Western Nevada, 1933–1944.* University of Utah Anthropological Papers 114.

Fowler, C. S. 1990. Ethnographic perspectives on marsh-based cultures in western Nevada. In *Wetland Adaptations in the Great Basin,* edited by J. C. Janetski and D. B. Madsen, pp. 17–32. Brigham Young University Museum of Peoples and Cultures, Occasional Papers 1.

Fowler, D. D. 1968. *The Archaeology of Newark Cave, White Pine County, Nevada.* Desert Research Institute Technical Report Series S-H, Social Sciences and Humanities, Publication 3.

Fowler, D. D. 1973. Biographical sketch of S. M. Wheeler. In *The Archaeology of Etna Cave, Lincoln County, Nevada,* edited by D. D. Fowler, p. 7. Desert Research Institute Publications in the Social Sciences 7.

Fowler, D. D., and C. S. Fowler. 1991. The use of natural man in natural history. In *Columbian Consequences,* Volume 3: *The Spanish Borderlands in Pan-American Perspective,* edited by D. H. Thomas, pp. 37–71. Smithsonian Institution Press, Washington, D.C.

Fowler, D. D., and D. B. Madsen. 1986. Prehistory of the southeastern area. In *Handbook of North American Indians,* Volume 11: *Great Basin,* edited by W. L. d'Azevedo, pp. 173–182. Smithsonian Institution Press, Washington, D.C.

Fowler, D. D., and J. F. Matley. 1979. *Material Culture of the Numa: The John Wesley Powell Collection, 1867–1880.* Smithsonian Contributions to Anthropology 26.

Fowler, D. D., D. B. Madsen, and E. M. Hattori. 1973. *Prehistory of Southeastern Nevada.* Desert Research Institute Publications in the Social Sciences 6.

Frémont, J. C. 1845. *Report of the Exploring Expedition to the Rocky Mountains in the Year 1842, and to Oregon and California in the Years 1843–1844.* Goles and Seaton, Washington, D.C.

Frémont, J. C. 1887. *Memoirs of My Life.* Belford, Clarke, New York.

Frison, G. C. 1973. Archeology of the Casper site. In *The Casper Site: A Hell Gap Bison Kill on the High Plains,* edited by G. Frison, pp. 1–111. Academic Press, New York.

Frison, G. C. 1991. *Prehistoric Hunters of the High Plains.* Second edition. Academic Press, San Diego.

Fry, G. 1976. *Analysis of Prehistoric Coprolites from Utah.* University of Utah Anthropological Papers 97.

Furgurson, E. B. 1992. Lake Tahoe: Playing for high stakes. *National Geographic* 181:112–132.

Gaines, D. 1989. Mono Lake Guidebook. Kutsavi Books, Lee Vining, California.

Gale, H. S. 1915. Salines in the Owens, Searles, and Panamint Basins, southeastern California. *U.S. Geological Survey Bulletin* 580:251–323.

Gehr, K. D. 1978. Preliminary note on the late Pleistocene geomorphology and archaeology of the Harney Basin, Oregon. *The Ore Bin* 40:165–170.

Gehr, K. D. 1980. Late Pleistocene and Recent Archaeology and Geomorphology of the South Shore of Harney Lake, Oregon. M.A. thesis, Department of Anthropology, Portland State University, Portland, Oregon.

Gibbons, A. 1992. Mitochondrial Eve: Wounded, but not dead yet. *Science* 257:873–875.

Gilbert, B. 1983. *Westering Man: The Life of Joseph Walker.* University of Oklahoma Press, Norman.

Gilbert, G. K. 1890. *Lake Bonneville.* U.S. Geological Survey Monograph 1.

Gillette, D. D., and D. B. Madsen. 1992. The short-faced bear *Arctodus simus* from the late Quaternary in the Wasatch Mountains of central Utah. *Journal of Vertebrate Paleontology* 12:107–112.

Gillette, D. D., and D. B. Madsen. 1993. The Columbian mammoth, *Mammuthus columbi,* from the Wasatch Mountains of central Utah. *Journal of Paleontology* (in press).

Gleason, H. A., and A. Cronquist. 1964. *The Natural Geography of Plants.* Columbia University Press, New York

Gobalet, K. W., and R. W. Negrini. 1992. Evidence for endemism in fossil tui chub, *Gila bicolor,* from Pleistocene Lake Chewaucan, Oregon. *Copeia* 1992:539–544.

Godfrey, W. E. 1966. *The Birds of Canada.* National Museums of Canada Bulletin 203, Biological Series 73.

Goebel, T., R. Powers, and B. Bigelow. 1991. The Nenana complex of Alaska and Clovis origins. In *Clovis: Origins and Adaptations,* edited by R. Bonnichsen and K. Turnmire, pp. 49–79. Center for the Study of the First Americans, Oregon State University, Corvallis.

Goodwin, H. T. 1989. *Marmota flaviventris* from the central Mojave Desert of California: Biogeographic implications. *Southwestern Naturalist* 34:284–287.

Goodwin, H. T., and R. E. Reynolds. 1989a. Late Quaternary Sciuridae from Kokoweef Cave, San Bernardino County, California. *Bulletin of the Southern California Academy of Sciences* 88:21–32.

Goodwin, H. T., and R. E. Reynolds. 1989b. Late Quaternary Sciuridae from low elevations in the Mojave Desert, California. *Southwestern Naturalist* 34:506–512.

Goss, J. H. 1968. Culture-historical inference from Utaztecan linguistic evidence. In *Utaztecan Prehistory,* edited by E. H. Swanson, Jr., pp. 1–42. Occasional Papers of the Idaho State University Museum 22.

Goss, J. H. 1977. Linguistic tools for the Great Basin prehistorian. In *Models and Great Basin Prehistory: A Symposium,* edited by D. D. Fowler, pp. 49–70. Desert Research Institute Publications in the Social Sciences 12.

Graham, R. W. 1985a. Diversity and community structure of the late Pleistocene mammal fauna of North America. *Acta Zoologica Fennica* 170:181–192.

Graham, R. W. 1985b. Response of mammalian communities to environmental changes during the late Quaternary. In *Community Ecology,* edited by J. Diamond and T. J. Case, pp. 300–313. Harper & Row, New York.

Graham, R. W. 1986. Plant-animal interactions and Pleistocene extinctions. In *Dynamics of Extinctions,* edited by D. K. Elliot, pp. 131–154. Wiley, New York. Graham, R. W. 1990. Evolution of new ecosystems at the end of the Pleistocene. In *Megafauna and Man: Discovery of America's Heartland,* edited by L. D. Agenbroad, J. I. Mead, and L. W. Nelson, pp. 54–60. The Mammoth Site of Hot Springs, South Dakota, Inc., Scientific Papers 1.

Graham, R. W., and M. A. Graham. 1993. The Quaternary biogeography and paleoecology of *Martes* in North America. In *The Biology of Martens, Sables, and Fishers,* edited by S. W. Buskirk, A. S. Harestead, M. G. Raphael, and R. A. Powell. Cornell University Press, Ithaca, New York (in press).

Graham, R. W., and Lundelius, E. L., Jr. 1984. Coevolutionary disequilibrium and Pleistocene extinctions. In *Quaternary Extinctions: A Prehistoric Revolution,* edited by P. S. Martin and R. G. Klein, pp. 223–249. University of Arizona Press, Tucson.

Grayson, D. K. 1975. *A Bibliography of the Literature on North American Climates of the Past 13,000 Years.* Garland, New York.

Grayson, D. K. 1977a. On the Holocene history of some Great Basin lagomorphs. *Journal of Mammalogy* 58:507–513.

Grayson, D. K. 1977b. Pleistocene avifaunas and the overkill hypothesis. *Science* 195:691–693.

Grayson, D. K. 1979. Mt. Mazama, climatic change, and Fort Rock Basin archaeofaunas. In *Volcanic Activity and Human Ecology,* edited by P. D. Sheets and D. K. Grayson, pp. 427–458. Academic Press, New York.

Grayson, D. K. 1981. A mid-Holocene record for the heather vole, *Phenacomys* cf. *intermedius,* in the central Great Basin, and its biogeographic significance. *Journal of Mammalogy* 62:115–121.

Grayson, D. K. 1983. The paleontology of Gatecliff Shelter: Small mammals. In *The Archaeology of Monitor Valley. 2. Gatecliff Shelter,* by D. H. Thomas, pp. 98–126. American Museum of Natural History Anthropological Papers 59(1).

Grayson, D. K. 1984. The time of extinction and nature of adaptation of the noble marten, *Martes nobilis.* In *Contributions in Quaternary Vertebrate Paleontology: A Volume in Memorial to John E. Guilday,* edited by H. H. Genoways and M. R. Dawson, pp. 233–240. Carnegie Museum of Natural History Special Publication 8.

Grayson, D. K. 1985. The paleontology of Hidden Cave: Birds and mammals. In *The Archaeology of Hidden Cave, Nevada,* edited by D. H. Thomas, pp. 125–161. American Museum of Natural History Anthropological Papers 61(1).

Grayson, D. K. 1986. Eoliths, archaeological ambiguity, and the generation of "middle-range" research. In *American Archaeology: Past and Present,* edited by D. J. Meltzer, D. D. Fowler, and J. A. Sabloff, pp. 77–133. Smithsonian Institution Press, Washington, D.C.

Grayson, D. K. 1987a. An analysis of the chronology of late Pleistocene extinctions in North America. *Quaternary Research* 28:281–289.

Grayson, D. K. 1987b. The biogeographic history of small mammals in the Great Basin: Observations on the last 20,000 years. *Journal of Mammalogy* 68:359–375.

Grayson, D. K. 1988a. *Danger Cave, Last Supper Cave, Hanging Rock Shelter: The Faunas.* American Museum of Natural History Anthropological Papers 66(1).

Grayson, D. K. 1988b. Perspectives on the archaeology of the first Americans. In *Americans before Columbus: Ice-Age Origins,* edited by R. C. Carlisle, pp. 107–123. Ethnology Monographs 12.

Grayson, D. K. 1989a. Bone transport, bone destruction, and reverse utility curves. *Journal of Archaeological Science* 16:643–652.

Grayson, D. K. 1989b. The chronology of North American late Pleistocene extinctions. *Journal of Archaeological Science* 16:153–165.

Grayson, D. K. 1990. Donner Party deaths: A demographic assessment. *Journal of Anthropological Research* 46:223–242.

Grayson, D. K. 1991a. Alpine faunas from the White Mountains, California: Adaptive change in the late prehistoric Great Basin? *Journal of Archaeological Science* 18:483–506.

Grayson, D. K. 1991b. Late Pleistocene mammalian extinctions in North America: Taxonomy, chronology, and explanations. *Journal of World Prehistory* 5:193–232.

Grayson, D. K. 1993. The Alta Toquima vertebrate fauna. In *The Archaeology of Monitor Valley. 4. Alta Toquima and the Mt. Jefferson Complex,* by D. H. Thomas. American Museum of Natural History Anthropological Papers (in press).

Grayson, D. K., and S. D. Livingston. 1989. High-elevation records for *Neotoma cinerea* in the White Mountains, California. *Great Basin Naturalist* 49:392–395.

Grayson, D. K., and S. D. Livingston. 1993. Missing mammals on Great Basin mountains: Holocene extinctions or inadequate knowledge? *Conservation Biology* (in press).

Green, J. S., and J. T. Flinders. 1980. *Brachylagus idahoensis. Mammalian Species* 125.

Greenberg, J. H. 1987a. *Language in the Americas.* Stanford University Press, Stanford, California.

Greenberg, J. H. 1987b. Language in the Americas: A CA book review. *Current Anthropology* 28:647–667.

Greenspan, R. L. 1988. Fish remains. In *Preliminary Investigations in Stillwater Marsh: Human Prehistory and Geoarchaeology,* edited by C. Raven and R. G. Elston, pp. 313–327. U.S. Department of the Interior, U.S. Fish and Wildlife Service, Region 1, Cultural Resource Series 1. Portland, Oregon.

Griffin, J. B. 1964. The Northeast Woodlands area. In *Prehistoric Man in the New World,* edited by J. D. Jennings and E. Norbeck, pp. 227–258. University of Chicago Press, Chicago.

Griset, S., ed. 1986. *Pottery of the Great Basin and Adjacent Areas.* University of Utah Anthropological Papers 111.

Gruhn, R. 1961. *The Archaeology of Wilson Butte Cave, South-Central Idaho.* Occasional Papers of the Idaho State College Museum 6.

Gruhn, R. 1979. Excavation in Amy's Shelter, eastern Nevada. In *The Archaeology of Smith Creek Canyon, Eastern Nevada,* edited by D. R. Tuohy and D. L. Rendall, pp. 90–161. Nevada State Museum Anthropological Papers 17.

Gudschinsky, S. 1956. The ABCs of lexicostatistics (glottochronology). *Word* 12:175–210.

Guilday, J. E., H. W. Hamilton, E. Anderson, and P. W. Parmalee. 1978. The Baker Bluff Cave Deposit and the Late Pleistocene Faunal Gradient. *Bulletin of the Carnegie Museum of Natural History* 11.

Guthrie, R. D. 1968. Paleontology of the large-mammal community in interior Alaska during the late Pleistocene. *American Midland Naturalist* 79:346–363.

Guthrie, R. D. 1982. Mammals of the mammoth steppe as a paleoenvironmental indicator. In *The Paleoecology of Beringia,* edited by D. M. Hopkins, J. V. Matthews, Jr., C. E. Schweger, and S. B. Young, pp. 307–326. Academic Press, New York.

Guthrie, R. D. 1984. Mosaics, allelochemics, and nutrients: An ecological theory of late Pleistocene megafaunal extinctions. In *Quaternary Extinctions: A Prehistoric Revolution,* edited by P. S. Martin and R. G. Klein, pp. 259–298. University of Arizona Press, Tucson.

Guthrie, R. D. 1985. Woolly arguments against the mammoth steppe—A new look at the palynological data. *Quarterly Review of Archaeology* 6(3):9–16.

Guthrie, R. D. 1990a. *Frozen Fauna of the Mammoth Steppe.* University of Chicago Press, Chicago.

Guthrie, R. D. 1990b. Late Pleistocene faunal revolution: A new perspective on the extinction debate. In *Megafauna and Man: Discovery of America's Heartland,* edited by L. D. Agenbroad, J. I. Mead, and L. W. Nelson, pp. 42–53. The Mammoth Site of Hot Springs, South Dakota, Inc., Scientific Papers 1.

Gwynn, J. W., ed. 1980. *Great Salt Lake: A Scientific, Historical, and Economic Overview.* Utah Geological and Mineral Survey Bulletin 116.

Hale, K. 1958. Internal diversity in Uto-Aztecan: I. *International Journal of American Linguistics* 24:101–107.

Hall, E. R. 1946. *Mammals of Nevada.* University of California Press, Berkeley and Los Angeles.

Hall, E. R. 1981. *Mammals of North America.* Wiley, New York.

Hall, S. A. 1985. Quaternary pollen analysis and vegetational history of the Southwest. In *Pollen Records of Late-Quaternary North American Sediments,* edited by V. M. Bryant, Jr., and R. G. Holloway, pp. 95–123. American Association of Stratigraphic Palynologists, Dallas.

Halsey, J. H. 1953. Geology of Parts of the Bridgeport, California and Wellington, Nevada Quadrangles. Ph.D. dissertation, Department of Geology, University of California, Berkeley.

Hanes, R. C. 1988a. Early cultural traditions of the Owyhee Uplands as seen from Dirty Shame Rockshelter. In *Early Human Occupation in Far Western North America: The Clovis-Archaic Interface,* edited by J. A. Willig, C. M. Aikens, and J. L. Fagan, pp. 361–372. Nevada State Museum Anthropological Papers 21.

Hanes, R. C. 1988b. *Lithic Assemblages of Dirty Shame Rockshelter.* University of Oregon Anthropological Papers 40.

Hansen, C. G. 1956. An Ecological Survey of the Vertebrate Animals on Steens Mountain, Harney County, Oregon. Ph.D. dissertation, Oregon State College, Corvallis.

Hansen, H. P. 1947. Postglacial vegetation in the Northern Great Basin. *American Journal of Botany* 34:164–171.

Hansen, R. M. 1978. Shasta ground sloth food habits, Rampart Cave, Arizona. *Paleobiology* 4:302–319.

Hardesty, D. L. 1987. The archaeology of the Donner Party tragedy. *Nevada Historical Society Quarterly* 30:246–268.

Hardesty, D. L., and S. Lindstrom. 1990. *Archaeology of the Donner Family Camp.* Tahoe National Forest, USDA Forest Service, Nevada City, California.

Harding, S. T. 1965. *Recent Variations in the Water Supply of the Western Great Basin.* Water Resources Center Archives Series 16. University of California, Berkeley.

Harington, C. R. 1980. Faunal exchange between Siberia and North America: Evidence from Quaternary land mammal remains in Siberia, Alaska, and the Yukon Territory. *Canadian Journal of Anthropology* 1:45–49.

Harper, K. T., and G. M. Alder. 1972. Paleoclimatic inferences concerning the last 10,000 years from a resampling of Danger Cave, Utah. In *Great Basin Cultural Ecology: A Symposium,* edited by D. D. Fowler, pp. 13–24. Desert Research Institute Publications in the Social Sciences 8.

Harper, K. T., D. L. Freeman, W. K. Ostler, and L. G. Klikoff. 1978. The flora of Great Basin mountain ranges: Diversity, sources, and dispersal ecology. In *Intermountain Biogeography: A Symposium,* edited by K. T. Harper and J. L. Reveal, pp. 81–104. Great Basin Naturalist Memoirs 2.

Harrill, J. R., J. S. Gates, and J. M. Thomas. 1988. *Major Ground-Water Flow Systems in the Great Basin Region of Nevada, Utah, and Adjacent States: Regional Aquifer Systems of the Great Basin.* U.S. Geological Survey Hydrologic Investigations Atlas HA-694-C.

Harrington, M. R. 1933. *Gypsum Cave, Nevada.* Southwest Museum Papers 8.

Harrington, M. R. 1957. *A Pinto Site at Little Lake, California.* Southwest Museum Papers 17.

Harrington, M. R., and R. D. Simpson. 1961. *Tule Springs, Nevada with Other Evidences of Pleistocene Man in North America.* Southwest Museum Papers 18.

Harris, A. H. 1985. *Late Pleistocene Vertebrate Paleoecology of the West.* University of Texas Press, Austin.

Harris, E. W. 1980. *The Overland Emigrant Trail to California.* Fourth printing, revised. Nevada Emigrant Trail Marking Committee, Nevada Historical Society, Reno.

Harris, G. A. 1977. Root phenology as a factor of competition among grass seedlings. *Journal of Range Management* 30:172–177.

Harrison, G. A., J. M. Tanner, D. R. Pilbeam, and P. T. Baker. 1988. *Human Biology.* Third edition. Oxford University Press, Oxford.

Hart, J. 1991. *Hiking the Great Basin: The High Desert Country of California, Oregon, Nevada, and Utah.* Revised edition. Sierra Club, San Francisco.

Harvey, L. D. D. 1989. Modelling the Younger Dryas. *Quaternary Science Reviews* 8:137–149.

Hastings, L. W. 1845. *The Emigrants' Guide to Oregon and California.* Conclin, Cincinnati.

Hattori, E. M. 1982. *The Archaeology of Falcon Hill Cave, Winnemucca Lake, Washoe County, Nevada.* Nevada State Museum Anthropological Papers 18.

Hattori, E. M. 1985. The first Nevadans: Pleistocene humans in Nevada. *Halcyon* 1985:105–117.

Hattori, E. M., P. H. Shelley, and D. R. Tuohy. 1976. Preliminary Report on a Techno-Functional Examination of Flaked Stone Artifacts. Paper presented at the 1976 Great Basin Anthropological Conference, Las Vegas, Nevada.

Hattori, E. M., M. E. Newman, and D. R. Tuohy. 1990. Blood Residue Analysis of Great Basin Crescents. Paper presented at the 1990 Great Basin Anthropological Conference, Reno, Nevada.

Haury, E. W., E. B. Sayles, and W. W. Wasley. 1959. The Lehner Mammoth Site, southeastern Arizona. *American Antiquity* 25:2–30.

Hawkins, B. R., and D. B. Madsen. 1990. Excavation of the Donner-Reed Wagons: Historic Archaeology along the Hastings Cutoff. University of Utah Press, Salt Lake City.

Haynes, C. V., Jr. 1967. Quaternary geology of the Tule Springs area, Clark County, Nevada. In *Pleistocene Studies in Southern Nevada,* edited by H. M. Wormington and D. Ellis, pp. 15–104. Nevada State Museum Anthropological Papers 13.

Haynes, C. V., Jr. 1971. Time, environment, and early man. *Arctic Anthropology* 8(2):3–14.

Haynes, C. V., Jr. 1973. The Calico Site: Artifacts or geofacts? *Science* 181:305–310.

Haynes, C. V., Jr. 1980a. Paleoindian charcoal from Meadowcroft Rockshelter: Is contamination a problem? *American Antiquity* 45:582–587.

Haynes, C. V., Jr. 1980b. The Clovis culture. *Canadian Journal of Anthropology* 1:115–121.

Haynes, C. V., Jr. 1987. Clovis origins update. *The Kiva* 52:83–94.

Haynes, C. V., Jr. 1990. The Antevs-Bryan years and the legacy for Paleoindian geochronology. In *Establishment of a Geologic Framework for Paleoanthropology,* edited by L. F. Laporte, pp. 55–68. Geological Society of America Special Paper 242.

Haynes, C. V., Jr. 1991a. Geoarchaeological and paleohydrological evidence for a Clovis-age drought in North America and its bearing on extinction. *Quaternary Research* 35:438–450.

Haynes, C. V., Jr. 1991b. More on Meadowcroft radiocarbon chronology. *Review of Archaeology* 12(1):8–14.

Haynes, C. V., Jr. 1992. Contributions of radiocarbon dating to the geochronology of the peopling of the New World. In *Radiocarbon after Four Decades,* edited by R. E. Taylor, A. Long, and R. S. Kra, pp. 355–374. Springer-Verlag, New York.

Hayssen, V. 1991. *Dipodomys microps. Mammalian Species* 389.

Hayward, C. L., C. Cottam, A. M. Woodbury, and H. H. Frost. 1976. *Birds of Utah.* Great Basin Naturalist Memoirs 1.

Heald, W. F. 1956. An active glacier in Nevada. *American Alpine Journal* 10(1):164–167.

Heaton, T. H. 1985. Quaternary paleontology and paleoecology of Crystal Ball Cave, Millard County, Utah: With emphasis on mammals and description of a new species of fossil skunk. *Great Basin Naturalist* 45:337–390.

Heaton, T. H. 1987. Initial investigation of vertebrate remains from Snake Creek Burial Cave, White Pine County, Nevada. *Current Research in the Pleistocene* 4:107–109.

Heckmann, R. A., C. W. Thompson, and D. A. White. 1981. Fishes of Utah Lake. *Great Basin Naturalist Memoirs* 5:107–127.

Heizer, R. F. 1951. Preliminary report on the Leonard Rockshelter site, Pershing County, Nevada. *American Antiquity* 17:89–98.

Heizer, R. F., and M. A. Baumhoff. 1970. Big game hunters in the Great Basin: A critical review of the evidence. *University of California Archaeological Research Facility Reports* 7:1–12.

Heizer, R. F., and L. K. Napton. 1970. Archaeology and the Prehistoric Great Basin Lacustrine Subsistence Regime as seen from Lovelock Cave, Nevada. *University of California Archaeological Research Facility Contributions* 10.

Heizer, R. F., M. A. Baumhoff, and C. W. Clewlow, Jr. 1968. Archaeology of South Fork Shelter (NV-El-11), Elko County, Nevada. *University of California Archaeological Survey Reports* 71: 1–58.

Herr, P. 1987. *Jessie Benton Frémont.* University of Oklahoma Press, Norman

Hester, T. R. 1973. *Chronological Ordering of Great Basin Prehistory.* Contributions of the University of California Archaeological Research Facility 17.

Hester, T. R., M. P. Mildner, and L. Spencer. 1974. *Great Basin Atlatl Studies.* Ballena Press Publications in Archaeology, Ethnology, and History 2.

Hickerson, H. 1965. The Virginia deer and intertribal buffer zones in the upper Mississippi valley. In *Man, Culture, and Animals,* edited by A. Leeds and A. P. Vayda, pp. 43–66. American Association for the Advancement of Science Publication 78.

Hidy, G. M., and H. E. Klieforth. 1990. Atmospheric processes and the climates of the Basin and Range. In *Plant Biology of the Basin and Range,* edited by C. B. Osmond, L. F. Pitelka, and G. M. Hidy, pp. 17–46. Springer-Verlag, Berlin.

Hiebert, R. D., and J. L. Hamrick. 1983. Patterns and levels of genetic variation in Great Basin bristlecone pine, *Pinus longaeva. Evolution* 37:302–310.

Hill, W. E. 1986. *The Oregon Trail: Yesterday and Today.* Caxton, Caldwell, Idaho.

Hintze, L. F. 1988. *Geologic History of Utah.* Brigham Young University Geology Studies, Special Publication 7.

Hockett, C. F. 1958. *A Course in Modern Linguistics.* Macmillan, New York.

Holmer, R. N. 1986. Common projectile points of the Intermountain West. In *Anthropology of the Desert West: Essays in Honor of Jesse D. Jennings,* edited by C. J. Condie and D. D. Fowler, pp. 89–116. University of Utah Anthropological Papers 110.

Holmer, R. N. 1990. Prehistory of the Northern Shoshone. In *Fort Hall and the Shoshone-Bannock,* edited by E. S. Lohse and R. N. Holmer, pp. 41–59. Idaho State University Press, Pocatello.

Hooke, R. Le B. 1972. Geomorphic evidence for late-Wisconsin and Holocene tectonic deformation, Death Valley, California. *Geological Society of America Bulletin* 83:2073–2098.

Hopkins, D. M. 1975. Time-stratigraphic nomenclature for the Holocene Epoch. *Geology* 3:10.

Hopkins, D. M. 1982. Aspects of the paleogeography of Beringia during the Late Pleistocene. In *The Paleoecology of Beringia,* edited by D. M. Hopkins, J. V. Matthews, Jr., C. E. Schweger, and S. B. Young, pp. 3–28. Academic Press, New York.

Hopkins, D. M., J. V. Matthews, Jr., C. E. Schweger, and S. B. Young, eds. 1982. *The Paleoecology of Beringia.* Academic Press, New York.

Houghton, J. G. 1969. *Characteristics of Rainfall in the Great Basin.* Desert Research Institute, Reno, Nevada.

Houghton, J. G., C. M. Sakamoto, and R. O. Gifford. 1975. *Nevada's Weather and Climate.* Nevada Bureau of Mines and Geology Special Publication 2.

House, J. S., C. Robbins, and H. L. Metzner. 1982. The association of social relationships and activities with mortality: Prospective evidence from the Tecumseh Community Health Study. *American Journal of Epidemiology* 116:123–140.

Houston, D. C. 1983. The adaptive radiation of the Griffon vultures. In *Vulture Biology and Management,* edited by S. R. Wilbur and J. A. Jackson, pp. 135–152. University of California Press, Berkeley and Los Angeles.

Howard, H. 1932. Eagles and eagle-like vultures of the Pleistocene of Rancho La Brea. *Carnegie Institute of Washington Publication* 429.

Howard, H. 1935. A new species of eagle from a Quaternary Cave deposit in eastern Nevada. *The Condor* 37:206–209.

Howard, H. 1946. A review of the Pleistocene birds of Fossil Lake, Oregon. *Carnegie Instititute of Washington Publications* 551:141–195.

Howard, H. 1952. The prehistoric avifauna of Smith Creek Cave, Nevada, with a description of a new gigantic raptor. *Bulletin of the Southern California Academy of Sciences* 51:50–54.

Howard, H. 1955. *Fossil Birds from Manix Lake, California.* U.S. Geological Survey Professional Paper 264-J.

Howard, H. 1962. A comparison of avian assemblages from individual pits at Rancho La Brea, California. *Los Angeles County Museum Contributions in Science* 58.

Howard, H. 1964a. *A New Species of the "Pigmy Goose,"* Anabernicula, *from the Oregon Pleistocene, with a Discussion of the Genus.* American Museum Novitates 2200.

Howard, H. 1964b. Fossil Anseriformes. In *The Waterfowl of the World,* Volume 4, by J. Delacour, pp. 233–326. Country Life, London.

Howard, H. 1972. The incredible teratorn again. *Condor* 74:341–344.

Howard, H., and A. H. Miller. 1939. The avifauna associated with human remains at Rancho La Brea, California. *Carnegie Institute of Washington Publications* 514:41–48.

Howard, R., and A. Moore. 1991. *A Complete Checklist of the Birds of the World.* Second edition. Academic Press, London.

Howe, K. M., and J. E. Martin. 1977. *Investigation of the Paleontological Resources of Fossil Lake, Lake Co., Oregon, with Recommendations for Their Management.* Bureau of Land Management, Lakeview, Oregon.

Hubbs, C. L., and R. R. Miller. 1948. The zoological evidence: Correlation between fish distribution and hydrographic history in the desert basins of western United States. *Bulletin of the University of Utah* 38(20), *Biological Series* 10(7):17–166.

Hubbs, C. L., R. R. Miller, and L. C. Hubbs. 1974. *Hydrographic History and Relict Fishes of the North-Central Great Basin.* Memoirs of the California Academy of Sciences 7.

Hughes, R. E. 1986. *Diachronic Variability in Obsidian Procurement Patterns in Northeastern California and Southcentral Oregon.* University of California Publications in Anthropology 17.

Hunt, C. B. 1966. *Plant Ecology of Death Valley, California.* U.S. Geological Survey Professional Paper 509.

Hunt, C. B. 1967. *Physiography of the United States.* W. H. Freeman, San Francisco.

Hunt, C. B. 1976. *Death Valley: Geology, Ecology, Archaeology.* University of California Press, Berkeley and Los Angeles.

Hunt, C. B., and D. R. Mabey. 1966. *Stratigraphy and Structure, Death Valley, California.* U.S. Geological Survey Professional Paper 494-A.

Hunt, C. B., T. W. Robinson, W. A. Bowles, and A. L. Washburn. 1966. *Hydrologic Basin, Death Valley, California.* U.S. Geological Survey Professional Paper 494-B.

Hutchinson, P. W. 1988. The prehistoric dwellers at Lake Hubbs. In *Early Human Occupation in Far Western North America: The Clovis-Archaic Interface,* edited by J. A. Willig, C. M. Aikens, and J. L. Fagan, pp. 303–318. Nevada State Museum Anthropological Papers 21.

Hymes, D. H. 1960. Lexicostatistics so far. *Current Anthropology* 1:3–44.

Imbrie, J., and K. P. Imbrie. 1979. *Ice Ages.* Enslow, Hillside, New Jersey.

Irving, W. N., and C. R. Harington. 1973. Upper Pleistocene Radiocarbon-dated artefacts from the northern Yukon. *Science* 179:335–340.

Ives, R. L. 1946. Glaciation in the desert ranges, Utah. *Journal of Geology* 54:335.

Jackson, D., and M. L. Spence, eds. 1970. *The Expeditions of John Charles Frémont,* Volume 1: *Travels from 1838 to 1844.* University of Illinois Press, Urbana.

Jackson, R. H., and D. J. Stevens. 1981. Physical and cultural environment of Utah Lake and adjacent areas. *Great Basin Naturalist Memoirs* 5:3–23.

Jacobsen, G. L., Jr., T. Webb III, and E. C. Grimm. 1987. Patterns and rates of vegetation change during the deglaciation of eastern North America. In *The Geology of North America,* Volume K-3: *North America and Adjacent Oceans during the Last Deglaciation,* edited by W. F. Ruddiman and H. E. Wright, Jr., pp. 277–288. Geological Society of America, Boulder, Colorado.

Jacobsen, W. H., Jr. 1986. Washoe language. In *Handbook of North American Indians,* Volume 11: *Great Basin,* edited by W. L. d'Azevedo, pp. 107–112. Smithsonian Institution Press, Washington, D.C.

James, S. R. 1983. Surprise Valley settlement and subsistence: A critical review of the faunal evidence. *Journal of California and Great Basin Anthropology* 5:156–175.

Janetski, J. C., ed. 1981. *Prehistoric and Historic Settlement in the Escalante Desert.* Report of Investigations 81-10. University of Utah Archaeological Center, Salt Lake City.

Janetski, J. C. 1991. *The Utes of Utah Lake.* University of Utah Anthropological Papers 116.

Janetski, J. C., and D. B. Madsen, eds. 1990. *Wetland Adaptations in the Great Basin.* Brigham Young University Museum of Peoples and Cultures, Occasional Papers 1.

Jarrett, R. D., and H. D. Malde. 1987. Paleodischarge of the late Pleistocene Bonneville Flood, Snake River, Idaho, computed from new evidence. *Bulletin of the Geological Society of America* 99:127–134.

Jefferson, G. T. 1982. Late Pleistocene vertebrates from a Mormon Mountain Cave in southern Nevada. *Bulletin of the Southern California Academy of Sciences* 81:121–127.

Jefferson, G. T. 1985. *Review of the Late Pleistocene Avifauna from Lake Manix, Central Mojave Desert, California.* Natural History Museum of Los Angeles County Contributions in Science 362.

Jefferson, G. T. 1987. The Camp Cady Local Fauna: Paleoenvironment of the Lake Manix Basin. *San Bernardino County Museum Association Quarterly* 34(3–4):3–35.

Jefferson, G. T. 1990. Rancholabrean age vertebrates from the eastern Mojave Desert, California. In *At the End of the Mojave: Quaternary Studies in the Eastern Mojave Desert,* edited by R. E. Reynolds, S. G. Wells, and R. H. Brady III, pp. 109–116. San Bernardino County Museum Association, Redlands, California.

Jefferson, G. T. 1991. Rancholabrean age vertebrates from the southeastern Mojave Desert, California. In *Crossing the Borders: Quaternary Studies in Eastern California and Southwestern Nevada,* edited by R. E. Reynolds, pp. 163–176. San Bernardino County Museum Association, Redlands, California.

Jefferson, G. T., J. R. Keaton, and P. Hamilton. 1982. Manix Lake and the Manix Fault Field Trip Guide. *San Bernardino County Museum Association Quarterly* 29(3–4):1–47.

Jehl, J. R., Jr. 1967. Pleistocene birds from Fossil Lake, Oregon. *The Condor* 69:24–27.

Jenkins, D. L. 1987. Dating the Pinto occupation at Rogers Ridge: A fossil spring site in the Mojave Desert, California. *Journal of California and Great Basin Anthropology* 9:214–231.

Jenkins, D. L., and C. N. Warren. 1984. Obsidian hydration and the Pinto chronology in the Mojave Desert. *Journal of California and Great Basin Anthropology* 6:44–60.

Jennings, J. D. 1957. *Danger Cave.* University of Utah Anthropological Papers 27.

Jennings, J. D. 1978. *Prehistory of Utah and the Eastern Great Basin.* University of Utah Anthropological Papers 98.

Jennings, J. D. 1989. *Prehistory of North America.* Third edition. Mayfield, Mountain View, California.

Jett, S. C. 1991. Split-twig figurines, early maize, and a child burial in east-central Utah. *Utah Archaeology* 4(1):24–32.

Johnson, D. M., R. R. Petersen, D. R. Lycan, J. W. Sweet, M. Neuhaus, and A. L. Schaedel. 1985. *Atlas of Oregon Lakes.* Oregon State University, Corvallis.

Johnson, L., and J. Johnson. 1987. *Escape from Death Valley.* University of Nevada Press, Reno.

Jones, G. T., and C. Beck. 1990. An obsidian hydration chronology of late Pleistocene–early Holocene surface assemblages from Butte Valley, Nevada. *Journal of California and Great Basin Anthropology* 12:84–100.

Jones, R. 1989. East of Wallace's Line: Issues and problems in the colonization of the Australian continent. In *The Human Revolution,* edited by P. Mellars and C. Stringer, pp. 743–782. Princeton University Press, Princeton, New Jersey.

Jorgensen, J. G. 1980. *Western Indians: Comparative Environments, Languages, and Cultures of Aboriginal Western North America.* W.H. Freeman, San Francisco.

Jorgensen, J. G. 1987. Political society in aboriginal western North America. In *Themes in Ethnology and Culture History: Essays in Honor of David F. Aberle,* edited by L. Donald, pp. 175–226. Folklore Institute, Berkeley, California.

Kaliser, B. N. 1989. *Water-Related Geologic Problems of 1983—Utah Occurrences by County.* Utah Geological and Mineral Survey Miscellaneous Publications 89-4.

Kaliser, B. N., and J. E. Slosson. 1988. *Geologic Consequences of the 1983 Wet Year in Utah.* Utah Geological and Mineral Survey Miscellaneous Publications 88-3.

Kelly, R. L. 1990. Marshes and mobility in the western Great Basin. In *Wetland Adaptations in the Great Basin,* edited by J. C. Janetski and D. B. Madsen, pp. 259–276. Brigham Young University Museum of Peoples and Cultures, Occasional Papers 1.

Kelly, R. L., and E. Hattori. 1985. Present environment and history. In *The Archaeology of Hidden Cave, Nevada,* edited by D. H. Thomas, pp. 39–46. American Museum of Natural History Anthropological Papers 61(1).

Kenagy, G. J. 1972. Saltbush leaves: excision of hypersaline tissues by a kangaroo rat. *Science* 178:1094–1096.

Kenagy, G. J. 1973. Adaptations for leaf eating in the Great Basin kangaroo rat, *Dipodomys microps. Oecologia* 12:383–412.

King, G. Q. 1978. *The Late Quaternary History of Adrian Valley, Lyon County, Nevada.* Department of Geography, University of Utah, Salt Lake City.

King, J. A. 1992. *Winter of Entrapment: A New Look at the Donner Party.* P. D. Meany, Toronto.

King, J. E., and T. R. Van Devender. 1977. Pollen analysis of fossil packrat middens from the Sonoran Desert. *Quaternary Research* 8:191–204.

King, T. J., Jr. 1976. Late Pleistocene–early Holocene history of coniferous woodlands in the Lucerne Valley region, Mohave Desert, California. *Great Basin Naturalist* 36:227–238.

Klein, R. G. 1989. *The Human Career: Human Biological and Cultural Origins.* University of Chicago Press, Chicago.

Klemmedson, J. O., and J. G. Smith. 1964. Cheatgrass (*Bromus tectorum* L.). *Botanical Review* 30:226–262.

Kodric-Brown, A. 1981. Variable breeding systems in pupfishes (Genus *Cyprinodon*): Adaptations to changing environments. In *Fishes in North American Deserts,* edited by R. J. Naiman and D. L. Soltz, pp. 205–236. Wiley, New York.

König, C. 1983. Interspecific and intraspecific competition for food among Old World vultures. In *Vulture Biology and Management,* edited by S. R. Wilbur and J. A. Jackson, pp. 153–171. University of California Press, Berkeley and Los Angeles.

Korns, J. R. 1951. West from Fort Bridger: The Pioneering of the Immigrant Trails across Utah 1846–1850. *Utah Historical Quarterly* 19:1–297.

Kroeber, A. L. 1953. *Handbook of the Indians of California.* California Book Company, Berkeley.

Kurtén, B., and E. Anderson. 1980. *Pleistocene Mammals of North America.* Columbia University Press, New York.

Kurzius, M. A. 1981. *Vegetation and Flora of the Grapevine Mountains, Death Valley National Monument, California-Nevada.* Contribution CPSU/UNLV 017/06. Cooperative National Park Resources Studies Unit, University of Nevada, Las Vegas.

Kutzbach, J. E. 1987. Model simulations of the climatic patterns during the deglaciation of North America. In *The Geology of North America,* Volume K-3: *North America and Adjacent Oceans during the Last Deglaciation,* edited by W. F. Ruddiman and H. E. Wright, Jr., pp. 425–446. Geological Society of America, Boulder, Colorado.

Kutzbach, J. E., and P. J. Guetter. 1986. The influence of changing orbital parameters and surface boundary conditions on climate simulations for the past 18,000 years. *Journal of the Atmospheric Sciences* 43:1726–1759.

La Rivers, I. 1962. *Fishes and Fisheries of Nevada.* Nevada State Fish and Game Commission, Carson City.

LaBounty, J. F., and J. E. Deacon. 1972. *Cyprinodon milleri,* a new species of pupfish (Family Cyprinodontidae) from Death Valley, California. *Copeia* 1972:769–780.

LaMarche, V. C., Jr. 1965. Distribution of Pleistocene glaciers in the White Mountains of California and Nevada. *U.S. Geological Survey Professional Papers* 525-C: C144–C146.

LaMarche, V. C., Jr. 1973. Holocene climatic variations inferred from treeline fluctuations in the White Mountains, California. *Quaternary Research* 3:632–660.

LaMarche, V. C., Jr., and H. A. Mooney. 1967. Altithermal timberline advance in western United States. *Nature* 213: 980–982.

LaMarche, V. C., Jr., and H. A. Mooney. 1972. Recent climatic change and development of the bristlecone pine (*P. longaeva* Bailey) krummholz zone, Mt. Washington, Nevada. *Arctic and Alpine Research* 4:61–72.

Lamb, S. M. 1958. Linguistic prehistory in the Great Basin. *International Journal of American Linguistics* 29:95–100.

Lambert, D. 1991. *Great Basin Drama.* Roberts Rinehart, Niwot, Colorado.

Lanner, R. M. 1981. *The Piñon Pine: A Cultural and Natural History.* University of Nevada Press, Reno.

Lanner, R. M. 1983a. The expansion of singleleaf piñon in the Great Basin. In *The Archaeology of Monitor Valley. 2. Gatecliff Shelter,* by D. H. Thomas, pp. 167–171. American Museum of Natural History Anthropological Papers 59(1).

Lanner, R. M. 1983b. *Trees of the Great Basin.* University of Nevada Press, Reno.

Lanner, R. M. 1988. Dependence of Great Basin bristlecone pine on Clark's Nutcracker for regeneration at high elevations. *Arctic and Alpine Research* 20:358–362.

Lao, Y., and L. Benson. 1988. Uranium-series age estimates and paleoclimatic significance of Pleistocene tufas from the Lahontan Basin, California and Nevada. *Quaternary Research* 30:165–176.

Larichev, V., U. Khol'ushkin, and I. Laricheva. 1988. The Upper Paleolithic of Northern Asia: Achievements, problems, and perspectives. I. Western Siberia. *Journal of World Prehistory* 2: 359–396.

Larichev, V., U. Khol'ushkin, and I. Laricheva. 1990. The Upper Paleolithic of Northern Asia: Achievements, problems, and perspectives. II. Central and Eastern Siberia. *Journal of World Prehistory* 4:347–385.

Laukhin, S. A., and N. I. Drozdov. 1991. Paleoecological aspect of Paleolithic man settling in northern Asia and his migration to northern America. In *The INQUA International Symposium on Stratigraphy and Correlation of Quaternary Deposits of the Asian and Pacific Regions,* pp. 133–144. CCOP Technical Secretariat, Bangkok, Thailand.

Lawlor, T. E. 1986. Comparative biogeography of mammals on islands. *Biological Journal of the Linnean Society* 28:99–125.

Layton, T. N. 1970. High Rock Archaeology: An Interpretation of the Prehistory of the Northwestern Great Basin. Ph.D. dissertation, Department of Anthropology, Harvard University, Cambridge, Massachusetts.

Layton, T. N., and D. H. Thomas. 1979. *The Archaeology of Silent Snake Springs, Humboldt County, Nevada.* American Museum of Natural History Anthropological Papers 55(3).

Lees, R. B. 1953. The basis of glottochronology. *Language* 29:113–127.

Lindskov, K. L. 1984. *Floods of May to June 1983 along the Northern Wasatch Front, Salt Lake City to North Ogden, Utah.* Utah Geological and Mineral Survey Water-Resources Bulletin 24.

Lindstrom, S. 1990. Submerged tree stumps as indicators of mid-Holocene aridity in the Lake Tahoe region. *Journal of California and Great Basin Anthropology* 12:146–157.

Lingenfelter, R. E. 1986. *Death Valley and the Amargosa: A Land of Illusion.* University of California Press, Berkeley and Los Angeles.

Livingston, S. D. 1986. Archaeology of the Humboldt Lakebed Site. *Journal of California and Great Basin Anthropology* 8(1):99–115.

Livingston, S. D. 1988a. Avian fauna. In *Preliminary Investigations in Stillwater Marsh: Human Prehistory and Geoarchaeology,* edited by C. Raven and R. G. Elston, pp. 292–311. U.S. Department of the Interior, U.S. Fish and Wildlife Service, Region 1, Cultural Resource Series 1. Portland, Oregon.

Livingston, S. D. 1988b. The Avian and Mammalian Remains from Lovelock Cave and the Humboldt Lakebed Site. Ph.D. dissertation, Department of Anthropology, University of Washington, Seattle.

Livingston, S. D. 1991. Aboriginal utilization of birds in the western Great Basin. In *Beamers, Bobwhites, and Blue-Points: Tributes to the Career of Paul W. Parmalee,* edited by J. R. Purdue, W. E. Klippel, and B. W. Styles, pp. 341–357. Illinois State Museum Scientific Papers 23.

Livingston, S. D. 1992. The DeLong Mammoth Locality, Black Rock Desert, Nevada. *Current Research in the Pleistocene* 8:94–97.

Lomolino, M. V. 1989. Interpretations and comparisons of constants in the species-area relationship: An additional caution. *American Naturalist* 133:277–280.

Lomolino, M. V., J. H. Brown, and R. Davis. 1989. Island biogeography of montane forest mammals in the American Southwest. *Ecology* 70:180–194.

Long, A., and P. S. Martin. 1974. Death of American ground sloths. *Science* 186:638–640.

Long, A., and A. B. Muller. 1981. Arizona radiocarbon dates X. *Radiocarbon* 23:191–217.

Loope, L. L. 1969. Subalpine and Alpine Vegetation of Northeastern Nevada. Ph.D. dissertation, Department of Botany, Duke University, Durham, North Carolina.

Los Angeles Department of Water and Power. 1989a. *Along the Owens River.* Los Angeles Department of Water and Power, Los Angeles.

Los Angeles Department of Water and Power. 1989b. *Los Angeles Aqueduct System.* Los Angeles Department of Water and Power, Los Angeles.

Lowie, R. H. 1939. Ethnographic notes on the Washo. *University of California Publications in American Archaeology and Ethnology* 36:301–352.

Lund, E. H., and E. Bentley. 1976. Steens Mountain, Oregon. *The Ore Bin* 38(4):51–66.

Lundelius, E. L., Jr. 1988. What happened to the mammoth? The climatic model. In *Americans before Columbus: Ice-Age Origins,* edited by R. C. Carlisle, pp. 75–82. Ethnology Monographs 12.

Lundelius, E. L., Jr. 1989. The implications of disharmonious assemblages for Pleistocene extinctions. *Journal of Archaeological Science* 16:407–417.

Lundelius, E. L., Jr., R. W. Graham, E. Anderson, J. Guilday, J. A. Holman, D. W. Steadman, and S. D. Webb. 1983. Terrestrial vertebrate faunas. In *Late Quaternary Environments of the United States,* Volume 1: The Late Pleistocene, edited by S. C. Porter, pp. 311–353. University of Minnesota Press, Minneapolis.

Lyman, R. L. 1991. Late Quaternary biogeography of the pygmy rabbit (*Brachylagus idahoensis*) in eastern Washington. *Journal of Mammalogy* 72:110–117.

Mabey, D. R. 1986. Notes on the historic high level of Great Salt Lake. *Utah Geological and Mineral Survey Survey Notes* 20(2):13–15.

Mabey, D. R. 1987. The end of the wet cycle. *Utah Geological and Mineral Survey Survey Notes* 21(2–3):8–9.

McAllister, J. A., and R. S. Hoffman. 1988. *Phenacomys intermedius. Mammalian Species* 305.

Mac Arthur, R. H., and E. O. Wilson. 1967. *The Theory of Island Biogeography.* Princeton University Press, Princeton, New Jersey.

McFadden, L. D., J. B. Ritter, and S. G. Wells. 1989. Use of multi-parameter relative-age methods for age estimation and correlation of alluvial fan surfaces on a desert piedmont, eastern Mojave Desert, California. *Quaternary Research* 32:276–290.

McGill, S. F., B. C. Murray, K. A. Mahler, J. H. Lieske, Jr., L. R. Rowan, and F. Budinger. 1988. Quaternary history of the Manix Lake fault, Lake Manix Basin, Mojave Desert, California. *San Bernardino County Museum Association Quarterly* 35(3–4):1–20.

McGlashan, C. F. 1880. *History of the Donner Party: A Tragedy of the Sierra.* H. S. Crocker, Sacramento (reprinted by Stanford University Press, Stanford, California, 1947).

McGlashan, M. N. 1977. *Give Me a Mountain Meadow: The Life of Charles Fayette McGlashan.* Pioneer, Fresno, California.

McGlashan, M. N., and B. H. McGlashan, eds. 1986. *From the Desk of Truckee's C. F. McGlashan.* Truckee-Donner Historical Society, Truckee, California, and Panorama West Books, Fresno, California.

McGuire, K. R. 1980. Cave sites, faunal analysis, and big-game hunters of the Great Basin: A caution. *Quaternary Research* 14:263–268.

Machette, M. N., ed. 1988. *In the Footsteps of G. K. Gilbert—Lake Bonneville and Neotectonics of the Eastern Basin and Range Province.* Utah Geological and Mineral Survey Miscellaneous Publication 88-1.

Mack, J. M., ed. 1990. Hunter-gatherer pottery from the far West. Nevada State Museum Anthropological Papers 23.

Mack, R. N. 1981. Invasion of *Bromus tectorum* L. into western North America: An ecological chronicle. *Agro-Ecosystems* 7: 145–165.

Mack, R. N. 1984. Invaders at home on the range. *Natural History* 93(2):40–47.

Mack, R. N. 1986. Alien plant invasion into the intermountain west: A case history. In *Ecology of Biological Invasions of North America and Hawaii,* edited by H. A. Mooney and J. A. Drake, pp. 191–213. Springer-Verlag, New York.

Mack, R. N., and J. N. Thompson. 1982. Evolution in steppe with few large, hooved mammals. *American Naturalist* 119:757–773.

McKenzie, D. 1982. The Northern Great Basin region. In *Reference Handbook on the Deserts of North America,* edited by G. L. Bender, pp. 67–102. Greenwood Press, Westport, Connecticut.

McLane, A. R. 1978. *Silent Cordilleras: The Mountain Ranges of Nevada.* Camp Nevada Monographs 4. Reno, Nevada.

MacMahon, J. A. 1988. Warm deserts. In *North American Terrestrial Vegetation,* edited by M. G. Barbour and W. D. Billings, pp. 231–264. California Native Plant Society Publication 9.

McManus, D. A., and J. S. Creager. 1984. Sea-level data for parts of the Bering-Chukchi shelves of Beringia from 19,000 to 10,000 14C years B.P. *Quaternary Research* 21:317–325.

MacNeish, R. S. 1964. Ancient Mesoamerican civilization. *Science* 143:531–537.

Maddison, D. R., M. Ruvolo, and D. L. Swofford. 1992. Geographic origins of human mitochrondrial DNA: Phylogenetic evidence from control region sequences. *Systematic Biology* 41:111–124.

Madsen, B. D., ed. 1990a. *Exploring the Great Salt Lake: The Stansbury Expedition of 1849–1850.* University of Utah Press, Salt Lake City.

Madsen, B. D. 1990b. Howard Stansbury's expedition to the Great Salt Lake, 1849–1850. In *Excavation of the Donner-Reed Wagons: Historic Archaeology along the Hastings Cutoff,* by B. R. Hawkins and D. B. Madsen, pp. 31–42. University of Utah Press, Salt Lake City.

Madsen, D. B. 1972. Paleoecological investigations in Meadow Valley Wash, Nevada. In *Great Basin Cultural Ecology: A Symposium,* edited by D. D. Fowler, pp. 57–66. Desert Research Institute Publications in the Social Sciences 8.

Madsen, D. B. 1975. Dating Paiute-Shoshone expansion in the Great Basin. *American Antiquity* 40:82–86.

Madsen, D. B. 1976. Pluvial–post-pluvial vegetation changes in the southeastern Great Basin. In *Holocene Environmental Change in the Great Basin,* edited by R. Elston, pp. 104–119. Nevada Archaeological Survey Paper 6.

Madsen, D. B., ed. 1980. *Fremont Perspectives.* State of Utah Division of State History Antiquities Section Selected Papers 7(16).

Madsen, D. B. 1982. Get it where the gettin's good: A variable model of Great Basin subsistence and settlement based on data from the eastern Great Basin. In *Man and Environment in the Great Basin,* edited by D. B. Madsen and J. F. O'Connell, pp. 207–226. Society for American Archaeology Papers 2.

Madsen, D. B. 1985. Two Holocene pollen records from the central Great Basin. In *Pollen Records of Late-Quaternary North American Sediments,* edited by V. M. Bryant, Jr., and R. G. Holloway, pp. 113–125. American Association of Stratigraphic Palynologists, Dallas.

Madsen, D. B. 1986a. Great Basin nuts: A short treatise on the distribution, productivity, and prehistoric use of piñon. In *Anthropology of the Desert West: Essays in Honor of Jesse D. Jennings,* edited by C. J. Condie and D. D. Fowler, pp. 21–41. University of Utah Anthropological Papers 110.

Madsen, D. B. 1986b. Prehistoric ceramics. In *Handbook of North American Indians,* Volume 11: *Great Basin,* edited by W. L. d'Azevedo, pp. 206–214. Smithsonian Institution Press, Washington, D.C.

Madsen, D. B. 1989. *Exploring the Fremont.* University of Utah Occasional Publication 8.

Madsen, D. B. 1993. Testing diet breadth models: Examining adaptive change in the late prehistoric Great Basin. *Journal of Archaeological Science* (in press).

Madsen, D. B., and M. S. Berry. 1975. A reassessment of northeastern Great Basin prehistory. *American Antiquity* 40:391–405.

Madsen, D. B., and D. R. Currey. 1979. Late Quaternary glacial and vegetation changes, Little Cottonwood Canyon area, Wasatch Mountains, Utah. *Quaternary Research* 12:254–270.

Madsen, D. B., and J. F. O'Connell, eds. 1982. *Man and Environment in the Great Basin.* Society for American Archaeology Papers 2.

Madsen, D. B., and D. Rhode. 1990. Early Holocene piñon (*Pinus monophylla*) in the northeastern Great Basin. *Quaternary Research* 33:94–101.

Madsen, D. B., D. R. Currey, and J. H. Madsen. 1976. *Man, Mammoth, and Lake Fluctuations in Utah.* Utah Division of State History, Antiquities Section Selected Papers 5.

Maher, L. J., Jr. 1969. *Ephedra* pollen in sediments of the Great Lakes Region. *Ecology* 45:391–395.

Malde, H. E. 1968. *The Catastrophic Late Pleistocene Bonneville Flood in the Snake River Plain, Idaho.* U.S. Geological Survey Professional Paper 596.

Mandryk, C. A. 1990. Could humans survive the ice-free corridor? Late-glacial vegetation and climate in west central Alberta. In *Megafauna and Man: Discovery of America's Heartland,* edited by L. D. Agenbroad, J. I. Mead, and L. W. Nelson, pp. 67–79. The Mammoth Site of Hot Springs, South Dakota, Inc., Scientific Papers 1.

Manly, W. L. 1894. *Death Valley in '49.* Pacific Tree and Vine, San Jose (reprinted by Chalfant Press, Bishop, California, 1977).

Markgraf, V., J. P. Bradbury, R. M. Forester, G. Singh, and R. S. Sternberg. 1984. San Agustin Plains, New Mexico: Age and paleoenvironmental record reassessed. *Quaternary Research* 22: 336–343.

Marr, J. W. 1977. The development of movement of tree islands near the upper limit of tree growth in the southern Rocky Mountains. *Ecology* 58:1159–1164.

Martin, P. S[chulz]. 1963. *The Last 10,000 Years: A Fossil Pollen Record of the American Southwest.* University of Arizona Press, Tucson.

Martin, P. S. 1967a. Pleistocene overkill. *Natural History* 76:32–38.

Martin, P. S. 1967b. Prehistoric overkill. In *Pleistocene Extinctions: The Search for a Cause,* edited by P. S. Martin and H. E. Wright, Jr., pp. 75–120. Yale University Press, New Haven, Connecticut.

Martin, P. S. 1973. The discovery of America. *Science* 179:969–974.

Martin, P. S. 1984. Prehistoric overkill: The global model. In *Quaternary Extinctions: A Prehistoric Revolution,* edited by P. S. Martin and R. G. Klein, pp. 354–403. University of Arizona Press, Tucson.

Martin, P. S. 1990a. 40,000 years on the planet of doom. *Palaeogeography, Palaeoclimatology, Palaeoecology* 82:187–201.

Martin, P. S. 1990b. Who or what destroyed our mammoths? In *Megafauna and Man: Discovery of America's Heartland,* edited by L. D. Agenbroad, J. I. Mead, and L. W. Nelson, pp. 109–117. The Mammoth Site of Hot Springs, South Dakota, Inc., Scientific Papers 1.

Martin, P. S., and R. G. Klein, eds. 1984. *Quaternary Extinctions: A Prehistoric Revolution.* University of Arizona Press, Tucson.

Martin, P. S., B. E. Sabels, and D. Shutler. 1961. Rampart Cave coprolite and ecology of the Shasta ground sloth. *American Journal of Science* 259:102–127.

Martin, P. S., R. S. Thompson, and A. Long. 1985. Shasta ground sloth extinction: A test of the blitzkrieg model. In *Environments and Extinctions: Man in Late Glacial North America,* edited by J. I. Mead and D. J. Meltzer, pp. 5–14. Center for the Study of Early Man, University of Maine, Orono.

Martin, P. S[idney], G. I. Quimby, and D. Collier. 1947. *Indians before Columbus.* University of Chicago Press, Chicago.

Marwitt, J. P. 1970. *Median Village and Fremont Culture Regional Variation.* University of Utah Anthropological Papers 95.

Marwitt, J. P. 1980. A Fremont retrospective. In *Fremont Perspectives,* edited by D. B. Madsen, pp. 9–12. State of Utah Division of State History Antiquities Section Selected Papers 7(16).

Marwitt, J. P. 1986. Fremont cultures. In *Handbook of North American Indians,* Volume 11: *Great Basin,* edited by W. L. d'Azevedo, pp. 161–172. Smithsonian Institution Press, Washington, D.C.

Marwitt, J. P., G. F. Fry, and J. M. Adovasio. 1970. Sandwich Shelter. In *Great Basin Anthropological Conference 1970: Selected Papers,* edited by C. M. Aikens, pp. 27–36. University of Oregon Anthropological Papers 1.

Mawby, J. E. 1967. Fossil vertebrates of the Tule Springs Site, Nevada. In *Pleistocene Studies in Southern Nevada,* edited by H. M. Wormington and D. Ellis, pp. 105–129. Nevada State Museum Anthropological Papers 13.

Mead, E. M., and J. I. Mead. 1989. Snake Creek Burial Cave and a review of the Quaternary mustelids of the Great Basin. *Great Basin Naturalist* 49:143–154.

Mead, J. I. 1987. Quaternary records of pika, *Ochotona,* in North America. *Boreas* 16:165–171.

Mead, J. I., and E. M. Mead. 1985. A natural trap for Pleistocene animals in Snake Valley, eastern Nevada. *Current Research in the Pleistocene* 2:105–106.

Mead, J. I., and L. K. Murray. 1991. Late Pleistocene vertebrates from the Potosi Mountain packrat midden, Spring Range, Nevada. In *Crossing the Borders: Quaternary Studies in Eastern California and Southwestern Nevada,* edited by R. E. Reynolds, pp. 124–126. San Bernardino County Museum Association, Redlands, California.

Mead, J. I., R. S. Thompson, and T. R. Van Devender. 1982. Late Wisconsinan and Holocene fauna from Smith Creek Canyon, Snake Range, Nevada. *Transactions of the San Diego Society of Natural History* 20:1–26.

Mead, J. I., P. S. Martin, R. C. Euler, A. Long, A. J. T. Jull, L. S. Toolin, D. J. Donahue, and T. W. Linick. 1986. Extinction of Harrington's Mountain Goat. *Proceedings of the National Academy of Sciences* 83:836–839.

Mead, J. I., C. J. Bell, and L. K. Murray. 1992. *Mictomys borealis* (northern bog lemming) and the Wisconsin paleoecology of the east-central Great Basin. *Quaternary Research* 37:229–238.

Meek, N. 1989. Geomorphic and hydrological implications of the rapid incision of Afton Canyon, Mojave Desert, California. *Geology* 17:7–10.

Mehringer, P. J., Jr. 1965. Late Pleistocene vegetation in the Mojave Desert of southern Nevada. *Journal of the Arizona Academy of Science* 3:172–188.

Mehringer, P. J., Jr. 1967. Pollen analysis of the Tule Springs Site, Nevada. In *Pleistocene Studies in Southern Nevada,* edited by H. M. Wormington and D. Ellis, pp. 130–200. Nevada State Museum Anthropological Papers 13.

Mehringer, P. J., Jr. 1977. Great Basin late Quaternary environments and chronology. In *Models and Great Basin Prehistory: A Symposium,* edited by D. D. Fowler, pp. 113–167. Desert Research Institute Publications in the Social Sciences 12.

Mehringer, P. J., Jr. 1985. Late-Quaternary pollen records from the interior Pacific Northwest and Northern Great Basin of the United States. In *Pollen Records of Late-Quaternary North American Sediments,* edited by V. M. Bryant, Jr., and R. G. Holloway, pp. 167–190. American Association of Stratigraphic Palynologists, Dallas.

Mehringer, P. J., Jr. 1986. Prehistoric environments. In *Handbook of North American Indians,* Volume 11: *Great Basin,* edited by W. L. d'Azevedo, pp. 31–50. Smithsonian Institution Press, Washington, D.C.

Mehringer, P. J., Jr., and C. W. Ferguson. 1969. Pluvial occurrence of bristlecone pine (*Pinus aristata*) in a Mojave Desert mountain range. *Journal of the Arizona Academy of Science* 5:284–292.

Mehringer, P. J., Jr., and C. V. Haynes, Jr. 1965. The pollen evidence for the environment of early man and extinct animals at the Lehner Mammoth Site, southeastern Arizona. *American Antiquity* 31:17–23.

Mehringer, P. J., Jr., and C. N. Warren. 1976. Marsh, dune, and archaeological chronology, Ash Meadows, Amargosa Desert, Nevada. In *Holocene Environmental Change in the Great Basin,* edited by R. Elston, pp. 120–151. Nevada Archaeological Survey Paper 6.

Mehringer, P. J., Jr., and P. E. Wigand. 1987. Western juniper in the Holocene. In *Proceedings of the Piñon-Juniper Conference, Reno, Nevada, January 13–16, 1986,* compiled by R. L. Everett, pp. 109–119. General Technical Report INT-215. U.S. Forest Service Intermountain Research Station, Ogden, Utah.

Mehringer, P. J., Jr., and P. E. Wigand. 1990. Comparison of late Holecene environments from woodrat middens and pollen: Diamond Craters, Oregon. In *Packrat Middens: The Last 40,000 Years of Biotic Change,* edited by J. L. Betancourt, T. R. Van Devender, and P. S. Martin, pp. 294–325. University of Arizona Press, Tucson.

Mehringer, P. J., Jr., E. Blinman, and K. L. Peterson. 1977. Pollen influx and volcanic ash. *Science* 198:257–261.

Meier, M. F. 1962. Proposed definitions for glacier mass budget terms. *Journal of Glaciology* 4:252–263.

Meighan, C. W. 1989. Further comments on Pinto points and their chronology. *Journal of California and Great Basin Anthropology* 11:113–118.

Meltzer, D. J. 1989. Why don't we know when the first people came to North America? *American Antiquity* 54:471–490.

Meltzer, D. J. 1988. Late Pleistocene human adaptations in eastern North America. *Journal of World Prehistory* 2:1–51.

Merola, J. A., D. R. Currey, and M. K. Ridd. 1989. Thematic mapper laser profile resolution of Holocene lake limit, Great Salt Lake Desert, Utah. *Remote Sensing of Environment* 28:233–244.

Merriam, J. C. 1915. An occurrence of mammalian remains in Pleistocene lake deposits at Astor Pass, near Pyramid Lake, Nevada. *University of California Publications, Department of Geology, Bulletin* 8(21):377–384.

Metcalfe, D., and L. V. Larrabee. 1985. Fremont irrigation: Evidence from Gooseberry Valley, central Utah. *Journal of California and Great Basin Anthropology* 7(2):244–254.

Mifflin, M. D., and M. M. Wheat. 1979. *Pluvial Lakes and Estimated Pluvial Climates of Nevada.* Nevada Bureau of Mines and Geology Bulletin 94.

Miller, A. H. 1946. Vertebrate inhabitants of the Piñon association in the Death Valley region. *Ecology* 27:54–60.

Miller, L. 1931. The California Condor in Nevada. *The Condor* 33:32.

Miller, L., and I. DeMay. 1942. *The Fossil Birds of California.* University of California Publications in Zoology 47(4).

Miller, R. F., F. A. Branson, I. S. McQueen, and C. T. Snyder. 1982. Water relations in soils as related to plant communities in Ruby Valley, Nevada. *Journal of Range Management* 35:462–468.

Miller, R. R. 1945. Four new species of fossil cyprinodont fishes from eastern California. *Journal of the Washington Academy of Sciences* 35:315–321.

Miller, R. R. 1948. *The Cyprinodont Fishes of the Death Valley System of Eastern California and Southwestern Nevada.* University of Michigan Museum of Zoology Miscellaneous Publications 68.

Miller, R. R. 1965. Quaternary freshwater fishes of North America. In *The Quaternary of the United States,* edited by H. E. Wright, Jr. and D. G. Frey, pp. 569–582. Princeton University Press, Princeton, New Jersey.

Miller, R. R. 1981. Coevolution of deserts and pupfishes (genus *Cyprinodon*) in the American Southwest. In *Fishes in North American Deserts,* edited by R. J. Naiman and D. L. Soltz, pp. 39–94. Wiley, New York.

Miller, S. J. 1979. The archaeological fauna of four sites in Smith Creek Canyon. In *The Archaeology of Smith Creek Canyon, Eastern Nevada,* edited by D. R. Tuohy and D. L. Rendall, pp. 272–331. Nevada State Museum Anthropological Papers 17.

Miller, W. E. 1976. Late Pleistocene vertebrates of the Silver Creek Local Fauna from north central Utah. *Great Basin Naturalist* 36:387–424.

Miller, W. E. 1982. Pleistocene vertebrates from deposits of Lake Bonneville, Utah. *National Geographic Society Research Reports* 14:473–478.

Miller, W. E. 1987. *Mammut americanum,* Utah's first record of the American mastodon. *Journal of Paleontology* 61:168–183.

Miller, W. R. 1983. Uto-Aztecan languages. In *Handbook of North American Indians,* Volume 10: *Southwest,* edited by A. Ortiz, pp. 113–124. Smithsonian Institution Press, Washington, D.C.

Miller, W. R. 1984. The classification of Uto-Aztecan languages based on lexical evidence. *International Journal of American Linguistics* 50:1–24.

Miller, W. R. 1986. Numic languages. In *Handbook of North American Indians,* Volume 11: *Great Basin,* edited by W. L. d'Azevedo, pp. 98–106. Smithsonian Institution Press, Washington, D.C.

Miller, W. R., J. L. Tanner, and L. P. Foley. 1971. A lexicostatistic study of Shoshoni dialects. *Anthropological Linguistics* 13:142–164.

Minckley, W. L., and J. E. Deacon, eds. 1991. *Battle Against Extinction: Native Fish Management in the American West.* University of Arizona Press, Tucson.

Minckley, W. L., D. A. Hendrickson, and C. E. Bond. 1985. Geography of western North American freshwater fishes: Description and relationships to intracontinental tectonism. In *Zoogeography of North American Freshwater Fishes,* edited by C. H. Hocutt and E. O. Wiley, pp. 519–613. Wiley, New York.

Minckley, W. L., G. K. Meffe, and D. L. Soltz. 1991. Conservation and management of short-lived fishes: The cyprinodontoids. In *Battle Against Extinction: Native Fish Management in the American West,* edited by W. L. Minckley and J. E. Deacon, pp. 247–282. University of Arizona Press, Tucson.

Moffit, J. 1934. Mule deer study program. *California Fish and Game* 20:52–66.

Moir, W. H., J. F. Franklin, and C. Maser. 1973. Lost Forest Research Natural Area. In *Federal Research Natural Areas in Oregon and Washington,* by J. F. Franklin, F. C. Hall, C. T. Dryness, and C. Maser, Supplement 3, pp. 1–17. USDA Forest Service, Pacific Northwest Forest and Range Experiment Station, Portland, Oregon.

Mono Basin Ecosystem Study Committee. 1987. *The Mono Basin Ecosystem: Effects of Changing Lake Level.* National Academy Press, Washington, D.C.

Moore, P. D., J. A. Webb, and M. E. Collinson. 1991. *Pollen Analysis.* Second edition. Blackwell, Oxford.

Moratto, M. J. 1984. *California Archaeology.* Academic Press, Orlando, Florida.

Morgan, D. L. 1964. *Jedediah Smith and the Opening of the West.* University of Nebraska Press, Lincoln.

Morgan, D. L. 1985. *The Humboldt: Highroad of the West.* University of Nebraska Press, Lincoln.

Morlan, R. E. 1987. The Pleistocene archaeology of Beringia. In *The Evolution of Human Hunting,* edited by M. H. Nitecki and D. V. Nitecki, pp. 267–307. Plenum, New York.

Morrison, R. B. 1964. *Lake Lahontan: Geology of Southern Carson Desert, Nevada.* U.S. Geological Survey Professional Paper 401.

Morrison, R. B. 1965. Quaternary geology of the Great Basin. In *The Quaternary of the United States,* edited by H. E. Wright, Jr., and D. G. Frey, pp. 265–286. Princeton University Press, Princeton, New Jersey.

Morrison, R. B., and J. C. Frye. 1965. *Correlation of the Middle and Late Quaternary Successions of the Lake Lahontan, Lake Bonneville, Rocky Mountain (Wasatch Range), Southern Great Plains, and Eastern Midwest Areas.* Nevada Bureau of Mines Report 9.

Mosimann, J. E., and Martin, P. S. 1975. Simulating overkill by Paleoindians. *American Scientist* 63:304–313.

Mozingo, H. N. 1987. *Shrubs of the Great Basin.* University of Nevada Press, Reno.

Murphy, V. R. 1980. *Across the Plains in the Donner Party: A Personal Narrative of the Overland Trip to California 1846–1847.* Outbooks, Golden, Colorado.

Musil, R. R. 1988. Functional efficiency and technological change: A hafting tradition model for prehistoric North America. In *Early Human Occupation in Far Western North America: The Clovis-Archaic Interface,* edited by J. A. Willig, C. M. Aikens, and J. L. Fagan, pp. 373–389. Nevada State Museum Anthropological Papers 21.

Musil, R. R. 1992. Adaptive Transitions and Environmental Change in the Northern Great Basin: A View from Diamond Swamp. Ph.D. dissertation, Department of Anthropology, University of Oregon, Eugene.

Nagy, J. G. 1979. Wildlife nutrition and the sagebrush ecosystem. In *The Sagebrush Ecosystem: A Symposium,* pp. 164–168. College of Natural Resources, Utah State University Press, Logan.

Naiman, R. J. 1981. An ecosystem overview: Desert fishes and their habitats. In *Fishes in North American Deserts,* edited by R. J. Naiman and D. L. Soltz, pp. 493–531. Wiley, New York.

Naiman, R. J., and D. L. Soltz, eds. 1981. *Fishes in North American Deserts.* Wiley, New York.

Napton, L. K., and R. F. Heizer. 1970. Analysis of human coprolites from archaeological contexts, with primary reference to Lovelock Cave, Nevada. *University of California Archaeological Research Facility Contributions* 10:87–130.

Nathanson, C. A. 1984. Sex differences in mortality. *Annual Review of Sociology* 10:191–213.

Neal, D. M., J. B. Perry, Jr., K. Green, and R. Hawkins. 1988. Patterns of giving and receiving help during severe winter conditions: A research note. *Disasters* 12:366–377.

Negrini, R. M., and J. O. Davis. 1992. Dating late Pleistocene pluvial events and tephras by correlating paleomagnetic secular variation records from the western Great Basin. *Quaternary Research* 38:46–59.

Nelson, D. E. 1991. A new method for carbon isotopic analysis of protein. *Science* 251:552–554.

Nelson, D. E., R. E. Morlan, J. S. Vogel, J. R. Southon, and C. R. Harington. 1986. New dates on northern Yukon artifacts: Holocene not Upper Pleistocene. *Science* 232:749–751.

Nelson, E. W. 1983. *The Eskimo about Bering Strait.* Smithsonian Institution Press, Washington, D.C.

Nelson, M. E., and J. H. Madsen, Jr. 1978. Late Pleistocene musk oxen from Utah. *Kansas Academy of Science Transactions* 81:277–295.

Nelson, M. E., and J. H. Madsen, Jr. 1979. The Hay-Romer camel debate: Fifty years later. *University of Wyoming Contributions to Geology* 18:47–50.

Nelson, M. E., and J. H. Madsen, Jr. 1980. A summary of Pleistocene, fossil vertebrate localities in the northern Bonneville Basin of Utah. In *Great Salt Lake: A Scientific, Historical, and Economic Overview,* edited by J. W. Gwynn, pp. 97–114. Utah Geological and Mineral Survey Bulletin 116.

Nelson, M. E., and J. H. Madsen, Jr. 1983. A giant short-faced bear (*Arctodus simus*) from the Pleistocene of northern Utah. *Transactions of the Kansas Academy of Science* 86:1–9.

Newman, D. E. 1988. Paleoenvironments of the Late Archaic and Formative Periods in Central Utah. Paper presented at the 21st Great Basin Anthropological Conference, Park City, Utah.

Nials, F. L. 1990. Geology. In *Archaeological and Paleoenvironmental Investigations in the Ash Meadows National Wildlife Refuge, Nye County, Nevada,* edited by S. D. Livingston and F. L. Nials, pp. 49–85. Technical Report 70. Quaternary Sciences Center, Desert Research Institute, Reno.

Norris, R. M. 1988. Eureka Valley sand dunes. In *Plant Biology of Eastern California,* edited by C. A. Hall, Jr., and V. Doyle-Jones, pp. 207–211. Natural History of the White-Inyo Range Symposium Volume 2. White Mountain Research Station, University of California, Los Angeles.

Nunis, D. B., Jr., ed. 1991. *The Bidwell-Bartleson Party.* Western Tanager Press, Santa Cruz, California.

O'Connell, J. F. 1975. *The Prehistory of Surprise Valley.* Ballena Press Anthropological Papers 4.

O'Connell, J. F., and J. E. Ericson. 1974. Earth lodges to wickiups: A long sequence of domestic structures from the northern Great Basin. *Nevada Archaeological Survey Research Papers* 5:43–61.

O'Connell, J. F., and K. Hawkes. 1981. Alyawara plant use and optimal foraging theory. In *Hunter-Gatherer Foraging Strategies: Ethnographic and Archaeological Analyses,* edited by B. Winterhalder and E. A. Smith, pp. 99–125. University of Chicago, Chicago.

O'Connell, J. F., and K. Hawkes. 1984. Food choice and foraging sites among the Alyawara. *Journal of Anthropological Research* 40:504–535.

O'Connell, J. F., and P. S. Hayward. 1972. Altithermal and Medithermal human adaptations in Surprise Valley, northeast California. In *Great Basin Cultural Ecology: A Symposium,* edited by D. D. Fowler, pp. 25–42. Desert Research Institute Publications in the Social Sciences 8.

O'Connell, J. F., K. T. Jones, and S. R. Simms. 1982. Some thoughts on prehistoric archaeology in the Great Basin. In *Man and Environment in the Great Basin,* edited by D. B. Madsen and J. F. O'Connell, pp. 227–240. Society for American Archaeology Papers 2.

O'Connell, J. F., P. K. Latz, and P. Barnett. 1983. Traditional and modern plant use among the Alyawara of central Australia. *Economic Botany* 37:80–109.

Oetting, A. C. 1989. *Villages and Wetlands Adaptations in the Northern Great Basin: Chronology and Land Use in the Lake Abert–Chewaucan Marsh Basin, Lake County, Oregon.* University of Oregon Anthropological Papers 41.

Oetting, A. C. 1990. Aboriginal settlement in the Lake Abert–Chewaucan Marsh Basin, Lake County, Oregon. In *Wetland Adaptations in the Great Basin,* edited by J. C. Janetski and D. B. Madsen, pp. 183–206. Brigham Young University Museum of Peoples and Cultures, Occasional Papers 1.

Ore, H. T., and C. N. Warren. 1971. Late Pleistocene–Early Holocene geomorphic history of Lake Mojave, California. *Bulletin of the Geological Society of America* 82:2553–2562.

Orr, P. C. 1952. *Preliminary Excavations of Pershing County Caves.* Nevada State Museum Department of Archaeology Bulletin 1.

Orr, P. C. 1956. *Pleistocene Man in Fishbone Cave, Pershing County, Nevada.* Nevada State Museum Department of Archaeology Bulletin 2.

Orr, P. C. 1969. *Felis trumani,* a new radiocarbon dated cat skull from Crypt Cave, Nevada. *Bulletin of the Santa Barbara Museum of Natural History Department of Geology* 2:1–8.

Orr, P. C. 1974. Notes on the archaeology of the Winnemucca caves, 1952–1958. *Nevada State Museum Anthropological Papers* 16:47–59.

Osborn, G. 1989. Glacial deposits and tephra in the Toiyabe Range, Nevada, U.S.A. *Arctic and Alpine Research* 21:256–267.

Osmond, C. B., L. F. Pitelka, and G. M. Hidy, eds. 1990. *Plant Biology of the Basin and Range.* Springer-Verlag, Berlin.

Oviatt, C. G. 1987. Lake Bonneville stratigraphy at the Old River Bed, Utah. *American Journal of Science* 287:383–398.

Oviatt, C. G. 1988a. Late Pleistocene and Holocene lake fluctuations in the Sevier Lake Basin, Utah, USA. *Journal of Paleolimnology* 1:9–21.

Oviatt, C. G. 1989. *Quaternary Geology of Part of the Sevier Desert, Millard County, Utah.* Utah Geological and Mineral Survey Species Studies 70.

Oviatt, C. G. 1991a. *Quaternary Geology of the Black Rock Desert, Millard County, Utah.* Utah Geological and Mineral Survey Special Studies 73.

Oviatt, C. G. 1991b. *Quaternary Geology of Fish Springs Flat, Juab County, Utah.* Utah Geological Survey Special Study 77.

Oviatt, C. G., and W. D. McCoy. 1988. The Old River Bed. In *In the Footsteps of G. K. Gilbert—Lake Bonneville and Neotectonics of the Eastern Basin and Range Province,* edited by M. N. Machette, pp. 60–65. Utah Geological and Mineral Survey Miscellaneous Publication 88-1.

Oviatt, C. G., D. R. Currey, and D. M. Miller. 1990. Age and paleoclimatic significance of the Stansbury shoreline of Lake Bonneville, northeastern Great Basin. *Quaternary Research* 33:291–305.

Page, B. M. 1935. Basin-Range faulting of 1915 in Pleasant Valley, Nevada. *Journal of Geology* 43:690–707.

Palmer, R. S., ed. 1962. *Handbook of North American Birds,* Volume 1: *Loons through Flamingos.* Yale University Press, New Haven, Connecticut.

Parenti, L. 1981. A phylogenetic and biogeographic analysis of cyprinodontiform fishes (Teleostei, Atherinomorpha). *Bulletin of the American Museum of Natural History* 168:335–557.

Paterson, W. S. B., and C. U. Hammer. 1987. Ice core and other glaciological data. In *The Geology of North America,* Volume K-3: *North America and Adjacent Oceans during the Last Deglaciation,* edited by W. F. Ruddiman and H. E. Wright, Jr., pp. 91–110. Geological Society of America, Boulder, Colorado.

Patterson, B. D. 1987. The principle of nested subsets and its implications for biological conservation. *Conservation Biology* 1:323–334.

Patterson, B. D. 1990. On the temporal development of nested subset patterns of species composition. *Oikos* 59:330–342.

Patterson, B. D., and W. Atmar. 1986. Nested subsets and the structure of insular mammalian faunas and archipelagos. *Biological Journal of the Linnean Society* 28:65–82.

Patterson, L. W. 1983. Criteria for determining the attributes of man-made lithics. *Journal of Field Archaeology* 10:297–307.

Pendleton, L. S. 1979. Lithic Technology in Early Nevada Assemblages. M.A. thesis, Department of Anthropology, California State University, Long Beach.

Peteet, D. M., J. S. Vogel, D. E. Nelson, J. R. Southon, R. J. Nickman, and L. E. Heusser. 1990. Younger Dryas climatic reversal in northeastern USA? AMS ages for an old problem. *Quaternary Research* 33:219–230.

Peterson, P. M. 1984. *Flora and Physiognomy of the Cottonwood Mountains, Death Valley National Monument, California.* Cooperative National Park Resources Studies Unit, University of Nevada, Las Vegas.

Pettigrew, R. M. 1985. *Archaeological Investigations on the East Shore of Lake Abert, Lake County, Oregon.* University of Oregon Anthropological Papers 32.

Phillips, F. M., L. A. Peeters, M. K. Tansey, and S. N. Davis. 1986. Paleoclimatic inferences from an isotopic investigation of groundwater in the central San Juan Basin, New Mexico. *Quaternary Research* 26:179–193.

Phillips, K. N., and A. S. Vandenburgh. 1971. *Hydrology and Geochemistry of Abert, Summer, and Goose Lakes, and Other Closed Basin Lakes in South Central Oregon.* U.S. Geological Survey Professional Paper 502-B.

Piegat, J. J. 1980. Glacial Geology of Central Nevada. M.S. thesis, Purdue University, Lafayette, Indiana.

Pippin, L. C. 1986. Intermountain brown wares: An assessment. In *Pottery of the Great Basin and Adjacent Areas,* edited by S. Griset, pp. 9–21. University of Utah Anthropological Papers 111

Pister, E. P. 1981. The conservation of desert fishes. In *Fishes in North American Deserts,* edited by R. J. Naiman and D. L. Soltz, pp. 493–531. Wiley, New York.

Pister, E. P. 1991. The Desert Fishes Council: Catalyst for change. In *Battle Against Extinction: Native Fish Management in the American West,* edited by W. L. Minckley and J. E. Deacon, pp. 55–68. University of Arizona Press, Tucson.

Porter, S. C. 1977. Present and past glaciation threshold in the Cascade Range, Washington, U.S.A.: Topographic and climatic controls, and paleoclimatic implications. *Journal of Glaciology* 18:101–116.

Porter, S. C. 1988. Landscapes of the last ice age in North America. In *Americans before Columbus: Ice-Age Origins,* edited by R. C. Carlisle, pp. 1–24. Ethnology Monographs 12.

Porter, S. C., K. L. Pierce, and T. D. Hamilton. 1983. Late Wisconsin mountain glaciation in the western United States. In *Late-Quaternary Environments of the United States,* Volume 1: *The Late Pleistocene,* edited by S. C. Porter, pp. 71–111. University of Minnesota Press, Minneapolis.

Powers, W. R., and J. F. Hoffecker. 1989. Late Pleistocene settlement in the Nenana Valley, central Alaska. *American Antiquity* 54:263–287.

Price, B. A., and S. E. Johnston. 1988. A model of late Pleistocene and early Holocene adaptation in eastern Nevada. In *Early Human Occupation in Far Western North America: The Clovis-Archaic Interface,* edited by J. A. Willig, C. M. Aikens, and J. L. Fagan, pp. 231–250. Nevada State Museum Anthropological Papers 21.

Quade, J. 1986. Late Quaternary environmental changes in the Upper Las Vegas Valley, Nevada. *Quaternary Research* 20:261–285.

Quade, J., and W. L. Pratt. 1989. Late Wisconsin groundwater discharge environments of the southwestern Indian Springs Valley, southern Nevada. *Quaternary Research* 31:351–370.

Quaife, M. M., ed. 1966. *Kit Carson's Autobiography.* University of Nebraska Press, Lincoln.

Quaife, M. M., ed. 1978. *Adventures of a Mountain Man: The Narrative of Zenas Leonard.* University of Nebraska Press, Lincoln.

Rabenold, P. P. 1983. The communal roost in Black and Turkey Vultures—An information center? In *Vulture Biology and Management,* edited by S. R. Wilbur and J. A. Jackson, pp. 303–321. University of California Press, Berkeley and Los Angeles.

Ramenofsky, A. F. 1987. *Vectors of Death.* University of New Mexico Press, Albuquerque.

Raven, C. 1990. *Prehistoric Human Geography in the Carson Desert,* Part II: *Archaeological Field Tests of Model Predictions.* U.S. Department of the Interior, U.S. Fish and Wildlife Service, Region 1, Cultural Resource Series 4. Portland, Oregon.

Raven, C., and R. G. Elston, eds. 1988. *Preliminary Investigations in Stillwater Marsh: Human Prehistory and Geoarchaeology.* U.S. Department of the Interior, U.S. Fish and Wildlife Service, Region 1, Cultural Resource Series 1. Portland, Oregon.

Raven, C., and R. G. Elston. 1989. *Prehistoric Human Geography in the Carson Desert,* Part I: *A Predictive Model of Land-Use in the Stillwater Wildlife Management Area.* U.S. Department of the Interior, U.S. Fish and Wildlife Service, Region 1, Cultural Resource Series 3. Portland, Oregon.

Ray, V. F. 1963. *Primitive Pragmatists: The Modoc Indians of Northern California.* University of Washington Press, Seattle.

Raymond, A. W. 1986. Experiments in the function and performance of the weighted atlatl. *World Archaeology* 18:153–177.

Raymond, A. W., and V. M. Parks. 1990. Archaeological sites exposed by recent flooding of Stillwater Marsh, Carson Desert, Churchill County, Nevada. In *Wetland Adaptations in the Great Basin,* edited by J. C. Janetski and D. B. Madsen, pp. 33–62. Brigham Young University Museum of Peoples and Cultures, Occasional Papers 1.

Rea, A. 1983. Cathartid affinities: A brief overview. In *Vulture Biology and Management,* edited by S. R. Wilbur and J. A. Jackson, pp. 26–54. University of California Press, Berkeley and Los Angeles.

Rea, J. A. 1958. Concerning the validity of lexicostatistics. *International Journal of American Linguistics* 24:145–150.

Rea, J. A. 1973. The Romance data of the pilot studies for glottochronology. *Current Trends in Linguistics* 11:355–367.

Reisner, M. 1986. *Cadillac Desert: The American West and Its Disappearing Water.* Penguin Books, New York.

Reneau, S. L., and R. Raymond, Jr. 1991. Cation-ratio dating of rock varnish: Why does it work? *Geology* 19:937–940.

Rennie, D. P. 1987. Late Pleistocene Alpine Glacial Deposits in the Pine Forest Range, Nevada. M.S. thesis, Department of Geology, University of Nevada, Reno.

Reveal, J. L. 1979. Biogeography of the intermountain region: A speculative appraisal. *Mentzelia* 4:1–92.

Reveal, J. L., and J. L. Reveal. 1985. The missing Frémont cannon—An ecological solution? *Madroño* 32:106–117.

Reynolds, R. E., J. I. Mead, and R. L. Reynolds. 1991a. A Rancholabrean fauna from the Las Vegas formation, north Las Vegas, Nevada. In *Crossing the Borders: Quaternary Studies in Eastern California and Southwestern Nevada,* edited by R. E. Reynolds, pp. 140–146. San Bernardino County Museum Association, Redlands, California.

Reynolds, R. E., R. L. Reynolds, and C. J. Bell. 1991b. The Devil Peak sloth. In *Crossing the Borders: Quaternary Studies in Eastern California and Southwestern Nevada,* edited by R. E. Reynolds, pp. 115–116. San Bernardino County Museum Association, Redlands, California.

Reynolds, R. E., R. L. Reynolds, C. J. Bell, and B. Pitzer. 1991c. Vertebrate remains from Antelope Cave, Mescal Range, San Bernardino County, California. In *Crossing the Borders: Quaternary Studies in Eastern California and Southwestern Nevada,* edited by R. E. Reynolds, pp. 107–109. San Bernardino County Museum Association, Redlands, California.

Reynolds, R. E., R. L. Reynolds, C. J. Bell, N. J. Czaplewski, H. T. Goodwin, J. I. Mead, and B. Roth. 1991d. The Kokoweef Cave faunal assemblage. In *Crossing the Borders: Quaternary Studies in Eastern California and Southwestern Nevada,* edited by R. E. Reynolds, pp. 97–103. San Bernardino County Museum Association, Redlands, California.

Rhode, D. 1993. Plant macrofossil assemblages from Alta Toquima. In *The Archaeology of Monitor Valley. 4. Alta Toquima and the Mt. Jefferson Complex,* by D. H. Thomas. American Museum of Natural History Anthropological Papers (in press).

Rhode, D., and D. H. Thomas. 1983. Flotation analysis of selected hearths. In *The Archaeology of Monitor Valley. 2. Gatecliff Shelter,* by D. H. Thomas, pp. 151–157. American Museum of Natural History Anthropological Papers 59(1).

Rich, P. V. 1980. 'New World vultures' with Old World affinities? In *Contributions to Vertebrate Evolution 5.* S. Karger, Basel.

Rich, P. V. 1983. The fossil history of vultures: A world perspective. In *Vulture Biology and Management,* edited by S. R. Wilbur and J. A. Jackson, pp. 3–25. University of California Press, Berkeley and Los Angeles.

Richerson, P. J., and R. Boyd. 1992. Cultural inheritance and evolutionary ecology. In *Evolutionary Ecology and Human Behavior,* edited by E. A. Smith and B. Winterhalder, pp. 61–92. Aldine de Gruyter, New York.

Richmond, G. M. 1964. *Glaciation of Little Cottonwood and Bells Canyons, Wasatch Mountains, Utah.* U.S. Geological Survey Professional Paper 454-D.

Richmond, G. M. 1986. Stratigraphy and correlation of glacial deposits of the Rocky Mountains, the Colorado Plateau, and the ranges of the Great Basin. *Quaternary Science Reviews* 5:99–127.

Richmond, G. M., and D. S. Fullerton. 1986a. Introduction to Quaternary glaciations in the United States of America. *Quaternary Science Reviews* 5:3–10.

Richmond, G. M., and D. S. Fullerton. 1986b. Summation of Quaternary glaciations in the United States of America. *Quaternary Science Reviews* 5:183–196.

Rickard, P. A. 1989. *A History of French Language.* Second edition. Unwin Hyman, London.

Riggs, A. C. 1991. Geohydrologic evidence for the development of Devils Hole, southern Nevada as an aquatic environment. *Proceedings of the Desert Fishes Council* 20–21:47–48.

Ritchie, J. C. 1984. *Past and Present Vegetation of the Far Northwest of Canada.* University of Toronto Press, Toronto.

Ritchie, J. C., and L. C. Cwynar. 1982. The Late Quaternary vegetation of the north Yukon. In *The Paleoecology of Beringia,* edited by D. M. Hopkins, J. V. Matthews, Jr., C. E. Schweger, and S. B. Young, pp. 113–126. Academic Press, New York.

Rivers, J. P. W. 1988. The nutritional biology of famine. In *Famine,* edited by G. A. Harrison, pp. 57–106. Oxford University Press, Oxford.

Rivers, J. P. W. 1982. Women and children last: An essay on sex discrimination in disasters. *Disasters* 6:256–267.

Rogers, G. F. 1982. *Then and Now: A Photographic History of Vegetation Change in the Central Great Basin Desert.* University of Utah Press, Salt Lake City.

Rolston, H. 1991. Fishes in the desert: Paradox and responsibility. In *Battle Against Extinction: Native Fish Management in the American West,* edited by W. L. Minckley and J. E. Deacon, pp. 93–108. University of Arizona Press, Tucson.

Romer, A. S. 1928. A "fossil" camel recently living in Utah. *Science* 68:19–20.

Romer, A. S. 1929. A fresh skull of an extinct American camel. *Journal of Geology* 37:261–267.

Roosma, A. 1958. A climatic record from Searles Lake, California. *Science* 128:716.

Roust, N. L. 1967. Preliminary examination of prehistoric human coprolites from four western Nevada caves. *University of California Archaeological Survey Reports* 70:49–88.

Ruddiman, W. F. 1987. Northern oceans. In *The Geology of North America,* Volume K-3: *North America and Adjacent Oceans during the Last Deglaciation,* edited by W. F. Ruddiman and H. E. Wright, Jr., pp. 137–154. Geological Society of America, Boulder, Colorado.

Ruhlen, M. 1991. The Amerind phylum and the prehistory of the New World. In *Sprung from Some Common Source,* edited by S. M. Lamb and E. D. Mitchell, pp. 328–350. Stanford University Press, Stanford, California.

Rush, F. E. 1972. Hydrologic reconnaissance of Big and Little Soda Lakes, Churchill County, Nevada. In *Water for Nevada: Hydrologic Atlas, Map L-5.* Division of Water Resources, State of Nevada, Carson City.

Russell, I. C. 1885a. Existing glaciers of the United States. In *Annual Report of the U.S. Geological Survey, 1883–1884,* pp. 303–355.

Russell, I. C. 1885b. *Geological History of Lake Lahontan, A Quaternary Lake of Northwestern Nevada.* U. S. Geological Survey Monograph 11.

Ryser, F. A., Jr. 1985. *Birds of the Great Basin.* University of Nevada Press, Reno.

Sack, D. 1989. Reconstructing the chronology of Lake Bonneville: An historical review. In *History of Geomorphology: 19th Annual Binghamton Geomorphology Symposium Volume,* edited by K. J. Tinkler, pp. 223–256. Unwin Hyman, London.

Sack, D. 1990. *Quaternary Geology of Tule Valley, West-Central Utah.* Utah Geological and Mineral Survey Map 124.

Sampson, C. G. 1985. *Nightfire Island: Late Holocene Lakemarsh Adaptation on the Western Edge of the Great Basin.* University of Oregon Anthropological Papers 33.

Schaedler, J. M., L. Krook, J. A. M. Wootton, B. Hover, B. Brodsky, M. D. Naresh, D. D. Gillette, D. B. Madsen, R. H. Horne, and R. R. Minor. 1992. Studies of collagen in bone and dentin matrix of a Columbian mammoth (late Pleistocene) of central Utah. *Matrix* 12:297–307.

Scharf, E. A. 1992. Archaeobotany of Midway: Plant Resource Use at a High Altitude Site in the White Mountains of Eastern California. M.A. thesis, Department of Anthropology, University of Washington, Seattle.

Schlesinger, W. H., E. H. DeLucia, and D. W. Billings. 1989. Nutrient-use efficiency of woody plants on contrasting soils in the western Great Basin, Nevada. *Ecology* 70:105–113.

Schneider, S. H. 1989. *Global Warming.* Sierra Club Books, San Francisco.

Schramm, D. R. 1982. *Floristics and Vegetation of the Black Mountains, Death Valley National Monument, California.* Contribution CPSU/UNLV 012/13. Cooperative National Park Resources Studies Unit, University of Nevada, Las Vegas.

Schroedl, A. R. 1991. Paleo-Indian occupation in the eastern Great Basin and northern Colorado Plateau. *Utah Archaeology* 4(1):1–15.

Schroth, A. 1992. Preliminary results of dating the Stahl site and the Pinto Basin site. Paper presented at the 1992 Great Basin Anthropological Conference, Boise, Idaho.

Scott, B. R., ed. 1971. Average annual evaporation. In *Water for Nevada: Hydrologic Atlas, Map S-5.* Department of Water Resources, State of Nevada, Carson City.

Scott, W. E. 1988. Temporal relations of lacustrine and glacial events at Little Cottonwood and Bells Canyons, Utah. In *In the Footsteps of G. K. Gilbert—Lake Bonneville and Neotectonics of the Eastern Basin and Range Province,* edited by M. N. Machette, pp. 78–81. Utah Geological and Mineral Survey Miscellaneous Publication 88-1.

Scott, W. E., W. D. McCoy, R. R. Shroba, and M. Rubin. 1983. Reinterpretation of the exposed record of the last two cycles of Lake Bonneville, western United States. *Quaternary Research* 20:261–285.

Seaman, J., S. Leivesley, and C. Hogg. 1984. *Epidemiology of Natural Disasters.* S. Karger, Basel.

Service, E. R. 1962. *Primitive Social Organization.* Random House, New York.

Shafer, C. L. 1990. *Nature Reserves.* Smithsonian Institution Press, Washington, D.C.

Sharp, R. P. 1938. Pleistocene glaciation in the Ruby–East Humboldt Range, northeastern Nevada. *Journal of Geomorphology* 1:298–323.

Shaul, D. L. 1986. Linguistic adaptation and the Great Basin. *American Antiquity* 51:415–416.

Shreve, F. 1942. The desert vegetation of North America. *Botanical Review* 8:195–246.

Shutler, D., Jr., M. E. Shutler, and J. S. Griffith. 1960. *Stuart Rockshelter: A Stratified Site in Southern Nevada.* Nevada State Museum Anthropological Papers 3.

Sigler, W. F. 1962. *Bear Lake and Its Future.* Utah State University Press, Logan.

Sigler, W. F., and J. W. Sigler. 1987. *Fishes of the Great Basin.* University of Nevada Press, Reno.

Simms, S. R. 1983. Comments on Bettinger and Baumhoff's explanation for the "Numic Spread" in the Great Basin. *American Antiquity* 48:825–830.

Simms, S. R. 1984. Aboriginal Great Basin Foraging Strategies: An Evolutionary Analysis. Ph.D. dissertation, Department of Anthropology, University of Utah, Salt Lake City.

Simms, S. R. 1986. New evidence for Fremont adaptive diversity. *Journal of California and Great Basin Anthropology* 8:204–216.

Simms, S. R. 1990. Fremont transitions. *Utah Archaeology* 3(1):1–18.

Simms, S. R., and M. C. Isgreen. 1984. *Archaeological Excavations in the Sevier and Escalanate Deserts, Western Utah.* University of Utah Archaeological Center Reports of Excavations 83-12.

Simms, S. R., and L. W. Lindsay. 1989. 42Md300, an early Holocene site in the Sevier Desert. *Utah Archaeology* 2(1):56–66.

Simms, S. R., C. J. Loveland, and M. E. Stuart. 1991. *Prehistoric Human Skeletal Remains and the Prehistory of the Great Salt Lake Wetlands.* Department of Sociology, Social Work, and Anthropology, Utah State University, Logan.

Simpson, B. B., ed. 1988. *Mesquite: Its Biology in Two Desert Scrub Ecosystems.* Dowden, Hutchinson, and Ross, Stroudsburg, Pennsylvania.

Simpson, J. H. 1983. *Report of Explorations across the Great Basin of the Territory of Utah.* University of Nevada Press, Reno.

Simpson, R. D. 1989. An introduction to the Calico Early Man Site lithic assemblage. *San Bernardino County Museum Association Quarterly* 36(3):1–91.

Slemmons, D. B. 1957. Geological effects of the Dixie Valley–Fairview Peak, Nevada, earthquakes of December 16, 1954. *Seismological Society of America Bulletin* 47:353–375.

Smales, T. J. 1972. Existing lakes and reservoirs. In *Water for Nevada: Hydrologic Atlas, Map L-1.* Division of Water Resources, State of Nevada, Carson City.

Smart, W. B. 1988. *Old Utah Trails.* Utah Geographic Series, Salt Lake City.

Smiley, T. L. 1977. Memorial to Ernst Valdemar Antevs, 1888–1974. *Geological Society of America Memorials* 6:1–7.

Smith, E. A., and B. Winterhalder, eds. 1992. *Evolutionary Ecology and Human Behavior.* Aldine de Gruyter, New York.

Smith, G. 1988. The story behind the story of Eureka Sand Dunes: What happened when scientists jumped down from their pedestals into rough-and-tumble politics. In *Plant Biology of Eastern California,* edited by C. A. Hall, Jr., and V. Doyle-Jones, pp. 195–298. Natural History of the White-Inyo Range Symposium Volume 2. White Mountain Research Station, University of California, Los Angeles.

Smith, G. I. 1979. *Subsurface Stratigraphy and Geochemistry of Late Quaternary Evaporites, Searles Lake, California.* U.S. Geological Survey Professional Paper 1043.

Smith, G. I. 1984. Paleohydrologic regimes in the southwestern Great Basin, 0–3.2 my Ago, compared with other long records of "global" climate. *Quaternary Research* 22:1–17.

Smith, G. I., and F. A. Street-Perrott. 1983. Pluvial lakes of the western United States. In *Late-Quaternary Environments of the United States,* Volume 1, edited by S. C. Porter, pp. 190–212. University of Minnesota Press, Minneapolis.

Smith, G. I., L. Benson, and D. R. Currey. 1989. *Quaternary Geology of the Great Basin: Field Trip Guidebook T117.* American Geophysical Union, Washington, D.C.

Smith, G. I., V. J. Barczak, G. F. Moulton, and J. C. Liddicoat. 1983. *Core KM-3, a Surface-to-Bedrock Record of Late Cenozoic Sedimentation in Searles Valley, California.* U.S. Geological Survey Professional Paper 1256.

Smith, G. R. 1978. Biogeography of intermountain fishes. In *Intermountain Biogeography: A Symposium,* edited by K. T. Harper and J. L. Reveal, pp. 17–42. Great Basin Naturalist Memoirs 2.

Smith, G. R. 1981. Late Cenozoic freshwater fishes of North America. *Annual Review of Ecology and Systematics* 12:163–193.

Smith, G. R. 1985. Paleontology of Hidden Cave: Fish. In *The Archaeology of Monitor Valley. 2. Gatecliff Shelter,* by D. H. Thomas, pp. 171–178. American Museum of Natural History Anthropological Papers 59(1).

Smith, G. R., W. L. Stokes, and K. F. Horn. 1968. Some late Pleistocene fishes of Lake Bonneville. *Copeia* 1968:807–816.

Smith, M. L. 1981. Late Cenozoic fishes in the warm deserts of North America: A reinterpretation of desert adaptations. In *Fishes in North American Deserts,* edited by R. J. Naiman and D. L. Soltz, pp. 11–38. Wiley, New York.

Smith, R. S. U. 1978. *Pluvial History of Panamint Valley, California: A Guidebook for the Friends of the Pleistocene, Pacific Cell.* Friends of the Pleistocene, Pacific Cell.

Smith, S. D., and R. S. Nowak. 1990. Ecophysiology of plants in the intermountain lowlands. In *Plant Biology of the Basin and Range,* edited by C. B. Osmond, L. F. Pitelka, and G. M. Hidy, pp. 179–242. Springer-Verlag, Berlin.

Smith, W. K., and A. K. Knapp. 1990. Ecophysiology of high elevation forests. In *Plant Biology of the Basin and Range,* edited by C. B. Osmond, L. F. Pitelka, and G. M. Hidy, pp. 87–142. Springer-Verlag, Berlin.

Snyder, C. T., G. Hardman, and F. F. Zdenek. 1964. *Pleistocene Lakes in the Great Basin.* U.S. Geological Survey Miscellaneous Geological Investigations Map I-416.

Soltz, D. L., and R. J. Naiman. 1978. *The Natural History of Native Fishes in the Death Valley System.* Natural History Museum of Los Angeles County Science Series 30.

Southworth, J. 1987. *Death Valley in 1849: The Luck of the Gold Rush Emigrants.* Pegleg Books, Burbank, California.

Spaulding, W. G. 1977. Late Quaternary vegetational change in the Sheep Range, southern Nevada. *Journal of the Arizona Academy of Science* 12(2):3–8.

Spaulding, W. G. 1980. *The Presettlement Vegetation of the California Desert.* Desert Planning Staff, Bureau of Land Management, Riverside, California.

Spaulding, W. G. 1981. The Late Quaternary Vegetation of a Southern Nevada Mountain Range. Ph.D. dissertation, Department of Geosciences, University of Arizona, Tucson.

Spaulding, W. G. 1983. Late Wisconsin macrofossil records of desert vegetation in the American Southwest. *Quaternary Research* 19:256–264.

Spaulding, W. G. 1985. *Vegetation and Climates of the Last 45,000 Years in the Vicinity of the Nevada Test Site, South-Central Nevada.* U.S. Geological Survey Professional Paper 1329.

Spaulding, W. G. 1990a. Vegetation dynamics during the last deglaciation, southeastern Great Basin, U.S.A. *Quaternary Research* 33:188–203.

Spaulding, W. G. 1990b. Vegetational and climatic development of the Mojave Desert: The last glacial maximum to the present. In *Packrat Middens: The Last 40,000 Years of Biotic Change,* edited by J. L. Betancourt, T. R. Van Devender, and P. S. Martin, pp. 166–199. University of Arizona Press, Tucson.

Spaulding, W. G. 1991. A middle Holocene vegetation record from the Mojave Desert of North America and its paleoclimatic significance. *Quaternary Research* 35:427–437.

Spaulding, W. G., and L. J. Graumlich. 1986. The last pluvial climatic episodes in the deserts of southwestern North America. *Nature* 320:441–444.

Spaulding, W. G., and T. R. Van Devender. 1980. Late Pleistocene montane conifers in southeastern Utah. In *Cowboy Cave,* by J. D. Jennings, pp. 159–161. University of Utah Anthropological Papers 104.

Spaulding, W. G., E. B. Leopold, and T. R. Van Devender. 1983. Late Wisconsin paleoecology of the American Southwest. In *Late Quaternary Environments of the United States,* Volume 1: *The Late Pleistocene,* edited by S. C. Porter, pp. 259–293. University of Minnesota Press, Minneapolis.

Spaulding, W. G., J. L. Betancourt, L. K. Croft, and K. L. Cole. 1990. Packrat middens: Their composition and methods of analysis. In *Packrat Middens: The Last 40,000 Years of Biotic Change,* edited by J. L. Betancourt, T. R. Van Devender, and P. S. Martin, pp. 59–84. University of Arizona Press, Tucson.

Spencer, R. J., M. J. Baedecker, H. P. Eugster, R. M. Forester, M. B. Goldhaber, B. F. Jones, K. Kelts, J. Mckenzie, D. B. Madsen, S. L. Rettig, M. Rubin, and C. J. Bowser. 1984. Great Salt Lake, and precursors, Utah: The last 30,000 years. *Contributions to Mineralogy and Petrology* 86:321–334.

Stafford, T. W., Jr., and R. A. Tyson. 1989. Accelerator radiocarbon dates on charcoal, shell, and human bones from the Del Mar Site, California. *American Antiquity* 54:389–395.

Stafford, T. W., Jr., P. E. Hare, L. Currie, A. J. T. Jull, and D. Donahue. 1990. Accuracy of North American human skeletal ages. *Quaternary Research* 34:111–120.

Stafford, T. W., Jr., P. E. Hare, L. Currie, A. J. T. Jull, and D. Donahue. 1991. Accelerator radiocarbon dating at the molecular level. *Journal of Archaeological Science* 18:35–72.

Stanley, D. A., G. M. Page, and R. Shutler, Jr. 1970. The Cocanour site: A western Nevada Pinto phase site with two excavated "house" rings. *Nevada State Museum Anthropological Papers* 15:1–46.

Steadman, D. W., and P. S. Martin. 1984. Extinction of birds in the late Pleistocene of North America. In *Quaternary Extinctions: A Prehistoric Revolution,* edited by P. S. Martin and R. G. Klein, pp. 466–477. University of Arizona, Tucson.

Steele, W. K. 1991. Paleomagnetic evidence for repeated glacial Lake Missoula floods from sediments of the Sanpoil River valley, northeastern Washington. *Quaternary Research* 35:197–207.

Stegner, W. 1981. *The Gathering of Zion: The Story of the Mormon Trail.* Westwater Press, Salt Lake City, Utah.

Stern, T. H. 1966. *The Klamath Tribe: A People and Their Reservation.* University of Washington Press, Seattle.

Stevens, G. C., and J. F. Fox. 1991. The causes of treeline. *Annual Review of Ecology and Systematics* 22:177–191.

Steward, J. H. 1933. Ethnography of the Owens Valley Pauite. *University of California Publications in American Archaeology and Ethnology* 33:233–350.

Steward, J. H. 1937. Linguistic distributions and political groups of the Great Basin Shoshoneans. *American Anthropologist* 39: 625–634.

Steward, J. H. 1938. *Basin-Plateau Aboriginal Sociopolitical Groups.* Bureau of American Ethnology Bulletin 120.

Steward, J. H. 1970. The foundation of Basin-Plateau Shoshonean Society. In *Languages and Cultures of Western North America: Essays in Honor of Sven S. Liljebad,* edited by E. H. Swanson, Jr., pp. 113–151. Idaho State University Press, Pocatello.

Stewart, G. R. 1953. *The Opening of the California Trail.* University of California Press, Berkeley and Los Angeles.

Stewart, G. R. 1960. *Ordeal by Hunger: The Story of the Donner Party.* University of Nebraska Press, Lincoln.

Stewart, J. H. 1980. *Geology of Nevada.* Nevada Bureau of Mines and Geology Special Publication 4.

Stine, S. 1984. Late Holocene lake level fluctuations and island volcanism at Mono Lake, California. In *Geologic Guide to Aspen Valley, Mono Lake, Mono Craters, and Inyo Craters,* pp. 21–49. Friends of the Pleistocene, Pacific Cell. (Reprinted by Genny Smith Books, Palo Alto, California, 1991).

Stine, S. 1990. Late Holocene fluctuations of Mono Lake, eastern California. *Palaeogeography, Palaeoclimatology, Palaeoecology* 78: 333–381.

Stinson, S. 1985. Sex differences in environmental sensitivity during growth and development. *Yearbook of Physical Anthropology* 28:123–147.

Stock, C. S. 1920. Origin of the supposed human footprints of Carson City, Nevada. *Science* 51:514.

Stock, C. S. 1925. Cenozoic gravigrade edentates of western North America. *Carnegie Institute of Washington Publications* 331.

Stock, C. S. 1931. Problems of antiquity presented in Gypsum Cave, Nevada. *Scientific Monthly* 32:22–32.

Stock, C. S. 1936. A new mountain goat from the Quaternary of Smith Creek Cave, Nevada. *Bulletin of the Southern California Academy of Sciences* 35:149–153.

Stock, C. S. 1956. *Rancho La Brea: A Record of Pleistocene Life in California.* Los Angeles County Museum of Natural History Science Series 20, Paleontology 11.

Stokes, W. L., G. R. Smith, and K. F. Horn. 1964. Fossil fishes from the Stansbury level of Lake Bonneville, Utah. *Proceedings of the Utah Academy of Sciences, Arts, and Letters* 41:87–88.

Stout, B. 1986. Discovery and dating of the Black Rock Desert mammoth. *Nevada Archaeologist* 5(2):21–23.

Street-Perrott, F. A. 1991. General circulation (GCM) modelling of palaeoclimates: A critique. *The Holocene* 1:74–80.

Strömberg, B. 1985. Revision of the late glacial Swedish varve chronology. *Boreas* 14:101–105.

Stuart, A. J. 1991. Mammalian extinctions in the late Pleistocene of northern Eurasia and North America. *Biological Reviews* 66:453–562.

Stuiver, M., and R. Kra, eds. 1986. Proceedings of the Twelfth International Radiocarbon Conference: Calibration Issue. *Radiocarbon* 28(2B):805–1030.

Sturm, P. A. 1980. The Great Salt Lake brine system. In *Great Salt Lake: A Scientific, Historical, and Economic Overview,* edited by J. W. Gwynn, pp. 147–162. Utah Geological and Mineral Survey Bulletin 116.

Sutton, D. A., and C. F. Nadler. 1969. Chromosomes of the North American chipmunk genus *Eutamias. Journal of Mammalogy* 50:524–535.

Sutton, M. Q. 1986. Warfare and expansion: An ethnohistoric perspective on the Numic spread. *Journal of California and Great Basin Anthropology* 8:65–82.

Swadesh, M. 1950. Salish internal relationships. *International Journal of American Linguistics* 16:157–167.

Swadesh, M. 1952. Lexico-statistic dating of prehistoric ethnic contacts. *Proceedings of the American Philosophical Society* 96:452–463.

Swadesh, M. 1955. Algunas fechas glotocronologicas importantes para la prehistoria nahua. *Revista mexicana de Estudios Antropologicos* 14:173–192.

Swadesh, M. 1959. Linguistics as an instrument of prehistory. *Southwestern Journal of Anthropology* 15:20–35.

Sweet, A. T., and R. G. McBeth. 1942. Soil survey of the Klamath Reclamation Project. *Carnegie Institute of Washington Publications* 538:145–147.

Tadlock, W. L. 1966. Certain crescentic stone objects as a time marker in the western United States. *American Antiquity* 31: 662–675.

Talbot, R. K., and J. D. Wilde. 1989. Giving form to the Formative: Shifting settlement patterns in the eastern Great Basin and northern Colorado Plateau. *Utah Archaeology* 2(1):3–18.

Tankersley, K. B., and C. A. Munson. 1992. Comments on the Meadowcroft Rockshelter radiocarbon chronology and the recognition of coal contaminants. *American Antiquity* 57:321–326.

Tanner, W. W. 1978. Zoogeography of reptiles and amphibians in the intermountain region. In *Intermountain Biogeography: A Symposium,* edited by K. T. Harper, and J. L. Reveal, pp. 43–53. Great Basin Naturalist Memoirs 2.

Taylor, R. E. 1987. *Radiocarbon Dating: An Archaeological Perspective.* Academic Press, Orlando, Florida.

Taylor, R. E., and L. A. Payen. 1979. The role of archaeometry in American archaeology: Approaches to the evaluation of the antiquity of *Homo sapiens* in California. *Advances in Archaeological Method and Theory* 2:239–283.

Taylor, R. E., L. A. Payen, C. A. Prior, P. J. Slota, Jr., R. Gillespie, J. A. J. Gowlett, R. E. M. Hedges, A. J. T. Jull, T. H. Zabel, D. J. Donahue, and R. Berger. 1985. Major revision in the Pleistocene age assignment for North American human skeletons by C-14 accelerator mass spectrometry: None older than 11,000 C-14 years B.P. *American Antiquity* 50:136–140.

Thomas, D. H. 1971. A cybernetic modeling of historic Shoshoni economic patterns. In *Great Basin Anthropological Conference 1970: Selected Papers,* edited by C. M. Aikens, pp. 119–134. University of Oregon Anthropological Papers 1.

Thomas, D. H. 1972a. A computer simulation model of Great Basin Shoshonean subsistence and settlement pattterns. In *Models in Archaeology,* edited by D. L. Clarke, pp 671–704. Methuen, London.

Thomas, D. H. 1972b. Western Shoshone ecology: Settlement patterns and beyond. In *Great Basin Cultural Ecology: A Symposium,* edited by D. D. Fowler, pp. 135–153. Desert Research Institute Publications in the Social Sciences 8.

Thomas, D. H. 1973. An empirical test for Steward's model of Great Basin settlement patterns. *American Antiquity* 38:155–176.

Thomas, D. H. 1974. An archaeological perspective on Shoshonean bands. *American Anthropologist* 76:11–23.

Thomas, D. H. 1978. Arrowheads and atlatl darts: How the stones got the shaft. *American Antiquity* 43:461–472.

Thomas, D. H. 1981. How to classify the projectile points from Monitor Valley, Nevada. *Journal of California and Great Basin Anthropology* 3(1):7–43.

Thomas, D. H. 1982a. An overview of central Great Basin prehistory. In *Man and Environment in the Great Basin,* edited by D. B. Madsen and J. F. O'Connell, pp. 156–171. Society for American Archaeology Papers 2.

Thomas, D. H. 1982b. *The 1981 Alta Toquima Village Project: A Preliminary Report.* Desert Research Institute Social Sciences Center Technical Report 27.

Thomas, D. H. 1983. *The Archaeology of Monitor Valley. 2. Gatecliff Shelter.* American Museum of Natural History Anthropological Papers 59(1).

Thomas, D. H., ed. 1985. *The Archaeology of Hidden Cave, Nevada.* Anthropological Papers of the American Museum of Natural History 61(1).

Thomas, D. H., ed. 1986. *A Great Basin Shoshonean Source Book.* Garland, New York.

Thomas, D. H. 1988. *The Archaeology of Monitor Valley. 3. Survey and Additional Excavations.* American Museum of Natural History Anthropological Papers 66(2).

Thomas, D. H. 1993. *The Archaeology of Monitor Valley. 4. Alta Toquima and the Mt. Jefferson Complex.* American Museum of Natural History Anthropological Papers (in press).

Thompson, G. A., and D. E. White. 1964. *Regional Geology of the Steamboat Springs Area, Washoe County, Nevada.* U.S. Geological Survey Professional Paper 458-A.

Thompson, R. S. 1978. Late Pleistocene and Holocene packrat middens from Smith Creek Canyon, White Pine County, Nevada. In *The Archaeology of Smith Creek Canyon, Eastern Nevada,* edited by D. R. Tuohy and D. L. Rendall, pp. 363–380. Nevada State Museum Anthropological Papers 17.

Thompson, R. S. 1983. Modern vegetation and climate. In *The Archaeology of Monitor Valley,* Volume 1: *Epistemology,* by D. H. Thomas, pp. 99–106. American Museum of Natural History Anthropological Papers 58(1).

Thompson, R. S. 1984. Late Pleistocene and Holocene Environments in the Great Basin. Ph.D. dissertation, Department of Geosciences, University of Arizona, Tucson.

Thompson, R. S. 1985a. Palynology and *Neotoma* middens. In *Late Quaternary Vegetation and Climates of the American Southwest,* edited by B. F. Jacobs, P. L. Fall, and O. K. Davis, pp. 89–112. Contributions Series 16. American Association of Stratigraphic Palynologists, Dallas.

Thompson, R. S. 1985b. The age and environment of the Mount Moriah (Lake Mohave) occupation at Smith Creek Cave, Nevada. In *Environments and Extinctions: Man in Late Glacial North America,* edited by J. I. Mead and D. J. Meltzer, pp. 111–120. Center for the Study of Early Man, University of Maine, Orono.

Thompson, R. S. 1988. Vegetation dynamics in the western United States: Modes of response to climatic fluctuations. In *Vegetation History,* edited by B. Huntley and T. Webb III, pp. 415–458. Kluwer, Dordrecht, The Netherlands.

Thompson, R. S. 1990. Late Quaternary vegetation and climate in the Great Basin. In *Packrat Middens: The Last 40,000 Years of Biotic Change,* edited by J. L. Betancourt, T. R. Van Devender, and P. S. Martin, pp. 200–239. University of Arizona Press, Tucson.

Thompson, R. S. 1991. Pliocene environments and climates in the western United States. *Quaternary Science Reviews* 10:115–132.

Thompson, R. S. 1992. Late Quaternary environments in Ruby Valley, Nevada. *Quaternary Research* 37:1–15.

Thompson, R. S., and E. M. Hattori. 1983. Paleobotany of Gatecliff Shelter: Packrat (*Neotoma*) middens from Gatecliff Shelter and Holocene migrations of woodland plants. In *The Archaeology of Monitor Valley. 2. Gatecliff Shelter,* by D. H. Thomas, pp. 157–167. American Museum of Natural History Anthropological Papers 59(1).

Thompson, R. S., and R. R. Kautz. 1983. Paleobotany of Gatecliff Shelter: Pollen analysis. In *The Archaeology of Monitor Valley. 2. Gatecliff Shelter,* by D. H. Thomas, pp. 136–151. American Museum of Natural History Anthropological Papers 59(1).

Thompson, R. S., and J. I. Mead. 1982. Late Quaternary environments and biogeography in the Great Basin. *Quaternary Research* 17:39–55.

Thompson, R. S., T. R. Van Devender, P. S. Martin, T. Foppe, and A. Long. 1980. Shasta ground sloth (*Nothrotheriops shastense* Hoffstetter) at Shelter Cave, New Mexico: Environment, diet, and extinction. *Quaternary Research* 14:360–376.

Thompson, R. S., L. Benson, and E. M. Hattori. 1986. A revised chronology for the last Pleistocene cycle in the central Lahontan Basin. *Quaternary Research* 25:1–9.

Thompson, R. S., E. M. Hattori and D. R. Tuohy. 1987. Paleoenvironmental and archaeological implications of early Holocene–late Pleistocene cave deposits from Winnemucca Lake, Nevada. *Nevada Archaeologist* 6(1):34–38.

Thompson, R. S., L. J. Toolin, R. M. Forester, and R. J. Spencer. 1990. Accelerator–mass spectrometer (AMS) radiocarbon dating of Pleistocene lake sediments in the Great Basin. *Palaeogeography, Palaeoclimatology, Palaeoecology* 78:301–313.

Thompson, R. S., C. Whitlock, P. J. Bartlein, S. P. Harrison, and W. G. Spaulding. 1992. Climatic changes in the western United States since 18,000 yr B.P. In *Global Climate since the Last Glacial Maximum,* edited by H. E. Wright, J. E. Kutzbach, T. Webb III, W. F. Ruddiman, F. A. Street-Perrott, and P. J. Bartlein. University of Minnesota Press, Minneapolis (in press).

Titmus, G. L., and J. C. Woods. 1991. Fluted points from the Snake River Plain. In *Clovis: Origins and Adaptations,* edited by R. Bonnichsen and K. Turnmire, pp. 119–131. Center for the Study of the First Americans, Oregon State University, Corvallis.

Topping, G. 1990. Overland emigration, the California Trail, and the Hastings Cutoff. In *Excavation of the Donner-Reed Wagons: Historic Archaeology along the Hastings Cutoff,* by B. R. Hawkins and D. B. Madsen, pp. 9–30. University of Utah Press, Salt Lake City.

Townley, J. M. 1977. *Turn This Water into Gold: The Story of the Newlands Project.* Nevada Historical Society, Reno.

Townley, J. M. 1984. *The Lost Fremont Cannon Guidebook.* Jamison Station Press, Reno.

Trimble, S. H. 1989. *The Sagebrush Ocean: A Natural History of the Great Basin.* University of Nevada Press, Reno.

Tucker, W. T., C. D. Zeier, and S. Raven. 1992. Perspectives on the ethnohistoric period. In *Changes in Washoe Land Use Patterns: A Study of Three Archaeological Sites in Diamond Valley, Alpine County, California,* edited by C. D. Zeier and R. G. Elston, pp. 189–201. Monographs in World Archaeology 5.

Tuohy, D. R. 1970. The Coleman Locality: A basalt quarry and workshop near Falcon Hill, Nevada. *Nevada State Museum Anthropological Papers* 15:143–205.

Tuohy, D. R. 1982. Another Great Basin atlatl with dart foreshafts and other artifacts: Implications and ramifications. *Journal of California and Great Basin Anthropology* 4(1):80–106.

Tuohy, D. R. 1985. Notes on the Great Basin distribution of Clovis fluted and Folsom projectile points. *Nevada Archaeologist* 5(1):15–18.

Tuohy, D. R. 1986. Errata and additional notes on the Great Basin distribution of Clovis fluted and Folsom projectile points. *Nevada Archaeologist* 5(2):2–7.

Tuohy, D. R. 1988. Paleoindian and early Archaic cultural complexes from three central Nevada localities. In *Early Human Occupation in Far Western North America: The Clovis-Archaic Interface,* edited by J. A. Willig, C. M. Aikens, and J. L. Fagan, pp. 217–230. Nevada State Museum Anthropological Papers 21.

Tuohy, D. R., and T. N. Layton. 1977. Towards the establishment of a new series of Great Basin projectile points. *Nevada Archaeological Survey Reporter* 10(6):1–5.

Turk, L. J. 1973. *Hydrogeology of the Bonneville Salt Flats, Utah.* Utah Geological and Mineral Survey Water-Resources Bulletin 19.

Turnmire, K. L. 1987. An Analysis of the Mammalian Fauna from Owl Cave One and Two, Snake Range, East-Central Nevada. M.S. thesis (Quaternary Studies), University of Maine, Orono.

U.S. Department of Commerce. 1983. *Climatic Atlas of the United States.* Environmental Data Service, U.S. Department of Commerce, Washington, D.C. (reprinted by the National Oceanic and Atmospheric Administration, Washington, D.C.).

Unruh, J. D., Jr. 1979. *The Plains Across: The Overland Emigrants and the Trans-Mississippi West, 1840–1860.* University of Illinois Press, Urbana.

Utah Wilderness Coalition. 1990. *Wilderness at the Edge.* Utah Wilderness Coalition, Salt Lake City.

Uyeno, T., and R. R. Miller. 1962. Relationships of *Empetrichthys erdisi,* a Pliocene cyprinodontid fish from California, with remarks on the Fundulinae and Cyprinodontinae. *Copeia* 1962:520–532.

Van Devender, T. R. 1977. Holocene woodlands in the southwestern deserts. *Science* 198:189–192.

Van Devender, T. R. 1988. Pollen in packrat (*Neotoma*) middens: Pollen transport and the relationship of pollen to vegetation. *Palynology* 12:221–229.

Van Devender, T. R. 1990a. Late Quaternary vegetation and climate of the Chihuahuan Desert, United States and Mexico. In *Packrat Middens: The Last 40,000 Years of Biotic Change,* edited by J. L. Betancourt, T. R. Van Devender, and P. S. Martin, pp. 104–133. University of Arizona Press, Tucson.

Van Devender, T. R. 1990b. Late Quaternary vegetation and climate of the Sonoran Desert, United States and Mexico. In *Packrat Middens: The Last 40,000 Years of Biotic Change,* edited by J. L. Betancourt, T. R. Van Devender, and P. S. Martin, pp. 134–165. University of Arizona Press, Tucson.

Van Devender, T. R., and W. G. Spaulding. 1979. Development of vegetation and climate in the southwestern United States. *Science* 204:701–710.

Van Devender, T. R., P. S. Martin, R. S. Thompson, K. L. Cole, A. J. T. Jull, A. Long, L. J. Toolin, and D. J. Donahue. 1985. Fossil packrat middens and the tandem accelerator mass spectrometer. *Nature* 317:610–613.

Van Devender, T. R., R. S. Thompson, and J. L. Betancourt. 1987. Vegetation history of the deserts of southwestern North America: The nature and timing of the Late Wisconsin–Holocene Transition. In *The Geology of North America,* Volume K-3: *North America and Adjacent Oceans during the Last Deglaciation,* edited by W. F. Ruddiman and H. E. Wright, Jr., pp. 323–352. Geological Society of America, Boulder, Colorado.

Van Valkenburgh, B., F. Grady, and B. Kurtén. 1990. The Plio-Pleistocene cheetah-like cat *Miracinonyx inexpectatus* of North America. *Journal of Vertebrate Paleontology* 10:434–454.

Van Winkle, W. 1914. *Quality of the Surface Waters of Oregon.* U.S. Geological Survey Water-Supply Paper 363.

Vander Wall, S. B., and R. P. Balda. 1977. Coadaptations of the Clark's Nutcracker and the Piñon pine for efficient seed harvest and dispersal. *Ecological Monographs* 47:89–111.

Vasek, F. C. 1966. The distribution and taxonomy of three western junipers. *Brittonia* 18:350–372.

Vasek, F. C., and R. F. Thorne. 1988. Transmontane coniferous vegetation. In *Terrestrial Vegetation of California,* edited by M. G. Barbour and J. Major, pp. 797–832. California Native Plant Society Publication 9.

Vaughan, S. J., and C. J. Warren. 1987. Toward a definition of Pinto points. *Journal of California and Great Basin Anthropology* 9:199–213.

Vaughan, T. A. 1990. Ecology of living packrats. In *Packrat Middens: The Last 40,000 Years of Biotic Change,* edited by J. L. Betancourt, T. R. Van Devender, and P. S. Martin, pp. 14–27. University of Arizona Press, Tucson.

Verbrugge, L. M. 1989. The twain meet: Empirical explanations of sex differences in health and mortality. *Journal of Health and Social Behavior* 30:282–304.

Verbrugge, L. M. 1985. Gender and health: An update on hypotheses and evidence. *Journal of Health and Social Behavior* 26:156–182.

Verosub, K. L. 1988. Paleomagnetism of Quaternary deposits. *Geological Society of America Bulletin* 227:123–136.

Vigilant, L., M. Stoneking, H. Harpending, K. Hawkes, and A. C. Wilson. 1991. African populations and the evolution of human mitochondrial DNA. *Science* 253:1503–1507.

Waitt, R. B., Jr. 1984. Periodic jökulhlaups from Pleistocene glacial Lake Missoula—New evidence from varved sediment in northern Idaho and Washington. *Quaternary Research* 22:46–58.

Waitt, R. B., Jr. 1985. Case for periodic, colossal jökulhlaups from Pleistocene Lake Missoula. *Geological Society of America Bulletin* 96:1271–1286.

Waldron, I. 1983. Sex differences in human mortality: The role of genetic factors. *Social Science & Medicine* 17:321–333.

Wallace, R. E. 1984. *Faulting Related to the 1915 Earthquakes in Pleasant Valley, Nevada.* U.S. Geological Survey Professional Paper 1274A.

Wallman, S., and D. S. Amick. 1992. Cody Complex occupation in the Black Rock Desert, Nevada. *Current Research in the Pleistocene* 8:51–53.

Warren, C. N. 1967. The San Dieguito Complex: A review and hypothesis. *American Antiquity* 32:168–185.

Warren, C. N. 1968. *The View from Wenas: A Study in Plateau Prehistory.* Occasional Papers of the Idaho State University Museum 24.

Warren, C. N. 1980. Pinto points and problems in Mojave Desert archaeology. In *Anthropological Papers in Memory of Earl H. Swanson, Jr.,* edited by L. B. Harten, C. N. Warren, and D. R. Tuohy, pp. 67–76. Idaho Museum of Natural History, Pocatello.

Warren, C. N., and R. H. Crabtree. 1986. Prehistory of the southwestern area. In *Handbook of North American Indians,* Volume 11: *Great Basin,* edited by W. L. d'Azevedo, pp. 183–193. Smithsonian Institution Press, Washington, D.C.

Warren, C. N., and J. De Costa. 1964. Dating Lake Mohave artifacts and beaches. *American Antiquity* 30:206–209.

Warren, C. N., and H. T. Ore. 1978. Approach and process of dating Lake Mohave artifacts. *Journal of California Anthropology* 5:179–187.

Warren, C. N., and C. Phagan. 1988. Fluted points in the Mojave Desert: Their technology and cultural context. In *Early Human Occupation in Far Western North America: The Clovis-Archaic Interface,* edited by J. A. Willig, C. M. Aikens, and J. L. Fagan, pp. 121–130. Nevada State Museum Anthropological Papers 21.

Wayne, W. J. 1984. Glacial chronology of the Ruby Mountains–East Humboldt Range, Nevada. *Quaternary Research* 21:286–303.

Webb, R. H., and J. L. Betancourt. 1990. The spatial and temporal distribution of radiocarbon ages from packrat middens. In *Packrat Middens: The Last 40,000 Years of Biotic Change,* edited by J. L. Betancourt, T. R. Van Devender, and P. S. Martin, pp. 85–102. University of Arizona Press, Tucson

Webb, R. H., J. W. Steiger, and R. M. Turner. 1987. Dynamics of Mojave Desert shrub assemblages in the Panamint Mountains, California. *Ecology* 68:478–490.

Webb, T., III. 1988. Eastern North America. In *Vegetation History,* edited by B. Huntley and T. Webb, III, pp. 385–414. Kluwer, Dordrecht, The Netherlands.

Webb, T., III, P. J. Bartlein, and J. E. Kutzbach. 1987. Climatic change in eastern North America during the past 18,000 years: Comparison of pollen data with model results. In *The Geology of North America,* Volume K-3: *North America and Adjacent Oceans during the Last Deglaciation,* edited by W. F. Ruddiman and H. E. Wright, Jr., pp. 447–462. Geological Society of America, Boulder, Colorado.

Weiss, P. V., and B. J. Verts. 1984. Habitat and distribution of pygmy rabbits (*Sylvilagus idahoensis*) in Oregon. *Great Basin Naturalist* 44:563–571.

Wells, P. V. 1976. Macrofossil analysis of wood rat (*Neotoma*) middens as a key to the Quaternary vegetational history of arid America. *Quaternary Research* 6:223–248.

Wells, P. V. 1983. Paleobiogeography of montane grasslands in the Great Basin since the last glaciopluvial. *Ecological Monographs* 53:341–382.

Wells, P. V., and R. Berger. 1967. Late Pleistocene history of coniferous woodland in the Mojave Desert. *Science* 155:1640–1647.

Wells, P. V., and J. H. Hunziker. 1976. Origin of the creosote bush (*Larrea*) deserts of southwestern North America. *Annals of the Missouri Botanical Garden* 63:843–861.

Wells, P. V., and C. D. Jorgensen. 1964. Pleistocene wood rat middens and climatic change in Mojave Desert: A record of juniper woodlands. *Science* 143:1171–1174.

Wells, P. V., and D. Woodcock. 1985. Full-glacial vegetation of Death Valley, California: Juniper woodland opening to *Yucca* semidesert. *Madroño* 32:11–23.

Wells, S. G., L. D. McFadden, and J. C. Dohrenwend. 1987. Influence of late Quaternary climatic changes on geomorphic and pedogenic processes on a desert piedmont, eastern Mojave Desert, California. *Quaternary Research* 27:130–146.

Wells, S. G., R. Y. Anderson, T. Enzel, and W. J. Brown. 1990. An overview of floods and lakes with the Mojave River drainage basin: Implications for latest Quaternary paleoenvironments in southern California. In *At the End of the Mojave: Quaternary Studies in the Eastern Mojave Desert,* edited by R. E. Reynolds, S. G. Wells, and R. H. Brady III, pp. 31–38. San Bernardino County Museum Association, Redlands, California.

West, N. E. 1988. Intermountain deserts, shrub steppes, and woodlands. In *North American Terrestrial Vegetation,* edited by M. G. Barbour and W. D. Billings, pp. 209–230. California Native Plant Society Publication 9.

West, N. E., R. J. Tausch, K. H. Rea, and P. T. Tueller. 1978. Phytogeographical Variation within Juniper-Piñon Woodlands of the Great Basin. In *Intermountain Biogeography: A Symposium,* edited by K. T. Harper and J. L. Reveal, pp. 119–136. Great Basin Naturalist Memoirs 2.

Wetmore, A. 1959. Birds of the Pleistocene in North America. *Smithsonian Miscellaneous Collections* 138(4).

Wetmore, A. 1965. The birds of the Republic of Panama. Part 1: Tinamidae to Rynchopidae. *Smithsonian Miscellaneous Collections* 150.

White, J. M., R. W. Mathewes, and W. H. Mathews. 1985. Late Pleistocene chronology and environment of the "ice free corridor" of northwestern Alberta. *Quaternary Research* 24:173–186.

White, J. P., and J. F. O'Connell. 1979. Australian prehistory: New aspects of antiquity. *Science* 203:21–28.

Whitebread, D. H. 1969. *Geologic Map of the Wheeler Peak and Garrison Quadrangles, Nevada and Utah.* U.S. Geological Survey Miscellaneous Investigations Map I-578.

Whitley, D. S., and R. I. Dorn. 1988. Cation-ratio dating of petroglyphs using PIXE. *Nuclear Instruments and Methods in Physics Research* B35:410–414.

Widdowson, E. M. 1976. The response of the sexes to nutritional stress. *Proceedings of the Nutrition Society* 35:175–180.

Wigand, P. E. 1985. Diamond Pond, Harney County, Oregon: Man and Marsh in the Eastern Oregon Desert. Ph.D. dissertation, Department of Anthropology, Washington State University, Pullman.

Wigand, P. E. 1987. Diamond Pond, Harney County, Oregon: Vegetation history and water table in the eastern Oregon desert. *Great Basin Naturalist* 47:427–458.

Wigand, P. E. 1990a. The study of links between climate and human activities in the Lahontan Basin. In *Studies of Climatic Variations and Their Impact on the Great Basin.* Final Report on Contract NA878A-D-CP114, National Climatic Program Office, National Oceanic and Atmospheric Administration, Rockville, Maryland.

Wigand, P. E. 1990b. Vegetation history. In *Archaeological and Paleonenvironmental Investigations in the Ash Meadows National Wildlife Refuge, Nye County, Nevada,* edited by S. D. Livingston and F. L. Nials, pp. 15–48. Technical Report 70. Quaternary Sciences Center, Desert Research Institute, Reno.

Wigand, P. E., and P. J. Mehringer, Jr. 1985. Pollen and seed analyses. In *The Archaeology of Hidden Cave, Nevada,* edited by D. H. Thomas, pp. 108–124. Anthropological Papers of the American Museum of Natural History 61(1).

Wilde, J. D. 1985. Prehistoric Settlements in the Northern Great Basin: Excavations and Collections Analysis in the Steens Mountain Area, Southeastern Oregon. Ph.D. dissertation, Department of Anthropology, University of Oregon, Eugene.

Wilde, J. D., and D. E. Newman. 1989. Late Archaic corn in the eastern Great Basin. *American Anthropologist* 91:712–720.

Wilke, P. J., T. F. King, and R. Bettinger. 1974. A comparative study of late Paleo-Indian manifestations in the western Great Basin. *Nevada Archaeological Survey Research Papers* 5:80–90.

Willden, R. 1964. *Geology and Mineral Deposits of Humboldt County, Nevada.* Nevada Bureau of Mines Bulletin 59.

Williams, P. A., and R. I. Orlins. 1963. *The Corn Creek Dunes Site: A Dated Surface Site in Southern Nevada.* Nevada State Museum Anthropological Papers 10.

Williams, T. R., and M. S. Bedinger. 1984. *Selected Geologic and Hydrologic Characteristics of the Basin and Range Province, Western United States: Pleistocene Lakes and Marshes.* U.S. Geological Survey Miscellaneous Investigations Map I-1522-D.

Willig, J. A. 1988. Paleo-Archaic adaptations and lakeside settlement patterns in the Northern Alkali Basin, Oregon. In *Early Human Occupation in Far Western North America: The Clovis-Archaic Interface,* edited by J. A. Willig, C. M. Aikens, and J. L. Fagan, pp. 417–482. Nevada State Museum Anthropological Papers 21.

Willig, J. A. 1989. Paleo-Archaic Broad Spectrum Adaptations at the Pleistocene-Holocene Boundary in Far Western North America. Ph.D. dissertation, Department of Anthropology, University of Oregon, Eugene.

Willig, J. A. 1991. Clovis technology and adaptations in far western North America: Regional patterns and environmental context. In *Clovis: Origins and Adaptations,* edited by R. Bonnichsen and K. Turnmire, pp. 98–108. Center for the Study of the First Americans, Oregon State University, Corvallis.

Willig, J. A., and C. M. Aikens. 1988. The Clovis-Archaic interface in far western North America. In *Early Human Occupation in Far Western North America: The Clovis-Archaic Interface,* edited by J. A. Willig, C. M. Aikens, and J. L. Fagan, pp. 1–40. Nevada State Museum Anthropological Papers 21.

Wingard, D. L. 1984. The sex differential in morbidity, mortality, and lifestyle. *Annual Review of Public Health* 5:433–458.

Woodcock, D. 1986. The late Pleistocene of Death Valley: A climatic reconstruction based on macrofossil data. *Palaeogeography, Palaeoclimatology, Palaeoecology* 57:272–283.

Wormington, H. M., and D. Ellis, eds. 1967. *Pleistocene Studies in Southern Nevada.* Nevada State Museum Anthropological Papers 13.

Wright, S. J. 1981. Intra-archipelago vertebrate distributions: The slope of the species-area relation. *American Naturalist* 118: 726–748.

Wuerthner, G. 1992. Nevada Mountain Ranges. American and World Publishing, Helena, Montana.

Yi, S., and G. Clark. 1985. The "Dyuktai culture" and New World Origins. *Current Anthropology* 26:1–20.

Yohe, R. M., II, M. E. Newman, and J. S. Schneider. 1991. Immunological identification of small-mammal proteins on aboriginal milling equipment. *American Antiquity* 56:659–666.

Young, D. A., and R. L. Bettinger. 1992. The Numic spread: A computer simulation. *American Antiquity* 57:85–99.

Young, J. A., and R. A. Evans. 1973. Downy brome—Intruder in the plant succession of big sagebrush communities in the Great Basin. *Journal of Range Management* 26:410–415.

Young, J. A., and R. A. Evans. 1978. Population dynamics after wildfires in sagebrush grasslands. *Journal of Range Management* 31:283–289.

Young, J. A., and B. A. Sparks. 1985. *Cattle in the Cold Desert.* Utah State University Press, Logan.

Young, J. A., R. A. Evans, and J. Major. 1972. Alien plants in the Great Basin. *Journal of Range Management* 25:194–201.

Young, J. A., R. A. Evans, and R. A. Weaver. 1976. Estimating potential downy brome competition after wildfires. *Journal of Range Management* 29:322–325.

Young, J. A., R. E. Eckert, Jr., and R. A. Evans. 1979. Historical perspectives regarding the sagebrush ecosystem. In *The Sagebrush Ecosystem: A Symposium,* pp. 1–13. College of Natural Resources, Utah State University Press, Logan.

Youngman, P. M., and F. W. Schueler. 1991. *Martes nobilis* is a synonym of *Martes americana,* not an extinct Pleistocene-Holocene species. *Journal of Mammalogy* 72:567–577.

Zancanella, J. K. 1988. Early lowland prehistory in south-central Nevada. In *Early Human Occupation in Far Western North America: The Clovis-Archaic Interface,* edited by J. A. Willig, C. M. Aikens, and J. L. Fagan, pp. 251–272. Nevada State Museum Anthropological Papers 21.

Zeveloff, S. I., and F. R. Collett. 1988. *Mammals of the Intermountain West.* University of Utah Press, Salt Lake City.

Ziegler, A. C. 1963. Unmodified mammal and bird remains from Deer Creek Cave, Elko County, Nevada. In *Deer Creek Cave, Elko County, Nevada,* by M. E. Shutler and R. Shutler, Jr., pp. 15–24. Nevada State Museum Anthropological Papers 11.

Zielinski, G. A., and W. D. McCoy. 1987. Paleoclimatic implications of the relationship between modern snowpack and late Pleistocene equilibrium-line altitudes in the mountains of the Great Basin, western U.S.A. *Arctic and Alpine Research* 19: 127–134.

Zigmond, M. 1986. Kawaiisu. In *Handbook of North American Indians,* Volume 11: *Great Basin,* edited by W. L. d'Azevedo, pp. 389–411. Smithsonian Institution Press, Washington, D.C.

○○○

Index

Entries suffixed by an f denote citations within figure captions; those suffixed by a t, within tables; those suffixed by an n, within end-of-chapter notes. Organisms are indexed solely by common name. A concordance of common and scientific plant names will be found in the Appendix, page 305.